STANISLAW KOT
Polish Ambassador to the U.S.S.R.
1941–1942

Conversations
with the Kremlin
and Dispatches
from Russia

Translated and Arranged by
H. C. STEVENS

London
OXFORD UNIVERSITY PRESS
NEW YORK   TORONTO
1963

Oxford University Press, Amen House, London E.C.4

GLASGOW NEW YORK TORONTO MELBOURNE WELLINGTON
BOMBAY CALCUTTA MADRAS KARACHI LAHORE DACCA
CAPE TOWN SALISBURY NAIROBI IBADAN ACCRA
KUALA LUMPUR HONG KONG

Printed in Great Britain by
Northumberland Press Limited
Gateshead on Tyne

CONTENTS

INTRODUCTION

The documents presented in this book consist chiefly of translations of reports of various conversations which I, as Ambassador of the Republic of Poland to the U.S.S.R., had with various members of the Soviet Government during the period of my mission. They date from the day after my arrival in Moscow, on 4 September 1941, to my departure from the U.S.S.R. on 13 July 1942. In addition there are extracts from my reports to General Sikorski, the Prime Minister of Poland, and to other ministers of the Polish Government in London, which throw further light on the course of Polish-Soviet relations during my period as ambassador.

As the main documents consist of reports of conversations, it is necessary to explain how they came to be recorded. In each of my conversations with Soviet ministers I was accompanied by a secretary. As I did not speak Russian (though, because of my knowledge of Old Slavonic, I did to some extent understand it) my secretary also acted as translator, translating my remarks into Russian for the Soviet representative, and his into Polish for me. In order to accomplish this task satisfactorily he had to make copious notes. These were not taken down in shorthand; but every sentence and, when the talking speed of the conversation allowed, every word, was written out in full. Immediately after each conversation, while the proceedings were still fresh in his memory, the secretary made a complete transcript, to which I added from my own recollection of the talk.

When writing his report, intended primarily for the Polish Government in London, the secretary added brief notes on the duration of the conversation, the atmosphere in which it took place, and the behaviour of those who took part. As these comments are in the nature of direct observations they have been retained in this book.

Needless to say, the word 'Kremlin' in the title of the volume is intended simply to indicate the headquarters of the Soviet Government. The Soviet organ in the sphere of foreign affairs, with which I had mostly to deal, was the 'Narcomindiel', the People's Commissariat for Foreign Affairs. So long as the Embassy was situated in Moscow the conversations did in fact take place in the Kremlin; but after the Diplomatic Corps was evacuated to Kuibishev, on the river Volga, only the conversation with Stalin recorded on pp. 106-15 was held in the Kremlin.

The documentation of Polish-Soviet relations during my mission could be completed only by the publication of the numerous official notes exchanged between the two Governments through their embassies; very valuable information concerning the Soviet treatment of Polish deportees was embodied in these notes. Unfortunately, the wartime archives of the Polish Ministry for Foreign Affairs have been dispersed, and at present there is no likelihood of their being reassembled in a condition fit for publication.

The Polish Embassy in Moscow was reopened in August 1941 as the direct result of the Polish-Soviet Treaty concluded on 30 July 1941 in London, with the help of the British Government.

As soon as he foresaw an end to the German-Soviet collaboration which the Ribbentrop-Molotov Pact of August 1939 had brought into being at Poland's expense, the Polish Prime Minister, General Sikorski, was alive to the possibility of reaching an understanding with Soviet Russia. His prime concern was to rescue the approximately one and a half million Polish citizens who had been deported to Russia, and put in prison or held in forced labour camps. He also proposed to organize detachments of the Polish armed forces from the prisoners of war whom the Soviet Government had deported to Russia, and from the Polish civilians working in forests, on collective farms, and elsewhere.

When Sir Stafford Cripps was preparing to go to Moscow as British Ambassador, at the end of May 1940, he visited France to discuss the Polish case with General Sikorski, and the General asked him to investigate the situation in Russia along the lines he, Sikorski, had in mind. When, twelve months later, the Germans invaded Russia and the question of a Polish-Soviet understanding came to the forefront Sikorski announced that the Polish Government was perfectly ready for negotiations. The moment the treaty was signed, in the presence of the British Prime Minister, Mr. Winston Churchill, the question of appointing an Ambassador to the U.S.S.R. was bound to arise. But I had no premonition that General Sikorski would at once turn to me with the request that I should undertake the mission. I was dumbfounded.

'You can't refuse,' Sikorski said. 'The Soviets have made the release of the Poles dependent on the restoration of diplomatic relations, and in particular on the exchange of Ambassadors. I have just been informed that they are nominating Bogomolov (the former Ambassador in Vichy), and are asking the name of our Ambassador. I want to let them have it this very day. I'm afraid they will use any delay in nominating an Ambassador as an excuse for holding our citizens longer in prison. I should never forgive myself if that continued for a single day just because the Government could not find an Ambassador.'

'But I've never been in Russia, I hardly know Russian, I have difficulty even in reading it. And there is more than one professional diplomat in the Ministry for Foreign Affairs, and even among our ministers, who has greater qualifications for the mission.'

'Nobody in the Ministry for Foreign Affairs wants to go, I don't know whether they all solidly oppose the pact, or whether they're afraid. Sosnkowski . . . has become the biggest opponent of the treaty and has left the Government. I have no one. Even if I forced one of our diplomats to go to Moscow, what certainty should I have that he would follow my political line. . . ? There's no help for it, you've got to agree. . . . You'll only be there a short time and you'll remain a member of the Government. In six weeks I shall be in Moscow and we'll come back together. By then someone will be found to replace you.'

So I had to agree, and the General passed my name to the Soviets through Mr. Churchill. Moscow's agreement came by return, while the Polish Government at once accepted Bogomolov.

However, the Soviet Government did not display any great enthusiasm in concluding the treaty with Poland. It announced that the treaties with Germany dating from 1939 were annulled, but refused to make any formal recognition of the Polish frontiers as demarcated by the Riga Treaty of 1921. It agreed to the formation of a Polish Army on Soviet territory, but during the negotiations to this end it would only admit the existence of 30,000 Polish prisoners of war in Russia. It promised to release all Polish citizens, but only by way of an amnesty. On all these points the Soviet Government was inflexible and flatly rejected the Polish desiderata. The British Government, which acted as intermediary, admitted that it saw no possibility of breaking down this opposition. The Soviet Government made only one concession: it withdrew its former condition that the treaty between Poland and the U.S.S.R. was to be concluded on the Polish side by a (non-existent) National Polish Committee in the U.S.S.R., which Committee was to take over the organization of the Polish Army in Russia. This was on the lines of similar agreements concluded with Czechoslovak and Yugoslav committees.

Even at this early stage Stalin had a plan for dealing with the nations adjacent to the Soviet Union; it consisted of setting up pro-communist committees functioning under nationalistic names, but in reality acting as instruments of the Soviet Government. However, the Association of Patriots which had already been planned as a means of dominating Poland could not be brought into existence at that time, since General Sikorski's Government was not only recognized by all the other Allied Governments, but enjoyed their highest respect.

From the beginning Sikorski realized what the Soviet Government was fundamentally aiming to achieve; if, none the less, he signed the treaty, it was because he was afraid that otherwise the million and a half Polish exiles would be wiped out; moreover, he hoped that the formation of a Polish Army in the U.S.S.R. to fight in the common struggle against Germany would give weight to the Polish desiderata and create a basis for co-operation in the future. He considered that something could be won from the Soviet Government only if the war went badly for them, and that if they had military successes they would prove inflexible. He also counted on the support of the Western Allies, to whom the Soviet Government was already looking for aid.

My task as Ambassador was to watch over the Soviet Government's fulfilment of the various articles of the treaty, to rescue the Polish exiles, and to give aid to the Command of the Polish Army, which came into being in the Volga region as the result of a separate agreement concluded on 14 August 1941 and signed on the Polish side by Generals Anders and Szyszko-Bohusz.

I arrived in Moscow on 4 September 1941. After an exploratory talk with Generals Anders and Tokarzewski, with several Poles already released from prison or work camps, and with the friendly British and United States Ambassadors, Sir Stafford Cripps and Mr. L. Steinhardt, I presented my credentials and entered into conversations with representatives of the Soviet Government. On 8 September I had a talk with the Commissar for Foreign Affairs, Molotov; on 9 September with the Chairman of the Council of People's Commissars, Kalinin; on the 10th with the Vice-Commissar for Foreign Affairs, Vyshinsky, and with various other officials. On 20 September I had the first of my regular conversations with Vyshinsky. Contacts with members of the Diplomatic Corps enabled me to acquire a good deal of information concerning the Soviet Government's tactics; in this direction I was indebted most of all to the doyen of the corps, the Ambassador of Iran, Mohammed Saed, who later became Prime Minister of Iran, and to the Yugoslav minister, Milan Gavrilović.

In my earliest conversations I considered it important to get the Soviet authorities to realize that the Sikorski Government regarded Polish-Soviet co-operation seriously—and sincerely—that their Polish ally wanted to see victory for the common cause, and that we were confident this victory would be achieved. I tried to dispel the inveterate Russian prejudices against the Polish Government, and to stress the outstanding historic mission which had fallen to General Sikorski in the war; I emphasized the heroism of the Polish forces on all fronts, the sacrificial resistance of our people living under the German occupation, and the sympathy and prestige which all these factors were winning for the Polish nation among the other nations of the free world. I also urged the extraordinary propaganda value for them, both in America and elsewhere, of a reconciliation between the Russians and the Poles and their alliance with the Polish Government.

I held no trumps of a material nature. The State of Poland had been defeated and was under occupation. The Government was in exile, and without resources. I had to put all my emphasis on the Polish moral contribution, to make this an effective argument in advocating our desiderata. At the same time I tried to discover the Soviet Government's intentions in regard to Poland, how sincere and loyal it would be towards us, and what views it held in regard to our role in the war and after, to our relations with our Allies, and to the Polish-Soviet Treaty.

As the Embassy files accumulated a mass of information based on the experiences of Polish citizens in all parts of the Soviet empire, I had no illusions, and fully realized what I was up against. But in order to obtain the results we desired I had to apply a suitable tactic, to restrain our thoroughly justified indignation, to avoid continual disputes, irritants, wrangles, pinpricks, and yet at every opportune moment to advance our view of the truth in opposition to the false picture presented by the Soviet authorities. In short, on no account must I lose my self-control. To this end I had to prepare for each conversation by cultivating calm and patience, briefing myself on all aspects of the questions to be raised, assembling information as exact as possible—not an easy task in the prevailing conditions. And I had to choose between problems which called for inflexibility and those which it was advisable or necessary to postpone. All this involved me in tremendous difficulties. On the burning question of the Soviet failure to liberate Polish officer prisoners of war I was warned (by General Anders on the inspiration of General Zhukov, of the Soviet Commissariat for Internal Affairs—the Narcomvnudiel) that if the Embassy raised this issue it would prove a serious misfortune; the only hope of recovering these prisoners of war, whose fate was then unknown, but who were thought to be concealed somewhere in the far north of Russia, was through the intervention of the military authorities. But as I was urged on all hands to take action on the question—by London, by men serving in the Polish Army in Russia, and by the families of the missing officers—I had to raise the matter, if only indirectly, by inquiring after the fate of particular groups of prisoners: doctors, professors, engineers, priests, etc. In the end, when I learned that Zhukov's suggestion was no more than a diversionary manœuvre, I raised the matter directly.

Through these prudent tactics, at all costs avoiding any breach of relations, I definitely achieved certain results, above all the release of thousands of Polish citizens from camps and prisons, a certain degree of legal protection for them, and the possibility of organizing welfare work among them, as well as obtaining food and living accommodation. The result was that hundreds of thousands of Poles were rescued, and that despite the rupture of relations in 1943 they survived to return by one road or another to their native land.

These tactics were all the more necessary since I became convinced quite early on that we could not count on any serious support from our Western Allies. I saw this quite clearly by the end of September 1941, during the Allied Conference in Moscow. When the Polish Government set about the creation of the Polish Army in the U.S.S.R. we reckoned that it would be equipped and armed by Great Britain. This had been the subject of earlier conversations in London, and promises had been made to this effect. Meanwhile, when Stalin astonished the Allied delegates to the Conference with unforeseen demands for supplies, the head of the British Delegation, Lord Beaverbrook, was not willing to reserve separate supplies for the equipment of the Polish divisions, and left the matter entirely to the goodwill of Stalin: a decision that surprised his own British generals at the conference.

Now Stalin felt sure that the British Government was leaving the fate of the Polish Army—and of Polish affairs generally in the U.S.S.R. —to his unfettered decision. When the Allies granted aid to the extent of many millions of pounds in the most valuable forms of war supplies (over 11 billion dollars on Lend-Lease) without any conditions, without even drawing up a draft statement of their common aims and obligations for the future, Stalin began to treat their wishes and views with scant respect, and to consider that he could not do better than by blackmailing them.

That September 1941 conference was the first of a series of important conferences which Stalin was bound to win, because he was prepared for them and knew exactly what he wanted, whereas the Allies were not in the least prepared to postulate their own demands. It has even been stated that Stalin asked Lord Beaverbrook about the British peace plan and that Beaverbrook promised to let him have information later, but forgot to do so.[1]

In those days the Narcomindiel, the People's Commissariat for Foreign Affairs, was ostensibly run on a 'collegium' basis, i.e., with a controlling group of high Soviet personalities in charge. It was headed by Molotov as Commissar for Foreign Affairs. His deputies were Andrei Vyshinsky for international affairs and for relations with the Allied States in particular; Dekanozov for relations with other states; Mikoyan for economic problems; Lozovsky for information and propaganda. Each deputy commissar had assistants, usually trainees drawn from the Diplomatic School, and as a rule confidants of the Narcomvnudiel (People's Commissariat for Internal Affairs). They included several who after the war became well known in the satellite countries and in international organizations: Valerian Zorin, Kiril Novikov (who was the real rapporteur on Polish affairs), and Georgii Pushkin.

In reality Molotov was not so much senior to the Vice-Commissars as their liaison with Stalin and the Communist Party's Politbureau. During his conversations with foreign diplomats Stalin usually kept Molotov at his side, ostensibly to observe the collegium principle in the conduct of foreign affairs. But in reality Molotov was only the instrument of Stalin's will, acting as his secretary during conversations. None the less, because of his position he was of much greater importance in the internal organization of the Soviet Government than Vyshinsky, who was far more capable.

[1] Henry G. Cassidy: *Moscow Dateline 1941-43* (Boston, 1943), pp. 138-9.

B

Neither the Commissar nor his deputies had any independence within the scope of their specific functions. It was obvious in all their arguments that they were governed by instructions from 'above', and that they had to turn to 'above' for a decision even on the most insignificant point.

Molotov was the most important authority in the Narcomindiel, yet he was the least interesting. Wooden and unctuous, constantly repeating the same phrases, always inflexible, he was the incarnation of banality. As a Pole I found it unpleasant to have anything to do with him. For he had been the co-author of the agreement with Hitler which decided the partition of Poland in 1939. And in the Supreme Soviet he had publicly proclaimed his delight at the elimination from the map of Europe of this 'bastard of the Versailles Congress.' My talks with him were useless; not merely did nothing positive ever result from them, they were not even enlivened by any incident worth remembering. Only once was there anything in the nature of a scene, during a conversation with Stalin. When I maintained that there ought to be no restriction on the development of the Polish Army in Russia the Soviet side took refuge behind the text of the Military Agreement, in which, they alleged, it was laid down once for all that the Polish Army was to consist of not more than two divisions. As Molotov ran his finger along the document to emphasize his point I took the liberty of snatching it from his hand and glancing at the text. I at once pointed out that it contained no such condition, and that it only said the Poles were to form two divisions by 1 October 1941. That by no means connoted that there was to be any restriction on the size of the army even in 1941. Stalin gave Molotov a furious look, and the Commissar had to drop his argument.[1] Molotov's face reflected his anxiety at having laid Stalin open to the charge of being inaccurate, and forcing him to withdraw.

After Molotov had organized the transference of the Narcomindiel and the Diplomatic Corps to Kuibishev he returned to Moscow to be at Stalin's side during the German military threat to the capital. Vyshinsky, who was a deputy premier, was left to run the Commissariat, and from that time my conversations were confined to meetings with him, apart from occasional invitations to Moscow. I was received by Vyshinsky with unusual courtesy, and thus began a collaboration which included twenty-six official conversations and frequent personal meetings in various circumstances. These meetings

[1] See B13, p. 109.

were particularly frequent during the week when he accompanied General Sikorski on his visits to detachments of the Polish forces in camps between the Volga and the Ural mountains. In private conversation Vyshinsky was very affable, good-humoured, and fond of a joke. In official conversations he resorted to a wide range of argument and unexpected changes of mood, from good manners, laughter, and jest, through civility and chilly courtesy to petty spite, sarcasm, positive rudeness, cynicism, and brutal attacks. It all depended on whether I was making claims which he could meet more or less or whether I mentioned some indubitable wrong done to the Polish people, its prisoners of war (especially those involved in the case known later as the Katyn affair) or the unfortunate civilian exiles. His behaviour also obviously depended on whether Stalin's tactic at the moment aimed at good and conciliatory relations with the Poles, or at deliberately worsening those relations.

Vyshinsky devoted all his mental agility, intelligence, knowledge, and eloquence to Stalin's service. In this abnegation of his own individuality there was a large element of opportunism : all his youth he had been a Menshevik; he joined the Bolshevik party belatedly, and he had to win his way by his zeal. He gave me an interesting reason for his fervour in the cause. I vividly remember one of his bursts of eloquence, after we had said good-bye in Saratov to General Sikorski, who was flying to Teheran on 15 December 1941. We returned to Kuibishev in a Red Army aeroplane. There was a severe frost. Vyshinsky took a flask of vodka out of his document case; when I refused to have a nip, he regaled a group of British who were shivering on the opposite side of the plane and then, returning to me, disposed of the rest in one gulp. It loosened his tongue considerably.

'Are you satisfied with your visit to the Polish Army?' I asked.

'It has been the finest week in my life,' he replied. 'Didn't you notice that I was always on hand during the meetings and conferences, and was always the last to leave?'

'And what did you find to like so much?'

'I felt so much at ease among you, it was so good to observe your social life. Your people laugh. That was a great inspiration to me. I love cheerfulness and laughter.'

'But surely the Russians laugh and make merry too?'

'You're wrong, Ambassador. You don't know the Russians.'

Vyshinsky's face flushed heavily; he leaned across to me, and said in a strained tone:

'I assure you the Russians are a gloomy people; sluggish, lazy, dull, dirty, without initiative, hostile to any form of cultural progress.'

'But you're exaggerating, Commissar,' I interrupted, suspecting that he was trying to provoke me into some indiscretion.

'Never! Nothing can be got out of this people by ordinary means. It can be raised to a higher level only by such a form of government as Stalin applies. Only by force and compulsion! And that's why I'm such a fervent adherent of Stalin and defend his system.'

He was always exceedingly polite to me, and when we met privately and alone he referred to subjects which he evaded in official conversations, for instance, his Polish origin. One day when only the two of us were present, I reminded him that his Polish name was borne by petty gentry who came from a locality named Wyszyn in Mazowia and Podlasie. 'But in your features and the shape of your head you're a pure-blooded Polish farmer,' I said jokingly, and added: 'You must know Polish well, for when I'm talking in Polish, sometimes if you're irritated you reply at once, without waiting for the interpreter to put it into Russian.'

Only later did he explain his origin. 'My father', he said, 'was a Pole, but fate flung him into the purely Russian milieu of the Caucasus, where he worked as a pharmaceutical chemist. He married my mother there, and she only knew Russian, so I too, born in Baku, was educated solely in Russian. But when I went to Kiev University and came into contact with Polish colleagues I joined a Polish society, and there I learned to speak Polish not too badly, and to write it and make speeches in it.' 'But why don't you talk with me in Polish?' 'You see, because of my revolutionary activities I was exiled to Siberia, and spent several years in a district where I had no opportunity to speak Polish. I still understand it, but I can't talk it without mistakes.' So we conversed with each other in French.

A third high official of the Narcomindiel with whom I had much to do was the Vice-Commissar for Propaganda, Solomon Lozovsky. Only our early conversations were recorded, for later I did not use an interpreter, as we talked in French. I knew that Lozovsky, who was of Jewish origin, had been a worker when quite young and a member of the Bolshevik party from his youth, using the pseudonym Dridzo. He had escaped from a Tsarist prison, had got to France, and had worked there till his return to Russia in 1917.

As director of the Information Bureau, Lozovsky demanded that he should be supplied with all kinds of documents illustrating the

Polish people's struggle against the Hitlerite occupation, and he used the material supplied by the Embassy extensively in his propaganda activities.

Lozovsky was natural and unaffected in his manner, and he aroused considerable trust. Now he is dead—he was arrested during Stalin's post-war anti-Semitic drive, and perished in mysterious circumstances —I can relate part of a conversation I had with him in the autumn of 1941. I had hopes of obtaining a large loan from the Soviet Government for the maintenance of the Polish exiles who were eking out a wretched existence, but Vyshinsky told me they intended to pay us only a few million roubles, possibly three. I happened to call on Lozovsky one day on some journalistic question, and found him sitting alone, half concealed by a great writing bureau. During the conversation I deviated from my subject to remark: 'What am I to do? Our Polish exiles are dying of hunger, but instead of a loan of a hundred million your Government is giving me only a few million. I refused to accept such a pittance today. Don't you agree I was right to do so?'

He behaved as though he hadn't heard my remarks and continued to talk about anti-German propaganda. A few minutes later a telephone rang at the far end of his large room, and a secretary whom I hadn't seen before rose from behind the desk at Lozovsky's side and went to answer it. Glancing at the telephone, Lozovsky leaned across to me and said in a lower voice, 'I advise you to take the three millions and at once demand more.' As we said good-bye I squeezed his hand warmly, though I had no intention of taking his advice. Evidently he did not feel sure whether the secretary, who was undoubtedly a Narcomvnudiel man, had heard any part of his remark, and he later safeguarded himself against denunciation by telling Vyshinsky that the loan had been mentioned during our talk and he had advised me to accept the small amount.[1]

I saw Stalin for the first time on 14 November 1941, when I was unexpectedly summoned from Kuibishev to present myself in the Kremlin. This invitation had come because I was opposed to General Sikorski's visit to Moscow before the most important points of the Polish-Soviet Agreement had been carried out by the Soviet Government. I realized that Stalin attached great importance to the Polish Prime Minister's visit. My conversation with him lasted over two hours.

[1] See below, document B16, conversation with Vyshinsky on 25 November 1941.

I was surprised to note that there was nothing in the form and demeanour of the Communist dictator to remind one of the old type of Russian revolutionary. Short, stocky, with calm, cold eyes, well-tended, plump hands, his tunic of half-proletarian and half-military cut buttoned up to the chin, and made of very fine greyish-blue cloth, his trousers thrust into legboots, a thick crop of hair, heavily grizzled and brushed up—only his bushy black eyebrows indicated its original colour. On the whole he gave the impression of a self-satisfied Armenian merchant.

His look, at times calm and controlled, then glinting with cunning and suspicion, then again cold, steely, almost cruel, witnessed to his craftiness but also to his wisdom, and above all to great strength. Whatever may be said about Stalin since Krushchov's revelations, it must not be forgotten that it was not Krushchov or Bulganin, nor Molotov or Malenkov, who made Soviet Russia a power felt by the Germans during the war, and by all the world later. Stalin alone was responsible for that. He achieved it by ruthless, frequently savage methods, but undoubtedly he possessed unusual intelligence, incredible energy, and could make a brilliant analysis of Russian society and of neighbouring and international relations. He was a monster, but he was also a powerful personality, one of the greatest in the list of Russia's despots. His achievement consisted in concentrating and canalizing all the forces of Russian society through the centralized executive rule of the party and the Government, and in creating an enormous administrative machine which withstood the sternest of tests.

He received me with a calm courtesy. Fully aware of the wrong he had done my nation, and of the brutal system which he dominated, I did not feel free in his company, but forced myself to remain calm and self-controlled. During every minute of our conversation I found it necessary to maintain intense vigilance both in order to repel false charges and to put forward irrefutable arguments. This conversation made it clear that every decision depended not on the Politbureau, not on the Party Central Committee, not on the General Staff, not on Molotov or any other Commissar, but on Stalin alone. So I had to try to wrest from him decisions furthering Polish interests, or at any rate to ensure that the situation was not worsened.

There was one moment, after I had mentioned the 'lost' officer prisoners of war, when he resorted to obvious play-acting: he ran to the telephone and called for the 'Narcomvnudiel' in a very loud voice, clearly intent on convincing me, at the other end of the room, that he really was sure they had been set free as the result of the amnesty.

'This is Stalin. Have all the Poles been released? I have the Polish Ambassador with me now, and he tells me they haven't.' Of course I did not hear the answer. When the phone rang again he went to it, listened, and replaced the receiver without saying a word. As he walked slowly back to me he muttered under his breath but so that I could hear it: 'They say they've all been released.'

On a second occasion I had the opportunity to study Stalin for a much longer time and in easier conditions. This was during Sikorski's visits to the Kremlin. On his first visit the conversation lasted two and a half hours, and next day there was a four-hour banquet in the Kremlin, after which there was an informal chat, and a film show, ending with the signing of the Declaration of Friendship on 5 December 1941.

Conversation was freest during the banquet, when Stalin had Sikorski sitting on his right and me on his left hand. Opposite us were several commissars and marshals. Stalin's speeches stood out by contrast with Molotov's banal toasts. Even when he said something offhand, without standing up, dead silence fell at the table, perhaps not so much because everybody wanted to hear what he was saying as because they were afraid of annoying him by talking when he was speaking.

I remember very well his lengthy answer to my question: 'Have you ever been in Poland?' 'Yes,' he said, 'I have, and I well remember my stay.

'A year or so before the first World War the Party ordered me to travel to see Lenin,[1] who was staying in Cracow. It was necessary to obtain his decision in regard to a certain difference of opinion which was causing confusion in the Party. I agreed to go, but I was not at all sure how to make the journey. At that time I was "illegal", I couldn't apply for a foreign passport. I was told to travel to a certain railway station, Dąbrowa Górnicza, and then find some means of smuggling myself across the frontier. I deliberately chose to take a train that arrived at Dąbrowa early in the morning, so as to avoid the gendarmes at the station in the semi-darkness. As soon as the train slowed down I jumped out of the last carriage and, avoiding the station buildings,

[1] For Stalin's contemporary story of this incident, see Isaac Deutscher, *Stalin: A political biography* (O.U.P., 1949, p. 115).

ran through the darkness in a southerly direction, which I had been told was the way to Austria and Cracow. I came to a road which seemed to be going the right way, and hurried along it, though still feeling rather uncertain. I saw a light in a peasant's hut at the road-side. I stole cautiously up to it and through the window saw a cobbler mending boots. I decided to risk it and knocked on the window. The cobbler opened and asked: "Who's there?" Without thinking twice I replied: "A revolutionary." "And what do you want?" I saw his face by the light and felt rather more confident.

'I asked him if he could show me the road to the frontier, because I had to get to Cracow, and had no passport. "I'll take you to the frontier if you're a revolutionary," he answered. I wasn't at all sure that he wouldn't take me to the gendarmes, but what could I do? We went southward, and after an hour's walking the road ran into a forest. Now it was growing light. I still expected the cobbler to hand me over to the gendarmes. But he led me into the forest and, pointing to a track, said: "There's the frontier. I won't go with you any farther. Follow that direction for a good hour, then go westward till you see a railway station, named Trzebinia. There get into a train going to Vienna and you'll arrive at Cracow."

'I wanted to give him several roubles for his trouble, but he wouldn't take them, he couldn't accept anything from a revolutionary. I reached Trzebinia and saw a large restaurant. I was terribly hungry. I ordered some food and sat down at a table. The waiter carted a lot of food around, but he continually gave me a miss, and then I heard a bell. Some of the people got up and ran to a train going westward. I went up to the buffet and said sharply: "This is scandalous; everybody else has been served except me." The waiter filled a plate with soup and handed it to me. Then there was another bell, a train for Cracow arrived and everybody rushed to get in. In my fury I threw the plate on the floor, flung a rouble at the waiter and flew out. I arrived at Cracow. I had a card with Lenin's address on it. The drozhki driver took me to the right number. A few moments later I was with Lenin. We had hardly greeted each other when I burst out:

'"Lenin, give me something to eat at once, for I'm half dead; I've had nothing since yesterday evening." Lenin replied: "Why didn't you eat at Trzebinia; there's a very good restaurant there?" "The Poles wouldn't give me anything to eat." And I told him the whole story. "But what language did you order the food in?" he asked. "Why, in Russian of course. I don't know any other."

' " What a fool you are, Stalin! " All the commissars goggled at Stalin in amazement, as though indignant that anyone could speak so blasphemously. " Don't you know that the Poles think of Russian as the language of their persecutors? " " But how could I order anything when I don't know Polish? " " How? Why, just point to what you wanted and you'd have got it." I remembered that advice, and whenever I went to a shop for cigarettes I pointed and put down my money and always got what I wanted.'

Lenin's remarks served as a peg for Stalin to talk about the persecutions of the Poles under the Tsars. But he tried to treat the issue on a broader basis and said there had been conflicts between Poland and Moscow for centuries. 'Once the Poles occupied Moscow, then the Russians occupied Warsaw.' I broke in: 'The Poles were only a few months in Moscow in the seventeenth century, but the Russians remained in Poland for over a hundred years. Why did you stay with us so long? '

I was struck by the circumstance that in political conversations Stalin had a very clear and sober understanding of the issues; he expressed himself pithily and concisely, frequently in phrases formulated in programmatic terms: obviously the result of many years of party discussion.

As though he already felt sure the western world did not trust the sincerity of Bolshevik assurances Stalin strongly emphasized that the Soviets for their part strictly observed treaties and agreements, and always kept their word. Molotov and Vyshinsky were even more emphatic about this, but, unfortunately, especially so when they had obviously failed to keep their word or had broken an agreement. To facilitate their evasive tactics the Soviet diplomats formulated the texts of agreements with the utmost care, couching particular clauses and phrases in a manner that made it possible for them to place their own one-sided construction on the text.

In their adroitness and equivocation Stalin and Soviet diplomats generally had inherited the diplomatic methods of the Tsars. They were the very methods which the British minister, Giles Fletcher, had noted in the days of Queen Elizabeth I, in his work: *Of the Russian Common Welth or Manner of Government by the Russ. Emperor . . . with the manners and fashions of the people of that country* (London, 1591).

At the same time Soviet diplomacy was outstanding for its very thorough preparation of every question, considering every aspect, and assembling all the sources and texts connected with the question at issue. For instance, I learned that Stalin, who took a special interest in the Polish question, ordered all the Soviet diplomatic posts abroad to collect and send in all kinds of material drawn from conversations, and even from gossip; he himself studied all this material and read every scrap sent from abroad on the subject.

In this respect Stalin stood head and shoulders above the Allies, just as today Soviet diplomacy is superior to Allied diplomacy, in that it has at its disposal a very wide acquaintance with the appropriate material, is carefully briefed as a preliminary to every issue, foresees every eventuality and formulates solutions to meet various contingencies. But above all, it is superior in being always fully aware of its objectives, whereas its opponents have no clear idea of their aims, and do not prepare thoroughly for the discussions.

Consequently, Stalin was able again and again to blackmail the Western Allies with threats, such as that he would conclude a separate peace with Hitler. He also succeeded in putting across various fantastic ideas to the Western Allied Governments; for instance, he managed to persuade even Churchill that there were pro-Hitlerite sympathizers among the Polish Government in London.

My stay in Soviet Russia lasted ten and a half months, from 4 September 1941 to July 1942.

The Soviet Government were not constant in their attitude to Polish issues throughout this period. At times even I did not understand the reasons for their changes of attitude, though each change called for an instant reaction.

The first week of my stay in the U.S.S.R. could well be described as a honeymoon. All the members of the Government were overflowing with goodwill and optimism concerning the general development of Polish-Soviet relations, and the satisfactory settlement of all the Polish Ambassador's desiderata. But after the Beaverbrook conference in Moscow in October 1941, during which the American delegation showed no interest in the Polish case (Harriman justified his passive attitude by saying he had been sent only to support the British delegation) the Soviet Government began to make light of the Polish demands and to reject every intervention I made. Molotov rejected all the demands I had put forward in connection with General Sikorski's proposed visit to the U.S.S.R.

In view of the Soviet Government's reluctance to meet my requests,

I asked Sikorski not to continue his journey from Cairo, and in a sharp note informed them of what I had done. Not wishing to push matters too far, especially as Harriman sent Stalin a telegram in Roosevelt's name hoping for a favourable settlement of Polish affairs, the Soviet side adopted a different tactic. I was summoned urgently to the Kremlin, and on 14 November 1941, in a conversation with me, Stalin promised to withdraw his demand that the Polish Army be reduced in strength, and to accelerate the release of Polish citizens; and he agreed in principle to the Embassy establishing delegatures in districts where the Polish refugees were concentrated.

General Sikorski's visit to Russia in 1941 was the culminating point of friendly Polish-Soviet relations. He was received with great honour, and during his visit a Declaration of Joint Polish-Soviet Friendship was signed by him and Stalin. But after his departure Soviet tactics took two lines. The first was to show warm feeling for the Poles; the radio broadcast reports of Sikorski's visit, his speeches were translated into forty languages, and so on. From then on the various republic and local authorities knew they were to be favourable to Polish requirements, and the Embassy's delegates were to be given every consideration. A loan of 100 million roubles was granted for aid to the Polish people in Russia. Social welfare was extended to Polish war wounded, the aged, sick, etc., and Poles were not compelled to work during Christmas and Easter. The Polish Army was transferred to southern Asia, to areas chosen by General Anders and his chief of staff in agreement with the Soviet staff. The ranks of the armed forces were enlarged by recruitment.

But some weeks later a second tactic began to be applied: especially in regard to the army and military affairs generally. Recruitment was restricted, payments already agreed were held up, petty objections were made to various steps taken by the Polish military authorities, and solemn protests about these steps were made to the Embassy. This culminated in the removal of the Polish armed forces from Russia to Iran, at Stalin's own request, and the harassing and arrest of Polish Embassy delegates in Vladivostok and Archangel, restrictions on Embassy personnel in Kuibishev, and other petty tricks.

My appointment as Ambassador to the U.S.S.R. was terminated on 13 July 1942. Owing to my poor health I had been recalled by a decision of the Polish Government on 22 May 1942, but I postponed my departure for nearly two months in the hope of being able to hand over directly to my successor.

Henryk Sokolnicki, who in pre-war days had been councillor to the Embassy in Moscow and later Minister to Finland, took over the Embassy as chargé d'affaires, and he fought vigorously for the restoration of the delegatures and the welfare of the Polish people until the arrival of Tadeusz Romer, who had been appointed Ambassador. Despite their efforts and their conciliatory tactics, in February 1943 Stalin began to organize Polish military forces dependent solely on the Soviet Government. In March he revealed that a body known as the Association of Patriots had been set up. This organization was destined to act as the future Polish Government, and meanwhile was required to organize an army and to care for the Polish civilians in Russia. Thus something which had been adumbrated as the intention of the Soviet Government even during the negotiations in London in July 1941, but which because of the Agreement with Sikorski had been postponed for nearly eighteen months, now came to pass. Relations between the Soviet Government and the Polish Government in London were only nominal when, arising out of the Katyn Affair, they were formally broken off by the U.S.S.R. in April 1943.

STANISLAW KOT.

London, 1961.

TRANSLATOR'S NOTE

The documents presented in this volume have been selected from two publications in Polish, issued in London. These are:

A. *Listy z Rosji do Gen. Sikorskiego*, edited with a preface by Professor Stanislaw Kot, and published under the imprint of Jutro Polski, 1955. 75 pp. introduction, + 369 pp. of documents, + 122 pp. appendix of supplementary documents and polemical material.

B. *Rozmowy z Kremlem*. Edited with a preface by Professor Stanislaw Kot, issued under the imprint of Jutro Polski, 1959. 30 pp. introduction, + 267 pp. of documents, + 38 pp. of supplementary matter and additional notes.

The main text of the first volume consists of 274 letters, cables, and reports sent by or to Professor Kot as Polish Ambassador to the U.S.S.R. The second volume consists in its main text of 34 precis' of conversations between Professor Kot and various members of the Soviet Government. The volume now presented in English draws upon nearly 60 documents from the first volume, and reproduces all the 'Conversations'. To facilitate reference to the original Polish volumes, in which each document is numbered, every document presented in this English version is prefixed with the number of the original Polish document, the first volume being referred to as A, the second as B.

In order to keep the dimensions of the book within reasonable limits, and in view of the fact that almost all the official agreements and other documents referred to in the text have been published in translation elsewhere, no documents of this nature have been included, much as they would have added to its usefulness.

The selection of documents and excerpts from documents has been made by Professor Kot and the translator jointly. The basis of selection has been to throw light on relations between the two Governments, of Poland and the U.S.S.R., during the months in which Professor Kot was Ambassador to the U.S.S.R. Except in so far as they impinge on these inter-state relations, internal Polish issues have been eliminated. Where excisions have been made from a document, these are indicated in the usual manner. Here and there the translator has thought it helpful to insert a word or a phrase in parenthesis, where the Polish text has been abbreviated. All interpretations not in the original text are enclosed in square brackets. Unsigned footnotes are taken from the original text.

As certain of the documents here published from *Rozmowy z Kremlem* have already appeared in translation in other publications, the translator wishes it to be clearly understood that he alone is responsible for the translations in this volume. It may also be of importance to mention that all the documents published in the main body of the two original Polish publications were printed from copies in the possession of Professor Kot, i.e., his own copies made at the time in the U.S.S.R.

H. C. STEVENS.

A2. Letter to General Sikorski.
Moscow. 5 September 1941

I am sending my first message from Moscow to you, to assure you that you have not made such great efforts and got run down in vain. We can already see great results arising from the deed of 30 July so far as the armed forces are concerned, and the people who are being systematically released bless Poland and you.

I arrived yesterday afternoon, and haven't yet been able to go into anything very thoroughly; but one important question, my relations with General Anders, I regard as settled. They will be of the best, of that you can rest assured. He is a plain and sincere fellow; he himself promised that he would discuss every question with me, and will refer everything to me—possibly I shall have to take more interest in this question[1] than I myself would like. In his views he reflects your mind just as if he had talked with you. . . .

He looks wretched, but declares that he feels well in himself. He impresses everybody. I am told this applies most of all to the [Soviet] people here, among whom he has enormous authority. It looks as if there will be more men for the army than can be used. To rescue the young men he is issuing call-up notices from the age of seventeen and organizing officers' training.

General Anders and I have discussed the question of the Jews: normally they are being taken into the army if they apply, and when I explained to him the importance [of this question] for America, etc., he promised that whenever possible he would emphasize that they were to be treated favourably. . . . Ukrainians are accepted if they themselves apply to join the army as our citizens. . . . Buzuluk, the centre of the army organization, situated between Samara [Kuibishev, Tr.] and Orenburg is well chosen from the future aspect. . . . [Anders] has gathered 20,000 from camps of prisoners of war, and some 10,000 more have already come in, while every day brings or promises yet more. Any man intending to join our forces has freedom of movement, their families have the right to settle close to Orenburg.

Anders will be allowed to join the Allied Conference[2] whenever

[1] i.e. the question of the Polish armed forces. *Tr.*
[2] The Anglo-American-Soviet conference on war resources, held in Moscow October 1941.

I

the needs of the Polish forces are under discussion; there is equipment here for only two divisions; all the rest must be supplied from America. . . . If there—and also among our closest friends—a long view is taken, they should decide this as quickly as possible. . . . Anders is contemplating bringing the strength up to 100,000 under arms. Of course the people must have a rest and time to recover. The officers he has rejected because they had previously volunteered for the Soviet forces do not number more than twenty, among them only one captain.

Yesterday, on the occasion of my arrival the government agreed to Retinger's suggestion to set free all the prisoners in Moscow. . . . In practice this will sometimes be difficult, for the authorities here themselves know very little about the deportees from Poland and in general have no lists. Their agreement to committees[1] will allow this to be done rapidly, but the extraordinary distances are at times an insuperable obstacle. They take a gloomy view of the prospect that the earliest moment aid can arrive from America will be in the new year. Today I shall send a very detailed cable to the Embassy in Washington, indicating what is needed and urging haste. . . .

Among politicians I have so far seen Grabski, Szczyrek, Komarnicki, and Mastek, Szczyrek is taking over the chairmanship of the Welfare Committee. Grabski has aged, but his mind is active and he will be of value in the National Council[2] in dealing with problems of the future.

. . . . Kwapinski has been found among the exiles in Yakutsk. It has not yet been possible to find any others, so far none of the well-known Peasant Party leaders. . . .

> A3. Cable to the Polish Embassy in Washington, and to the Ministry for Foreign Affairs in London.
> Moscow. 5 September 1941

There are about one and a half million Poles in Russian territory. Several hundred centres from Archangel to Tiflis and Sakhalin. Only the swiftest possible mass aid can save them. I ask for the most energetic efforts to organize large shipments of indispensable supplies, in conjunction with American Poles and the American Red Cross. . . .

---

[1] Citizens' committees for care of released prisoners.
[2] The National Council in London, drawn from representatives of all parties, as a substitute for the Polish Parliament. *Tr.*

> *B1. Conversation between Professor Kot, Polish Am-*
> *bassador, and Viacheslav Molotov, Vice-President of*
> *the U.S.S.R. and People's Commissar for Foreign*
> *Affairs.*
> *8 September 1941*

KOT. Never before has a Polish Ambassador presented himself in the Kremlin in such circumstances as these. Our two countries have known many difficult experiences with each other, we have known times of alliance, and even friendship, but only now, for the first time in history, are our forces preparing for the common struggle shoulder to shoulder against the one enemy. This fact is of tremendous importance not only for the present day but also for the future of both our countries. . . . The Polish Government and its head, General Sikorski, have decided that the Poles will go with you into a merciless fight against the Germans, who wish to wipe out the Polish people. We are watching with appreciation the Soviet Government's organizing efforts and the valour of the Russian soldier. General Anders has informed me that his first steps towards the formation of a Polish army are meeting with the goodwill and assistance of the Soviet authorities.

At the present time my nation is in an unbelievably difficult situation: its territory is entirely under enemy occupation. The government is abroad. And yet everybody knows that Poland is an ally of great value to Russia. The name of Poland carries enormous weight. This is due to the heroic, steadfast conduct of the Polish people, who have not shrunk from any sacrifice under the occupation. . . . If the new Hitlerite order is universally hated, it is because it has revealed all its infamy in its treatment of occupied Poland. But the Poles have also won the sympathy of all the world through their sufferings. . . . The side on which the Poles are fighting is regarded as representing morality and justice. The American people especially feel and admit this. And so the conquered Poles are contributing a great fund of fighting and moral strength to the Allied camp. As I have been able to confirm since my arrival here, the Soviet Government is showing goodwill in regard to the agreement with Poland and is fulfilling its promises. That makes our joint co-operation possible. We judge that the difficulties and delays arising from local conditions can be adjusted.

. . . .

MOLOTOV. I am delighted to welcome the representative of the Polish

nation, to welcome the representative of the government led by
General Sikorski, whose readiness to co-operate with us we value very
highly. I am delighted that you, sir, are that representative, for we
know your value well both as a man and as a statesman in Poland.
(KOT: that's exaggeration!) The fact that Poland and Russia will be
acting jointly against Hitlerite Germany will have inestimable significance for both our countries in the future. We are aware of the
suffering and the heroic conduct of the Polish nation. We believe that
the Polish nation will recover its independence. Most profoundly we
believe that despite all the difficulties we shall gain the victory over
Hitler and his hordes. I assure you we shall not shrink before war to
the uttermost. We are ready to co-operate in all sincerity with the
Polish Government. On your arrival, what have been your observations, what have you noticed in regard to the war?

KOT. Already during my short stay I have observed the enormous
energy and authority of the Soviet Government, the first-class valour
of the Russian soldier, and the notable determination of the Russian
people. I am absolutely convinced of victory.

MOLOTOV. What do you think of the way in which our agreement
is beginning to work in practice?

KOT. The formation of a Polish Army is proceeding excellently. As for
the civilians, I confirm that the arrangements made by the Soviet
Government are satisfactory. But there are difficulties in carrying
them out. We realize many of these difficulties, especially as a war is
being fought and there is the problem of communications. None the
less the local authorities, especially those in remote parts, are not
always properly carrying out the instructions of the central authorities.
Every Pole in Soviet Russia, whether a prisoner or a deportee, even in
the most remote corner of Siberia, should feel that the Soviet Government's attitude towards him has changed, that the Polish Government
now has its representative here, and that it is watching over him and
will improve his conditions. I have met newly released prisoners, still
staggering on their feet, who . . . are at one with the Polish Government in its attitude and desire to fight, because they know that
only this struggle against the Germans will ensure an independent, just and democratic Poland. Those incapable of bearing
arms, and also the women, will work, either in war industry
or agriculture. . . . Every Pole wants to aid you in the common
struggle.

MOLOTOV. What is the position in regard to the arming of the Polish army? What aid are Great Britain and America giving in this direction?

KOT. That is a new question to me. When I left London I understood that only equipment was to be supplied from abroad, and that Russia would supply the arms. On my arrival here I learned that this is not possible, and so I am trying by cables to inform and influence [my Government] accordingly.

MOLOTOV. We cannot supply arms, any more than equipment. After all, we are passing through a most terrible war, and suffering enormous losses. We are losing not only masses of soldiers, but masses of arms. We have lost a certain number of factories, while we must transfer others elsewhere, and this will reduce our production capacity. Great Britain and America must realize that we are shedding our blood for them, that we are bearing all the burden of the sacrifice. In exchange for their peace they must provide us with arms.

KOT. Agreed. The Polish Government is already raising this matter with the United States, appealing to the fact that after a conversation with General Sikorski President Roosevelt added Poland to the list of countries entitled to take advantage of Lend-Lease. But we must draw your attention to one point: very strong propaganda must be undertaken in America . . . we must get the [American] Poles moving, for there are five million of them, and we can move them above all by a call to humanitarian aid for the Poles in Russia. To achieve this certain facilities must be granted by your government. . . .

MOLOTOV. None the less armaments are the most urgent necessity of all, and America and Great Britain must supply these both to us and to you. As they are not fighting at present they have the less need of arms.

KOT. Undoubtedly; but so far as America is concerned we must engage in more intensive propaganda. Immediately before my departure from London a representative of the American Poles arrived to warn us that there is still opposition to us in America, even in governmental circles. If anyone thinks that American public opinion is stabilized he is making a mistake. On more than one question they say ' yes ' today but tomorrow they will say ' no ', since public opinion is uncertain and vacillating. . . . We mustn't forget that so far the American people have not had any experience of war.

MOLOTOV. That is so, unfortunately. . . . Please count on me on all questions and I shall gladly help you.

KOT. I want to point out that as I am not a diplomat by profession I have Mr. Sokolnicki as my assistant; he was here for several years [before the war] as councillor of Embassy, and I ask that his work, too, may be facilitated. . . .

The conversation began at 6 p.m. and ended at 7.10 p.m. At first official, it later grew very animated. Kot spoke in French, Molotov in Russian; the secretary translated for both sides. The Ambassador had been prepared only for the ordinary formal call, and so he arranged to have a conversation with Vice-Commissar Vyshinsky the next day.

B2. Private Audience of the President of the U.S.S.R. Supreme Soviet, Michael I. Kalinin.

9 September 1941

After the Ambassador had presented his credentials, Vice-Commissar Vyshinsky being present:

Kalinin expressed his pleasure at the arrival of the Polish Ambassador, welcomed him in the name of the Soviet Government, and expressed the hope that his arrival would initiate a new period of co-operation between the two nations.

KOT: thanked Kalinin for the welcome and emphasized that he fully appreciated the historical importance of this renewal of relations between the two states. The past has known many Polish-Russian agreements and treaties, but never before in history has a Polish army fought shoulder to shoulder with a Russian army against the greatest barbarian known to history. Everybody today recognizes and marvels at the heroism and valour of the Soviet army.

KALININ. The enemy is not only unprecedented and barbarian, he is also very strong. He has got to be fought with his own weapon, which is force. The Ambassador has referred to the valour of the Soviet soldiers. One can say of them, though only briefly, that they are fighting, and fighting well. The enemy is powerful, but the Soviet soldier is learning the methods of struggle from him and is inflicting blows on him with his own methods.

As for the past, the President wishes to speak frankly, because he is a simple man and not a diplomat. He has a great appreciation of the Polish people, the workers, peasants, and intelligentsia. If the once Polish town of Królowiec later became Königsberg, the Poles were not entirely blameless. The government circles in Poland proved deceitful. Coming to more recent times, some five or six years ago, in this very room I told Beck: 'A Polish-German understanding is impossible. The Germans have only one aim: to make the Poles their stable-boys.' When I said that Litvinov's eyes nearly dropped out of his head. . . .

кот. The political orientation adopted by the present Polish Government never did have and has not now anything in common with the policy of co-operation with the Germans. I myself belong to a group which did not cease for one moment to condemn and combat the policy of an understanding with Hitler. That group always resolutely opposed Beck's policy. . . . For that matter all Polish public opinion, following the voice of its deepest national instincts, was opposed to co-operation with Hitler. . . . I would like it to be understood in the Soviets that the policy of General Sikorski's Government is a completely new one, and it is not calculated for a short term. The understanding with the U.S.S.R. and the struggle against the common enemy, which undoubtedly will be crowned with victory, will not be the end of Polish-Soviet co-operation. It is the determination of the Polish Government that that co-operation should be solid and enduring. Hitler is a great teacher: he has taught both us and you a good deal. The terrible lesson which the catastrophe of September 1939 constitutes for the Polish nation will not go in vain. The result of German arrogance, of the transportations and the destruction of the Polish nation will be that Königsberg will once more become Królowiec.

KALININ. I have no doubt of the heroism of the Poles and their endurance in the struggle against the enemy, but Hitlerite Germany is a power against which heroism alone is not sufficient, one needs also to know how to fight it. I hope the Polish divisions in the U.S.S.R., which, it appears, are not being organized swiftly enough, will be able at the front to demonstrate that they have learnt to fight not only heroically but intelligently. I am delighted to hear what you say concerning the new Polish policy, I am delighted that the Polish people have poured into the great Slavonic sea, since the danger is common to all. The Germans regard both Poles and Russians as a racially lower element, they want to turn all the Slavs into their stable-boys. . . . I want the Polish intelligentsia to understand well the difference between the attitude of the Russians and the Germans to the Polish people. . . .

кот. Thank you for your frankness. I, too, am not a professional diplomat, and so I want to, and I will, speak openly and freely. If Poland did not go hand in hand with Russia, that was the fault of

Tsarist policy. The policy initiated by the present Polish Government is not concerned with looking backward. There is no intention to recall the wrongs suffered, but to look to the future. But as there is talk of the past, I cannot forget that the Polish nation was in an exceptional difficult situation. The choice between German and Tsarist Russian domination was difficult, for it is difficult to decide whether to go with the devil or Satan. . . .

Present-day Poland and its government are also advocating close co-operation among the Slavonic nations. The best proof of this is the project for a federation of Poland and Czechoslovakia, which is being advanced as one of the basic Polish desiderata. The Polish nation will never renounce its national individuality, its complete independence and the State's independent activity. We know that post-war Europe will not resemble the Europe of 1939. After this terrible war there must and will be a complete reconstruction of Europe; we wish, together with the U.S.S.R., to take our appropriate part in that work, we wish to aim at such a reconstruction of the structure of Europe as will free our continent once for all from the danger of a new war, and make it impossible in the future.

As for our army now being organized in the U.S.S.R., I want to emphasize that the spirit of the men who will make that army is magnificent. When they emerge from the prisons and camps, emaciated, undernourished, sometimes still staggering on their feet, they have only one thought: to get arms into their hands and to take part in the fight against the German invader as quickly as possible. Obviously, after their terrible experiences they must recover their strength. They must . . . receive the appropriate equipment and outfit. Therefore the speed at which our army is formed depends also on the Soviet authorities. I ask you, Mr. President, to act as patron to our joint co-operation.

. . . President Kalinin, an old revolutionary, plays no political role, and so the conversation with him was of a rather formal nature, to observe protocol. The Ambassador, who replied to every point the President made concerning Poles, did so chiefly in view of the presence of Vyshinsky.

The audience began at 1.40 p.m.

B3. Conversation with Andrei J. Vyshinsky, Vice-Commissar for Foreign Affairs.
10 September 1941

кот. Sir, I am the representative of General Sikorski's government, which has resolved to co-operate with the Soviet Government to ensure victory over the Germans despite our many traditional conflicts. The Polish nation today is in a particularly difficult situation, since its territory is occupied by the Germans, and the government is abroad. None the less, as an ally it represents a great force. The Germans themselves know well that in Poland it is not they who govern the souls of the people, but General Sikorski. The entire nation, organized militarily and civilly, is only waiting for the moment when it can settle accounts with the invader . . .

But in the international field also Poland possesses enormous influence and authority. A number of bourgeois societies who take a distrustful view of the Soviet system are adjusting their sympathies in the light of Poland's attitude to the Soviets. . . . Poland's presence in the Allied camp is of far reaching importance to the entire Catholic world. If the Vatican, despite all the pressure of the Germans as well as the Italians and certain cardinals, has not allowed itself to be drawn into the anti-Soviet crusade which the Axis powers have proclaimed, this is partly due to the influence of the Order of Jesuits, which is headed by a Pole, Father Ledochowski, whose opinion is valued by the Pope and many prominent Catholics. Wherever Jesuits are to be found they are combating Hitlerite influences; for instance, in Spain they are restraining tendencies towards military action on the side of the Axis.

Poland's agreement with Russia has exerted a powerful influence on her friends, and it has influenced the formation of their own attitude to Russia. So far as America is concerned, we have five million Poles there (Vyshinsky: I thought it was seven millions). Truly, counting all those of Polish origin though Americanized, the figure is seven millions; but I am thinking of those who are active in defence of the Polish aims. But native Americans also are sympathetic to the Polish cause. The United States would like to be considered as a kind of protector of Poland. For it was Wilson who demanded her independence; later American governments readily and unreservedly recognized the Polish territory and frontiers, Paderewski is buried in the American National cemetery, President Roosevelt in General Sikorski's presence foretold the great role to be played by Poland in

the organization of Europe; the Americans are showing their gratitude, so to speak, for Pulaski and Kosciuszko. The Polish-Russian
agreement has had a very strong influence on American opinion in
regard to Russia, and the further course of Polish-Russian friendship
will undoubtedly greatly influence the extent of United States aid in
arms, etc. . . .

Wherever Poles are scattered, they are serving the national programme, and everywhere they are at the disposition of the government. . . . But the Polish Government's propaganda activities can
develop only in an atmosphere of confidence. Poles everywhere must
learn that their fellow-countrymen in Russia have been transformed
from prisoners and deportees into free citizens, that where previously
things were bad, now they are good.

So far as the Polish armed forces are concerned, co-operation with
the Soviet government is developing in the best possible way. . . . I
did not wish to reply yesterday to President Kalinin's doubts about
the slow rate of organization of the army. After all, it was only the day
before yesterday that the first transport arrived at the concentration
centre. Troops cannot be shaken out of one's sleeve. At the present
time I am chiefly concerned with arranging fundamentals, with improving the existence of the mass of Polish civilians. . . . Every
Polish citizen in the most remote corner of Asia must be convinced
that the Polish Government's protecting arm will reach him. In this
direction I ask for effective assistance.

I have to notify you that today I have decided to set up a Polish
Welfare Committee with the well-known workers' leader, Jan Szczyrek, at its head, and with regional and local committees, and men of
trust wherever there are less than fifty Polish families. The Committee's task will be care in the strict sense of the word, it will ascertain
the needs and distribute assistance. . . . In this connection I ask
you, sir, what is the Soviet Government's attitude to the question of
supplying material resources for meeting the needs of the Polish
citizens? . . . .

Next, we must decide in which districts to concentrate the civilian
population, taking into account climatic conditions, the possibility of
providing work for the healthy, maintenance for those incapable of
work, and the satisfaction of medical and educational needs. Embassy
delegates will be visiting these concentrations of Polish people; as
these visits must be carried out speedily, I am asking for aeroplanes.

For the representatives of the local committees I ask for travelling facilities, and in particular for free railway tickets.

The Soviet Government has issued an order that the Polish citizens are to be provided with Polish documents within three months; but it is impossible for them to travel to Moscow to get these, so I wish to organize provisional passport-consular posts, which will have the task of investigating and confirming their Polish citizenship, providing them with provisional passports, and controlling the activities of the Welfare Committees. These will be a kind of consular post, which obviously will be closed down when the Polish population is removed from the given area.

To undertake certain welfare activities the Polish Red Cross will be brought into action, but as it is poor we must obtain the co-operation of the American and possibly the British Red Cross. Supplies from the American Red Cross will be augmented by the collections of the American Poles, for which a spacious warehouse is already waiting in New York. As the Soviet Government has not so far allowed the American Red Cross to enter the country I raise this issue definitely and ask for an assurance that the Soviet authorities here will authorize the aid of the American Red Cross, will free its gifts from customs duties and ensure them free transport, as well as for the gifts of the American Poles. . . .

In addition, turning to another sphere, the Poles must have their own newspaper, which could also be sent to Poland. What an impression it will make all over the world, and especially in occupied Poland, when it is known that . . . in Moscow itself a free Polish newspaper is being issued, which can be dropped to the Polish people living under the occupation. . . . We also wish to issue some brochures which are needed to inform the Polish people here and to shape their attitude, above all an informative brochure explaining what has been happening to the Polish cause, the Polish Government and Army in the West during the past two years. I would also like to issue a Black Book in Russian and Polish, under the Polish Government imprint, dealing with the German administration of Poland.

We must have freedom to speak on the radio both to Poles in Russia and to Poles at home, we must broadcast General Sikorski's speeches. I shall speak, and also prominent Polish citizens in the U.S.S.R. as they turn up here. The auditions so far arranged in Moscow are of no use to the Polish people here, it is a pity to waste time on them, since they reveal ignorance of Polish psychology (Vyshinsky assents). Our auditions will have a great effect in Poland. This would also help us to seek out our kinsmen and to pass on information. At this moment we haven't the forces available for carrying out a more extensive programme, but I would like to have a short period on the air at my disposal quickly. The same applies to the newspaper; we haven't adequate resources as yet, but technical preparations, in regard to printery, Polish printers, and paper, need to be started at once.

Two other requests relate to a different important sphere. In connection with the release from Moscow prisons of Poles who at present are being accommodated in luxury hotels, and in the hope that Polish citizens will be arriving from the provinces, I ask for a separate, modest but large hotel to be set aside for them, with a large number of beds and a common kitchen. That will be cheaper than the present arrangement, and more sensible too. The sudden jump from prison to luxury is rather a shock, and if people were to arrive from the provinces to magnificent hotels, and then return to primitive provincial conditions they might feel bitter. The Polish soldiers who come to Moscow would also be accommodated in this hotel.

Second question: The Embassy Consular department in Moscow has been occupying a separate building furnished with furniture which is the property of the Polish State. However, it is a long way from the Embassy. We must have a second large house close to the Embassy for an office, and especially for the Welfare Committee. I know from the military authorities that owing to evacuation there are many empty houses in Moscow, so I ask for our consular building to be exchanged for another, furnished. I must apologize for raising so many practical questions, but it is of great importance to us today to have them settled; others will be regulated by the Mixed Commission.[1] . . .

VYSHINSKY. In reply to your points, with the salient features of which I wholly agree, I wish to emphasize that, forgetting the past, we shall work jointly, in the most friendly relations possible, since our common aim is victory over the Germans; and without that victory, which must be decisive and final, it will not be possible for our two

---

[1] The Mixed Commission, brought into being on the Embassy's initiative, consisted of Novikov as representative of the Narcomindiel, one commissar from the Narcomvnudiel, and two representatives of the Polish Embassy, one of them from the Welfare Department. At its first meeting, on 9 September, the Polish side put forward desiderata which were submitted to joint discussion; but the Soviet replies were vague, and did not go beyond what Commissar Vyshinsky had already said. The Commission stopped meeting, and even petty questions had to be handled through the normal diplomatic channels.

nations to develop in peace. I subscribe to your proposition that for the sake of our common interests we initiate sincere and friendly co-operation on new bases. So far as the problem of organizing the life of Polish citizens on U.S.S.R. territory is concerned, I ask you to count on the goodwill of the Soviet Government. None the less we must take into account the enormous difficulties which confront us, since, both because of the size of the U.S.S.R., and the communications difficulties arising out of the war, these problems will require a great deal of labour. In the name of the Ministry[1] for Foreign Affairs I assure you we shall resolve those problems as swiftly as possible and with full co-operation. On the matter of care for Polish citizens, we have sent you a list of candidates for men of trust, in the sense of Mr. Retinger's note,[2] in various centres, from which you can select your delegates. I shall refer the question of a Polish Welfare Committee to the Soviet Government, but I am afraid this will lead to duplication in the work of the Embassy's delegates and the Committee's representatives; in war-time the election of committees may be undesirable, nor would we wish to revive certain unfortunate experiences of the first world war. However, we shall go entirely hand in hand with you and shall afford every facility to the delegates appointed by you. So far as we are concerned the Committee need not exist, Mr. Szczyrek and others can be appointed Embassy delegates, we wish to have to deal only with the Embassy.

KOT. I am anxious to have the Committee, since it is a question of facilitating the distribution of food and all kinds of aid in a non-bureaucratic manner, in accordance with the wishes of the interested persons themselves. It will be carried on best of all by persons knowing local needs and enjoying the confidence of the citizens. . . . The committees will occupy themselves exclusively with welfare questions, and will be controlled by the Embassy's delegates.

VYSHINSKY. I propose that after I have referred this question to my government it should be discussed by the mixed Polish-Soviet Commission.

KOT. I agree.

VYSHINSKY. As for the Red Cross entering the U.S.S.R., I have to say that the Soviet Government is in negotiation with the American Red Cross for the supply to our army of all kinds of aid, and we are shortly

---

[1] As in the Polish text. Presumably a slip on the part of the note-taker. *Tr.*
[2] Dr. Retinger had been acting as Chargé d'affaires for three weeks while awaiting Professor Kot's arrival as Ambassador.

expecting transports; aid from the American Red Cross to Poles will be accommodated within this framework, and if the American Poles add anything further we have nothing against it. Supplies sent by the Red Cross are free of duties here, and the question of transport and charges will be settled as a whole, following on the decision as to Red Cross activity on Soviet territory.

KOT. I take it that any possible contributions made by the American Red Cross for Poles . . . will be handed over in their entirety to the Polish Committees, although transported together with those destined for the U.S.S.R. I must remark, however, that from the propaganda aspect it is very important that American Poles should participate in this activity, openly and publicly, and even with some resort to publicity. So . . . it is important to ensure that their delegates may travel . . . to the three main distribution points for example, so that they may witness the distribution and inform the American people about it.

VYSHINSKY. That can be arranged, within strictly defined limits. As for newspapers, propaganda publications and the radio, I suggest you have a conversation with the head of our Press Department, Mr. Lozovsky. During the report which I made on this subject to Stalin as Chairman of the Council of Ministers [sic], he gave instructions that the wishes of the Polish Embassy in regard to starting a Polish newspaper were to be met. Mr. Lozovsky will provide the technical assistance. On the question of an hotel for Polish citizens I entirely share your viewpoint and we shall consider the matter favourably. As for the question of a building, we shall meet your wishes completely and Director Novikov will deal with it.

KOT. I would not wish to abuse the diplomatic bag by using it for private letters, but I consider it very necessary that the Poles in the U.S.S.R. should know that they can write to their families in Great Britain, America, and elsewhere. Letters sent to the embassy would, of course, be carefully censored here and forwarded to their destinations. Could the radio be used to inform Poles that they are to send their letters to the embassy?

VYSHINSKY. It would be better not to make a public announcement, for then other embassies would want to demand the same for themselves. We shall not interfere with what you do with your citizens' letters.

KOT. Thank you; we shall inform Poles confidentially through the committees. Finally, sir, I ask you kindly to indicate whom I should approach concerning certain Polish citizens who are of particular interest to us, and who so far have not been found. There are many such. Of members of my own Party, the Peasant Party, so far not one has turned up. . . . I know for certain they are here somewhere. The Jews are asking the same about several of their prominent members, and so far it has been impossible to obtain any information concerning them.

VYSHINSKY. We shall occupy ourselves with these questions, and if you will indicate the persons in whom you are interested we shall settle the matter as favourably and swiftly as possible.

KOT. Great affairs are decided by great gestures. If we begin discussing small details too long we shall not have time for the great affairs. I would like to talk with you not only officially but privately, so I ask you to accept my invitation to call on me.

VYSHINSKY. I am very glad to have your invitation. I shall always be pleased to talk with you unofficially, but in this office too we can talk frankly, openly, and unofficially always, removing the diplomatic mask, co-operating in friendship for the good of our two countries.

During the conversation, which lasted from 12.30 to 2.30, Vyshinsky took detailed notes of all the Ambassador's desiderata, not waiting for their translation into Russian: he obviously knew Polish. He is a typical Polish nobleman in features, fair-haired, short and stocky, about fifty. In his replies he ignored certain points. . . . Besides Vyshinsky, Novikov, the director of the Narcomindiel IVth Department (Poland and the Balkan States), also took notes all through the conversation; he did not make a friendly impression. . . .

A5/6. To General Sikorski.
10 September 1941

I have already had my first conversations; I shall include reports on these when they are of prime importance. They are giving me a very friendly reception, and at present I am praising the way they are keeping their promises; but any day now we may come to sharper conversations. They admit to my officials that there are 38,000 prisoners to be released, and they calculate the number of deportees as not quite 400,000. We must have rather more frank discussion as to why they reckon the remainder, as it would appear, as Soviet citizens; there will be a scene over this—for it is obvious that they at once accept military personnel as Polish. I still don't know how to take their emphatic insistence on speed in the creation of our army, whether it is out of fear at the Germans' swift advance, or whether they're concerned with their own skins, because they hear that we prefer them to any other form of government—which for that matter even their bitterest enemies among our own people admit.[1]

I have appointed Szczyrek chairman of the Polish Welfare Committee and am transferring all the welfare work to civilians. They are setting up local, regional, and other committees. To tell the truth, here in the centre we are still very short of responsible people; those released are too weak, or to select them would be one-sided. . . .

There was only a handful of prisoners, less than forty, left in Moscow, for they had already been dispersed to other prisons. . . . Cables are arriving from Asia, but so far not from any of the well-known people we are seeking. Evidently they cannot yet respond.

We are discussing with General Anders the great problem of communications with the Homeland and other occupied countries.[2] The local people [i.e. Soviet authorities. *Tr.*] are extraordinarily interested in this and I expect to obtain much in return for these services. Of course, we emphasize that any agreement must be with you. But you must reckon with the fact that in certain regards their pressure is justified, and we cannot ignore it; this refers to military reconnaissance and certain urgent diversionary activities, for instance oil in Rumania, so they urge that the Poles in Rumania shall aid their agents; aid and protection in Boryslaw,[3] etc. . . . When tomorrow we establish our radio contact with London—the Soviet people are to put up the antennæ, to provide what we lack, and are handing over our wireless telegraphists to us some time today—you will receive many proposals for approval. . . . I ask you to emphasize that I have

---

[1] The opinion was being expressed that if the Soviet Government broke down pro-German Russian elements would come to the forefront. In the conditions of the time the Bolsheviks provided a greater guarantee of resistance to Hitler than any other government.

[2] General Zhukov of the Narcomvnudiel was negotiating with Anders for co-operation with the Soviets' underground activities in various parts of German-occupied Europe, inter alia, by helping the individuals the Soviet authorities were parachuting into these areas. It was in the Polish interest to ensure that agreements and decisions on this question were achieved with the Polish Government in London, and that supervision of the corresponding steps in Russia was in the hands of the embassy as that government's representative.

The initiating and directing of non-military activities and preparations, such as the concentration of personnel, information, and the propaganda of the Polish underground organization on the European continent belonged, by a decision of the Polish Government and agreement with the British Ministry for Economic Warfare, to the Polish Ministry for Internal Affairs in London, working through a special department.

[3] The Polish Oilfield in Eastern Galicia. *Tr.*

authority here over all anti-German activities in Poland and else-where. . . . I shall be able to fight for political concessions in return for every military service we render. . . . The Soviet people admit that there are many things they are ignorant of, that their espionage contacts are ruined—Rumania, Spain—they are ready to reveal their agents to us, and even to remove them if we demand it. . . .

A6. To General Sikorski (continued).
10 September, evening

I have now had a conversation with Vyshinsky. I took care to ensure that the beginning was warm, we have time in which to quarrel. Nor do I want to rely on incomplete information. Yesterday it was confirmed that people from the Eastern Borders[1] are not being released although all are joining the army regardless, while today the Cracow socialist Szumski arrived here from Sverdlovsk—he says you're worshipped by the Poles in Siberia—and is amazed that you may have difficulties with the emigrés. He says he has even met released Ukrainians. . . .

Some moving details are arriving from the army. In one camp of 12,000 soldiers fifty officers with a chaplain have been concealed right till now, and no one betrayed them—the Soviets can't believe it. The peasants behaved best of all. . . .

A7 To the Minister for Internal Affairs, S. Mikołajczyk.
Moscow. 10 September 1941

. . . How things are going perhaps the Premier will inform you from the letter I am writing him in my own hand—for we have only one typewriter so far—and from the enclosures.

Almost everybody we meet here—only a few dozen people were being held in prison in Moscow recently, and almost all have been released—and who arrive from the east in response to our summons, cannot find words to express their appreciation and gratitude for the Agreement. Today S[zumski] arrived from Sverdlovsk, and he says the Poles in Siberia worship Sikorski. He was quite amazed when someone here mentioned critics of the pact in England.

The organization of the army is proceeding with extraordinary rapidity, although it will take some time to restore the men to strength; but the enthusiasm is beyond words. Of course they have no

---

[1] The territories lying roughly east of the River Bug, ceded to Poland by the Riga Treaty of March 1921. *Tr.*

equipment until some arrives from England, and things are bad in regard to armaments. Today we were notified that not two but only one division will be able to receive arms from the Soviets, so it becomes all the more necessary to urge America to recognize the need for armaments. Two divisions—here a division is reckoned at about 12,000 men—are being formed between the Volga and the Urals.

. . . So far it has not been possible to find any of our people.[1] I shall take the most energetic steps. . . . There is very good news concerning the behaviour of the peasants, both from the forests of Siberia and from the farms around Vologda, and of their conduct in the prisoner of war camps; everywhere they are displaying unusual strength of character and integrity. They are convinced that Providence brought about their deportation to the East in order to save them from the German-Ukrainian fury.

. . . .

A9. Letter to General Sikorski.
15 September 1941 Evening

. . . .

Anders has left for the army camp, so the whole question of work in Poland must wait till his return. He is conducting consultations on this, very discreetly, but the people here are naïvely cunning and think they can get along without us. They are constantly training parachutists, some of them reliable, who should be used at once . . . others completely suspect, they will either go into hiding or work for the enemy. Unfortunately, I cannot so far get access to the authorities who are sending them. . . . They still try to bind released prisoners to report to them [anyone] ' who is against the Pact,' and so on. Apart from a few scoundrels the majority report this to us, thus exposing themselves to danger.

There is a dead silence on the war—we listen to the foreign radio. Things are bad with Leningrad, but they say they still have access to the railway line running eastward, and on the other side to the sea; but they do not deny the danger. Judging from the way they insisted on arms from America, I understand that things are very bad. Yet I think it certain that the government and the organization will withstand everything. . . .

There are two leaders of the Bund, too emaciated for us to show

---

[1] Both Kot and Mikołajczyk were members of the Peasant Party. *Tr.*

them,[1] highly intelligent, I want to employ them for the time being, until Schorr turns up. It is strange how they're hiding the Jews and politicians somewhere. We cannot discover any Peasant Party men. News is coming in that the bulk of our prisoners, judges, priests and officers—there are 1,300 but there ought to be about 7,000—were carried off to camps in the Polar circle—at Piechora—and to the Primoria region of Siberia [Vladivostok area. *Tr.*] to which access was frozen as early as August. . . .

Work is boiling in the Embassy, but when the number of letters in today's post exceeds one thousand what can one do? We are looking for candidates for delegates and above all for secretaries in the Welfare office; I have sent a request to Anders to lend me twenty people to deal with this flood of letters, as well as several for delegates. . . .

A10. To the Military Attaché to the Polish Embassy in Turkey.
16 September 1941

I take the opportunity to communicate some very confidential and urgent information to you.

The organization of our army in Russia is going forward. There are very many volunteers, great enthusiasm, perfect spirit. General Anders enjoys extraordinarily high authority both among the troops and with the Soviet authorities. The area in which the army is being organized is the Czkalov region, with headquarters at Buzuluk; the assembly point for those coming to join the army is Totskoe, near Buzuluk. There are still great organizational difficulties, communications and climatic conditions have to be overcome first and foremost, and this means that it will be impossible to draw in a considerable proportion of those capable of service before the winter. The Soviet Government is taking a favourable attitude to affairs connected with the organization of the Polish army. . . .

For the time being two divisions are anticipated, with Generals Boruta-Spiechowicz and Karasiewicz-Tokarzewski at their head; at a later stage a third with General Szyszko-Bohusz. . . .

But now a matter of great importance. The Soviet people would like

---

[1] When Henryk Ehrlich and Wiktor Alter were released from prison it was planned to send them to Great Britain and the U.S.A. to organize an international Jewish Anti-Fascist Committee there. But they emerged from prison in such a wretched state that it was highly unlikely that the Narcomvnudiel would give permission for them to leave the country. Moses Schorr, a professor of Warsaw University, was intended to be the Embassy referee on Jewish affairs. Professor Schorr was never found. *Tr.*

to develop a broad diversionary activity in our occupied country, and have already begun vigorous attempts on their own account. . . . Their lack of success, or relatively small results . . . will undoubtedly open their eyes to the nonsensical nature of these attempts and will lead to activities carried on exclusively by Polish elements.

Of course, communication to them of the most urgent information as well as [the undertaking of] certain pressing activities will have to be carried out directly from here, and that not only in regard to Poland but in certain other areas. . . .

B4. Conversation with Dekanozov, Vice-Commissar for Foreign Affairs.
16 September 1941

. . . . Kot tells of the perfect liaison with Poland which the Polish Government has had first in France, and now in London. For instance, we have received information not yet published anywhere concerning the burning down of the German district of Warsaw, the district from which the Polish population has been evicted. We have not yet made contact with Poland from Moscow.

Dekanozov asks how the people in Poland have received the Polish-Soviet Agreement.

Kot tells of the favourable reaction of the National Committee, consisting of representatives of all the former parties, from left to right. The Government Delegate in Warsaw has sent the government this information.

DEKANOZOV. Which is the strongest party in Poland? Is it the socialists, as I have heard?

KOT. As a member of the Peasant Party, which considers itself the strongest, I cannot confirm that. It is true that in the towns and industrial areas the socialists occupy the leading place, but seventy per cent of the population are peasants. Today the two parties are working hand in hand.

Dekanozov asks whether the Ambassador is Minister for Internal Affairs.

KOT. I was until recently. For our Government in London internal affairs means liaison with our mother country. I am still a member of the Government, but Mikołajczyk, a member of my party, has become Minister for Internal Affairs. General Sikorski's government was anxious that someone should come to Moscow who is working in close co-operation with the General, knows his mind, and can represent his position even if all connections were to be broken. I shall be in contact with Poland from here, but I am no longer director of liaison.

Dekanozov expresses his satisfaction that General Sikorski's government has sent to Moscow an Ambassador so close to it and in its confidence. Polish questions come within the competence of Vyshinsky and Novikov. Is the Ambassador satisfied at the way things are going?

KOT. The military side is going well, but so far as the Polish civilians are concerned there are many deficiencies. There is a lack of drive in settling questions, and now winter is coming on and there are a number of localities, such as the Primoria and Piechora districts, where help is needed at once, because later on it will not reach them. That is of great importance to the people of Poland. It has nothing to do with military successes or failures, for them the decisive question is the Soviet attitude to the deported people. In this regard the U.S.S.R. Government's conduct should be wise and swift.

Dekanozov interjects that military success is always of importance. He asks about the German plans and their attitude to the Poles.

KOT. Since the beginning of the Soviet-German war the situation in the so-called *General-Gouvernement* has begun to improve a little. Mass arrests and street round-ups are no longer occurring. But terror has begun in the eastern part of Poland. The Germans have officially incorporated Eastern Malopolska in the *General-Gouvernement* in order to win over Polish opinion. On the outbreak of the German-Soviet war they even issued a manifesto to the Polish population, but all these attempts have met with no success whatever. The Poles have suffered seriously from Soviet persecution; now the Soviet government's policy must be wise and swift in regard to the arrested and deported Poles.

DEKANOZOV. Are the Germans attempting to form a Polish government?

KOT. The Germans have tried to enter into relations with the Poles. At present it is being said in Madrid and Lisbon that there will be a change in their attitude to us. Poland, they are saying, must lose a little in the west, but first of all General Sikorski's government must resign. They are making proposals through Italy and Hungary.

Dekanozov asks why through Hungary, and who is acting as intermediary for them.

KOT. Without doubt they have turned to Hungary because of our

Polish-Hungarian friendship. It is being undertaken by one of the Hungarian parties which passes as anti-German. . . .

> B5. *Conversation with the Vice-Commissar for Foreign Affairs. Salomon Lozovsky.*
> *17 September 1941*

Kot congratulates Lozovsky on beating Goebbels in propaganda.

Lozovsky says the success of Soviet propaganda is due to their telling the truth. He is ready to help and co-operate with us. He values highly Poland's propaganda value, because there are Poles all over the world.

кот. Even in Denmark there is a considerable Polish element at present, and it consists not only of agricultural workers but teachers and other members of the intelligentsia.

In the U.S.S.R. there are a great number of Poles who because of their recent experiences must be unfavourably disposed towards the Soviets. They have got to be turned into friends, they must be informed, and the process of changing their outlook must be accelerated. At present Poland is a very important area, there is not only a concentration of German military forces in our country, but also various kinds of industry have been transferred there because of the bombing of western Germany, new factories have been built, and so on. The workers in Poland have asked us in London what they are to do : they are ready for sacrifices. Today the situation is clear : we are allies. But it is necessary to have a plan, to inform, etc. There are many ways of carrying on activity : 1. through the Polish element wherever it is to be found; 2. with the help of other resources : (*a*) through the radio. . . . Several weeks have already been lost, because you here prefer a slower method. A programme of activity must be drawn up, in general outline to begin with. (*b*) Through the press. This affords the possibility of Poles influencing Poles. We have a million and a half of Polish people here. This figure may be increased still further. It isn't difficult to turn them into an active element. All the pain Russia has inflicted on them must be got out of them. The Poles are ready to do anything. . . . We must have a Polish newspaper. . . . I have already spoken to Mr. Vyshinsky about this, and he has agreed and said that the question is to be discussed with you, so far as the site, paper, etc are concerned. So now we ask for permission, for initiative, for machinery, etc. Now we must raise the matter of the Soviet press. It is maintaining a strange silence. Everything must be done to introduce a certain warmth, through the radio, in articles, in the speeches of well-known persons, etc. There may have been good reasons for silence at one time. On our side we have writers who will write.

Lozovsky asks their names.

кот. I am accrediting Mr. Jan Tabaczynski on organizational matters, and Mr. Ksawery Pruszynski on the question of articles and subjects.

It is necessary to take further action (c) by publishing brochures for Poles. To inform them of the deeds of our airmen, sailors, etc. We would like to publish in Russia a Polish Black Book telling of the German persecutions and terror in Poland. We have information and written materials concerning German economic questions. These materials should be used as a weapon in the struggle both in the Polish and in the Soviet press. The brochures and newspaper etc. issued here should also be transported to Poland. That would make a great impression. Of course, it will cost money.

Finally we must work (d) through information sent to America and England. I must ask you to name the office through which correspondents can send information abroad.

At present I am receiving about one thousand letters every day from Poles scattered about the U.S.S.R. I cannot answer them all. Here the radio can help. Especially in the distant provinces, which are not reached by newspapers. There is a chaotic movement of Polish people going on, and it must be stopped. Through the radio we should also give a picture of the present reality, should tell how the Polish Government came into being, etc. I ask for your suggestions in regard to details of the various points I have raised.

lozovsky. I would like to reply to twelve points which I have noted down. . . . The Poles and the Russians both know how to make propaganda. . . . Propaganda must not be too general. It must penetrate to all strata and should have a different approach to each group. The object is to defeat the Germans. All the forces of both States must be organized. . . . The Poles have many possibilities which history has created. . . . They are in America, in various countries of the East and the Near East. They can carry out work which will help the Allies. After all, we are allies. For the liberation of your country and mine. There are problems which affect you equally with us. We shall begin with the practical problems. But first they must be formulated. As for the radio, on the 18th at 5 a.m. General Sikorski is to speak. His speech will be transmitted on all the Soviet wavelengths. I think that from our [Soviet] side there should be talks once or twice a week. We must decide which days and for how many minutes. The broadcasts will have significance for those abroad as well as for those here [in Russia]. As for a newspaper, we shall help, but there are difficulties. We must start with a weekly. There is the problem of distribution, of paper, of circulation.

KOT. We must aim at its reaching the broad masses.

LOZOVSKY. I think it should begin with a small issue, and then we shall see.

KOT. Can it be transported by aeroplanes?

LOZOVSKY. I doubt it, but there are communications, and facilities will be provided.

KOT. I think the size of the issue depends on the communications. Better a smaller issue, but it must be dispatched without delay after publication.

LOZOVSKY. I don't think that is so important, because it will be a weekly. Practice will show best of all. . . . *Pravda* has now been reduced from six pages to four. Let us keep to the practical side and we shall certainly agree.

As for the Soviet press, I have spoken on Poland at press conferences. The greatest difficulty is that we haven't got the documentary material.

Kot promises to send it to him.

LOZOVSKY. I am glad I shall get documentary material from London. We'll put a Bureau of Documentation to work, also great writers. We shall make films, etc., from it. Documentation plays an enormous role; for instance, recently there was a meeting of Slavs in order to unmask German policy. Januszajtis and Wasilewska spoke.

KOT. Our press reported only Januszajtis' speech.

LOZOVSKY. That meeting revealed a serious lack of documentation. During this talk I have become convinced that there are many things I haven't heard of. For instance, the transfer of factories to Poland as the result of the bombing of Germany.

KOT. That has its military aspect too. In the district from which I come, between Przemyśl and Cracow, to be exact between Dębica and Kolbuszowa, villages have been demolished in order to build certain works with underground aerodromes and underground communication with the COP.[1]

LOZOVSKY. Turning to Polish journalists, please let me have a list.

[1] Central Industrial Region. *Tr.*

They should make contact with the Press Department, of which Mr. Palunov is head, and articles and cables sent abroad should pass through the censorship of that department. As for a Black Book, it should be published as quickly as possible. It is important to show all the evil the Germans have done. It must be printed in a large edition for abroad and for our country. It's all a question of paper. . . .

KOT. It must be printed here. We already possess many of the texts. I shall cable London for more texts.

LOZOVSKY. I can provide about ten Russian co-workers, writers, professors, journalists, translators. We shall exploit it on the radio too.

KOT. The book consists of documents, reports, and letters, all of them reliable. I also have many specimens, between thirty and forty, of the secret press published in Poland.

Lozovsky asks to borrow them for a week or so, he wishes to photograph them.

KOT. We also have miniature film, it can be enlarged.

LOZOVSKY. Of course that can be done, I'd like to have that too for a time, then I'll hand it back. As for brochures, they can be printed in the same works as the newspaper. I've received various brochures concerning Poland which the English have published.

KOT. I have some general sketches already written: two years of struggle since the beginning of the war, the organization of the army, the government, etc., and on the Polish-Russian Agreement, a brochure on the fight put up by our airmen, a brochure on our navy. We need to tell the future Polish soldiers here in Russia what the Polish soldiers have already achieved, as airmen and in the fleet. It will increase their self-confidence.

LOZOVSKY. I would like to know how many brochures there will be; I shall give instructions as to the size of issue. I think the military must discuss how these brochures can be transported to Poland. The paper should be specially light. As for the supply of information, I repeat again that it should pass through the Press Department.

Kot raises the question of [Polish] journalists making excursions with others to the front.

LOZOVSKY. First they must be registered in the Press Department, on all such questions specific proposals must be put forward. On the press and radio, to the Press Department.

KOT. I raise also the question of Soviet broadcasts for Poles. In view of the development of friendly relations these broadcasts should be in the hands of the Polish Government. That is of great political significance. And besides, the broadcasts so far have not been adapted to Polish psychology.

LOZOVSKY. Before I could discuss this question I need to inform myself.

KOT. The broadcasts are not scrupulously careful either in form or in regard to the Polish language. They must be attractive. After all, in Warsaw the people are threatened with the death penalty for listening to the radio, and besides, they cannot listen at any time of the day.

LOZOVSKY. That question will be investigated too.

KOT. They are complaining of this in London and we have difficulty in explaining it to the people at home [in Poland].

LOZOVSKY. Are these broadcasts in bad taste?

Kot speaks further of the difficulties of listening in Warsaw to broadcasts from abroad. The game has to be made worth the candle. He thinks that in future he and Mr. Lozovsky should stand together in front of a map and discuss propaganda in every country with pencils in hand.

LOZOVSKY. We have to begin from the beginning. The journalists should go to the Press Department. Proposals must be put forward in regard to the radio and newspaper, and the brochures, etc., will follow.

B6. Conversation with the Vice-Commissar for Foreign Affairs, A. J. Vyshinsky.
20 September 1941

KOT. I propose to discuss a number of practical problems which have arisen since our last talk ten days ago. Undoubtedly much is happening in the field of Polish affairs in the U.S.S.R., but the information being supplied to the Embassy by the Soviet authorities is quite inadequate.

Action is proceeding smoothly in the military sector, but the situation in regard to care for the civilians is worse. We need news from this field not only in order to inform the Polish Government in London . . . but also for the Polish people in Poland, England, and the U.S.A. Quite a lot has certainly been done which has not yet been brought to the knowledge of the Polish people here. Data are still lacking concerning the numbers and distribution of Poles in particular republics and regions.

To prove how badly the Soviet authorities are keeping the Embassy informed the ambassador produces a list of thirteen people released from prison, which was sent by the Narcomindiel on 10 September. In reality many more persons on the Polish list to which this was a reply have been released.

VYSHINSKY (recognizes the necessity for supplying the Embassy with the data required). The Soviet authorities themselves are in a difficult position in this respect, since they do not possess exact statistical material. In addition the Polish people [in Russia] are shifting about in masses, and this makes it difficult to cover them. None the less, in the immediate future, within not more than five days for certain, the Embassy will receive a statement of the number of Poles released from prisons, camps, and places of exile, according to republics, lands and *oblasts*, in thousands, if closer approximations are not possible. I don't guarantee that this term will be kept so far as concerns more distant regions, from which we still haven't had reports; in any case as we receive the details I shall give instructions for them to be communicated to the Embassy every few days.

KOT. This is a friendly request on our part, for it is a question of making propaganda use of the information and the broad lines of what the Soviet authorities have done for the Poles in the U.S.S.R. I am particularly anxious because of the lack of information regarding liberation of Poles in the north, in a climate which they find murderous—the regions of Kolyma, and Piechora, north of the Yenesei *oblast*. They ought to be released and transferred to a more suitable locality immediately.

VYSHINSKY. I promise to take up this matter myself and to do everything possible to have the people transported out of these unsuitable conditions. But what is to be done with them after they have been released and shifted from the north? . . . .

KOT. I shall take the liberty of returning to this question. But as we are talking of releases, I would like to find out where the peasants deported from Poland have been settled. (In an ironic tone) So far we've been told of the release of officials, counts, and Jews, but we have been given no news of the peasants who were deported from Poland by entire villages. I raise this matter because I am anxious to see a proper exploitation of their attachment to the land, of their industry and professional capacity. Now the Germans have been deported from the Volga Republic it would be possible to settle Polish peasants there. That would be of enormous propaganda value: the Germans are expelling the Poles from their own land, but the Soviet Government is handing over to Polish peasants lands from which it has evicted the Germans. The moral significance of such a step would move the whole world. I know that two large collective farms there have been handed over to Poles already, but that was quite by chance, it was simply that a group of Polish civilians had arrived in the area together with men journeying to join the armed forces, and they were accommodated on these collective farms. I am thinking of a broader plan, of ensuring that the Polish peasant, who is a fine agriculturist, should stop chopping down trees in Siberia, which is only a waste of his capabilities. I ask for facilities to discuss this question with a competent person in the Commissariat for Internal Affairs, who would be capable of fully appreciating the political value of the plan.

VYSHINSKY. I don't know whether the inhabitants of any Polish village have been deported, and if so, where to. I've heard of the deportation of settlers[1] and foresters, who figure as separate groups in the Soviet authorities' compilations. It must first be confirmed that incidents of this kind did actually take place.

KOT. From Malopolska . . . entire villages have been deported. The matter was decided by local committees consisting of Ukrainians, who thus got rid of the Poles. There were far fewer settlers than deported peasants, who had been living in those parts in many cases for hundreds of years.

VYSHINSKY. I am not responsible for internal affairs, but I do know that the collective farms left empty by the Volga Germans were at once occupied by agriculturists evacuated from the front-line zone. In any case, these are not the Germans the Soviet Union is fighting at present, they are being removed from the Volga not because the Soviet administration is at all hostile to them, but simply as a precautionary measure.

KOT. The Poles know the Germans well and don't deceive themselves that it is easily possible to divide them into bad and good.

VYSHINSKY. Undoubtedly there are not a few million people in Germany who are enemies of the Hitler régime.

KOT. The experience of the Poles, who know the Germans well, who have frequently travelled to Germany and who had relations or friends there, but above all had a large number of kinsmen in Westphalia and other parts of the Reich, shows that only the older people, those over forty, are discontented with Hitlerism. The young people are

---

[1] ' Settlers ' comprised roughly Polish people who had settled in Malopolska after 1918. *Tr.*

completely dominated by it. To believe in a German revolt against Hitlerism is to fall for an illusion.

VYSHINSKY. As the conversation has turned to these subjects I would like to say that in my conviction two forces will decide the defeat of Hitlerism : the first external, the armed forces of the Soviet Union, England, America, and the fraternal nations such as Poland, Czechoslovakia, Yugoslavia, who have now joined in with the Soviet Union. When military defeat comes, a second force, internal discontent, will begin to operate. Hitlerism is opposed not only by Rauschnigg and Strasser, but by the peasants, workers, and millions of the people, who will take up arms against Hitler and finish off the military defeat. That is not an illusion, but a realistic view.

KOT. When I spoke of illusions I had in mind the naïve views of certain English lords and even professors concerning the existence of good Germans. When I was given the degree of doctor *honoris causa* by Oxford University one eminent scientist said to me : ' I'm sure Hitler doesn't know what his administration is doing in Poland.'

VYSHINSKY. (laughing). I don't believe the lords and professors. And I am at liberty to say that, because I myself am a professor of penal law and a member of the Academy of Sciences. However, you, as an historian, know better than I that the past provides ample proofs that tyranny, which doesn't seek support in the broad masses of society, always falls in the end.

KOT. Of course I agree, but one must not delude oneself that a *bouleversement* may come quickly in Germany.

VYSHINSKY. I am of the same opinion, though defeat at the front may radically change the internal situation in Germany in quite a short space of time.

KOT. Returning to the question of the Polish people in Russia, I would like to draw attention to the lack of planning and the chaos which is arising in connection with the release of Polish citizens from prisons, camps, and places of compulsory settlement. We have got to work out together a detailed plan for solving this problem. I count on the Soviet Government presenting definite proposals. They should be worked out jointly in the Mixed Commission. It might be possible to set aside certain areas, or to gather part of our people into special camps . . . in which they could work with all the rights of free citizens.

VYSHINSKY. We have no camps except the compulsory labour camps of a punitive character. With us the system of administrative restriction of freedom provides for three degrees: 1. Individual exile to a definite locality, in which the given person lives quite freely and works entirely as he chooses, but has no right to leave the given locality and remains under police supervision; 2. Settlement in special husbandries, frequently equipped with farming stock and implements, the so-called ' special settlements ' (*spetsialnoe posielenie*) where work is performed in normal conditions, and the deportee enjoys complete freedom of movement in the given locality. 3. Confinement in compulsory labour camps, in which the inhabitants work for their living, with total deprivation of liberty. I repeat that camps in which the inhabitants don't work don't exist at all in the U.S.S.R.

KOT. In any case I ask that a plan may be drawn up and presented to us quickly.

VYSHINSKY. I shall occupy myself with it at the earliest moment.

KOT. I ask for a joint consideration of a plan for settlement and employment. Unfortunately, the Embassy doesn't possess the requisites for formulating its own plan, since the information obtained from the Soviet authorities is quite inadequate.

(As he says this, the Ambassador presents a summary statement of the number and distribution in particular *oblasts* of Polish scientists, specialists, and artists, which was passed to the Polish representatives on the Mixed Commission on 17 September.)

KOT. Information of this kind is quite useless to us; nothing can be deduced from the statement that in a certain *oblast* there is a certain number of doctors, so long as their names and addresses and even the locality where they are residing are not given. The figures relating to lawyers are strikingly low, and where are the public prosecutors, the judges, the police officers? The statement is not merely incomplete, it is quite valueless.

VYSHINSKY. I have spoken to the Commissar for Health concerning the possibility of making use of Polish doctors. Maybe the figure we have given is incomplete.

KOT. Obviously. In Volhynia alone some 800 were arrested. . . . It isn't a question only of doctors, but of other professions too. For instance, town councillors and public prosecutors. After all, Russia can have no claims on these, but we certainly have (he laughs).

VYSHINSKY (laughing). I shall try to obtain detailed information as soon as possible. I shall also concern myself with the question as a whole.

KOT. I would like to raise two other matters of a quite fundamental nature: the organizational aspect of care for the Polish people, and material resources. Allow me to begin with the second point. . . . During the initial stage of the Soviet Government's release of Polish citizens from prisons and camps they were paid a rate of 15 roubles a day, and were given tickets for travel to the chosen place of residence. In certain areas this was applied only to persons intending to join the army, in others no money was paid at all. Some were paid a kind of bonus when they left, others got nothing. We are receiving telegrams and letters reporting more and more instances of our people having no means whatever and being unable to travel anywhere when they are released. I would like you to tell me how the Soviet Government thinks of settling these questions, who has to provide material resources for these purposes, and in what manner.

VYSHINSKY. Those released get free railway travel and an issue of 15 roubles per day, in accordance with the government's instructions. If payment has not been made in any locality we shall take it up.

(Novikov intervenes to say that the instruction to pay fifteen roubles and to issue tickets applies only to persons released from prisons and labour camps.)

But there is another category of payments for travel and maintenance to enable the person to carry on till he is earning in his new place of work; this covers the category of Polish citizens who have not been shut away in camps or prisons, but were settled in 'special settlements'. The first group of payments is borne by the Soviet Government, the second should be undertaken by the Polish Government.

KOT. The Polish Government? But we have no resources, we have no money, one part of Poland was occupied by the Germans, the other part by you. Our Government is abroad. We haven't got the property of the Polish state at our disposition. The Polish people didn't go to the U.S.S.R. of their own free will. You tore them away from their organized normal life, their farms, their workshops; you flung masses of human beings into incredibly difficult conditions. The Soviet Government bears the responsibility for the Polish people being in this country at all. So it should provide the resources for aid to those people.

VYSHINSKY. We have borne the payments associated with the liberation of Polish people, but we cannot pay for their removal from place to place.

KOT. In Switzerland there are some 18,000 Polish citizens, who were not brought there by the government of that country, but who found themselves there as political refugees or interned prisoners of war, and yet the Swiss Government not only spends on their maintenance but even makes it possible for them to study and work.

VYSHINSKY. I cannot accept the way you put this matter, or your charging my Government with responsibility for the changes that have taken place and your condemnation of its measures. . . . If we start to survey the past at this stage we shall find many reciprocal claims. We do not regard the attitude taken by the U.S.S.R. Government as unjust and we do not recognize the obligation to support the Polish citizens who found themselves here. In any case, the Soviet Government is not the successor to the Polish Treasury and has not taken over any of its obligations. If the Polish Government wished to raise the question in this form it should have done so during the negotiation of the Agreement, not now. What we did in 1939 was solely the result of strategic considerations. The Germans were threatening our frontier, we had to keep them as far away from it as possible. In occupying Polish soil we did not commit any act of aggression. The present war has completely confirmed this argument. For that matter, we have given expression to it, both then and now, quite openly, even in the press. If it hadn't been for what happened then the Germans would have been in Moscow today, and possibly would even have reached the Urals.

(During the translation of this passage of his statement Vyshinsky, who had grown heated and was speaking very emphatically, interrupted the translator, and added:) For that matter it is just as well that the question of the alleged guilt of the Soviet Government in the year 1939, which we do not and would not recognize, was not raised during the negotiation of the Agreement. As for the merits of the financial problem, after all, the Soviet Government is bearing the expenses of railway and river transport, it will be able to supply agricultural implements and seed for sowing, for instance; but we cannot accept the argument that for political reasons it now has to bear the financial burdens. The Soviet Government has taken political steps which were necessary, and will never agree with the statement that it has committed excesses against one or another group of people.

KOT. I have not raised the question of aggression or non-aggression at all. These are not questions for present discussion. I haven't come here to raise them; but when my Government concluded the Agreement it refrained from opening this discussion, in order not to make the negotiations difficult. I did not make any political commentary on the financial questions. I stated the undoubted fact that the Polish people found themselves in the U.S.S.R. against their own choice; surely you will not maintain that the prisoners, or persons sent to labour camps, came here of their own accord as tourists.

VYSHINSKY. But you have touched on the question of aggression by saying that one half of Poland was occupied by Germany and the other half by the U.S.S.R. I cannot agree to such a formulation. We are not on the same plane as they. If there is to be talk of anyone's guilt, then it must refer to the German Government. I hope the Soviet Government together with the Polish Government will bring this matter up again in Berlin.

KOT. The discussion took a political turn owing to an inexact translation. I said that the Polish Government has no money because one part of Poland was occupied by the Germans and the other by the U.S.S.R., and this caused the disappearance of Polish State property. The translator omitted the first part of this sentence. In future he should translate at shorter intervals.

Vyshinsky confirms that this obviously does change the sense of the statement and twice emphasizes that in view of this he regards the discussion as not having taken place.

KOT. The Polish Government wishes to undertake part of the obligations of coming to the people's help, because they are our people; but we have no resources available for this purpose, so we must find a way out of the situation. . . .

VYSHINSKY. Of course, we shall think about it. I shall speak to our financial experts on these matters, but I ask you also to consider a number of other sources from which the Polish Government could draw money.

KOT. Part of the payments for immediate needs is already covered or is being covered by the Soviet Government. Now it's a question of further payments for the maintenance of people incapable of work, or those who still have to find work, and of more extensive assistance. So I propose that the Soviet Government should make the Polish Government a loan for these purposes. Unfortunately, the material resources of the Polish Government enable us only to cover the cost of maintaining the Embassy and its personnel.

VYSHINSKY. I shall discuss this proposal with the government and our financial experts, and shall return to it in our next conversation.

KOT. I have no trust in financial experts, I prefer to have to deal with politicians, with the governing heads. It would be desirable to lay the question before Vice-chairman Molotov or Chairman Stalin. We must confine our thinking to the political aspect if we are to solve this question satisfactorily. After all, fiscal considerations should not cause any difficulties in the *rapprochement* of our two countries.

VYSHINSKY (laughing). Our financial experts don't function on their own, but strictly carry out the Government's instructions. You can trust them.

KOT. Now I would like to turn to the question of the form the organization of care for our people in the U.S.S.R. must take. Unfortunately, the despatch of delegates from the Embassy is not achieving serious results owing to the lack of people. I could send three or four persons travelling round the areas to get an idea of the needs of our people and to inform me on those needs. Such journeys are important and should be undertaken as swiftly as possible, but they will not solve the problems of care for the people on the spot. The Embassy delegates permanently residing in any locality would have to be people deserving of complete confidence; the difficulty is that at present we don't know these people.

VYSHINSKY. The list of candidates for men of trust or delegates which we sent to the Embassy came into being in this way: at our request the local Soviets sent us the names of people with whom they had been in contact. . . . I am of the opinion that we should begin in a small way and, not using the word 'committee', select from the people who make contact with the Embassy those who appear to be most active. If in the course of correspondence it transpires that someone is capable of presenting the needs of his locality, and can send in statistical data, he can be entrusted with certain matters for settlement. After all, no man of trust has to be appointed for ever and ever, he can be changed. In addition, the Embassy may already have various people known by name in the areas, and can appoint them as men of trust. It would be better to begin with ten to fifteen people, and then the business will develop automatically. I am not afraid of committees, I have had plenty to do with them in my lifetime (he laughs), but I think it a pity to waste time discussing the form of organization.

KOT. I too realize the need for selecting the active element, but the question of confidence does arise. The people we are talking about may well be men trusted by the local Poles, but if they are not known to the Embassy the Embassy is not in a position to trust them. I ask you to see to it that in cases where the men of trust select a few of the local

Poles to assist them, consulting with them on the problems of the given group and jointly deciding on the fairest method of distributing aid in kind or in money, the local authorities do not intervene under the pretext that no permission has been given to set up committees or organizations.

VYSHINSKY. That can be done. We have no reservations against the idea of men of trust, since it does not create organizational complications. If a committee is set up such questions as its competence, its relations with the local government organs, and its scope of activity arise immediately, and complications can ensue. I myself, however, think it better to work at once with the people who are available. Let the Embassy be the central committee, and yourself the chairman (he laughs) with men of trust as representatives of the committee. As for the list of candidates we have presented, of course it needs to be filled out. We must ascertain the profession of each individual and get a brief character sketch of him. . . .

KOT. Now one more question of a formal nature. The final date by which Polish passports can be obtained was fixed as 22 November, but this date cannot be observed. So far the provisional passports have not even been printed. I ask for an assurance that the necessary paper will be forthcoming.

VYSHINSKY. What sort of paper must it be, some special quality? (He asks Novikov how the matter stands in regard to the printing of passports and says it must be accelerated.)

KOT. It must be strong paper which won't tear or wear out. Although the form of the passport is purely an internal Polish matter, we have decided to include a Russian text, for the convenience of the Soviet administrative organs. I ask you to see that the selection of suitable places for the passport-consular agencies which are to issue the passports is discussed with representatives of the Embassy.

VYSHINSKY. I shall deal with these questions myself. Obviously the date of 22 November cannot be kept and the period will be extended.

KOT. One very important question is that of aid from America for our people: a large quantity of food and aid of all kinds has been collected. Now it is a question of the Soviet authorities granting facilities. I have heard that a delegation of the American Red Cross has arrived here; we must see that the gifts intended for the Poles do reach us and that their distribution is in Polish hands.

VYSHINSKY. I give you my assurance that this will be arranged.

KOT. . . . There is also the problem of their transport. If transport is

E

free there will be a considerable increase in the Americans' generosity. Such a gesture on the Soviet Government's part would be fully appreciated by American opinion.

VYSHINSKY. For transport of such goods we provide reduced tariffs. After all, free transport would mean that the Soviet Government would be paying the charges. We have already agreed to free these consignments from customs duty.

KOT. Is that finally settled? None the less I ask you to arrange free transport.

VYSHINSKY. So far as release from customs duty is concerned a decision to that effect has already been taken in essence. It is a question only of its formal application. Free transport will be a difficult question.

KOT. Individual parcels are a special form of American aid which has considerable propaganda value. Can this type of consignment be allowed into the Soviet Union?

VYSHINSKY. I think so. We shall discuss the question with the Commissariat for Communications (Post and Telegraph).

KOT. Polish organizations in America have collected a large quantity of used clothing. It had already been decided to send this to the U.S.S.R. when the Soviet Ambassador in Washington began to make difficulties. The clothing given by Americans is in very good condition and of good materials. Hygienic questions should not come into consideration.

VYSHINSKY. It can be disinfected.

KOT. That might ruin the clothing.

VYSHINSKY. I promise to send the Ambassador in Washington an instruction not to make any difficulty.

KOT. The large amount of correspondence reaching the Embassy makes it necessary to add to the staff. In addition I must bring the people who are to act as Embassy delegates to Moscow in order to get to know and to brief them. I ask that the formalities involved in granting permission for them to come may be settled as quickly as possible.

VYSHINSKY. There is a state of war in Moscow. Arrivals of all kinds must be restricted as much as possible. I don't ask you to specify the exact number of people who are to arrive, but to take into account the state of war and the fundamental restrictions in force here.

KOT. In conclusion I wish to hand you two lists of people whom I am anxious to trace. The first list consists of political persons. We would like to send certain of them to London to add to the National Council.

This list includes the names of several Ukrainians, men whom we know with certainty to be anti-German. Now that lands inhabited by Ukrainians are under German occupation it is necessary to challenge her monopoly to a decision of the Ukrainian problem. The world must be told that there are other Ukrainians who are opposed to the Germans. The Ukrainian people and their local Germanophiles know this. The second list consists of private individuals, of no political significance, several families of officials in our Embassy and other Polish organizations.

Vyshinsky takes the lists and promises to deal with them.

KOT. Finally, I would like to convey my official, but also my private wish. Namely, could I have an audience with President Stalin in order to mention certain matters to him? The propaganda value of such a conversation would be a very positive factor in our relations and would have strong repercussions abroad.

VYSHINSKY. I see from the way you raise the matter that you realize how fully President Stalin is occupied, but of course I shall put your proposal to him.

KOT. I shall be very grateful to you. If I go on occupying so much of your time as I have today you will come to dislike me. Perhaps we could see each other more often but not so long. (He laughs.)

VYSHINSKY. Why more often and not so long? Oftener and longer. (He laughs.) It is very good for us to meet, for we ought to discuss all these problems with each other.

KOT (pointing to Novikov). It's all his fault. If the Mixed Commission were functioning properly and swiftly, if it consisted of people who could make decisions, I should not need to come to you with all these issues. Really they are their concern.

The conversation was very lively, in a free, and sometimes joking spirit, and lasted from 18.00 to 20.30 hours.

A11. Letter to General Sikorski.
22 September 1941

. . . . Certain conversations are trying. Yesterday's[1] two and a half hours exhausted me so much that for five hours I could not get over it. But it can't be helped, the beginning is hard.

It would be very desirable for you to visit Moscow, but you cannot

[1] Really the previous day, 20.9. *Tr.*

come until the most urgent issues have been settled. I shall even urge
that everything must be achieved by the time you arrive. . . . Everything here goes slowly. The day before yesterday Stalin said to Cripps:
'What is to be done with these Russians? They never are able to do
anything to time.'—But please don't repeat this to gossips.—We were
moved as we listened to your speech over the radio; at times it was
rather faint; so far we have not been able to get the full text from the
government; apart from fragments—and those according to Reuter—
they [the Soviets] have not issued anything. . . .

I am expecting Anders to arrive tomorrow, and we shall discuss
details [in regard to] Poland. The news you gave of the failures of the
emissaries[1] is having an excellent effect. Only a couple of weeks ago
they sent a small group with . . . a lot of money. They are still training others; some of these honestly keep us informed of everything.
Even at the end of August they forced one man to sign a statement
that he would report everything to them, in secret from the Polish
authorities, about what is happening in our ranks, especially with an
eye to the future. I think all this will soon be stopped.

It appears that many had to sign documents in prison under threat
of not being released. In certain conditions, in the provinces it has been
impossible to get out otherwise (even now!) and no one can be condemned for doing it. . . . I think that in order to ease the consciences
of these people you will have to find some opportunity to tell them
that anyone who informs our authorities he was forced into making
a declaration has done his duty and will not be subjected to reproach
as a Polish citizen.

. . . .

Owing to war needs Anders will ask you to let us have news of the
movements of German troops behind the front as early as possible; in
exchange for this service it may be possible to gain much in other
directions. . . .

PS. The list of prisoners I presented to Vyshinsky includes Jews,
and Ukrainians, and members of the Sanatza [Régime].[2] I shall
present more. Please show it to Mikołajczyk and Lieberman.

---

[1] Parachutists dropped in Poland by Soviet planes. *Tr.*
[2] The pre-war government bloc. *Tr.*

*A12. Letter to Edward Raczynski, Minister for Foreign
Affairs.
Moscow. 22 September 1941*

. . . .

Things are not going easily, but I am convinced that the majority
of issues will be regulated in accordance with our way of thinking.
The military forces now being created are filled with such a remarkable spirit that everybody is amazed at the valuable national quality
which is evident in these emaciated and ragged forms. . . . A second
indubitable fact is the release of prisoners and internees, amounting
to hundreds of thousands; although this is occurring chaotically and
their resettlement is exposing them to fresh difficulties—at first even
to hunger—none the less soon everything will be brought into order
and the great mass of Poles will be saved.

The work of the Embassy is still not as fruitful as it should be. We
are really working cut off from the Polish masses, who are living in
very distant spots from here. The Poles we do get here are a handful
either of people imprisoned in the worst of conditions in Moscow,
and so still incapable of work of any importance, or persons whom we
have discovered by chance and brought here. Every day we get an
incredible number of letters and telegrams, so many that it is impossible even to open them all or to answer those we do open. . . .

As for a network of consular posts, there is no hope of achieving
this. In this direction not even Cripps has managed to obtain anything. In the eyes of the Soviet people a consular service is identical
with espionage. I am asking only for consular passport agencies of a
provisional nature, in those areas where there are Poles; and I hope
to obtain so much, but only because of the necessity for every
individual to possess documents.

It would be a good idea if you could communicate certain of our
desiderata to Ambassador Bogomolov, putting stress on their urgency.
For instance, the more prominent political prisoners are not being
released; the Soviets themselves seem unable to find certain of
them, while they don't want to hand over others; more than one of
these would be very useful in London. . . . The incomprehensible
chicanery that goes on, such as the refusal to allow worn clothing to
be sent from New York for the exiles, or difficulties in sending
individual parcels, or their reluctance to waive transport charges completely on American aid, and in general their strictly fiscal approach
to the question—a charge of 38,000 roubles for railway trucks coming

from Archangel with material for Poles—doubtless Bogomolov could throw light on all this from his observation post. I get the impression that they take him seriously here.

A.14 Cable from General Sikorski.
London. 25 September 1941

Please let me have your view on the question of sending Bishop Gawlina to our army in Russia. At the moment the English are interested in this. Bishop Gawlina himself has asked me to agree to his going, giving me solemn assurances of his utter loyalty. . . .

A14. To General Sikorski.
25 September 1941

The bishop's arrival is quite impossible for the time being. We must have conversations with them concerning religion—with America in mind—propaganda among the Catholics of the world, and so on. They must not be taken by surprise. Stalin's personal attitude on the question must be sounded. First we must get our priests out of prison.

A16. Conversation with Representatives of the American Red Cross

Report of a conference between the Polish Ambassador, Prof. St. Kot, and the representatives of the American Red Cross, Mr. Allen Wardwell and Mr. James C. Nicholson, in the National Hotel, Moscow. 2 October 1941.

Kot gives a broad outline of the situation of Poles deported to Russia, and information as to their numbers and distribution. According to figures supplied by the Soviet Government the total number of persons deported does not exceed 350,000, which figure, however, is completely at variance with the reality, since according to information received by the Embassy the total figure of deportees exceeds one and a half million. In proof the Ambassador presents several telegrams from various areas, on the basis of which:

1. In one small locality, Tajszet, there are 10,000 Poles.
2. In the Autonomous Republic of Komi there are 181,000 resettled persons, not including those in camps.
3. In many other localities there are from two to four thousand Polish citizens.

There are many localities in which Poles are living, such as the

Yakutia Republic, the district of Kolyma, other places in the far north, even Franz Josef Land, from which we have received no information at all so far.

In summary, the situation is as follows:

1. Refugees from the western part of Poland deported to Russia number about 600,000.
2. Resettled peasants, some 400,000.
3. State officials and functionaries, with their wives and children, some 100,000.

In addition, there are those who were put in prison and labour camps. In southern European Russia there are many Poles employed on the land, digging infantry trenches, constructing defensive lines, etc.

The situation of all the Polish citizens so far released is wretched. Their debility, total lack of clothing and footwear, and the complete lack of funds make their desperate position still worse.

The Soviet Government has stated that it is unable to give any help at all, and so the entire burden falls on the Polish Government. In view of this the Ambassador, in the name of the Polish Government, appeals to the American Red Cross for help, and especially for help in food, clothing, and above all else, medical goods.

Mr. Wardwell asks several questions concerning the numbers exiled to free settlements, the possibilities of supplying foodstuffs, etc.

In reply the Ambassador gives exhaustive explanations.

Kot explains that he has already conferred with the Soviet Government on the questions of forming a Polish organization of welfare committees, to which, however, he has received a discouraging reply, since it is not in line with the system here. However, the Soviet Government sees no obstacle whatever to the Ambassador appointing delegates and assigning them to assist local men of trust among the exiles. The Ambassador declares that he has also gained the impression that the Soviet Government would not put difficulties in the way of the Polish Red Cross being active in Russia, but he has not wished to raise this question in detail before acquainting himself with the opinion of the American Red Cross delegates. The Ambassador indicated that in the event of the American Red Cross providing aid to Polish citizens in Russia he considers it fundamental to separate help to the Poles from the proposed help to Russia. . . .

Mr. Wardwell says he can assure the Ambassador that all aid intended for the Poles would be sent separately, to the disposition of the delegatures set up by the Embassy. Probably a delegation of the American Red Cross will be established in Moscow, aid could be sent to it, and it would then allocate all consignments earmarked for the Poles direct to the disposition of the Polish Committee or the Embassy delegature. Owing to the binding 'neutrality act' America cannot make use of her own ships for supplies to countries at war, she will have to make use mainly of Soviet ships for the transport of aid; but he sees no difficulty in distinctly stating in the shipping consignment notes whom the goods are intended for. Even the packaging could be different and provided with special labels. The American Red Cross has no possibility of sending a numerous staff for the distribution of aid, and has complete confidence in the Polish organization to which the Polish Government will entrust the matter.

Finally, Mr. Wardwell asks the Ambassador to treat today's conversation as an expression of his personal view, and so as not binding, since he must present the plan in its entirety and the desiderata to the American Ambassador in Moscow and must discuss it with the Red Cross headquarters in Washington, and only thereafter will it be possible to give a final and official reply. . . .

A17. To General Sikorski.
Moscow. 3 October 1941

Your letter of 18 September received 29 September.

As we must close the mail today I send a provisional review of the situation, as I have not yet got results on questions which will only come up for consideration during the day.

The past week has slipped past while we wait for the most important decisions. The news of the German advances in the south has completely absorbed the authorities here, and to this has been added the arrival of guests, and conferences. In this atmosphere it has been difficult to press our affairs. Although Vyshinsky has not so far given answers on my main desiderata—especially on the financial question —I have decided to renew pressure only after the conference.

All forces have been concentrated on preparing material for the members of the conference. General Anders, who flew here on 25 September, together with Bohusz has formulated our military desiderata, and handed them confidentially to General MacFarlane. An official copy was to have been handed to Harriman; unfortunately, immediately on their arrival the guests were so fully occupied with an intensive programme of consultations and work that, despite all the promises given in London and here, they did not make contact with us immediately they arrived. As a matter of form I mentioned this and yesterday morning handed Ambassador Steinhardt Anders' memorial, though the Americans already knew it from a copy which MacFarlane had given them. The conference continued unbrokenly through Monday, Tuesday and Wednesday in several commissions and special evening consultations with Stalin. It was wholly occupied in consideration of the Soviet demands, which enormously exceeded anything for which the visitors were prepared. It became necessary to prepare for aid on such a considerable scale that it calls for extraordinary efforts and restrictions.[1]

At my insistence, yesterday at 2.30 there was a conference on our affairs at Ambassador Steinhardt's. In addition to our host, those present were Beaverbrook, Harriman, Cripps, Ismay, MacReady, MacFarlane, Burns, the American general concerned with armaments, and myself with Anders and Bohusz. MacFarlane spoke most sympathetically on Anders' programme. Its normal consideration was rendered impossible by Beaverbrook, who is despotic by nature, knew everything better [than anyone else] and had settled everything in advance. He argued that even if it were possible to supply us separately with some material there wouldn't be any transport resources for it, for already there are insufficient to enable them to fulfil the obligations entered into with Russia, and it will be her business to allocate something from this for the Polish Army. He is prepared to talk about this to Stalin. It will be possible to achieve part of the programme for Poland, but part not (tanks). Harriman made a timid intervention, saying that America wants to supply the Poles to some extent with armaments over and above the Russian programme. All three British generals argued sympathetically in favour of the necessity and possibility of providing for the Poles separately. Beaverbrook did not make a final decision. I put in the remark that in the uncertain conditions exist-

---

[1] The conference on the question of Western aid to Russia took place on 28 to 30 September. The chief role was played by the British delegate, Lord Beaverbrook, and an auxiliary role by President Roosevelt's delegate, Averell Harriman. Stalin presented such a huge list of requirements that it astonished the visitors. However, Stalin won Beaverbrook to his side, and despite the observations of the members of the British Military Mission he accepted all Stalin's demands (Robert E. Sherwood: *The White House Papers of Harry L. Hopkins*, vol. 1, London, 1948, p. 392) and did not agree to reserve even equipment for the Polish Army. The first confidential Protocol of 1 October promised the Soviets materials to a sum of over 11,000 million dollars.

ing here the Polish element provides the greatest guarantee of certainty,[1] [an argument] which MacFarlane supported later.

After Beaverbrook's departure with Harriman I did not conceal my disillusionment from the British generals and my scepticism as to Beaverbrook's goodwill towards us[2] and his eager confidence in the people here. The generals declared that Beaverbrook is a fortress which they cannot take by storm, but they will endeavour to outflank it. I think our troops will get equipment for six divisions. Perhaps the question will be cleared up today, since we shall learn what was agreed in the evening in the Kremlin and what the British generals have managed to get through in the privacy of their own delegation.

From Beaverbrook's remark that the Polish Army numbers only 40,000 Anders rightly deduces that the Kremlin would like to stop at this figure for the present, to avoid being forced to agree to too great a concession in regard to the allocation of armaments for us, and that this explains the unexpected hold-up of transports for the Polish Army during the past few days, also their persistent failure to release or even to reveal the place of confinement of many thousands of our officers, shut away in forced labour camps in the far north.

I asked Steinhardt to arrange for me to have an opportunity of talking with Harriman as quickly as possible, with a view to my getting a clear idea of Washington's views on the Russian attitude, *inter alia* on the religious issues. I would like this to come off today. I am afraid that too many principal guests will be departing tomorrow. The American delegation has behaved far from independently, only noting desiderata of various kinds. Beaverbrook dominated everything. I only hope he has not succumbed to the illusion that he is controlling the fate of the world in agreement with Stalin! I am afraid he completely fails to understand and doesn't even want to understand the peculiarities of Russian conditions, and that he thinks of the people here as like western people even in regard to their sincerity and the keeping of obligations.

I have devoted much effort to convincing the American Red Cross Delegation of the need, the extent and form of aid for us. . . . The first conference was held yesterday. . . . I had Minister Sokolnicki

---

[1] Certainty in regard to the Germans.
[2] Lord Beaverbrook never concealed his views as to the fate of the enslaved nations. In the *Sunday Express* of 31 March 1940, he wrote that the British were not interested in raising Poland and Czechoslovakia out of the gutter, dusting them down, and putting them on pedestals with arms in their hands, only for them to be overthrown again.

and Evgeniusz Lubormirski as translator with me—he had just turned up from hard labour, and was still in his ragamuffin attire. . . .

I gave them an oral report on the needs, illustrating the figures with certain original [copies of] telegrams; we established the main areas of settlement on a map. . . . Wardwell is convinced of the need for help and of its vast extent, and also allowed himself to be convinced that it must be independent of Russian factors. The main trouble is that in practice it may be sent in Russian vessels, mainly through the Persian Gulf; but every consignment destined for us will have a distinguishing mark, and our receiving points will receive direct from American hands. . . . A permanent American delegation in Moscow will watch over the distribution.

I insisted that their delegation must include American citizens who speak Polish. Nicholson was taken aback, but after I had explained that this was required only by practical lingual considerations, and that it would repay them, he promised to consider it. Lubomirski's appearance and his cheerful references to his tragic experiences made a great impression on them. I took it as an opportunity to emphasize that despite all the wrongs done to them the Poles are capable of sincere co-operation with Russia for victory over Germany.

Among real achievements I can put first and foremost the dispatch of the first travelling delegation to the exiles. After long arguments we obtained places in a plane, but only to Novosibirsk, for Heitzman as a delegate, and Szumski—a Polish Socialist Party deputy from Cracow—as his deputy. From that town they are to visit by rail the main centres of Kazakhstan and southern Siberia. We haven't yet had a cable advising of their arrival at Novosibirsk. The flight takes three days. . . . They are taking specific instructions, and some money.

We are posting delegates in separate districts in several provinces of European Russia.[1] . . . In view of the fact that in the Volga Basin a large number of refugees are concentrating close to the army, there will be a permanent delegate in certain of the larger towns, and possibly also a central welfare and consular office, as it is much nearer to Asia from there than from Moscow. We are sending Gruja as delegate to Archangel, and also to take over civilian transports, and with him a skilled office worker, to deal with the problems of our

[1] Although the Narcomindiel had not yet given their agreement, the Ambassador tried to send out delegates under various pretexts. Kwapinski had gone as delegate to Tashkent, although the formal approval of the Soviet authorities had not been obtained.

refugees in that part of the north. We are preparing to send a delegate to Vologda, Viatka (Kirov) and the Komi republic.

I have prepared a speech for the radio, and so has Anders; we are waiting for permission for our national anthem to be played after the speeches, and for a communiqué to be read giving detailed instructions to Polish citizens. I have not hurried with this speech, for I wanted first to obtain from the authorities a general picture of the releases to date. So far I haven't received it. It is true that releases are being carried out on quite a mass scale, but there is still no arrangement for the release either of the more prominent individuals we are asking for, or of the mass groups which are still shrouded in secrecy, several thousand officers, judges, police, etc. From one of the less important prisoners released I have learnt that in a prison at Balashov, not far from Saratov, are the former Sejm deputies Sommerstein and Celewicz, the latter an Ukrainian, also the Bialoruthenian Luckiewicz. I shall see whether, by stating exactly where they are being held, I shall be able to obtain their release. For they—the Soviet authorities —still assure us of their goodwill and that the decision is made, only it is difficult to say where any particular individual is being held.

. . . . We heard your radio speech, but with interruptions. In the army only one section of it was heard; but this proves that it was in fact transmitted in Russia. With some difficulty I wrested a copy of the text from the Narcomindiel a week later; we have had it cyclostyled and are distributing it. We all think it is splendidly fitted to the situation. We shall include it in a brochure Naglerowa[1] is preparing as a collection of documents on the Pact; unfortunately, we are not receiving any material whatever from London, to enable us to finish the brochure.

. . . . Our army which has been formed here with such enthusiasm consists of first-class material, but they are in dire material need. In order to meet their cultural requirements it will be necessary to create some auxiliary organization. Best of all would be a Polish YMCA, which would open libraries and reading rooms, would try to provide the most modest of cultural amusements, would get hold of paper and ink, thread and buttons, gramophones and music, etc. There is a small group of good YMCA personnel in Scotland, where they are a luxury; it might be possible to form a group for our people here, pro-

---

[1] Herminia Naglerowa, a well-known Polish woman novelist who had been deported to the U.S.S.R. *Tr.*

vided it was supplied with material which no one here can get hold of. The work in the camp calls for really devoted people, since they lack the most primitive conveniences, and thousands of people are having to camp under the bare sky in snow and rain.

A19. Cable from General Sikorski.
London. 3 October 1941

I attach great importance to obtaining reinforcements for our forces from the U.S.S.R. . . . Please explain to the Soviet authorities that it is in the common interests of the Allies to maintain the existence of the Polish forces in Great Britain and Egypt at full strength, unbrokenly. I request you to demand the evacuation to Archangel of the Polish soldiers in various camps in Vologda and similar districts. . . .

B7. Conversation with the Vice-Commissar for Foreign Affairs, A. J. Vyshinsky. 6 October 1941
Present: Director K. N. Novikov. Embassy Secretary W. Arlet (interpreter).

. . . . KOT. You cannot complain that I am being importunate, for during our last conversation you assured me that I would receive data of fundamental importance for us within five days, but already fifteen days have passed. But I realize that both you personally and the Soviet Government have had a number of urgent and important matters to settle, and that this explains the delay.

VYSHINSKY. The delay has been due in fact solely to that reason.

KOT. We, too, have not been idle in the meantime, we have been trying for our part to ease the situation of our allied Soviet Government in those directions where we have considerable possibilities.

(During these remarks the Ambassador shows Vyshinsky dispatches from the Polish Telegraph Agency in London, reporting a *Times* interview with J. Retinger, and from New York concerning a letter from Ciechanowski[1] to Cordell Hull on the restoration of religious freedom to the Poles in the U.S.S.R., which President Roosevelt referred to in a press conference. The Ambassador also explains the protests that Roosevelt's declaration has provoked in isolationist circles and groups hostile to rapprochement with the U.S.S.R.)

So you have proofs of our propaganda activity in the spirit of the Polish-Soviet understanding. In this war we are trying to help our Allies all we can.

---

[1] Polish Ambassador to Washington. *Tr.*

VYSHINSKY. I greatly appreciate these activities, the more so as they accord with the reality.

KOT. Unfortunately, not in all spheres. So far as religious questions are concerned our troops have certainly been afforded the possibility of observing religious practices, but the civilian population is completely deprived of religious care, since they don't have a single church or a single priest. The Soviet Constitution guarantees freedom of religious practice, but in reality it is impossible. I would like to discuss this problem with you, of course without interfering in the U.S.S.R.'s internal affairs; and I ask you to consider a separate conversation with me on this subject.

VYSHINSKY. I agree to the matter being put in that way, especially as you have no possibility of interfering in the Soviet Union's internal affairs. I shall readily receive any proposal you have to make on the subject.

KOT. I can put certain proposals into definite form, but first I would like to discuss this problem with you unofficially, in a sense privately. We cannot allow those circles who attacked Roosevelt for his declaration on religious freedom in the U.S.S.R. to charge us with lying.

Vyshinsky expresses his agreement to such a conversation.

Kot asks whether at least some of the subjects raised in the conversation of 20 September have been settled.

VYSHINSKY (looking through his notes of 20 September). The project for settling Polish citizens in the German Volga Republic does not arise, because on the very day you raised the question, 20 September, the Government confirmed another basic plan for those areas. I reported your proposal to the Government, but was informed that the areas were already disposed of.

KOT. Would it not be possible to allot part of these areas to our people? A high official of the Narcomvnudiel who was in those parts last month promised to allocate two cantons in the German Volga Republic for accommodation of Polish people. . . .

VYSHINSKY. The Polish citizens who have been accommodated in the Republic of Volga Germans happened to be there by chance. By the end of this week at the latest a new plan for dealing with the question of settling Polish citizens will be confirmed.

KOT. I ask that before the plan is finally formulated and presented to the Government it may be discussed with us. Once it has been confirmed it will be difficult to make changes in it. And yet I, too, will be held responsible for the way in which this very important matter is handled.

VYSHINSKY. The final plan will be presented to you and your wishes will be taken into account as far as possible. I passed on your inquiry concerning the judges, procurators, and former members of town councils to the appropriate quarters and I expect to have a reply shortly. The same applies to the statistics on the Polish population according to regions and categories. . . .

VYSHINSKY. We have issued regulations for counteracting the mass unorganized movement of Polish people. For instance, in Molotov region we have stopped the mass movement of Poles, as we have already informed you.

(In fact the Embassy had received no information whatever concerning mass movements of Polish people in the Molotov region, and so Vyshinsky's statement obviously embarrassed Novikov.)

KOT. So long as that is not tantamount to restricting the freedom of movement of Polish citizens over a long period!

VYSHINSKY. Of course not. This week you will not only receive a plan for settling the Polish population, but also definite data as to the localities from and to which Poles are moving.

KOT. I ask yet again for all these matters to be expedited.

VYSHINSKY. I am personally dealing with the problem of the form of welfare organization for Polish citizens, and the committees, and men of trust. And I hope that my scheme will satisfy both sides and will be accepted by you. I am also working on the question of financial arrangements in order to achieve definite results. . . .

VYSHINSKY. In our previous conversation, although at first you did not recognize the Polish Government's obligation to bear the financial burdens, you agreed with this principle by the very fact that you suggested credits.

KOT. My conviction of what justice requires cannot be reconciled with that. But I cannot argue about justice when people are dying of hunger. Without entering into discussions on the subject, I want a practical solution that will provide resources for financing the most urgent necessities.

VYSHINSKY. I am concerned to establish the most fundamental aspect of the problem; the extent of the credit; on what principles the money is to be issued, how to settle the question quickly so as to provide you with resources. The plan will be ready in four or five days.

KOT. Thank you very much, but I am not a financier, so I would ask that before the plan is presented to the Soviet Government it may be examined by my specialist on financial affairs.

VYSHINSKY. When the plan is ready, in four or five days, I shall hand it to director Novikov, who will discuss it with your representative.

KOT. This is such a serious matter that I must of course first discuss it with my Government. After all, I am not taking a loan for myself, but on behalf of the Polish Government.

VYSHINSKY. Of course; but you will be able to inform your Government by telegraph. You will present the plan to the Polish Government, I to the Soviet Government. When both Governments have expressed their opinion it will be possible to settle the question.

KOT. I'm afraid that will drag it out. In view of our people's urgent needs would it not be possible to consider an advance payment on the loan?

VYSHINSKY. I see no objections in principle to an advance, but I think we shall be able to settle the question finally within a week. After all, we shall not haggle over the details. After deciding what sum is involved, and for what purposes, we shall hand it all over to the financiers and lawyers. The question of the text will be a detail. . . .

Kot raised the issue of the slow release of Polish citizens, showing Vyshinsky a cable from the World Jewish Congress concerning Professor Schorr and Sejm Deputy Sommerstein. There was a short discussion. Vyshinsky and Novikov affirmed that many Polish citizens were not reporting to the Embassy. The Ambassador replied that Sommerstein, Celewicz, and Luckiewicz were being held in prison at Balashov.

VYSHINSKY. I want you to believe that I shall personally gladly ensure the release of these men you are interested in, for I know it is not a question of any fundamental obstacles, only of technical difficulties. But there are certain categories of people who in our common interests cannot be released.

KOT. I realize that, and you can be sure I shall not intervene in such cases. But among the people who are still definitely in prison are some for whom I would give my soul that they have done nothing to justify their detention. I am afraid that fatal mistakes might be committed, which could have a tragic reaction on those interested.

VYSHINSKY. I agree that such accidents are possible, and so we must investigate them all in detail.

KOT. Apart from the category of individual releases and the search for well-known persons, scientists, politicians, who are of public interest as individuals, there are other matters of a similar nature which we find very painful. I refer to a certain group of people, to certain facts, which I shall communicate to you because I am sure they are not known to you.

VYSHINSKY. The lack of information from prisons is sometimes due to the circumstance that because part of the Soviet territory came under German occupation prisoners were evacuated separately from the prison archives. (Novikov intervenes with examples of several such prisons.)

KOT. Then ignoring for the moment that I cannot meet London's instructions to discover a number of well-known people in order to add them to our National Council, I would like to quote the following figures. In round figures 9,500 officers were imprisoned in Poland and deported into the U.S.S.R.; but in the army we have only 2,000. What has happened to the other 7,500?[1]

Vyshinsky and Novikov attempted to maintain that this was impossible, but produced no arguments.

KOT. We have tried to find these men everywhere. We thought they might have been handed over to the Germans, and we sought them in German prisoner of war camps, in occupied Poland, everywhere where they could conceivably be. I could understand it if a few dozen men were missing, or even a few hundred, but not several thousand.[2]

Vyshinsky and Novikov are embarrassed; they themselves ask ' what has happened to them? '

KOT. In the autumn of 1940 a transport of about 1,500 of our officers was sent by ship from Archangel northward.

VYSHINSKY. That information is indubitably inaccurate. Where did you get it from?

KOT. From Archangel. In Moscow region there was a prisoner of war camp in the locality of Ostashkov, in which only gendarmerie and

---

[1] The Soviet Army newspaper, *Krasnaya Zviezda*, for 17 September 1940 announced that Soviet Russia had taken on Polish territory 181,000 prisoners of war, including 12 generals, 55 colonels, 72 lieutenant-colonels, and 9,227 officers of lower rank, in addition to civilians.

[2] On 4 September 1941 General Anders passed to me a warning from General Zhukov of the Narcomvnudiel that the Embassy should not interfere in the matter of the ' lost ' officers, and that any intervention should be made by the military, otherwise insuperable difficulties might arise. This prevented my making direct reference to the question in my early conversations with the Narcomindiel. I was also waiting for a list of names of the lost officers, which the staff had drawn up, and which Anders promised me. See also *The Katyn Forest Massacre, Hearings before the Select Committee to conduct an investigation of the Facts, Evidence, and Circumstances of the Katyn Forest Massacre.* Eighty-second Congress. Washington, 1952.

police were held. It is true this camp no longer exists, but among the tens of thousands of men who have reported to the army there is not one prisoner of war from that camp. And how about the camps which are still holding our officers, on the Sosva, in Kolyma, in the Omsk district?

VYSHINSKY. I am sure they are among the upwards of 300,000 Polish citizens released.

KOT. There is not one prisoner of war from these camps in the army. And where are the doctors and the university professors?

VYSHINSKY. During our last conversation I told you of 591 Polish doctors. 600 doctors are the lot, surely? But perhaps some of them reported a different profession?

KOT. At present we have only thirty in the army. The soldiers' health leaves much to be desired, and there is nobody to treat them.

VYSHINSKY. I promise to act on your request to direct a larger number of doctors to the army.

The end of the conversation was very hurried, as Vyshinsky had another conference following. The Ambassador also raised the point of announcing the names of released Poles over the radio; . . . . the plan to transfer part of the Embassy offices to Cheliabinsk or Sverdlovsk (Vyshinsky was unfavourable to this suggestion, the Ambassador said he would return to it); the question of Mr. Gruja's departure to Archangel as the embassy delegate (Vyshinsky agreed, and took the opportunity to speak unfavourably of the proposed consulate); and expressed the hope that the dates Mr. Vyshinsky had promised would be kept.

The conversation lasted from 6.30 to 7.45 p.m.

A20. To General Sikorski.
Moscow. 8 October 1941

. . . . We are affected by Hitler's offensive. It is not far from Viazma to here; the pessimists consider that it may be necessary to evacuate Moscow in a few days, the optimists think, not for a month. But maybe the city will be defended. Evacuation will be very easy for the Embassy, we have so little to shift. Obviously we cannot take any initiative on the matter. When during a conversation with Vyshinsky I mentioned the necessity to transfer part of our offices (welfare and consular) to Cheliabinsk or Sverdlovsk in order to be close to a large concentration of Poles, he protested vigorously; so it is all the more difficult to raise the question of a transfer for any other reason.

The serious defeats reveal the existence despite everything of a so-called fifth column. Undoubtedly all the collective farmers belong to it. I have been told of one locality where they are openly scoffing at the war, and soldiers called up for the front are seen off by the whole village with genuine funeral rites. The religious factor is playing a great part. The view is being spread around that Hitler will restore the church and the priest. The German radio has exultantly reported that in Smolensk the Slavonic Orthodox service has been restored in the cathedral, which previously had been used as an anti-religious museum. It has also been announced that the Ukrainian Eparch—a higher Slavonic Orthodox cleric, though, to tell the truth, nobody knew he existed, unless this relates to Polish territories—has thanked Hitler for restoring religion. The families of the many who are perishing in prisons and work camps can hardly be enthusiastic for victory, and these prisoners are reckoned in millions.

My informant read out a 'Secret Military Order' issued three weeks ago, which announces that commanders and all who voluntarily surrender or commit acts of treachery will bring punishment on their families and all their relations also; they will be imprisoned, and their property confiscated. It appears that four generals failed in the defence of Minsk and were shot, and their families have, in fact, been imprisoned. It is noteworthy that in Smolensk the Narcomvnudiel ordered the people to evacuate, but they went into hiding in order not to leave the town. None the less there are no signs of germs of revolt. The Narcomvnudiel is not only not sending its troops to the front —there are an enormous number of them—but is strengthening them numerically in the country.

Ambassador Steinhardt has been profuse in his explanations of the fact that, despite his promise, he did not arrange a conversation between me and Harriman on the political issue. He explained that on the day of their arrival by plane the delegation received a cable that it must return by the sixth day, and so all subsidiary conferences had to be abandoned. Steinhardt assures me that we have lost nothing by this, because he informed Harriman in the fullest detail of our military requirements, which in any case could not be officially settled. Harriman was of the opinion that to start with one must not adopt a distrustful attitude towards Russia and burden her with any binding obligations. If the Russians fail to hand over to the Polish army that which it should have from the war materials dispatched, then it will be necessary to make our claims publicly, and Washington will see that they are taken into account. Supplies will be sent every week, so with their aid it will be possible to bring all kinds of pressure to bear. In two or three weeks the United States Government will appoint a representative to Moscow to supervise supplies and everything will have to be discussed with him. This attitude of the American delegation is undoubtedly the result of Beaverbrook's suggestion.

. . . . The transport of aid for the people will be quite free, and will be undertaken by the Russians from the American port, but it has to be delivered to the American Delegation in Russia. However, so far agreement has not been reached on the number of members and workers in the Delegation, especially shorthand-typists.

On the religious question he and Harriman were informed of Roosevelt's wishes, but not of definite proposals. So in their last conversation in Moscow they mentioned Roosevelt's wishes concerning religious freedom to Stalin, Molotov, and Lozovsky. They consider they could not do more, and are satisfied that in a press interview Lozovsky confirmed Roosevelt's own view that there is in fact freedom both of religion and non-religion in Russia. Ambassador S. considers it is now my turn to take definite action. As things turned out, referring to Ciechanowski's letter to Cordell Hull, I was able to ask Vyshinsky how he thought our religious desiderata should be put into effect; but he evaded the question, demanding that I should put forward proposals, and we are to have a separate conference on the subject.

I take the opportunity to emphasize yet again the extraordinarily friendly behaviour of the British generals. When MacFarlane presented our troops' requirements and mentioned that 50,000 complete sets of equipment were on their way here Beaverbrook broke in violently: 'On what basis and who sent them? I know nothing of this, has there been parliamentary agreement?' This irritated Mac-Ready and he murmured to me: 'Our command surely has the right to send anything at its disposal, and we shall go on doing so.'

Yesterday we had a cable from Novosibirsk announcing the safe arrival of our delegates Heitzman and Szumski. They are making a three-day journey to Omsk. They praise the local authorities' friendly attitude. Tomorrow a delegate will set out for Archangel. The authorities here were less friendly to this journey, for instance they refused a place in a plane. We are planning further journeys, especially in Tashkent direction.

Our relations with the military camp are too loose so long as General Anders himself is not here. Liaison with Buzuluk is minimal. A 'lightning' telegram takes 30 hours to get there. The telephone doesn't function at all; although the Command has been granted one hour daily for telephoning, not one conversation has been successful so far. Train takes five days at least from Moscow (to Buzuluk), a plane takes nine hours, but it cannot be done in one day. Liaison between Buzuluk and the two divisions is also difficult; from Buzuluk to Totskoe, 45 kilometres, by car through the mud two hours . . . . to Kuibishev (Samara) 160 kilometres, by car seven hours, by train twelve hours; from there to Saratov it is 300 kilometres. In practice one can only communicate by air in that region. From Buzuluk to Ulianovsk, headquarters of the regional command, takes three days by train. It is not surprising that in these conditions it takes an unheard-of time to settle any question. Added to this is the shortage of trucks, which causes delay in meeting every kind of requirement.

I mention these details in order to explain much of the chaos which reigns here. I don't think it will be possible to shift any larger number of people out of Russia at present. None of us can determine who is in the Archangel area, or if anyone is there at all, and the Soviet authorities also don't know very much. So far we have no indication that a compact military prisoner camp exists there. The people coming from that area are a mixed lot: soldiers, refugees, women, old people, children. No one can segregate or even control them, so long as this mass of wandering groups, here and there held up by the authorities, does not arrive in Buzuluk or some other point in the south which is to be designated as a new encampment (near Tashkent).

Out of this chaotic mass who will be able to arrange for the transport of soldiers to Great Britain in any brief space of time? How long it will be before some order emerges from the chaos it is still difficult to foresee, since transport difficulties are increasing as the result of the military defeats. The one camp from which it would be possible to take people ready—i.e. trained—is Buzuluk, or the first two divisions; but to take 10,000 young men from them would be tantamount to destruction of the basis on which the entire military structure can be built up. I think General Anders, who is fretting and fuming over how to carry out your order and not undermine his own basis, will not find any judicious solution. Not to mention the fact that when he sounded the question with the authorities here he at once met with unpleasant surprise [on their part]. They are very suspicious and at

the moment it is necessary to avoid everything which seems unintelligible to them. They understand the dispatch of airmen and
sailors. Their numbers can be increased if we add a certain number
of candidates for the air and the navy. General Anders fully recognizes the necessity for our army in the West to be added to numerically
with a view to an offensive, but I have the impression that only when
spring has arrived will it be possible to talk of any considerable
transshipment of men. Then everybody capable of service will be
prepared and classified in the camps.

A21. To General Sikorski.
Moscow. 10 October 1941

It is possible that today may be my last good opportunity, so I write
hurriedly concerning various matters. On the one hand the German
offensive, on the other the difficulties of air flight, threaten the loss of
swift communications. So far as we have heard, the next convoy from
Archangel will not be sailing for a fortnight, and it will reach London
about 20 November.

Today for the first time official circles betrayed anxiety. The press
has carried articles preparing for any eventuality. The evacuation of
women and children has been quietly arranged. They fear an offensive
from Oriel towards Riazan, which would sever the main motor
traffic artery to the south, leaving only one road—to the east. In
diplomatic circles evacuation plans are being drawn up. No one is
mentioning the question to the Government as yet. Nor shall we be
the first to do so, although in the opinion of the British Embassy
priority in evacuation ought to go to the representatives of states not
recognized by Germany. Meanwhile we have prepared a list of people
who are not necessary in Moscow, with a view to sending them in the
direction of Tashkent.

Yesterday Kwapinski arrived from Yakutia in very good shape.
Today I shall decide whether to appoint him delegate to Tashkent.
There we shall have the largest concentration of Poles—especially
Jews, who are moving there *en masse*. There, also, further divisions
will probably be organized. Kwapinski has good personal conditions,
knowledge of the [Russian] language and methods, also great audacity
and self-confidence. . . . We at last have some delegates available for
the nearest areas, but it is not easy to obtain the approval and agreement of the authorities, who are now beginning to lose their heads,

while our Poles are more and more wandering *en masse* from north to south, though in tragic conditions.

When General Anders and I spoke over the radio on Saturday it was not agreed that the [Polish] state anthem should be played—they declared that no national anthem of any foreign state is ever played here—but a Soviet speaker astonished us by crying at the beginning and the end: 'Proletarians of all countries.' When my speech was repeated on Wednesday—it was read by Pruszynski—this was omitted because of our protest. If it were not for the serious situation it would be possible to begin regular radio speeches. . . .

I don't know whether in the present conditions they will agree to have a conversation with me on religious questions. I must demand an appropriate number of priests, so that services can be arranged for the larger concentrations of Polish citizens. If in fact few of them were deported from Poland I shall try to advise the release of priests imprisoned earlier,[1] otherwise they would have to agree to allow priests in from abroad. How many Polish priests have we available in Palestine and elsewhere? I would like to have the figure before the conversation, just in case.

. . . .

Through me Ehrlich and Alter have made an official inquiry of the [Polish] Government whether it foresees the Bund's participation in the National Council. In that case one of them will have to settle in London. I have informed them of the actual state of affairs, that there is no decision on this question, but that there are possibilities. I strongly request a definite answer. Meanwhile I have sent Alter as delegate to Sverdlovsk for a short time.

. . . . In two or three days General Anders will be leaving Moscow, presumably after waiting for and receiving a final decision of the Supreme Soviet, confirming the staff proposals: formal agreement to further divisions, the granting of 70,000 rations and the designation of a new area for the army—near Tashkent, possibly for Bohusz's division in Uralsk. Without these decisions the chaos will continue.[2]

Ambassador Steinhardt, who had delayed his flight owing to the weather, today decided to remain. During the last few days anxiety in Moscow is very keen. In any case our Embassy will remain, with a smaller staff of twenty persons—together with chauffeurs and porters. All the others I am removing, without using the term 'evacuation'.

---

[1] i.e., during pre-war anti-religious drives. *Tr.*
[2] Anders did not obtain this decision.

Everyone is going to Buzuluk under the pretext of military service, but it is planned that a group of aged and sick are to go on to Tashkent, and we would like the social welfare section to be settled in Novosibirsk. Unfortunately, I could not obtain the agreement of the authorities here, who are incapable of making any decision whatever, to the transfer of the welfare department outside the Embassy, so we are doing this in fact, but secretly. . . .

If General Zhukov travels [to London] it would be desirable to have conversations on various subjects with him; but in general you as Premier should raise only essential matters with him, and arrange for sensible persons to undertake conversations on details. The original object of his journey was to organize anti-German co-operation in Poland. Afterward this object was enlarged, apparently, into an investigation of Polish conditions in their entirety: *inter alia* the position of the Government and yourself, in view of the enormous quantity of news and gossip which they are receiving from their investigations and espionage. So I ask you to be thoroughly sure who is to inform him and on what. He is completely in Stalin's confidence, well up both on matters of external espionage—a specialist on Polish conditions—and as military expert—he controls the Moscow anti-aircraft defences—he is the *rapporteur* on matters concerning the Polish Army. As a confidant, quite high in the Narcomvnudiel hierarchy, he can influence the progress of our affairs within the Soviet state. . . .

In general you must stress the necessity for sincere co-operation with the Poles, based on confidence, so that so far as we are concerned they should cease to apply their police methods, which are ridiculous and do not yield any result. After all, they have lists of all our prisoners, but they are not releasing either political persons or whole groups of civilians and officers. Please do not believe their assurances that they do not know the whereabouts of those whom we are seeking. Every one of them [the prisoners] has been interrogated several times over by the Narcomvnudiel, and they know by heart where every one is confined, they only want to have us in their hands by detaining those we are interested in, and possibly in certain cases they are also afraid to admit that the individual is no longer alive. If they were really anxious to meet our desiderata honestly and with appropriate speed they would put me in touch with the head of the Narcomvnudiel, Beria, as I suggested to Vyshinsky in the Narcomindiel and in the presence of Zhukov himself; but apparently neither of them wanted to hear and understand what I said. Of course the Narcomindiel prefers that I should make contact with genuine government authorities, but in present conditions that has a delaying effect on every little detail of our requirements.

Activities intended for Poland have been largely put aside owing to the German advance. Soon it will be more difficult to fly to Poland from here than from London. It is necessary [for you] to emphasize that the organizations already functioning there will be able to do everything needed even without a numerous dispatch of people from here. With the exception of the Eastern Border areas. For various reasons we must insist that our people should be sent by plane to those areas, and to this end we must get hold of many politically active individuals from there who so far have not been released (for instance, the Boryslaw workers) and must make it clear that in face of Ukrainian pro-Germanism only Poles can be used.

. . . .

They [the Soviet authorities] seem to think that if they compel many Poles to sign declarations of service—which they are still forcing out of our people in the provinces—and assign them to this activity, they will have us encircled. That is absurd: every honest Pole is reporting to us in accordance with orders, despite the forced declarations. . . .

. . . . General Zhukov should honestly reveal to us the entire set up of his own organization in Poland, so that we can control whatever is rotten in it. For it is impossible for our people to co-operate with such types. A group they enrolled for pay and sent by plane in August consisted of a quite worthless lot of individuals, daring though some of them were. . . . And what is the object of putting before certain Poles a declaration binding them to watch what is happening in our army, to keep observation on certain generals . . . what is the object in sending into our ranks *provocateurs* who when in exile betrayed their fellow Poles? . . .

Naturally, it must be emphasized that secret activity in Poland must be based on a general move towards a realization there of the favourable position of our affairs in Russia, which will not be achieved if our radio speeches from Russia and ultimately our newspaper in Russia do not inform them. Regular broadcasts from our radio in Russia of lists of people who have been released will keep the listeners in Poland glued to their wireless sets despite all the dangers.

How varied the Narcomvnudiel activities are is indicated by a story which has been told me personally and in confidence by Ehrlich and Alter. They were summoned to a discussion of Jewish propaganda, especially in America, in favour of help to Russia under the guise of anti-Hitlerism. A central committee would be set up here, including representatives of Jews from Poland, Austria, Rumania, etc., and also Russia; in America a second, similar committee. Here Alter would be at the head, in America Ehrlich. As the result of their express proviso, as Polish citizens, this activity must have our approval, which would take the form, e.g., of appointing the Polish Ambassador and possibly others as honorary members of the committee. Beria held consultations on this question some days ago, and generals Fiedotov and Zhukov took part. It will be worth while making some reference to this activity, saying that in this direction too it will be better to co-operate openly with the Polish Government.

A22. To S. Mikołajczyk, Minister for Internal Affairs. Moscow. 10 October 1941

Communication is growing more and more difficult. From London I have had only one mail dated 18 September, I am still awaiting the next. From now on there are to be no further flights from here owing to the snow and ice in the North Sea; in other words, letters will go only by convoys, taking over a month. Apart from cables in cypher we are learning absolutely nothing. I have grown quite unused to newspapers and daily news, we pick up only what can be obtained from the radio. Undoubtedly Moscow is threatened and may fall in ten days or so. Yet here there is no knowledge whatever of what and if so how strong a defence is being prepared. There are hardly any raids, but who is to say whether that is not to lull vigilance, so that the capital should not be evacuated too soon? We here have split up, in preparation for any eventuality. A group of former prisoners is travelling to Tashkent. Those occupied with welfare will go for the time being to the army, then, if I obtain permission for their legal settlement in Novosibirsk, will be transferred there. About twenty of us will remain here until the last moment.

I have not advanced a single step in the search for our people, despite my persistence. . . .

Please go thoroughly into the question with Minister Liebermann of taking the Bund into the National Council. Ehrlich and Alter have expressed their desire for this. True, at the moment they are occupied with the organization of a Jewish anti-Hitlerite committee, but in full loyalty to the Polish Government. I do not believe that the authorities here would very sincerely favour this committee if it was not prepared to become their submissive instrument. Both these gentlemen well understand the situation and are firm, also they know the negative features of the Soviet system better than we do. The committee will in fact attempt to function in America, and I expect Ehrlich will go there. Alter was to become head of the committee here and simultaneously work in our welfare organization, but I get the impression that if a Bund representative was invited to join the National Council he would very readily travel to London. Please cable your reply on this question, since the hot situation here makes a speedy decision necessary.

. . . .

So far there are no political conflicts in sight among us. The situation does not allow of that. Among the delegates and men of trust we have all kinds of trends, including socialists and Jews; the decisive factors are personal energy and whoever can be found.

A24. To General Sikorski.
Moscow. 11 October 1941

(Things may be bad here at any moment now.) We shall manage somehow. On the other hand, you might discreetly ask Bogomolov where and how diplomatic posts will be organized in the event of the loss of Moscow. . . . It might be best if the Czechs and Yugoslavs asked about this, and not we.

Here there is an everlasting lack of decision. Today Cripps complained that he cannot even extort the signature of an agreement in which Britain gives Russia everything for nothing, without a soul! . . .

The threat to Moscow will undoubtedly make Zhukov's departure impossible and hold up the plans for work in Poland. Maybe as time passes it will be easier for us to gain something here. For the time being the monstrous centralization renders it impossible for even high officials to obtain a decision. . . .

If Moscow is lost it will be some time before the chaos is brought under control, the snapping of the threads of central government authorities will facilitate disorder. Our people are now wandering and camping quite arbitrarily, and of course are paying for it with hunger and disease.

As the authorities here will require more and more aid, those who give it would be able to obtain many conditions by bargaining, but they would also have to give real aid and dictate the conditions. If we could co-operate well with Washington that would give the greatest results. . . .

A26. To S. Mikołajczyk.
Moscow. 11 October 1941

I am making an addition to yesterday's letter. The military situation is very unclear, we hear alarming rumours that Moscow is encircled, which afterwards turn out to be somewhat exaggerated. Tomorrow two trucks of our people will set off for the [army] camp. . . . I feel some scruples whether parting from the welfare office is not premature, but as certain rather impressionable individuals are getting unnerved I prefer to send them away earlier rather than have to stand their continual fears. . . .

Difficulties are arising over the Jewish question: because of the Pact and the releases the Jews are fervently emphasizing their Polish citizenship. We must remember that if not a third, at least a fourth of our citizens here are Jewish. For the Soviets carried off about 400,000 Jewish refugees from the Hitlerite occupation, but if any of them had Russian sympathies they have been cured of them completely. There has been an enormous influx into the army, in certain formations forty per cent. Our military . . . are already wanting to introduce a *numerus clausus* in the military institutions. Both our anti-Semites and the Jewish nationalists (the followers of Jabotinsky[1]) are putting forward the idea of purely Jewish detachments under Polish command. Politically this is very undesirable and it would be good if London did not encourage the idea. In the future, when the eastern frontier comes up for consideration, this influx of Jews will be a great political argument, especially in view of the Ukrainians' systematic hatred for everything Polish—despite this they gladly avail themselves of the provisions of the Pact.

A27. (a) Cable to General Sikorski.
Moscow. 12 October 1941

Although it would be the greatest of festivals for the Poles, I decidedly consider your visit here as purposeless at the moment. It can have no effect in reinforcing the Russian masses, since they live in the secret

[1] Leader of the group of Zionist Revisionists to the left of the orthodox Zionist organization. *Tr.*

hope that the régime will fall, and they dislike the Poles.[1] The officials here are too arrogant, secretive and petty to open their ears to suggestions and genuinely to allow a joint analysis of the situation. Because of their equivocation Polish affairs have not developed to such an extent that your arrival might give them a fundamental push forward. The government is absorbed in defence and evacuation and has no time for anything else.

When the front is stabilized, when a planned reorganization of activity in every field begins, your arrival may be beneficial and triumphant. . . .

A27. (b) To General Sikorski.
Moscow. 13 October 1941

On the eleventh a convoy arrived at Archangel with uniforms and men. Unloading has begun.

Today I handed Vyshinsky a firm note asking for the Pact to be carried out in respect of the release of prisoners, accommodation of those released, assurance of accommodation for the troops; I appended a list of prisoners, and camps where thousands are still held.

B8. Conversation with A. J. Vyshinsky, Vice-Commissar for Foreign Affairs.
14 October 1941
Present: Pushkin, deputy head of a Narcomindiel Department; the Embassy secretary, W. Arlet.

Kot . . . asks whether Vyshinsky knows of the plan for the Premier, General Sikorski, to visit Russia. The Ambassador would like to devote today's conversation to this question.

VYSHINSKY. The Soviet Ambassador in London, Bogomolov, has already informed the Soviet Government of this and has received appropriate instructions.

KOT. When was this?

VYSHINSKY. I don't remember the date. (He sends Pushkin to get information on the point.)

Kot indicates that the plan for a visit arose in understanding with Premier Churchill.

Vyshinsky confirms that he knows this.

KOT. I would like to explain General Sikorski's intentions in making

---

[1] Because of the Polish determination to go on fighting.

such a visit to the U.S.S.R. It is for the purpose of emphasizing and demonstrating to all the world the fighting readiness of all Poles for the struggle now being waged in Eastern Europe. At this moment, when German and isolationist propaganda all over the world is vociferously declaring that the war against the Soviet Union is already ending in victory, General Sikorski wishes to show all the world that he not only ardently desires the victory of the Soviet Union but profoundly believes in that victory.

He also wishes to contradict the Hitlerite propaganda that the war on the Soviet Union is a war for religious freedom, that it is in the interests of Catholicism. The arrival of the Head of Government of a nation known all over the world as a Catholic nation will be a living refutation of this propaganda. It will also be of far-reaching importance for public opinion in all the Slavonic world as well as in the United States and the Anglo-Saxon world generally. The press of America and Great Britain will undoubtedly comment on the fact that the Head of the Polish Government is making such a visit at this time, and will give it great publicity.

So far as Polish affairs are concerned, General Sikorski's visit is of very great importance. The Germans are beginning to make up to the Poles and are developing certain activities aimed at winning them over, for instance, they are returning estates and other real property to Poles who fled from the Soviet annexed area, or to those originating from Eastern Poland who found themselves in German prisoner of war camps. This activity is being accompanied by corresponding propaganda. General Sikorski's arrival in the U.S.S.R. will be a serious blow to German propaganda in Poland and a summons to our nation not to give ear to this German activity. . . . I would like to hear your views on General Sikorski's proposed visit.

VYSHINSKY. The Soviet Government will be very glad of his coming. (Vyshinsky had made detailed notes of the Ambassador's statement, but he had shown some signs of nervousness.)

KOT. But in the present state of Polish affairs General Sikorski's visit could not achieve full results. We cannot allow him to be met on U.S.S.R. territory only by complaints from the Polish people. For his stay to be of significance the obligations arising from the Polish-Soviet Agreement should be loyally executed by the Soviet side. Already two months have passed since the Supreme Soviet proclaimed an amnesty, yet there are still many Poles in prison, in work camps and exile. We have a number of practical desiderata which we think it vitally important should be realized as swiftly as possible. In addition to completing the work of freeing the prisoners, there is the question of effecting the transference [of the Polish people], but in a planned manner that will be beneficial to them. Further, there are the questions of providing them with work according to their qualifications, of settling the problem of organizing care and aid for those who are without means of existence.

VYSHINSKY (in a somewhat agitated tone). The problems you are now raising are all very difficult and complicated, they cannot be solved in a short space of time in such difficult conditions as exist at present.

KOT. A number of problems demand immediate settlement. In Tashkent, in the south, to which spot the Polish people have been trekking in order to improve their lot, Polish citizens are camping out in the streets under the bare sky, without means of existence, and driven by the militia from place to place. Large groups of our citizens are camping out in the railway stations without any oversight or means of existence whatever being provided. They are not receiving even the bread and other food supplied to refugees from the Soviet territories occupied by the Germans.

The second great section of our affairs which is not proceeding in accordance with our interests is the army. The accommodation provided is completely inadequate. Two camps, and summer camps at that, are so overfilled that thousands of men have to remain in the open, and are even spending the nights there. The Polish Army has undertaken to build eighty dugouts, each with room for 300 people. But to do this it needs two thousand spades; so far not one has arrived, and the timber is in a forest some 100 kilometres away, with no means of communication whatever. Owing to the lack of accommodation and the horrible hygienic conditions spotted typhus and typhoid have made their appearance in the army. General Anders waited two weeks in Moscow for a decision as to the formation of further divisions and then was forced to leave, unable to wait any longer.

VYSHINSKY. What army are you referring to? To the one which was to be formed in accordance with the Agreement?

KOT. Yes, of course.

VYSHINSKY. But the Agreement provides for two divisions and one reserve brigade. These have been formed.

KOT. The basic Agreement does not make any restriction of that kind, it states that the numerical size of the army will depend on the numbers of the contingents available.

VYSHINSKY. Why are you mentioning this to me? After all, it is not for me to form the new divisions. Let the military settle these matters among themselves.

KOT. But the military are running into difficulties. General Anders presented definite plans long ago, and he cannot get an answer. That is why I am raising these issues. If the war is to be conducted seriously all the human resources must be mobilized.

VYSHINSKY (agitated, in a rather discourteous tone). What is the purpose of all your remarks? You have presented your complaints to us, we have received a note which I am inquiring into, now you raise it all again. What is it really all about?

KOT. Only to ensure that all the defects and shortcomings in Polish-Soviet relations should be eliminated as quickly as possible. It's a matter of issuing definite instructions and orders to the local authorities, so that by the time General Sikorski arrives all these disputed issues should no longer disturb Polish-Soviet relations.

VYSHINSKY. I cannot guarantee that they will be settled before General Sikorski's arrival. Especially as they are so complicated, and their settlement is difficult because of the war.

KOT. I quite understand that, but none the less there are certain things which are fundamentally important, for instance, release. Not one Polish citizen should be left under arrest by the time General Sikorski arrives.

VYSHINSKY. As a matter of fact I wanted to talk to you about the releases. (He takes statistics on the released Poles from Pushkin, and quotes:)

Of the 387,932 former Polish citizens deprived of freedom in the U.S.S.R. the various categories were made up as follows:

1st Category: put in prison or held in prison under investigation: 71,481.
2nd Category: settled in special settlements and deported to places of compulsory residence: 291,137.
3rd Category: prisoners of war: 25,314.

Of the total, on 1 October 1941, 345,511 had been released. . . .

KOT (challenges the accuracy of these figures). That is impossible. The camp in Starobielsk alone held more prisoners than the total you have given.

VYSHINSKY. I can give you only the figures I possess.

KOT. According to Soviet sources there were 9,600 officers alone in prisoner of war camps.

VYSHINSKY (replies, and a long discussion follows, carried on at great speed, at times without the interpreter, on the question of the figures' accuracy. The conversation takes on a note of irritation). I sincerely admit that we did deport certain definite groups: officials, officers, police, gendarmes; but after all, not the entire population.

KOT. But the settlers?

VYSHINSKY. The settlers are included in these figures.

An argument follows over the term 'deportee'. Vyshinsky and Pushkin explain that the figures do not include citizens, formerly Polish, who, by force of the Soviet decree of 1 October 1939 acquired Soviet citizenship.[1] Vyshinsky produces another statistical compilation, according to the above three categories, but divided into regions (*oblasts*), and indicates that the Ambassador will be receiving this compilation tomorrow. An argument follows as to the accuracy of the numbers of Poles in the respective regions.

VYSHINSKY. . . . Is the settlement of these questions a condition of General Sikorski's visit, or only a desire?

KOT. Obviously, only a desire.

VYSHINSKY. As the representative of the People's Commissariat for Foreign Affairs, and *ipso facto* of the Soviet Government, I should be very glad if all these questions could be settled. I am dealing with them myself, but I wish to emphasize that we concluded the Polish-Soviet Agreement more from sentimental motives (*dogovor po chustvu*) than rational ones. And it is difficult to say that it involved advantages for us, rather the reverse. After all, we too are interested in putting the situation of Polish citizens in order and organizing work for them.

KOT. This question is of serious sentimental importance for us also. We would like all the issues which still divide us to be brought to a successful conclusion, so that when General Sikorski arrives they should not burden our relations. At the moment he cannot find even

---

[1] The U.S.S.R. Supreme Soviet decree dated 1 October 1939, incorporating Eastern Malopolska and Volhynia in the Soviet Union, under the name of 'Western Ukraine'. Also the Supreme Soviet decree dated 29 November 1939, declaring Soviet citizens (1) citizens formerly Polish, who were on the territories of Western Ukraine and Bielorussia on the day these territories became part of the U.S.S.R. (i.e., 1/2 October 1939); (2) persons who arrived in the U.S.S.R. on the basis of the agreement with Germany dated 16 November 1939.

close officer friends of his who are in the U.S.S.R., among them even his own adjutant.[1]

VYSHINSKY. I shall do everything possible in the present situation, but perhaps the Mixed Commission could occupy itself with the details?

KOT. The Commission is a dead institution and will settle nothing. The Soviet side doesn't include anyone who could make a decision on even the tiniest point.

VYSHINSKY. In that case, send me the data on the local authorities' shortcomings in writing. Let one of the six first secretaries of the Embassy occupy himself with writing out these points, or at least send us the originals of the complaints the Embassy has received.

KOT. We have three first secretaries, of whom one is returning to England for reasons of health. Of course we shall send you all the Polish citizens' complaints, but I would not like the local authorities to utilize them afterwards against the persons concerned.

VYSHINSKY. We don't even require to know the names of the individuals making the complaints. It is only a question of the facts, and we shall bring pressure to bear on the local authorities. In your note[2] you write that the situation of the released Polish citizens is worse than before. On this point I have received a statement from the Narcom-vnudiel, also in writing, to the effect that wherever Polish citizens have remained behind in order to work they enjoy the same basic rights possessed by free Soviet citizens. . . .

KOT. Turning to other matters, has the question of a credit made any progress?

VYSHINSKY. I have been held up on this question. But I expect to be in a position to give you an answer during the next few days.

KOT. Really the object of my visit today was not to discuss all these issues. The conversation has departed somewhat from its real subject. I would like to clear up certain other matters connected with General Sikorski's visit. I hope that, turning to the formal aspect, he will be sent an official invitation.

VYSHINSKY. Of course. Bogomolov has already received instructions on that point.

KOT. Can General Sikorski count on being received immediately by the Head of the Government?

---

[1] Major Jan Fuhrman, one of the Katyn victims.

[2] In a note to the Vice-Commissar for Foreign Affairs, of date 13 October 1941, the Ambassador, after citing details on the situation of Polish citizens, declared: ' In no case could the Polish Government agree to a state in which the result of the 30 July 1941 agreement was to be a worsening of the fate of Polish citizens in the U.S.S.R. . . .'

VYSHINSKY. That goes without saying.

KOT. Has the Soviet Government any wishes in regard to the date of his arrival?

VYSHINSKY. We leave that entirely to the choice of General Sikorski, who will be received in accordance with international law and the etiquette appropriate to this kind of visit.

KOT. I hope that when he arrives he will find all his officers.

VYSHINSKY. We are handing over to you all the people we have, but we cannot hand over people who are said to be in the U.S.S.R. but who in reality have never been here.

KOT (laughing). We ask only that you should hand over the people you have, that will be quite enough for us.

The conversation lasted from 20 to 21.15 hours, to the accompaniment at times of anti-aircraft fire. It was carried on in a more animated tone than any previous conversation. Vyshinsky was agitated, at times discourteous. Towards the end of the conversation he calmed down and adoped a conciliatory, and finally a joking tone.

A27. (c) Cable to General Sikorski.
Moscow. 14 October 1941

Discussing the question of your visit with Vyshinsky today, I started from the premiss that the situation of the Poles here must be so ordered that they will welcome their Premier as their saviour and will not overwhelm him with reproaches concerning their difficult lot, and I further emphasized the necessity for release from the camps and of the people still detained, the improvement of the lot of those who have been shifted elsewhere, regulation of labour and welfare, the creation of better housing and sanitary conditions for the army. I explained that these were not prerequisites to your visit, but that without improvements your visit will be made difficult, as, for instance, it will be unpleasant for the General not to see many of his officers, and even his own adjutant, who so far have not been released.

There were also sharp exchanges over details, when, for instance, he assured me there were only 25,000 prisoners of war, and the total number of deported Polish citizens amounted to 380,000. I stressed the importance of your visit for the Poles, the Slavs, the Catholics, and America. I consider it necessary to wait to see whether they show goodwill to improve the difficult situation.

For some time we have been conscious of a complete hold-up in our

affairs. This has been evident since the beginning of the Moscow
Conference, when doubtless they became convinced that the Allies
are not supporting us.

A28. To General Sikorski.
Moscow. 15 October 1941

This evening, the 15th, we are all travelling by train to Kuibishev—
Samara. There are some seventy of us; yesterday as many more went
off. Moscow is to be defended desperately, order continues, railway
damage is swiftly repaired, but the population is waiting passively
and is criticizing aloud. I hope the system of centralization may hold
out outside Moscow too. Our journey will take three days, that is
certain. . . .

A29. To General Sikorski.
Kuibishev. 20 October 1941

We detrained at Kuibishev today, 20th, we have a tolerable building.
The government hasn't yet made itself known to us, though without
doubt it is here. In the train during the night of the 18th we picked
up part of the cable referring to the date of the Premier's intended
arrival, but without any further details, so I don't know what attitude
to adopt. I await Anders' arrival, but I know that so far no accommodation has been granted for further detachments, and so the
soldiers and volunteers are travelling *en masse* further into Asia.

Please repeat the details of your arrival in a cable. I do hope it will
not be premature. *En route* I saw crowds of our wretches, sick and
hungry, sent off without plan.

The atmosphere here is unwarlike, with no blackout.

A30. To General Sikorski.
Kuibishev. 21 October 1941

I am afraid the government here will not be in such a state of reorganization within ten days as to be able to welcome you appropriately, and especially to make good use of your visit.

I advise postponement of the date, and in the meanwhile that we
press for the fulfilment of our desiderata. If they accept them and issue
corresponding decisions here, then on arrival you will be able to give
a strong push towards their realization. If they don't make any
decision before your arrival, that will be a sign that they welcome your
visit only in so far as it fits their own interests, and will continue to be

evasive towards us. They are still not releasing the more prominent individuals despite our indicating definite addresses.

I have had talks with peasants who have travelled down from the North, they believe unshakably in the defeat of the Germans and tell of the diametrically opposite attitude of the Russian peasants.

> *B9. Conversation with the Vice-Chairman of the U.S.S.R. Supreme Soviet, and People's Commissar for Foreign Affairs: V Molotov.*
>
> *In the Narcomindiel at Kuibishev. 22 October 1941*

(Ambassador's note: Today I requested an audience with Molotov; shortly afterward I received notification that he had asked me to see him at 21 hours. He gave me the impression of being incredibly overworked, obsessed with the seriousness of the situation, but endeavouring none the less to master his exhaustion during the conversation, which throughout was of a friendly nature.)

KOT. In coming to see you I begin by expressing both in the name of the Polish Government and on my own behalf our wishes for victory over Germany, which, I hope, will occur while the Soviet Government is in its new headquarters, Kuibishev.

MOLOTOV. Thank you for those words. But I must emphasize that none of us is losing heart and the fight is continuing with all our inflexibility.

KOT. We Poles realize the difficult situation, but, as history has shown, our national character is such that it is in the difficult moments that we are able to develop our forces most thoroughly, and in every sector we put up increasing resistance. During the last few days I have talked with hundreds of Poles and they are all of the one opinion, that we must jointly co-operate in our task so as not to be weakened in the struggle against the common enemy. The feeling among the Poles is so strong that the Soviet Government may be sure they will constitute an organic force resisting any currents which might weaken the struggle with the enemy. Part of Hitler's plan counts on the possibility of the Soviet Union weakening not only on the external but also on the internal front, and here the Poles, who are all without exception absolutely opposed to the Germans, will be an active ally.

MOLOTOV. I must state that the masses of the people of the Soviet Union are as solid as possible and in all sectors and with all their strength are supporting the Soviet Government's efforts in its struggle with the enemy. When Hitler started the war he reckoned that the solidarity of the Soviet Union would weaken, he counted on a weakening of its centripetal force, and also on differences among the nationalities. These calculations have completely failed, and today Hitler clearly realizes that he will not win the struggle on this front. The representatives of the Soviet Union have vital contact with the masses, they are conscious of their will to victory. The Polish citizens who have contact with the masses of the Soviet population should certainly aid them.

KOT. If you deem it necessary we are perfectly ready to put ourselves at your Government's disposition, in order to aid it on the propaganda front. We can arrange for a number of transmissions, auditions and speeches of Polish citizens at present in the Soviet Union, who would tell the whole world of their inflexible determination in the fight against our common enemy and would emphasize Poland's co-operation with the Soviets. That would upset even more Hitler's hopes of the emergence of differences of opinion in the Soviet Union and of utilizing these in propaganda abroad.

MOLOTOV. Only before the outbreak of war did Hitler count on disintegrating forces operating in the Soviet Union; now he doesn't count on such possibilities even one per cent. But I thank you for your proposal: if we need help, of course we shall take advantage of it.

However, our most important problem arises in connection with the shortage of tanks and aeroplanes. A very large part of our war industry has had to be evacuated, and at present we are installing factories and war industry plants in the Caucasus, in Asia, and in various parts of the Soviet Union's eastern territories. I must tell you that the Germans have a very considerable preponderance of tank weapons, and even modern infantry cannot hold out against the Germans' blows; and, because of their numerical superiority, they break through and make withdrawal necessary. Of course we have great possibilities of organizing war industry, and not only [for production of] tanks and aeroplanes, but also of artillery, all of which we shall manufacture, if not today then tomorrow and even later—but for this we need time.

KOT. You know, of course, of General Sikorski's intention to visit the U.S.S.R. (MOLOTOV: Yes.) This visit is intended to emphasize his faith in victory. . . . After all, so-called official visits are not made at times when the situation is difficult. But this visit is of a totally different nature. Its purpose is to demonstrate the solidarity between the Soviet Union and the Polish Republic to all the world.

MOLOTOV. I well understand the objects of the General's and Commander in Chief's visit . . . and fully realize the role he will play. Obviously we would prefer to receive General Sikorski in Moscow, in better conditions, and showing him all the honours to which he is entitled. You realize that in the local conditions here a number of technical difficulties will arise; but these are not so important. I leave it to General Sikorski to choose the most suitable moment for fixing the date of his arrival.

KOT. But we are not concerned with outward decorum. As a soldier, General Sikorski is accustomed to the modest conditions of a soldier's life, and will realize the local difficulties. General Sikorski would like to leave London on 28 October, as he has notified me in a cypher cable, asking at the same time whether that is suitable to the Soviet Union, and also emphasizing that he could postpone the date.

MOLOTOV. I shall inform the Chairman of the Supreme Soviet of this, and will let you know the result immediately. But even now I can say that I see no obstacles so far as the date of the visit is concerned, which we can already regard as fixed.

KOT. The date I have given you is that of his departure from London; but the exact date of his arrival in Kuibishev cannot be fixed since that depends on the means of communication, but in any case it will take about a week.

MOLOTOV. I realize that. . . .

KOT. Arising out of General Sikorski's visit, I wish to raise some problems connected with the situation of the Polish citizens in the U.S.S.R. A positive solution to these problems will facilitate General Sikorski's visit and prepare his welcome by the Poles. You realize that the visit of the Head of the Polish Government has two aspects : first, the external effect which I mentioned to you at the beginning and which does not raise any difficulties; second, the problem of the Polish citizens. If this is solved satisfactorily the Poles, who, because of the experiences they have undergone during the past two years, are nervously sensitive, as soon as they are conscious of a change for the better in their existence will be grateful to General Sikorski. But if there were to be complaints it would be unpleasant for us.

MOLOTOV. Of course.

KOT. First, the amnesty question. The instructions of the central authorities have very evidently not reached a number of centres, they should be carried out a hundred per cent, so that General Sikorski can see our Agreement is quite real.

MOLOTOV. Please give me a precise account of how this matter stands.

KOT. I have given Mr. Vyshinsky a number of instances of centres which the amnesty instructions have not reached, as well as categories of our citizens, for instance officers, public prosecutors, police, who have not been released. Mr. Vyshinsky promised to take up the question, but has not done so. I'm afraid the oncoming winter will make it impossible for them to leave such remote areas as Kolyma, for example.

MOLOTOV. All the Polish citizens have been released as the result of the amnesty, but doubtless in a number of districts they have remained in their previous places of residence, since, owing to the course of events great transport and administrative difficulties have arisen, for instance the problem of evacuating the Soviet population from areas occupied by the Germans. But please accept my assurance that we shall give the Polish Government full help in this matter within the bounds of our possibilities.

KOT. Thank you very much, and we ask for a list of those centres where Polish citizens freed so far are remaining for the present. We realize the Soviet Government's difficulties, but if we have information about our citizens we shall be able to wait patiently for the possibility of their being transferred.

MOLOTOV. We shall take every step to see that you are informed.

KOT. I want to raise the question of accelerating the discovery of a number of my political friends, of whom so far we have no information. You have released (in a joking tone) several princes, counts, two Pilsudskis,[1] but so far I have seen no representatives of the Peasant Party and I have been unable to make any contact with them. (Molotov laughs.) In London we have a National Council which is our reduced parliament. The Peasant Party, of which I am a member, still has an unfilled quota of seats. I would like to send several members of the Peasant Party from Russia to London. In 1939 the representatives of the opposition in Poland did not have the facilities to go abroad that the governing circles had, and so there are hardly any of them in the West.

MOLOTOV. The persons you have referred to are better known than many other sections of the population and so it was easier to find them. But we shall endeavour to obtain news of the persons you have in mind, and I hope there will be no difficulties, provided they are living in the U.S.S.R. under the names they had in Poland.

---

[1] Relations of Marshal Pilsudski. *Tr.*

KOT. Could I perhaps make an appeal over the radio to my fellow citizens, citing a number of names?

MOLOTOV. Not everybody has a radio. The best thing would be to give us lists of the names, and I shall try through the Narcomvnudiel to have full instructions issued on the question.

KOT. It would be very helpful if I could make direct contact with a representative of the Narcomvnudiel on a number of issues which don't really concern foreign affairs and only burden your office. Not that they are difficult to resolve, but they're complicated. As an example I cite the impossibility of discovering General Sikorski's adjutant, to whom the General is deeply attached.

MOLOTOV. Is he here?

KOT. He was in a prisoner of war camp in the U.S.S.R., and afterwards was transferred into the heart of Russia.

MOLOTOV. What is his name?

KOT. Major Jan Fuhrman.

MOLOTOV. Everything will be done to find him. (He instructs the interpreter, a Narcomindiel official, to make a note of the name.)

KOT. If by chance, unfortunately, he is no longer alive, please let us know, for uncertainty is worst of all. I mention also the names of two eminent Polish generals: Orlik-Łukoski and Kmicic-Skrzyński, of whom so far we've had no news whatever, as well as a number of other names, which I shall not burden you with now.

MOLOTOV. Please send me a list.

KOT. General Anders has already presented one such list to the competent authorities. I ask for instructions to be issued for the matter to be settled speedily. General Sikorski attaches great importance to it in connection with his visit.

MOLOTOV. We shall try to do everything possible.

KOT. On the question of care for the Polish population, arising out of their transfer to other districts and the difficult living conditions there is a high mortality rate among the children, and illness and want among the people generally. I have neither the technical nor the financial possibility of helping them. I want to discuss how to improve this state of things with the Narcomvnudiel, and I ask for a competent representative to be appointed with appropriate plenipotentiary powers and empowered to settle a number of practical questions without resort to diplomatic channels. In your present situation I dare not ask for a conversation on points of detail either with you or with commissar Vyshinsky.

MOLOTOV. Please do not feel under any constraint, but come to me or Mr. Vyshinsky, for I feel myself under obligation to adjust this question. It is impossible to arrange for a Narcomvnudiel delegate, since he would be competent only in regard to affairs connected with his commissariat. But if it is a question of adjusting the existence of Polish citizens, there are other, equally competent commissariats, for example Health, Trade and Industry, and Transport. I hope we shall delegate a competent official of the Commissariat for Foreign Affairs to adjust these questions, but in any case I shall raise the problem with the Narcomvnudiel.

KOT. I suppose when you talk with other representatives of the Diplomatic Corps accredited to the Soviet Government you discuss subjects arising out of problems of foreign policy. I am in a worse situation than my colleagues. I have to burden you with a number of points of detail. I emphasize once more that this is not the moment for such things, and I well realize the seriousness of the time. But if you empower me to do so I shall certainly raise such issues as the supply of milk for children. (They both laugh heartily.)

MOLOTOV. I am always at your disposal, but if I am not available, since I anticipate visits to Moscow, with which we have good communications, then Vyshinsky will always act in my place.

KOT. I ask you to put in a good word to speed up the question of a welfare loan for the Polish people. That is a burning question for us. Mr. Vyshinsky has promised to send me an outline agreement. I realize that the delay has arisen because of the situation. But I am very anxious to get the matter of the loan settled before General Sikorski arrives.

MOLOTOV. Yes. . . .

KOT. There remains one final question, namely, the army. As you know, General Sikorski is not only Chairman of the Council of Ministers, but the Commander in Chief of the Polish Armed Forces. In Soviet Russia we possess an enormous reserve of men capable of bearing arms. It is only a question of utilizing it properly. We have put forward a plan, which the Staff of the Soviet Forces has received favourably, for the creation of three new divisions. You fully realize that the war will go on for a long time yet and will exhaust many forces. The Poles want to fight, and they will certainly put all their energy and enthusiasm into the struggle. I am anxious to obtain a speedy decision from the Soviet Government as to the place where the camps for these three divisions can be established.

MOLOTOV. Great organizational difficulties arise in the creation of these divisions. Above all, armaments are necessary, and these are lacking in the U.S.S.R., nor does Poland possess them. After all, we haven't armaments even for those divisions already organized. What are the prospects of the Polish Government receiving armaments from America and England?

KOT. As a military man General Sikorski will give a full answer to this question. Obviously, so far as armaments are concerned there are no prospects at present of tanks, armoured weapons and anti-tank weapons, but so far as other categories are concerned they will undoubtedly be forthcoming. The most important immediate issue is that of bringing the soldiers within an organizational framework, of preparing their training and forming cadres. We have many militarily seasoned soldiers here in the Soviet Union, many of them are from armoured forces, and it would be a pity not to make full use of them. In addition, by forming these three divisions before equipment for them has arrived we shall have time to bring them up to strength. Moreover, if the soldiers are brought under a certain discipline, and not forced to seek work on their own account, they will remain good soldiers and preserve their moral and physical strength. Of course General Anders anticipates that these soldiers will not only undergo military training, but will be at the Soviet Government's disposal for carrying out works in the area where their camps are situated.

MOLOTOV. Will they receive food rations from England or America?

KOT. No. By the terms of the Military Agreement the question of their rationing falls to the Soviet authorities.

MOLOTOV. The Agreement mentions a definite number of divisions, and these have already been formed. We have lost the most fertile Ukrainian lands, and the Germans are outside Moscow, so the situation is very difficult in regard to food supplies. The Poles will be able to earn their keep among us by working.[1]

KOT. The Agreement provides for the formation of two divisions and one brigade at first, but it foresees the further formation of new

---

[1] This part of the conversation aroused fears on the Polish side that the Soviets were wanting to hold up the further development of the Polish Army. This explains why I referred the matter to the United States Ambassador, Mr. Steinhardt, and also his report to the State Department on 22 October, and Cordell Hull's suggestion, in a letter to Steinhardt on 7 November, that the troops should be sent to Iran for feeding and training, and thence return to the Soviet front. (Diplomatic Papers, 1941, as above; pp. 254-258.) Also Harriman raised the matter with Stalin, Sikorski mentioned it to Ambassador Bogomolov, and Ambassador Ciechanowski sent a note to the State Secretary on 10 November. (ibid., pp. 260-261.)

divisions. So far as uniforms, etc., for these three additional divisions are concerned, the English will supply them, but on the question of food rations General Sikorski must talk to the English about it. In any case I am not empowered to discuss these matters in detail, but I wish to notify you that General Sikorski will want to raise them. If difficulties do arise in the organization of a certain number of new divisions, there is the idea of sending for example 20,000 soldiers from here to England, where we have many officers who, owing to the lack of soldiers, cannot be properly utilized. I wish to inform you that the Polish Army in England is intended as an army of descent on the continent. (Molotov noted down this part of the conversation.)

MOLOTOV. So far as military issues are concerned, the English are unfortunately not in a state to make any descent today, and so cannot form a second front which would relieve us of some of the burden in the struggle against the Germans. So far as we are concerned, owing to the lack of armaments we ourselves are holding up the formation of new military units. At the conference of the three States in Moscow the question of food supplies for the Soviet Union was raised *inter alia*, and they were assured to us by both England and America. America and Canada must supply us with flour. In regard to the soldiers whom you plan to draw upon to form new divisions, if it is a question of solving the problem of feeding them, in my opinion the only solution, if England does not supply food, is to place them in factories, industrial establishments or elsewhere. Returning again to the question of a descent, we must face the fact that the English are not in a position to accomplish this, nor unfortunately to transfer their forces to U.S.S.R. territory. This state of affairs obviously does not coincide with the interests of either the U.S.S.R. or Great Britain.

KOT. I ask that the Soviet Government do not decide prematurely on the question of forming three new divisions. The Poles are excellent soldiers. After all, the war will last a long time yet, and select troops will certainly be required.

MOLOTOV. I spoke in such detail of the difficulties in forming three new divisions because I wished you to be exactly informed of those difficulties, as well as the conditions in which the Soviet Government is placed, so that you may take it all into consideration.

KOT. The Poles are preparing energetically for a descent. You know that the Poles are the finest of airmen, you know of their exploits over the Germans, and what a spirit animates every Polish soldier. (Molotov makes a note.) I don't know whether it would be a good thing to use soldiers as unskilled workers, not much benefit would accrue from them that way, and a reserve of energy and enthusiasm for the struggle would be dissipated. I ask very strongly that the door may remain open for a settlement of this question.

MOLOTOV. In any case we shall have to take the actual facts of the situation into account. We shall be delighted if something can be achieved, bearing in mind whether we have the possibilities. I again stress that I am concerned that you should get a clear picture of our situation. (Molotov quotes the Russian proverb corresponding to ' cutting your coat to fit your cloth '.) If we could do more to provide our own army with what it needs obviously we would.

The conversation lasted from 20.52 to 22.14 hours.

A31. Cable to General Sikorski.
Kuibishev. 23 October 1941

Would it not be possible for you to travel direct from here to Washington? Then the people here will treat our potentialities differently. By Liberator it would take a week from here to America via Cairo. Via India it is ten days. We must start trying to get not only arms but food.
. . . .

A32. Cable to General Sikorski.
Kuibishev. 24 October 1941 7 a.m.

Your arrival must be postponed. The Government here will not be functioning quickly. Molotov flew to Moscow yesterday to see Stalin. The others are wandering around unpacked; even if they wished to they would not be in a condition to receive you properly, despite their promises. . . .

A34. Cable to Polish Embassy in Washington.
Kuibishev. 27 October 1941

For some time now transports of Polish people have been routed to Uzbekistan and they are being employed on the cotton plantations and on irrigation and construction works. The Soviet authorities are settling 100,000 Poles in the districts of Nukus and Novo-Urgench on the Amu-Daria river and at Bokhara, Samarkand, and Fergana. The labour conditions are very hard. Earnings are sufficient only for very poor nourishment. People are dying of hunger *en route*. There is a danger of malaria in the localities. The greatest tragedy is the lack of clothing, footwear, and children's clothing. You must urge the speed up of aid in kind. Please stir up Polonia[1] and the Red Cross.

35. Cable to General Sikorski. 29 October 1941

I was tremendously glad of your cable No. 110. I shall use the possibility that your arrival may be postponed to obtain concessions. Today we are conscious of improvement in details, but the absence of the heads of Government makes it difficult to clear up fundamental problems. . . .

Can I inform the Soviet Government that England gives an official assurance as to the equipment and provisioning of our forces? The area to which the excess of soldiers and volunteers is being directed—Uzbekistan—is situated most favourably for British supplies. The Caucasus cannot be taken into account. A great increase in transport from England via Archangel is technically out of the question, it is more possible though not prepared through Iran, but this must be expressly decided by the British authorities. England's attitude to our sending soldiers out from here is not clear so far, even as regards the sending of airmen; instructions from London restrict them only to trained crews. After a definite British decision we can start negotiations with the Soviets for sending soldiers in larger numbers. When do you expect to end your stay in Egypt?

B10. Conversation with the Vice-Commissar for Foreign Affairs. A. J. Vyshinsky.

In the Narcomindiel, Kuibishev. 2 November 1941

(In the presence of M. Pushkin. W. Arlet interpreted and took notes.)

KOT. I haven't come today to bother you with current issues which we have already had the opportunity to discuss several times over, if only because I think that meanwhile many of these have been settled. I wish today to discuss another question. With reference to conversations I have had with yourself and with Mr. Molotov I would like to raise the question of General Sikorski's visit to the U.S.S.R. According to information from London General Sikorski left England on 31 October and at present he should be in Egypt. After inspecting the Polish troops, part of which, as is well known, hold an important sector in the defence of Tobruk, and after discussion of practical problems, he will be able to set out for the U.S.S.R. about 7 November. In accordance with his instructions I bring you a note for the

---

[1] Americans of Polish origin. *Tr.*

Commissar for Foreign Affairs, Mr. Molotov, which touches on certain problems; their detailed discussion, if the Soviet side expresses its agreement to this course, could be the subject of conversations between General Sikorski and the Soviet Government. I ask you to transmit the contents of this note to Chairman Molotov, by telephone. For I await a very speedy reply to it. Liaison with General Sikorski is now rendered difficult, we have to cable from here to London, and only from there are my dispatches transmitted to the Premier. I ask you to take this circumstance into account.

VYSHINSKY (promises to transmit the note quickly to Molotov, and in any case this same day). Of the various questions you have raised during our conversations, I can reply on two problems today. 1. The transfer of the Polish population; 2. The loan. Unfortunately, on both questions our answer is a refusal. I would like to explain the reasons for this. At the present time the transfer of a large number of Polish people must be held up owing to transport difficulties. Masses of Soviet people are being transferred from the west and south to the east, because the Hitlerite invaders have occupied great areas of our country. In these conditions the organization of transports of Polish citizens in the opposite direction, from the east and north to the west and south, is quite impracticable. Of course this does not exclude the journeys of individuals or particular groups of Polish citizens who are able to set out at their own expense and to pay for railway tickets. In these cases the Soviet authorities are inclined to direct them to the southern areas of the Kazakh Soviet Republic. In view of this the loan, which was to be granted for the purpose of their transfer, no longer has any point.

In this connection I wish to deal with the conversation which Mr. Sikorski has had with our Ambassador in London, Mr. Bogomolov. The General said that in conversation with you Mr. Molotov had declared that the Soviet authorities prefer to retain the Polish citizens in their places of work and in factories rather than see them in the Polish forces. I would like to emphasize that if Commissar Molotov did in fact say something of that kind, he had in mind Polish citizens who have not been called up for the Polish Army and so must, of course, work in agriculture or industry. That is perfectly clear. If the problem is put as though we have to support Polish citizens who are not serving in the army and not working, that would not be just, and not even possible of achievement. They must work for their maintenance just like Soviet citizens. In regard to those citizens who have

material resources enabling them to travel, so far as technical transport possibilities allow they will be enabled to make those journeys.
I ask you to bear in mind that this position arises out of the general
situation.

KOT. You know very well from all our previous conversations that I
have never demanded any privileges for Polish citizens. On the contrary. . . .

VYSHINSKY (interrupting). I know that well and I'm not saying at all
that you have demanded privileges for Polish citizens, but they would
be given a privileged status as the result of the actual state of affairs.
Soviet citizens must travel on the railways at their own expense and
must earn their keep. The same applies to Polish citizens.

KOT. On the contrary, I have always said that those who are capable
of military service should go into the army, and those capable of work
should work. I have never put forward any plan for a loan to be
granted to the Polish Government for the purpose of transferring
people. It was a question of finding means of supporting people
incapable of work, old people, children, all those in general unable to
maintain themselves by labour, and also of feeding up for several
weeks those released from prison and camps in a state of hunger, until
they regain sufficient strength to work. I would like to remind
you that I have always divided the Polish citizens into three categories: 1. Those fit for the army; 2. Those fit for work; 3. Those
unfit for work. The first should be in the army, the second should
work.

So far as the first category is concerned, we are still unable to obtain
agreement to the incorporation of these individuals in further divisions. I raised this problem in my conversation with Commissar
Molotov, but I received the answer that while the Soviet Government
would not oppose their formation, it was on the condition that we
ourselves take steps to secure their armaments and even food supplies.
I was astonished by the statement that we had got to feed our forces,
but we have taken appropriate steps and I can inform you today that
we have received Great Britain's positive assurance on this matter. We
have received equipment, arms, and food for further large units[1] on
condition that they are accommodated in a locality to which it will be
possible to send these supplies. We know the war will be a long and
burdensome one and so we want our soldiers to be in the army, so that

---

[1] *Sic.* Presumably the précis or the actual statement omitted the words ' the promise
of ' before ' equipment '. *Tr.*

this fine fighting element should not go to waste in civilian labour. We are now waiting for a clear decision from the Soviet Government on this question.

As for the second category, from the beginning of my activity I gave instructions that anyone who has work in more or less tolerable conditions, who can manage even in a harsh climate, should not move from the spot, but go on working. It is the will of the Polish Government that the Polish citizens in the U.S.S.R. should voluntarily contribute their labour to the common war effort. Those not fit for military service should work, but in an appropriate fashion, in accordance with their professional qualifications. The doctor and engineer should not be employed in tree felling. The best proof of my intentions and instructions on the question is the activity of my delegate Professor Heitzman, who is at present in Novosibirsk. In agreement with the local organs of the Narcomvnudiel he has even issued a call to the Polish people not to move elsewhere and not to expose themselves to the burdens of travelling in the present difficult war conditions. Professor Heitzman is satisfied with the co-operation he is getting from the local authorities.

I myself can only regret that the Soviet authorities have not so far settled the question of sending out further delegates, which, as the example of Novosibirsk shows, is in the interests of both sides. Right from the beginning I have asked for us to work out a plan and detailed instructions jointly on the question of who are to remain at their places of work and who can travel, in what conditions, and where to. See to it that someone takes up this matter and really gets it settled. Obviously, I want to avoid some local factor using this pretext to make it impossible for Poles to travel to join the army.

VYSHINSKY. You are raising the question of local authorities not detaining Polish citizens travelling to join the army. What citizens are you referring to, those travelling to the divisions already in being, or to those proposed?

KOT. Both the one and the other. Unfortunately, thousands of those who have been taken into our army are proving physically unfit for service. So it is a question of replacing them by physically suitable individuals. As for the units to be formed, General Anders has agreed a project for an additional three divisions with the Red Army General Staff, and of these three, two would be purely labour divisions. In addition to two or three hours of professional training each day these soldiers would be employed in labour.

H

(Vyshinsky takes detailed notes, as though this were the first time he had heard of these plans.)

KOT. For that matter, the Soviet authorities themselves favour the concentration of Polish citizens in an area where it will be possible to realize these proposals. Numerous centres receiving Poles are already scattered between Nukus on the Aral Sea and Ferghana, and in this connection the figure of 100,000 Polish citizens has been mentioned as to be settled there.

VYSHINSKY. This is a special problem, one I have no knowledge of, nor do I quite understand it. Of course I shall raise it in the appropriate quarter.

KOT. Please do so as soon as possible.

VYSHINSKY. This is essentially a new problem, which must be dependent on the government's decision. Obviously it is quite a different issue from the one previously raised, of shifting great masses, tens and even hundreds of thousands, of Polish citizens. That plan must be dropped.

KOT. And yet in one of our conversations you said the Poles would be transferred from the northern regions to the south.

VYSHINSKY. But now it's winter time.

KOT. I beg your pardon, but you said distinctly that if the Soviet authorities wished, means could be found of shifting people from the north even in the depths of winter by utilizing special means of transport.

VYSHINSKY. It's true I did say that, but there have been many changes since then. Almost two months have passed. You yourself know what serious events have occurred since then.

KOT. If only you would at least provide us with information as to where these people are, and would facilitate our communicating with them, if only by telephone!

VYSHINSKY. Of course I will do that.

KOT. You see, we must get help to them, must make it possible for them to survive the harsh winter, and must send things that may have a decisive effect in keeping them alive, vitamin preparations, warm clothing.

VYSHINSKY. You can count on all help from us. As soon as I ascertain where these people are I shall inform you exactly and conscientiously.

(Several minutes' discussion follows on the subject of Poles still held in camps in various parts of the Soviet Union, despite assurances that all the Poles have been released.)

VYSHINSKY. The figure of 9,500 Polish officers alleged to be in the U.S.S.R. has never been confirmed. The Narcomvnudiel records have never shown such a number of officers, and the People's Commissar for Defence denies its exactitude. But I shall go on trying to obtain the data you have asked for.

KOT. You promised to take a personal interest in the question of the lawyers, judges, procurators and police. We still lack many generals, eminent military men, and even personal friends.

VYSHINSKY. Unfortunately, procurators, judges, and police are not classified separately in the Narcomvnudiel files. We just haven't any information.

KOT. So much time has passed since the agreement was signed, and yet so many of our people have not gained the freedom to which they are entitled by law. We are not getting any letters or telegrams. We haven't even their addresses. Meanwhile, in our conversation of 14 October you promised to get me these details within a day or so.

VYSHINSKY. I know I did, but on the 15th there was the departure from Moscow, as the result of which contacts between the various departments have grown looser. That of course makes for delay in the obtaining of data. Not only are the local organs of the Narcomvnudiel co-operating well with your delegate, Heitzman, but the central Narcomvnudiel is also working well with us. And they declare that there never was such a large number of Polish officers in the U.S.S.R.

KOT. I don't stand by the figure of 9,500, but over 4,000 officers were carried off from the camps in Starobielsk and Kozielsk. Right till now a kind of impenetrable wall has been raised between us and these deported people. I ask you to make it possible for us to cross that wall. The Central Authority of the Narcomvnudiel or the Central Camps Administration (*Glavnoye Upravlenie Lagierov*) possesses the requisite data. Please make it possible for me to send delegates accompanied by Narcomvnudiel officials to travel round the camps containing these people, to take them aid and give them comforts enabling them to survive the winter.

VYSHINSKY. You are putting the case as if we wanted to conceal certain Polish citizens. But where are they?

KOT. How about Kolyma? The Behring Straits? It has been confirmed that whole transports of our people were sent to these parts. They are even in Franz Josef Land. I myself have talked with a youngster who had come back from Novaya-Ziemlia.

VYSHINSKY. From the way you put it it follows that there is a need for our authorities to be controlled by emissaries of the Embassy. We have records of everybody, living or dead. I have promised the details and I shall supply them.

KOT. I am extremely anxious to get details relating to certain people.

VYSHINSKY. But do take into account the fact that there must have been many changes since 1939. People have shifted from place to place, many of them have been released, many are working, many have returned home. Why, quite recently in the former Perm *Oblast* thousands of Poles set out in every possible direction. They scattered, and now they are giving no sign of their existence.

KOT. If any of the people I am concerned about had in fact been released they would have reported at once. I am not speaking of people without name, there are hundreds of prominent people, for instance : the Generals Stanislaw Haller, Skierski, Skuratowicz, Kowalski, Lukoski, Skrzynski. After all, these people aren't children, it's impossible to hide them. If any of them have died, please inform us. I cannot believe that they don't exist any longer.

VYSHINSKY. I ask you to let me have the names, and then it will be easier to find them. You have mentioned the name of general Haller for the first time today.[1] These people aren't trees, they must be somewhere, possibly some of them themselves did not state that they were generals, possibly they figure under other professional categories. After all, I am not in a position to travel all over the Soviet Union looking for them.

KOT. The data I possess I have received from eyewitnesses, from written statements and protocols. At one time or another they have seen a certain number of our officers taken off in some unknown direction. If I had obtained exact data from you I should have used them. These people are not steam, which can fly away, or like those melting flakes of snow (he points to the window).

(There is a further brief exchange of views as to the accuracy or inaccuracy of the data.)

VYSHINSKY. If I had lists of the people you are concerned about that would facilitate my task.

---

[1] It would appear that Vyshinsky was confusing two generals of the same name. General Stanislaw Haller, formerly chief of the Polish General Staff, had been asked for by General Sikorski through Sir Stafford Cripps, as the General considered him the most suitable candidate for the task of organizing and commanding the Polish armed forces in Russia. When he was not found, Sikorski decided on General Anders. Vyshinsky appeared to be thinking of General Josef Haller, who after escaping from Russia through Murmansk to France during the first world war, became head of the Polish Army formed in France, and returned to Poland in 1918.

KOT. I've already handed over such lists, but so far I've had no answer to them. The most important thing for me is that I should be able to send these people aid and care. I realize that you cannot personally occupy yourself with these questions, as your competence covers foreign and not internal affairs. But both from you and from Commissar Molotov and the Soviet Government generally we have had assurances of co-operation in this direction.

VYSHINSKY. A certain number of the people on the lists you have handed us have already been found, we are looking for the others. When I have the definite names I can approach the competent authorities and say, for instance, ' Please report to me on the case of General Haller.' If as the result something unsatisfactory comes to light, I shall even be able to punish where necessary. But you're wrong in thinking these matters are not within my competence. In the Commissariat for Foreign Affairs we have three Vice-Commissars. I am the first of the three, and Polish affairs are under my personal care. That is a measure of the importance we attach to these questions. Within my competence come Great Britain, the United States, Poland, Czechoslovakia, and Yugoslavia.

KOT. In other words, friends!

VYSHINSKY (laughing). The friendly states: Great Britain and the United States, and our brother Slavonic nations: Poland, Czechoslovakia, and Yugoslavia.

KOT. From the very beginning of my contacts with you I have had no doubt of your friendly attitude towards us. As for myself, I have always put issues openly and frankly. . . .

As for the financial question, I would like again to stress that not only is the interest of the Polish citizens at stake, but also the prestige of the Soviet Union, which is involved in seeing that Polish citizens unfit for work should not die of starvation. I have lived through more than one war, and I know what importance paper money has. The question of a loan should not be approached from a fiscal standpoint. You as a politician are perhaps in the best position to appreciate what future political importance the granting of a loan might have, at the cost of putting a printing machine quickly into motion and issuing a still larger quantity of paper money.

I have yet other matters to raise, e.g., the religious question, but I shan't trouble you with them today. The most urgent issue so far as we are concerned, the one I have come about, is contained in that note (he points to the letter to Molotov). I ask for this letter to be sent quickly.

VYSHINSKY. As it is not addressed to me I cannot myself deal with its contents, but I shall send it to commissar Molotov this very day.

The conversation lasted from 13. to 14.30 hours. Vyshinsky's tone was not too friendly. The Ambassador was very calm and conciliatory.

A40. To the Minister for Foreign Affairs.
Kuibishev. 2 November 1941

Today I have handed Vyshinsky a note for Molotov on the conditions of the Premier's visit.

During the conversation Vyshinsky stated:

1. The Government is stopping the transfer of Polish citizens from the north to the south, with the exception of small groups. The reason: transport difficulties caused by the war.

2. In view of this the loan to the Polish Government has also been refused.

3. Referring to the General's conversation with Bogomolov, he denied that the Soviet Government was detaining our people in work instead of sending them to the army.

On 1. I made the reservation that this must not cause the hold up of people journeying to join the army and unable to stand the northern climate, and demanded that I should be enabled to make contact with the alleged liberated northern camps.

On 2. We did not need the loan for the purpose of transferring people, but in order to keep alive people unfit for work, women, children, for whom, independently of the loan, we are seeking help from abroad. I regard this question as still open to discussion.

On 3. Vyshinsky is not properly informed on our plans for the development of the armed forces. He treated it as a new problem, but at once precipitantly pointed out the difficulties in transporting arms and food from abroad.

Throughout the hour and a half of conversation I tried to formulate my replies and desiderata in a manner conducing to their favourable settlement, always emphasizing my faith in the goodwill of both sides.

My general impression: an intensification of the unfriendly relationship. None the less I expect a reply to the note which will make the Premier's visit possible. But if in the present situation Molotov were to reject the Premier's four points I regard the visit as impermissible.

> B11. *Conversation with A. J. Vyshinsky in the Narcomindiel. 5 November 1941*
> (Mr. Pushkin present; W. Arlet, Embassy secretary, noting and interpreting.)

VYSHINSKY. I have asked you to come and see me in order to acquaint you with the contents of the U.S.S.R. Government's resolution on the question of credits for the Polish Army, which has been passed during the last few days. As a basis the state of the Polish forces in the U.S.S.R. is accepted at a strength of 30,000. In accordance with point 13 of the Polish-Soviet Military Agreement, expenses on the commissariat, maintenance, and equipment of the Polish Army are covered by a non-interest bearing credit, granted by the U.S.S.R. to the Polish Government. Down to 31 December 1941 the credit amounts to 65 million roubles, allocated as follows:

Maintenance of forces from 1 Nov. to 31 Dec.	47.5	million
Maintenance of forces down to 31 Oct. 1941	9	,,
Building works for forces	5	,,
Aid for civilian population	3	,,

This credit is to be extinguished in ten years from the end of the war.

The arrears in rank and file and officers' pay for October must have arisen through the oversight of the Polish and Soviet Military authorities. However, in order to eliminate these arrears as quickly as possible, instructions have been given for the immediate payment this day of four million roubles, which will be taken up by General Anders.

KOT. I am not fully informed on the financial affairs of the forces. They come within the competence of the Military Mission and the High Command of the Polish Armed Forces. So I cannot adopt any definite attitude to your statements. General Anders is in Kuibishev at present, so I shall ask him to deal with the matter. . . . But the item specifying three millions for aid to the civilians is not clear. I would like you to explain the purpose for which this sum is assigned.

VYSHINSKY. I know these problems concern the military primarily, and so General Anders will be notified of them by the Staff. But I have received a special instruction from Mr. Molotov to communicate the Government decision to you personally, not only because it concerns the army, and so an institution very dear to us, but because of the item of three million roubles for the civilian population in most urgent need, which is placed at your disposition. Also, on the question of arrears in payments due to the forces Mr. Molotov has given personal instructions and instructed me to communicate his decision to you.

KOT. The arrears of pay to men and officers did not arise through any fault of our military. They presented all the requisitions betimes and sent the claim in to the Soviet Army Chief Intendancy, but they were told that although there were no fundamental reservations as to the amount of the quotas demanded, the decision of the Supreme Soviet was necessary before payment could be made. The high morale of our troops is testified to by the fact that although they had not received a single farthing for two months they made no claim on the Command for payment, but trained, exercised, and carried out their daily military duties. In no circumstances can I agree that the fault for the arrears lies with them.

VYSHINSKY. I agree our military were to blame. I see that the Narcomindiel will have to take more interest in these questions, and I personally will handle them, so that this kind of occurrence should not happen in future.

KOT. The figure you mentioned of the number of soldiers, 30,000, is also open to question. So far as I remember the number is 44,000. To what date do your figures refer?

VYSHINSKY. I have obtained the data from the Staff. They correspond to the Agreement position, namely:

Two infantry divisions, each of 11,000	22,000
Reserve pool	5,000
Officers' School	2,000
Staff and auxiliary services	1,000

KOT. To tell the truth, this is all outside my competence. I shall clear it up with my military.

At the moment I am interested in another question: the quota of three million. If this is intended to have some connection with my request for a loan, obviously I cannot accept it. It has no relation whatever to the needs.

VYSHINSKY. On the question of a loan, during our last conversation I explained that the Soviet Government's decision was in the negative, *inter alia* owing to the necessity to abandon the plan for transfer of the people.

KOT. I have just received information from Tashkent that already some 300,000 Polish citizens have arrived in Uzbekistan. Of this figure 100,000 are not fit for the army or for paid labour and have no means of subsistence. They consist of war wounded, women, old people, children. On comparing these two figures you will see that three millions is a figure which helps me not at all.

VYSHINSKY. I have already clearly defined the Soviet Government's position. If the Polish Government wants to help these people it must seek resources from elsewhere, perhaps from some form of social fund.

KOT. I repeat that such a sum settles nothing. Perhaps, as it comes out of military credits, it is intended for payments to the families of military personnel. Perhaps the Soviet Government would retain it at its own disposition, using it to assist persons whom it releases from prisons and camps?

VYSHINSKY. How you arrange things with your military is your affair. That is all I wished to communicate to you today.

KOT. Can you say anything on the question of a reply to my note to President [*sic*] Molotov?

VYSHINSKY. I am expecting the reply this evening and I shall communicate it to you at once.

KOT. I shall be greatly obliged to you.

VYSHINSKY. In accordance with your wish, I telephoned the note to Moscow the day you handed it to me. Yesterday I had a telephone conversation with Mr. Molotov, who said he would not delay with the reply. The aeroplane from Moscow bringing our official post takes off about noon and is here before the evening, and if nothing unforeseen occurs, such as a landing and stopping the night *en route*, I expect the reply this evening, or tomorrow morning at latest. . . .

Vyshinsky was much more equable than during the previous conversation. Apparently he expected the Ambassador to thank him for arranging the matters he talked about, and seemed to be disillusioned. The Ambassador was restrained and cold. The conversation lasted half an hour.

A42. To the Minister for Foreign Affairs.
7 November 1941

Notes of a private conversation between Professor Kot and the Vice-Commissar for Foreign Affairs, Mr. Vyshinsky, during a reception given by Mr. Vyshinsky to the Diplomatic Corps on the anniversary of the October Revolution, 7 November 1941.

. . . . Mr. Vyshinsky came up to the Ambassador accompanied by the Embassy secretary, Mniszek, with whom he had been talking. He brought with him a glass of wine and proposed to drink to the common victory. A lively and friendly talk followed in French, Polish, and Russian.

The Ambassador stressed the common qualities which linked the Polish and Russian nations, qualities characteristic of all the Slavonic nations, namely great capacity, great vigour, and devoted zeal for the struggle. On the other hand, these nations lacked the characteristics of organizing ability and the gift for selling the successes gained from work achieved, qualities which distinguish the German nation.

Vyshinsky answered that so far as the Russian nation is concerned the Bolshevik Party under Lenin and Stalin had been able to graft these organizational characteristics into the new generation and had overcome the lack of organizational intellect.

The Ambassador strongly emphasized that when talking of the German nation we must not only fight and defeat Hitlerism, but destroy all the evil forces which inhere in the German race.

Vyshinsky indicated that he hoped the Germans were strong only so long as they retained their organizational capacity, but that when the decisive blow was struck against Germany, and he was profoundly convinced it would be struck, they would disintegrate together with all their organization.

The Ambassador jokingly told Vyshinsky that as he looked at him he saw in his profile a reflection of a Polish rural squire—*un hobereau* —and asked whether he was of Polish origin. Vyshinsky said his mother had been Russian, but his father was indeed a Pole. He himself was born in Baku and felt that he was Russian, and also, of course, a Slav.

The Ambassador also asked Vyshinsky whether he had received a reply from Moscow to the note handed in some days before. Vyshinsky replied that he had been expecting a special courier from Moscow in the evening of the 6th, but owing to communications difficulties the plane had not yet arrived; but he should have a reply on the eighth. . . .

A45. To the Minister for Foreign Affairs.
Kuibishev. 8 November 1941

After two months of observation and work in the U.S.S.R. I wish to make certain general remarks:

1. The Polish-Russian Agreement has proved a good fortune and salvation for the Poles in Russia. To it at the present moment several hundred thousand Poles owe their release either from prison or from forced labour camps or from semi-forced stay in settlements in circumstances so menacing to their existence that their release has brought them salvation. Without regard to the degree of tolerable living conditions they are now succeeding in obtaining, the very fact of their release is decisive for their future. Many of them had reached the last bound of nervous and physical endurance.

The releases effected as the result of the Agreement have evoked an amazingly positive reaction among the Polish people, a kind of mystical faith in the *raison d'être* of the Polish State. They are convinced that although they are outside their country and without means, somewhere afar off exists a representation of that State, incarnated in the Government, which is not only taking care of citizens shut away at the other end of the world and [previously] condemned to extermination, but also has sufficient authority and strength to restore these citizens to conditions of very modest yet human existence. The fact that among the [Soviet] prisoners drawn from various States only the Poles, who were the objects of their persecutors' greatest spite, have gained their freedom, has raised the authority of Poland incommensurably high in the eyes of the Russian people and all the other nations imprisoned here. When the national anthem 'Not yet has Poland Perished' sounded out on the first ship carrying prisoners released from the Polar Sea area along the Piechora River, it caused a tremendous shock among the groups working on the banks and a powerful reaction among those Poles who did not yet know about the Pact, yet felt that their rescue by the Polish Government was imminent.

They had no idea where this Government was and who constituted it. Only the name of General Sikorski was known everywhere, and among the masses fleeing from the north, so mails from the junction stations report, it acquired the features of a religious cult. This consciousness of the strength of the Polish Government in exile has aroused faith in the great future of the Polish State. This faith has conduced to an intense moral atmosphere among the civilian population and the forces.

2. The moral value, endurance, and allegiance to their State of the Polish citizens are making a great impression on the Russians, and on governmental circles above all. When the Agreement was signed there was fifty per cent tacit insincerity and equivocation on the part of those circles. After comparing various details and admissions, I can state today that at the beginning of July the Soviet Government, when it decided on the Agreement, took various deliberate steps to ensure that its effects did not take on dimensions which they considered undesirable.

Although a year ago some 8,000 officers, several thousand non-commissioned officers and rank and file, and a great number of judges, procurators, and police, whose existence in the U.S.S.R. Vyshinsky still denies, were carried off mysteriously from camps in Starobielsk, Kozielsk, and Ostaszkov,[1] and although, with the exception of a few officers, it has been impossible so far to make any contact with these men, none the less as late as last July steps were taken to distribute transports of Polish citizens to various inaccessible areas so as to effect a definite diminution in the number of Poles officially admitted [to exist]. Likewise considerable numbers of Poles were evacuated eastward from many prisons, from some of course under the pressure of the war (Bielorussian and Ukrainian prisons), but also with the intention of concealing them. Of the large number of Polish citizens forced into [Soviet] military service, the great majority were isolated from the front line forces, to avoid the charge that they were taken into the army, and they were formed into labour battalions, at first behind the front lines. As time passed they were shifted eastward.

The figure of 20,000 fit for the Polish Army which Ambassador Maisky has mentioned, and which at the end of July was raised to 30,000, is the figure which the Soviet Government allowed for our forces in their plans at that time, and they still resist its increase. At first they imagined that this force would be susceptible of being coloured strongly red, that the influence of communists such as Wanda Wasilewska, dressed in colonel's uniform, as well as a certain number of professional officers won over in prison and in camps to co-operation with the Communists, plus a considerable number of

---

[1] Places in western border areas of the U.S.S.R. *Tr.*

individuals who were forced to sign declarations of service to and espionage for the Narcomvnudiel, would be very great; also that its national and psychological composition could be given a tendentious slant by directing an excessive number of Jews to this force. In this connection, during July death sentences were pronounced in large numbers in the prisons, in order to obtain declarations of service by resort to terror. The release from camps of both physically and morally healthier Polish elements was delayed in various ways, and war wounded and Jews were sent out; the Poles were very often forced to sign contracts to engage in free labour, and in their [the Soviets'] view this signature makes it impossible for the signatory to leave for the army; their miserable payments for work performed were held back, their personal effects were not handed over, and thus by various petty tricks large numbers of people were retained in the camps. Those who left were directed to very numerous parts of Russia, and the fact that the army was being organized as well as the locality of its headquarters were usually concealed from them.

Contact with the Embassy was rendered difficult, and in many instances impossible, by the mass confiscation of letters and telegrams sent to it. Very often there was incitement against the Polish Government and the Embassy because of their alleged negligence, charging them with responsibility for the fact that the Poles were left abandoned and in need. In Moscow itself the authorities at first tried to lull our vigilance by politeness and promises; for instance, their release of Poles from Moscow prisons on the occasion of the Ambassador's arrival was represented as a great event, but we know that there were only some thirty such prisoners. The promise was also given to facilitate the sending of Embassy delegates everywhere, but in practice they are making this impossible. The Narcomindiel, both Mr. Vyshinsky and Mr. Molotov, has opposed the Ambassador having contact with the Narcomvnudiel for the purpose of ordering the position of Polish citizens, and has not given a really favourable decision on any essential question.

3. The situation is developing in such a way that Polish issues cannot be confined within the very narrow bounds which the Soviet authorities have designed for them. They have been broken above all by the mass influx to the Polish Army, which is so great that undoubtedly it would be possible to create an army of 150,000, and even more, if agreement and supplies could be obtained. On the other hand the perfect behaviour, spirit, enthusiasm and moral level of those

who have been gathered into the army so far are so imposing that not
even hostile forces can find any serious argument for holding up its
organization. All the training of spies and workers for disintegration
has gone for nothing. In the army this element was stifled at once by
the general atmosphere. High officials of the Narcomvnudiel, who
without doubt are highly sensitive to negative phenomena, apprecia-
tively testify to the excellence of the ragged soldiers' bearing, to
the outstanding quality and trustworthiness of the generals, the
enthusiasm of everybody to fight the Germans. Even the Soviet
Government reckons with the authority of General Anders, and his
insistence on the release of his fellow officers still detained—insistence
which is complemented by the Ambassador's incessant, vehement
pressure for the genuine fulfilment of the Agreement and the release
of all Polish citizens—may lead to a change of the Soviets' July
decisions.

We are trying to exploit the announcement of General Sikorski's
visit in order to obtain the release of those still detained, and agreement to further formations of Polish forces. While the Narcomindiel
cynically assures us that all the Polish citizens have been released, the
Narcomvnudiel is disposed to admit that this is not so, and promises
to send officials to clear the arrears. But the question of the forces
will have to be handled on both sides by the highest instances. And
so we attach the utmost importance to the Premier's arrival. If the
Soviets take the path of loyalty, which must be decided during the
next few days, General Sikorski's presence will lead to a genuine
fulfilment of the Agreement, and possibly to its extension, especially
in military respects.

4. My greatest troubles arise from the situation of our civilians.
The Soviet authorities' equivocal attitude has meant that we have
never been told the numbers and distribution of the Polish people or
any instructions affecting its changes. The Soviets declare they
deported about 400,000 citizens from Poland. It is clear that in this
figure they do not include an unknown number whom they have
taken into their army, at least several dozen thousands in round
figures, and possibly several times as many. It is impossible to obtain
even an approximate basis for calculating how many Poles there were,
and how many have now changed their places of settlement.

From the very beginning the Embassy adopted the attitude that
where free settlers have a roof over their heads and the possibility of
at least minimum earnings, they should not move. This applied to

a large part of Kazakhstan, certain districts of the Urals, and in northern Russia a large part of the Republic of Komi and the district of Vologda, where our peasants, being accustomed to heavy physical labour, have successfully survived forest work despite the deep frosts. I was of the opinion that a southward move should be made by soldiers travelling to join the army, those released from prison or forced labour, and the inhabitants of climatically difficult districts, irrespective of whether we have any prospect of creating tolerable living conditions for them in the south.

The drive to join the army and the desire to flee from the north put in motion a great avalanche of Polish transmigration. Anyone who had no resources (the Soviets have paid the cost of the journey only to those released from prisons and camps, and even then only for a journey of several days' duration, unfortunately quite inadequate in the present confusion, when every journey lasts some three weeks) sold his surplus clothing, and especially boots, in the hope that in the south he would be able to survive without warm clothes. The journeys of these people are marked by tragedy. Above all, they are being decimated by hunger and disease, a kind of hunger dysentery. Deaths occur in many of the transports, and the travellers bring with them seriously ill cases, who often end their lives at the railway junctions. In one of the transports from the north there were sixteen corpses.

The crowds released from forced labour in the north, who have no means to enable them to travel, are in despair. The despair is even greater among those whose release is delayed for unknown reasons. Among such there have been cases of hunger strikes in Solikamsk, the Molotov *Oblast* (Perm) and this led to the transfer of some thirty persons to neighbouring camps.

So there is tragedy on the journey, and more tragedy after arrival in the south. In principle, for three weeks now everybody has been directed to Uzbekistan, to the vicinity of Tashkent, whence they are distributed to the east and west. At first we thought it would be possible to influence the control of transports and the settlement of the people. Unfortunately war events, which have caused a mass evacuation of Soviet citizens from the west and south, have rendered all planned operations impossible. At present everybody is being unorganizedly directed towards Tashkent, and as, because of this influx, nobody is able to prepare or is capable of preparing living conditions, the starving crowds, unprovided for, are mechanically

being distributed to various inhabited zones in the desert, where
work far more hard than they had in the north awaits them (work on
cotton, dangerous to the sight) and also starvation. Only the climate
is more favourable.

Despair is greatest among the soldiers who are directed thither in
the hope that new formations will be established around Tashkent,
and who frequently have left more tolerable living conditions and are
now being driven to work in unpleasant conditions. Some time ago
General Anders handed the [Soviet] Staff a plan for forming three
divisions there, two of them labour divisions (i.e., employment in
groups on various works, but spending two or three hours daily in
military training). Unfortunately, this plan has not yet received
approval, and here again General Sikorski's visit may lead to a favourable decision.

5. All efforts to organize care of the Polish community come up
against lack of understanding and downright difficulties from the
Soviet side. Our forces have sent a certain number of officers to direct
military groups to the appropriate termini and to care for them at the
junctions. These emissaries, who are provided with some resources,
have brought some help, but they have a difficult time because of the
trickery of the local authorities; sometimes they are simply thrown
out.

The Government is not prepared even to discuss the introduction
of a consular service for care of the Polish citizens; here a consul is
a synonym for a spy. Under the pretext of the necessity to issue passports I was able to obtain agreement to passport-consular agencies of
a temporary nature; unfortunately the passport books have still not
arrived from London and the printing of provisional certificates, for
which I pressed in Moscow, has now lost all practical meaning owing
to the evacuation.

The Government has flatly rejected my plan for forming welfare
committees from among the people themselves, on the ground that it
is impermissible in the local system; but it has agreed to the sending
out of delegates, for whom the Ambassador is personally responsible,
as well as for the selection of men of trust from among the people, to
report on their requirements. The Government has adopted a favourable attitude only to our sending delegates to Novosibirsk and part of
Kazakhstan. They grant the delegate in Archangel only the right to
supervise the transport of materials arriving in the port, but they are
not prepared to allow him to have contact with the people.

The delegates I have proposed for various other areas have so far not been officially acknowledged. None the less, I am sending out nominations and people in order at least to collect information and to provide indications: the authorities ignore them and many cables do not reach them; one of them has been interned, though the Government denies it. Where co-operation is achieved between the delegates and the local authorities many difficulties have been ironed out and settled.

I wait anxiously for the longed for moment when greater material aid will arrive; but what difficulties will arise in its distribution! Yet perhaps that will be a convenient opportunity to show the authorities the absurdity of not recognizing delegates, and the benefits to be derived from their co-operation.

. . . . In the opinion of all of us here, including the British Embassy, it is the Soviets' obligation to care for the maintenance of the Polish citizens whom they wrested from their reasonable existence and transported here by force. The Soviet Government is not prepared to recognize that obligation, and so, not willing to let the Polish people die, I asked for a loan to cover aid to those who are not fit for the army or for paid labour. I asked for work for all who have the strength, provided it was in climatic conditions tolerable for Poles and took account of their qualifications . . . emphasizing that in directing to labour all who were fit for it the Polish Government wanted to help the Soviets in their war effort. But monetary aid is needed for those who are quite unfit for work, for many women, old people, war wounded, sick, children, and for the temporary feeding and restoration to strength of those who have come out of prison and forced labour camps.

Mr. Vyshinsky promised affably to draw up a plan for a loan to meet this need; but he has now notified me that the Polish Government is not to be granted any loan, as the war situation does not allow of transferring the Polish population. I declared that we have never asked for money to meet the transfer of population and that this refusal sentences to death all the Poles unfit for work. Who is to feed them, and on what? He replied that means must be sought for from social sources.

This appears to be a form of pressure to extract dollars and pounds and bring them here. For down till now my efforts to obtain aid in kind from outside have not been regarded favourably. The American Red Cross, which told us that it was ready to give great help, as

I

also to all the Soviet people, has yet not obtained agreement to its proposal to open a delegate's office in the U.S.S.R. to control distribution. In Vladivostok, where we were expecting transports to arrive from America, we have been refused permission to open a post which could have been organized from suitable persons in Tokio. To our request for a guarantee of transport from India through Ashkhabad so far there is only silence. In addition, we are alarmed by the chaos and the slowness of transport: trucks coming from Archangel (even with uniforms for the troops) take weeks, and it is impossible to wait for them. We have no idea how much material is lost. We have no idea what sums are demanded in payment for the trucks.

Unexpectedly, in our last conversation Mr. Vyshinsky informed me that in connection with the loan for the forces the Soviet Government had granted three million roubles for the civilian population's most urgent needs; I refused to accept this butt end; according to our estimates we require about 100 million roubles yearly to meet the most urgent needs. Ambassador Cripps also was of the opinion that we should demand this sum, and in conversation with Vyshinsky he strongly emphasized the duty of the Soviet Government to see to the feeding of the Poles.

Unfortunately, the negotiations are dragging on and the people are not getting any aid on any large scale, with the exception of what the Embassy pays either directly or through delegates, but which is too small to satisfy the needs. I mention with appreciation the fact that our [military] Staff has shown great understanding of the needs of the civilians, and in various ways expended a considerable sum in aid, so long as it had ready money at its disposal. Now that, after several weeks of ' fast ', the army is again receiving money, part of this also will be directed to the same end, either direct or through the Embassy.

We keep the people in the hope that midway through winter great help in kind will arrive from America: clothing, medicines, and even food. For our part we have sent a list of all the urgent requirements both to the [Polish] Ministry for Foreign Affairs and direct to the American Red Cross Delegate, Mr. Wardwell, and through him, when he left, copies also for our Embassy in Washington. . . . So I ask most urgently for the development of propaganda of all kinds and pressure in America both officially and through public opinion, to collect all sorts of material, and to emphasize the possibility of transporting it here. For this problem still troubles us: yesterday Mr.

Litvinov, who is flying to the Embassy in Washington, expressed the view in my presence that he doubted the possibility of transporting aid for civilians, since so far the difficulties of transporting military materials have not been overcome. . . .

7. The Polish people of whom we get reports and with whom we have contact here in groups during their transit through Kuibishev eastward deserve our admiration. The majority of them are ordinary people, the families of foresters, settlers, workers. They are all emaciated, overworked, but extraordinarily patient, calm, enduring, dignified, making no reproaches. They are all confident of a happy future and are filled with faith that they will get back to Poland. Many of them have tiny savings and refuse aid; they require directions, a kind word, but manage without financial help. Help is asked for families who have been plundered, the seriously ill, mothers with numerous children, or rather, their fellow travellers ask help for them.

Groups travelling together have grown into communities and help one another. The leaders, who are thrown up during the journey, are always amazingly responsible and solicitous, they look after all the members of the group and they distribute the resources received from us with great scrupulosity.

They receive the representatives of the Polish Government with deep feeling and tears, they respond enthusiastically to the greetings and short speeches. To my amazement, among them are many men who, despite their hard experiences, are physically in good shape and are enthusiastic for any physical effort. They all welcome the idea of service in the army : anyone who fails to get into the army has a feeling of injury.

Naturally, there is not a trace of sympathy for communism, they are all full of contempt for a system which they know well from personal experience. The intelligentsia are fired with great determination, they have learnt to adapt themselves to the situation, even to physical labour, especially the youth, and the opinion is expressed that they must apply their experience here to education in Poland, so that, if deprived of work in an office, they should be able to fend for themselves.

The moral level is high, cases of bad behaviour are very rare, and are condemned by public opinion, the longing for religious life is great. In general, tendencies for everything to be arranged differently from here. . . .

8. There is a very high percentage of Jews among the Polish citizens

in the U.S.S.R.; there may be as many as one third, because the Soviets deported masses of Jews who fled eastward before Hitler, while in addition many Jews from our Eastern Border lands went voluntarily to Russia in search of work, while many were called up for military service; certain labour battalions are exclusively Jewish. In the present shift of population the percentage seems to be even higher, because it is not balanced by the mass of peasants deported from Poland, who, burdened with families, are in general unwilling to abandon the little villages into which they have grown.

. . . . Representatives of the Jabotinski [Zionist] Revisionists . . . have put forward a proposal to form separate Jewish detachments with Polish officers, which later on would go to Palestine. After their release the representatives of the Bund have opposed this. The Bund leaders, M. Ehrlich and M. Alter, obtained from the Narcomvnudiel the release of the leading members of their party, thanks to which this trend seems to be the main one among the Jews here; on the other hand, despite all endeavours, the Soviets do not want to release the Zionists.

In harmony with his personal attitude, General Anders has rejected the plan to separate the Jews from the army, and has forbidden anti-Semitic agitation. Every Jew who in September 1939 was serving or had had military training belongs to the army. . . .

The bulk of the Jews flows most swiftly to the south, and Uzbekistan already has a high percentage of them; but many of them manage to find a place on their own account and to avoid heavy labour. Because of the great need among the Jews pressure should be brought to bear on wealthy spheres in America and aid obtained for them. But this must pass through the Embassy. I can select plenty of delegates and men of trust from among the Jews of all trends.

> *B12. Conversation with the Vice-Commissar for Foreign Affairs, A. J. Vyshinsky.*
> *In the Narcomindiel. 12 November 1941*
> Present: Departmental Head K. N. Novikov; W. Arlet, first secretary to the Embassy, as interpreter.

VYSHINSKY. Forgive me for bothering you again, but today I have received materials on the subject you raised with me in the letter dated 31 October. I refer to your list of persons, mentioning localities and names, a document of nine pages, containing much detailed material. I gave instructions for the list to be considered at once, and today I can make certain explanations to you. I take one by way of example: you said that in the Altai District, Topczynski Region, Chyshchunek locality, there were three Polish citizens . . . who were said to have been refused their release. Meanwhile, according to documents in the Narcomvnudiel they were released at the time specified by the amnesty, and they left this locality in an unknown direction in the early days of October. Your letter makes mention of a group of Polish citizens who were to remain there. The Narcomvnudiel organs state that in reality there is not one Polish citizen there. You see, when we have definite names it immediately makes it easier for us to investigate the case.

KOT. Thank you for this information.

VYSHINSKY. And now a second example. According to your letter some 3,000 Polish citizens from Vilejka were transported to the prison in Riazan in July. I gave instructions for this to be investigated through the Narcomvnudiel and through the local procurator's office, and it was confirmed that a certain number of Polish citizens were in fact transferred to Riazan, but not 3,000, only 937. . . . They have all been released. I realize that because of the great distance and the slowness of communications the news of this had not reached you at the time you drew up your list. In one of the localities of the Komi Republic you report the presence of 66 Polish citizens; according to information received there were not 66, but 22 or 23. . . . Out of the 66 names we have found 17, all released; the search for the others is still going on. And now, the prison in Gorky. You report that a group of Polish citizens was still being held in the prison on 16 October; . . . meanwhile, all the Polish citizens were released from the Gorky prison on 6, 7, and 8 September.

KOT. But how about Jakub Hoffman? And Father Kucharski?

VYSHINSKY. Their presence there has not been confirmed; undoubtedly they have been released, but I haven't yet received full details concerning them.

KOT. Thank you very much for this information, though I would ask for an answer in writing. It's a pity to waste your time and mine in dealing with individual instances.

VYSHINSKY. Of course we shall reply in writing, but I was particularly anxious to speak to you personally on the question, since we have had several long discussions on it. I gave you assurances, and I have tried to prove that I am a man of my word. In future of course we shall reply to all these matters in writing. But perhaps you for your part have some question to raise?

KOT. I have very many, but I don't want to discuss them haphazardly. I would prefer first to see the Narcomindiel's reply to our letter. Of late so many questions have accumulated that it might be best if I sent you a list of them.

VYSHINSKY. By all means. I shall deal with them, and take steps personally to see that you have the answers. But perhaps you have some other questions?

KOT (reluctantly). Well, so far as Commissar Molotov's reply is concerned, I cannot, unfortunately, say anything yet. We have not received General Sikorski's answer. These military questions are so important for us that I must wait for the arrival of General Anders, whom I am expecting today.

VYSHINSKY. But it is not a question of the forces already in existence, but of forming new units. Surely, as a new problem, that cannot be made a pre-condition of General Sikorski's visit. Mr. Molotov did not prejudge the matter negatively. It was the Polish side that laid down certain conditions in the form of an ultimatum.

KOT. There can be no suggestion of our putting conditions in the form of an ultimatum. General Sikorski is not a diplomat but a soldier, and he put the issue quite clearly. It is simply that, if on a question which he considers important the Soviet Government sees no possibility of expressing its fundamental agreement, then he has no reason to come here.

(Vyshinsky, by assenting, gives to understand that he takes cognizance of this declaration.)

KOT. I repeat, General Sikorski is a soldier, a politician of spirit. If he were to learn of all the difficulties we have here, and of how reluctantly the Soviet Government received his proposal, there would be trouble. (Vyshinsky laughs.) After all, General Sikorski's proposed visit is no longer a secret. All the world knows of it. What would be the state of Polish-Soviet relations if his visit didn't come off? I personally regard it as a turning point for the future of those relations. If General Sikorski doesn't visit the U.S.S.R. now, commentaries will appear all over the world, [to the effect] that relations between the two countries are deteriorating. We Poles would find ourselves in a disadvantageous position, since we have pledged ourselves to take the road of rapprochement with the Soviet Union. General Sikorski has imposed the idea of an understanding with the

Soviet Union on circles which opposed it, and he wants to come here in order to put that idea into practice. But have I myself come for any other purpose? . . . Am I not constantly putting forward definite proposals, so far waiting in vain for their realization?

VYSHINSKY (nodding). You have expressed your readiness to go to Moscow to discuss these matters. Do you still hold to that intention?

KOT. Of course. I am ready to go at any moment.

VYSHINSKY. You once expressed a wish to meet Stalin. I think you could discuss certain questions with him.

KOT. I shall consider that an honour. But I would like to stress the urgency of the matter. . . . I must draw your attention to the fact that the time General Sikorski will remain in Egypt is limited. If he finishes his work there and flies off it may be too late.

VYSHINSKY. I shall phone Moscow this very day and discuss the question directly with Stalin. Returning to the question of the officers whose release General Sikorski has referred to you, does the Narcomindiel possess a separate list of their names? Perhaps Mr. Arlet could supply one to Mr. Novikov?

KOT. The Narcomindiel has two lists of politicians and more important individuals. One I handed to you personally, the other I gave instructions to send. As for the officers, General Anders has presented a list to the Narcomvnudiel, but only in regard to Starobielsk. The list of officers at Kozielsk, Ostashkov, and other camps is still being compiled in the army.

VYSHINSKY. I ask you again about this because I am convinced these people have already been released. It is only a matter of ascertaining where they are. If any of them haven't yet been freed of course they will be released. So far as I'm concerned this problem simply doesn't exist.

KOT. The position is quite clear. The commands of the camps at Starobielsk, Kozielsk, Ostashkov and elsewhere possessed exact lists of the names of the Polish military held in the camps. It is simply a matter of issuing an instruction for these military men to be released according to the list.

VYSHINSKY. Obviously, if they were there.

KOT. In any case, before my departure [for Moscow] I would like to see General Anders, since I am not acquainted with military affairs, and these are particularly important. If he arrives today I'm prepared to leave tomorrow morning. . . .

The conversation lasted 35 minutes. At first Vyshinsky was smiling and affable, towards the end he grew even more heated [than on previous occasions]. At first the Ambassador was more than restrained, unconcerned; in the second half of the conversations he, of course, completely changed his tone.

A47. Cable to the Polish Mission in Cairo.
For Sikorski. 13 November 1941

Today, Wednesday, at 16 hours, I saw Vyshinsky, who after tactical evasions proposed that I should fly to Moscow to discuss the conditions of your visit with Stalin. I hope to do so tomorrow, if the weather permits. This is an obvious *volte-face*, since hitherto Vyshinsky had avoided this idea and had made difficulties over various problems.

. . . .

B13. Conversation with Stalin.
In the Kremlin. 14 November 1941
Present: Molotov with interpreter, and W. Arlet, Embassy first secretary.

KOT. I consider it a real honour to be presented, Mr. President, to you, whose name is associated with the historic deed of re-establishing friendly relations between Poland and the U.S.S.R.

STALIN. I welcome you gladly, Mr. Ambassador. The Soviet people, all of us, consider that the very best of relations should exist between the Soviet and the Polish people. I hope that, in so far as this depends on the Soviet people, we shall succeed in doing everything necessary. I think we may begin a new page of history and that we should base our relations on friendship.

KOT. I have listened to your remarks with great pleasure, and for my part I can assure you that the leaders of the Polish State and nation are advocates of lasting and profound Polish-Soviet co-operation. We simply do not see any reason for conflicts, or any problems which could be the source of conflicts between us who are neighbours.

STALIN. Not only neighbours, but of the same blood.

KOT. In face of the terrible lesson Hitler is giving us and all the world you and we must demonstrate that kinship.

Stalin (agrees).

KOT. But meanwhile a war is being waged which has absorbed every Pole. We wish to contribute all our powers, all our possibilities. Our situation is not easy, the Polish lands are occupied by the Germans.

None the less, the Germans themselves have to admit that the Poles constitute a great force. They themselves know and are afraid that, when the decisive moment arrives, every Pole under their occupation will know how to do his soldierly duty. The Polish nation is playing its part in the struggle today by its resistance and endurance, which command it to fight always loyally and to the last breath on the side where all the democratic peoples are ranged. Without doubt you, Mr. President, know of the Polish nation's love of freedom. The Germans have not found any Quisling in Poland, they are unable to form a puppet government.

There is one other characteristic feature which Poland contributes to the democratic camp: the Poles are the only Catholic nation standing together with the Allies, namely the Anglo-Saxon powers and the Soviet Union. This is of great significance. Hitler cannot proclaim that he is the defender of religion. Poland's attitude also renders it impossible for the Vatican to take up a position on the Axis side.

But our most serious ambition is to form as large a Polish army as possible abroad. After all, this war is not only your war, but ours. And for that reason we ask you to take a friendly attitude to the development of our great army. The Poles have proved that they want to and know how to fight against Hitler to the last drop of their blood. Our troops are to be found in Egypt, Palestine, Great Britain, on the seas and in the air; but the greatest reservoir of vital Polish forces is in the Soviet Union. I would like to discuss this serious problem with you.

General Sikorski is a politician of great spirit, a soldier who breaks down all barriers. His character is marked by resolution, one of the proofs of which is our conclusion despite opposition of an understanding with the Soviet Union. He enjoys great respect among the leaders of the Allied States. And there is every indication that together with you, Mr. President, and Churchill and Roosevelt he will be a member of that group who will decide the future of world organization.

STALIN. I realize the necessity for the formation of a Polish army. I have come into contact with the Polish soldier on many fronts, and I know how to value him. I am ready to give every assistance. Would you care to say just what you are dissatisfied with, what the Poles in Russia are dissatisfied with and what they want? If General Sikorski wishes to come to the Soviet Union he will be our guest, and I hope we shall be able to understand one another.

KOT. So you would like to hear our requests and complaints?

STALIN. Exactly.

KOT. The basis of good relations and co-operation between us must be a friendly atmosphere. The Poles, who have suffered much at Russian hands, beginning with the sixteenth century, genuinely need that atmosphere. I am not referring simply to views, but also to emotional relations, to warmth. False ideas of the Poles as a nation of gentry (*panów*) are widely spread among the Russian people. This simply does not correspond with the reality. We are a nation of peasants, workers, and labouring people, a nation profoundly and sincerely democratic. I have to say that this false view is deeply rooted among the lower Soviet executive organs[1] and it gives rise to a number of difficulties for Polish citizens. We should be very grateful to you, Mr. President, if by exercising your authority you conduced towards a change of these views, as for that matter you have already done by your gesture to co-operate with us.

STALIN. For the sake of historical truth I would like to clear up one point. Beginning from the sixteenth century, not only have Poles suffered at the hands of the Russians but Russians also at the hands of Poles. After all, since that date you have occupied Moscow twice. We ought to be done with the past. I don't doubt that in certain organs there are instances of an unsatisfactory attitude to Poles. But that atmosphere will be changed. I know that Poland is a nation of peasants and toilers. All the conditions exist for finishing with the story of mutual hostility and for going forward in a joint campaign against the common enemy: Hitlerite Germany.

As for the question of the Polish army, in 1941 we are under obligation to put 30,000 soldiers into formation, made up of two infantry divisions, a reserve regiment, an officers' school, and staff. The first division is to be armed by the Soviet Union, the second by the Poles. Both these divisions, or rather, the entire 30,000, roughly speaking, must be fed by the Soviet people. The U.S.S.R. has entered into an obligation to do this and will keep its obligation. Is that right?

KOT. There is a mistake here. As many Polish troops have to be organized in the U.S.S.R. as the human reserves permit. If they are all made use of, we can have an army of 150,000. It could be even larger, but here I take into consideration only physically fit elements. We shall endeavour to obtain equipment from abroad.

---

[1] This was my way of protesting against instructions sent out by the Soviet Government after the Ribbentrop-Molotov Pact to all the Soviet civil and military organs, in which this opinion of the Poles was repeated.

STALIN. But a protocol stipulating 30,000 in 1941 exists. I don't regard that as our last word, but I stress the existence of this protocol.

KOT. There are other protocols too. For instance, one dating from the first session of the Polish-Soviet Military Commission, dated, if I remember aright, 12 August. This protocol expressly says that two divisions are only the first stage, the force which was to be created at once. The very next month further protocols covering further units were drawn up.

MOLOTOV. But the later protocols were not signed or confirmed by the Government. Here (he has the protocol in his hand) I have the protocol we are talking about (He runs his finger over part of the protocol, on which the date 1 October 1941 is visible.)

KOT (pointing to this date on Molotov's copy). Please tell me where it says that only two divisions are to be formed in 1941. All it says is that the first two divisions are to achieve military readiness by 1 October 1941. But that means something quite different. There is no quantitative restriction on the troops in 1941.

MOLOTOV. Hm, you're right. But in any case the later protocols were not ratified by the Government.

STALIN. The Russians have not violated the protocol. If the Poles are dissatisfied they can put forward proposals for further agreements. The Russians have not violated their obligations.

KOT. Three divisions were to be formed from further units, of which to begin with two were labour divisions, intended for building works on behalf of the troops, constructing winter quarters.

STALIN. But so far, on the contrary, you have only one division.

KOT. We have two divisions, of which only one is equipped, despite assurances that equipment would be provided for both. Only in September did the Soviet military authorities notify us that they could not provide arms for the second division.

STALIN. Ah yes, that is so; I remember now.

KOT. I am not a soldier and I don't feel called upon to discuss technical details. I am concerned with the principle, not the details.

STALIN. We Soviet people desire to see the Polish army as large and militarily well prepared as possible. We shall share with you all we possess and which we feel under obligation to share, but I ask the Poles to bear in mind that the Russians are waging a war and must arm their reserves. After all, we have military losses. I ask you to bear in mind that possibly we shall not have sufficient equipment and provisions to satisfy the requirements of the front, the [Soviet] complements, and the Polish army. We have many millions under arms: they have to be fed.

We can equip two Polish divisions. One of them is already ready. I don't oppose the formation of five, six, or seven Polish divisions on Soviet territory, as many as you have men and material for; but I repeat that we are waging a war, we're fighting on a great front, and possibly we shan't have sufficient material to equip this army. The Poles themselves must endeavour to equip and arm it. Maybe after a time the situation will improve, and then things will be different.

KOT. I thank you very much for that statement. So if I have understood you aright, we can form as many divisions as we have people for, on condition that we obtain equipment and food supplies from abroad.

STALIN. You have understood me perfectly.

KOT. So all the candidates capable of bearing arms will be allowed to enter the service, and all that remains is to indicate the place where we can proceed with the formation of detachments, a spot chosen so as to facilitate the transport of equipment and food supplies from abroad.

STALIN. I agree in principle. Such a spot will be designated. But it will not be Uzbekistan, to which place Polish citizens are travelling illegally.

KOT. Uzbekistan was not our idea, but was indicated to our military authorities by the Soviet military authorities. I have always been against the unorganized transference of the Polish people, but despite many requests that I should be presented with a plan for their transfer I could not get hold of one. The Soviet authorities themselves directed the people to Uzbekistan. I even have a telegram testifying to this.

STALIN. Where is the telegram from?

KOT. From Novosibirsk, where the local Soviet authorities are compelling our people to travel to the south. The people released in the north have made their way to the south because they feared the harsh winter, and this explains their influx into those areas. I consider that mass wandering in wartime is impermissible, but I have been impotent in face of the way the situation has developed.

STALIN. A suitable district will be indicated tomorrow.

KOT. I again ask that the factor of a suitable climate and one favourable to the transport of supplies from abroad be taken into consideration.

STALIN. Are you referring to the centre where the further military forces are to be organized, or to the places where the civilian population is to be accommodated? Are they not already indicated?

KOT. An excessive number of candidates for the forces flowed into the district where the first Polish divisions were being formed. The Polish military authorities had to direct these people somewhere, so they obtained guidance from the Soviet military authorities to send transports to the spot where it was anticipated the further divisions would be organized, to Vrevskoe station in Uzbekistan, where there were said to be suitable large barracks.

MOLOTOV. This place was not confirmed by the Government, and so there was no justification for sending people there. The Embassy and its officials even sent telegrams to various localities where Poles were living, recommending them to go to Uzbekistan.

KOT. The Soviet authorities directed these transports to the south. For instance, to Faraba station. The Soviet authorities' representatives even requested General Szyszko-Bohusz to send a telegram on the subject.

STALIN. I ask you again whether you are talking of a centre for formation of the Polish army or of a centre for settlement. Are these two questions, or one?

KOT. This is a very difficult problem.

STALIN. So what districts am I to designate tomorrow?

KOT. The designation of both the one and the other is obviously a question which the Soviet Government will decide. I have already mentioned our wishes in regard to centres where the army can be formed. So far as the civilians are concerned I ask that in addition to the climatic factor the possibility of assuring them work on the spot may be taken into consideration. But there is no need to designate them definitely tomorrow. I would ask you to delay a decision on this question until General Sikorski arrives and you have a conversation with him.

STALIN. Good! I repeat that we wish to see the largest and best possible fighting fit Polish army; but we are waging a war and we're not in a position to maintain further Polish divisions. Maybe in three months' time the material situation will have improved, but now we're organizing large numbers of our own divisions. Possibly the situation will have improved even as soon as two months' time.

KOT. Thank you, Mr. President. I shall inform General Sikorski of this.

STALIN. After all, we are allies. Who wishes to have a weak ally? We shall share everything fraternally with the Poles. We shall do all we can.

KOT. I fully realize your difficulties. But if it is a question of food supplies to further units of our forces I would ask for an assurance that they will be supplied at least during the initial phase.

STALIN. Everything possible will be done.

KOT. After all, there can be no comparison between the enormous requirements of your army and of our few divisions.

STALIN. And yet there are times when a man will shift twenty poods[1] but will collapse under a single pound. We shall endeavour to do all that lies in our human power, but I don't want to make promises that cannot be fulfilled.

KOT. I have one other question of a military character. General Anders, the commander of the Polish Armed Forces in the U.S.S.R., an energetic and spirited general, three times wounded in the campaign of September 1939, has been ordered by the Soviet military authorities to send out of the camp all men in excess of 30,000. Surely that cannot be demanded of him?

STALIN. Who has issued such an order?

KOT (handing Molotov a copy of a letter from the Red Army Plenipotentiary for the formation of the Polish Army, under date 8 November 1941). Here is a copy of the order.

(Molotov hands the document to Stalin, who passes it on to the Secretary.)

STALIN. What is this letter? Who signed it?

INTERPRETER. Panfilov.

STALIN He has no right to issue such instructions. (In an obviously dissatisfied tone.) This is not an order.

KOT. I have already taken up much of your time, which is occupied with highly important matters. But I have one other question I would like to raise.

STALIN (affably). By all means, Mr. Ambassador.

KOT. You are the author of an amnesty for Polish citizens in the U.S.S.R. You made that gesture, and I should be very grateful if you would bring influence to bear to ensure that it could be carried out completely.

STALIN. Are there still Poles not yet released?

KOT. We still have not seen one officer from the camp in Starobielsk which was dissolved in the spring of 1940.

[1] One pood = 36 lb. *Tr.*

STALIN. I shall go into that. But all sorts of things happen to the released people. What was the name of the commander of the Lwów defence? General Langner, if I am not mistaken.

KOT. That's right.

STALIN. Yes, General Langner. We released him as long ago as last year. We brought him to Moscow, and talked with him. But then he fled abroad, possibly to Rumania. Our amnesty provides for no exceptions, but the same may have happened to certain other military individuals.

KOT. We have names and lists; for instance, so far General Stanislaw Haller has not been found. We lack the officers from Starobielsk, Kozielsk, and Ostashkov, who were transferred from those camps in April and May 1940.

STALIN. We have released everybody, even people whom General Sikorski sent to us to blow up bridges and kill Soviet people. . . . However, it was not General Sikorski who sent them, only his Chief of Staff, Sosnkowski.

KOT. He has already resigned. As for the people General Sikorski has sent, you can count on them most of all, they're a first-class element.

STALIN (laughing). I know that.

KOT. And so I ask for an order to be issued that the officers whom we need for the organization of the army are to be released. We have details of when they were transferred from the camps.

STALIN. Do exact lists exist?

KOT. All the names are registered with the Russian camp commanders, who summon all the prisoners to a roll call every day. In addition the Narcomvnudiel interrogated each man separately. Not one officer on the staff of General Anders' army, which he commanded in Poland, has been handed over.

(Stalin for a minute or two has been pacing slowly up and down by the table, smoking a cigarette, but listening closely and answering questions. Suddenly he goes swiftly to the telephone on Molotov's desk and connects with the Narcomvnudiel. Molotov gets up and also goes to the telephone.)

MOLOTOV. This is the way. (He moves the connection, then returns, to sit at the conference table.)

STALIN (at the telephone). NKVD? This is Stalin. Have all the Poles been released from the prisons? (He listens to the answer.) Because I have the Polish Ambassador with me and he tells me they haven't all been released. (He listens again, then replaces the receiver and returns to the table.) I would like to ask you, Mr. Ambassador, when and where the Polish forces wish to go into action against the Germans. Have you any material on this subject? If so, please let me have it.

KOT. I am not a military man. That is really a matter for General Sikorski. I can say that we Poles are not turning the army into a stage performance. But we don't want to send to the front just one or two divisions, which would be lost among the masses of Red Army divisions. We wish to be entrusted with some important sector of the front so that Poles can demonstrate their answer to Hitler. We want our forces to fight here in the east, so that our agreement may be sealed with the brotherhood of arms.

STALIN. The Czechs assembled a battalion and wanted to fight, but I wouldn't allow it. I understand your attitude. The Poles should act as a corps or as an army.

KOT. I venture to emphasize that every Polish division formed, and of which news is conveyed to Poland, is of great importance in developing friendly feelings among the people at home towards the Polish-Soviet *rapprochement*.

STALIN. Of course. I realize that. (The telephone rings, and he goes to it and listens. He replaces the receiver and returns, saying in an undertone as though to himself, ' They say they've all been released.')

KOT. I wish to thank you for your promise concerning the further formations for our army and the release of our citizens. The Army and release: those are two great words. Before taking my leave I wish to say that I hope the aureole of the defender of Moscow which surrounds you today will change as the war proceeds into the aureole of the final victory over Hitler.

STALIN. Thank you. Could you tell me when General Sikorski is expected to arrive?

KOT. Unfortunately we are not able to make direct contact with Egypt from here. I shall be able to do so on my return to Kuibishev. I would say it is a matter of several days yet. I shall not occupy any more of your valuable time. I would like to assure you that the Poles remember and will not forget that the agreement with us, and the amnesty, are linked with your name.

STALIN. As for myself, I personally am anxious to contribute to the restoration of an independent Polish State without regard to its internal régime.

KOT. Thank you very much for that declaration. May I make a note of it and announce it publicly? It would be of enormous importance. Or perhaps you would like to announce it publicly?

STALIN. I shall do so willingly at the first opportunity. . . .

KOT. One other question. I know you have already given your decision on the matter of starting a Polish periodical. Unfortunately we are meeting with difficulties.

STALIN (half turning to Molotov). Hasn't a Polish periodical been started yet?

KOT. Unfortunately not. The authorities in Kuibishev tell us they have no printing works, no type, etc.

STALIN (not hiding his dissatisfaction). Who said that?

KOT. I prefer not to mention names. But I shall be grateful if you will issue an instruction on this question also.

STALIN. Of course I shall (laughing). They have Polish type there. A Polish printing works was got ready some time ago at Wanda Wasilewska's request. Do you know Wanda Wasilewska?

KOT. Of course; she was a student of mine in Cracow. You see, by profession I am a university professor.

STALIN. About a year ago—yes—I remember it exactly. Exactly a year ago I had a talk here with Wasilewska.

KOT. What about?

STALIN. I talked with her about the need to form a Polish force in the U.S.S.R. I emphasize that this was a year ago, and so at a time when the Pact of Non-aggression with Germany was still in force. Wasilewska undertook to find Polish officers for these detachments.

KOT. Well, and what did she achieve?

STALIN. Enough willing officers came forward.

KOT. Then why didn't the force come into being?

STALIN. Not one general could be found prepared to put himself at its head.

KOT. You see, Mr. President, these Polish generals have their value and strong character. They refused because they had taken an oath of allegiance to the Polish State and Government. And you can be sure that now the situation has changed and we have the Polish-Soviet Agreement the Polish generals will not fail, and on the command of their Commander in Chief, General Sikorski, they will march together with you into the fight against Hitler.

(Kot thanks Stalin, takes leave of him, and asks Molotov for an audience next day, which is agreed to.)

K

Mr. Arlet, who wrote out the foregoing conversation from his notes, observed that it contained far more pronouncements than he succeeded in noting down. The conversation lasted from 19 to 21.10 hours. The Ambassador spoke in French, Stalin and Molotov in Russian. The whole time Stalin was very calm and self-controlled, and spoke quietly. More than once he showed his dissatisfaction when it transpired from the Ambassador's arguments that he [Stalin] had not been kept adequately informed by the Soviet authorities. At first he maintained a shade of reserve or caution, but as the discussion proceeded he seemed to speak more calmly. He always addressed the Ambassador with perfect courtesy. During the conversation he got up several times and walked along the conference table at which the Ambassador was sitting.

A50A. *Cable to the Minister for Foreign Affairs.*
Moscow. 14 November 1941

Today a conversation of over two hours with Stalin. The tone was very friendly. Fundamental agreement to the formation of further divisions in the U.S.S.R., but for the time being impossible to provide them with arms and food because of their own great effort. He understands the amnesty as unconditional and general, promised to look into the matter. At the end he declared that he personally is interested in helping in the rebuilding of an independent Polish State without regard to its internal system. On my request he promised to repeat this publicly.

The Premier's visit will undoubtedly yield important results; he asked concerning the date.

A50B. *Cable to the Minister for Foreign Affairs.*
Moscow. 14 November 1941

Undoubtedly the people here count very much on the Premier's visit. I ask for his arrival to be delayed; during these days there are very great chances of settling the difficulties outstanding.

B14. *Conversation with the Commissar for Foreign Affairs, Molotov.*
In the Kremlin. 15 November 1941
W. Arlet, interpreter.

KOT. I would like first of all to deal with a certain question which I didn't want to raise yesterday [with Stalin]. In one of my conversations with Mr. Vyshinsky, and also in conversations General Anders has had with the Soviet military authorities, we have heard the remark that in connection with General Sikorski's proposed visit the Polish side has put certain conditions in the form of an ultimatum. This is obviously a misunderstanding, which I would like to clear up in the interests of mutual good relations. The position is simply that before General Sikorski's arrival I would like to settle a number of current issues which otherwise would lead to difficulties. . . . During the last few weeks, and even days, certain issues have arisen, such as the refusal of a loan, the stopping of civilian transfers, the difficulties placed in the way of delegates, and even difficulties of a local nature in Kuibishev, which have seemed to indicate that General Sikorski's visit is not desired.

On the military question, the attempt to restrict our armed forces to two divisions was incomprehensible. For from the very beginning of the military conversations no quantitative restrictions were introduced. If it is intended to introduce them, why did the Soviet side bind itself in the first protocol to announce through all the military commissariats all over the Soviet Union that all Polish citizens are to enter the ranks of the Polish Army? Also, what would be the object of the order to transfer to the Polish Army Polish citizens in the Red Army who express the wish to serve in the Polish Army? I present you with the texts, in order to put an end to this misunderstanding.

MOLOTOV. You're right, there has been some misunderstanding. But to associate these misunderstandings as well as various petty matters, such as the question of accommodation in Kuibishev, with the supposition that we do not wish General Sikorski to visit us is incorrect. If General Sikorski wishes to come to the Soviet Union he will be our guest. As for the protocols on military questions, there are protocols confirmed and protocols unconfirmed by the Government. Nobody ever thought of restricting the organization of the Polish Army, but in regard to the further organization of the Army decisions were not taken simply because of difficulties of a material nature. Similarly, so far as proposals originating from the Command of the Russian [*sic*] Army are concerned, we are not in a position to confirm them all. After yesterday's conversation with Stalin this question is to be regarded as cleared up.

KOT. There are four protocols, not one; namely, from 16 August 1941 and later. But that question no longer arises. Yesterday I didn't wish to mention the name of the person who gave Uzbekistan to us as the area to which transfers were to be made. But today I would like to clear up the question completely. When proposing the formation of a further, third division, General Anders put forward a plan to base it on Uralsk, and in regard to the fourth and fifth divisions he only expressed a wish for them also to be accommodated not far from the Command headquarters. When no decision on the question of Uralsk arrived, and the number of persons applying to join the army was continually increasing, General Fiedotov indicated Uzbekistan to General Anders as the area in which our further units were to be organized. That was the reason why the military, and we too, directed Polish citizens to the south. In this question also I present you with the texts, for it was unpleasant for me to listen yesterday to the charge that the Embassy was directing Polish citizens wherever it wished, to places chosen off our own bat without discussion with the Soviet authorities. We were empowered to do so.

MOLOTOV. The journeys to the south were not permitted. The fact that there was discussion of them does not settle the question, for they were not confirmed by the Government. Meanwhile the Polish side took it as a question already decided. The Embassy telegrams gave instructions for journeys without the authority of the Soviet authorities.

KOT. As early as September, in conversations with Mr. Vyshinsky, I vainly demanded that a plan should be presented to me covering the distribution of the Polish population. Meanwhile life has moved on. The tragedy was that the people released had set out for the south, and so we could not wait for a decision from the Soviet side. I pointed out that this kind of mass wandering is particularly dangerous in wartime, but we for our part could not do anything about it without Soviet co-operation. Some days ago I gave Mr. Vyshinsky a list of the important issues which we ourselves have raised with the Narcomindiel and which have not been settled to date. I shall be grateful if you will give instructions for this list to be presented to you and if you will take an interest in these questions.

MOLOTOV. I am not only ready, but obliged to help you. I would ask you none the less to take our military situation and the circumstances arising from it into account. At present thousands and even millions of human masses, who are in a very serious position, are being transferred on a great scale. But from history we ought to turn to the future, and I have no doubt that my deputy Vyshinsky and I will do everything possible to order all these questions.

KOT. When I paid my first visit to you you expressed the conviction that my stay here and co-operation with you and your colleagues would bring success. I answered then that it would be a joint success. I deliberately recall this now and ask you to be ready to assist in achieving this reciprocal success. I have with me a note listing our basic needs and desiderata. This note was ready yesterday, so it includes various points which have already been decided in a positive sense by President Stalin (he hands Molotov the note). That applies to the first and second points, namely, the release of all Polish citizens and enrolment in the army. I turn to the third point. The question of a planned distribution of the Polish people was to have been handled by the Mixed Commission, but it has simply ceased to exist.

MOLOTOV. What is this Commission?

KOT. It consisted of one representative from the People's Commissariat for Foreign Affairs, one from the People's Commissariat for Internal Affairs, and two representatives from the Embassy. Its purpose was to discuss desiderata put forward by both parties, and to achieve the solution of various burning questions. I don't mention this in order to propose the revival of the Commission, since it did not have authority to decide important and urgent matters; but for our part we tried from the beginning to put issues on practical bases and not to allow difficulties and confusion to arise.

MOLOTOV. Today there are far greater difficulties than there were some months ago, so far as the question raised in point three is concerned.

KOT. We had a promise on the question of the procurators, judges, and police, who had been deported to particularly difficult localities in the north; but these promises have not been kept.

MOLOTOV. That is a physical problem. Many hundreds of thousands, and even millions of people will abandon their previous places of residence, but we require of them that they should provide themselves with monetary resources, that they should earn that money to the requisite amount. This point has been considered, but the material and transport difficulties are great.

KOT. But I hope it will be possible to do it. Our people are in a particularly difficult position: on release they have nothing whatever in their hands.

MOLOTOV. It's difficult, but they must work for it themselves. In the credits for Polish military purposes we have included a quota of three million roubles for cases of exceptional need.

KOT. I cannot take the risk of accepting that sum. We are anxious to obtain a serious loan. I count on a magnanimous gesture. The next question is that of utilizing our citizens' professional qualifications, which at present are being completely wasted. After all, a doctor or a chemist chopping down trees in a forest, or an outstanding designer of submarines working as a brickmaker is a pointless waste of our citizens' energies.

MOLOTOV. That will be done, undoubtedly, but it will be possible to achieve it only by degrees. We don't help even our own people, though they are shifting from spot to spot in a genuinely difficult situation. In this connection I would like to raise the question of General Sikorski's conversation with our minister Bogomolov, to whom General Sikorski declared that the governing authorities of the Soviet Union prefer to use Polish citizens on forced labour rather than have them as soldiers in the Polish Army. I was simply amazed at this statement, since it is without basis. I also had to state that I had never spoken on this subject with you. In reality I said something different, that Poles not embodied in the army should work where they are at any given moment and earn for their own needs on the spot.

KOT. There was no talk of forced labour. I simply asked you what was to be done with soldiers who applied to join the army and who could not be accepted in view of the over-complementation of the existing units. I stated that these people, instead of being soldiers, would have to work. Meanwhile, in fact we need soldiers above all else. Of course I shall clear up this question with General Sikorski.

MOLOTOV. The Polish Army is being organized, but there is bound to be a certain period before the units are formed. Stalin assured you that two divisions will be armed and maintained; the people who are to join the further divisions should work for the time being, or else the Polish Government should take them on to its own account, or transfer them as Polish citizens to new areas. I would ask you to eliminate all misunderstandings with Sikorski on the idea that the Soviet Government prefers forced labourers to soldiers.

KOT. Of course I shall do so, but for our soldiers the problem of working instead of fighting still exists.

MOLOTOV. The army will be organized, but by degrees. Therefore, in the interim either the Polish Government should assist them or they must work as workers, engineers, employees. . . .

KOT. For its part the Polish Government is endeavouring to help its citizens in material respects. Already certain transports sent from Great Britain to Archangel have arrived. Great collections are being organized in America. We are to receive the aid of the Red Cross from India. We expect the Soviet authorities to provide transport facilities for consignments of this kind, but there can be no question of comparing the situation of Soviet citizens forced by the war to change their places of residence with that of Polish citizens released from prison, work camps, and places of compulsory residence, without any monetary resources and even without clothing. Your people have plentiful resources. The situation of our people calls for material resources, hence our request for a loan. It isn't a question of aiding people who can work, but children, war-wounded, women burdened with small children. . . .

MOLOTOV. I shall report your remarks to the Government.

KOT. But I for my part ask you to be our advocate with the Government. The loan which you give us will in future yield fruits a hundred-fold.

MOLOTOV. I see that, but you must bear in mind that all our efforts are directed to waging the war.

KOT. If I don't make contact with our Polish citizens in this country my role will be quite absurd. For I must keep them informed, I must explain the nature of the Polish Government's new policy and its co-operation with the Soviet Union. To do this I need delegates, who must also issue passports to them, must take care of them, must bring them help. I have proposed a plan for forming local committees consisting of representatives of the interested Polish citizens to the People's Commissariat for Foreign Affairs. This plan was rejected; but agreement was given for Embassy delegates and men of trust, and an assurance that the local authorities would be given instructions to co-operate with them and facilitate the functions entrusted to them. But in practice a number of difficulties are arising. I was promised that representatives of the People's Commissariat for Internal Affairs would travel with the Embassy's travelling delegates. But this has happened in only one instance. Meanwhile it transpires that wherever we have co-operation from the Soviet authorities the results are of the best. The Embassy delegates don't want anything and don't do anything which might not be to the liking of the Soviet authorities. On the contrary, they try together with them to eliminate difficulties and arrange things which are in the general interest. In this respect my situation cannot be compared with that of other Ambassadors, who don't have masses of their citizens here. Among definite examples I cite the case of our delegate in Archangel, Mr. Gruja. He cannot make contact with the local authorities on any question whatever with the sole exception of transport, he cannot provide the Polish people with the clothing which is arriving from Great Britain, although it is in the north, in the harsh winter conditions, that it is particularly needed.

MOLOTOV. The case of Gruja is certainly well chosen. Mr. Gruja went to Archangel to deal with transports. . . . The opening of consulates would be incorrect. We have adopted the principle that we shall not start consulates. It would not be in order to agree to the extension of functions which were originally arranged within a definite restricted sphere.

KOT. My note, presented to the People's Commissariat for Foreign Affairs in connection with Mr. Gruja's departure, left no doubts as to the scope of his activity, which was not in the least restricted to transport questions. Give instructions for this note to be shown to you. From the beginning I demanded a definition of delegates' rights and duties, among which in any case was the collection of all kinds of data and information concerning Poles, as well as providing them with passports. How can we act on the instructions issued by the Soviet Government itself for furnishing the Polish people with passports within a definite period and what you yourself said, that we are to occupy ourselves with the Polish people, if simultaneously you render it impossible for me to make contact with the people? . . . How am I to escape from this dilemma?

MOLOTOV. So far as Gruja is concerned, so far as I remember, his tendency to extend the functions originally entrusted to him is not in order. But I shall check that, since what was decided must be adhered to. But I must emphasize that the sending out of plenipotentiaries is one thing, and the question of consulates another, since they can be opened only by agreement with the Government. Functions must be defined clearly and fixed, but there must be no creation of *faits accomplis*.

KOT. Where are these consulates? I'm not insisting on them in the least, I am not a professional diplomat and I am not concerned with formal titles. In the present difficult war conditions the traditional consulates might not perhaps be able to fulfil the functions I want to see in being. We must have people from the local milieu, from those who are interested. The only consular question they would have to facilitate is the issuing of passports. As regulation of this matter is to the benefit of both Governments I ask you to take interest in it and to understand that such functions can be entrusted only to people in whom I have complete confidence.

MOLOTOV. Of course it is necessary to establish the delegates' rights and duties and clear up the whole question.

KOT. I can give instructions to our citizens to co-operate only if I maintain contact with them through my emissaries, adherents of the policy I represent. Only then can I undertake the responsibility of informing and guiding them. I shall present an appropriate plan covering delegates' rights and duties to the Narcomindiel, we shall discuss it and shall regulate the matter as swiftly as possible to our mutual benefit. In conclusion I would like to congratulate you on the magnificent way you are holding out, as I have seen with my own eyes in Moscow. . . . I would even be very ready to say on the radio how excellent the spirit is here and how very different the situation is from that painted by German propaganda.

MOLOTOV. Certainly the military situation of Moscow has changed for the better. We don't wish to conceal from ourselves or others that the situation is serious, but I am glad to be able to assure you that Moscow's situation today is much stronger than one month ago, when we were compelled to evacuate the Embassy. During this past month we have made very serious preparations to strengthen our defensive possibilities.

KOT. I would like in conclusion to assure you that I left this room yesterday impressed by the great authority and extraordinary affability of President Stalin.

The conversation lasted from 18 to 19.45 hours. The Ambassador spoke in French, Molotov in Russian.

A51. Cable to General Sikorski.
Kuibishev. 16 November 1941

I returned to Kuibishev on Sunday afternoon. Yesterday a long conversation with Molotov on our desiderata, namely: 1. planned distribution and employment of civilian Poles; 2. material security for those not fit for the army or labour, possibly in the form of a loan; 3. transport facilities for aid from abroad; 4. development of the Embassy delegations.

Atmosphere favourable, though few definite promises. They take shelter behind their own difficulties. Conclusion from both conversations: the Premier's visit necessary. We shall use the next few days for partial elimination of the outstanding difficulties. Please let me have the date of journey and names of the party.

A52. To General Anders in Buzuluk.
Kuibishev. 17 November 1941

The course of the conversations in Moscow was such that their results are not suitable for telephonic transmission, yet I think it very important that you should know of them before your arrival in Kuibishev. The atmosphere was very good and friendly. The audience with Stalin lasted two hours ten minutes and was largely occupied with military questions.

It has proved unfortunate that I did not know the protocols of all the Polish-Soviet military conferences. From what I learned from General Bohusz the day after the conference, I see that acquaintance with this material would have had a very strong influence on the course of the conversation.

Naturally, above all else I put the problem of organizing further divisions. There is very definite agreement, but with reservations which make it rather theoretical. 'On the territory of the U.S.S.R. you can create not two, but three, four, five, six, seven divisions,' however with the emphasis that they haven't enough arms and food. After a time, possibly in three months, the situation may change for the better. On my insistence that for a start, so long as we do not receive our own commissariat supplies, we should be fed from here, I obtained a kind of agreement in the words: 'I am of the opinion that Russia should share with you all she has,' but as things are difficult, try to seek food abroad. It stopped at the point that this question is to be given precise formulation in conversation with General Sikorski. As for arms, when I mentioned that at first agreement had been given for two divisions, but afterwards one was withdrawn, I received the declaration: if that is so, the second also will get arms.

When I complained of the restriction to 30,000 and the order to discharge the excess, at first this was not believed. Fortunately I had a copy of the document, which I handed to him, and it evoked the rough statement: 'Whoever signed this had no right to do so, it is illegal.' I thanked him. On the other hand, a difficulty arose from their statement that the protocol recognized only the figure of 30,000 for 1941. Unfortunately I did not have this document, but fortunately it was produced by Vice-President Molotov, who was assisting at the conversation. Even my poor acquaintance with Russian sufficed to convince them that the date 1941, [which he] pointed to with the finger involved only the obligation to form the first two divisions by 1 October 1941, nothing more. . . . It was proposed that an order should be issued tomorrow, in which the district assigned for the concentration of human material for further divisions would be named. In view of the fact that I was informed that it cannot be Uzbekistan, where the Poles are gathering illegally, I asked for the needs of the climate and easy transport conditions from abroad to be taken into account. Being afraid of too hasty a decision, I obtained agreement to postpone the issue until the conversation with General Sikorski.

The same applies to indicating the areas for our civilians. I remarked that the journeys to Uzbekistan are causing irritation and the profound conviction that we are directing people there against the Soviet authorities' wishes. I claimed to have proofs that we were authorized to do so. This did not find credence. I think it necessary to send telegrams stopping at once all transports directed there, as it may be very detrimental to our Poles. . . .

To the question, put to me very delicately, whether and when our troops will be ready to fight, I answered that only the military could reply to that. As for myself, I know that our troops take the war with the Germans seriously, and not theatrically, that the war with Germany is our war, but if we throw in one or two divisions they will be drowned in the sea of the Soviet Army and they will not be distinguished as a Polish effort. I was answered: 'Perfectly sound, there should be a corps, or an army.'

I mentioned the people not yet released, speaking very energetically. I also mentioned that so far you have not seen one of the officers of your staff in the September campaign. This provoked astonishment and the statement: 'The amnesty was general and unconditional; I ask for names, I shall look into the matter.' At this point I was painfully conscious of the fact that despite my many requests I had not obtained extensive lists from the military. I am convinced that if I could have presented them nothing could have held up the issue. But now I am afraid the counter-action of elements hostile to us can bog down the matter by supplying information unquestionably false.

I implore you to collect within a week lists of all whose names can be remembered by those who were held in Starobielsk, Kozielsk, and Ostaszkow. If the officers of the individual formations only noted down their colleagues, and the same was done by the doctors, the

lawyers, military judges, priests, chaplains, and the judges, procurators, and police, mass lists would be drawn up which would be very
close to reality. An opportunity may arise during the next few days
when it may yet be possible to hand over such a list. . . .

. . . General Sikorski will not be able to arrive until about the
25th; his tour starts from Kuibishev.

A51A. Cable from Minister for Foreign Affairs.
London. 19 November 1941

After acquainting himself with your report on your conversations
with Stalin the Premier asks you to notify the Soviet Government
that he will arrive in the U.S.S.R. at the end of the current
month. . . .

B15. Conversation with the Vice-Commissar for Foreign
Affairs, A. J. Vyshinsky.
Kuibishev, in the Narcomindiel. 19 November 1941
Present: An employee taking notes on behalf of the
Narcomindiel, and Embassy secretary Arlet
as interpreter.

Kot began by mentioning the results of his visits to Stalin and
Molotov, thanking Vyshinsky for his aid in bringing about these
visits, and emphasizing that he was satisfied with the course of the
conversations.

On the two questions fundamental for us, the army and the releases,
President Stalin gave me assurances completely in line with our aims.
President Stalin emphasized that the amnesty is general, uncondi-
tional and does not allow of exceptions.

VYSHINSKY. Of course the amnesty has been fully observed by us and
it is only a question of checking that it has been carried out in
individual instances. Certain elements, such as criminals, Hitlerite
agents, Rumanians, Hungarians, and Finns had to be excluded from
it.

KOT. It would appear that in fact you released criminal prisoners first
of all, whereas we are not interested in them.

VYSHINSKY (laughing). Then we can take them back. In any case we
did not release serious criminals, only those sentenced for petty
offences. This problem arises for us only as a check on the fulfilment
of the amnesty by the governmental lower organs. Stalin said firmly
that all are to be released, and for us Stalin's word is a command.

KOT. President Stalin also made a general declaration on the Polish question, saying that he personally was anxious to take part in the restoration of an independent Polish State without interfering in its internal affairs. President Stalin even promised to use this sentence in one of his speeches at an early date.

VYSHINSKY. Of course, that corresponds completely with the Lenin-Stalinist principles of respect for the sovereignty of other nations, and non-interference in their internal affairs. Undoubtedly, as the result of victorious military activities against Hitler a situation will arise in which we shall jointly liberate the Polish lands also. I am very glad you're satisfied with the results of the conversations, and that your stay in Moscow has led to the elucidation or definition of a number of fundamental issues whose development is in the interests and for the prosperity of both the U.S.S.R. and Poland.

KOT. I add that Moscow made a good impression on me. It was evident that the people were remaining calm, and the military spirit is perfect. For us who are accustomed to raids on London, the complete absence of destruction was particularly striking. . . .

VYSHINSKY. Obviously the German raids mean as much to Moscow as the bite of a mosquito. For we have magnificent artillery, especially anti-aircraft guns. But all the same, things are not happening without casualties among the civilian population.

KOT. But those casualities are not numerous, especially if they are compared with the war casualties generally.

VYSHINSKY. In view of General Sikorski's forthcoming visit, and in view also of the extension of the Embassy's sphere of activities, during the past few days I have occupied myself with the question of accommodation. (Jokingly.) So you see, I am not only a diplomat but also the quartermaster for diplomats. . . . (They both laugh.) The house I have managed to reserve for the Embassy's needs is in Leo Tolstoy Street, not far from the present building.

KOT. Thank you very much; but are there enough rooms and are they big enough?

VYSHINSKY. Quite definitely. In any case, somebody will be able to look them over, and if they proved too small we'd have to try for something else. . . . But I've asked you to call in connection with a more important problem. We now have a reply to the *aide-memoire* which you presented to Commissar Molotov on the fifteenth.

KOT. That fits in perfectly, for this very day I have given instructions to refer to you one of the important matters we discussed with Com-

missar Molotov. Commissar Molotov wished to have a definition of
the rights and duties of the Embassy's delegates and the principles
governing their co-operation with the Soviet authorities. I have sent
you my plan, which I worked at yesterday and today.

VYSHINSKY. The reply devotes a separate section to this question, and
according to it, because of the war our Government does not think it
possible to establish consulates in the U.S.S.R.; but it has no reservations against Embassy plenipotentiaries who would go to localities
where Poles are residing in order to issue passports to them and to
give aid to the Polish citizens. Their functions would be defined by
the People's Commissariat and the Embassy jointly.

KOT. I am glad the reply corresponds with our wishes. In my conversation with Commissar Molotov I emphasized that Embassy delegates cannot create any difficulties for the Soviet authorities, that there
is nothing in our instructions to them which would not be beneficial
to the Soviet authorities as well as to us. So far as my delegates are
concerned, I have absolutely nothing to hide; on the contrary, all our
instructions to them should be agreed with the Soviet authorities, to
establish the very best co-operation with them.

VYSHINSKY. Out of this arises a question which I think Mr. Sokolnicki
raised in conversation with me, concerning Kwapinski, the Embassy
delegate in Tashkent. I sent a telegram to Tashkent yesterday to the
effect that not merely were difficulties not to be put in his way, but, on
the contrary, he was to be given assistance and co-operation and nothing was to be done to hinder his activities until further instructions
on this question arrived.

KOT. Thank you very much. This very day I have received a telegram
from Kwapinski (he hands it to Vyshinsky) which conveys the desperate plight of our people.

VYSHINSKY (reads the telegram). And so today or tomorrow we shall
thoroughly discuss the details of the delegate problem. We shall send
a plan to Moscow, and after it has been settled within two or three
days the matter will be under control.

On the question of a loan I have already notified you of the Soviet
Government's reply; in view of the hold up in the plan for resettlement the question was decided negatively. I recall that at that time
you put forward the argument that a loan is needed also for providing
aid to the Polish citizens unfit for work and having no means of
existence. Commissar Molotov's reply states that your proposal to
maintain Polish citizens at the cost of the Soviet Government or for

a loan to be granted to the Polish Government for this purpose has been communicated to the Soviet Government and will be considered with all due attention.

KOT. I ask you once more to give this matter your warm support. After all, the money you lend us now will bring you interest in the future in Polish-Soviet relations. I ask for a broad gesture on your part, and no small-mindedness.

VYSHINSKY. Of course. The government will take these points into consideration. But did you raise the question with President Stalin?

KOT. No, because I wanted to discuss with him the questions of most importance to us, namely the army and the releases. In addition, in view of the great range of President Stalin's occupations and duties, with so many important matters on his shoulders, I could not burden him with such an activity as counting money (he laughs).

VYSHINSKY (also laughing). Well, of course, I quite understand.

KOT. But I did raise with him one small question, namely, that of a newspaper for the Poles. President Stalin asked who had told us there was no paper, printing works, or printers. Of course I didn't answer that, not wishing to mention names, but I asked him to take an interest in the matter and received a corresponding promise. . . .

VYSHINSKY. The evacuation from Moscow has held up the whole affair. I remember it was very near to being put into effect. I have already received instructions from Moscow on the subject and have issued the appropriate orders. Other problems are dealt with in detail in the reply.

KOT. As for points one and two, referring to the releases and the formation of further divisions, I now have President Stalin's positive assurance, but I ask you personally once more to take up the question of releases. I disliked having to burden President Stalin with this in Moscow. I want to ensure that when General Sikorski arrives and talks to Stalin he will not need to return to the subject.

VYSHINSKY. I have already said that the problem consists simply in checking that the appropriate orders are being carried out. On all the cases you have referred to us I personally endeavour to obtain detailed explanations. But when there is a divergence between the data the Embassy sends us and those in our possession it is due to the difficulties of communication and the general situation, which impedes the transmission of information.

KOT. But I have President Stalin's word, and I think it is binding on the Soviet authorities and that it will be acted upon. I ask you to watch over its fulfilment. The northern winter is terrible for our people. Why should many of them lose their lives unnecessarily? The nightmare of those deaths would be bound to burden our future relations.

VYSHINSKY. I understand. I shall do all that is within the competence of the People's Commissariat for Foreign Affairs.

KOT. I thank you again for arranging my journey to Moscow. And I must admit that my meeting with President Stalin made a great impression on me. . .

The conversation lasted from 14.30 to 15.05 hours.

> B16. *Conversation with the Vice-Commissar for Foreign Affairs, A. J. Vyshinsky.*
> *In the Narcomindiel, 25 November 1941*
> Present: K. N. Novikov and W. Arlet.

KOT. I have asked you to receive me today on a difficult and urgent matter. I have received news from several sources that during the period 25 November to 5 December 36,000 Polish citizens are to be transferred from Uzbekistan to the north and directed to the *oblasts* Dzambulsk, Southern Kazakhstan and Siemipalatinsk. I also know that the Soviet authorities in the *oblasts* I have mentioned are not in the least prepared for the suitable reception of such a large number of people. There is no accommodation for them, nor food, nor work, nor feeding points at the railway stations. The travellers are to receive only bread for the road, but no other kind of food. A very considerable number of them consists of children, women, and old people. They lack suitable clothing, as they had to dispose of it when they travelled to the south, and many of them are ill. These thousands of Polish citizens went to Uzbekistan absolutely legally, in circumstances which I have already communicated to the Soviet Government. What results this sort of transportation has on our people are indicated by the figures for deaths from hunger and exhaustion. During the week from 7 to 14 November there were seventy deaths among Polish citizens travelling to Uzbekistan. What is now being done with the Polish citizens is inhuman and cruel. I don't understand why and for what purpose it is occurring. This question was raised in my Moscow conversations with President Stalin and Commissar Molotov on 14 and 15 November, and President Stalin agreed that the final decision as to the designation of regions in which the new Polish divisions are to be formed and the Polish civilian population settled could be postponed until General Sikorski's arrival. When talking of the needs of the Polish people President Stalin told me in so many words: 'We, Russians, will share everything we have in brotherhood with the Poles.'

The Polish community will undoubtedly put the responsibility for what is now happening to the Polish people transported from Uzbekistan on my Government; they will say it allowed this treatment of its citizens at the very moment when the Premier, General Sikorski, is arriving on an official visit to the Soviet Union and is being received by the Soviet central authorities with all the honours due to him. At this very same moment Poles will be flung in masses, like cattle, in horrible conditions, from a warm climate to the north. I get the impression that someone is anxious to mar the effects of General Sikorski's visit. Things which at any rate would be intelligible if there were war between us, when people would be perishing as the result of the war, are quite inexplicable in view of the present alliance between the Soviet Union and Poland. That is not the way to wage war on Hitler. If our people are to perish like this, then everything loses all sense and I consider that my mission in the U.S.S.R. will not achieve its end. I ask you to do everything to stop these deportations. I am forced to declare that I present a protest against this action, since for me and the Embassy, for the Polish Government and the Polish Nation it constitutes an unfriendly act.

VYSHINSKY. I have received three letters, dated 23, 24, and 25 November, on the question you raise. The first of them yesterday, the last two this morning; two in the form of verbal notes, one in the form of a personal note from yourself to me. I passed the contents of the verbal note of 23 November immediately to the information of the Government in Moscow, and I already have a reply, which I shall hand to you. In that note you asked the Soviet Government to hold up the order given for the transfer of 6,500 Polish citizens to the Siemipalatinsk *oblast*, motivating your request by saying that this transfer will have a negative reaction on their situation. I have also communicated the notes received today to my Government, and you will receive a reply to them. As our reply to the note of the 23rd cannot touch on the matters which you have now raised, since we simply had no knowledge of them, before handing it to you I must make a number of observations on them. You have called the transportation an unfriendly act and have presented a protest on the subject.

L

KOT. Not against the transportation, only against the circumstances and the horrible conditions in which it is taking place.

VYSHINSKY. I shall report that to my Government immediately. But I would like to explain how my Government sees this problem. In speaking of the transfer of Polish people from Uzbekistan already ordered, you evidently had in mind the conditions in which the Polish people travelled from the north to the south, which resulted, *inter alia*, in incidents such as you have already reported to me. The Polish people's wanderings from north to south took place in a completely chaotic, unorganized fashion. There can be no suggestion that those journeys are to be compared with the plan for transferring 36,500 Polish citizens from Uzbekistan. The first movement was an elemental, unplanned urge, hence the mortality cases which you have reported to us. If their number or the very fact of their happening at all corresponds with the reality, I can only express my regret. But I cannot refrain from declaring that a number of Polish official individuals sent out precise instructions, frequently on a mass scale: 'travel to Uzbekistan.' I think (he turns to Novikov) we even had to raise this question in a conversation with Sokolnicki. (Novikov assents.) Many thousands of people cannot make such journeys without various tragic incidents. As the result very serious difficulties have arisen in the Uzbekistan area. The new arrivals were faced with lack of accommodation, of work, even the possibility of existence. You doubtless remember that we did not undertake any obligations to assure work to all the Polish citizens, and yet our authorities endeavoured and are endeavouring to do everything to ensure that every Pole fit for work obtains it. Starting from the assumption that finding paid work for such a great mass of Polish citizens is not possible in Uzbekistan, the Soviet Government has given orders for their transference to other districts. The difference between the transfer of the Polish people from north to south and the present transfer consists in the circumstance that it is not in the least an elemental drive or unorganized wandering. The Soviet Government has assured food on the journey to all who travel. The People's Commissar for Trade, Mr. Lubicev, has been instructed to organize feeding points along their route. The People's Commissar for Health, Mr. Mitiorov, has been obliged by the same instruction to organize medical help along the route.

KOT. But what of assuring clothing to the travellers? That is an even more urgent question than food, for at a pinch one can go several days without food, but what good will the medical aid be if the people, having no suitable clothing, simply die of the cold?

VYSHINSKY. There are no special instructions in regard to clothing, but as the authorities of the Kazakh Republic have been put under obligation by the Government to receive these Polish citizens and assure help to them, obviously that problem will be solved too. In addition the Government has assigned monetary resources for the transfer. You surely realize that the costs of this kind of action run into millions. You have expressed a wish for it to be postponed till later. After all, the settlement of this issue is just as important for us as for you. We simply must eliminate this blockage, and as swiftly as possible, hence the speed with which it is being carried through. The situation really is difficult in Uzbekistan. Cases of mass stealing and even pillage have begun to multiply, which after all is quite understandable, since there is such a heavy concentration of people without roofs to their heads or means of existence. It seems to me that the very speed with which we are operating testifies to our determination to get a satisfactory settlement of this vital problem. So the objective the Soviet Government has set itself in ordering the transfer cannot affect relations with the Polish Government or disturb our friendship in the least. I categorically declare that such assumptions are quite unrealistic. I think that when you have given it quiet consideration you will share my view. I'm sure that to leave these people in Uzbekistan would not lead to any good, but on the other hand in their own interests it is only possible to transfer them swiftly from there at the present moment. December and January are a very unhealthy period of winter, and so the transfer has to be carried out now. I repeat that I shall pass on the protest you have presented to my Government, and I shall let you have the reply, just as I am now replying to the note of the 23rd on the question of the 6,500 Polish citizens.[1] (He hands over the note.) Of course, in this note only the one subject is dealt with.

KOT. Thank you. May I for my part make certain observations?

VYSHINSKY. By all means.

KOT. Ever since September, from the beginning of our conversations I have demanded that a joint plan should be drawn up for the settlement of the Polish people. Do you recall that?

VYSHINSKY. Of course.

KOT. Yet I have received no reply to any of my requests on the subject,

[1] The figures 36,000, 6,500 and 36,500 are as in the Polish text. The first was evidently a round figure, the second referred to a first batch. *Tr.*

though if such a plan had been drawn up we should have been able to avoid all that has happened since.

VYSHINSKY. I too wanted to draw up a plan, and gave it my personal attention; but in face of the changed situation, which you know all about, the Soviet Government was forced to decide to hold up the transfers. It was not pleasant for me to inform you of this on 2 November, but I had to do it.

KOT. But two months passed from September to the moment when you told me. The shift of population occurred chiefly in September and October, and in a completely unplanned manner at that.

VYSHINSKY. At the present time and in the given conditions there can be no talk of transfers. When I had my conversation with you on 2 November I mentioned the *oblasts* of Siemipalatinsk, Southern Kazakhstan, and Dzambul as places for settling people who were already *en route*, or individuals who wished to travel at their own risk. You made no protest against that.

(A short discussion follows, to which both Novikov and Arlet contribute a few words; it transpires that the *oblasts* were mentioned by Mr. Pushkin in a conversation with Mr. Arlet, with reference to 10,000 Polish citizens who were staying in the area where the Polish army was being formed. These names were first mentioned in writing to the Polish side in Molotov's note dated 19 November.)

KOT. When the *oblasts* named were first presented to me in writing I gave instructions to be informed on the climatic conditions and the possibility of earning a living from exclusively Soviet sources in those areas. It appears that north of the mountains separating Kazakhstan from Uzbekistan the climate is much harsher. Agriculture is poorly developed, and there are no prospects of earnings with the exception of work in copper and zinc mines, which is very unhealthy.

VYSHINSKY. The climatic difference between the *oblasts* of Southern Kazakhstan and Dzambul and Uzbekistan is not great. In any case the Poles will be able to work there.

KOT. Is there any possibility of settling them in other districts of Kazakhstan, in a climate more suited to them, and of assuring them work corresponding with their qualifications and capacities?

VYSHINSKY. I shall send your proposal to my Government, and as soon as I have the reply I shall communicate it to you. In any case I assure you there is not a great difference in climate. As for employment corresponding to their qualifications, it is possible that those professions which the transferred Polish citizens represent will be in demand precisely in Kazakhstan.

KOT. In Alma Ata *oblast*, for instance, the climate is much more suited to our people.

VYSHINSKY. I shall inform my Government of your request.

KOT. I want to emphasize again that I don't attach any special importance to Uzbekistan, it is only a question of postponing the transfer to a time when it will be possible to organize it satisfactorily.

VYSHINSKY. I cannot reply to that suggestion. Of course I am ready to report on all this to Stalin and Molotov in Moscow.

KOT. I have the very worst of information from Siemipalatinsk *oblast*. The situation of our people there is difficult beyond words. Many of them are appealing to us for help because they won't survive the winter [otherwise]. Work on the collective farms has finished, they don't need our people any more, so they not only have nothing to eat, they are not only suffering from need and hunger, but they don't even have anywhere to live. In such circumstances nobody should be sent to Siemipalatinsk.

VYSHINSKY. The Government of the Kazakhstan Republic will be under obligation to organize everything. As for aid from outside, you know about the ten millions which the Soviet Government has assigned for these purposes. Lozovsky has informed you of this. It is not a large sum to meet the most urgent needs, but I think it would be well if the Polish Government agreed to accept it. This money will be useful just for help in exceptional cases, and, after all, aid will come from abroad. For instance, I can inform you that orders have already been issued in regard to the transport from India to the effect that the six lorries are to be passed through, the members of the expedition are to be given visas, and no difficulties are to be put in their way. These six lorries will certainly be followed by others. After all we, too, need help from abroad. If your and our friends set about the task properly, if we jointly assemble all our forces, it will be possible to eliminate many difficulties and needs. But do please bear in mind that our own requirements are enormous, that some 100 kilometres from Moscow a fight is going on in which millions are taking part, and many of them are perishing.

KOT. In the fight being waged outside Moscow all the desires of the Polish Nation, all its wishes are for you. We desire your victory no less than you. But I ask that action such as the transfer from Uzbekistan should not [be allowed to] cool the Polish Nation's feelings towards you. For it is only a matter of purposeful and orderly organization of the transfer. A good end can be achieved at the same cost as a bad one. I am concerned to ensure that the greatest good should be achieved, but what will happen if our people arrive in the north in rags, naked? From the Altai Land and other regions I am receiving information indicating that wherever our delegates and men of trust co-operate with the authorities after those authorities have received appropriate instructions from the central authorities, the very best of results are achieved. In connection with this transfer particularly the delegates could play a very valuable part. I ask you to ensure that the question of delegates is settled finally and fundamentally.

VYSHINSKY. I well understand that. I have personally gone through the plan you sent me some days ago, have proposed changes in several points, have furnished the whole with my observations and sent it to Moscow. I hope that in the very near future, in not more than two or three days I shall have a reply, and the matter will be finally settled.

KOT. As for the loan, I thank you for informing me about it, but I would ask for an instruction for me to receive the money as quickly as possible, so that I can get help going now, at the beginning of the winter.

VYSHINSKY. I believe that in your conversation with Molotov he used the phrase: cut your coat according to your cloth. After all, we are allies, and we make a point of speaking the truth to our allies and friends. Our situation is difficult, our possibilities are restricted, we put the matter sincerely and frankly. You know very well in what diplomatic phraseology and evasive forms we could invest the question of a loan, for instance. We don't do that, we speak the truth. We help you as far as we are able.

KOT. The quota we are receiving is truly small. Nor would there be any sense in not paying it out as quickly as possible, so that we can go to the aid of the people at once. . . . But I would like to take this opportunity to raise another matter: help from abroad. I have news from America of transports of food and clothing which are to be directed to Vladivostok. They are even asking me who will take them over. They are demanding that I should give names. I have asked the Narcomindiel for visas for several of our people who are to leave Tokio because of the close-down of our post. Unfortunately, so far I haven't received visas for them. They are people who have been engaged exclusively in welfare and have never had anything to do with the consular service, and in Vladivostok they would be concerned only with taking over the goods and sending them on to us. I ask you to make a positive recommendation on this matter.

VYSHINSKY. I shall put it before my Government.

KOT. I return again to the fundamental issue on which I came to see you today. It is in both our interests either to hold up the transfer of our people from Uzbekistan or to restrict it, but above all to make it possible to supply the people with clothing, to assure them living accommodation and work. If that is not done, there will be a tragedy which can never be mended. Do you realize what effects this may have in connection with General Sikorski's visit? I wanted to send telegrams to all the Polish centres informing them of his visit, in the hope that telegrams would be sent from the Polish people to General Sikorski, gratefully greeting him as the man who has initiated a Polish-Soviet *rapprochement*. But what would happen if I were to send out telegrams now? I cannot do it, because curses, reproaches, requests will be coming back. In such a situation people forget the great and important matters. They are so overwhelmed by their primitive vital needs.

VYSHINSKY. I hope you will send the telegrams.

KOT. Judging by all that is happening I see I shan't. For that matter I don't believe there is any objective possibility of the local authorities carrying out the instructions of the central authorities. Any instructions to ensure the adequate organization of transport, the reception of the people and accommodation for them as well as living conditions will simply not be carried out below.

VYSHINSKY. On the contrary, I haven't the least doubt that the central authorities' instructions will be carried out precisely. Besides, what would the Polish citizens do in Uzbekistan? In Kazakhstan they will be able to obtain better living and labour conditions. That is what moved the Soviet Government in organizing the transfer.

KOT. But the most urgent question of all is warm clothing. For they cannot live without suitable clothing in the climate to which they are going. If only you would hold up their transfer until we have supplied them with clothing; several trucks have arrived from Archangel during the last few days.

VYSHINSKY. Nothing could be simpler than to send the trucks on at once.

KOT. Not at all! First the bales have to be opened, their contents sorted; after all, you cannot send only stockings, or only sweaters or underwear. The thing to do would be to postpone the transfer until we can get help to them.

VYSHINSKY. That's impossible.

KOT. Couldn't at least some of those going be held back?

VYSHINSKY. Their situation can only get worse with every day in Uzbekistan.

KOT. It would only be a question of getting clothing to them, and financial aid immediately you pay us the money.

VYSHINSKY. I shall mention that to my Government.

KOT. In Molotov's note of 8 November we had official agreement to the evacuation of 20,000 of our soldiers to reinforce the Polish Army in Great Britain and the Near East. Isn't that number to be found among the people now travelling northward? And if they were to have to travel through the south it would be quite inexpedient to transport them to the north now and back again later.

VYSHINSKY. I have no details on this question, and I cannot say whether such people are included among these 36,000, but I shall try to find out.

KOT. But how many Polish citizens are there altogether in Uzbekistan, according to the Soviet Government's calculation?

VYSHINSKY. Unfortunately I have no data.

KOT (noticing that Vyshinsky is glancing at his watch). I shall not occupy your time any longer.

VYSHINSKY. I'd never allow myself to look at my watch if some private matter were involved. But I have another visitor at eleven.

KOT. I would prefer to settle everything with you in five minutes. I'd like to come and discuss some question and obtain a positive decision at once.

VYSHINSKY (laughing sourly). Well yes, but not when you come with protests.

KOT. That's all very well, but I too would prefer not to have to come with a protest.

The conversations lasted from 21.30 to 22.50 hours. After the Ambassador's opening statement, ending in the protest, Vyshinsky was very conciliatory and polite, he uttered his main reply in a gentle tone such as he had never used before, as though excusing himself to the Ambassador. As the conversation proceeded, and especially in its final section, he clearly grew nervous, but all the time he remained in control of his choice of words and tone.

A56A. Cable from the Minister for Foreign Affairs.
London. 30 November 1941

For the Premier.

Harriman has acquainted me with a long reply from Stalin, handed to him by Maisky yesterday, to his telegram of 12 November, in which he put forward the plan for transporting the Polish Army out of Russia to be equipped and armed, and at the appropriate moment returning it to the Russian front. Stalin refers to a satisfactory conversation with Ambassador Kot and ends as follows: 'For your information I communicate that in conversation with me Mr. Kot did not raise the question of sending the Polish troops to any other country.' I explained to Harriman that Stalin's interpretation is undoubtedly based on a misunderstanding. In line with my suggestion H. intends (leaving the final text dependent on the President's agreement) to tell Stalin in reply that the proposal put forward in his first cable corresponded with the emphatic desideratum of the Polish Government and also with that of the United States Government. Harriman will say that, as he knows, the Polish Government has not changed its attitude.

RACZYNSKI.

A56B. Cable to the Minister for Foreign Affairs.
Kuibishev. 30 November 1941

In conversation with Stalin I did not raise the evacuation of the Polish troops as a whole from the U.S.S.R., since at that time I had not received any instructions to this effect. I was instructed only to intervene for the transfer of fifteen to twenty thousand, to which I received written agreement before I left Moscow.

In my conversation I confined myself to obtaining basic agreement for a limited number of divisions, for that is the most important thing to achieve if only for the sake of the many thousands of officers and soldiers still not released and the great number of our citizens called up into the Red Army and now constituting labour battalions. I left all definitely military matters to be raised in the Premier's conversation.

By obtaining Stalin's agreement that everybody should be handed over to the army and his admission that they cannot feed and equip everybody I prepared the way for the proposal to move troops abroad. That must follow from Russia's admission of her inability to organize our troops adequately on her own territory. It is also the opinion of

Cripps and MacFarlane that Russia's sensitivity in regard to this question is enormous and dangerous. Under foreign pressure they agree to the transfer, but in practice they will release no more than those already in freedom and awaiting call up into the ranks. Restriction to this small number and loss of the remainder would be a terrible disaster for us. Great caution is necessary. I propose that Harriman should delay his intervention until the Premier's conversation.

KOT.

At this moment the Ambassador and Diplomatic Corps are waiting at the airfield for the Premier. (Secretary's note.)

> B17. *Sikorski meets Stalin.*
> *Conversation between General Sikorski and the Chairman of the U.S.S.R. Council of People's Commissars, Stalin, in the Kremlin, 3 December 1941*[1]
> Present: Professor Kot, Polish Ambassador; Molotov, Commissar for Foreign Affairs; General Anders, Commander of the Polish Armed Forces in the U.S.S.R., (interpreting) also Molotov's secretary.

SIKORSKI. I am glad beyond measure that I can greet one of the genuine creators of contemporary history and congratulate you, Mr. President, on the heroism of the Russian Army in the struggle against the Germans. As a soldier I must express my admiration for the valiant defence of Moscow, which you are directing so effectively yourself from the capital. At the same time I thank you for the very great hospitality which I have experienced from the very first moment I set foot on Soviet soil.

STALIN. I thank you for what you have said and I am very glad to see you in Moscow.

SIKORSKI. I begin by saying that for the past twenty years I have never conducted any policy and have never agreed with any policy directed against the Soviet Union. In view of this I had a moral right to sign the Agreement, since it may be the crown of all I have long subscribed to. Moreover, in this matter, so important for the future, I have behind

---

[1] The protocol of this conversation was drawn up in Kuibishev on 6 December 1941 by General Anders, with the aid of my notes. I can guarantee that Stalin's words are noted exactly, as I made a careful note of them. The protocol was written in a hurry, and was to have been looked over by General Sikorski; unfortunately his illness prevented his doing so. Profiting by the fact that a courier was travelling, I had to send it to London in this state, though, in my opinion, it does not always faithfully reflect Sikorski's thoughts and words. S. Kot.

me the Polish nation, both at home and wherever Poles are concentrated, in the larger settlements, such as America, where there are four and a half million Poles, in Canada, in France, where there are six hundred thousand of them, and in the other, smaller concentrations. Against me I have those who did not pursue a policy similar to mine.

I would not like the slow realization of the Agreement to weaken the policy of *rapprochement* and friendly co-existence between our two States. On the full and loyal fulfilment of the Agreement depends whether we have in fact come to a turn in history. That depends on you, Mr. President, since in this country your decisions are final. So it is necessary to fulfil the Agreement, it is necessary that an end should be put to the vexatious annoyances to our people. I know perfectly the difficulties in which Russia finds herself. Four fifths of all the armed forces of the German Reich have been flung against you. Realizing this, I am an advocate of your case in London and the United States. Already several months ago I presented memoranda arguing the necessity to form a second front in the West.

STALIN. Thank you, Mr. Premier. That is sound and good.

SIKORSKI. But that is no easy task. There are great difficulties, especially in regard to shipping. The crossing of the Channel by any large number of troops, the occupation and development of corresponding positions on the continent are not a simple task. That kind of operation needs to be prepared very thoroughly, precisely, and solidly; one must not force it, lest there should be a second Dakar.

MOLOTOV. Correct. If such an operation were not successful it would have very bad moral effects.

SIKORSKI. But I return to our question. I have to tell you, Mr. President, that your declaration of an amnesty is not being put into effect. Many, and those some of our most valuable people, are still in labour camps and prisons.

STALIN (making notes). That is impossible, since the amnesty concerned everybody, and all the Poles have been released. (These last words are addressed to Molotov, who nods.)

ANDERS (at Sikorski's request handing over details). That is not in accordance with the true state of affairs, for we have absolutely exact data that the first to be released from the camps have been those least physically fit for work, especially the urban Jewish element, and only later the rather stronger Ukrainian and Polish peasant element. The strong have been held back, only a small proportion of them have been released. In the Army I have people who have been released from such camps only a few weeks, and they declare that in certain camps there are still hundreds and even thousands of our fellow countrymen. The [Soviet] Government's orders are not being carried out there, because the commandants of the particular camps, being under obligation to fulfil their production plan, don't wish to lose their best workers, without whom at times it would be impossible to fulfil the plan.

(Molotov laughs and nods.)

ANDERS. These people have no understanding of all the importance of our common cause, which is suffering terribly great detriment in consequence.

STALIN. Those individuals should be brought to trial.

ANDERS. I agree.

SIKORSKI. It is not our business to supply the Soviet Government with detailed lists of our people, but the camp commandants have complete lists. I have with me a list of some 4,000 officers who were carried off by force and who even now are still in prisons and labour camps. And even this list is not complete, for it contains only the names which it has been possible to set down from memory. I gave instructions to check whether they are not back in Poland, with which we have constant contact. It turned out that not one of them is there, nor are they in the camps of our prisoners of war in Germany. Those men are here. Not one of them has come back.

STALIN. That's impossible. They've fled.

ANDERS. But where could they flee to?

STALIN. Well, to Manchuria, for instance.

ANDERS. It isn't possible that they have all fled, especially as from the moment of their transfer from prisoner of war camps to labour camps and prisons their correspondence with their families ceased completely. I know quite definitely from officers who have already returned even from Kolyma that many of our officers are being held there, and they are even known by their names. I know there were transports of Poles all ready for release and travel, but they were stopped at the last moment. I have information that our people are to be found even in Novaya Ziemlia. The majority of the officers named in this list are known to me personally. Among them are my staff officers and commanders. These people are perishing and dying there in terrible conditions.

STALIN. They must have been released, only they haven't arrived yet.

SIKORSKI. Russia is a large country, and the difficulties are equally great. Possibly the local authorities have not acted on their instructions. Those who have been released and have arrived confirm that the others are vegetating and working. If any of them had got across the Russian frontiers he would undoubtedly have reported to me.

STALIN. Please understand that the Soviet Government has no reason whatever for detaining even a single Pole : I have even released the Sosnkowski agents who organized attacks on us and murdered our people.

ANDERS. None the less, information is coming in concerning people exactly known to us, together with the names of the prisons and even the numbers of the cells in which they are locked up. I know the names of a large number of camps in which an enormous number of Poles have been detained and are forced to go on working.

MOLOTOV. We've detained only those who after the war [began] committed crimes, provoked diversions, set up radio stations, etc. I'm sure you won't be concerned about them.

KOT. Of course not; but I have already asked again and again for us to be given lists of these people, for very often this charge is made against people whom we know to be fervent patriots and absolutely innocent.

(Molotov assents.)

SIKORSKI. Don't let us discuss cases arising in wartime. It would be a good thing now if you, Mr. President, were to give public explanations of this question, so as to bring about a fundamental change [of attitude] in Soviet Russia to Poles. After all, these people are not tourists, but were carried off from their homes by force. They didn't come here of their own choice, they were deported, and endured tremendous suffering.

STALIN. The people of the Soviet Union are well disposed towards the Poles. But officials can make mistakes.

ANDERS. It isn't a question merely of officials not acting properly on their instructions, but that the population should realize that it isn't of their own choice that the Poles are concentrating in large groups in certain localities. We attach particular importance to good relations with the [local] population.

SIKORSKI. In Kuibishev I saw a transport of our people which made a horrible impression on me. Of course they must be helped swiftly. I divide our people into two categories : The one category can work, and these should be given work in as good conditions as possible.

STALIN. In the same conditions as Soviet citizens.

SIKORSKI. It isn't even a matter of the same conditions, but simply of tolerable conditions. It is in the interest of the common military effort that our people should be made use of appropriately. You will realize, Mr. President, that a specialist on tank construction is not being used properly if he is chopping down trees in a forest, or an eminent chemist doing physical labour in agriculture. The other category of our people consists of those unfit for work, the old people, women, children, who should be collected in localities where there are suitable conditions and climate, so that the Embassy could concern itself with them. Everybody should be released from the labour camps, and only those living in settlements where there are tolerable conditions should be left where they are. The uncoordinated transfer of people this way and that only causes bad feeling, since they are living in very difficult conditions, and then it transpires that by my Agreement with you I have only done them harm. People are even dying as the result of the terrible conditions. Those corpses are a heavy burden on our future relations. These people must be helped, and it is not worth chaffering over a few million roubles, which, especially in wartime, have no serious significance. A large-scale loan should be granted to the Polish Government. The Embassy delegates must also be allowed to visit all the places where Poles are concentrated and be granted genuine and not fictitious rights. For instance, our delegate in Archangel is not able to help the people there at all, and his work is confined to the dispatch of transports. He cannot even distribute warm clothing to the local Polish population. I am anxious to see an Embassy delegation brought into operation in Vladivostok also, for the American Poles have collected many things for the Poles in Russia, but they have made dispatch conditional on their being able to hand them over into Polish hands, to delegates of the Embassy.

STALIN. Agreed on the delegates, including Vladivostok.

MOLOTOV. Surely it is not possible that any of your people can still be in camps?

ANDERS. None the less I state with the utmost precision that they are! I repeat that it is the strongest who are being held in the camps, because workers are needed. This failure to release our people is a poor service to the common cause.

STALIN. That will be settled. Special instructions will be issued to the executive authorities; but you must realize that we are waging a war.

SIKORSKI. And you are waging it well.

STALIN. Well no, just average. Our transport has been terribly overloaded. We have transported wounded, we have evacuated the population, we have transferred seventy large factories. We have had to transport troops in one direction and another. The Poles must realize the enormous difficulties we have had to face. But things will be better.

SIKORSKI. The Polish population must be settled in a province with a better climate.

STALIN. We must give consideration to the allocation of districts for the Poles. Normally we import grain into Ferghana and Uzbekistan, because we produce cotton there, and we have even issued special instructions forbidding the cultivation of grain. From that angle these areas are disadvantageous. But the southern areas of Siemipala-tinsk would be more pleasant. For that matter we can see how it looks on the map (everybody rises and goes to a map; Stalin points to various places). Thus Tashkent, Alma Ata, and all southern Kazakhstan.

KOT. For those from the Far East possibly the Barnaul and Novosi-birsk districts would be better.

STALIN. It's cold there, but there's plenty of grain.

KOT. But where to send those who are in the Archangel *oblast* and Komi?

STALIN. To southern Kazakhstan too. (They resume their seats at the table.)

SIKORSKI. In regard to the loan, I consider that one hundred million roubles would settle the problem for a long time, if only because it would not leave a bad impression, and so you would not be exposed to the charge that you are making difficulties over such petty things.

MOLOTOV. But we've already given sixty-five millions.

KOT. But that was for the army.

SIKORSKI. Hitler has taught everybody how it is possible to achieve great things without gold and only with labour. Mr. Commissar, don't imitate the Finance Ministers in the West, who to begin with haggled over every million.

STALIN (nodding). Good!

SIKORSKI. That is all I wish to say concerning the Polish civilian popu-lation. Now I have to raise military matters. Am I to speak at once about the problem as a whole, or shall we discuss its component parts in turn?

STALIN. As you wish, General.

SIKORSKI. We Poles see the war not as a symbolic, but as a genuine struggle.

(Stalin gestures his agreement.)

ANDERS. We want to fight for the independence of Poland here, on the continent.

SIKORSKI. In Poland we possess a strong military organization to which I have forbidden all publicity, since the Germans shoot for every [hostile] word. (Stalin assents. General Sikorski gives a number of instances of the methods the Polish Nation is using to fight the Germans.) Our troops are fighting everywhere. In Great Britain we have a corps which requires reinforcements. We have a navy, which is functioning perfectly. We have in operation seventeen air divisions, which are being given the very latest British machines and are fighting magnificently. Polish pilots have accounted for twenty per cent of the losses of German aircraft over England.

STALIN. I know the Poles are brave.

SIKORSKI. When they are well led. Thanks to Providence and to you, Mr. President, we have here General Anders, my best soldier, whose eight stars for wounds testify to his valour. You shut him in prison because he wanted to link up with me. He is a loyal commander, not a politician, and he will not allow his subordinates either to engage in any politics.

STALIN. The finest politics is to fight well. (Turning to Anders) How long were you in prison?

ANDERS. Twenty months.

STALIN. And what sort of treatment did you receive?

ANDERS. In Lwów exceptionally bad. In Moscow rather better. But you can realize for yourself what 'better' means in prison, when you've been there for twenty months.

STALIN. Well, it couldn't be helped; such were the conditions.

SIKORSKI. I have one brigade, in Tobruk, which is to be transferred to Syria and reorganized into a motorized division with two tank battalions. If the need arose, I could transfer it here to the East. We have several naval vessels. When I decorated the sailors of our submarine stationed at Malta, which sank an Italian cruiser and one transport ship, the crew were so enthusiastic that the vessel sailed into a Greek port and despite a damaged periscope sank yet another cruiser and one Greek transport. It returned without loss. That's how the Polish soldier will fight when he is well led.

Our country is under occupation, and the only reserve of youth we have is here. I want you to send some 25,000 to Scotland and Egypt to make up complements; with those left it would be desirable to form some seven divisions. That is extremely important for Poland, which has its eyes fixed on the Polish Army as a symbol of its resistance and its independence. We want to fight, and so the troops in Scotland will be used as an advance guard for the formation of a second front, or transferred here, to the East. In that case I would take over the command personally.

The present difficulties in regard to commissariat, equipment and training are causing me some anxiety, lest the formations organized in such conditions should be completely useless. Instead of devoting their health and life to the common cause the men are vegetating or are perishing pointlessly. The war will be a long one. Great Britain and the United States have disarmed themselves overmuch, and their war industry, especially that of America, will require a long time to achieve full production capacity. In time an avalanche of war material will be poured in. But I already have Roosevelt's and Churchill's assurance that they will arm our divisions parallel with yours, without affecting your supplies, but on the condition that our army will be formed in areas which supplies can reach without great difficulty. The present state of equipment of our divisions is completely inadequate. Divisions in such conditions are unfit for battle. . . . General Anders will explain this to you in detail. (Anders explains the state of the equipment received, stressing the insurmountable difficulties which arise every day.)

STALIN. (inquires about certain details concerning artillery). Russia entered the war with divisions consisting of some 15,000 men, but in practice they proved too heavy, so we have gone over to a type of lighter division consisting of about 11,000 men.

SIKORSKI. The conditions in which the Polish Army is now being formed are quite unsatisfactory. The soldiers are freezing in summer tents, they feel the lack of food and are simply condemned to slow death. For this reason I propose to transfer all the troops and all the human material fit for military service to Persia, for example, where the climate and the guaranteed British and American aid would enable us in a short time to restore their health and form a strong army, which would return to your front, to occupy its own sector there. This is agreed with Churchill. For my part I am ready to make a declaration that these troops will return to the Russian front and that they might even be reinforced by several British divisions.

ANDERS (continues with his exposé of the situation of the troops already in formation, and declares that in these conditions of food, housing, sanitation and medical care and in the hard climate it is quite impossible to organize units capable of waging war). This is only a state of wretched vegetation, in which all efforts are put into maintaining existence, and that very badly. But we want the Polish Army to be ready for battle as quickly as possible and to fight for Poland together with her allies; in these conditions this is quite impossible. So it is necessary to transfer the troops to climatic, food and supplies conditions which will enable us to go ahead on these lines. In view of the difficulties with which Russia is faced we must take the facilities for Anglo-American supplies into account. All the actual serving soldiers and all the men fit for military service should be sent there. When we take part in battles our army's blow should not be merely symbolic, but should serve the end for which we are fighting all over the world, the fight for Poland.

SIKORSKI. I would like the Soviet Government to have confidence in my proposal. I am a man who, when he says ' yes ' means ' yes ', and when he says ' no ' means ' no ', and when I say nothing, I either cannot or don't wish to tell the truth.

STALIN (in an irritated tone and obviously dissatisfied). I am an old and experienced man. I know that when you go to Persia you will not return here. I see that England has much work and needs the Polish soldiers.

SIKORSKI. We are linked with Great Britain by an alliance which she is observing loyally. Also in Great Britain we have genuine sovereignty. I can even bring a corps here from Scotland, and they certainly won't make difficulties for me in England in consequence. Similarly, I can add the forces in Tobruk to our troops here.

KOT. The Pole fights particularly well if he is close to his homeland.

STALIN. Iran isn't all that far, but the English can force you to fight the Germans in Turkey, or tomorrow Japan may enter the war.

ANDERS. We want to fight for Poland. We believe that even the strongest of airforces and navies will not finish the war. It will be ended by battles on the continent. We all without exception love our Fatherland, and we want to be the first to enter it, we want to be ready for the fight as quickly as possible, but in the conditions we have now it is impossible to prepare for it.

SIKORSKI. England today and formerly are as different as heaven and earth. At present the English have enough troops to defend their islands, so they have no reason to stop our corps from going.

(Molotov proposes to call General Panfilov into the conference and gives instructions to his secretary, who goes out.)

ANDERS (explains the difficulties of army formation and the living conditions in Koltubiansk, Tatishchev, and Totskoe, the [Soviet] failure to observe the dates fixed for supplies of food, fodder, equipment, instruments, etc.) Such a life is only a wretched vegetation and the months are wasted. In these conditions it is quite impossible to form an army.

STALIN (irritably). If the Poles don't want to fight let them go. We cannot detain them. If they want to go, let them go.

SIKORSKI. If we could have created our formations we should have been fighting already, but how much time has been wasted here through no fault of our own! In the present areas of location we have no prospects of any conditions for training soldiers. (A moment of silence.) In that case I ask for another solution.

STALIN. If the Poles don't want to fight here, let them say so straight out, yes or no. I am sixty-two and I know that where an army is formed, there it remains.

SIKORSKI (in a sharper tone). Then please suggest some other solution to me, for conditions for organizing our army don't exist here, and I don't want the people to perish uselessly. I'm not presenting any ultimatum, but when there is a severe winter, wind, and frosts, from which people are dying, I cannot look on and say nothing.

ANDERS. The frosts have already reached thirty-three degrees [Centigrade] in our area. The men are living in single tents, the majority of them without stoves, which are being supplied to us in inadequate quantities. They wake up in the morning with frostbitten noses and ears. That's not forming military forces, that's wretched vegetation.

SIKORSKI. We cannot fling an untrained soldier against the Germans. We must not expose ourselves to the risk of being compromised. The Polish Army must be well armed and must fight as a whole.

ANDERS. As it is I'm amazed at our soldiers, who despite their great sufferings during the past two years and the horrible conditions in which they are now living—they received an issue of boots only a few weeks ago, and before that sixty per cent had been going barefoot—yet they made no complaint though they've never received all the food due to them, and for a long time not even their pay.

SIKORSKI (resolutely). You have annoyed me, Mr. President, by saying that our soldiers don't want to fight.

STALIN. I am blunt, and I want to know clearly whether you want to fight or not.

SIKORSKI (resolutely). That we do is shown not by words but by the facts.

ANDERS. That's what we are forming an army for, in order to fight here, and we realize that our struggle must be waged on the continent. According to my calculations I can have 150,000 soldiers, in other words, the equivalent of eight divisions. Meanwhile we have only two divisions and those not up to full strength. We are not getting the requisite food, and none of the promises to settle this question are kept.

STALIN (to General Sikorski). It's as you wish.

SIKORSKI. I don't want the issue to be put like that. I'm still waiting for a new formula, and I'm ready to accept any equitable solution.

STALIN (with a touch of sarcasm). I see the English need good soldiers.

SIKORSKI. That is not a correct appreciation [of the situation]. The English value us, but don't exploit us. Also I know Churchill well; I know he wants to do everything to help Russia.

ANDERS. Sixty per cent of my men are reservists, but after two hard years these men must be put on their feet and retrained. The volunteers also are arriving in a very bad state and must be given the requisite training, for which time and suitable conditions are necessary.

STALIN (irritated). That means we're savages, we cannot put anything right now. It seems to imply that the Russian can only strangle a Pole, but is not capable of doing anything for him. But we shall manage without you. We can hand over the lot. We'll shift for ourselves. We shall conquer Poland and then we'll give it to you. But what will people say to all this? The world will sneer that we here cannot do anything.

SIKORSKI. I have not received any answer to the question where I am to create an army so that it can take part in the war and not perish in terrible climatic conditions. I ask for a definite counter-proposal. I assert once more categorically that we want to fight for Poland and at your side.

STALIN. If you go to Iran you may have to fight in Turkey against the Germans; if Japan enters the war tomorrow then against Japan. Just as the English order. Maybe in Singapore.

ANDERS. We want to fight on the continent against the Germans and for Poland. Our people have not seen their country for a long time, and no one loves his Fatherland like the Pole. The nearest route for us is from here.

SIKORSKI. The patriotism of the Poles does not need attestation. I maintain that I still have no definite counter-proposal.

STALIN. If you must have it, then one corps, two to three divisions can go. But if you wish, I shall assign a place and resources for the formation of seven divisions. But all the same I see the English need Polish soldiers. For I have received a demand from Harriman and Churchill to evacuate the Polish Army.[1]

SIKORSKI. Things aren't going so badly for the English that the Polish Army formed here will decide their fate. They are slow, but today they already constitute a considerable force. It was I myself who demanded that Churchill should take action on the question of evacuating our troops. But I demonstrate my good will and am ready to leave the Army in Russia if you indicate a favourable concentration area and assure us of supplies and accommodation creating conditions in which their training is possible.

MOLOTOV. Panfilov is ready. Do you object to his coming in? (They all agree; a moment later General Panfilov, Deputy Chief of Staff of the Red Army, enters.)

(A conversation ensues between Stalin, General Anders, and General Panfilov on the conditions necessary to the creation of a Polish force, in which the two sides cite contradictory details.)

ANDERS. I categorically state that I am not receiving adequate food, or fodder for the horses. The divisions have not received all the requisite food, nor even such necessary articles of equipment as heating stoves for the tents. Several months have passed since the promise was made to send tractors, but they still have not arrived. All our requests have no effect and the promises made by the Soviet military authorities are not fulfilled. I have typhus in the divisions, and I cannot get agreement to my request for a hospital train. The soldiers have not received any soap, building materials, boards, or nails, for several months. A large number of food products are not included in the diet at all. The means of transport are quite inadequate and are in very bad shape. A few weeks ago the number of rations was suddenly reduced from 44,000 to 30,000, and despite the promise you yourself gave, Mr. President, to our Ambassador that the rations would be restored to 44,000, this has not yet been done. On 1 December

---

[1] On 7 November 1941 Mr. Cordell Hull informed the U.S. Ambassador to the U.S.S.R., Steinhardt, that Harriman had intervened with Stalin to secure his agreement to sending the Polish Army to Iran for equipment, etc., returning afterwards to the Soviet front. A note from Ambassador Ciechanowski to the State Department, dated 10 November, put forward the same suggestion. (Diplomatic Papers, p. 258.) The starting point of all these activities was Prof. Kot's report of Molotov's statement that the Soviet Union could not feed more than 44,000 Polish soldiers, which Steinhardt reported to Washington, 25 October. (ibid., p. 257.)

the entire camp at Totskoe got no food at all. (He goes on to specify a number of other shortages of food and supplies.) It is not correct that we have not mentioned these things. I have appealed again and again to the liaison officer, Colonel Volkovyski, and have myself sent telegrams and letters. I have travelled personally to get these matters put right many times.

STALIN (very sharply to Panfilov). Who is to blame for all this?

PANFILOV. The requisite orders have been issued, General Khrulov issued the instructions.

STALIN. When did I give the instruction to increase the number of food rations?

PANFILOV. Two and a half weeks ago.

STALIN. Then why hasn't the instruction been acted on yet? Have they got to eat our instructions?

(All this part of the conversation is carried on by Stalin in a very sharp tone. Panfilov stands to attention, going red and white.)

SIKORSKI. Only the excessively great difficulties which we are meeting with here, and the bad conditions, have forced me to raise this issue.

STALIN. We can give the Polish Army the same conditions we give the Red Army.

SIKORSKI. In present conditions not even a corps will result.

STALIN. I realize that they're bad. Our own forces are being organized in better conditions. I say this honestly, that if they can give you better conditions in Iran, so far as we're concerned we can only give you the same as our Army gets. But our food nourishment is better than what the Germans get.

ANDERS. If I get full nourishment such as is due to soldiers I regard it as sufficient, but it should be supplied without the continual shortages we suffer from. I must have the possibility of running my own commissariat, creating our own reserves, and not living from day to day, with the result that if transport breaks down the men frequently go hungry.

SIKORSKI. I declare yet again that we want to fight together with you against the Germans as our common enemy.

STALIN. But I have got the impression that the English need your soldiers.

SIKORSKI. No, it was I who, seeing the difficulties we are up against here, asked the English and Americans to feed our soldiers in better conditions.

ANDERS (hands over a detailed statement of the numbers of Polish soldiers in the southern areas of Russia, mentioning the respective localities. A discussion follows as to the places in which further forces are to be formed. The names Uzbekistan, Turkestan, Trans-Caucasia, are mentioned). I reckon on 150,000 men, i.e., eight divisions, together with auxiliary services. There may be even more of our people, but this includes a strong Jewish element which does not want to serve in the army.

STALIN. The Jews are rotten soldiers.

ANDERS. Many of the Jews who have applied to join are speculators or people who have been punished for smuggling; they will never make good soldiers. The Polish Army doesn't need these. Two hundred and fifty Jews deserted from Buzuluk on the false report that Kuibishev had been bombed. Over sixty deserted from the fifth division on the eve of an anticipated distribution of arms to the soldiers.

STALIN. Yes, the Jews are poor soldiers.

(A discussion follows, Stalin, Anders and Panfilov taking part, on the question of armaments and their shortages.)

SIKORSKI. When shall we be given the new area and learn other details concerning the [new] formations?

Stalin (confers aloud with Panfilov and gives the names Uzbekistan, Turkmenistan and Trans-Caucasia as indications).

SIKORSKI. After formation and training it will be necessary to concentrate the units in a single whole for striking as an army, for that alone will have the necessary impact on the imagination of the Polish nation.

STALIN. That will take a long time.

ANDERS. Not if everything is carried out properly; after arms have been received the formation will not take long.

Stalin (raises the issue of forming an army not based on the corps as a unit).

SIKORSKI. Perhaps that would be better. We'll agree to that, only then the divisions must be equipped and armed more powerfully.

STALIN. Organization without a corps basis is better, for where you have the existence of corps the army commander throws all the responsibility on to the corps commanders, and in the end no one is responsible for anyone. It would be better for your army simply to have divisions, the same as we have.

SIKORSKI. I shall watch to ensure that equipment arrives for you from abroad in a greater flow. Given good will it will be possible to do this.

STALIN. We supply a part. The English should send the rest. But sea transports don't always reach us in time. They can be delayed, and that has to be taken into account.

SIKORSKI. Twenty-five thousand men must be evacuated from here, because I need them for the airforce, the navy, and armoured detachments. Apart from these we can form seven divisions. After all, our sole human reserve is here. Have you enough aeroplanes?

STALIN. There are never enough aeroplanes. Quantitatively we are no worse off than the Germans. Qualitatively we even have predominance. But the situation in regard to tanks is much worse.

SIKORSKI. Part of the German airforce has already been destroyed in Libya.

STALIN. We have not been conscious of German air superiority for two months. They have very inexperienced young pilots now. Their planes are relatively slow. But how many planes do you have to a division?

SIKORSKI. Twenty-seven; eighteen in the first and nine in the second line.

STALIN. That is equal to our air regiment.

SIKORSKI. We shall be able to send several air divisions from England for our army. Our people there are burning to come.

Stalin (praises the British airmen now in Russia).

SIKORSKI. Our airmen have perfect sight and swift orientation.

STALIN. The Slavs are the finest and bravest of all airmen. They react very quickly, for they are a young race which hasn't yet been worn out.

SIKORSKI. The present war is rejuvenating the Anglo-Saxons. The British are not the French, who have ended their role in this war.

STALIN. I don't agree with that opinion.

SIKORSKI. The lower strata are good, but the majority of the top stratum are of no great value. (a long conversation on the subject of Pétain and other generals)[1]

STALIN. The Germans are strong, but the Slavs will defeat them.

SIKORSKI. Now I would like to go and review the Army and visit the

---

[1] General Sikorski, who was a friend of the French and admired France, was disillusioned by the breakdown of the French command in June 1940. His bitter judgement was modified when 'Free France' began to organize resistance in the colonies. In December 1942 Sikorski ardently supported the French effort during a visit to Roosevelt, who distrusted General de Gaulle.

centres of the civilian population, and then return to Moscow to see you once more.

STALIN. By all means; I am at your service.

SIKORSKI. Tomorrow I am making a speech over the radio in the name of the nations under German occupation. Commissar Vyshinsky was to have sent you the text of my speech.

STALIN. Yes, I have read it, it will be very good if the transmission takes place.

SIKORSKI. I think it will make an impact on the world. The B.B.C. and America are also taking the transmission.

STALIN. I have given instructions for your speech to be translated into forty languages.

SIKORSKI. I ask that my speech may be announced beforehand. I make the suggestion that we should sign a joint political declaration. I don't really insist on it, but I leave you a draft for your consideration. (Handing Stalin the draft.)

STALIN. I agree in principle. I shall read it and tomorrow we shall settle the question jointly.

SIKORSKI. And now I regard the military issue as agreed and settled. In the Mixed Commission, which should meet as soon as possible in order to give these questions finality, General Anders will take my place. Perhaps you would like to nominate your men of trust for the visit to the camps.

STALIN. I agree. (He names Vyshinsky and Panfilov, asking whether they meet with Sikorski's approval.)

Sikorski (answers affirmatively and takes his leave, with the Ambassador and General Anders. Stalin detains Anders.)

Stalin (questions Anders concerning co-operation with Panfilov; Anders declared that it had gone amicably, but General P. could not do much).

ANDERS. Now you have promised to eliminate the difficulties I'm sure the development of our army will be handled properly.

STALIN. I greatly regret I haven't seen you before.

ANDERS. It is not my fault that I have not been summoned by you, Mr. President.

STALIN. I shall be very pleased to see you again.

ANDERS. Mr. President, I am at your disposition at any time.

(The main conversation lasted two hours. That between Stalin and Anders several minutes.)

*B18. Conversation with the Vice-Commissar for Foreign
Affairs, A. J. Vyshinsky.
In the Narcomindiel. Kuibishev. 6 December 1941*
Present: Director K. N. Novikov. W. Arlet as
interpreter.

In the first part of the conversation, lasting over forty-five minutes:

Kot acquainted Vyshinsky with the course of the Moscow conversations, stressing the atmosphere of understanding in which they
were conducted, and President Stalin's favourable attitude to all the
Polish issues put before him. Next the Ambassador presented and
agreed the plan for General Sikorski's further stay in the Soviet
Union. Vyshinsky, replying to the Ambassador's statement, expressed
his appreciation of General Sikorski's speech, indicating that he
regarded it as a special honour to have been able to acquaint himself
with its text before it was broadcast.

VYSHINSKY. Personal meetings between statesmen are more conducive
than the normal exchanges of diplomatic correspondence to the
elimination of difficulties and all possible misunderstandings. So
far as I am concerned, from the very beginning I declared I would
do everything to ensure that Polish affairs went as well as possible in
the People's Commissariat for Foreign Affairs. On the basis of the
recent conversations and the Declaration of Mutual Friendship relations should develop even more favourably in every respect. I can
assure you that not only General Sikorski and yourself, but, as I know
from telephone conversations, the Soviet Government also are very
satisfied with the results of the Moscow conversations and take an
optimistic view of the future of Soviet-Polish relations. We hope that
the former misunderstandings between us will not be repeated, and
will yield place to profound friendship. I can assure you with the
utmost sincerity that I and all my co-workers in the People's Commissariat for Foreign Affairs will carry out to the full the task of
co-operation with Poland which has been laid upon them. With us a
situation cannot arise such as sometimes occurs in other systems,
where one or another official sabotages his government's policy and
acts according to his own whims. For me personally, as a man linked
for many years with the Party, Stalin is all, and his word is law. And
it is from this angle that I shall conduct my co-operation with you,
Mr. Ambassador. In view of this I take an optimistic view of the
future.

KOT. I would fervently ask you for one thing: I should be glad if you would direct requisite attention to the problem of the Polish civilians. I believe that military affairs will go well, but, if only out of regard for the spirit and fighting value of the troops, we should do all we can to improve the lot of the civilian population. These questions are bound together indissolubly. The soldiers with families cannot after all get rid of their anxieties for the fate of their dear ones, and the better footing this issue is put on the more beneficial will be the spirit and work of the army.

(Vyshinsky agrees and asks the Ambassador for his impressions of Moscow, both from the general and from the military aspect.)

KOT. I am not a specialist on these matters, but my impressions are favourable. One is sensible of the fact that the front is closer than when I was in Moscow a month ago, but the population remains calm. From talks with the Head of the Soviet Government I see that they possess a good and consequentially applied plan of defence, while I regard the lack of official optimism as an especially encouraging feature. They don't underrate the enemy, but they are not afraid of him, and that can be regarded as a guarantee of success.

VYSHINSKY. Certainly the news from the front is good. The struggle is tense, but we are mounting more and more offensive operations. It is obvious that Hitler has boiled himself a brew. I expect that about 20 December we shall begin to drive the Germans back from Moscow, and when spring comes our troops will go forward in earnest, exploiting the winter production, and they will be able to put into practice the old slogan of the Polish revolutionaries: 'for our freedom and yours'.

KOT. After these great and important matters I would like to raise several current issues.

(He asks for a decision on the matter of instructions for the Embassy's travelling delegates. Vyshinsky proposes that in a few days' time an Embassy representative should discuss the [Polish] amendments to the Narcomindiel proposals with director Novikov.)

(Kot in turn raises the necessity of settling the formal and accountancy aspects of the sixty-five million rouble credit for the army, reminding Vyshinsky that he has appointed the Embassy financial counsellor as his representative on these questions. Vyshinsky admits the necessity for it to be discussed by experts, but he indicates that in view of the anticipated development of the Polish Army, credits for military purposes must in any case be subjected to a very considerable extension.)

KOT. But what about the loan for the needs of the civilian population?

VYSHINSKY. What do you think, should we conclude a single financial agreement for the military and the civilians jointly, a general agreement on credit questions?

KOT. I think that would be inexpedient. After all, the problems are completely different. Aid for the civilian population is a simple matter: the Soviet Government will lend us a definite sum of money. On the other hand, expenditure on the army covers a number of items calling for discussion, calculations, checking of tables, prices, etc. You see supplies have to cover equipment, provisions, supplies in kind.

VYSHINSKY. Good, then we'll have two agreements: one dealing with finances for the civilians, the other for the military. I have already given instructions to our appropriate authorities to draw up a preliminary statement of expenditures for an increased number of Polish divisions. But so far as the quotas mentioned hitherto are concerned, I have definite knowledge of only sixty-five millions, assigned for the Army till the end of the current year. How did this matter finally stand in Moscow?

KOT. General Sikorski understood that his request for a loan of 100 millions for aid to the civilians had been met favourably.

VYSHINSKY. I shall communicate your statement to Molotov and ask him for an answer.

KOT. Thank you. The next current issue is a note to you on the question of the Ukrainians, Jews, and Little-Ruthenians, whom you do not regard as Polish citizens. I don't want to discuss this question now, but we shall deal with it and fundamentally at that.

VYSHINSKY. We start from a perfectly clear point of departure. The Ukaze [sic] of 29 November 1939 is the legal basis for conferring Soviet citizenship on the inhabitants of lands incorporated in the Soviet Union.

KOT. It isn't merely a question of the strictly legal aspect. The question of Polish citizenship is to a large extent a practical problem. In the last resort not all Ukrainians and Jews are of identically equal value to us, but the viewpoint adopted by the Narcomindiel has led us into a blind alley. The plebiscite to which you appeal is no argument. We know what to think of wartime plebiscites. If they are to be taken seriously then all the plebiscites Hitler has organized in the states he has annexed must also be recognized.

VYSHINSKY. We aren't appealing to the plebiscite at all, only to the Ukaze of 29 November 1939, which for us is the law. It concerned the areas which came to us then.

KOT. But I don't understand! Your Agreement with us cancels the Agreement with Germany, and yet the next day you put forward this kind of argument over the question of citizenship?

VYSHINSKY. This question will have to be studied. After all, various things happened on the Polish side.

KOT. In any case, we never took your people into our army.

VYSHINSKY. We must deal with it at an early date. It's difficult now because of my departure. But when I return I shall speed up the matter.

KOT. A few days ago two Polish citizens were arrested who had been working in close co-operation with the Embassy. Alter and Ehrlich. I should be very glad if this matter could be cleared up. Above all, they are men very well known in circles abroad, they're leaders of the Jewish Socialist organization, the Bund. Your arresting them is very unpleasant, especially just at this moment, during General Sikorski's visit. Alter is a member of the Executive of the Socialist International. We were intending to send Ehrlich to London as the Bund representative to the [Polish] National Council. On making inquiries, the Embassy was informed that the arrests had taken place in connection with new material implicating them, so pretty clearly it is a question of something that occurred before the amnesty. It is very important for them to be released now. For that matter, when they were released from prison last September they were not issued provisional certificates, like all other Polish citizens. Just think what a hullabaloo the American Jewish organizations will raise over these arrests.

VYSHINSKY. We cannot be guided by the possibility that Jewish organizations abroad will kick up a fuss. They have been arrested for an exceptionally important reason. It is a very unpleasant business, which has come to light in a very stupid fashion. It has been established beyond all doubt that they were working on behalf of Germany. Of course I cannot foretell the final results of the investigation. But the crime they have committed is very serious.

KOT. That is quite incredible. Jews holding such important positions, yet you say they are German agents!

VYSHINSKY. And yet Trotsky turned out to be a German agent.

KOT. After they were released from prison they had conversations with the Narcomvnudiel on the question of forming a Jewish Anti-

Fascist Committee, with headquarters in Moscow. How could they do that, if they were German agents?

VYSHINSKY. The Anti-Fascist Committee may be only a kind of camouflage. I cannot give you any detailed explanations. But I will give instructions for the matter to be investigated thoroughly.

KOT. We know both of them perfectly. The charge is absolutely fantastic. It is my conviction that erroneous evidence or false accusations have led to the arrests. After all, sometimes it is quite sufficient for inexpert investigating officials to have suspicions. I personally knew a man, I talked to him some days ago, who as late as 2 August was sent to prison for activities on Russian soil against the Germans. The case had been investigated, the affair had taken its official course, and five weeks after the beginning of the [German] war against you you sentenced a man for anti-German activities committed before the [outbreak of] war.

VYSHINSKY. Such mistakes do occur. But I can assure you it was not a subordinate official who took the decision to arrest Alter and Ehrlich, only central authorities.

KOT. I fervently request that the matter may be cleared up.

VYSHINSKY. But supposing the interests of our common cause demand that this kind of German agent should be rendered harmless?

KOT. Mr. Commissar, if I had the least doubt of Alter and Ehrlich's innocence I should not intervene in the case.

VYSHINSKY. The arrests took place only two days ago, the reasons are serious, the investigation cannot be carried through in a moment.

KOT. I am convinced that these arrests are mistaken.

VYSHINSKY. If they have been accused unjustly, you can be sure they will be released.

KOT. I ask again for the matter to be cleared up.

From the beginning the conversation was carried on in a friendly tone on both sides. Vyshinsky was affable and smiling as never before.

A58. Cable to the Minister for Internal Affairs.
Kuibishev. 7 December 1941

. . . The General's stay here has put a large number of issues on a favourable basis, though unfortunately there will always be difficulties.

The General has fallen ill with a kind of gastric flu, owing to the changes of climate (in four days by seventy degrees) and because of this delay he will not be going to Moscow again, and also in order not to create a difficult situation for himself in view of Minister Eden's visit.

> *B19. Conversation with the Vice-Commissar for Foreign Affairs, A. J. Vyshinsky.*
> *Narcomindiel. 8 December 1941*
> Director Novikov present. Polish translator: Embassy secretary A. Mniszek.

KOT. I want to thank you very warmly and sincerely for your kindness in being present at our reception yesterday; it was a great pleasure to me to have you as our guest.

VYSHINSKY. How is General Sikorski today? We are greatly concerned about his health, and I hope it will quickly be restored.

KOT. General Sikorski feels better today, the fever has fallen, he is only rather weak, and besides the flu he is troubled by pains in the stomach. Tomorrow the doctors will decide when he will be able to fly off. His programme for visiting the centres of the Polish Army will be modified in dependence on that. (The Ambassador reads out the revised programme.)

VYSHINSKY. During the reception yesterday General Anders and Dr. Retinger expressed the opinion that presumably in view of Mr. Eden's forthcoming visit to Moscow General Sikorski's simultaneous visit would not be convenient.

KOT. They had instructions only to ask whether General Sikorski's arrival at the same time would be inconvenient to the Soviet Government. Because of General Sikorski's state of health, his fatigue with long journeys and an anticipated journey for the purpose of meeting President Roosevelt in Washington, after visiting the Polish troops in the U.S.S.R. he would travel direct via Teheran to London. However, in order to discuss a number of questions associated with his visit to the Army, and also certain questions postponed to a second interview with President Stalin, he wishes that I and General Anders should travel together to see President Stalin, if the President agrees.

VYSHINSKY. I communicated this question to Molotov at once, and today at five a.m. Stalin personally telephoned to me. I repeat his words verbatim:

(Vyshinsky reads out the text with obvious piety, watching attentively to ensure that the translator takes it down verbatim.)

' I do not go back on my word and am ready to receive the Chairman of the Council of Ministers, General Sikorski, irrespective of the simultaneous stay in Moscow of both General Sikorski and Minister Eden, and dependent only on whatever may be most convenient to the General.'

KOT. I ask you to express our warm thanks to President Stalin and to stress that General Sikorski attaches great importance to seeing him, and if during the present visit his state of health should not allow him to travel to Moscow he will take advantage of the invitation to visit the Soviet Union a second time. For General Sikorski is considering the intention, when the Polish Army is formed in the U.S.S.R., to take over its personal command. General Sikorski's health is a matter of particular importance to us, since he is Poland's man of Providence and there is no one to replace him.

VYSHINSKY. I shall inform Moscow of your wish that you and General Anders should see President Stalin, if it proves impossible for General Sikorski to go to Moscow.

KOT (after a moment's silence hands Vyshinsky a note on the arrest of Alter and Ehrlich). I warmly ask you to intervene in the case of Alter and Ehrlich, who were arrested some days ago. In the note I am now presenting to you all the factors connected with this affair are expounded in exact detail.

During this short, fifteen-minute conversation Vyshinsky was in a friendly mood, and he repeated Stalin's words twice, stressing that Stalin had telephoned him at five a.m. and that he was repeating his words exactly.

A59. Cable to the Minister for Foreign Affairs.
10 December 1941

Two leading members of the Bund, Alter and Ehrlich, were arrested during the night of 4 December in Kuibishev. The Embassy intervened at once, I personally with Vyshinsky. I warned against the negative impression [this would cause] in America and England. I demanded their release, permission for them to see a representative of the Embassy, and for us to supply food and clothing parcels.

Vyshinsky's reply, that they had been working on behalf of Germany, I regard as a frivolous excuse.

Today permission has been granted for us to supply parcels.

KOT.

A60. To Minister for Foreign Affairs.
Kuibishev. 10 December 1941

A glance back over the course of our affairs during the past month reveals a fundamental change.

Difficulties and chicanery came to a climax on 12 November, when the liquidation of our delegations was announced on the ground that they were unauthorized, while the army was to be reduced to 30,000, the transport of civilians from the north was held up, and those who had been allowed to travel were refused food. Molotov's reply to the conditions precedent to General Sikorski's visit was practically a refusal. A change took place in the afternoon of the very same day: an invitation arrived for the Ambassador to go to Moscow for a conversation with Stalin. Harriman's cable had some influence on this invitation, but only partial, the real influence being the fear that General Sikorski would abandon his visit.

The Ambassador's conversation in Moscow on 14 November cleared up certain difficulties (basic agreement to delegates, withdrawal of the order to reduce the army, an acceleration of some of the releases) and guaranteed bases for the Premier's visit through Stalin's precise statement that he wishes to take part in the work of restoring the Polish State without regard to its system, and that he agrees to the formation in the U.S.S.R. of seven divisions, which all Polish citizens under obligation to serve in the Army are to join. But it was not possible to eradicate Stalin's suspicions concerning the illegal irruption of Poles, against the Government's agreement, into Uzbekistan; and from 25 November onward a forced, violent evacuation of 45,000 Poles began from there. The Ambassador's sharp protest secured a partial hold up of the evacuation, an improvement in its technical and sanitary conditions, and withdrawal of the transfer to Siemipalatinsk.

Looking back over the situation of recent months, one can specify the following causes of the difficulties in the way of full realization of the Pact:

1. First and foremost, of course, the fundamental reluctance to allow extensive changes in conditions here in full view of Soviet citizens, for whom nothing will change, but rather for whom the situation will grow worse; the fear of 'privileges' for the Poles; and, among many authorities, lack of psychological preparation for further far-reaching changes in regard to the Poles; the commands of many camps for forced labour were in no hurry to release the prisoners, because they were among their better workers.

N

2. The hold up in the development of the Army, and, too, the intensification of a suspicious attitude towards Poles are partly the result of the boundless garrulity of many people, especially officers, who extensively and vociferously proclaimed the necessity to settle accounts with the Soviets; certain among them, especially in the Asiatic south, even talked of the necessity to co-operate with revolting Turkmens and Kazakhs, and proposed a march by force across the Persian frontier. The NKVD agents collected all this sort of boasting talk as proof that it was impossible to co-operate loyally with the Poles.

3. Internal, transport, and provisioning difficulties associated with the progress of the war were not favourable to solicitude for the tragic situation of the Polish people. Millions of Russian citizens evacuated from the West have met with no better treatment, frequently even worse. And in addition, nothing has been done by the press and radio to warm the atmosphere towards the Poles.

4. Among governing circles, who are still filled with distrust of Great Britain, there was a profound conviction that the Poles are not politically independent, but are an instrument of British policy and political game.

The Premier's arrival led to a fundamental clearing up of the position. The Soviet Government did not conceal its great pleasure at this visit, which it regards as increasing its own prestige in the world. It was announced that General Sikorski would be received with the honours shown to heads of state. Not one such head of state has been received as a guest here for a very long time. The official foreigners, even very influential ones, have been treated rather with coolness, as though to demonstrate that here no one will impose on us [the Russians]. In this respect the reception given to the Polish Premier caused a sensation among both Russians and foreigners. The presentation of guards of honour, Polish flags, and the playing of the Polish national anthem everywhere, constituted the outward expression of hospitality. In personal relations it was quite extraordinary.

The reception in the Kremlin, which lasted over four hours (and to which all the Polish suite were invited) took place in an atmosphere of freedom and *rapprochement*. Molotov's toasts ran from the Ambassador down to Captain Klimkowski, General Anders' adjutant, as a representative of Polish military youth. Stalin's toast, long, detailed, and frank, and ending with a cry in honour of a Poland not only independent but powerful, was marked by involuntary recognition and respect for everything Polish. Recalling how the Poles had boycotted him at the station of Trzebinia in 1913, when he ordered food in Russian, and how Lenin had scolded him for this insult, he admitted that Poles had every right to feel dislike of Russia for her annexationist imperialism. One of the Soviet officials present at the reception, who already had relations with us, declared that no one had been shown such regard in this place as the Poles.

In conversations with the Premier Stalin did not conceal that he counts on a common struggle with the Poles, such as has been unknown in history since Grunwald,[1] and that he would regard the departure of the Polish troops from Russia as an affront to himself and to Russia. Consequently the General's decision to leave the troops here—if he had not taken this decision, undoubtedly their departure would have been sabotaged by the system—at once created a clear situation and a basis for a definite policy. With General Anders the Soviet staff immediately worked out conditions for the transfer of the existing forces and the organization of new ones on the principle of complete equality with the Soviet army's conditions of accommodation, training, and provisioning, and partially in equipment also, taking into account help from abroad for us.

For the civilian population Stalin at once assigned the warmest lands of the South, with part of the same Uzbekistan—the Tashkent district—from which our people had only just been evacuated. Telephone messages yesterday and today from Tashkent and Alma Ata confirm all along the line an immediate improvement in conditions for our people, among other things the warm co-operation of the local authorities, and the supply of provisions and accommodation; for instance, the government in Alma Ata has sent several tons of fats to Dzambul and Chimkent for the Poles, something which is never done for the local population.

We do not know how far the release of the hitherto secretly detained military and civilians in the far north and the east is being carried out, but we know already that every day groups of several dozen persons are being released from prison (in Gorki, and Saratov) that those detained in camps in the north are on the move, and even in Siberia groups of people released from Kolyma have already been met with. Out of the lists of political and prominent persons handed over on the occasion of the General's visit, several people have already reached us from prison. . . .

---

[1] Battle of Grunwald or Tannenberg, 1410, in which a combined Polish-Lithuanian army with a small Russian force defeated the Teutonic knights. *Tr.*

The solemn signing of the Joint Declaration was the signal for an improvement of the atmosphere in regard to Poles all over Russia: the publication of the General's speech, the introductory articles dealing with the Declaration, interviews concerning the Polish Army, etc., have been taken by the Russian community as the essential beginning of a new policy in regard to the Poles and as a signpost for themselves. Everybody arriving from various parts during the past few days confirms the change in conditions, and especially the courtesy of the authorities everywhere. Astonished at this turn in affairs, the foreign Embassies are treating everything connected with the General's stay in the U.S.S.R. as an incredible phenomenon, for which not one of them was prepared; they regard it as an expression of the moral and political influence of the Polish nation, thanks to its heroism and political wisdom; they have all sent reports to their Governments referring to the importance and prestige of the Poles.

It is noteworthy that at the Premier's desire Stalin appointed Vyshinsky as assistant during the tour round the Polish camps, which meant that the Narcomindiel virtually suspended operations for these five days. This meant that the highest ranking Government representative available in Kuibishev was assigned to accompany General Sikorski.

We must not succumb to the delusion that from now on all our desiderata will be conceded loyally and successfully. Undoubtedly there will be difficulties and chicanery, and more than one promise will be modified. But the essential gains of General Sikorski's visit will remain, and for the rest it will be necessary to wage a stubborn, systematic fight. No one can cancel out the authority which the Premier's visit has assured to our cause in the eyes of the foreign communities, the Slavonic on the one hand and the Anglo-Saxon on the other.

> B20. *Conversation with the Vice-Commissar for Foreign Affairs, A. J. Vyshinsky.*
> *In the Narcomindiel. 16 December 1941*
> Present: Mr. Pushkin, deputy departmental head; W. Arlet as interpreter.

. . . .

кот. Many of the matters I am raising today I have already discussed with you on the way back from Saratov. But I have asked you to receive me today because I wish to repeat them officially. First and foremost I ask you to express my thanks to President Stalin for delegating you in particular to General Sikorski's tour of our military forces, and secondly I wish to thank you personally for the pains you undertook all through this time, your care for us, and for coming to our aid in every respect, and for speaking three times to our officers and men. All your speeches were extremely valuable and really were of great assistance. I would like in turn to hear your impressions of the tour, for I should inform my Government.

VYSHINSKY. First and foremost I thank you for your kind words. I see from them that I carried out the task for which I made the journey. But so far as pains are concerned, I suffered none, since the entire journey was a genuine pleasure for me. I regard the spirit that reigns among men and officers as very good. The most striking thing was the militant spirit of the troops, obviously intensified by the presence of General Sikorski and yourself. But I hope this enthusiasm and spirit are just as evident in the everyday round. I fully realize the sufferings and difficulties these people have passed through. I recognized the still painful situation of the sixth and to some extent the fifth division, and so I liked all the more the magnificent bearing of these men, their fighting spirit, and I would even say their maturity, their political development. I was able also to come into contact with instances of Polish culture; both during the functions organized by the forces and in contact with the soldiers I was enabled to appreciate the high level of that culture.

KOT. But I would like to ask you definitely whether you did not find it strange and foreign.

VYSHINSKY. Oh no; true, during the last twenty-five to thirty years I have not had any opportunity to make contact with manifestations of Polish culture. I can assure you that I brought back from this journey one of the strongest impressions I have had for several years.

KOT. Did you get the impression that this fighting spirit is a friendly and allied one?

VYSHINSKY. Certainly! I felt both the one and the other. Perhaps history does work in such a manner that many difficulties and hard experiences must be accumulated so as to lead to a true understanding.

KOT. Sometimes a violent shock is necessary to achieve that. In the faces of many of the soldiers and officers you could read the harsh experiences which they had known in the camps and prisons. Did you see even on one face, or even in one pair of eyes any glint of dislike or unfriendliness towards you?

VYSHINSKY. In fact, not once.

KOT. You heard the ovations with which your speech was interrupted and ended. They were not organized, but sprang out of the listeners' genuine appreciation. And the spontaneous shouts in honour of President Stalin.

VYSHINSKY. Yes, undoubtedly they expressed a genuine friendship and alliance.

KOT. I am convinced that the more often this kind of meeting could take place the closer would be our co-operation. It is of tremendous importance for people abroad to see how well co-operation between us is working out. For the Americans and British, who lack an explosive temperament, this contact with our troops must have been a genuine revelation.

VYSHINSKY. I transmitted General Sikorski's letter to Stalin in Moscow yesterday evening by wireless. Today I have sent the original by air.

KOT. Have you any information concerning the General's flight from Baku to Teheran today?

VYSHINSKY. Yes, I have received news from our airline authorities that the aeroplane has left. . . .

KOT. The Polish Government had no foreknowledge of General Sikorski's speech or the draft of the Declaration. After the speech and the signature of the Declaration had been announced the Government assembled for a special session. They passed a resolution, which has been sent to me for information, proclaiming that after detailed study of the Declaration and General Sikorski's speeches and acquainting themselves with the results of the conversations, the Polish Government have taken them into cognizance with satisfaction. The Government have also expressed the conviction that these acts, and also General Sikorski's visit as a whole, will conduce to a further ordering of Polish-Soviet relations, laying down a road to the settlement of the issues of the Polish forces and civilian population in the U.S.S.R., and strengthening the Polish forces in the struggle against Germany while preserving them for future liberated Poland.

. . . .

KOT. But now, Mr. Commissar, to turn to the prose of life. I have here a cable from the World Jewish Congress, signed by Rabbi Wise. He raises the case of Professor Rabbi Schorr. I have already mentioned his case to you some time ago. I shall hand the cable to you, for what else can I do with it? (He hands Vyshinsky the cable.)

VYSHINSKY. I recall the case. . . . I remember that I gave instructions for a search to be made for him.

KOT. It was three months ago.

VYSHINSKY. I hope he will be found during the next few days.

KOT. I have now received certain information concerning people whose names I have previously handed in to be searched for. It concerns a number of people. One is Franciszek Wilk, a young man from my Peasant Party; he is in Uchta camp. During my visit to Buzuluk I saw with my own eyes a petition he had handed in to the camp commandant, in which, together with many other Poles, he demanded to be incorporated in the Polish Armed Forces. All the others have been released. But he is still held locked up.

VYSHINSKY. But perhaps he's dead?

KOT. Oh no; he's a young man. The other three are Waclaw Grubinski, a well-known Warsaw writer, who has never had anything to do with politics. He fled before the German army from Warsaw to Lwów and was arrested there. Finally, there are the university lecturer Jurkiewicz and the engineer Lang. All three are in the camp at Vierkhnie Uralsk.

VYSHINSKY (taking the paper from the Ambassador). I shall give instructions for this to be cleared up.

KOT. Finally, there is the question of Alter and Ehrlich. I have forbidden other members of the Bund at present in Kuibishev who came to ask my advice to cable abroad; none the less the news has already leaked out. I myself have not sent any notification of these arrests and have forbidden the acquaintances of the two men to cable concerning them. This affair is badly compromising me. Yet news of the arrests is already known abroad. (He hands Vyshinsky a cable from New York.)

VYSHINSKY. It must have got out through journalists.

KOT. I strongly request you to clear up this case. I have asked for a representative of the Embassy to be allowed to see the arrested men.

VYSHINSKY. I shall endeavour to get the matter cleared up.

. . . .

KOT. The greatest holiday in Polish life is Christmas. In the evening of 24 December everybody, even the poorest, gathers for a supper in common, and on 25 December, Christmas Day, no work whatever is done. It would be a kindly gesture on the part of the Soviet Government if this year the Poles could be freed from all labour on the afternoon of 24 December and all day of the 25th.

VYSHINSKY. I don't quite understand what work you are referring to.

KOT. Every kind of work, both in camps where there are still Poles, and wherever they are working as free men. I don't want to bring any pressure to bear, but the Poles would be very grateful to the Soviet Government if of its own accord, as though of its own initiative, it issued an instruction that our people were not to work on this their greatest festival.

VYSHINSKY. Obviously I cannot settle this question without reference to the Government. I'll communicate your request to Moscow.

KOT. Certain difficulties are arising in connection with the dispatch of a transport of airmen and sailors through Archangel. For inexplicable reasons difficulties have arisen, it would appear, in the Narcomindiel itself, over the issue of visas for 250 men of the forces. They have been issued individual passports, but really quite unnecessarily, for military transports should travel on a collective list.

VYSHINSKY. Obviously in such cases a collective passport is sufficient. But where are these airmen and sailors now?

KOT. On the way to Archangel, whence they are to sail in a special vessel paid for by the Polish Government, during the present month.

VYSHINSKY. But what is the date of their sailing?

KOT. 29 December. Dr. Lieutenant Straszynski, who is to be the commandant of the transports, has remained here in order to obtain a passport with visas for them.

VYSHINSKY. Where is this officer to be found?

KOT. He is in the Embassy. The question of his departure is already settled formally, of course he has an individual passport and visa. So I would ask your assistance on two matters: a visa for those who are going, and air flight for Lieutenant Straszynski.

VYSHINSKY. I shall give instructions for this matter to be dealt with.

KOT. The last question is that of the delegates. In view of the basic agreement of the Polish and Soviet texts on the instructions for delegates, this matter could be settled at once if we could come to a final decision on certain minor details.

VYSHINSKY. I haven't had time to deal with this. It does appear that, as you say, there is no fundamental difference of opinion. (He turns interrogatively to Pushkin. Pushkin assents.) It could be settled in fifteen minutes. I shall deal with it tomorrow. . . . And so, some time tomorrow, or the next few days, we shall confirm the contents of the instructions and establish the places of residence of the Embassy representatives.

KOT. With the general question of delegates is linked the matter of Vladivostok. A delegation with a restricted sphere of activity in that locality will not be sufficient for us.

VYSHINSKY. I know. We have received a note on your attitude to this question.

KOT. People are coming away from Kolyma in a terrible state, insufficiently fed, without clothing.. It would be bad if they had to travel right across Siberia in such a state. Our delegate in Vladivostok will be able to give them the requisite aid. When there was talk in Moscow about the delegations General Sikorski and I particularly inquired concerning Vladivostok, and President Stalin agreed to this delegation without any restrictions.

VYSHINSKY. Both here and in Moscow, whenever there has been talk of Vladivostok the Embassy has particularly emphasized the importance of the aid which is to come through that port, and therefore of the transport problems. I must obviously inform Moscow of your present standpoint. Or perhaps, when we draw up a list of the delegations and send the plan to Moscow, we shall simply add Vladivostok to the list and thus the question will go through.

The conversation lasted fifty minutes.

> B21. *Conversation with the Vice-Commissar for Foreign Affairs, A. J. Vyshinsky.*
> *Narcomindiel. 24 December 1941*
> Present: Director K. N. Novikov and Embassy first Secretary W. Arlet.

Kot opened by expressing his thanks to Vyshinsky for making arrangements to allow the Poles to celebrate Christmas. He would be glad if he could be enabled to announce the news on the radio, but he did not know exactly how the arrangement had been made, so he could only arrange for mention of it in the press.

VYSHINSKY. The instruction was issued in the normal form.. The same day that we had our conversation I made contact with Moscow and gained the Government's agreement to your request. The People's Commissariat for Internal Affairs sent a telegraphic instruction to the competent authorities, saying that any Poles who wished could celebrate this festival.

KOT. Next I wish to thank you for the final settlement of instructions to the Embassy delegates. I hope their co-operation with the local authorities will develop favourably.

VYSHINSKY. I feel that the text agreed between us provides a real basis for beneficial and positive co-operation.

KOT. So far as I am concerned, I see this document as confirming the argument I have long advocated, that co-operation between the Embassy organs and the Soviet authorities is beneficial to both sides. What is good for us will be of benefit equally to the Soviet Government.

VYSHINSKY. On the spot, in the provinces, in view of the precise definition of the delegates' competence the instruction will make it possible to avoid misunderstandings between the delegates and the local authorities.

KOT. Today I have two requests to make. First, the question of the distribution of our delegates, decisions as to where their headquarters will be situated. We have presented a list containing proposals for the localities, but bearing in mind that the geographical distribution of delegates will not be according to some rigid scheme, but that it will be subject to changes. In certain localities, after all the Polish citizens have left, delegates will be unnecessary; on the other hand it may be necessary to arrange for delegates in other places, of which we have had no knowledge until recently. For instance, during the last few days I have received information that there are a large number of Poles residing in the Caucasus. You have promised me that a scheme of instructions for the delegates and their distribution in the various areas will be decided upon during the next few days.

VYSHINSKY. It is quite true that I did make that promise, but precisely in order to distribute the delegations appropriately I have given instructions for data to be collected on the numbers of Poles residing in the particular *oblasts*. It is a matter of finally establishing the localities where there is a genuine need for the delegates. This is the reason for the delay in deciding. But I expect it will be finally settled during the next few days, especially now Novikov, who is working on the question, has returned.

KOT. Now for my second request. Some months ago I raised the subject of a loan for aid to the Polish population. It is now becoming a terrible necessity. The fifth point of the instructions to delegates lays on us obligations which we are not in a position to carry out owing to the lack of material resources.

VYSHINSKY. If you are referring to a credit for the Polish Government, after my conversation with you I took the matter up with Molotov and received the reply that General Sikorski had correctly understood President Stalin's statement concerning the granting of a credit of 100 million [roubles]. I think the matter will be settled formally very shortly.

кот. I am very grateful for this information. But unofficially I would like to stress that when General Sikorski raised this question of 100 millions with President Stalin the President said ' *da* '. In Polish ' *da* ' derives from the verb ' *dać*, to give ', so I took it to mean that it really would be given to us and given at once! We need the money very urgently. In Poland people give one another presents at Christmas time. But I have not received a Christmas present, so I have come to remind you, though that isn't really done. (They all laugh.)

novikov. Well, it will be for the New Year.

vyshinsky (following this up). Exactly; it will be a New Year's present.

кот. It would be better if we received the loan in 1941, and not in the coming year.

vyshinsky. I shall try to get the business settled this year. Yesterday I sent a preliminary draft of a credit agreement to Moscow. I couldn't do it before, for there is the other question of a credit for military purposes.

кот. That is quite a different problem.

vyshinsky. But we must get it worked out simultaneously. Novikov has returned now, and he will deal with it. I hope that by tomorrow, or in a few days at most, the matter will be settled finally.

The conversation lasted over fifteen minutes. It was carried on in a friendly, affable, and at times a ' merry ' tone.

> B22. *Conversation with A. J. Vyshinsky, Vice-Commissar for Foreign Affairs.*
> *Narcomindiel. 28 December 1941*
> Present: Director K. N. Novikov and W. Arlet.

Vyshinsky informed the Ambassador that he had asked him to call in order to hand him the texts of the draft agreements on loans: for the needs of the civilian population a sum of 100 million, and for the army, 300 million roubles.

Kot expressed his thanks for Vyshinsky's swift preparation of the drafts and studied the texts of the two drafts and their annexes. The Ambassador directed special attention to the question of the terms of repayment, asking whether there was no possibility of formulating this point differently.

Vyshinsky replied that this had been arranged on the same lines as the loans which the Soviet Union had obtained from the Allies, and remarked that the possibility of cassation of the obligations arising out of the loan by repayment in goods provided a solution allowing the Polish Government a more convenient form of repayment if, five years after the end of the war, any difficulties existed in regard to payment in monetary terms.

Prof. Kot next stressed the urgent need for concluding the loan agreement during the next day or two, depicting the serious situation of the Polish civilians and the extent of their requirements. In view of the terms of the note regulating the method of putting the loan into force, twenty millions on the day of signing and ten millions on the first of each month thereafter, at Novikov's suggestion Vyshinsky declared his readiness to sign the agreement within the current year, which in effect would bring half the loan into operation during the winter period : thirty million in January and ten each in February and March.

Kot stated that he would present both drafts at once to his Government and he expected a decision in the affirmative, at least so far as the loan for the civilians was concerned, during the next few days. But because of the length of the texts he was forced to ask Vyshinsky whether the Narcomindiel would send them in cypher to Bogomolov to pass to the Polish Government, since the Embassy's technical facilities for communication would not be capable of dealing with the task swiftly.

Vyshinsky agreed to this suggestion, suggesting for his part that the Polish Government should pass to Bogomolov plenipotentiary powers for the Polish Ambassador to sign the agreements. In that case the Soviet Government would not wait for receipt of the text of the plenipotentiary powers for Ambassador Kot, but would be satisfied with a cable from its Ambassador in London confirming the text of those powers.

Kot then asked if Vyshinsky would cause instructions to be issued for the sale of provisions and other necessities at official prices in order to aid the Polish people, since their possession of money would not in itself solve the question if they were not afforded the possibility of buying. Vyshinsky promised to go into this.

Turning to the loan for the armed forces, Kot stated that owing to its nature and the inclusion of supplies of military equipment in kind in the calculations he must talk over the question with General Anders before adopting any attitude. So he could not indicate the date by which the Polish side would be ready to sign, not to mention the possibility that we would have amendments to put forward.

Vyshinsky remarked that in the military agreement it is proposed to transfer the appropriate sums to the account of the Commander of the Polish Forces in the U.S.S.R., but if the Polish Government considered that the quotas for military purposes should be transferred to the Ambassador's account the Soviet side would have no objections. Kot made his reply on this point, as on the draft agreement as a whole, dependent on the decision of General Sikorski and the opinion of General Anders.

The conversation was friendly, and ended with the assurance that both sides would make every endeavour to sign the agreements as soon as possible.

A71. Cable to General Sikorski.
29 December 1941

Unofficially a colonel of the Narcomvnudiel, Volkovyski, has handed over details of the instructions for organizing further units of the Polish Armed Forces; among these instructions is a reservation reading as follows: 'Only the levying of Poles from Western Ukraine and Western Bielorussia is permitted.. Other nationalities are not to be included in the levy.'

I wait for an official formulation before making an immediate protest. So far I have not informed anyone of this.

A73. Cable to Deputy Premier, S. Mikołajczyk.
Kuibishev. 3 January 1942

During his farewell call, Cripps mentioned that Stalin has a feeling of great success, believes the Germans will be completely shattered, and above all is concerned that Russia, even at this stage, should be assured of strategically secure frontiers and such as will guarantee the annihilation of the Ukrainian movement. Cripps confirmed that in Moscow they[1] had recognized that Russia should have all the

---

[1] The pronoun here presumably refers to Mr. Eden's visit to the U.S.S.R. in December 1941, and possibly to Lord Beaverbrook's in September 1941. *Tr.*

Baltic States and the Rumanian frontier of 1940, i.e., with Bessarabia and part of the Bukovina. As for Poland, he reckons that Russia counts on the Curzon Line, but in exchange is prepared to recognize to Poland as much as possible from a shattered Germany. He is of the opinion that on the question of a frontier with Lithuania, and in regard to Lwów, we should make haste to seek the support of America, for Russia will press for a speedy decision. After a rest Cripps will devote himself to a study of the problem of frontiers and the problems of peace.

A75. To the Minister for Foreign Affairs.
Kuibishev. 5 January 1942

The last month of 1941 has brought the Soviet Union a greatly increased feeling of strength. The repulse of the German invasion, connected on many parts of the front with the capture of a considerable number of prisoners and military material, has taught them that the German soldier not only allows himself to be beaten, but is also poorly equipped and seriously demoralized. There has been such a growth of belief in victory among the men of the Soviet Army that wounded and sick soldiers in the rear hospitals are demanding to be sent back to the front more quickly. Among the civilian population the increasing shortages and restrictions are being borne more patiently, and the atmosphere of criticism and disbelief, which was particularly noticeable in October, has been restrained. Eden's visit and the great concessions he has made to Russia have increased the self-confidence of Soviet circles, though they expressed quite clearly their distrust, suspicion, and almost dislike of Great Britain. Kalinin's return to Moscow was an expression of the conviction that the military situation is secure for a long time to come.

It is not without significance that during this period there has also been an improvement in the Soviet Government's attitude to the Polish population. This is undoubtedly the consequence of certain political calculations, but above all of General Sikorski's visit and the impression he personally made. The Soviet Press is still maintaining its warm tone towards the Poles now he has gone, and this finds expression especially in numerous articles about the Polish Army. The influence of this change in the press and radio makes itself felt over wide expanses of the U.S.S.R., as is shown by the circumstance that in such remote spots as Syktyvkar (Komi), Novosibirsk, and Alma Ata, the local radio authorities proposed to the Polish delegates that they should broadcast to the Polish citizens. In Novosibirsk delegate Maliniak began by reading the Polish text of General Sikorski's Moscow speech, which had reached Siberia only in the Russian version. Only during December did the Soviet authorities genuinely begin to meet our desiderata, which had been subjected to procrastination ever since September.

Despite the winter and difficulties in communications the rate of release of Polish citizens from the northern camps has been speeded up, especially from the Archangel *oblast*, and a considerable number of Poles deported from settlements in the Archangel, Vologda, and Komi *oblasts* and from Siberia are being transported. All these transports are moving down to southern Kazakhstan and are being allotted passenger carriages, heated, with provisions for fourteen days. For such a long journey this is really inadequate, but it is a great advance over the previous ban on food supplies to evacuated Poles. Settlers travelling from the north are mainly deportees from the [Polish] districts of Lomza, Vysokie Mazovieckie, and similar areas; they are being distributed over the district of Dzambul, where there are already over 30,000 Poles. The mortality in the transports is certainly high, but this is because the people were exhausted before they set out on the journey, and because of fresh epidemics; children especially are falling victim to a fatal form of measles which develops into inflammation of the lungs.

Unfortunately there is still no word concerning the military and civilian prisoners deported from Starobielsk and Kozielsk in 1940, concerning whom General Sikorski handed a list of 4,000 names to Stalin. They are probably so far north that the question of transporting them elsewhere simply cannot arise during the winter season. Ambassador Cripps has intervened on behalf of some Englishmen who Poles indicated were in the camps; he received the reply that it is impossible to release them before the summer, for they are in a locality which a cable would not reach. Undoubtedly imprisonment for a second winter will have a tragic effect on the health and vital strength of our people.

One expression of the authorities' friendliness towards the Polish population was their instruction—on my initiative—freeing Polish citizens, no matter where they are, from work during Christmas. All the various kinds of work centres were notified of this by cable from Moscow; we know from Soviet Farms that this concession was in fact put into effect, and during this period Poles were supplied with exceptional rations of food; the natives were shown no consideration whatever during their holiday period.

An important step has been taken with the obtaining of agreement as to the sphere of activity of Embassy delegates. This sphere is very wide and quite adequate. It includes almost everything appertaining to consular administrations, and much more in addition. The regulations as to the delegates' sphere of activity are published in the issue of *Polska* dated 1 January.[1]

The discussion over the distribution of delegates is now drawing to its end. In these conversations we have agreed twenty places where there are to be delegates, in dependence on the numbers and distribution of Polish citizens. The Soviet authorities have not been over favourable to the settlement of delegates in capitals of remote republics, it is rather as if they did not wish them to become intimate with the heads of racially foreign territories, who have in fact at times shown far-reaching friendliness to the Poles: for instance, the Kazakh government in Alma Ata, or the Kirghiz in Frunze. They also opposed their being allowed in certain large cities, as they are afraid the existence of a delegation would attract a larger number of Polish people to these cities. In regard to several places they withdrew their opposition after hearing our arguments. They maintained their opposition to Sverdlovsk, Novosibirsk, and Tashkent: the delegates to these places will have to reside in other localities, which, however, are convenient. . . . Sometimes a single delegate will be in charge of several *oblasts*, but in every *oblast*, as also in the more important regions, men of trust will be in charge with a somewhat diminished sphere of activity, but recognized [by the authorities].

There have been difficulties over Vladivostok; they have agreed to it only for transport reasons. . . .

Of all this network, so far only the delegate for Archangel, Gruja, has been recognized; many weeks of hard struggle have gone on over others, especially Tashkent.

. . . . The granting of a loan of 100 millions for the needs of the civilian population was arranged in a friendly atmosphere. So that it could still be signed last year, and we could thus obtain ten millions more at once, the Narcomindiel apparatus worked until late in the night of New Year's Eve; the signing took place at eleven p.m. This loan is to last for eight months, without prejudice to whether it is followed by another. It is a great loss that we did not get it before

---

[1] A Polish periodical published by the Embassy. See later in this report. *Tr.*

the winter, but now everything is ready for using the money effectively and rapidly.

Independently of providing concentrations of Poles with ready money, I have given instructions to prepare for the opening of shelters and sanatoria for those incapable of work, war wounded, sick, etc, and also children's homes, kindergartens etc. . . .

At last aid in kind is beginning to arrive; in addition to transports from Archangel supplies by lorries from India. Unfortunately the difficulties in regard to internal communications are so great that there is extensive delay in distributing the resources that have arrived. Our efforts are now directed towards dealing with these transports.

The decision to form new large units and to transfer the Army to the south is the result of General Sikorski's intervention. The establishment has been fixed at six infantry divisions each of 11,000, plus the 30,000 already in the army. A total of 96,000 men. Our Command further reserves the cadres for a seventh division. Both the existing divisions, and the Command with auxiliary services and reserve forces will very soon be leaving the Volga basin area and will be transported to the south. In designating the headquarters larger cities have been avoided, but good communication points are assured; the whole will be distributed between Alma Ata and Bokhara, along the main railway line and its two southerly branches.

. . . . Arms are to be issued for yet another division—so far only the fifth has been armed—and the equipment and armaments as a whole are to be distributed among all the units and used for training purposes. Sappers', liaison, medical, and other equipment is to be issued in quantities necessary for training. Motor vehicles, horses and carts in the quantity to meet economic needs. It follows from this that the supply of arms and equipment must be undertaken from outside, in principle from Great Britain, and partly assured from the U.S.A. . . .

Recruiting commissions will shortly be travelling to the various concentrations of Poles. In accordance with General Sikorski's demand the Soviet authorities agree to the evacuation of 25,000 to Iran, but they make the reservation that this can take place only after the army has reached its full complement, namely 96,000. I judge that it will be possible to obtain agreement to an earlier evacuation in groups as soon as the recruitment supplies a large number of soldiers to the new divisional headquarters.

The Soviets have granted us sixty-five million roubles for the maintenance of the Polish Army in the past year, and this sum is now being included in the loan, to a total of 300 millions, proposed to us for the Army. This loan would have to suffice for six months. The military recognize that the Soviet authorities include provisions, arms, and equipment supplied by them at extremely low prices.

The Ambassador has the right to speak over the radio four times a week for ten minutes a time. These speeches are broadcast simultaneously in the territory of the U.S.S.R. and on short waves abroad, mainly with Poland in mind; so far we have no data as to the extent of their range, beyond the immediate vicinity of Kuibishev. . . .

Polish broadcasts made by the Soviet radio, which we regard with less favour, are still being put out from Kuibishev, and a little group of Polish-Jewish communists is responsible for them. They endeavour to obtain material from us, because they themselves possess almost nothing, and they try not to inflame Polish feelings in any way and not to draw down on them the criticism of the Embassy. The point is simply that the members of this group want to have something to live on here, and later to have the possibility of returning to Poland. In these circumstances we do not make any immediate reservation concerning the existence of these broadcasts, *inter alia* because we haven't the means to run a larger programme.

During the period under review Polish press activity has begun in the U.S.S.R. The Embassy has undertaken the issue of a periodical called *Polska* [Poland]. It is to be a weekly, but various technical difficulties have prevented us from issuing it regularly so far; three numbers have appeared, each of 10,000 copies. The difficulties made by the Propaganda Department of the Narcomindiel (the lack of a printing works, of paper), were broken down only after intervention with Stalin; permission has been given to print in the only works here which has Latin type (so far Polish type has not been brought in, but it has been promised), provided for the official bulletin, *Moscow News*; but this printing works is seriously overloaded, it keeps manuscripts for a long time before setting them up, but demands them usually urgently and very early; owing to the lack of Polish printers the proof reading is horrible. The censorship is carried out in accordance with Soviet regulations by the Narcomindiel Press Bureau; it is not pestiferous, but as it is not independent and waits for guidance on many a ticklish point, the publication of each issue is delayed for several days. There are difficulties with paper also; in principle we obtained agreement to a twelve page number, but they are continually insisting that we do not extend to this size owing to the lack of paper. The distribution of the periodical is a difficult problem; there can be no question of using the post, not only because it functions slowly—letters take several weeks—especially to such remote provinces as those in which the Poles are settled, but also owing to the uncertainty whether the packets might get lost. So we use only individuals travelling to one or another of the Polish groups for sending large parcels, and from there they are distributed further.

The Polish Forces Command has founded the weekly *Orzel Biały* [White Eagle]. As long ago as August it had the Soviet military authorities' agreement to the issue of a periodical and the promise of a printing works and paper. Paper was not received till December, but then not in any large quantity, also a wretched little printing machine run by two soldiers who are printers. The paper is issued only for the forces and is censored by our military authorities, so it has greater freedom of speech than *Polska*; but its issue is small and it circulates only in the camps.

. . . . Russian writers and publicists are slowly beginning to make contact with the Embassy, asking for material on the Polish forces and the situation of the Poles, and also proposing to place articles written by Poles. The editor of the monthly *Istoricheskii Zhurnal* [Journal of History] has made most vital contact; he has writing for him: Parnicki on Polish literature of the past twenty years; Pruszynski on Narvik; Weissblum, a survey of the course of the Polish-German conflict in history. Military periodicals especially are asking for articles and would accept the unlimited collaboration of professional pens in England.

Catholic services are held in the forces quite regularly; there are forty-five chaplains, and, given the full military complement envisaged, eighty will be needed. Outside the army there are only some half a dozen priests. These include Father Kucharski in the Embassy; he is still ill, but holds services, attended by individuals from the diplomatic corps. . . . Five in Polish civilian concentrations in Kazakhstan hold services wherever they happen to be, but only privately so far. In agreement with the delegates the Embassy is making preparations for the formation of religious societies to conform with Soviet laws, so that they can apply for the use of church buildings and liturgical equipment. Unfortunately, this activity is being held up by the lack of priests. I have presented a note asking for the release of several dozen imprisoned priests whose names we have collected;

to this list we have added about ten names of Poles, Soviet citizens, long held in prison, in order to try to raise the question of their position.

Although we have a priest, Dean Kurylas of Lwów, and some 3,000 soldiers, Orthodox services cannot be celebrated so far owing to the lack of missals and equipment. We are negotiating for these with the Russian Church . . . but if its agreement indicates even a hint of uncertainty we shall make use of a set purchased in Istanbul. A rabbi provides for the religious needs of Jewish soldiers.

A76. To the Minister for Foreign Affairs.
Kuibishev. 5 January 1942

The amnesty granted on the basis of the Pact made no distinction of nationality among Polish citizens. Above all, Jews were released first and foremost and almost to the last man; a mass of Ukrainians and all the Bielorussians have been released. Only prominent political individuals [of these nationalities] have been detained in prison, or sometimes in camps. . . .

Not only were no obstacles put in the way of national minorities reporting to the Polish Armed Forces, but the first group of Jews was directly sent there; it included many wretched elements arrested for smuggling and speculation. During the early days the position of the Jews in the Polish Armed Forces won some notoriety; it was the subject of observation by the Narcomvnudiel and the particular concern of Jewish foreign correspondents; the suggestion was spread about that Jews would not be able to find a satisfactory atmosphere and do service in the Polish Army because of Polish anti-Semitism. On the other hand, observations came from the Narcomvnudiel that the Jews were the worst element in the troops, cowardly and everlastingly dissatisfied, and that it would be desirable to get rid of this element. To this were added the attempts of the Jabotinsky group to have the Jews organized in separate detachments, with the idea of assigning them sooner or later to Palestine. The excess of Jews was reduced by the removal of the physically less fit.

In the 5th Division in Tatishchev there are quite a number of Jews; certain detachments have up to thirty per cent, and General Boruta has no reservations in regard to them. On the other hand, the majority of the Jews in the 6th Division have been separated and a battalion formed from them has been sent to work at Koltubïansk. The Jews complain that a young captain ordered: Jews, join the detachments formed from national minorities; and thus the entire Jewish element in these detachments has been eliminated from the forces without regard to the value of individuals.

The number of Ukrainians in the forces has been greatly reduced; to some extent pro-Hitler propaganda spread among them, but mainly they were demoralizing the detachments by continually complaining about all kinds of shortages. The Bielorussians' behaviour is without reproach.

The nationality question entered an entirely new phase during November and December. When several Jews, Polish citizens living in Alma Ata, were incorporated in the Soviet forces I handed in a note of protest on 10 November. On 1 December the Narcomindiel rejected the note, declaring *inter alia*, as follows:

' In connection with the decree of the Presidium of the Supreme Soviet of the U.S.S.R. dated 29 November 1939, all citizens of the Western lands of the Ukrainian and Bielorussian S.S.R. who were on the territory of the said area on 1-2 November 1939 acquired citizenship of the U.S.S.R. by virtue of the law " On citizenship of the U.S.S.R. " dated 19 August 1939.

' The Soviet Government's readiness to recognize as Polish citizens those individuals of Polish nationality who on 1-2 November 1939 were residing on the above specified territory testifies to the Soviet Government's good will and conciliatory spirit. But in no case can it form any basis for similarly recognizing as Polish citizens persons of other nationalities, and in particular: Ukrainian, Bielorussian, and Jewish, because the problem of the frontiers between the U.S.S.R. and Poland has not been resolved and is subject to decision in the future.'

The Embassy replied with a note on 9 December, very firmly emphasizing that Polish law does not distinguish citizens according to race or nationality, that only Polish law decides as to the possession of Polish citizenship, and that the law ' On citizenship of the U.S.S.R.' cannot have any application to Polish citizens, since it would be contrary to the decision of the fourth Hague conference of 1907.

To this note came a reply maintaining the importance of the ' plebiscite '. However, when a passport was applied for for persons of Jewish origin the Soviet authorities again indicated their attitude: on 29 December they refused to allow the well-known paper merchant Aleksandrowicz of Cracow with his family to leave for Palestine, defining them as Soviet citizens in accordance with the above note.

Similarly Polish passports were not granted for the writer Anatol Stern and his wife, because 'they have acquired Soviet citizenship on the basis of the order of the Presidium of the U.S.S.R. Supreme Soviet dated 29 November 1939, and as persons of non-Polish nationality they retain their citizenship etc.' I must add that the Sterns took a Soviet passport in Lwów, as for that matter the mass of the population had to if they wished to remain gainfully occupied, whereas the Aleksandrowiczes never accepted a Soviet passport and always declared their Polish nationality, not even agreeing to be listed as Jews.

From our conversations it follows that at present the Soviet authorities will not grant an exit visa on a Polish passport to any Jew, in view of which their families' endeavours to secure their departure to Palestine or anywhere else lack all realistic basis.

On such a fundamental issue we obviously cannot make any compromise, especially as it would set a precedent for the demarcation of frontiers. When I discussed these claims with commissar Vyshinsky he was embarrassed, admitted that it raises many complications, but took refuge behind the Supreme Soviet resolution. Evidently he had been ordered to take this attitude. During our tour of the forces, when he spoke at the reception in Totskoe, Vyshinsky forecast friendship between the nations of Russia under the leadership of the Russians and the nations of Poland under Polish leadership. Asked later in a conversation for an explanation, he declared that without regard to the settlement of frontiers Poland will always have Jews, Ukrainians, and Bielorussians in her midst. During the tour, in front of Vyshinsky and representatives of the Narcomvnudiel General Sikorski always stressed the far-reaching importance for Poland of the Eastern areas and their peoples, drew their attention to the march past of a company from Lwów, and children from Lyczakow. And in his speeches the Ambassador extolled the Polish patriotism of Vilna and Lwów and their links with Katowice, Poznan, and Torun.

Ambassador Cripps comments on this subject as follows: Russia has already decided to ensure to herself the demarcation of frontiers, but as she must come to an understanding with the Polish Government in regard to the Polish-Russian frontier she wishes until then to treat the Polish eastern areas occupied by her in 1939 as a neutral zone, not to allow them to pass as areas to which she can have no claim, and she secures this neutrality by recognizing Polish people from those parts as ours, but the non-Polish as hers.

We shall have to work on this question painstakingly, step by step. In practice conflicts will occur over the issue of passports to Polish citizens from the national minorities. On the question of a levy for the new divisions the Soviet staff has received instructions for its liaison officers with the Polish Armed Forces, and these have been unofficially communicated to our staff:

'The new divisions are permitted the levy of Poles originating from anywhere in Poland, also from Western Ukraine and Western Bielorussia. Other nationalities are not to be included in the levy.'

The news that every Jew who has been in the Soviet-occupied areas is to be regarded as a Soviet citizen has already circulated among the Polish Jews, and has caused fear and depression among them. A certain proportion of the Jews behaved well as Polish citizens, a certain proportion and, as some declare, the majority, welcomed the entry of the Russian forces, and during the occupation co-operated fervently with the Soviet authorities, using unpleasant expressions concerning Polish statehood; and during the transportations and in the camps they sometimes caused trouble for the Poles. None the less the feeling of injury and humiliation which they have suffered from Russia despite their sympathies is so strong among them that it has provoked a feeling of affliction, dislike, contempt, and even hatred of Russia. Their attitude to Russia today is very much sharper and more inflexible than that of pureborn Poles, who had no illusions that Russia would give them friendly treatment. And so the Polish-Soviet Pact and the recognition of the Polish state evoked loud protestations of attachment to the Polish state and Polish nationality even among the Jews previously most anti-Polish, and a desire at all costs to return to the little border towns as to Polish State territory.

. . . . Today it would appear to be anything but easy to find even among the Jewish communists anyone who would defend Russia's claims to these areas. The Jews do not wish to be under Russian domination at any price. The authorities here have clearly realized that this is their mood, and I think this is one of their reasons for refusing to allow Jews outside the U.S.S.R. frontiers. The Jews are indignant at the fact that from the beginning of the occupation the Soviets were not prepared to allow them to declare Polish nationality and forced them to state their nationality as Jewish, although in the U.S.S.R. Russian nationality is declared almost without exception and the Soviet regulations absolutely forbid the statement of nationality according to any other criteria whatever—for instance, birth, origin, language—except on the basis of the given individual's own feeling of nationality.

As for the Ukrainians, it follows from the hints of governmental circles that Russia wishes as far as possible to concentrate the entire Ukrainian element within her own borders, in order to destroy it for ever, in order to rid herself of the spectre of internal disintegration. It would be of interest to us here to see whether the Jews and Ukrainians who have influence in the Western democracies will change their previous attitude of reserve or even hostility to Poles, as the result of this new turn in affairs. For it is becoming clear that only the will to co-existence with the Poles within the frontiers of the Polish State, which is stressed everywhere among them, can save them from being wiped out.

The same question arises in regard to the Lithuanians. Russia, having obtained Great Britain's agreement to the incorporation of Lithuania as well as Latvia and Estonia, will leave the Lithuanians no prospect whatever of any form of Lithuanian state existence. It is more probable that she will strive to create a frontier barrier from purely Russian elements, which will mean the evacuation of millions of people from along the frontier zone into the heart of Russia. This trail has already been marked out by the transports of masses of Ukrainians and Germans to central and northern Siberia.

A78. To General Sikorski.
Kuibishev. 6 January 1942

. . . . Cripps is preparing himself for the great role of referee of war aims. He may be a little dangerous for us, despite all his criticism of Russia he none the less believes in the Curzon Line, or rather, that England cannot oppose Russia's demand. He regards Lithuania's case as hopeless, for Russia will never surrender it, and therefore the question of Vilna also! This again emphasizes the necessity for your journey to America. . . .

If you glance through my report of yesterday's date, you will see how much improvement there has been as the result of your visit. Your authority is enormous. In addition, operating with our forces here, you will have the future in your hands. . . .

According to Cripps, the creator of the annexationist-nationalist policy, the one who insists on the importance of the ' plebiscite ' in Lwów etc, is Molotov—not Stalin. It would be good to encourage

England a little so that she doesn't humble herself excessively. In the spring the war may have altered prestige values. . . .

I end because it is time for me to say good-bye to Cripps at the aerodrome. I shall miss him very much; he has been a good counsellor.

A85. Cable to the Minister for Foreign Affairs.
14 January 1942

I suggest you make a special intervention with Bogomolov for the release of at least four prominent Ukrainians, whose solid anti-Germanism has been confirmed by their Polish fellow prisoners. The argument can be used that their speeches would smash the Germanophile policy of the Ukrainians at home, or possibly the pretext of intervention by American Ukrainians could be used.

[Four names follow, with their places of detention]

Or perhaps you will regard intervention in Washington as more expedient? After all, Ukrainians of lesser value, rather Germanophile if anything, have been released, but these prominent, notoriously anti-German Ukrainians are obstinately held prisoner.

KOT.

B23. Conversation with the Vice-Commissar for Foreign Affairs, A. J. Vyshinsky.
In the Narcomindiel. 16 January 1942
Present: Director K. N. Novikov and W. Arlet.

The Ambassador began by thanking the Soviet Government and Commissar Vyshinsky for the hospitality shown to the Polish Premier. He emphasized that in all the General's interviews with the international press and others he had expressed his confidence not only in the fighting strength of the Red Army but also in the solidity and might of the Soviet Government. . . . As for the loan of 100 millions for the Polish civilians, its importance in the eyes of the Polish Government was indicated in the statements of the Minister for Information, Mr. Stronski, to the press and in broadcasts intended for Poland, in which he presented the loan as a proof of the thought the Soviet Government was showing for the fate of the Polish citizens.

Vyshinsky expressed the Soviet Government's satisfaction at this estimate of the effects of General Sikorski's visit.

The Ambassador turned to discussion of the loan for military purposes. He explained that he personally was anxious to give the speediest

possible reply on the Soviet Government's plan, but the chief of
staff had been absent from London, and without him the Ministry
for Finance could not take a decision, as it could in the case of the
loan for the civilians. . . . In addition there had been a breakdown
in the Embassy's liaison with London. 'We cannot communicate
directly, everything has to go through Ankara, which is overloaded.
I received my Government's instruction yesterday and I present our
counter-plan to you today.'

Presenting in more detail the attitude of the Polish Government
as indicated in the remarks appended to the Polish counter-plan (which
he handed to the Minister), the Ambassador made particular mention
of the following points which had induced the Polish Government to
put forward a counter-proposal. 1. The necessity to base the loan agreement on para. thirteen of the Military Agreement of 14 August 1941,
which provides for the conclusion of a special military-finance agreement. Such a solution would ensure continuity of supplies of finance
to the troops, instead of the present irregularity. 2. The problem of
repayment; he explained that there is a fundamental difference between the loan for military purposes and that for civil purposes,
both because of the comparatively small amount involved in the
latter, and of the nature of the expenditures. Poland during the post-
war period will be in a very difficult financial and economic situation,
and the postponement of the repayment by five years in relation to
the repayment of the loan for aid to civilians would give our finances
some relief. The same applies to the proposed postponement of the
fixing of the rate of payment till later.

Vyshinsky replied that he must first study the Polish counter-
proposal and send it on for the information of his Government, but
he wished to make certain preliminary observations at once. The
Soviet plan stipulating a definite sum of 300 millions is in every
respect more practical than the Polish plan. The Soviet Government's
obligation to finance the Polish Army is completely covered by para.
thirteen of the Agreement of 14 August 1941, and the plan for an
understanding put forward by the Soviet Government is only a technical agreement, not a political one. He simply does not see any necessity for concluding any new basic agreement, and he thinks the Polish
interpretation of para. thirteen unsound. As for the date and conditions of repayment, the Soviet Government proposed only exactly
what it had taken upon itself as an obligation in relation to the Allies,
and to the United States in particular. Similarly, failure to determine

now the rate of repayment to bind both parties would leave too many points unclarified. It is not expedient to create open questions and to leave to the future the decision of matters which in the interests of both sides should be settled at once. Repayment according to the official rate, dependent on the situation on the international money market, is the most expedient and practical solution.

Kot reminded him that the state of affairs existing hitherto, which in the event of acceptance of the Russian plan would not suffer any change, creates constant practical difficulties in the supply of finance. The forces have received finance irregularly, sometimes at very long intervals. The Soviet intendancy does not settle these matters too scrupulously, so that hitherto our forces have not been informed how much in reality, and above all for what purpose, the money has been supplied. The quota of sixty-nine million roubles, which we were notified consisted of expenditure on the forces down to the end of 1941, so far consists of a number of unknown quantities. At the moment, as the result of the negotiations on the loan agreement, our forces have not received any money at all. This is not a very encouraging prognostication for the future, when conversations on a new loan agreement come up. The Polish plan sought to avoid such a situation.

When Vyshinsky explained that on 31 December 1941 not sixty-nine but seventy-five million roubles had been paid out for the Polish forces, Mr. Kot said:

Then pay out eighty-five millions! After all, the army cannot go without money, especially when it is transferring to a new centre. After all, these sums will be set against the loan account, and although our soldiers are accustomed to getting by without money, if only because the Soviet authorities have already held up payment once for a period of over one and a half months, the payment of a quota of ten million roubles now is an urgent necessity.

Vyshinsky, after a discussion of the Ambassador's arguments without introducing any new factors, promised to deal with the question of paying out a sum for current needs to the Polish command in the U.S.S.R., stating that he had not been informed that the payments had been held up.

The conversation, carried on in a friendly spirit, lasted about forty-five minutes, but it was not without petty pinpricks on Vyshinsky's part over the delay in our reply to the Soviet plan, which the Ambassador did not allow to pass unrequited.

B.24. Conversation with Vice-Commissar A. J. Vyshinsky.
Narcomindiel. 17 January 1942
Present: Director Novikov and W. Arlet.

Vyshinsky stated that already yesterday he had sent, or rather telephoned to his Government the contents of the Polish counter plan, and the Ambassador's remarks. After making a close study of these documents the Government sees no possibility of changing its original plan.

Kot replied that he regretted the Soviet Government had not thought it possible to take the Polish wishes into account, though they were completely justified, and that he would pass the reply to his Government. But in any case he was forced to ask for an explanation of how the Soviet Government conceived of the financing of the troops after the 300 millions had been exhausted. The conclusion of fresh understandings every few months would be very inconvenient.

VYSHINSKY. It goes without saying that after the 300 million roubles have been spent the Soviet Government will supply further resources. After all, you don't play about with an army. That is a serious matter. But today it is difficult to say what quota will come under consideration. It may be 200, or it may equally well be 400 millions, dependent for instance on the prices which will then be in force. After all, the present quota of 300 millions also will consist partly of supplies in kind. In putting forward the plan to conclude an agreement with a fixed quota we stand on a definite position, which cannot be said of the Polish plan. Today is 17 January. There is no military financial agreement in existence, but the Polish Army exists and is receiving resources. That is the best proof of our good will.

KOT. And yet unpleasantness and difficulties of various kinds are arising. The Soviet authorities responsible for securing supplies to our forces treat these matters arbitrarily, as if they were trying to tell our troops: 'If we want to we'll give, but if we don't want to we shan't.' After all, the signing of an agreement based on the Polish plan would not mean a single rouble more in our payments than the signature of an agreement based on your plan. Our plan aimed to avoid the difficulties which could arise, by establishing certain permanent principles for the supply of money. It is superior to an immediate settlement of these matters. It was from these prerequisites that the Polish Government started when it put forward its plan.

VYSHINSKY. The difference between the Soviet and the Polish Government's attitude is not fundamental. It concerns first and foremost the interpretation of para. thirteen of the Military Agreement of 14 August. We regard the terms of this paragraph as an obligation by the Soviet Government to maintain the Polish Army. It is clear that there cannot be any talk of organizing an army without material resources. It is only a matter of their being issued in definite sums for a definite term. We consider that the August agreement is of a military-political nature. It was supported by the declaration for friendly co-operation signed in Moscow in December. At this moment there is no need to conclude any fresh basic agreement, only an understanding of a technical nature, for six months as planned by us. When this term has elapsed obviously a further understanding for a further six months will be concluded. It is for both sides to ensure that this understanding is prepared betimes. Only two problems will undergo any change in the next understanding. These will be the amount, obviously other than 300 millions, and the new term for which the understanding will be valid. I don't understand how difficulties can arise, given good and friendly relations between the two states which, I profoundly believe, will permanently build a road into the future. We are condemned by history to friendship, and that should eliminate all difficulties.

кот. I don't doubt for one moment that there will not be and cannot be difficulties of a political nature. As you are already issuing resources without a military financial agreement, so with stronger reason will you continue to issue them. But the Polish Government's concern is about something different. You mentioned the sum of sixty-nine millions. To this day there have been no calculations showing how much has been issued and for what purposes. Despite the Polish Command's repeated requests no invoices can be obtained from the Soviet Intendancy, nor any specifications of the equipment, supplies, and provisions handed over. Hence there is chaos. There is no information whatever what thirty, sixty, or eighty millions have been paid out for. The Polish plan was intended to put an end to this situation and to avoid its repetition in future. The quota of 300 millions may be sufficient to last till 1 July, but it may equally well last to 1 May or 1 June. Meanwhile, we were anxious to avoid any preclusive term, after which in dependence on possible external factors there could easily be an interruption in the supply of material resources for the forces. The terms of para. thirteen of the August Agreement provided for the conclusion of a skeleton military financial agreement which would order these issues. Money would be passed to the forces regularly, but independently of this the Intendancy would, at later dates, at leisure, in the course of a few months, agree the accounts for the past periods and would strike a final balance. Such emergency short-term loans do not conduce to continuity in the forces' activities. Under this system it will be altogether difficult to prove how much has been paid out for what.

VYSHINSKY. If I tried to answer your arguments as a whole, I should be compelled to repeat again our view of para. thirteen of the August Agreement. I have already done that once. But let us consider the difference between the Polish and the Soviet plans. It consists above all in the fact that our plan foresees an agreement for a definite sum, while the Polish is for an undefined quota. Article three of the Polish plan presents the same position as point six of the draft note, which has to be exchanged at the moment of signing the understanding. Like article three, point six of this note speaks of bringing financial resources into use every month on the basis of the Polish Command's applications agreed with the Red Army Command. In further points of this note there is reference to the supply of provisions and supplies, taking the [Soviet] non-front ration number three as the basis, also energy fuel, fodder, training ammunition, etc, for six divisions, i.e. 96,000 men, to the formation of which number the Soviet Government agrees. In what circumstances could the quota we propose not last till 1 July? Only if there were to be changes in prices and standards. An agreement for a definite quota binds both the intendancies to a diligent settlement of financial matters, to a strict issue of every rouble. The Soviet Intendancy will present statements and accounts to the Polish Command, which has the right to approve them or to put forward objections in the event of their not agreeing with the Polish figures. An agreement without a stated sum would be a blanket agreement. The Soviet plan is more definite and establishes a means of controlling the sums expended. Therefore the Soviet Government considers its plan should be accepted, and not the counter plan.

KOT. I take note of that and will communicate it to my Government. Nor do I consider that an understanding according to the Soviet plan would be detrimental to us. So I shall send on my own account a proposal that as the Soviet Government has not considered it possible to change its attitude we should sign the understanding on the lines of the original Soviet plan.

VYSHINSKY. Thank you very much.

KOT. Although my Government would have preferred to conclude a fundamental skeleton understanding I don't think we'll take the matter to court. Nevertheless, when the present agreement is approaching its end we must conclude the next rapidly. That will be the inevitable consequence of the piecemeal settlement of the question. . . . None the less my fears concerning a possible lack of continuity in financing the forces, and therefore in their work have not been dispelled. It was precisely this fear which moved the Polish Government to instruct me to put forward our desiderata.

VYSHINSKY. You have surely been convinced of my Government's, and in particular Chairman Stalin's attitude to Polish questions. You know how warm is his attitude to the Army. His attitude is the best guarantee of a happy development of the Polish Army, and that all its requirements, including finances, will be covered.

KOT. I am of the same opinion. When Premier General Sikorski was here President Stalin recognized that we could leave Russia if we wished. General Sikorski decided that the army would remain, on which President Stalin guaranteed that 'we give whatever the army needs'. That is an assurance which of course the Soviet Government will observe. Yet not a single rouble more would be issued under the Polish plan. It is simply that the Polish Government regards its plan as more expedient. We have some experiences in this sphere. Previously in France, and now in England, financial agreements were concluded on bases closely approximating to our plan. There the settlement of accounts between the intendancies took place every quarter or half year and it did not hold up the army's work in the least.

VYSHINSKY. Be so good as to bear in mind the circumstance that I personally shall be very deeply anxious to ensure that difficulties do not arise on this account. . . .

KOT. I, too, am concerned for the same thing. I hope I shan't find it necessary to come to you in a few months' time and complain that the army's work is being rendered difficult or held up because we are carrying on discussions over further money.

VYSHINSKY (jokingly). That is exactly what I am concerned to avoid, Mr. Ambassador.

KOT. But now another question. I would greatly like your collaborators and the Soviet Government organs generally with whom we have contact to realize that if the Polish Ambassador turns to them with some question, especially relating to care of the Polish civilians, it can and should be dealt with in a favourable sense, and above all, quickly. The situation today is such that after exhausting the normal official channels I am forced to turn to you on purely technical details, and in every instance you settle the matter satisfactorily. But this is a thoroughly inexpedient loss of energy and time. I have really difficult work, and very difficult problems to solve. I would like a friendly attitude to our affairs to exist at all rungs of the ladder, and not only at the top. Delay in settling certain problems threatens irreparable losses for our people.

VYSHINSKY. Oh, I have very few collaborators, really only Novikov and Pushkin. I have direct influence with them and straightforward relations. The difficulty isn't that either of them takes an unfriendly attitude to your affairs. It arises from the nature of these problems, which almost always involve the competence of various other departments. They must have discussions with the military authorities, the militia, the authorities of the various republics. Take the question of delegates, for instance. It called for agreement not only with the instances mentioned, but with the authorities of the Tadjik, Uzbekistan, and other republics. Sometimes a question appears to be simple, but in fact the highly democratic system of the Soviet Union means that the central authorities cannot take a decision without inquiring the opinion of the governments of the Uzbekistan, the Kazakh, and the Tadjik republics. After all, we are a Union of Republics; the Government of Great Britain asks the Dominions for their opinion before it takes a decision on any important matter.

KOT. So far I have not raised and I do not intend to raise any question which would shatter the unity of the Soviet Union, or set its republics at loggerheads. I come to you with much simpler issues, which although they are small, are of very great importance to us. You yourself best of all know the language you have to use when talking to the governments of the Union republics. (They all laugh.) I am concerned that the aid in the form of a loan which the Soviet Government has put at the Polish Government's disposal should be distributed in the areas swiftly and efficiently and supplied to those who need it. For otherwise, if every journey and every petty detail is turned into a fundamental issue the result will be of such a nature that I shall bring this money back and lay it on the table before you.

VYSHINSKY. You can be assured that for my part I am doing and shall do everything to facilitate settlement of your affairs.

The conversation lasted fifty minutes. Friendly tone.

B25. Conversation with A. J. Vyshinsky.
Narcomindiel. 22 January 1942

Present: Director Novikov, Director Pavlov, Arlet,
Financial Counsellor Marian Strumiłło,
and Pavlovich, a Narcomindiel official. A.
Mniszek, Embassy secretary, as interpreter.

KOT. I congratulate you on the victories which the Soviet forces have just won on the western front. I hope that the victories will grow bigger and bigger with every day.

VYSHINSKY. Thank you, Mr. Ambassador. I hope your words will come true. If our forces move forward at this rate we shall reach Minsk before long, well and—(he stopped short, evidently not wishing to say that the Soviet forces would then enter territories hitherto Polish).

(A moment or two later the other persons listed above and present at the signing enter the room. Director Pavlov and Arlet, the Embassy first secretary, set seals to the agreement covering military finances.)
. . . .

VYSHINSKY. . . . . By signing this agreement I have legalized the hitherto unformalized financing of the Polish Army in the U.S.S.R. Thus in this sphere the past is now put in order.

KOT. But, Mr. Chairman, not everything in the past is susceptible of being legalized by means of a seal.

I wish to notify you, with a view to your informing the Soviet Government, that I have received news from London that the present Embassy delegate in Tashkent, Mr. Kwapinski, has been appointed a minister in the Polish Government in London, his functions to be defined after his arrival. . . . Minister Komarnicki[1] with Minister Kwapinski will represent the Polish citizens residing in the Soviet Union. Owing to the difficulties of staffing the delegations through our shortage of people I shall have to retain Minister Kwapinski on the spot for the time being, until I find a suitable candidate to take over from him.

VYSHINSKY. Thank you for notifying me of this. The local authorities in Tashkent will be informed of Mr. Kwapinski's nomination. I shall issue full instructions for his journey to be facilitated.

Kot thanks the Soviet Government in the name of the Polish Government for the loan.

---

[1] Professor Komarnicki, who had left Moscow for London in September 1941, had been appointed Minister of Justice.

The visit lasted from 15.45 to 16.30 hours. The conversation was conducted in an atmosphere of cool courtesy.

B26. Conversation with A. J. Vyshinsky.
Narcomindiel. 23 January 1942
Present: Arlet and Novikov.

кот. I have called on you today on a matter which is not very serious, but which possesses practical importance for us. It is a question of the Embassy delegates. I should have no reason to raise it with you, since the delegates' sphere of competence and administrative centres have been agreed, if it were not for the statement Mr. Pushkin has presented in the name of the People's Commissariat for Foreign Affairs on 19 January.

. . . .

кот. From the beginning of the discussion of this question with the People's Commissariat, away back in Moscow, we agreed that the delegates could be selected from among Embassy officials. Actually the People's Commissar himself made reservations against the appointment as delegates of persons drawn from people on the spot. In any case, it was clear to me that the officials going out would be endowed with the full rights due to them. Later, in practice it transpired that we haven't sufficient people to act as representatives of the Embassy, and, as happened in Tashkent, Alma Ata, and elsewhere, I appointed people from among the Polish population at present in the U.S.S.R. In regard to every one of them I considered it perfectly natural to assure them such rights as, above all, personal inviolability, inviolability of the archives, and the possibility of the delegates' corresponding with the Embassy, such correspondence also being inviolable. After all, these rights constitute the indispensable minimum, without which all work would be impossible. In view of this, Mr. Pushkin's statement of 19 January, raising certain objections even in regard to diplomatic officials of the Embassy, is not clear to me. I could not agree that Embassy officials possessing diplomatic privileges are to lose them because I send them to carry out official functions, which, after all, are among the duties coming within the Embassy's sphere of activity. Similarly, individuals who act as delegates but are not members of the Embassy must be assured the same rights. This was so obvious that I did not even enter into correspondence with the People's Commissariat in regard to these rights, not considering that this question could meet with any objections. When I delegated Heitzman to travel about, and Gruja to Archangel, or Zmigrodzki to Askhabad, it was and is obvious that there had been no change in their formally legal position. I cannot believe that the People's Commissariat could adopt the position that an official working in the Embassy building in Moscow or Kuibishev possesses diplomatic rights, while if he carries out exactly the same functions outside the Embassy he loses those rights. I should be glad if you would explain the attitude of the People's Commissariat and dispel my doubts.

VYSHINSKY. If I have understood you aright there are two questions involved here: 1. Whether diplomatic rights and privileges can be granted to persons, outside the diplomatic personnel, whom the Ambassador has designated as delegates. 2. Whether Embassy officials carrying out functions entrusted to them outside the Embassy retain their diplomatic privileges and rights.

In regard to the first question, concerning the diplomatic rights and privileges of local people, the Soviet authorities, when formulating and considering the sphere of competence of Embassy delegates, were bound also to anticipate what their official character would be. The creation of twenty representations with the special aim of aid to the Polish people cannot be synonymous with the bringing into being of twenty consulates. The official character of the Embassy officials is assured by instructions issued to the local authorities, based on the agreed regulation concerning the delegates' spheres of competence. It is clear that the persons of the delegates will enjoy full rights assuring them the possibility of doing their work. In particular, so far as personal immunity is concerned—immunity of residence and correspondence—the Soviet Union constitution guarantees these to all citizens of the Union, and it is understandable that representatives of the Embassy of a foreign state must all the more enjoy them to the full.

But now for the second question, in which connection you mentioned the cases of Gruja and Heitzman, in other words diplomatic officials whom you had sent out for these or other tasks. Obviously they remain diplomats. In this or any other instance they fulfil functions belonging to the representatives of the Embassy, but their going on a journey affords no basis for depriving these temporary Embassy representatives of diplomatic rights or questioning their rights. If Mr. Pushkin's statement on this subject was taken to mean that Embassy diplomatic officials are to lose their diplomatic rights the moment you give them instructions to travel to carry out official duties, that state-

ment was erroneous and went beyond the instructions given to Mr.
Pushkin.

KOT. I must explain that the officials whom I delegate from the
Embassy will not be leaving permanently. None of them will remain
permanently delegates of the Embassy in one or another spot. Certain
of them, when they come to know the area well and find a suitable
candidate for delegate among the local people, might return quite
quickly. . . .

VYSHINSKY. Perhaps you would be good enough to explain whether
you intend to fill the posts of twenty Embassy representations with
new people or with members of the Embassy?

KOT. I cannot answer with one or the other. Certain delegations will
be taken over by new people, to others I shall send persons from among
my own staff. I can have and obviously do have more confidence in
my own officials. They have worked in the Embassy over a long
period, they know my wishes and the attitude and views of the
government, they know how to carry on the welfare work. Some time
will pass before local people are found. But I don't possess sufficient
staff to fill all the delegations. And there are the elements of chance,
of sickness. For instance, I shall have to recall Zmigrodzki; whether
anyone will be found at once to fill his place I don't know. Altogether
these personnel questions are not easy.

VYSHINSKY. So the problem is as follows: diplomatic officials who
have possessed this character hitherto, as notified to the People's
Commissariat, and who possess diplomatic papers, do not lose their
rights when you appoint them representatives. To new persons such
rights will not be granted. You know the Soviet Government's fundamental stand on this issue: it is a question of relations not only with
the Polish Government but also with others. If we were to open so
many Polish consulates the representatives of other states would be
calling on me tomorrow; indeed, they are already raising the question.
After all, each of them has certain interests, some justification for
setting up consulate posts. If we allowed Poland to do so they would
demand equal treatment. I ask you to take our point of view into
account.

KOT. You have had the opportunity during our past co-operation to
convince yourself that I take that point of view very thoroughly into
account. That for us is a prejudged question. I am always concerned
not with one or another formality, but with the possibility of practical work. If in the present war period the Soviet authorities see

no possibility of bringing consulates into being, there is nothing to discuss. But if, in Djambul for instance, someone turns up as my delegate, as a representative of the Polish Embassy, his non-possession of the necessary personal rights will not only render it difficult for him to co-operate satisfactorily with the authorities, but may prejudice the authority of his office and that of the Embassy. I am concerned with rights only in connection with that function and so long as the given individual is fulfilling it. After all, during the present war difficulties even such matters as a residence, supplies, journeys, are more easily arranged for diplomatic officials than for others. Therefore if I aimed to furnish all the delegates with diplomatic rights I had in mind precisely these practical considerations. It seemed to me that to grant them diplomatic rights would be the simplest solution of the question.

VYSHINSKY. When we considered the question of Embassy delegates we realized that these people, as representatives of the Embassy, would have to have a special position *vis-a-vis* the local authorities. This was given expression in the instructions which we sent to the authorities of all the *oblasts* in which delegates will reside. Apart from informing them of the details of the agreed decisions concerning the sphere of competence of Embassy delegates, we obviously issued guiding lines on how to deal with delegates as the representatives of a foreign Embassy and on their treatment as official government persons. The *oblast* executive committees, the organs of the Narcomvnudiel, and all the Soviet institutions which are involved in co-operation with the delegates have been informed how they are to behave towards them. Apart from instructions in writing, I have personally had conversations with the chairmen of the Councils of People's Commissars of the Uzbek and Kazakh Soviet Republics, they being regions in which very many Polish people have been concentrated. You can be sure that the People's Commissariat instructions will be fulfilled strictly. The local authorities will give the Embassy representatives such conditions as will enable them to perform their functions thoroughly, those functions for which they have been brought into being. In the final section of the 'Decisions on the Sphere of Competence of Embassy Delegates' there is reference, in points one and two, to co-operation between Embassy delegates and the local authorities (he reads these two points). In harmony with these decisions, the People's Commissariat has for its part done everything to ensure that the local authorities will facilitate the delegates' activities.

KOT. So can I regard your statement as a guarantee that the delegates will enjoy personal inviolability of their archives and official correspondence, also the possibility of organizing an office and selecting personnel, as well as freedom of travel? After all, we are foreigners, and so the Soviet Constitution benefits which you have been kind enough to mention don't apply to us. I regard your statement as of equal value to the 'Decisions' in regard to our delegates. Where our people are concerned I must receive a guarantee from you and they from me. I repeat this yet again, since on such an important question I am anxious to avoid any misunderstandings and to ensure that my delegates should not come up against any difficulties in their perfectly normal activities.

VYSHINSKY. You can be quite confident that the People's Commissariat for Foreign Affairs has done everything to assure them those conditions. Whether it be Kwapinski or anyone else, the Soviet authorities will make every endeavour to facilitate his work. If any difficulties of a local nature should arise, please inform me and they will be removed.

Kot thanks Vyshinsky for his statement and asks whether he for his part has any wishes or suggestions in connection with the delegates' activities just beginning.

VYSHINSKY. Certainly, in the interest of smooth co-operation I would like to propose that every delegate should be given some kind of certificate attesting his official character, which he could show to the local authorities. It would be very useful if this certificate referred to the 'Decisions on the Sphere of Activity of the Delegates of the Polish Embassy' and indicated that these 'Decisions' have been agreed with the People's Commissariat for Foreign Affairs.

On the Ambassador's instructions Arlet explained that certificates of this nature had already been prepared, and that reference was made in them to the 'Decisions'.

. . . .

The conversation lasted some fifty minutes. On both sides the atmosphere was friendly, the tone affable and calm.

A89. Cable to the Minister for Foreign Affairs.
25 January 1942

For Montreal if the Consul thinks fit, but the source of the information should not be broadcast.

Please discreetly inform Mme Ehrlich, 5579 Park Avenue, Montreal, that in the matter of both the arrested men I have made the strongest intervention three times. We have succeeded only in obtaining permission to hand in underwear, nothing more so far. The authorities know they are both the object of the Embassy's particular solicitude, so I do not think they will meet with any serious unpleasantness. They are in the prison here. When I wanted to provide them with food I was assured that they are well fed.

The charges against them are absurd, but behind them is rather a hidden hatred for Jews, who are regarded as responsible for the critical attitude of American opinion towards the Soviets. Arrests of Soviet Jews are going on at the present time. Polish [Jews] are flatly refused permission to journey beyond the frontiers of the U.S.S.R., on the pretext that they are regarded as Soviet citizens, because in the autumn of 1939 all the then inhabitants of so-called Western Ukraine and Bielorussia were incorporated in the U.S.S.R.[1]

> B27. *Conversation with A. J. Vyshinsky.*
> *Narcomindiel. 26 January 1942*
> Present: Novikov and Arlet.

VYSHINSKY. I have asked you to see me today in regard to two questions. Many instances of Polish citizens abandoning their places of residence, and even their work, in the north of the U.S.S.R. and shifting in an unorganized manner to the south have come to the knowledge of the People's Commissariat for Foreign Affairs. These incidents have occurred in the *oblasts* of Archangel, Novosibirsk and Vologda. I have to ask you to bring influence to bear on the local population through your delegates and men of trust to ensure that Polish citizens do not move from their places of residence and work, this being above all else in their own interests. By way of illustration I want to cite the following facts. Representatives of the Polish Army Staff in the persons of a Polish Military Commission, consisting of Kręzel, Gaj, and Jan Iłowanczyk, have caused 800 Polish citizens in one locality of the Vologda *oblast* to leave their work in order to go to Kazakhstan. By abandoning their work these people have ceased to earn, have left their place of residence, and have concentrated at the railway station in order to travel south. Ignoring the fact that in the south of the U.S.S.R., in Kazakhstan to be precise, there are already a

---

[1] The Narcomindiel reassured the Embassy as to the fate of the arrested men, and the Narcomvnudiel accepted parcels for them which Ludwik Seideman, Ehrlich's nephew, and the *rapporteur* for Jewish affairs in the Embassy, prepared and delivered.

large number of Polish citizens, who undoubtedly will be sufficient to make up the complement of the anticipated Polish military units, this kind of unorganized travel may have serious consequences for these Polish citzens. Even though their earnings were of the smallest, these and their places of residence provided them with a basis of existence; now they have lost it. Even if they succeed in getting to the south, who will be responsible for the sacrifices which this fact may bring in its train? Who will guarantee that they will get work in the south?

KOT. Does this refer to Polish citizens under obligation to do military service, or also people not capable of such service?

VYSHINSKY. It refers to men capable of military service, but at present in work. After all, the numerical composition of the Polish Army is limited to 96,000, and the number of Poles already in the south may be sufficient to meet this contingent. The journey from Archangel to Uzbekistan in present conditions really is a risky enterprise.

NOVIKOV. In addition, some of them are taking their families with them.

KOT. I have always taken the attitude and have personally ordered the issue of instructions that Polish citizens who have work appropriate to their qualifications and who are employed in climatic conditions enabling them to survive should not move from where they are. The Embassy has always restrained this kind of transmigration. For that matter this problem was the subject of discussions in Moscow. I told President Stalin about the state of certain of our citizens. He spoke of areas in the north where the climate is too hard for them to be able to survive. Archangel *Oblast* and the Republic of Komi are precisely such areas, and the work there is of such a nature that whole families are dying out, as they are unable to keep going. President Stalin said he agreed with our conclusions and asked how I thought this matter could be solved. I replied that the Poles in the northern part of Siberia could be directed to Altai Land, the district of Barnaul, and Novosibirsk, but as for the European part of the U.S.S.R. and especially the Archangel *oblast* and Komi, I said I did not know where they could be directed to. Then President Stalin decided that they too ought to travel to the south; he went over to a map and drew on it an arc from the Turkmen Republic through southern Kazakhstan and Uzbekistan as far as Alma Ata. None the less the Embassy has not directed any transports whatever from the Vologda *Oblast* to the south, but we have very numerous requests to get the people shifted from Archangel. We are continually being asked to transport them to a better district. Only recently, some two days ago, I received a telegram from a transport of over 200 persons released from a camp. They are journeying into the unknown and they're asking for help. After all I must direct them somewhere. Also a few days ago there was another request from Irkutsk *Oblast*, where the climate is hard, and there is starvation too and the earnings are such that the people cannot survive. I wanted to ask you for your advice, and to receive some indication where these people are to be directed to.

As regards military service, the numerical problem isn't quite as you put it. Ninety-six thousand are to be incorporated in the divisions formed here, but we shall send 25,000 as a complement to the Near East and to Great Britain, not speaking of the airmen and sailors who also are to go. President Stalin distinctly said: every Polish citizen who wishes to and can serve is to be in the Polish forces. And it was established that the formation of six divisions will not be the definitive end of our army formations. After these have been formed we shall talk of further divisions. We take the view that as many Polish citizens as are fit to bear arms should go into the army. The point was not that those at work are not to go into the army. Obviously we wish to achieve our objective in a certain order. Those first to enter must be former soldiers who are not supporters of families. Obviously these should not work. If former soldiers now under obligation to do military service were called up in Vologda, the commission acted correctly. If it also called up men not under obligation or men with families, obviously it acted incorrectly. . . . The Soviet military departments are to take some part in this, and as soon as I receive exact details from General Anders I shall be completely informed on the subject. Of course I shall do all in my power to restrain wild unorganized journeys.

VYSHINSKY. To clarify the situation I would like to remind you that at a certain stage, in the name of the Government I notified you that owing to the winter season and the military situation the mass transfer of Polish people must be stopped. But, as I said then, this does not exclude individuals or small groups from travelling to other places of residence, but in an organized manner, at the cost of the Embassy. For we are not concerned to detain Poles for ever in the places where they are at present, but we do want that they should not shift from the spot disorganizedly, without any order. If the Polish staff sends commissions to the Babinsky region of Vologda *Oblast* it must first discuss the matter with the Soviet military authorities. Meanwhile, a commission travels to the Babinsky region without notifying the appropriate command, people at once set out on their travels, and only when they have all abandoned their work and begun to sell off their belongings do the Polish military ask for trucks, provisions, and a travelling route. Meanwhile there are no trucks, no provisions, no travelling route. People without work or earnings have gathered in the station, and now what are they to do?

I am instructed to ask you to put an end to this sort of unorganized movement. After all, we are at war, and it is wintertime too. Wouldn't it be better for the Polish people to wait a month or two and thus avoid the sacrifices which in such conditions are unavoidable? You rightly say that in addition to the 96,000 a certain number are to leave the country, and that after this figure has been reached we shall talk of further units. But first it is necessary to take advantage of those people who are in the south, and if the contingent is not reached with them, then to draw in others in an organized manner.

KOT. I entirely share your view and I shall be very grateful if you will indicate to me how (1) to direct the travels of the civilians who must change their places of residence, or who have already set out. (2) How am I to proceed in military matters, whether to leave them exclusively to the competence of the Polish and Soviet military authorities, or to refer also to the People's Commissariat for Foreign Affairs? I myself don't intervene in military affairs, I am only kept informed of their course by General Anders. But I must point out that we are still uncertain how many of those who are still in the south are fit for military service.

VYSHINSKY. As for the military issue, I see no need for any change in the existing state of affairs. Let the Polish military settle things with the Soviet military. But I would ask you to use your influence with the Polish military to stop unorganized shifts of people.

KOT. Very willingly.

VYSHINSKY. As for civilian journeys, please discuss them with us. But I would like, not for the official record, but to show you the actual state of affairs, to state that personal journeys from Moscow to Kuibishev at present take ten to twelve days, because absolutely all railway transport has been subordinated to military needs. We are now pouring westward men, armour, tanks, ammunition, supplies of all kinds, and provisions. When I sent officials of the Commissariat to Moscow with important documents I had to couple a car to a special train:

even so the journey lasts seven or eight to ten days. Everything must wait on the passage of the military transports. If in such conditions unprepared groups of people were to travel from north to south, even if it was possible to indicate some definite route for them to follow they would be travelling for two months. How many of them would die of starvation, exhaustion, and cold? For no matter how hard their situation may be in their present places of residence one can say as a rule that it is better than travelling in such conditions.

KOT. I have that in mind, and I flatly don't inspire journeys of that kind. I know very well how many deaths it would involve before the transports arrived at their destination. But there are exceptional situations. We have reports of settlements where the Polish people are dying at an alarming rate. The people who remain there will be lost, whole families will die off. We must rescue them. With cases of this kind I shall come to the People's Commissariat for Foreign Affairs.

VYSHINSKY. Yet do bear in mind the present difficult conditions, and handle requests for travel with the utmost circumspection.

KOT. The situation created in Buzuluk at this moment for instance must be regarded as exceptional. Owing to the transfer of the military to the south several hundred Polish civilians must leave this locality and Totskoe. For the quarters evacuated by our troops have been taken over by the Red Army, and these people will have nowhere to live. In addition the military, who have been looking after them so far, cannot do so in future and they have informed me in so many words that they are directing the transport to Arys station, where the Embassy is to look after them. So naturally I turn to the Narcomindiel, asking for some indication of the locality to which they are to go.

VYSHINSKY. That will have to be considered as a separate question.

KOT. One reservation I wish to make in advance: it was precisely to appeal against the ban on the transfer of our people to the south that I raised the question with President Stalin, who decided that it was necessary to have regard to this request.

VYSHINSKY. Yes, of course, in cases deserving of special consideration it will be possible to settle the question, so long as it is in an organized fashion.

KOT. I agree.

VYSHINSKY. But now another problem from the same sphere of population shifts, but over a lesser distance. From the authorities of the Uzbek, Kazakh, and Kirghiz Republics we have received reports that

Polish citizens distributed among the collective farms, where they have some sort of existence and labour, are abandoning the villages and concentrating in the towns. I would like you through your delegates to instruct the Polish people not to abandon their places of residence and not to concentrate in the cities or towns, where homelessness and need will await them once more. Here, too, it is a question of introducing order which is constantly being violated.

KOT. It has always been my desire to stabilize the stay of the Polish citizens in conditions tolerable for them. But to achieve this I had to have my delegates. For instance, if an Embassy delegate had already been functioning in Vologda *Oblast* he would either have prepared those men who were to enter the army before the military commission arrived, or else, by supplying appropriate information, he would have restrained them from wild journeys. As for Uzbekistan and other southern republics, the local Mongol population are behaving very ruthlessly towards our citizens. Certain of them sent to collective farms have been refused living quarters, they have to camp under the bare sky, or instead of bread they are given gluey cakes in such a small quantity that it is quite insufficient to keep them alive. Is it surprising that in such conditions the people flee to the cities or towns? I am constantly receiving disturbing reports on the state of our people.

VYSHINSKY. We, too, realize the difficult situation and exactly two days ago, on the 24th, instructions were issued to the authorities of the Uzbek, Kazakh, and Kirghiz republics to improve the conditions of the Polish citizens both by making it possible for them to obtain more suitable work and also by improving living conditions. But I ask you to use your influence with the Polish citizens in the direction of persuading them not to abandon the work to which they have been assigned. Of course every man seeks a spot in which things are better for him, just as a fish seeks the deepest water; but in the present war period it is necessary to restrict all avoidable shifts of population.

In this connection the question arises of the Embassy organizing shelters and rest homes for the aged, war wounded, and persons unfit for work. There was some talk of this at one time. They are an urgent necessity. Let the Poles push ahead with establishing this type of institution more rapidly. For our part also, the day before yesterday we issued instructions to the above-mentioned authorities that at the cost of the Embassy they should supply everything necessary to meet the needs of institutions of the afore-mentioned type. When we discussed the question of a loan you said the money would not be sufficient, since there is no free market or the prices on that market are very high. For these reasons we have arranged that provisions, industrial articles and other articles necessary for the organization and existence of such institutions should be issued to the Polish institutions at the rates for corresponding Soviet institutions. Let the Embassy delegates get to work quickly, so that we may know in what places and for how many people homes for the elderly and war wounded will be organized.

кот. I take note with great gratitude of your statement that the Embassy delegates haven't so far had the support of the local authorities. A definite example: as long ago as 9 January a very detailed search was made in the quarters occupied by Kwapinski and his officials, in search of one knows not what. How can the Embassy delegates work if they are treated by the local organs as suspect or quite harmful persons?

(Vyshinsky started with anger.)

кот. But we have not had assistance in other matters too. For instance, Powierza's journey.[1] I sent him out for the very purpose of investigating the situation of our people on the spot. He was to compare particular districts from the viewpoint of the expediency of setting up just this type of institution. But what happened to his journey? He had to wait a long time, and finally set out by rail, and now is dragging along to his destination in a slow train.

From various foreign countries very large and valuable transports of provisions, clothing and medicines are being sent to us. And these consignments are in your interest too. When a Polish citizen obtains provisions, clothing or medical goods from us he will not require these things [from you] which you need for your own citizens. Even more unpleasant things happen: for instance, a transport from India was rifled *en route*, on Soviet territory. I don't want to have our people travelling around as convoys to trains, but I shall have to ask for this if the Soviet authorities are not able to assure security to our transports.

vyshinsky (turns to Novikov for an explanation). Novikov will investigate that. In any case there will be a guard. If the transport has been rifled we shall succeed in finding and returning what has been lost. In any case there will be no repetition of such incidents in

[1] Andrzej Powierza, an Embassy secretary, had been sent in January to travel round areas in Uzbekistan and Kazakhstan; he accomplished his misson despite many difficulties.

the future. Novikov has demanded an explanation through the Nar-comvnudiel. We know that large consignments are due to arrive for the Poles, and I have suggested that the Government should appoint a special official of the Narcomtorg,[1] whose task it will be to make arrangements with the Embassy and to settle all questions connected with aid in kind from abroad for the Polish people.

Kot expresses his thanks.

VYSHINSKY. But now one other not very pleasant matter. Though in fact the first matter was not pleasant. In the Polish Army a weekly, the *Orzeł Biały* (White Eagle) is being published. We have read carefully through eight numbers of this weekly, and noted a whole series of remarks, expressions, themes, explanations which are not conducive to good co-operation between the Polish Army and the Red Army.

KOT. I, too, have noticed certain awkward phrases, and I can assure you I have raised the matter. I have spoken about it to General Anders, and he, too, was dissatisfied with certain articles. But you see, neither General Anders nor I have read this paper from cover to cover. I should be grateful if you would give me an extract of those parts of the weekly to which you object, and I shall send them to General Anders, who will issue instructions as to what may and may not be written.

VYSHINSKY. General Anders will receive a letter on this subject, together with an extract, from General Panfilov. So I have no need to give you one. By way of example I cite a few passages, which Mr. Arlet will note down. In the first issue of this newspaper we have an article on the Commander in Chief of the Polish Forces, General Sikorski. In it we read that during the Polish-Russian war General Sikorski, fighting against us, shattered a large number of Bolshevik divisions.

KOT. Of course it's stupid to write about such things now. But I know how it came about. In connection with General Sikorski's visit to Russia an article giving his biography was needed in the very first issue of the periodical, something all ready to hand. The editors simply took an article written some eighteen months or two years ago in France, and reprinted it.

VYSHINSKY. We, too, have journalists who write historical memoirs of this kind and propose that they should be printed. Only we throw their articles into the waste-paper basket. But in the second number is

[1] People's Commissariat for Trade. *Tr.*

an article on Polish participation in the war. In it we read how a brigade was formed under the command of General Szyszko-Bohusz, and how this heroic Polish General was to take it to Finland to fight against us.

KOT. That's not true. The Podhalan [Highland] Brigade was not formed for any such purpose.

VYSHINSKY. If it isn't true, then there is all the less point in writing such things on 14 December 1941 in a journal published for the Polish Army in the U.S.S.R. Yet in the fourth number of this periodical there is a sketch of General Anders' life, telling what a bad time he had in the Lubianka prison. Of course it isn't pleasant to be in the Lubianka, but what is the point of writing about it now for the soldiers under General Anders' command? In the eighth number is an article on the new British uniforms which the Polish Army has received: and lo! The Buzuluk lice are besieging this good British cloth.

I don't want to multiply my examples, but I must state that this periodical is not fulfilling its task satisfactorily. It says nothing about the military successes on the German-Russian front, or the defeats we have inflicted on the German army; it says nothing about the organizational and other aid which indisputably we have given to the formation of the Polish Army in the Soviet Union. The periodical is not serving the spirit of co-operation, and on the Soviet Government's instructions I am empowered to draw your attention to the fact that the weekly *Orzeł Biały* is not appropriate reading for the Polish forces and cannot be reconciled with the brotherhood in arms and spirit of friendliness between the two armies which we should be glad to see. As I have said, General Panfilov will be taking up the matter with General Anders.

KOT. I have no influence over military affairs, but of course I shall do all in my power to ensure that such incidents are not repeated. But please believe me, Polish psychology is very distinctive. These matters must not be treated as if they were written for Russians. Poles like to talk a lot, to chew things over, or to write something in order to relieve their feelings; but that doesn't mean that it is to be taken as indicating their attitude, or that anything serious is likely to come of it.

VYSHINSKY. All the same I ask you to take this statement into consideration. For my part I have dealt with everything for today and must apologize for taking up so much of your time.

. . . .

(The conversation lasted over an hour. The tone was affable on both sides, despite moments of very rapid crosstalk.)

B28. Conversation with A. J. Vyshinsky.
Narcomindiel. 20 February 1942
Present: Novikov and Arlet.

VYSHINSKY. I am troubling you again today unfortunately in regard to two cases of inappropriate action on the part of Polish military authorities. Namely, the commander of the Totskoe garrison has issued a certificate to a Lieutenant Jankowski which, contrary to the law, unsoundly declares that on the basis of a Commissariat of Justice regulation dated 22 June 1941, the Soviet authorities are burdened with obligations of a material nature to the afore-named person.

KOT. On what basis has this certificate been issued and what does it refer to?

VYSHINSKY. That's just it, I would like to know on what basis, since there was no decree or law dated 22 June 1941. That is the date of the outbreak of the Soviet-German war. The certificate states that in view of the fact that Lieutenant Jankowski is serving in the Polish Army his family is entitled to receive support from the Soviet authorities.

KOT. What are the date and number of this certificate, and who signed it?

VYSHINSKY. The certificate is not numbered; it is dated 27 October 1941, the signature is Polish, unfortunately illegible, but above it is the inscription: Commander, Totskoe Garrison.

KOT. Oh, it's a very old story if it dates from October. As you have raised the matter, I take the opportunity to ask what sort of certificate the Polish authorities have to issue to show that a man is serving in the Polish Army.

VYSHINSKY. I'm not questioning that, the certificate can be issued by the chief of staff, the commander, or garrison commander. Here I'm concerned with something else. Both in this case and in another concerning Rifleman Bierul, to which also I am forced to draw your attention, the Polish garrison commander issues a certificate that the Soviet Government is obliged to bear the military burdens connected with the families of Polish soldiers, and this is not in accordance with the correct state of affairs. In addition, the certificate is based on a non-existent law.

KOT. But who signed the second certificate?

VYSHINSKY. Here, too, the signature is illegible.

кот. But when was it issued?

vyshinsky. Also on 27 October 1941.

кот. Well, even if it was so long ago, none the less I shall of course ask our military authorities for an explanation; I hope that such incorrect certificates were not issued later.

vyshinsky. All the same I would like to draw your attention to the circumstance that the certificates are based on a non-existent regulation.

кот. But wasn't there perhaps some other regulation of that date? Perhaps it is simply a mistake, a wrong date, for the intentions were good.

vyshinsky. I don't exclude the possibility of some blunder. But there was no regulation issued on 22 June 1941, which was the very day of the outbreak of war. The garrison commander simply wanted to throw the responsibility on the Soviet Government for expenditures which the army ought to bear itself.

кот. Thank you for informing me of this. As I have said, I shall take up the matter. Now I take advantage of the opportunity to hear from you how the question of assistance for our soldiers' families does stand. I remember that on this issue there were certain joint decisions, probably in the Military Agreement or in one of the joint protocols of the Polish-Soviet Military Commission. Meanwhile our soldiers' families are receiving nothing.

vyshinsky. The Soviet Government undertook only to support the Polish Army. According to the relative decisions, the pay, etc, in the Polish and Soviet armies are equalized, but there is no provision for any obligation to support families. There are detailed provisions for expenditure of various kinds connected with the forces, but not expenditure on families.

кот. Maybe my memory of the matter isn't exact, since I was not expecting to raise the question; but I have read some decision in regard to this with my own eyes, perhaps in one of the protocols. I shall check my documents and then will return to the subject.

vyshinsky. I shall check it at once. (He calls in the secretary, Abramov, who opens a safe in the room and looks for the documents.) But I well remember the text of the Military Agreement. The sum of 300 million roubles provided for maintenance of the army covers various items, but nothing refers to expenditure on families. Here for instance is a note relating to the signed agreement on financing the forces. It says that the forces will be supplied according to the behind the front

ration number three, it also provides for expenditure on fuel for
motive power, accommodation for the staff, and barracks, etc. But
nowhere is there any mention of expenditure on families. So that is
the best proof that the Soviets are under no obligation on this score.
Yet another example: protocol number two of the conference of the
Mixed Polish-Soviet Commission, with Generals Panfilov, Zhukov,
Anders and Bohusz present. Various questions are raised, but not
this. And besides, the Embassy after all has 100 millions for aid to
the civilian population. There cannot be yet further debits on that
account.

KOT. It is difficult for me to discuss this at the moment. I know this
question was raised at conferences; I shall check it in the light of my
documents.

VYSHINSKY. Returning to the question of certificates, I must ask that
this kind of incident should not recur in future.

KOT. You have mentioned the military loan. In view of this I am
forced to inform you that the army is not yet receiving any money
from this loan. On 6 February it received 200,000 [roubles], and that's
the lot, not a kopek more. Meanwhile the money is urgently needed
and they are continually referring to it. For they are now organizing
in a new centre.

VYSHINSKY. This is the first I've heard of it. If you had raised the
subject with me earlier it would undoubtedly have been cleared up
already. For according to point six of the note the sums have to be
paid every month.

KOT. They ought to be paid every month, but nothing was handed
over in January or February. I didn't raise the question with you
because I assumed that certain documents hadn't arrived somewhere,
and that any day, today or tomorrow, our forces would receive the
money due to them.

VYSHINSKY. I don't understand this. The money had to be paid according to the monthly requirements. Perhaps the requirements were
not agreed in time?

KOT. On the contrary. I know everything has been done by the army
to receive the money due to it. They send reminders persistently, but
without result.

VYSHINSKY. This is not in order. Do you happen to know whom the
Polish Command handles this matter with?

KOT. With the Intendancy. With the general who regularly deals
with these matters.

VYSHINSKY. . . . . I shall see to it.

KOT. You remember that when we signed the loan for aid to the civilians I asked you to pay an advance for military purposes before the signing of the second agreement. Even then General Anders was completely without money, for he had received the last quota of several millions in the middle of December. And that's over two months ago.

VYSHINSKY. Yes, I remember. But as we signed the loan a week later I regarded that point as no longer applicable; the signed agreement had to be observed. There is obviously something wrong somewhere and I shall find out what has happened. But what is the position in regard to the transfer of quotas against the civilian loan?

KOT. Exemplary. That's in perfect order. But I would like to ask you to be so good as to look into the following matter. Namely, money transfers sent to our people sometimes for large sums are being held back; for instance, sums sent to Siemipalatinsk and Novosibirsk by telegraph on 31 January have not yet been handed over to the delegates. In Uzbekistan other complications are arising. The money is paid out to the addresses in small quotas, because the post offices haven't the requisite amount at their disposal.

VYSHINSKY. I would like to have details of this. Director Novikov will deal with it.

KOT. I have yet another current issue. . . . Very upsetting information is reaching us from Bokhara. The typhus epidemic has reached alarming dimensions. The numbers falling ill are up to thirty daily. The majority of the staff in my man of trust's office are sick. The man of trust's wife has died, and his deputy too. The Embassy has sent monetary resources, and a little food, soap, and medicines from the Indian consignment. But certain things are indispensable in combating an epidemic, and despite our vigorous endeavours these cannot be obtained on the spot. I refer to disinfectors, anti-typhus serums, and linen. Couldn't the local authorities provide the requisite quantity of these items? That is in the interests not only of our Polish citizens but of the local population.

VYSHINSKY. The Government has already taken the necessary steps. At the end of January we ourselves informed the Embassy that an epidemic is spreading in these areas, mentioning Bokhara *inter alia*. We have sent special sanitary expeditions, led by the Vice-Commissar for Health, Kolesnikov, to these areas to carry on anti-typhus activities.

It is to our common interest to stop the epidemic. Disease is no respecter of citizenship. All are menaced equally.

KOT. Nor do I raise the question for the sake of the exclusive interests of our citizens. But I must emphasize that my citizens' situation is worse, because their organisms are exhausted by their previous experiences and their prolonged starvation, hence the terrible mortality. The disease is spreading not only in Bokhara; the same thing is happening in Chimkent. There our man of trust, Zaleski, has had typhus, and now some of his staff are ill.

VYSHINSKY. The People's Commissariat for Health will direct its attention to this question again.

KOT. Our delegate in Pavlodar, who recently arrived there, reports that 600 Polish citizens incapable of work, the majority of them children and old people, are in a critical state. The local authorities cannot give permission for the allocation of food to them without the agreement of the central authorities.

VYSHINSKY. There is a decision of the Council of People's Commissars, dated 29 January 1942, empowering the Commissariat for Internal Trade, headed by Lubimov, to sell food at government prices to children's homes, shelters for old people, homes for wounded, etc. The competent internal authorities have been sent notification of this. But what is the date of the telegram from the Embassy representative at Pavlodar?

KOT. I think yesterday. But evidently there is a lack of contact between Lubimov and the local authorities in Pavlodar, if they cannot hand over food to the Poles without the permission of the central authorities, although they know the food is necessary.

VYSHINSKY. But that is already laid down. All that is necessary is to agree how many persons are entitled to benefit from the welfare homes, shelters, or dining-rooms, between the Embassy representative and the local authorities, and a corresponding quota will be allotted.

KOT. This has already been done in Pavlodar, where the number entitled to benefit from this form of help has been jointly fixed at 600. The authorities are asking our representative to obtain appropriate instructions from the central authorities through the Embassy.

NOVIKOV. Possibly the Embassy representative applied to the Regional Executive Committee and not to the Regional Department for Trade?

VYSHINSKY. We'll deal with the matter.

KOT. I ask for instructions to be sent by telegraph.

VYSHINSKY. Good. Novikov will see to that.

KOT. Recently the People's Commissariat raised the question of un-organized movements of our people from the Archangel *Oblast*. I have taken up this question and received various reports confirming my argument that the people there are frequently forced to leave, not only by circumstances, but even by the authorities. For instance in Vodopad settlement in Archangel *Oblast* the Narcomvnudiel representative advised 640 Polish citizens to travel to the south. When they replied that they hadn't any money he told them they were to travel free. They were taken to the railway station, but there payment was demanded for the tickets. When a representative of the group went to Archangel to obtain help from our delegate he was arrested for illegal residence. But afterwards he was released and on the delegate's intervention the transport left for the south. A second case: Zoria settlement: the Polish citizens are discharged from work and sent to Akmolinsk. This action was stopped only through the intervention of the Embassy delegate. Kiarnysh settlement: ten Polish families with numerous children were directed to the south. But the transport was stopped at Yemtse station, and as a result many children died. The Slavna forestry centre: although the Polish citizens wanted to remain and work, the authorities refused to allow bread to be sold to fifty-five Polish citizens, gave them a certificate and sent them to Chimkent. The Embassy has a copy of this certificate. In Vologda *Oblast* a transport of Polish citizens, ninety people in all, was held up at the station of Vozhega. Without tickets, without money, without documents, the people were simply thrown out of the station building. Surely something must be done about all this. They cannot be left to their fate. I have received information from my delegate that at least 30,000 Polish citizens can be accommodated on collective farms in Alma Ata, with work in relatively good conditions. Another 20,000 could be accommodated in Frunze *Oblast*.

VYSHINSKY. In the present conditions it is a crime to send people away, to discharge them from work, or force them to travel. I shall take up this question and bring the guilty persons to strict legal account. If you will let me have exact details I'll deal with it. As for the Alma Ata and Frunze *Oblasts*, I have diametrically contrary reports to yours. The authorities are complaining of the excess of poor population, and report that they are not in a position to take any more.

KOT. Our people have already suffered so much that they realize what conditions they will find in any particular place. If the delegate informs me the people can be accommodated we can be sure it corresponds with the reality. No doubt the authorities don't want to have the bother and declare that too many people are arriving. In those same two districts the situation is better than elsewhere. A lot of our people can still be accommodated with work on the collective farms.

VYSHINSKY. As you know, all travel must be stopped now.

KOT. But if someone is already on the road, if they have already been sent away, what is to be done with them?

VYSHINSKY. There are quotas of food, there is the regulation to assist in the organization of aid. To send people on the road today is nothing less than a crime. Those crimes must be brought to judgement. The Embassy can help in holding up these journeys by giving its delegates and men of trust instructions and indications. For there is a shortage of labour everywhere. There is more work than people. As you know, we have even given instructions for our families, our wives and sisters to be mobilized into the factories. Today people are doing physical labour who have never done that sort of work before. Meanwhile there are elements which are daring to say to the toilers: take yourself off to the south. They talk to them of pie in the sky instead of the bread already in their hands.[1] I repeat, it is necessary to organize everything possible on the spot. The local resources have got to be exploited. We for our part will deal with those who are thus deluding the people. They must answer for it.

KOT. But what is to be done with those already on their way? For Tashkent and Chimkent are overloaded. We cannot direct them there. Please indicate regions where there is work; let it be Ufa, or Kuibishev, it doesn't matter; but these people must be assigned a place of residence and labour somewhere if they are not to be driven out blindly.

VYSHINSKY. We must find out how many there are and take the necessary steps.

KOT. That's difficult to do, for the Embassy knows nothing of the majority of those who are travelling. We receive a telegram out of the blue.

VYSHINSKY. We aren't informed of them either. We must investigate this question, jointly collect information and resolve the problem.

KOT. I shall try to see that unorganized journeys are stopped. I have

[1] Literally: Cranes in the sky instead of titmice in their hands. *Tr.*

appointed Mr. Gorszczyk as deputy delegate in Archangel; on his way northward he was to stop in Vologda *Oblast* and organize aid there for our people, or find work for those of them who cannot remain in their present places of work. I think it must be easier to find work in Vologda *Oblast* than in Archangel *Oblast*. Only after he has carried out this task will Gorszczyk travel on to Archangel. But we have serious difficulties with these journeys of all our people.

. . . .

KOT. But now I want to discuss a matter affecting the work of the Embassy, putting it sincerely and frankly, how it seems to us. I must complain of director Molochkov, who a few days ago informed an Embassy representative that Narcomindiel plans to restrict the number of Embassy workers, on the ground that there are allegedly too many. The statement that we have an excess of Embassy personnel is a fairy tale. The staff is too small in relation to our actual needs. We receive about 1000 letters and 100 telegrams daily, and we have only a few people to handle all this correspondence. The actual state of the Embassy staff is as follows: diplomatic officials, twelve; non-diplomatic officials, thirty-three; total, forty-five. In the attachés' departments there are four officers with diplomatic rights, and four other officials: total, eight. Servants: eleven. To ensure the proper functioning of the office I need at least another thirty-five workers and six attaché workers. To meet this number of workers and employees we need at least twenty-six servants. Please also bear in mind that by recruiting personnel fresh from prisons and camps I take on people physically exhausted. We constantly have about ten people on the sick list. Finally, I cannot refuse to take into the Embassy people who are not members of the staff, but who must rest here after their hard experiences. I cannot refuse them a roof over their heads, and food, as well as permission to remain in a homely atmosphere for at least a time.

My request is in the direction of asking you to agree to the Embassy having such staff as is necessary within reasonable limits for the performance of its functions. The Search Department, for instance, alone requires a large number. The British have no citizens here at all, but their staff is larger than ours, without counting the military mission, and they have one servant for every two members of their Embassy. We make no claim to be served as well as the British; but after all, someone must work in the kitchen and on the domestic side. We have quite different tasks from Norway and Turkey. How many citizens have those states got in Russia?

VYSHINSKY. Molochkov didn't act on his own initiative, but on my instructions. And I shall explain to you at once the reason for our attitude.

KOT (jokingly). So I have to complain of Minister Vyshinsky to Commissar Vyshinsky. That's a good one.

VYSHINSKY. That's exactly it. Of course there can be no suggestion of comparing the scope of activity of the Polish Embassy with that of the Norwegian or Turkish Embassy. There are only three Turks in the Soviet Union: the Ambassador, his deputy, and his secretary. Nor have we any Norwegians. But certain standards do exist. The staff of the average Legation or Embassy amounts more or less to fifteen. The number employed in the Polish Embassy departs very considerably from this standard. What you said about the difficult conditions of residence and work in the Embassy only confirms our attitude. Life in Kuibishev also is not easy. We cannot allow the Polish Embassy staff to increase to enormous figures.

KOT. Mr. Commissar, we live very modestly, in exceptionally difficult conditions. We live rather a barrack life, but I do ask you to help us carry out the task for which we are here.

VYSHINSKY. It might seem that providing for the diplomatic corps is an easy matter. Meanwhile, with over 1,000 persons belonging to embassies and legations, and the very difficult transport conditions, this is a difficult problem. I cannot change our attitude. Especially as the Embassy work is not concentrated only here on the spot. No other Embassy has so many co-workers. Part of the work must fall on the delegations which have been set up in agreement with us. It would be very difficult to enlarge the personnel further.

KOT. So far as the delegates are concerned, they are completely absorbed in work on the spot and are no relief whatever to the Embassy. From the aspect of the Soviet authorities' interests this local activity of theirs is very beneficial. The delegations cause increased work for the Embassy, because they turn to us to settle a number of issues with the central authorities. In addition certain people should pass through a kind of stage in the Embassy before leaving for abroad or to go to provincial localities; they need a rest in good conditions.

VYSHINSKY. I have investigated this problem in great detail. I cannot and I don't wish to enter into the Embassy's internal affairs, but, looking at this problem from outside, I must ask you to have regard to our point of view.

кот. I know there are difficulties with the Diplomatic Corps, but we shall not increase them. We have special tasks here and spheres of work such as no other diplomatic resorts have. I must have people for our radio broadcasts; our periodical *Polska* must have personnel; the money we have received from you must not only be wisely distributed and handed out, but exactly accounted for. Please take all this into consideration.

vyshinsky. At the moment I cannot change the decision.

. . . .

B29. Conversation with A. J. Vyshinsky.
Narcomindiel. 6 March 1942
Present: Novikov and Arlet.

vyshinsky. I am again compelled to trouble you on a not very pleasant matter. On 14 February the chief of staff of one of the Polish divisions, Colonel Gielgud, sent the chairman of the District Executive Committee in Kermin a letter which reads as follows. (He hands the text to Arlet, who translates it.)

'Please set to work immediately to rebuild the wooden bridge on the high road from the railway station to the town of Kermin, prepare and transport gravel from the river Zeravshan for repairing the road, repair all the wooden bridges on the high road from Kermin to Kenimekh and set up road signs. Instruct the Soviet Farm to put the road Kermin-Napai which is in its charge into perfect order by 20 February, and the Town Soviet to put in order the section of street from October Street to the bakery, and to put the bakery in order within three days. Failure to carry out this present instruction will involve you in material and criminal responsibility for any possible accidents and for damage to motors during the war to the detriment of the Seventh Polish Motorized Infantry Division.'

The contents of this letter, as well as its form, are absolutely impermissible. I am instructed to inform you that the Soviet authorities have been issued an instruction that if they receive this kind of letter from commanders of Polish forces it is to be returned without further consideration. For that matter not only the chief of staff of the Polish division in Kermin but its commander, General Szyszko-Bohusz also, has acted incorrectly, since they have occupied the school at Kermin station as a military hospital, without the agreement of the competent authorities. This, too, is a quite impermissible act, and I bring it to your notice.

KOT. Are there any liaisons, any Soviet officers attached to the division in Kermin and to our divisions generally, through whom the divisional commander and his staff have to deal with the local authorities?

VYSHINSKY. Colonel Volkovyski is attached to the Polish Army command for liaison with the Soviet authorities.

KOT. Yes, that's true, but Colonel Volkovyski is in Yangi-Yul. To report to the Command on small local matters, so that it may raise the issues with Colonel Volkovyski, and he in turn to raise them with the Soviet authorities would lead to every question being dragged out, it would be necessary to wait terribly long for a result. I don't suppose even the Soviet authorities would wish Colonel Volkovyski to be referred to over every hole in a bridge or a road; that would be absurd.

VYSHINSKY. That's not the point. Of course the division can raise questions with the local authorities, but not in this form.

KOT. I would like to clear up this matter completely, so as to avoid misunderstandings. So the military authorities can turn direct to local instances?

VYSHINSKY. Of course they can, but note the impermissible form in which this is done. 'I order, I command at once, for non-performance', 'material and criminal responsibility', and the preclusive terminal dates. All this is impossible.

KOT. I must take it up with the military authorities.

VYSHINSKY. Letters of this sort are quite impermissible. It goes without saying that over small issues it is necessary to communicate directly with the local administrations, but in proper form, without usurping authority which is not possessed.

KOT. I certainly would never have written such a letter. Yet this letter from our forces to the authorities in Kermin could have been dictated by genuine anxiety for the condition of military equipment and a desire to get the matter settled quickly. Of course I shall take it up with the Command. But our tragedy is that since General Anders' departure from Buzuluk we have lost contact with him. It can't be helped, but it isn't even convenient to clear everything up by telegrams. Meanwhile we have insuperable difficulties in sending him mail by special messengers. We have to wait up to two weeks and to plead for a place in a train. You might do something about that.

VYSHINSKY. We can assure a place in a train on three days' notice.

KOT. I'd be very grateful for your help on this question. It is of importance to me that this kind of misunderstanding should not occur again, but in order to avoid them we must have contact.

VYSHINSKY. It is important for us too. The Polish Military Authorities must understand that the Soviet authorities are not abolished the moment they [the Poles] arrive in any spot and as the result of their arrival.

KOT. I share your view, but it is necessary, too, to reckon with the circumstance that the local authorities are not accustomed to the fact that a different army is in their districts. Our soldiers tell one another: if we were a Soviet division everything would be done for us at once. And so, after possibly an ineffectual appeal to the local authorities on questions they haven't settled, they wrote this letter thinking it would have its effect.

VYSHINSKY. But the effect is diametrically opposite to that intended.

KOT. I should be greatly obliged to you if you would facilitate my contacts with the Command of the Polish Armed Forces.

VYSHINSKY. I hope I shall be able to do that. I have an agreement with the Kuibishev railway administration that on three days' notice I can obtain several places for any part. Of course, provided nothing unexpected happens and provided the train goes at all.

KOT. Since General Anders' departure I haven't had a single courier from Yangi-Yul. Nor have I received three numbers of the *Orzeł Biały*. I have asked for explanations on the questions you've already raised with me, but so far I cannot come back to you with them because I haven't had any answer. Buzuluk was close, so the contact was more convenient.

VYSHINSKY. I shall find out just what are the difficulties in regard to travelling, and I shall try to help you.

Although at first the conversation was not too friendly, it was carried on by both parties in an affable and calm tone.

> *B30A. Conversation with Vice-Commissar A. J. Vyshinsky. Narcomindiel. 24 March 1942*
> Present: Novikov; Embassy secretaries A. Mniszek and W. Arlet.

KOT. I have brought Mr. Kwapinski, a minister member of the Polish Government, with me to introduce him officially before his departure for London. Mr. Kwapinski, President of the City of Łódz, was of

late the Embassy delegate in Tashkent. In his place I have nominated
Professor Heitzman, so there should be no interruption in the work
of caring for our people.

VYSHINSKY. I know, I know; I am acquainted with Professor Heitzman.

KOT. Mr. Kwapinski is a sincere advocate of Polish-Soviet co-
operation, and in London he will effectually oppose all the tendencies
fighting against our understanding.

VYSHINSKY. That's very good.

. . . .

Kwapinski takes very cordial leave of Vyshinsky, who shakes his
hand several times in a friendly fashion and wishes him a good journey.

B30B. Conversation with Vice-Commissar A. J. Vyshinsky.
Novikov and Arlet present.

After Kwapinski's departure together with Mniszek:

KOT. Despite the late hour I am compelled to trouble you with one
quite fundamental question and two minor ones. I am disturbed by
the way the problem of the Polish Army in the U.S.S.R. is developing. Both General Sikorski and the Polish Government, and I personally would most ardently desire to see the Polish Army now being
organized in the Soviet Union as large and powerful as possible. After
General Sikorski's conversation with President Stalin it seemed that
nothing stood in the way of our army becoming a real force which
might influence the course of military operations, that the Polish
soldiers could take part in as large numbers as possible in the struggle
against Germany, and that the blood shed in common would
strengthen the bonds of friendship between the two nations and would
constitute a foundation for the future historic development of their
co-existence. General Anders has told me of his recent conversations
in Moscow and the decision which has been taken to send abroad
any excess of troops over 44,000. He also informed me of the motives
causing these decisions. I am not called upon to evaluate those motives.
In view of General Sikorski's absence from London and the difficulties
in the way of discussing matters with him I cannot adopt any final
attitude on the question, and possibly I shall return to it. Today I
must confine myself to expressing, in the name of the Polish Government, our regret and sorrow that despite the will of that Government,
and not at all on its initiative, the development of the Polish Armed
Forces in the U.S.S.R. has taken this turn.

VYSHINSKY. Undoubtedly you are aware of the reasons for the situation which has arisen. Undoubtedly also you know that those reasons do not depend on us. The development of military events has made supplying the army with food one of our most difficult tasks. We had an assurance from parties abroad, chiefly the United States, that we would receive very important quantities of food, and above all grain, from abroad. Because of the United States' entry into the war these supplies have not reached us even to a small extent. You know that the main task in this sphere must be to provision the active fighting army. In my view the evacuation of part of the Polish forces will not modify the basic conception of joint struggle against German fascism. The number of Polish soldiers will be reduced, but qualitatively there will be no change, they will fight with us for the common cause. That was the first element of the problem, but there is also a second factor.

I personally have the impression that when our army approaches the frontiers of Poland not only will those 44,000 who are remaining with us be able to take active part in the war, but maybe also those thousands of Polish soldiers and officers who are being organized abroad will return to our front. The nearest road to Poland leads through the U.S.S.R. . . . . Although today America and Great Britain are suffering serious military failures, I regard them as temporary. And yet, although I believe in their success in the future, I am profoundly convinced that the road to Poland leads inevitably through our frontiers, and that the Polish forces will enter Poland together with our army. Mr. Stalin and General Anders have established all the details of the evacuation. I repeat, this change cannot affect the basic problem of Soviet-Polish co-operation. That is all I can say in reply to your statement.

KOT. The arguments put forward by President Stalin, and repeated by you, are known to us, nor is it a question of their evaluation, but of the fact that because of this evacuation the army will not constitute a genuine force at the front; that part which remains here will be rather only a political demonstration.

VYSHINSKY (assents).

KOT. President Stalin has agreed to a swift evacuation, because the quantity of food rations is to be reduced on 1 April. Every day of lost time causes complications, and so may lead to the emergence of serious difficulties. According to the plan, the first detachments are to leave Krasnovodsk already on 26 March. The British cannot prepare for their adequate reception and provisioning until the Soviet Ambassador in Teheran receives instructions and a plenipotentiary from the Red Army is appointed to handle evacuation questions on Persian soil.

VYSHINSKY. . . . . I have personally confirmed that the Narcomindiel instructions have been sent by telegraph to Smirnov, the Soviet Ambassador in Teheran, and to the Soviet Consul-general in Pahlevi on 22 March at six a.m.

KOT. As late as yesterday those instructions had not yet arrived. Nor do we know who has been appointed by the Red Army as plenipotentiary in Iran territory to settle the various petty difficulties which may arise, so that the central authorities don't have to be bothered with them. He would correspond to General Zhukov, who is handling it all in Russia.

VYSHINSKY. I only know that various instructions have been issued. I have not gone into the details. In view of this I cannot give you the name you ask for. Smirnov must have received the instructions of 22 March, but if in fact they were not to hand in Pahlevi yesterday I can only explain it as due to some technical liaison defect.

. . . .

KOT. If the British should not happen to get food supplies to Krasnovodsk in time, this would react on the course of the evacuation; the soldiers would be travelling hungry, it would leave a negative impression, and that can be avoided.

VYSHINSKY. Food should arrive at Pahlevi in time.

KOT. The food to be supplied by the British has to be transported to Krasnovodsk.

NOVIKOV. In Krasnovodsk we feed the troops; they will also get food rations from us for the journey, after they have gone on board.

VYSHINSKY. So far as I know, the British are to supply the food only from Pahlevi.

KOT. But the Soviet authorities themselves have demanded that the British shall transport 27,000 rations to Krasnovodsk. Meanwhile, down to yesterday, owing to the lack of instructions they could not start to deal with it.

VYSHINSKY. The instructions have been issued. The promise has been given that British and Polish officers will arrive in Pahlevi to prepare everything necessary to the evacuation.

KOT. Thank you. Now quite a different issue, of a comparatively small nature. You remember the Soviet Government once met the

Polish people halfway by allowing them to celebrate Christmas. Now. . . .

VYSHINSKY. Ah yes, I know: prosecutions for absenteeism.

KOT. Now Easter is coming. After Christmas that is the second most important festival in Polish life. For Christians it comes this year on 5 and 6 April, and for Jews on 2 and 3 April. I would ask the Soviet Government to show its good will on this occasion also and issue the appropriate instruction.

VYSHINSKY (favourably). I'll put the matter to the Government. There is certainly a precedent in Christmas.

KOT. Finally, a second, more important question. General Anders has asked me whether I could delegate General Wolikowski to Moscow for the Slavonic meeting. In doing so he indicated that General Panfilov had made this proposal, and that Panfilov indicated he was making it in the name of the Soviet Government. This is a political issue, and General Anders referred it to me. I confess I am in some difficulty, for I know nothing of this meeting, what sort of function it will be, and who is organizing it, or who is taking part in it, nor whether anyone apart from General Wolikowski is to act in the name of Poles. I would be grateful for an explanation of this question, which no one has raised with me before. If it is to be a show of Slavonic co-operation we should like to take part in it; but I must know the details, what decisions and resolutions will be proposed.

VYSHINSKY. I shall have to find out, for I don't know the details. But as the meeting is to take place in Moscow, and is being organized by us, one can be sure that it will not be detrimental to those taking part. The same applies to the question whether other Poles are taking part in it, or only those sent from the Embassy. I think the organizers of the congress cannot be bound by that sort of restriction. One can be sure, on the other hand, that participation will be a positive contribution to solid Slavonic co-operation, and no discord will arise. The object of the Slavonic Congress is to demonstrate the joint Slavonic struggle against German fascism. Anyone who has taken that road can and should take part in the congress. For that matter, one congress of this nature has already been held.

KOT. So far as non-Polish citizens are concerned obviously that point of view is sound. So far as Polish citizens are concerned, I could not agree with it.

VYSHINSKY. These meetings are not organized officially. It is difficult to restrict participation in them only to particular nationalities, or citizens of a given state; for there can be Polish citizens who are not Polish and Poles who are Soviet citizens.

KOT. I quite agree. Only it should be clearly stated who represents whom, in order that such a meeting should not have unfavourable repercussions in occupied Poland [to the effect] that someone is taking part as representative of the Polish nation who doesn't represent it at all. Try to imagine that this kind of show was organized somewhere abroad, in an allied country, and that people were invited to it as Russian representatives with whom the Soviet Embassy has and could have nothing in common. That would undoubtedly be of interest to you and the Embassy!

VYSHINSKY. . . . . I shall have a word with Lozovsky, though I can state in advance that the people taking part in this meeting simply represent themselves.

KOT. I shall be grateful to have the question cleared up, for I would like to avoid possible unfavourable reactions in Poland.

NOVIKOV. One thing isn't clear. What is the point in this question of holidays for Jews? What is this date: 2 and 3 April?

KOT. It concerns Polish citizens of Jewish nationality.

VYSHINSKY. Well, if it is a matter of persons of Jewish nationality who were living in the territory of Western Ukraine or Western Bielorussia on 2 November 1939, they are Soviet citizens, in accordance with our note of 1 December 1941.

KOT. I here, as Polish Ambassador, represent all Polish citizens. We make no distinction between Jews and non-Jews. When I ask for a holiday for Christians, I must also ask the same for Polish citizens of the Moses confession.

VYSHINSKY. So far as Poles are concerned there is a precedent in the Christmas holiday. As for the Jews, the issue is complicated by this question of citizenship.

KOT (laughing). But I couldn't ask for Christmas holidays for the Jews, who don't recognize that holiday. If you admit the possibility that Polish Jewish citizens exist, then I am asking for a holiday precisely for them.

VYSHINSKY. This question is complicated by the problem of citizenship; it would be better to have these holidays without the Jews.

KOT. I'm sorry, but here I represent all Polish citizens.

After Kwapinski's departure the conversation lasted half an hour. The mood was calm, the tone friendly.

A125. Cable to Polish Embassy in Washington.
13 March 1942

In regard to Dr. Rajchman's advice concerning Dr. Wroczynski I have to report that unfortunately he is among the prisoners of war of whom so far we have no trace.[1]

Last month on General Anders' instruction Josef Czapski travelled to the Narcomvnudiel in Moscow with a memorandum on the fate of 8,300 officers carried off in April 1940 from Starobielsk, Kozielsk, and Ostashkov, concerning whom all news has been lost. However, traces of them lead to the mines on the Franz Joseph Land islands, Novaya Ziemlia and the shores of northern Siberia. No answer whatever was given.

We need to obtain confirmation whether and if so where they are living, and whether we can send them at least medicine by aeroplanes. Among the twelve generals are Stanislaw Haller, Skuratowicz, Orlik-Lukowski, Plisowski, Smorawinski, and others.

About 100 colonels, about 150 lieutenant-colonels, etc. Also the military [religious] heads of all denominations: Father Wojtiniak among the Catholics, Rabbi Steinberg of the Jewish persuasion, and several pastors.

It would be desirable to inform the appropriate authorities confidentially of their tragic fate and the failure so far to release those who are still alive. We are afraid that the few who survive will be skeletons.

A133. Cable to Minister for Foreign Affairs.
22 March 1942

All the attempts to have Alter and Ehrlich released have come to nothing. Narcomindiel has now replied in a manner that renders it difficult to carry on the argument further, [saying] they are citizens of the U.S.S.R. in the sense of the Soviet thesis concerning the citizenship of national minorities. Of course, as a matter of principle the Embassy will continue to intervene; but the present situation does not allow us to count on a satisfactory settlement of the question without decided pressure from outside.

KOT.

---

[1] Ambassador Ciechanowski had passed on to us Dr. Ludwik Rajchman's good advice to entrust the supply of medicines to the Polish people to Dr. Wroczynski [a Katyn victim. Tr.]

R

A138. Cable to General Sikorski.
Kuibishev. 25 March 1942

The question of Polish citizens deprived of their liberty in the U.S.S.R.

To this date the Soviet Government have not carried out their obligations of 30 July 1941. The Embassy possesses lists of names of some 2,000 persons who, despite the Embassy intervention giving the exact places of their detention (prisons, and in certain cases even the number of the cell, or else camps, with indications of the so-called sections and camp points) have not yet been released. Five to ten thousand Polish citizens, to a large extent of non-Polish nationality, still remain in prisons and camps known to the Embassy.

Still more serious is the problem of individuals of whom all we know is that they were arrested in Poland and carried off into the heart of the U.S.S.R., but whose present fate and places of stay are still unknown. Among them frequently figure the names of very eminent persons: priests, political and social workers, the presidents and burgomasters of eastern [provincial] towns, higher officials of general and institutional administrations, public prosecutors, officers and junior officers of the police force, industrialists, landowners, etc. Their presence has not been signalled in any of the places of imprisonment (prisons and camps) known to the Embassy, from which, however, the ' amnestied' Poles are slowly being released.

The fate of these persons, who can be approximately estimated as from a dozen to several dozen thousand, remains unknown; this also applies to the fate of the 15,000 prisoners of war in Starobielsk, Kozielsk, and Ostashkov, among whom are 8,300 officers.

Being unable to assume that some 50,000 persons have been lost in the course of two years, or have died in prisons and camps, one must assume that they are concealed in camps situated in the far north and difficult of access, or in the strictly isolated political prisons (the so-called ' political isolators ') from which prisoners are never released, and which no information concerning the ' amnesty' and the releases has reached.

A149. Cable to Minister for Foreign Affairs.
Kuibishev. 10 April 1942

About midnight of Thursday-Friday the militia carried out a search to check the personal documents in quarters belonging to the Embassy, but situated outside its building. In the rental contract it figures as rented ' for accommodation of a Polish newspaper ', so it does not possess extra-territoriality. The quarters are used for the accommodation of lower officials of the Embassy and Polish citizens passing through Kuibishev.

During the search the communist Burg-Piwowarczyk was arrested. He was spending the night there before travelling on to the Polish Army, to which he had reported as a volunteer and had been accepted by the Military Mission.

Although ex-territoriality has not been violated, to search quarters belonging to the Embassy is an unfriendly act, as also is the arrest there of a Pole, whose Polish citizenship the Soviet side will undoubtedly question. Piwowarczyk's role is ambiguous, there is the possibility that he is a *provocateur*. I am intervening with the Chief of Protocol in the Narcomindiel.

KOT.

A168. Cable to General Sikorski.
8 May 1942

On 7 May I met Ambassador Clark Kerr, whom I informed that in May two years will have passed since the mysterious disappearance of 8,000 Polish officers. In view of the oncoming summer we must again intervene, since communications conditions allow of bringing people back from the far north. I expressed the hope that the Ambassador would not refuse to support us, just as in November Ambassador Cripps of his own accord took action in regard to the unreleased civilians, acting on the basis that the British Ambassador is a guarantee of impartiality.

Ambassador Kerr took a friendly attitude to this initiative, but obviously he has to communicate with his government. I ask for firm support on this issue. Kerr put forward the idea of sending a letter to Stalin on the matter. I indicated in my reply that for our part we have written enough about it, but if he writes obviously we shall agree.

As for the proposal to set up a mixed Polish-Soviet commission to investigate the camps, in the conditions here this idea is hopeless, though it would be sound in cultural conditions.

A173. Cable to the Polish Consulate in Jerusalem.
Kuibishev. 19 May 1942

Let the [Zionist] Revisionists get information from Beigin or Szeskin who have reached Teheran. The levy commissions were exclusively Soviet in the field with a Polish delegate present, and on the spot

rejected Jews, often tracing their heredity back to the grandmother
or examining for circumcision. A second examination took place in
our army, where the Narcomvnudiel delegate watched, and even
those Jews who had been passed in the field were rejected. The same
applied to Ukrainians, and Bielorussians. Even so a large number of
Jews were smuggled through under false names. While forbidding
us to accept Jews, the Soviets simultaneously spread through their
agents among the Jews the story that they were doing this on the
demand of the Polish authorities.

. . . .

> #### B31. Conversation with Vice-Commissar A. J. Vyshinsky.
> #### Narcomindiel. 31 May 1942
> Present: Mr. Valerian Zorin and Embassy secretary
> A. Mniszek.

VYSHINSKY. Mr. Ambassador, I have taken it on myself to trouble
you with two unpleasant questions.

KOT (interrupting). I would prefer any unpleasant questions to be
discussed after I have gone.

VYSHINSKY. Why do you want to go? We don't want you to go at all.

The first unpleasant question concerns the activity of Mr. Rola-
Janicki, an Embassy attaché (he emphasizes the word attaché) who in
his quality as Embassy delegate has undertaken activity hostile to the
Soviet Union. Consequently he should leave the U.S.S.R. at once.[1]

KOT (interrupts Vyshinsky, and a friendly exchange of opinions
develops on general Polish-Soviet political relations, with the
Rola-Janicki case as background). I share your view entirely. Immediately I received information of Mr. Rola-Janicki's activities I
myself decided that he cannot continue to perform his duties and
must leave the Soviet Union. You will remember I warned you that I
don't personally know the majority of our delegates, and that it was
not possible in so short a time to fill the posts with a staff of officials
for whom we can take full responsibility. That takes a long time. We
must get to know the people. I have talked to Mr. Rola-Janicki only
once in my life. He was reclaimed from the army because of his
knowledge of Russian. . . . After all, we don't need to collect
information concerning the internal life of the U.S.S.R.; that is a
useless and detrimental task. As soon as I was informed of the reports

---

[1] Rola-Janicki, embassy delegate at Aktiubinsk, left his document case behind in the
Narcomvnudiel hotel in Kuibishev. In it the Soviet authorities found not only reports on
the situation of Poles in his area but material on internal Soviet conditions. Tr.

Mr. Janicki had sent in I decided to recall him and empowered Mr. Freyd, an Embassy secretary, to communicate the foregoing to the People's Commissariat for Foreign Affairs, which he did on 29 May. I am intending to replace several delegates who are not suitable. I think it ridiculous that stupid details of this kind should spoil relations between Poland and the Soviet Union. For these relations must be friendly at their basis. I view their development in the perspective of thirty years and farther.

VYSHINSKY. I agree with you. Our relations must be friendly.

KOT. We must educate the present-day generation in this spirit, since this is a problem enjoined by the necessities of both our states. So far as Mr. Rola-Janicki is concerned, he will leave the U.S.S.R. immediately the transit visa formalities are settled. Before my departure and in connection with the changes of delegates I am planning, I would like to bring in a number of suitable people from abroad, and I ask your help in this.

VYSHINSKY. But there are so many Polish citizens already here.

KOT. Of course I'd like to fill the posts on the spot with the people here at present, but that is the more difficult since, as experience has proved, these people are worn out, sick. In any case, before appointing them I must get to know them, must have something in the nature of a session with them. I anticipate their staying on these lines in Kuibishev for a couple of weeks, and, as you know, we come up against a number of difficulties in bringing Polish citizens to Kuibishev. It is a paradoxical phenomenon that out of every two to three Polish citizens summoned here by the Embassy, on the average hardly any arrive, or they arrive after great delay; while on the other hand every day some thirty Polish citizens turn up in Kuibishev who have arrived illegally so far as the Soviet authorities are concerned, and often unnecessarily, so far as we are concerned. They have to be accommodated and fed. For instance, today there are some forty Polish citizens in the Embassy yard who have made their way to Kuibishev. I ask for your aid to bring in Polish citizens whom the Embassy has officially sent for.

VYSHINSKY. The difficulties in obtaining permits for through travel sometimes arise from the restrictions which have been introduced as the result of the war. The Narcomindiel for its part does everything possible to remove those difficulties.

MNISZEK. If you would allow me, we would ask for instructions to be issued to the Kuibishev militia to the effect that Polish citizens who get to Kuibishev, after reporting to the militia should be given permits to travel to the places of their permanent residence. In that way we would avoid overcrowding the Embassy.

Vyshinsky notes the suggestion and expresses his agreement.

VYSHINSKY. Now for the second unpleasant business. On the basis of materials in our possession, which I have myself read through, we have learnt that an illegal organization, making use of secret signs, is functioning on the territory of the Soviet Union and is occupied in the transport of correspondence. It must be liquidated.

KOT (interrupting). Mr. Chairman, at one time during the period when we were sending the first delegates out to the localities, there were plans for organizing a postal service between the Embassy and the delegations. I was even shown such a plan. I said it was to be destroyed at once, and flatly refused to agree to its being put into operation. Evidently, unfortunately my instructions have not been carried out, and this plan is still in existence. When the delegates send letters or reports they do so through Polish citizens who happen to be travelling to Kuibishev. The only code which has been introduced in the Embassy is the numeration of telegrams between the Embassy and the delegations. This has been done because certain telegrams don't reach the addressees, they are often confiscated *en route*. By numbering the telegrams we have exact control over them and can demand the repeat of those lost.

VYSHINSKY. Of course we have nothing against that. But I would like yet again to emphasize that if anyone is detained with this kind of correspondence, or with a packet suspiciously concealed and furnished with secret signs, or identifiable by agreed signs, he will be arrested at once and brought to trial.

KOT. Before my departure I would like to have a longer conversation with you, so that we can discuss a number of current and important questions. Would you have time tomorrow or the day after?

VYSHINSKY. I am very busy tomorrow. If you don't mind we'll meet the day after tomorrow at three p.m.

KOT. Agreed.

At the moment of their taking leave, while both were standing there was a further moment of conversation in a spirit of cordial good-will. Vyshinsky emphasized the superfluity of the kind of understanding of the delegates' role shown by Rola-Janicki, since after all we are allies and both the Polish and the Soviet forces can recipro-cally and on official ground exchange information of interest to both

Governments. For that matter, the best proof of this collaboration was General Sikorski's agreement to delegate a higher Polish officer to the Soviet staff, and this officer was co-operating closely with the staff.

The Ambassador paid some compliments to Zorin, stressing his special knowledge of Polish affairs and saying jokingly that sometimes he knew them even too well.

The conversation was conducted in a friendly tone, and lasted about twenty minutes. Both Vyshinsky and the Ambassador, but especially Vyshinsky, stressed the necessity for friendly Polish-Soviet relations at the present time and in the future.

B32. Conversation with A. J. Vyshinsky.
Narcomindiel. 2 June 1942
Present: Valerian Zorin and W. Arlet.

кот. I haven't had a talk with you about our affairs for over two months; so today I have come to trouble you with many current issues. Maybe I shan't even be able to deal with them all thoroughly today.

. . . . [1]

кот. And now a third important matter: the organization of religious care for Polish citizens in the Soviet Union. This is a very important problem which ought to have been settled long since. I think this is a politically suitable moment for us to institute pastoral oversight of our citizens. When I had the opportunity of talking with you in Moscow on this question you proposed that I should hand you a definite plan. In November last year Mr. Bogomolov told Premier Sikorski that Polish citizens can enjoy complete religious freedom. Statements and declarations to the same effect have also been made on other occasions. I remind you of the General's conversation with you in December last year.

. . . .

I am not a specialist on these matters and only now, owing to Bishop Gawlina's visit to the U.S.S.R., have we worked out a joint plan for solving the problem; it is contained in this short draft which I now give you. This is a minimal plan, extremely modest. (The interpreter reads the text.) At every step it takes account of the binding Soviet laws, since its basis is the creation of appropriate spiritual oversight of Poles without causing any difficulty or complication what-

---

[1] Here two or three paragraphs were devoted to the Polish underground press and its reactions to Polish-Soviet relations, etc. *Tr.*

ever for the Soviet authorities. The most difficult problem is undoubtedly that of the number of priests. If we attempted to assure our citizens pastoral oversight on the scale which existed in Poland we should need a thousand priests. We realize that it is impossible to bring in such a number, and have taken only ten per cent of the figure. After the most scrupulous calculations . . . of the localities in which they would have to work we find we need 105 pastors. Eleven of our priests are already at work in a number of localities, not taking military chaplains into account; they perform their functions more or less privately. But if we include these eleven in the total we still need ninety-four priests. I would like to hand you a list of fifty Polish Catholic priests who have not yet been released from prisons and work camps.

VYSHINSKY. We have one such list already.

KOT. But this one has been corrected. Our previous intervention related to fifty-seven priests. But then we learned that certain of them had died. This list is absolutely realistic. And so, in order to bring the number up to the necessary requirements, we need another ninety-four. If you let us have the fifty you're still holding in prison, there are two ways of making up the number we still require. And at this point I would like to hear [the view] and eventually have the help of the Soviet Government, either by its allowing us to utilize the priests who must still be here, to the number of about 100, for pastoral work, or else by allowing us to bring in the requisite number from abroad It is true that a number of priests who had been deported from Poland were released during last autumn and winter, but the army has absorbed them all. According to military regulations a large number of chaplains is required in certain units, and some twenty priests went with the troops evacuated to Persia. I don't raise the question of Protestant clergy today because so far no Protestant group has come to light. As for the Jews, I know that in a number of the localities synagogues already exist, to which they can resort, so their problem is not such a burning one; though I reserve the right to return to these questions and to make definite proposals in regard to them also.

Finally, I wish to draw your attention to the great increase in religious feeling among the masses of Poles in the Soviet Union. The hard experiences of recent years have influenced even many who formerly were indifferent to religion or showed no great interest in it to turn to it and demand the organization of spiritual oversight. It is in the interests both of the Polish citizens and of good Polish-

Soviet relations that these questions should be considered and decided favourably, along the lines of our plan.

This second list which I hand you gives the localities where we would like to place our priests. You will see that the distances between the localities are so great that no one priest could serve them. And so we really have restricted our requirements to the absolute minimum.

VYSHINSKY. The plan you have given me is by no means so simple as it might appear at first sight. It raises quite a number of highly important reservations and difficulties. Undoubtedly the Government will state its position on the matter, but I wish at once to clear up certain questions. It is true that in November 1941 Bogomolov had a talk with General Sikorski on these questions; so far as I remember he informed him at that time that the same conditions and rights to satisfy their religious needs were extended to the Catholic citizens of Poland as are enjoyed by all the citizens of the Soviet Union under the Stalin Constitution. What are those rights? Soviet citizens and, since Bogomolov's statement Polish citizens also, can form religious groups and on the basis of agreements with the Town Soviets can obtain accommodation for the performance of religious rites. In the Soviet Union the church is separate from the state, which has no possibility or legal right to support any religious group. In view of this the Soviet Government cannot undertake any obligations to support the religious life of Polish citizens. I am not prejudging what will be the final answer on the question, I merely cite the fundamental difficulties.

But what can the Government do in a country where the church is separate from the state? After all, our Russian Orthodox citizens also have their religious requirements and needs, and we don't give them any help, nor do we interfere in their religious questions in any way. If the issue is to be decided as the Embassy proposes it will be necessary to provide special facilities to all confessions. You have mentioned the Protestants. But there are more Soviet than Polish Protestants. All the confessions would start to send in similar demands—the Muslims and members of the Armenian Gregorian rite, and all the others. They would all appeal to the fact that the Soviet Government had given special help to the Poles. All these problems are very closely bound together, and in no case can I admit that they would be simple or easy to settle. I think that Polish citizens can organize their own religious life without any special decisions from the Government, which are impossible, but simply on the basis of the normal Soviet legislation and agreements with the Town Soviets. Where does the Government come in here, and possibly even the Supreme Soviet? Why are resolutions necessary? So long as no one puts any difficulties in the way of Poles taking advantage of the legally guaranteed religious freedoms Government instances have no cause to interfere at all. One of the points of the plan speaks of tax reliefs for Polish Catholic citizens. They would immediately provoke justified discontent among the other denominations, who don't enjoy such reliefs.

I shall not conceal from you that, unlike the growth of religious feeling among the Polish citizens, which you have mentioned, during the twenty-five years of the Soviet régime religious interest has dropped immeasurably among our population. No one wants to study to be a priest, the youth are not interested in it; they prefer to be educated as agronomists, or lately for instance as ' tankists ', whom we badly need.

You have spoken of bringing in priests from abroad. The Russian Orthodox also would gladly see clergy of their denomination coming into the Soviet Union, where there are now so few. For instance, they could bring in Russian Orthodox priests, knowing our language, from Bulgaria. And there are many Russian Orthodox clergy in the United States; in New York there is even a Russian Orthodox bishop, a respected, decent patriarch who is even organizing prayers for the success of the Soviet arms. But this has no meaning whatever for us. You can see that there would be a second group of difficulties. But you have also referred to the Jews. I simply don't understand that; for according to our standpoint, which you know, the Jews are Soviet citizens.

KOT. But surely no Soviet authority would maintain that there is no such thing as a Jew who is a Polish citizen?

VYSHINSKY (ironically). Even if there is, it's not worth talking about. The issue you have raised with us calls for consideration of a whole complex of problems (laughing). It is not desirable to hurry in questions of this kind. Of course we shall let you have our reply in due course.

KOT. I have the impression that things are just the reverse of how you see them. The difficulties are greater on paper than in reality, and with goodwill on the part of the Soviet authorities they can be removed. Each praises God in his own way. The Russian believes à sa façon, the Pole after his. The circumstance that during the past twenty-five years Soviet citizens have not shown any increase in religious feeling makes no difference whatever to the Poles' attitude to religion; and they, as I have said, are showing a definite increase in religious feeling, especially during this last, difficult period.

VYSHINSKY. I have already pointed out that the Soviet constitution guarantees religious freedom to the citizens of the U.S.S.R., and Mr. Bogomolov has told General Sikorski that these decisions will be applied equally to Polish citizens.

KOT. Please bear in mind what great importance religion possesses on the international plane, and what a positive reaction a settlement of this issue would evoke. Why, even when Roosevelt met Churchill, they joined together in worship with Bibles in their hands before they began their discussions. So even if these questions play no part in the Soviet Union it is different abroad.

VYSHINSKY. The question is handled in a quite normal way. The adherents of the various religions are at liberty to form groups of the faithful and can observe all their religious practices.

KOT. Well, yes, but the point at issue is that the Soviet authorities should permit Polish citizens to organize their religious life, that they should not be hindered in doing so. Eleven priests are already working in the field, but their position has not been put in order.

VYSHINSKY. If they are registered with the authorities and possess agreements with groups of the faithful everything is in order. If they are functioning on their own responsibility, without agreement, that is not in order. Functioning against the existing laws can cause difficulties.

KOT. Our programme is genuinely minimal. We do not demand the creation of an ecclesiastical hierarchy, without which, after all, the Catholic Church never functions. We are only concerned to ensure that Polish citizens should have religious oversight, which they themselves are demanding. We want an assurance that our citizens will not meet with political difficulties on this account, and that nobody will persecute them. After all, they are foreigners in the Soviet Union, they don't understand what they are free to do and what not. Let them know that in the religious sphere they possess quite definite rights.

VYSHINSKY. The Polish citizens can organize their religious life on the same principles as Soviet citizens, in accordance with the binding legislation. Please also take into account the circumstance that Catholic priests are in a special position; they have a constant dual dependence, on the state of which they are citizens and on the Holy Father (ironically) to whom they vow fidelity.

KOT. If there were any tendency for our priests to pursue some special policy I could guarantee that this simply would not happen if they were dependent on the Embassy. The situation isn't all that bad even with their dependence on the Holy Father; they observe fidelity to Him in their hearts, but that doesn't prevent their being subordinate politically to their own Government.

VYSHINSKY. But the Soviet Union doesn't maintain any relations with the Apostolic See.

KOT (jokingly). No; but I don't doubt that such relations will be entered into.

VYSHINSKY (laughing). I am of a different opinion; we have absolutely nothing to gain by such relations. However, despite your statements, the plan you have presented does not keep within the bounds of Soviet law. It contains mention of Embassy priests who would possess special rights in regard to their performance of functions as chaplains. That kind of demand is entirely without basis. No Embassy or diplomatic mission in the Soviet Union has its own priests; that institution is not known.

KOT. It is just this institution of chaplains which will enable us to control the priests' activities and will be a safeguard against their pursuing any policy of their own.

VYSHINSKY. I have already told you that your plan will be considered, and that the purpose of my remarks today is only to point to certain serious difficulties which it at once aroused in my mind. The very consideration of this plan puts the People's Commissariat for Foreign Affairs in quite a delicate position of [considering] separate treatment, of setting apart, so to speak, one group of believers and creating a privileged position for them. I personally consider that that is very difficult, and maybe quite impossible.

KOT. If the Soviet Government is prepared to take a positive approach to this question it can be settled quite easily in practice. Take into account the political aspect of the problem. I don't come here with a demand for any privileges, or to create difficulties for the Soviet authorities; I only appeal for a spirit of benevolent understanding and ask for a practical solution to the question. Theoretical assurances have no value whatever for us, and we are not concerned with them. Your fears as to the discontent of the Russian Orthodox population in the Soviet Union if Poles are granted freedom of religious practice don't seem justified to me. After all, there are priests in the Polish Army, and I haven't heard that this has caused any difficulties with the Soviet people (jokingly). Nor do I think the soldiers of the Red Army have begun to put forward demands to be assigned chaplains, using this argument as a basis.

VYSHINSKY. Let them try to put forward any such demands! (after a moment, calmly) The Red Army is an enlightened army and doesn't need religious care. That's exactly why it's called the Red Army.

KOT. Hitlerite propaganda is continually trying to give the world the impression that there is religious persecution in the Soviet Union. What a good counter-argument this would be to their propaganda.

VYSHINSKY. There are no restrictions on religious freedom in the Soviet Union, but—I repeat—your plan is altogether difficult to discuss. How are we to reply to it? By issuing a circular to the authorities that they are to support religious life among the Polish population?

KOT. A circular would be useful, but I don't insist on it in the least. Let the Polish citizens be given the certainty that they are free to try to organize their religious life and that their clergy will not be arrested, and with the aid of the Embassy they will organize spiritual ministrations within the requisite limits inside your country, quite quietly, without fuss, *ohne Pauken und Trompeten* [without drums or trumpets]. And in return you will gain great publicity abroad.

VYSHINSKY. Bogomolov gave the answer on this question away back in November. The present requirements go too far. The plan to bring in priests from abroad, for instance, is not realizable at all.

KOT. Then release those you're still holding. Then we shall not insist on bringing in priests.

VYSHINSKY. In November also the Embassy was informed that the Polish citizens who had been deprived of their freedom had been released.

KOT. But we have lists of priests who are still not free. The one I have just given you applies to them exactly.

VYSHINSKY. We shall check the lists we have already received as well as today's. We shall give you our reply.

KOT. I would ask for the check to be as brief as possible.

. . . .

KOT. Now to the next important question. Taking the Soviet Union's difficulties with food supplies into account, we would like to organize the mass transfer of Polish children abroad. According to calculations to hand so far, there are about 160,000 children, Polish citizens, in the Soviet Union. If this number, which is not complete, since we have not ended our calculations, were transferred abroad it would be a very considerable relief both for you and for us. For children are a non-working element, and so from the economic aspect their stay here at present is not expedient. But we are up against serious difficulties, because the world will not come to our aid very readily. It is difficult today to settle such large numbers of children abroad. So far we have obtained agreement to the settlement of only 50,000. The constant mortality among the children, their mass mortality, is a very painful thing. It would be a great relief to us if these children could be transferred abroad. I realize that in wartime there are difficulties in regard to communications but if resort were made to waterways, organizing transport along the Volga, the operation could go smoothly and quickly. To a large extent we could ourselves undertake the feeding of the children *en route*, we would ask you only for bread and groats. I strongly request that the Soviet Union agree to let these children go.

VYSHINSKY (in a reluctant tone). You have spoken of mass mortality among the children. I am forced to state that there is no such thing. The Embassy sent us data concerning mortality in the Uzbek Republic. I ordered these to be checked. Before long we shall let you have our reply. I have confirmed that the Embassy delegates, certainly the delegate in Samarkand, Kazmierczak, has simply deceived the Embassy. The data presented are based on competely false information. Kazmierczak has not done any visiting in his area, and in the best case has been taken in. The mortality relates to isolated incidents, which can almost be confirmed by name. As the result a sort of panicky mood has been created in the Embassy and an exaggeratedly pessimistic estimate of the situation. I think I shall let you have our reply during the next few days. The collective farms are not only providing food to the working Polish citizens, but are even feeding the lazy ones. The figure of 50,000 children is quite fantastic and unreal. How many of them were to go to India? I think 500. (Zorin confirms.) But so far they have not been transferred.

KOT. Unfortunately, mass mortality among the children is a confirmed fact. I shall take the liberty of presenting you exact statistics touching not only the far south but Kuibishev itself. You will see how many children have died here. I ask you to investigate this on the spot through your officials.

VYSHINSKY. I have heard nothing about it. There is no mass mortality. Where cases of death do occur the incidence is quite normal, not in the least higher than among Soviet citizens.

KOT. The Russian climate is particularly unfavourable to our citizens. They suffer both from the deep frost of winter and the great heat of the summer.

VYSHINSKY. The plan to transfer 50,000 abroad is quite fantastic. Why, we are waging a war, and a very hard one at that.

KOT. I take the liberty of saying that it was the Soviet Government that brought the Polish children here, not we. Now allow us to take them away.

VYSHINSKY (getting rattled). So you're making accusations again? What is the point of reminding anyone of the past, of constantly returning to the fate of these people, which was due to the international situation and various other events?

KOT. We must look after our youth.

VYSHINSKY (growing impatient). Our youth are equally valuable to us. (Recovering his control) We care for the Polish youth just as much as our own. We provide them with the same food as we give our own. As Stalin said, we share everything fraternally with them.

KOT. But please raise this question in the appropriate quarters all the same, and advocate it in a friendly manner.

. . . .

VYSHINSKY. From the aspect of food supplies it would obviously be desirable to rid ourselves of 50,000 people, which would mean having 50,000 pounds of bread more a day. But I don't see any real possibility of carrying out such an evacuation.

KOT. I have a better opinion of the Soviet Union's organizing ability. You can organize it if you want to. Over 40,000 Polish citizens were evacuated to Iran in five days, and there was no reason whatever to complain about the method of transport. Whenever you have the will to do something, you display astonishing powers of organization. After all, the enormous transport resources which the Soviet Government has at its disposal on the Caspian Sea are employed mainly in the importation of all kinds of supplies and goods from abroad, and they are not fully exploited on their return voyages. Our children could undoubtedly be transported by these means.

VYSHINSKY. That evacuation was carried out by the army.

KOT. But over 12,000 civilians went too. Why not let the army deal with this question?

VYSHINSKY. The army has quite different tasks, and this is not one of them.

KOT. I had not expected such a reaction to our plan. I had expected you to regard it favourably. If in fact the transport difficulties were to prove so great we could count, it appears, on the help of our army, which has now received sufficient motor transport for its needs. In the south certainly it will be possible to transport the children in that way. The plan fits in both with our and with your interests. In any case I ask for it to be presented to the Government, who perhaps will take a different attitude towards it.

. . . .

KOT. I shall take the liberty of troubling you in regard to various personal questions connected with the Embassy and delegatures, and I ask in advance for a separate conversation. But there are several urgent issues which I must raise today.

KOT. The Embassy delegate in Kustanai has sent me a telegram which I have brought with me. He reports that on 28 May the Vice-Chairman of the *Oblast* Executive Committee informed him that, in accordance with instructions he had received, Romanski is recalled from Kustanai and is to leave, handing over charge of the delegation to his deputy Ernst. From now on the authorities will discuss questions concerning Polish citizens exclusively with Ernst. The Embassy delegate replied that he could not take this statement into cognizance until he received instructions from the Embassy. You will admit that I cannot agree to this way of taking me by surprise in regard to delegates, and I ask for an explanation.

VYSHINSKY. I know nothing whatever about this. (He turns interrogatively to Zorin.)

ZORIN. Nor do I.

KOT. Romanski, a serious and reliable man, formerly director of a bank in Katowice, has been working in Kustanai for many months and enjoys the general respect of the Polish citizens and the Embassy.

VYSHINSKY. If we have any queries in regard to any delegate we definitely inform you of them, as we did, for instance, in Grygier's case. I must go into this.

KOT. Before Romanski became the Embassy delegate he was the registration officer in this area; you see, he was a captain on the reserve. Perhaps that is the reason for the demand the local authorities have made of him. But I emphasize that I have perfect confidence in this man, though I have had no contact with him at all, and from the moment he left for the area, four months ago, I have not received a single report from him. Even though I have had no correspondence with him over so long a period I feel certain that everything is in order. He is a man with an extraordinarily well developed social outlook. Even as registration officer he revealed so much understanding of the problem of social welfare that as soon as he arrived at the Embassy I applied to the military for him not to be sent on leave, but to be completely discharged. So from the moment he became the Embassy delegate he has had absolutely no connection with the army and is not interested in anything except the problem of caring for Polish citizens.

VYSHINSKY. But what were these registration officers?

KOT. Emissaries sent out by the staff to deal with recruitment questions; in agreement with the Red Army Command they were sent to the areas where Polish citizens were residing, because at that time the Soviet Military Command had not yet begun to occupy themselves with the levies of Polish citizens.

VYSHINSKY. That cannot have had any bearing on the local authorities' attitude to Romanski. Neither the Vice-Chairman of the *Oblast* Executive Committee nor anyone else has the right to address the Embassy delegate in such a manner, without agreement with the Commissariat for Foreign Affairs. I shall look into the question and get it cleared up this very day.

KOT. Thank you. Unfortunately there are other, similar cases. What do you think of this article? (He opens an issue of the newspaper *The Altai Bolshevik* in front of Vyshinsky, at an article entitled 'Dear Fellow Countrymen of Poland', but covering the author's name.)

VYSHINSKY (reading parts of the article aloud). Very well written. I'd be prepared to sign it myself.

KOT. Well, you see (revealing the author's name). But the man who wrote this article, Mr. Krzyzanowski, the Embassy's man of trust in Ust-Kamienogorsk, has been arrested by the local authorities there on the charge that he is hostile to the Soviet Union. Could a man who wrote that really be regarded as an enemy of the U.S.S.R.?

VYSHINSKY. The article is good, but that doesn't prove anything. A man can write one thing but be engaged in doing something quite different. Take Rola-Janicki's activities, for instance, only not on behalf of an ally, but on behalf of an enemy power.

KOT. That is completely excluded. Krzyzanowski is known for his reliability. But, strange to say, here too we have the same circumstances as in the Romanski case, for he also was a registration officer. But after his discharge from the army he joined our staff because of his great usefulness to the Embassy. Is it that the authorities con-

S

sidered he was trying to evade the order for registration officers to leave? That would be unjust, since he is the Embassy's man of trust and doesn't concern himself with military affairs.

VYSHINSKY. That cannot have anything to do with the question of his arrest. The authorities must have serious reasons.

KOT. A similar incident has occurred in the case of Bugajski, another reliable and serious social worker, our man of trust in Tashkent. He also again as a reservist was a registration officer for a time, but because of his age and qualifications he was taken over by the Embassy. He, too, has been arrested without prior notification either to myself or to the Embassy delegate in Samarkand. If we add two workers in the delegation at Syktyvkar, also arrested, and remember that all these incidents have occurred within a short period, almost simultaneously, one gets the impression that some kind of organized pressure and organized suppression of the Embassy's social welfare administration is being carried out. Including Ursula Muskus, at this moment six of our people are held under arrest by the Soviet authorities; and all our inquiries as to the reasons for these steps and our demands for their release remain unanswered.

VYSHINSKY (he has noted down the names). Was Krzyzanowski notified [to us as a delegate]?

KOT. Of course he was.

VYSHINSKY. But was he confirmed?

ZORIN. No, the appointment was not confirmed.

ARLET. But we sent in the notification over two months ago; and we received an answer in writing from the Commissariat for Foreign Affairs to the effect that Krzyzanowski's case would be elucidated supplementarily. Meanwhile he has been arrested, but we are still without any elucidation of his case.

VYSHINSKY. That is because he has been arrested by an entirely different authority, whereas the elucidation of his case was to be made by the Commissariat for Foreign Affairs.

ARLET. But so far none whatever has been made.

KOT. I strongly request that this matter be cleared up and the people unjustly detained released. After all, in this matter my prestige is also affected.

VYSHINSKY. But how can this affect your prestige? You are not in a position to answer for every one of the several hundred men of trust. In any case I cannot agree to your charge that Polish citizens have been arrested by the state security organs without cause. They arrest

Polish citizens, and especially the men of trust or Embassy delegates, with the utmost caution.

кот. All the same I strongly ask for an investigation of all these incidents and the release of these people. If something quite unforeseen has not occurred, I repeat that I can guarantee them. I ask you to give instructions for the following dozen and more people to be brought to Kuibishev (he hands Vyshinsky a list). I would like to nominate them either as delegates or deputy delegates before I leave, especially as I shall have to withdraw certain persons as unsuitable.

Vyshinsky takes the list and promises to deal with it.

кот. I also ask for instructions for the journey to Kuibishev of the Embassy delegate at Chimkent, Kosciałkowski, to be facilitated as quickly as possible. It is necessary to recall M. Wiecek from Alma Ata, and I want to appoint Mr. Kosciałkowski to that post. But I must see him first.

Vyshinsky makes a note and promises to arrange it.

кот. Finally, there is one other question which the Embassy has already raised more than once. I refer to Ehrlich and Alter, Polish citizens, councillors of the city of Warsaw, whom you are holding under arrest.

vyshinsky. I am not in a position to discuss that subject.

кот. Please do this for me and let me have these men for my journey. I shall take them with me, and I take full responsibility for their not conducting any kind of anti-Soviet agitation abroad. I am not speaking now from any other motive but the interests of the war we are waging jointly. For no one will ever believe that these men had any connection with pro-Hitlerite activity. (The Ambassador produces a leaflet and copies of correspondence with leading figures in the United States, reporting protests by Jewish workers' organizations in the U.S.A.) Why is this necessary to anyone? Does the joint struggle against Germany gain anything from it?

vyshinsky (not looking at the materials shown to him). I fully realize your intentions and feelings, but I cannot enter into discussions with you on the case of Ehrlich and Alter. You know our fundamental attitude, according to which they are citizens of the Soviet Union.

кот (in a joking tone). Well, then perhaps you want to occupy Warsaw after the war? For if you are right the people there are also your citizens! Why, these men were city councillors of Warsaw, who found themselves in your prison when you incorporated Eastern Poland in the Soviet Union.

VYSHINSKY. I must regard your remark about Warsaw as a joke. We don't want to occupy it in the least. But Warsaw will get along without Ehrlich and Alter.

KOT. I greatly regret that the Soviet authorities take this attitude, since it would be only to your good to release these men.

VYSHINSKY. I am not in a position to discuss this matter, or to have any influence on its course. I tell you that sincerely, though I could resort to subterfuge, could make some promise. The matter is closed.

KOT. I am very sorry. . . .

. . . .

The conversation lasted two hours ten minutes. The tone was friendly and calm except for part of the conversation concerning the evacuation of children, when Vyshinsky seemed openly unnerved and dissatisfied.

A189. To the Minister for Foreign Affairs.
Kuibishev. 12 June 1942

Solely for your exclusive information and eventual indirect utilization (perhaps through Washington), but the source is not to be revealed on any account.

Publicity and informative activity of Jewish organizations must be directed towards interesting public opinion in England and the United States in the situation which has developed as the result of the Soviet Government's trend towards a one-sided settlement of the problem of the Eastern borders. The Soviet Government's attitude on the question of the citizenship of national minorities (not Poles) must be publicized emphatically and clearly, and the connection of this question with that of the frontiers, which hitherto has not been generally understood, must be explained.

It is necessary to strive to ensure that all public opinion, including that section which would not wish to be involved in the fundamental dispute over the Eastern Borders, should demand that the Soviets should, in regard to the Jewish Polish citizens deported to the U.S.S.R., apply the individual consequences arising from the politically unresolved problem, at least until the issue has been settled.

In particular it is necessary to point out that the differential treatment meted out to the Jewish population is shown by (1) the non-application of the amnesty to those Jews, Polish citizens, who are still held in prisons, camps, and exile; (2) not allowing Jews to travel out of the U.S.S.R. even to their closest relations and families; (3) rendering it impossible for Jews to join the Polish Armed Forces, and thus to avail themselves of the care given to soldiers and their families, which would partially solve many difficulties of survival; (4) rendering it difficult for Jews to work in the social welfare administration of the Embassy; (5) by means of repressive measures against those issuing Polish passports to Jews and a ban on issuing [them] to these Jews, depriving them of the possibility of availing themselves of the help provided by the Embassy social welfare administration.

The fact that, despite the principle of self-determination which Soviet law has made propaganda use of hitherto, racial criteria are applied in doubtful cases needs stressing. For instance, information supplied to the press could be summarized as follows: In September and October 1941 Polish citizens were released from prisons, camps, and exile, and every person so released received a certificate on his release which simultaneously established his Polish citizenship. But many Polish citizens remained unreleased. In December 1941 the People's Commissariat for Foreign Affairs stated that Polish citizens —Jews, Ukrainians, and Bielorussians—had been deprived of Polish citizenship, although previously, precisely as Polish citizens they had been sent to prisons, camps, and exile, and had no wish to adopt Soviet citizenship.

The initial formal statement has now been transformed into practical persecution. To begin with Jews were not issued exit visas; next the Soviet Government stated that the Jews still in prisons, camps, and exile, would not be released, because they were not Polish citizens. In order to deprive them of proofs of Polish citizenship the amnesty certificates are now being taken from those already released from prisons, camps, and exile. In questioning the Jews' right to Polish citizenship the Soviet authorities are applying principles condemned by all who are fighting Hitler. This is forcing those involved to conceal their nationality, which, however, is not sufficient. Origin is investigated for three generations back; they are deprived of the right to avail themselves of the social care provided by the Embassy administration.

In one of the *oblasts*, where it had been possible to transfer Polish citizens from worse to better areas, the Narcomvnudiel excluded Jews from this charitable action. In Samarkand the Soviet authorities are taking away the Polish passports recently issued to Jews; for declaring their Polish citizenship Jews are fined and threatened with deportation and labour camps. In many instances Jews are even forbidden contact with the Embassy delegation. In Alma Ata, for instance, over a dozen Jews of Polish citizenship have been arrested for having contact with the Embassy delegation. The Narcomvnudiel demanded the delegate's recall because he was issuing passports to Polish Jews.

The Soviet authorities have formally forbidden the Polish Armed Forces to take in Jews; on the other hand, cases are known of Jews being forced to serve in the Lithuanian division which is being organized.

It would be desirable to develop discreet activity with the object of obtaining:

first: the release of those still held in prisons, labour camps, and exile;

second: complete equality of rights of citizenship;

third: withdrawal by the Soviet authorities of the ban on accepting Jews in the Polish Armed Forces;

fourth: equality of rights in regard to the possibility of leaving the U.S.S.R.; and,

fifth: equal benefit with other Polish citizens from the services of the Embassy social welfare organization.[1]

A190. Cable from General Sikorski.
London. 15 June 1942

In enlargement of Minister Raczynski's cable, I inform you that today I am sending to President Roosevelt a note with a resolute appeal for intervention in Moscow with the object (1) of [the Soviets] not putting obstacles in the way of officers returning to the army; (2) Renewal of the levy of the 49,000 still lacking, of which 19,000 to go to the Middle East and England, and the rest for their reinforcement; (3) If difficulties in regard to feeding them are raised, then the evacuation to Persia of all the newly enrolled; (4) I have demanded acceleration of the equipment of the forces in Russia. I have cited the fact that the airforce has recently lost several hundred valuable flying personnel, and the navy two ships and a vessel in convoys to Russia. Molotov is informed of all this, he should have carried my message back to Stalin.

---

[1] Drawn up by Ludwik Seideman, Embassy *rapporteur* on Jewish affairs.

B33. Conversation with A. J. Vyshinsky.
15 June 1942
Present: Director Novikov and Embassy secretary
Alexander Mniszek.

Kot congratulates the commissar on the signing of agreements with Great Britain and the U.S.A.[1]

VYSHINSKY. I am glad to hear you say that, Mr. Ambassador, for this agreement certainly introduces a new element into international politics; it strengthens the bonds between the states that wish to live and work in peace. I am convinced that this agreement will be in force not only for twenty years, but for longer.

KOT. The purpose of my visit today is not [to raise] great political questions but a number of current problems, which, so long as they are not settled, are holding up the work both of the Embassy and of its organizational links in the field. Their settlement will help forward labours which are of value for both the Polish and the Soviet side. I ask for a friendly attitude to these questions.

VYSHINSKY. We shall consider your desiderata in a friendly light within the bounds of our possibilities.

KOT. First and foremost the question of the personnel staffing the delegations. In its proposals so far the Commissariat for Foreign Affairs has laid down the stereotype figure of seven co-workers to each delegation. (VYSHINSKY. From three to seven, Ambassador.) I want to approach this question in the most realistic manner possible. For this reason in a moment I shall hand you a note with detailed proposals.

(The Ambassador went on to justify in detail the necessity for twelve workers in each delegation; emphasizing that certain delegations, because of the density of the Polish population, the delegation's remoteness from the centre, and other vital necessities, require a departure from the figure twelve. Certain delegations can manage with three or four officials, while others, Samarkand for instance, need as many as twenty-four. . . .)

Obviously the figure of twelve workers I propose does not include

---

[1] The treaty between the U.S.S.R. and Great Britain on their alliance in the war against Hitlerite Germany and co-operation and mutual aid after the war. Concluded for twenty years in London on 26 May 1942. Signed by Molotov and Eden. Also the agreement between the U.S.S.R. and the U.S.A. on the principles of mutual aid in the war against aggression, concluded in Washington 11 June 1942, between Litvinov and Cordell Hull.

workers employed in the delegation, nor the directors of shelters, hospitals, stores, kindergartens, dining-rooms, etc.

VYSHINSKY. Obviously (taking the note from the Ambassador). We shall consider these questions favourably, closely, and positively.

KOT. The second question is the problem of the men of trust. I ask you to bear in mind the enormous difficulties and the vast areas of the regions, the lack of means of communication, and finally the dispersal of the Polish population into small settlements, colonies, collective farms, etc. So I ask that each man of trust may have an assistant, who, in the event of the man of trust making a visit in the field, can take his place. The question of control also comes into this, for human beings are sinful and not every man of trust—as we know from experience—is equal to his task. There have been instances of abuses, and in these cases we have removed the people who have abused our confidence.

(A discussion developed with Vyshinsky, in which it transpired that he was completely out of touch with the problems of the men of trust. He was confusing them with the representatives of the Polish population chosen in the small settlements, and the Ambassador and Novikov had to explain to him the organizational network of men of trust.)

VYSHINSKY. On principle I cannot agree to such a solution to the question. Only in special cases, when justified by the Embassy in great detail, where the man of trust has a large area, a large number of Polish citizens, can the Commissariat for Foreign Affairs agree to the appointment of a deputy to the man of trust or to one office worker in the office of the man of trust.

KOT. Together with the question of the work of the delegations and the men of trust arises a burning problem—swifter recognition by the Narcomindiel of the candidates for men of trust nominated by the Embassy. The practice the Narcomindiel has adopted hitherto of dragging out the recognition of a number of men of trust sometimes for two or three months causes disorganization in the field and is troublesome both to the Embassy and to the local authorities. I ask strongly that in the interests of both sides the man of trust nominated by the Embassy may be able to begin his official activities provisionally from the moment of his nomination, independently of the question of his recognition by the Narcomindiel. This will ensure that there is no breakdown in the work of the organizational network. If for any reason a man of trust is not recognized he will cease to function and we shall nominate another in his place.

VYSHINSKY. I understand your attitude. I see the benefit to our common interests and take a favourable view of your proposal. But I must put the case before the Collegium of the People's Commissariat for Foreign Affairs (this is a kind of committee formed from the higher officials of the Commissariat; among the members is the former Ambassador to the U.S.A., Umansky).

KOT. In connection with aid to the people in cash and in kind, the necessity arises of controlling this activity; I ask you for permission to introduce three controllers, who would exercise control over financial expenditures, warehouses, aid in kind, and all the accounts, in the field. In order not to add to the personnel of the Embassy I would like these controllers to have their headquarters in Kirov, Samarkand, and Pietropavlovsk. Of course they would be reckoned as additional to the established figure for delegation staffs, but they themselves would have no office staff.

VYSHINSKY. Unfortunately I cannot agree to this kind of controller functioning in the provinces. But I see a way out if you will delegate the controllers from among the Embassy personnel.

KOT. I agree to that.

I would like to ask for permission to send one of the Embassy officials to the Caucasian Republics and to Stalingrad *oblast* for a tour of the areas. We are getting a number of letters from these areas, and news on the situation of the Polish people there, numbering several tens of thousands. We would like to establish contact with them and send them help.

VYSHINSKY (in an obviously reluctant tone). Have you exact information as to the distribution of these people?

KOT. The details are being formulated.

VYSHINSKY. I would like you to send them to me. Then we shall study the question.

KOT. They will be sent within the next day or two.

But now I turn to a subject which is painful for me, namely, the number of personnel in the Embassy. The figure of eighty officials is absolutely inadequate for normal Embassy work. In any case the figure is really smaller, since the eighty include 'twelve apostles' (jokingly), in other words, a number of our delegates registered with the Commissariat for Foreign Affairs but not actually in the Embassy.

VYSHINSKY. At one time you agreed to this quota.

MNISZEK. It was I who agreed, and I only did so, fixing this figure provisionally with the Director of Protocol, until the final settlement of the question between you and the Ambassador.

KOT. I would ask that these twelve 'apostles' of ours, while continuing to be counted as Embassy officials, should not be included in the quota of eighty officials; then we could register an additional twelve persons.

VYSHINSKY (in an unfriendly, dissatisfied tone). So you would like to increase the quota of Embassy personnel to ninety-two persons. Unfortunately I cannot agree to that. I wish confidentially to inform you that this kind of desideratum is put forward by the heads of all the diplomatic missions. Apart from the basic reason for not increasing the quotas of officials, and not only those of the Polish Embassy, there is the very difficult problem of food, and I ask you to put yourself in our place. You can strike delegates off the list of officials registered in the Commissariat for Foreign Affairs and nominate whomsoever you like in their place, in accordance with your own judgement. We shall not make the least objection.

KOT. That I cannot do.

MNISZEK. But these twelve delegates of ours don't figure in any diplomatic lists. It is purely an internal matter between the Commissariat for Foreign Affairs and the Embassy. The diplomatic representations will know only of the actual figure of eighty Embassy personnel, and therefore of the established quota.

KOT. The figure of the established quota is decidedly small. We have such enormous fields of activity that to cope with them we must increase the Embassy personnel. Independently of the question of increasing the personnel registered with the Narcomindiel we must and do have auxiliary personnel.

With this question, which I would like to put on a legal footing, is connected that of accommodating in the Embassy building the delegation officials and candidates for men of trust who visit us; also prominent Polish citizens, professors, writers, etc., who usually arrive with the agreement of the administrative authorities. I reckon the number of such persons as round about thirty. I would ask you to issue instructions to the Kuibishev militia that these people are to be given the right of residence in Kuibishev for a certain period.

VYSHINSKY. Of course the Kuibishev militia will receive instructions. But persons of this type will have the right of residence for only a very short period, about a week to ten days.

KOT. Some of them, especially those who are temporarily working in the Embassy, must be employed longer.

VYSHINSKY. While we have no reservations to make in regard to persons such as university professors, writers, etc., coming to Kuibishev and staying here for a short period, I cannot agree to your proposed and, as I understand it, 'illegal' additional group, additional Embassy personnel. What you are wanting to do in fact is to increase the Embassy personnel. . . .

KOT. You have previously explained that the main reason for refusing agreement to an increase in the Embassy personnel is the food problem. We shall not ask for additional rations for these people, we shall feed them ourselves. One of the reasons why we need a larger number of officials is that they are frequently ill.

VYSHINSKY. We also have people fall ill, but we manage so that one of the other officials takes the sick man's place.

NOVIKOV. May I point out in passing that the personnel of the Narcomindiel does not greatly exceed the figure of your eighty Embassy officials.

KOT (jokingly). But our brains trust is engaged in handling not only important but also petty questions which take up a lot of time. *A propos* of these seemingly small questions which none the less have to be dealt with: it needs four officials just to read the daily correspondence.

VYSHINSKY (interrupting). Reading correspondence, Ambassador, certainly is a difficult job.

KOT. In addition the editorial of *Polska* requires a large number of staff. The cashier's and accounts department also. And all the other Embassy departments, for that matter.

VYSHINSKY. As you know, travelling to Kuibishev is forbidden. But if some Polish citizen or other manages to smuggle himself into Kuibishev and the Embassy considers he must reside for a time in the Embassy, then either on the Ambassador's recommendation or on the basis of an Embassy note the Commissariat for Foreign Affairs will issue an instruction to the militia to register him for a short time, after which he must leave at once.

KOT. Leaving Kuibishev is a difficult matter too. Our co-workers sometimes wait for weeks for the possibility of leaving.

VYSHINSKY. But if you issue instructions to the Embassy officials to notify the arrival of any Polish citizen to the militia, we shall know in advance that his departure is to be expected; and then I guarantee that a place will quickly be obtained for him in a train or on a boat. But I must point out yet again that I cannot agree to so-called 'temporary' residence in the Embassy which, as I have defined, constitutes illegal, additional personnel, while the 'temporariness' may extend to a whole year.

KOT. I wish to notify you officially of the date of my departure, which I have fixed as starting from 5 July. In this connection I would ask for a speedy settlement of the questions I have raised and. . . .

VYSHINSKY (interrupting). We shall consider them favourably, but we don't want any speedy settlement if it means that you'll be leaving the U.S.S.R. more speedily.

KOT. Thank you. In any case before my departure I would like to make the acquaintance of the candidates for delegates whose arrival here I have already asked you to arrange.

VYSHINSKY (uneasy). Has the Embassy asked for the persons you have named?

KOT. I handed you the list during my conversation of 31 May.

VYSHINSKY (it is obvious that he and Novikov have both forgotten to deal with the matter). Yes, yes, we shall issue instructions immediately.

KOT. Can they arrive already?

VYSHINSKY. I shall inform the Embassy very shortly, and then it will be possible to send them summonses to come to Kuibishev.

KOT. In connection with my departure I would ask you to issue a recommendation to the competent authorities for a swift clearance of the departure formalities of a dozen or so persons (he hands Vyshinsky a list). Among them are prominent scientists, well-known writers, and journalists. At one time the Embassy made strong representations to secure their release, and these were crowned with success. In addition there are the families of governmental persons living abroad, such as the family of a member of the National Council, Zaręba, of the Polish Consul-general in New Zealand, Wodzicki, etc.

VYSHINSKY (taking the list and speaking without enthusiasm). I must first examine the list, and then we shall issue the appropriate instructions.

KOT. I would like some of these people to travel with me.

In connection with my departure I would ask you to inform President Stalin that I would like to see him to discuss questions of importance to both our Governments, the solution of which depends solely on his personal decision. I would like to raise problems which will be of importance to the development of our friendly relations, not only now, but in the future. I would strongly ask you to use your friendly influence in this direction.

VYSHINSKY. I shall not fail to inform President Stalin at once of your request. (After a moment's hesitation) But I wish to point out that, as you know, President Stalin is greatly occupied with the whole complex of questions connected with carrying on the war.

. . . .

The conversation was very lively, and at times was carried on at a very fast rate. It was obvious that Vyshinsky was not briefed in regard to certain questions. When discussing the problem of delegates one felt that he took a favourable view, but in discussing the question of Embassy personnel he not only flatly did not accept any of the Ambassador's desiderata, but categorically refused to agree to any compromise settlement of the question, at times in a downright unpleasant fashion.

During the discussion of the Ambassador's departure one was conscious of a friendly attitude towards the Ambassador himself, interest in the route he would take, and emphasis that all instructions would be issued for the formalities associated with his departure to be settled in detail and efficiently by the Narcomindiel Diplomatic protocol.

A206. Cable to Minister for Foreign Affairs.
Kuibishev. 30 June 1942

In organizing the first transport of children, I have given instructions to include a dozen or so Jewish children, but with great caution so as not to attract the attention of the authorities here. We must avoid the word 'Jewish' even in the telegrams which are our sole liaison with the delegate sending the children from Ashkhabad. In the first transport of children there were to be fourteen Jewish children and a woman doctor, out of 162 children; probably because of sickness their number fell to eleven.

B34. Conversation with Vice-Commissar for Foreign Affairs, A. J. Vyshinsky.
Narcomindiel, Kuibishev. 8 July 1942
H. Sokolnicki as interpreter.

Although this was a farewell visit, it came about as the result of Vyshinsky's initiative.

VYSHINSKY. The first question I want to raise with you on the authority of the Soviet Government is the evacuation of the Polish forces from the U.S.S.R. The military situation in the Near East, and in particular in Libya has led the Soviet Government to inform the British Government that it would not oppose the Polish divisions in Russia being used in the Near East for the common war aims.

KOT. I have been informed of this suggestion by my Government and by the British Government, but the decisions are outside the Embassy's competence and depend on direct conversations between the Polish and the British Governments. We created an army in Russia with the idea of fighting against the common enemy on Soviet soil. So far as the circumstances in which the Polish forces might be evacuated from Russia are concerned, this does concern the Embassy.

VYSHINSKY. When the Soviet Government agreed to this step it realized that it was to the detriment of its own interests. But as the Polish divisions can be used elsewhere for the common interests the Soviet Government has nothing against it.

KOT. I must stress that these are our finest divisions by comparison with the material previously sent out. It was our desire that for the first time in history we would have a brotherhood of arms with Russia, that the Polish soldiers would fight with the Russians against the common enemy. Of course the war is a joint affair and, wherever anyone fights, he is fighting for the joint cause. These three divisions of ours will fight well. They would have been ready for immediate participation in the war if they had all received arms for training betimes; but it is too late to discuss that now.

VYSHINSKY. Of course you're right. The Soviet Government considered that this is in the common interest; the situation there requires it.

KOT. I note that it is in Russia's interests that the Polish forces formed here should fight there too. I draw your attention to the circumstance that if Russia decided to permit a further levy of soldiers among the Polish citizens a second similar army could be formed here for fighting in the Near East. There is much splendid military material, especially among the Polish peasant population, scattered from Archangel, Vologda, as far as Krasnoyarsk and used unproductively in forestry and other labours, and mainly starving.

VYSHINSKY. That is a separate problem. Our attitude was defined in Stalin's answer of 13 May 1942 to General Sikorski's message on recruitment questions.

KOT. The war may take an unexpected course, and perhaps it is better not to decide on the future today; it may take such a turn that that attitude will have to be submitted to review.

VYSHINSKY. So far the Soviet attitude is negative. This question falls within the competence of the military. I cannot go into details. Of course it is possible that the question will be reviewed and our attitude changed in the future. A levy causes political difficulties. Wherever it is carried out it creates alarm among the people, it agitates the people.

KOT. I must stress that the levy to the Polish Army, which in any case was carried through by Soviet commissions, has so far taken place only in the three southern provinces. It was carried through swiftly and efficiently, complete calm reigned. Several days were sufficient.

VYSHINSKY. I turn to a second question. It is tied up with the Piwowarczyk question,[1] and the revealed facts of General Wolikowski's hostility to the U.S.S.R.; his recall from the U.S.S.R. has been demanded by the Soviet military authorities.

KOT. I don't know what this hostile activity consisted in. Piwowarczyk is a suspect, a *provocateur* sent in. When I learned he had talked with General Wolikowski I took very strong action and demanded his removal from the Embassy premises.

VYSHINSKY. General Wolikowski is leaving. I consider it would be pointless now to discuss the details of this issue. But during its course documents came to light against the Embassy first secretary, Mr. Arlet, confirming his hostile activity towards the U.S.S.R. And so I am empowered to present a demand for Mr. Arlet to be recalled and to leave the U.S.S.R.

KOT. I must ask for an explanation. Arlet was the first of us to come to the U.S.S.R. He has always been friendly to Russia and he influenced other Poles in the same sense. I cannot accept your statement of his hostile activity, and I ask for proofs. I could not personally receive all the people who came to see me; in such cases Arlet helped me, investigating who they were. If in doing this he inquired who had been left behind in camps, about the priests who remained there, that is quite natural. If we had been given the lists of all the Polish citizens who had been sent to camps and were released, which we asked you for again and again, it would not be necessary to question arrivals as to who still remained in the camps. From the very beginning I regarded Piwowarczyk as a *provocateur*. He is a

[1] See A149, pp. 228-9. *Tr.*

liar, and a *provocateur*'s lies cannot be set against Arlet's gentlemanly
conduct. His activities have always been open and inspired by the
necessity to defend our interests and individual citizens. I have the
impression that not everybody—I am not referring to you, who have
shown great feeling and understanding—understands the Poles' real
attitude to Russia. If someone openly speaks and refers to our citizens'
rights and wishes to harmonize their co-existence in the Soviet Union
he is regarded as being unfriendly to the Soviet Union. There have
been many cases of informing, *provocateurism*, and various proposals,
and anyone who rejected them was afterwards declared to be an
enemy of the U.S.S.R. Open activity, struggle to save his fellow
citizens from death, is no proof of an unfriendly attitude to Russia.
VYSHINSKY. Do you intend to make a general issue of this matter?
I must deny that there have been cases of improper behaviour on the
part of Soviet authorities towards Poles. If you have any details,
please let me have them, and we shall make an investigation and
establish what happened in reality.

KOT. I have numerous proofs that attempts have been made to de-
moralize and terrorize the workers in our outposts, that *provocateurs*
have been sent in, and some have even penetrated to me. But I did
not want to make an issue of these things, I wanted to avoid poison-
ing the atmosphere of co-operation. I deliberately played them down,
because I considered that my role was to do everything that would
conduce to a *rapprochement* between us, and not a cooling of relations.
VYSHINSKY. Returning to the case of Mr. Arlet, we cannot regard
Piwowarczyk as a *provocateur*, nor anyone else who occupies himself, as he did, in espionage activities in the U.S.S.R. on Mr. Arlet's
instructions. I have irrefutable proofs that Mr. Arlet wished to use
that person as an informer. This is indicated not only by Piwowarczyk's admissions, but also by documents which have unmasked certain persons. I consider that sufficient for you to take account of my
statement concerning Mr. Arlet. The circumstance that Mr. Arlet
was friendly in the Narcomindiel is not a proof of his real attitude.
All diplomats must be polite, I don't know any who are not. We
regard Mr. Arlet as *persona non grata*.

As for the general question of the Soviet authorities' attitude to
Polish citizens and the charges made, I can adduce proofs that no
injury has been done to them. This refers to the accusations handed
in with reference to the situation in Uzbekistan. A commission's investigations on the spot, with Mr. Kazmierczak, the delegate's deputy,

taking part, prove that the statements alleging the bad situation and the bad treatment of the Polish people are untrue. Is it necessary to go back to all these issues? It is not the Soviet organs, but the Embassy's local representatives who are guilty, for sending such provocative information as, for instance, that 400 people died in one collective farm. A second question: for instance, our treatment of Rola-Janicki. His hostile activity, and certain secret courier instructions, were brought to light, and yet no harm was done him, we only requested that he should leave. There are no bases for accusing the Soviet organs of being unfriendly. Frequently it is just the reverse. But Rola-Janicki and his kind have in fact been conducting unfriendly activity in regard to the U.S.S.R.

KOT. I admit that not all the information coming from various reporters in the field is always exact, sometimes it is exaggerated. We do our utmost to check it and to resist this tendency. For instance, Professor Heitzman dismissed one man of trust simply because he gave him inexact information. But here it is a question of the truth, and the truth is that on many collective farms in Uzbekistan no food is being issued. If certain Polish citizens contradicted their previous information when they came before the commission, and said that everything was in order, they did so, as they themselves confidentially declared afterwards, out of fear of the consequences with which they and others were threatened by the collective farm. The fact is that since 15 May on many collective farms there is nothing to eat, the people are living on berries and grass. Of course somebody could have exaggerated somewhere, but the situation is very difficult, and we find that painful.

Rola-Janicki is not hostile to the U.S.S.R., he is only stupid. He thought his information might be of use to one of us.

If Mr. Arlet is *persona non grata*, I take note of it; but I must express my reservation against his being charged with hostile activity, and I would want to have adequate proofs of that from you. After all, no importance whatever can be attached to the admissions of Piwowarczyk, a spy. I emphasize once more that I cannot agree with the suggestion that Mr. Arlet has engaged in hostile activity.

I have before me figures showing that, for instance, in the locality of Guzar, out of 521 Polish citizens thirty-eight died of starvation in the month of June. In face of such a situation I am compelled to ask that at least the minimum of food shall be laid down for the Polish population, whether working or not, and that it shall be supplied.

T

VYSHINSKY. I shall investigate the figures you have given. I must state that in the collective farms many capable of work are not working; for instance, in one collective farm one family consisting of four persons earned only twenty labour days in four months.

KOT. Not everybody can work; there are many war-wounded, people who haven't the strength for heavy labour. I shan't ever make mention of any who are capable of work but don't want to.

VYSHINSKY. I know your attitude. The war-wounded and incapable of work have been covered by special allocations.

KOT. In practice these allocations are provided only to a very small extent.

VYSHINSKY. But what is happening to the food which is being brought in from abroad?

KOT. It was distributed as soon as it arrived. At first, as the food situation was satisfactory, we appealed to our Government and abroad first and foremost to send clothing and medical supplies, which are now arriving. Recently we have also asked for food; it is coming, but not in the quantities necessary to feed all the Polish citizens properly.

VYSHINSKY. The third issue I wish to raise relates to an interview with President Raczkiewicz, published in the *Dziennik Polski*;[1] it appeared on 30 June, I think. In it are two sentences which taken together could give a wrong impression:

'The two years' suffering of the Poles in Russia has strengthened their will for action and no trace of exhaustion or apathy is left among them.

'Everywhere I met with only one desire: to avenge the wrong inflicted on Poland.'

KOT. Evidently there is a printer's oversight there. The President is a very tactful man, and is aiming at co-operation with Russia. Obviously the second sentence can only have Germany in mind. There must have been some fault in the proof-reading, a sentence must have been omitted. I shall try to clear up the question.

VYSHINSKY. I wish to emphasize that what I have said is not against the President, but against the newspaper and the juxtaposition of the two texts.

Those are the three issues I wished to raise.

KOT. Now I must raise one question with you. In Vladivostok the Embassy first secretary, Maciej Zalęski, has been arrested. You have been informed that he went there as delegate with the special task

---

[1] *Dziennik Polski*, issue for 30 June 1942, published in London.

of supervising the consignments of gifts arriving from the United States, and looking after the Polish people in those remote areas, for instance, those residing in Kolyma. The arrest of a diplomatic official is a violation of one of the main principles of international law. I don't know the circumstances in which this has taken place. In addition there must have been a violation of the inviolability of residence and archives. I request an explanation. Nor do I know the date on which it occurred. I am forced to make a very firm protest and to demand Mr Zaleski's immediate release.

VYSHINSKY. I know nothing about this arrest and I shall give orders for the matter to be inquired into at once.

KOT. But somebody must have allowed it. It is not credible that the Narcomindiel knew nothing about it and that the local authorities acted arbitrarily.

VYSHINSKY. I have been absent from Kuibishev and I know nothing of it. When I say the Narcomindiel is not informed of it you have no reason whatever to disbelieve me. If he has been arrested there must have been some reason.

KOT. There couldn't be any reason.

. . . .

VYSHINSKY. I repeat that I know nothing about it and I shall order the case to be investigated.

SOKOLNICKI. An investigation may last several days, but all that needs to be done in this case is to give instructions by telephone for his release.

VYSHINSKY (with a look of dissatisfaction). I have said that I shall look into it.

KOT. Now I wish to raise the question of the closing down of four delegations by your note of 3 July, and the question of the arrest of Mr. Gruja's co-workers and the removal of the archives in Archangel.

VYSHINSKY. I have received your note on this case and the Narcomindiel will consider it.

KOT. As you know, in Murmansk Mr. Loga was accused by the Narcomindiel of committing excesses, or engaging in speculation, and of selling to the port authorities certain articles derived from the American gifts. I have a report dated 2 May from Mr. Loga, in which he explains in detail that it was the port authorities who demanded payment from him in kind for the drying of goods which had suffered shipwreck, and that in addition he had to clothe the shipwrecked men out of this, and he complains bitterly that he had to hand over so much material.

VYSHINSKY. That is the private affair of Mr. Loga (he withdraws the charges); we simply wanted to inform you of the fact, but it is his concern what he does with it.

KOT. Although I was completely convinced of Mr. Loga's honesty and decency, so long as I did not have his report and had only the Narcomindiel accusations I had to clear up the matter, and I instructed Mr. Gruja to go to Murmansk for this purpose. Before his departure Mr. Gruja agreed with the local authorities that a member of the delegation, Mr. Kuczynski, would take his place. Four hours after Mr. Gruja's departure the authorities burst into the office, carried out a five-hour interrogation of the workers, arrested them, and removed the archives.

VYSHINSKY. All this is in the Embassy note, which we shall consider, as I have said.

KOT. These are very unpleasant facts; such behaviour is meted out only to enemies, not to friends. To arrest office workers is impermissible, and the archives were under diplomatic protection.

VYSHINSKY. I cannot agree that the archives were under diplomatic protection.

KOT. The close-down of the Archangel delegation on the pretext that it has fulfilled its task of welfare in the Archangel and Vologda *oblasts* is unintelligible when you consider the exact state of affairs. We have there already 15,000 persons registered as Polish citizens. Special difficulties arise in reaching these people and looking after them. In the Archangel *oblast* we have only seven men of trust for seventy-five localities scattered over three areas, and in Vologda not one. This is because of the difficulties which have been put in the way of the delegation by the local authorities. And yet at one time the Narcomindiel even mentioned Vologda and demanded that we should look after our Polish citizens there. The mortality figures are enormous. The people there are literally dying off. At one time I was assured by Stalin that the entire Polish population would leave those districts. Meanwhile, the very possibility of looking after them is now being taken from us.

As for transports, in April and May twenty-four vessels left America and England with food for us amounting altogether to 1516 tons. . . .

The Archangel outpost is of immeasurable importance to the

material maintenance of the Polish people in the U.S.S.R. Its elimination is contrary to the 'Regulations as to the sphere of activity of Delegates', and to the promise Stalin gave me that the Poles would be given favourable treatment, as brothers.

VYSHINSKY. I have received a note on the arrest of the office workers in Archangel and, as I have said, it will be considered, checked, and we shall give you our answer. I cannot agree that the charge that the Soviet authorities are not taking a brotherly attitude has any relation with the facts, when it is the behaviour of the other party that has necessitated their arrest. Is that not rather an abuse of hospitality? If they are accused, it is because they are not friends.

KOT. Such a statement without any proofs is empty talk. I am constantly hearing from the Soviet side that when someone is arrested there must have been a reason for it. . . . If we are to admit anyone's guilt, we must be presented with factual material, and that we don't get. Who now is going to look after the Poles in the Archangel and Vologda *oblasts*?

VYSHINSKY. What do you mean by 'looking after'? Here we have no 'looking after', what is due to the people is regulated by law. We cannot make special laws for Polish citizens.

KOT. For us, 'looking after' means providing the Polish citizens with clothes if they are ragged, with food if they are hungry.

VYSHINSKY. The Soviet authorities look after the people.

KOT. We get all our food from Great Britain and America. It is the custom in those countries for the donors to take an interest in the way the food is supplied and how it is distributed. . . . What can we tell them now? In my anxiety to account for the care of the Polish people I ask you, how are we to present this matter now that the delegation in Archangel has been closed down? What will happen to the goods transports? Answer me that question, how are we to present the matter? Perhaps you can make some suggestions?

VYSHINSKY. As I have already said, the Soviet State organs concern themselves with welfare. But we have nothing against men of trust being left in Archangel and Vologda *oblasts* or being appointed by the Embassy. A warehouse for re-expediting goods to the various addresses, in charge of a storekeeper, can remain in Archangel.

KOT. I think it possible to separate the warehouse from the delegation But the goods in Archangel have not only to be re-expedited but sorted. It would be quite inexpedient, for instance, to send goods to somewhere in the south only to have to send them back to Archangel,

Vologda, or Komi. That has to be done in Archangel, so as not to load the railways unnecessarily.

As for our difficulty in obtaining permission to have people sent out, I wish to quote the case of Mr. Marczewski, who was to go to take charge of the stores. But now he has been refused permission to leave, and the militia have ordered him to quit Kuibishev.

VYSHINSKY. In regard to the delegations, I must state that many facts have come to light that the workers in them are hostile to the U.S.S.R., they are slandering the Soviet regime, prophesying that it will collapse, that things are better in Germany; and they are having a demoralizing influence on the people.

KOT. So because someone bad has said something in the south the Soviet authorities arrest people in the north? If anyone utters criticism at times that is because of the difficult conditions, and it isn't in the least a proof that our citizens are hostile generally. After all, the local people also utter slanders, and how! They even attack the Polish people for co-operating with the ' Reds '. I agree that critics of this type must be suppressed, and our delegations are already operating in this direction. But not a shadow of such accusations can fall on Gruja and his co-workers.

I throw out the idea, which I haven't yet given precise formulation to, that it would be possible to have a delegation in Vologda to cover these two *oblasts*. That could be studied from the technical angle. The Polish people who are remaining there in very difficult conditions must be looked after.

VYSHINSKY. At the moment I am expressing my own point of view, but I'm sure the Soviet authorities will not agree to a delegation being established in Vologda.

KOT. In that case perhaps the man of trust in Vologda could be given permission to communicate with other men of trust and co-ordinate their work?

VYSHINSKY. That would be almost equal to a delegation, to which we don't agree.

KOT. The question of care in these *oblasts* must be considered from the technical aspect between yourselves and us.

VYSHINSKY. I agree with that.

KOT. The next question concerns the note cancelling the diplomatic privileges of certain delegates. It is very unpleasant that this note decides such questions one-sidedly, without discussion, despite previous agreements. I have no intention of combating this. When even an Embassy secretary is arrested it convinces me that in the U.S.S.R. diplomatic privileges are illusory, and so I renounce their necessity for the delegates. In view of this I shall recall certain of them, and the others will work without these privileges.

VYSHINSKY. It is a matter entirely for yourself whom you recall and whom you leave working without diplomatic basis, but I ask you not to generalize from the arrest of a diplomat.

KOT. Two cases are surely enough to justify my remarks.

VYSHINSKY. The case of Kuczynski and the other workers cannot be cited in this connection. Immunity is granted to diplomats' persons and their residences, but not to documents they leave behind.

KOT. The issue is the violation of principles, and then it is a matter of indifference whether it has occurred in one or in two instances.

VYSHINSKY. As for the delegations' archives, I cannot agree that they are covered by diplomatic rights. Our liberal treatment is proved by the case of Rola-Janicki, who was working to the prejudice of the U.S.S.R., and who retained his diplomatic status. We only asked for him to be recalled and to be sent out of the U.S.S.R.

KOT. I see you wish to make things thoroughly pleasant for me in various ways before I leave Russia. Now I ask for your sincere reply to these questions:

What will be the competence of the delegates in the future? What can they count on, what is their personal situation, what guarantee have they of their necessary liberty of action, in view of the fact that the existing state of affairs and the agreement have been violated?

How is the sending out of people and their communication with the Embassy to be effected? And how are the delegations to reach understanding with the men of trust in face of the many difficulties?

VYSHINSKY. The 'Regulations' define the rights and functions of the delegations. That is not changed. If the Embassy has any suggestions to make for changing that agreement we shall consider them. I cannot accept the charge that the Soviet authorities are violating it. If there has not been some misunderstanding, then there must have been criminal activity on the part of those arrested. The delegations do not enjoy diplomatic rights.

KOT. The agreement has been violated by the abolition of various representations. How can I recall and change delegates in such conditions? Will others be granted permission in their place? I have asked you to allow us to bring a dozen or more people here, for me to investigate whether they are suitable to be sent out as delegates or deputy delegates. So far only two or three have arrived in Kuibishev. How am I to organize anything in such conditions?

VYSHINSKY. Can you give me the names of those who haven't arrived yet, and we'll try to clear up the matter.

KOT (names three names). I don't recall all the names. I'll give instructions for them to be passed to the Narcomindiel. What is more, these two or three have been ordered to leave, since the militia have not granted them the right to remain in Kuibishev.

I ask you to reply frankly: if all this is being done in order to destroy what has been created, why make any pretence? There is no surety of the fate of either the individual or the institution.

VYSHINSKY. The people you have assigned to new spots can go there. If we have any reservations we shall communicate them later.

KOT. Yes, of course that is the only expedient way, but although their nomination has been notified to the Narcomindiel the militia sends them back to where they come from, without regard to what has been decided in the Narcomindiel.

VYSHINSKY. The militia must act in conformity with the Narcomindiel's instruction; evidently it has not been informed. There is no sense in people who have to travel in one direction being sent in another. Those you have selected can travel to the place to which they have been appointed. We shall endeavour to confirm their appointment quickly.

KOT (in a friendly tone, with feeling). On leaving Soviet Russia I wish to raise with you two questions which are of enormous importance for the future, for the development not merely of friendly but of cordial relations between us. There is the question of the evacuation of children, which has already been raised more than once. I turn to you with the request that you should for your part do everything to induce the Soviet Government to let the largest possible number of children leave the U.S.S.R. We must assure them elsewhere the good conditions of nourishment which they don't have here. At a time when the Germans are murdering enormous numbers of children every child life is of enormous value to us. We are concerned about all categories of children, irrespective of whether they are orphans or not, or whether they're in children's homes in which they are being Russified. After all, it cannot matter to the Soviet Union, which has such a large population. I ask you very warmly to let the greatest number of children possible go.

The second question is that of the Polish citizens not yet released, including thousands of judges, public prosecutors, police, and other officials; but even more particularly I have at heart the question of the 8,000 officers, of whom—I say this with a full sense of responsibility—not one has been released. Taking advantage of the summer season, which makes communications possible, I ask for the possibility of making contact with them. After all, they are not criminals, but prisoners of war, our finest officers. It is impossible that so many men should have disappeared all at once; no one will ever believe that. The failure to find them is a thorn in the side of Polish-Russian relations. I repeat again, with a full sense of responsibility, that not one of them has been released. I ask you not for an answer, not for a repetition of the stereotype [reply] which is in all the notes relating to this, for us painful, issue, but for assistance in finding them. I raise the matter particularly fervently before I take farewell of you and the Soviet Government.

VYSHINSKY. In regard to the children you know that there are various difficulties, and at present the Government will not consider it. I shall not fail to pass on your request. There cannot be any talk of the children being Russified, that would be contrary to all our principles. Their accommodation in children's homes is due to the desire to save some from death.

As for the continued detention of Poles in prisons, or camps, or doing hard labour, I can assure you that I have personally gone into this question, and have checked that they really are not there. I observe some tendency to regard our replies as purely formal, but I have judged that in fact that is not so, it does not correspond with the reality. Apart from a large group detained as Hitlerite agents, there are no others. There are no officers either in the far or near north, nor anywhere else. Maybe they are outside the U.S.S.R., maybe some have died. For instance, the Embassy itself in a recent note cancelled an earlier request to release someone, because he had been found in Poland; and possibly this applies to others. Everybody has been released. Some were released before our war with Germany, some after.

KOT. When I spoke of Russifying the children I had in mind the natural process which is the result of environment. For instance, recently a father who had had to put his child into a children's home wanted to take him away, but he couldn't talk to the boy, because he himself didn't know Russian. And he was terribly upset.

As for the officers, I must say that it is from Poland that I receive the greatest number of inquiries from their families, who are filled with anxiety for their fate, because they are not in Poland. Not a single one.

SOKOLNICKI. The case you have cited of finding one person testifies, on the contrary, that we know what is happening in Poland; and if so many of those we are seeking were there we should be all the more bound to know of it.

KOT. If our prisoners have been released, please let me have a list of those released and the dates when and places whence they were released. The Soviet Government has organized lists of prisoners in camps again and again, and there cannot be any difficulty in providing these lists.

VYSHINSKY. Unfortunately we have no such lists.

KOT. Finally I would like to raise one other question, the really small matter of registration. Of recent days the militia are constantly arresting our workers in the street; it is causing a very exasperated, unpleasant atmosphere. Recently the Embassy Minister Drohojowski, the *chargé d'affaires* in China, was detained for fifteen minutes right outside the Embassy, and he was interrogated and badgered in a very improper manner.

VYSHINSKY. I am sorry about Minister Drohojowski, but checks in the street are being made because of the proximity of the front, which in the air is right above Kuibishev. Were the detained officials registered?

KOT. Not all; there are also a certain number waiting for the vacation of posts which will occur soon after my departure together with the persons accompanying me, and other departures. The militia wants all these people to leave Kuibishev at once; but it would be nonsensical to bring them all back again.

VYSHINSKY. Obviously the best thing would be to draw up a list of these people who are waiting for offices to be vacated, and we will then deal with it.

KOT. We did present such a list several days ago, but the Narcomindiel Diplomatic Protocol refused to accept it.

VYSHINSKY. Please send us a list, and we'll consider the question.

KOT. For that matter not many remain to be registered after the recent departures; twelve persons, I think.

SOKOLNICKI. I think it is rather more; we must draw up this list again; we'll do so after you've gone, when many posts will be left vacant.

KOT. I must also raise the question of the officials and various friends who are travelling at the same time, and I would like them to accompany me. They haven't yet received exit visas, so I ask you to let them have their visas as quickly as possible.

VYSHINSKY. Where persons holding diplomatic passports are concerned the question of exit visas will be settled quickly; but the formalities may be protracted in other cases. But I see no reason why they should not all receive exit visas.

KOT. In addition there are various other persons who will not be ready by then, but whom we would wish to bring away from here. For these also I am asking exit visas. But I am coming up against difficulties with the authorities. For instance, I asked for an instruction that the local authorities should not detain Mrs. Krystina Szmanda, who so far has not arrived; she is detained not far from here, in Karakulin.

NOVIKOV. I recall that case. We have issued the necessary instructions.

KOT. But she still hasn't arrived, so I ask that she may be able to count on a visa. What could I say to her father, Kisielewski, the well known author of a work on the Polish substratum of German lands, who is working in the B.B.C. in London and has asked me to bring her out? Already his wife, Krystina's mother, has died here.

And now I wish to say goodbye. I am forced to leave my post and to leave Russia owing to the state of my health and lack of strength. I arrived here full of the good will with which General Sikorski's Government had concluded the Pact with the U.S.S.R. I am deeply grieved that not everything has been achieved; many petty obstacles lay in the way. In my conviction relations between Poland and the U.S.S.R. should be regulated according to great lines and not be disturbed by pettiness. I have the impression that my mission here has contributed to the creation of the foundations for this co-operation. The sole guarantee of smoothing out of friendly relations is that the Polish citizens and the Polish state should receive from Russia all that is due to them. Those are the true friends who aim at the clear settlement of these difficulties. When that comes about, there will be no heartier friends than Poland and the U.S.S.R.

I wish you success in the war, and valiant victories. I present my wishes for success to the Soviet Government, to its Chairman Stalin, and to Commissar Molotov.

I must thank you especially, Mr. Commissar, for your co-operation with me and for the understanding of Polish affairs you have shown. I wish that you may fulfil your tasks, which will be of great significance in history, with great success.

VYSHINSKY. I am very sorry your health has worsened, and I hope you will soon be better, so that you may continue to work fruitfully for your State. During your stay here as Ambassador it has not been possible to avoid many difficulties and not everything has gone smoothly, but there have also been many positive achievements. I hope that these will occupy more place in your memories than all the others. Our attitude to Poland, to the Polish nation and the Polish State is perfectly clear. It was formulated by comrade Stalin, and that is the law for all of us. That is both our desire and our view and aim. I am profoundly convinced that Poland will be great and free and independent, as Stalin said. I believe, too, that our relations will be strong and genuinely friendly; all of us in the U.S.S.R. wish to work in that direction, and I, too, will work in that direction. Thank you, Mr. Ambassador, for your wishes for our success, and for my part I wish the Polish nation, the Army and the Government success in their fight to restore independence to the Polish State and for the freedom of the Polish nation. I ask you to accept yet again my thanks for your good wishes, which I shall pass at once to Stalin and Molotov. I personally wish you health and the return of strength for future work.

KOT. I retain in my memory our journey together with General Sikorski to our troops, and our invitation to you to visit Poland. For my part, I would wish when the war is over to come here and see Russia happy, and to visit those spots I could not see before, such as the Caucasus and Siberia, and of course the Crimea also. As an historian I would like to study various Polish documents which are to be found here.

VYSHINSKY. We shall be very glad.

The conversation lasted from one to four ten p.m., three hours ten minutes. One sensed a desire not to exacerbate matters on Vyshinsky's part. The tone was calm and quite friendly.

POSTSCRIPT

A218. Cable from Minister H. Sokolnicki.
Kuibishev. 22 July 1942

For Ambassador Kot in Teheran.

Between the fifteenth and twentieth all the delegations were abolished
. . . [reporting many arrests.]

Vyshinsky has postponed a conversation until Monday; the same
night I sent him a personal note of protest, repeating your fundamental
questions and demanding their release. In conversation Vyshinsky
read out a statement that because all the delegations had engaged in
hostile activity and espionage instead of welfare they are to be liquidated and the authorities have been given instructions. I rejected these
charges most energetically, demanding the immediate release of those
arrested, and announced that I would refer it to my Government.
Unable to give any proofs, Vyshinsky took refuge behind a cloak of
mystery.

SOKOLNICKI.
Chargé d'affaires.

INDEX

INDEX

COUNSELING: DIRECTIONS IN THEORY AND PRACTICE

COUNSELING: DIRECTIONS IN THEORY AND PRACTICE

edited by

Gary S. Belkin
Long Island University

KENDALL/HUNT PUBLISHING COMPANY
Dubuque, Iowa

CREDITS

Wm. G. Perry, "On the Relation of Psychotherapy to Counseling." In *Annals of NYAOS*. New York: New York Academy of Sciences, 1955, pp. 396-407. Reprinted by permission.

N. A. Sprinthall, "Counseling: Its Dual Focus." From *Guidance for Human Growth*, by N. A. Sprinthall © 1971 by Litton Educational Publishing, Inc. Reprinted by permission of Van Nostrand Reinhold Company.

R. F. Aubrey, Misapplication of therapy models to school counseling. *Personnel and Guidance Journal*, 1969, 48 (4), 273-278. Copyright © 1969 American Personnel and Guidance Association. Reprinted with permission.

Gordon W. Allport, "Psychological Models for Guidance." *Harvard Educational Review*, 32, Winter 1962, 373-381. Copyright © by President and Fellows of Harvard College.

Arthur W. Combs, "Self-Actualization and the Teaching Function of Counselors." Reprinted by permission.

D. R. Cook, "The Change Agent Counselor: A Conceptual Context," *The School Counselor*, 1972, 20 (1), 9-15. Copyright © 1972 American Personnel and Guidance Association. Reprinted with permission.

L. E. Tyler, "Minimum change therapy." *Personnel and Guidance Journal*, 1960, 38 (6), 475-479. Copyright © 1960 American Personnel and Guidance Association. Reprinted with permission.

Lewis Wolberg, "Methodology in Short-Term Therapy." *American Journal of Psychiatry*, Vol 122, pp. 135-140, 1965. Copyright 1965 by the American Psychiatric Association. Reprinted by permission.

William J. Kirman, "Modern Psychoanalytic Counseling." Reprinted with permission.

Jacob Kesten, "Learning for Spite." Reprinted from *The Psychoanalytic Review*, Vol. 4, No. 1, 1955 through the courtesy of the editors and the publishers, National Psychological Association for Psychoanalysis, New York, N. Y.

Carl Rogers, "The Interpersonal Relationship: The Core of Guidance." *Harvard Educational Review*, 32, Winter 1962, 416-429. Copyright © 1962 by President and Fellows of Harvard College.

C. Gratton Kemp, "Existential Counseling." *The Counseling Psychologist*, 1971, II, (3) 2-30. Reprinted by permission of *The Counseling Psychologist*.

M. I. Garfinkle, Ellen Mendel, R. F. Massey, "Adlerian Guidelines for Counseling." Reprinted with permission.

T. W. Allen, "Adlerian interview strategies for behavior change." *The Counseling Psychologist*, 1972, III (1), pp. 40-48. Reprinted by permission of *The Counseling Psychologist*.

William Glasser, "Reality Therapy and Counseling." From *Philosophical Guidelines for Counseling*, by Carlton E. Beck, Wm. C. Brown Company Publishers, 1971. Reprinted with permission.

To Stephanie Abrams
and Alison M. Belkin

CONTENTS

PREFACE

When all is said and done—when the politician's dry rhetoric crumbles into flurries of dust like the fragile wings of night moths, and the social scientist's confusing jargon mutes itself into a blurr of meaningless sound, and the "good intentions" of the altruists appear as the futile platitudes they really are; when those who suffer in living find their salvation in suffering, and those who love, and love to love, find their freedom in love; when we, in moments of free flight, soar above the mundane concerns that burden so much of life's time—then still we shall rest uneasy upon this planet, cast in dubious battle against enemies we cannot understand.

What I want to suggest is that when this Mobius strip of a thing we call life, with its illusive dimensions of space and time confound and challenge us, we all feel a natural inclination to flee, to free ourselves from it, to escape, expand, expel, expunge, and exorcise the demons which infuse their devilish aims in the sound reason of our normal thinking. Sure, we suffer; but we also learn; we make mistakes; and then we start anew, bound to suffer, learn, and err again. But this cycle (although it is not a cycle in the geometric sense because it lacks the symmetry, predictability, and continuity of geometric cycles) is one that we learn to expect, and attempt to live with, as best as we are able. The solutions offered to us by the politicians, the explanations articulated by the social scientists, the alms of empathy gratuitously distributed by the altruists, are revealed for what they are: hollow expedients for the interminable traumas of living.

But what then? Should we succumb to the pervasive pessimism that weighs down the spirits and dampens the hopes of so many of our people? Or should we, as many choose to do, look only to the pleasures of each day ignoring the consequences of each tomorrow? Or, perhaps, we should forget the question entirely: "No need to trouble ourselves with 'ifs' and 'buts'." Or, are other alternatives available to us?

No man is an island, John Donne said, and yet many of us insulate ourselves from others, from the world around us, even from ourselves. This is recognized by most people in the mental health field: the existentialists call it "alienation"; the psychoanalysts call it "narcissism"; the behaviorists call it "response inhibition"; and I'm sure that others have different names for it. But whatever it is called, the phenomenon of retreating from life, overtly or covertly, intentionally or unintentionally, voluntarily or reluctantly, is a characteristic of most people.

This brings us to the point of this book: counseling. Frankly, I'm not sure exactly what counseling is, nor am I really that concerned. Rather, what interests me is something I've observed over the years, both in relation to my own growth and to the growth of those I know and love. At various times during the course of living, we experience profound changes in perception, reaction, behavior-in-general, and feeling states, as a result of some crucial interaction with another person. This person may be a lover, a parent, a teacher, a doctor, a friend, an enemy, a coworker, an heroic figure, or anyone else with whom we have some contact. In some cases, this Other Person has intentionally tried to change us, either for the better or worse; but in many cases the change is an incidental consequence of a situation more complex and multidimensional than we can fully grasp. In either case, we are still changed, and must then live as a changed person.

Later on, we will speak some more about this Other Person, trying to better understand what it is about some people that make them so influential in the shaping of our lives. But for the time being, let's concentrate on the mechanism involved in profound changes. I am referring to *feelings*.

It is difficult, if not impossible, for us to talk about feelings without talking about people. Certainly, we experience what we readily call feelings which involve no other person. But are these really feelings, or do the limits of our language give these experiences a designation that is not entirely appropriate? I mean we could have a "feeling" such as a pain in the stomach, or a feeling of self-satisfaction and pride, or a feeling of depression and worthlessness, or a feeling of boredom, but these are not the kinds of feelings I want to speak about. Actually, these are not full feelings, but feeling fragments, which cut off others and deny their complicity in the feelings.

Full feelings (or *fully experienced feelings*), on the other hand, are always the remnants of interactions between people. They are the natural by-products of being-in-the world. When we exist with others we feel, and the range of feelings that we are capable of experiencing is a direct consequence of the range of our interactions with others. "I feel beautiful," I cry out, only later to recognize who it is that makes me feel this way. Or, "I feel worthless," I moan, implying that someone has made me feel worthless. *Every feeling is a communion between the person who feels and those who make him feel.*

Counseling, it is generally agreed, is something that involves feelings between people. But what feelings? How are they involved in the process? Is counseling a science of *feelings* or an art of *feeling*? These are challenging questions, and no easy answers come to mind. But we have to find, at the very minimum, a starting point at which we can begin to answer these questions. Since the subject itself is so charged with emotions, and because feelings runs strong about feeling, it is both safer and better to open our investigations with a relatively objective, nonemotional issue, such as "In what contexts can counseling take place?" Part one of the book does just this. It attempts no more than to set the stage for the subsequent parts, each of which builds on the others. But it does so in a way that perhaps opens up more questions than it answers—and this is the way it should be. Here we come back again to the Mobius strip—the more you travel the closer you are to the starting point.

All right, so here we are, having now read the first part of the book and even more perplexed than we were before we cracked the binding. What to do? Part two, "The Counselor," turns our attention away from the abstract issue and on to the person who is intimately and intricately tied up with the issue; the critical variable in the counseling process. And what about the counselor—what does this tell us about the counseling process? Again, through turns and detours, answers begin to emerge, vaguely at first and then with greater clarity. Allport's paper, the first in that section, delves into the mind of the counselor, revealing how the counselor's perceptions influence his actions. The second paper makes a similar point through an objective study, while the third paper expands the point, applying a brilliant philosophical stroke to a traditionally psychological problem. Finally, the social, philosophical, and psychological perspectives merge in David R. Cook's concept of the counselor as a change agent.

By the end of part two it should be clear that the contexts of counseling, elaborated in the first part, are contexts created as much by the counselor as by the setting.

Now, having covered these issues, we get into the heart of the "feeling" matter. Part three, "Models of Helping" will certainly be the most controversial part of the book, and has traditionally been the most controversial part of counseling study. It presents, in ten chapters, ten diverse approaches to helping the client, ranging from the psychoanalytic approach, in which feelings have total priority, to the behavioral approach, where the behavior of the client subordinates feelings to second place. It shows, in panorama, the diversity of views about counseling, and highlights the perennial debates that dot the counseling literature. It is intended to jolt you, to make you think, to force you to question, to make you want to give up on it all, and then finally to conclude, ". . . . ."—well, the conclusion will be up to you.

Or, there may be no conclusion, and that too can serve as a conclusion. But putting together the first three parts of the book—"The Contexts of Counseling," "The Counselor," and "Models of Helping,"—something should begin to happen, whether that something is a picture of counseling that starts to emerge or a general dissatisfaction with all the nitpicking, or the germ of an understanding of where *you*, the potential counselor, fit into this whole complicated, involuted picture.

The next three parts—"Child Counseling," "Counseling Special Groups," and "Counseling Services"—are directed toward practical matters. The papers in these sections may be more immediately filling than the papers that precede them, but not necessarily more nourishing. For those who want answers, techniques, and practical applications, these parts will prove richly rewarding. For those who want more provocation, more challenge, more questions, read each of these papers deeply and intensively, and you will see that as the picture appears to become clearer, in a sense it has become even cloudier.

Each part of the book is prefaced by a short introduction that tries to organize the material and provide some avenues for question. Since the purpose of this book is not to provide "pat" answers, but to open up new possibilities for each reader, I have tried to avoid formulating any conclusions about the material. Instead, after each part there is a section called *Counterpoint* which presents some of the students', teachers', and reviewers' responses to the articles. These responses, in conjunction with the articles, may help crystallize some of the problems.

In putting together an anthology such as this one, an editor always feels a sense of loss at the excellent selections which could not be included because of limited space, permission problems, inaccessibility to some readers, and so on. Many of the selections were written specifically for this book. This was done wherever I felt a gap in the literature, and hopefully some of these original contributions will fill that gap. But in choosing from the existing literature and in selecting original material, I was guided by what I believe to be a fundamental principle of counselor training: the counselor develops professionally as he or she develops a personal sense of awareness, and as he or she begins to relate the domains of personal experience to the professional responsibilities. Thus, if each of these papers is treated as a stimulus to personal growth—whether that growth is in the areas of forming new ideas, trying out new strategies, or learning about oneself—then the book will have served its purpose.

Have fun with the book, and if you have any questions about anything you've read, any comments, any suggestions, any additions—*anything*, for that matter—please feel free to write to me c/o Kendall/Hunt Publishing Company, 2460 Kerper Blvd., Dubuque, Iowa 52001.

G. S. B.
Brooklyn, N.Y.

PART ONE

THE
CONTEXTS
OF
COUNSELING

CHAPTER 1. ON THE RELATION OF PSYCHOTHERAPY TO COUNSELING

William G. Perry

CHAPTER 2. COUNSELING: ITS DUAL FOCUS

Norman A. Sprinthall

CHAPTER 3. THE MISAPPLICATION OF THERAPY MODELS
TO SCHOOL COUNSELING

Roger F. Aubrey

We'll begin by examining the contexts that help define counseling. By contexts, I mean the kinds of situations, environments, interpersonal perceptions, and expectations that make certain types of interactions—which we call counseling interactions—possible. This is no easy matter. For when we come right down to it, counseling (in both its theoretical and operational senses) occurs in so many different kinds of circumstances, under so many variable conditions, with such diverse expectations, that it's a wonder we can define the term at all

What we will try to do in this part of the book is focus in on counseling by focusing out other related activities, such as psychotherapy. This has its pitfalls as an

analytic method, since parameters of exclusion in no way establish guidelines of inclusion, but until we do this we are sort of bogged down in terminology. Perry's paper, "On the relation of psychotherapy to counseling," serves as a starting point. While editors of "current practice" texts, such as this one, generally eschew articles which are twenty years old, Perry's paper is so important, and so current (in terms of its thinking), that I was happy to include it. The paper is useful not only in differentiating two closely related processes, counseling and psychotherapy, but in its attempts to define counseling by goal and process considerations. In much of the literature, as we shall see, "goal" and "process"—the ends and

1

means of counseling—serve as the pivotal points in the argument. While it is easy to argue against this practice, since the ubiquitous "goal and process" paradigm is in some conflict with the individuality and eccentricity of each client, this model serves as a convenient stepboard to more specific analyses. Perry's handling of the subject, now over twenty years old, is still the most articulate and incisive example in the literature.

The two other papers included in this part of the book, Norman Sprinthall's "Counseling: its dual focus," and Roger Aubrey's "The misapplication of therapy models to school counseling," are derivative positions that substantially expand and apply Perry's ideas. Each of these papers, in its own way, attempts to deal with the question, "How can counseling be used most effectively in the school setting?" But this question invariably takes into account the broader question, "What *really* is counseling, and what functions are peculiar to it?" It is the way that these two writers touch upon that broader question, the way they penetrate its

illusive difficulties, that makes reading these two papers a worthwhile investment.

SUGGESTED ADDITIONAL READING

Arbuckle, D. S. Kinds of counseling: Meaningful or meaningless. *Journal of Counseling Psychology*, 14, (1967):219-25.

———. The Counselor: who? what? *Personnel and Guidance Journal*, 50 (1972):785-90.

Belkin, G. S. *Practical counseling in the schools* (Chapter 1) (1975) Dubuque, Iowa: Wm. C. Brown Company Publishers.

Curran, C. A. *Counseling and psychotherapy*. (1968) New York: Sheed & Ward.

Morrill, W. H.; Oetting, E. R.; and Hurst, J. C. Dimensions of counselor functioning. *Personnel and Guidance Journal*, 52 (1974):354-59.

Parker, C. A. The new scope of counseling. *Personnel and Guidance Journal*, 52 (1974):348-53.

Shertzer, B. and Stone, S. C. *Fundamentals of counseling, 2d ed.* (Chapters 1, 2, and 4 especially). (1974) Boston: Houghton Mifflin.

Sprinthall, N. A. *Guidance for human growth*. (1971) New York: Van Nostrand Reinhold.

Zaccaria, J. S. Developmental tasks: Implications for the goals of guidance. *Personnel and Guidance Journal*. 44 (1965):372-75.

1. ON THE RELATION OF PSYCHOTHERAPY TO COUNSELING

William G. Perry, Jr.[1]

Peter Schwarzburg

Introduction

The movements that have brought five different professions to contribute to this monograph started almost simultaneously in the first decade of this century. In the year 1908 alone, the First International Congress of Psychoanalysis was held at Salzberg; G. Stanley Hall issued his invitations to Freud and Jung to lecture at Clark University; C. W. Beers launched the mental hygiene movement with *The Mind That Found Itself*; The Rev. Elwood Worcester published *Religion and Medicine: the Moral Control of Nervous Disorders* in connection with the Emmanuel Movement, the first explicit use of psychological theory in pastoral counseling; and Samuel Parsons in Boston and Eli Weaver in Brooklyn set up the quiet beginnings of formal vocational guidance. At the same time, guidance was entering the schools with the work of Wheatley and Boyden in Westport, Connecticut, and Jesse Davis in Detroit, and the Binet intelligence test was undergoing its first American revision. Two years later, in 1910, Dewey brought progressive education to the high school level with *How We Think.* Meanwhile, in 1906, the first classes graduated from the New York and the Simmons School of Social Work to enter a field in which Mrs. Adolf Meyer had made, only two years before, the first *reapproachement* of casework and psychiatry. Seen against the backdrop of a vast industrial and educational expansion leavened by the new theories of relativity in both the scientific and cultural sense, these events and the movements they furthered appear as efforts to develop new knowledge and new services to assist individuals who would otherwise be lost or wasted in a new and restless age.

In the years that have followed, these movements have tended to converge, in one respect at least. Guidance, applied psychology, education, social work, mental hygiene, and pastoral counseling have all looked more and more toward dynamic psychology[2] for the theoretical basis of many of their insights and procedures, while psychiatry, using the same theoretical systems, has emerged from areas of pure pathology into those of prevention and general social adjustment, particularly education. It is at this point that the five professions joined to contribute to this monograph, and the question before them may be phrased "Are we all trying to do the same thing or aren't we?"

Counseling (or guidance) is a process. It is performed in many settings by widely different kinds of people. The other commissions in this conference speak frequently of counseling by the internist, by the social worker, by the psychologist, and by the minister. This commission could have made similar comments for the educator or for specialists in marriage counseling, vocational counseling, industrial personnel work, and so on, and then we could have endeavored to consider the professional problems of these different groups under the general headings outlined as guides for this monograph. We represent, however, people with a common interest but without a common professional organization. The different groups have different problems, and professional standards are as often set by the institutional framework in which the counselor works as by the professional group to which he belongs. Therefore, we shall not examine these problems directly. We shall address ourselves instead to an issue common to counseling in all settings, the nub of so many professional and interprofessional problems, namely: *Is it possible any longer to distinguish theoretically and practically between counseling and psychotherapy?*

It seems to us that even a little clarification of this question would contribute to the solution of many problems of training, practice, and social policy in the many fields and specialties in which counseling and guidance are carried on.

Part 1

Thus far, at least, no one has succeeded in defining psychotherapy in a way satisfactory to anyone else (1). Nor do we know of an adequate definition of counseling. Most attempts to compare one with the other, furthermore, have been biased by an interest either in making one exclusive of the other, or in making the two entirely indistinguishable. Even less biased comparisons have not been very illuminating, for they have referred to peripheral matters of institutional setting, function, or training, seldom to process.

However, the differences of coloring and emphasis observable in the daily work of those we call psychotherapists and those we call counselors has led a few writers to attempt to differentiate the processes themselves through reference to psychological theory (2). This paper follows from the work of these writers.

We start with a hypothetical psychotherapist and a hypothetical counselor who are well-trained, experienced, and, in an ideal way, representative. We postulate that a systematic examination of their work would reveal the following: while (1) the psychotherapist sometimes does the kinds of things the counselor does most of the time, and while (2) the counselor sometimes does the kinds of things the psychotherapist does most of the time, nevertheless (3) there is, a large part of the time, a sensible difference in the character of what each does. Let us say of this difference that it is somehow a difference *in the direction of regard*, as if the counselor and the psychotherapist were, in their most characteristic moments, attending to matters nearer to different ends of some continuous dimension in the individual's function.

We can begin to outline what we are proposing as in figure 1. Here we distribute the working time of the psychotherapist and counselor along a continuous dimension, and find overlapping distributions of a shape, let us say, like the curves in the figure. The problem we have set ourselves is to define this dimension. If we can do so, and if we then assume that the activities most characteristic of the counselor are properly called "counseling" and those most characteristic of the psychotherapist are properly called "psychotherapy," we shall be in a position to compare these processes. At present our figure gives us only the form we presume our problem to take, the skeleton on which we plan to build.[3]

Let us start at some distance and approach the matter afresh. We consider that counseling and psychotherapy exist because of the need of a new function in our society. Our Western culture has added the ideals of

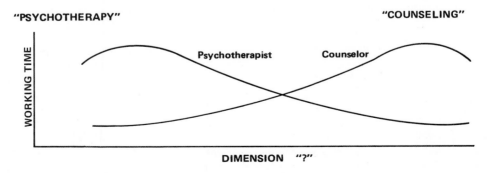

FIGURE 1. Overlapping distribution of process-time on "?" dimension.

"freedom" and of "equal opportunity for all" to a highly complex multivalued, multiroled society characterized by great economic and moral change. This has produced serious problems for everyone in his transitions from role to role, and in his efforts to cope with multiplicity of roles and with value conflicts. In this way of looking at things, counseling and psychotherapy have developed in our society for the assistance of individuals *in finding themselves in the relation of their personalities and roles.*[4] In figure 2 we therefore set forth tentatively this dimension linking the individuals personality and the roles in which it is manifest. The arrows indicate the interpenetrating nature of the two poles. To the left, at the "personality" end of the dimension are represented the individual's biology and temperament, the residues of his learned responses in past roles (especially those of early childhood), his present balance in respect to independence-dependence, dominance and submission, and other dynamic variables. At the other pole, we find the roles in which the individual has his social existence, lying in social describable areas such as education, vocation, marriage.

We should pause here to say that we do not find roles and individuality antagonistic but synergetic. We feel that roles, where they are reasonably loose-fitting, are to be looked upon not as a restriction on the individual, but rather as the cultural patterns or "roughed out" forms through which in-

dividuality can alone be finally expressed. Freedom is not, as it is frequently defined in adolescence, freedom "from" the responsibilities and expectations characterizing roles. The ultimate of freedom is the freedom to create an identity through an individual interpretation and use of available roles and through an individual integration of them.

Before going on, we might make our dimension a little clearer, by picturing in a perspective drawing in figure 2a, a part of the identity of John Doe, thought of as a circle. The center or core of the personality is represented to the left, and we see, radiating from the center, its different manifestations in various roles. Our dimension is a kind of radius that can be rotated through these roles, anchored to the left in the core of the personality from which each role permits, or demands, the expression of different aspects. It is the interaction along this dimension, when projected through time, that generates and confirms the individual's sense of selfhood.

It is, of course, when problems arise along this dimension that psychotherapy and counseling become useful. Problems may originate in the developmental processes of the personality, in the abandonment of personality to the demands of role, or in the wanton destruction of roles by the demands of temperament. They may arise in transition from role to role, or in role choice, or in conflicts among multiple roles, or in con-

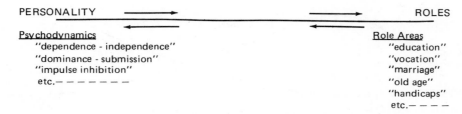

Figure 2. The dimension "personality-roles."

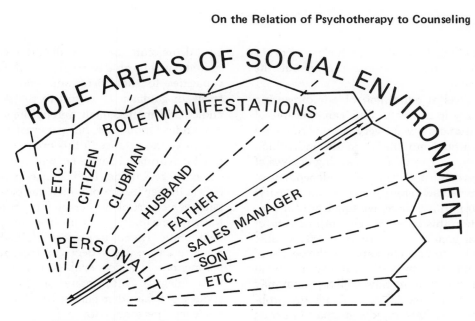

FIGURE 2a. Sector of identity John Doe on dimension "personality-roles." The dimension rotates around a core of personality through the roles in which personality is manifest.

tradiction of values and role expectations imposed by the complexity and fluidity of the social environment.

Since we conceive of counseling and psychotherapy as processes providing the optimal conditions in which individuals may deal with such problems in the dimension of personality and roles, we now reexpress our "dimension" in "problem" terms, as in figure 3. When individual psychodynamics are thought of as problems, we think in terms of intrapersonal conflicts, and we have in mind such problems as the person's intense am-

bivalences, his inhibiting guilts, or his self-defeating lack of inhibition. We think also of the problems of transition or fixation at different levels of psychic development, conflicts of need, *etc.* But when roles and role choices are thought of as problems, we think in socially describable areas such as vocational choice, marital adjustment, the reorientation required by the limitations of aging, the management of the roles of the physically handicapped, *etc.* At this end are all the specific learning problems posed by social development from role to role and by

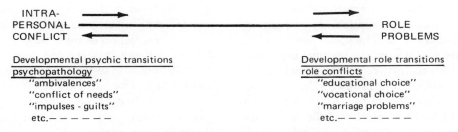

Figure 3. The dimension "personality-roles," problem aspects.

role conflict. Inevitably, each class of problem will affect processes throughout the dimension.

Conflicts at either end of our dimension may vary in intensity. One can conceive of circumstances posing very serious role conflicts through no "fault" in the individual. So, also, we can think of varying degrees of intrapsychic conflict largely independent of the immediate environmental complexity. For our purposes here, we single out for consideration this latter variable of intensity of internal conflict and, for simplicity's sake, we shall assume a constancy in the degree of environmental stress. We can say that what will most determine how well a person may use his own potential in resolving any problems of role, how rapidly he may integrate or learn, is the degree to which he is free from, or afflicted by, disrupting internal tendencies. In considering what kind of assistance a person can best use, therefore, the *focus* of any personality-role problem may be conceived as located in our dimension in accordance with the intensity of the internal disturbance. In figure 4 we plot, therefore, with the lower arrows, the variable of intensity of intrapsychic disturbance, starting with the so-called "normal" at the right, where some conflict may be supposed to exist in everyone, and moving to the left to extreme pathological cases merging into the psychoses and extreme behavior disorders. These difficulties, for our purposes, can stem from any of the psychic factors named and also from emotional difficulties resulting from organic disability and requiring special learning. The upper arrows plot, in inverse proportion, the learning capacities of the person, relative to his potential, *vis a vis* whatever role problems he may encounter. That is, we can make the rough statement that the less internally handicapped a person may be by pathological anxi-

ety, depression, or other disturbance, the more he will be able to respond with his full capacities to the briefer and more direct forms of guidance in regard to the skills of choice and management among life's roles. An understanding of his personality may still be of importance in this process, but to put his learning to use, he will not be required to reexamine, for instance, primitive beliefs the repression of which has become a pathogenic part of his personality structure. Rather, he rapidly picks up from his guide, be it family, friend, or professional, what he needs to know, with a degree of trust and experimentation which enables him to cope with integrity with many of life's vicissitudes. At the other end of the dimension, however, persons with a strong internal disturbance tend not to be able to make use of direct guidance in its own terms, no matter how kindly or skillful it may be. Instead, they more frequently require a very extended relationship with a single person, or small group of people, whom they test out over a period of time, before they can trust enough, or love enough, to learn effectively the emotional and social skills required for successful handling of the roles expected of them and desired by themselves. In the middle, we have people whose difficulties or disturbances are more reactive and acute than longstanding and imbedded. We may find also that the disturbance is less pervasive and more limited to particular roles or role areas. That is, they may be inadequate students or poor husbands but effective in some other area of life. The ameliorative instruction of these people can take a form midway between the two extremes because they have at least the potentiality of transferring successful integrative skills from one role area to another.(3)

We venture now to superimpose from figure 1 our curves which describe the

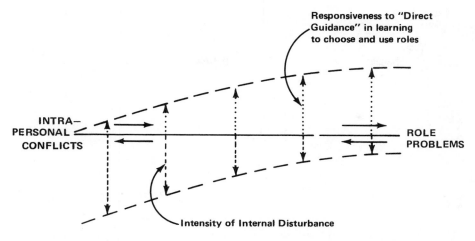

FIGURE 4. Location of a problem along dimension "personality-roles" determined by intensity of intrapersonal disturbance.

distribution of working time of counselor and psychotherapist. With these before us in figure 5, we can attempt to portray the different colors of counseling and psychotherapy as they facilitate a client's learning to realize his identity—a selfhood expressed as the creative interaction of his "personality," as we have designated it here, with the roles which are available, mandatory, or chosen in his life.

The psychotherapist, as we see it, spends the predominance of his time over a number of cases (or the predominance of his time in a given "typical" case) in areas of moderate to intense intrapersonal disturbance. Even though he may frequently find himself able to help his client or patient directly in learning to handle some role with maturity, his primary concern is with looking with his client more inward toward the process represented at the left end of our dimension and less outward toward the individual's point of immediate contact with the external world. For the psychotherapist, the role problems of his clients are of interest less for themselves and more for the light they throw on

inner conflicts. He requires time because his clients do not have, at the level of these conflicts, a prototype for genuine interpersonal trust, and he must start from scratch with his own relationship. Since his major tool must be this dyadic relationship itself, he is characteristically concerned with the dynamics of the client as they are projected on this relation.[5] It is here, in the contrast of fact with expectation, that his patient will learn both to trust another realistically and to distinguish better between objective and subjective experience.

The counselor must also be concerned with these projections, but the resources of his clients make it possible for him to use many teaching tools, and in his most characteristic work he need not depend primarily on the events of the transference.[6] He spends the predominance of his time over a number of cases (or the predominance of his time in a given "typical" case) in areas of minimal to moderate personal disturbance and in relation to some particular problem area in which he claims a competence, be it vocation, education, marriage, or the like. This is

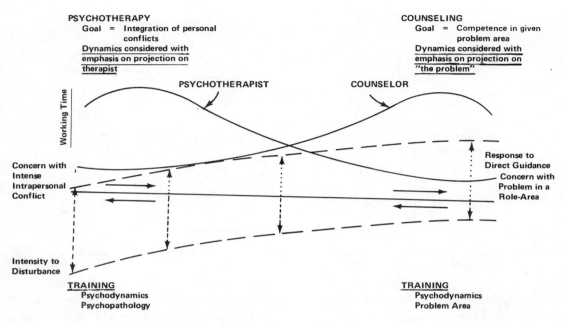

FIGURE 5. Diagrams showing the superposition of Figures 1, 3, and 4.

not to say that he never works with persons with intense disturbances. The counselor frequently works in mental hospitals and frequently finds himself, in other institutions, faced with severe behavior problems which have been deemed not suitable for psychotherapy or for whom there are no therapeutic facilities.

With his more typical clients, a counselor also may make extended excursions into problems of psychodynamics. But when he does so, it is for the most part with the question in mind "What does this tell us that will be useful in attaining a mature competence in the particular roles we are considering (vocation, marriage, *etc.*)?" More consistently than the psychotherapist, the counselor looks with the client outward toward a particular role area. It is this orientation that gives counseling its characteristically triangular rather than dyadic character, a sensed triangle of "client, coun-

selor, role-problem."(4) The felt presence of this "problem," even in the midst of exploration of some sector of deeper dynamics, gives counseling its particular "cast" or character.(5) This characteristic is manifest in action in the tendency of the counselor to be concerned with and to interpret the client's psychodynamics less as they project on the relationship itself and more as they are projected in a given role area. (6) That is, the client learns about himself through the contrast of expectancy and fact in this role area.[7]

We can express the difference in emphasis, then, by saying that counseling looks more often toward the interpretation and development of the personality in the relations characteristic of specific role-problems while psychotherapy looks more often toward the reinterpretation and reorganization of malignant conflictual elements within the personality through the relation with the therapist.

It is, we believe, from this difference in emphasis that other differences follow that have sometimes been mentioned in distinguishing the two processes—such differences as attention to "ego integration" as against the "analysis of infantile conflict or impulse," attention to "conscious and preconscious material" as against "unconscious" or "repressed," attention to the present as against the past, and so on. (We would rephrase this latter contrast by saying that counseling deals with the future "What shall I do about my problem?" while psychotherapy deals with the present "What am I doing that creates my problems?") The distinction as we have presented it does not, of course, immediately resolve such issues as "when" an internal disturbance shall be categorized as "disease," but the scheme suggests that marginal determinations can be made only in the light of the roles the individual's environment asks him to fill. In any case, the degree of overlap in the work of counselors and psychotherapists in the handling of both mild and more intense disturbances will vary with the institutional setting, training, and temperament of personnel, and perhaps even with their theoretical orientation.

Part 2

Some support for our scheme may be found, we think, in the nature of the interests and bones of contention favored among counselors on the one hand, and among psychotherapists on the other. From what we have been saying, we should be able to predict that the major professional divisions among counselors would be according to problem areas; and so indeed we have vocational counselors, marriage counselors, *etc.* Psychotherapists, on the other hand, would divide professionally according to schools or theories of personality, and so

indeed we have Freudians, Adlerians, Jungians, and Washington schools. In their formulations about practice we should expect counselors to differ on matters concerning the triangular relationship of client, counselor, and role-problems. We should expect concern regarding who was to say what about "what the client should do" in respect to his problem. And in fact we do hear debates about the "directive" and "nondirective" procedures. With psychotherapists, on the other hand, we should expect debate regarding the problem of handling the dyadic relationship, and indeed we find that differing views of the "transference" are the major concern.

It seems to follow too that on those regrettable occasions when therapists and counselors point in anger at each other's weaknesses, the psychotherapists should charge the counselor with blindness regarding the exploitation of this transference relationship both by their clients and themselves, while counselors should attribute to the therapists an unworldliness which causes them to impute psychological meaning to sociological variables and transference meanings to objective concerns.

Another interesting validation may be seen in the changes of vocabulary concurrent with the development of the Rogerian school, starting with Roger's book *Counseling and Psychotherapy*(7) in 1942. In this book, the average time reported for cases was 15 hours or less, and concern was mainly with the words "directive" and "nondirective" as illustrated by materials (with the exception of the long case) drawn from counseling in particular problem areas. In 1951, in the book entitled *Client-Centered Therapy,*(8) much longer cases are typical and excerpts from protocols focus on internal conflict. The phrase "client-centered" is of itself a relationship phrase referring specifically to the client-therapist relation, and the book contains an outline of a theory of personality. In 1954, Rogers and Dymond edited *Psychotherapy and Personality Change.*(9) In the index of this book, "Counseling," which had over 200 references indexed in the first book, has one reference followed by "see Therapeutic Relationship," which has 49. In the first book, "Therapy" has five references and "Relationship" three, only one of them long. In the first index, there are numerous references to role areas; in the last, none. We can say, then, that there seems to have been movement in the focus of interest of this school along the dimension we have postulated as central. An extension of interest in the other direction is evident in the writings of psychiatric groups discussing "preventive psychiatry" and the application of psychiatric knowledge to particular areas such as education.(10)

These illustrations suggest only that the two patterns of interests, concepts, and vocabulary we have postulated for persons attending to either end of our dimension do, in fact, appear in the talk of the professions. However, an empirical study of process itself is entirely possible. Large samples of protocols could be procured and analyzed for frequency of the variables we have mentioned, and norms could be described for therapy and counseling as they occur in various settings. We have hypothesized that one of the most distinctive among these variables will be the degree of concern with psychodynamics projected on the dyadic relationship compared to the degree of concern with psychodynamics projected onto a given problem area.

We ourselves should regret to see such a quantitive study of our scheme used to crystallize practice in a new science. We should be content, however, to have it point to useful clarifications in matters of professional relations and training and in all those issues listed as guides for this monograph. Psychotherapists necessarily must be trained in psychodynamics, in psychopathology, and in the handling of the intense strains placed on their persons in the therapeutic relationship. The counselor in his turn (from whatever other professional field he may come) should be trained in psychodynamics, in the special considerations relevant to his problem area, and in the use of his own person and role in the learning process. Since this role can often resemble that of the regular teacher at his best, teaching experience past or present can be a help to him.

In all professional issues, counselors and psychotherapists who are part of these converging movements can work at greater ease with each other where they can see that each approach has its own integrity, its own special direction of regard. Then this integrity need be neither overreaching nor exclusive, for the psychotherapist and counselor have more in common than an interest in dynamics. Together, their ultimate art lies in their capacity to put their training at the service of their humanity in providing a context where another can grow to know himself and to make the choices that affirm his being.

Ultimately, too, all of us who work in this field can share the feelings that follow on remembering how men have practiced this art (without claim to formal theory and certified training) for thousands of years. When we remember also how small our formal knowledge remains beside the complexity of a human being's concerns and resources, we can accept together the possibility that the recent prestige of our specialties may spring no more from the virtue of our knowledge than from the urgency of the times.

REFERENCES

1. Report of the Committee on the Evaluation of Psychoanalytic Therapy. 1950. *Bull. Am. Psychoanalytic Assoc.*: 17-19; G. F. Lehner *Am. Psychologist* 7 (1952):547.
2. Aptekar, H. H. *Jewish Social Service Quart* 27 (1950): 2; O. H. Mowrer, Minn. Studies Personnel Work 1 (1951):7-26; J. A. Rose. *Jewish Social Service Quart* 27 (1950):3.
3. Perry, W. G. and S. G. Estes. 1953. In *Psychotherapy, Theory, and Research.* O. H. Mowrer, Ed. Ronald Press. New York, N.Y.
4. Perry, W. G. and S. G. Estes. 1953. In *Psychotherapy, Theory, and Research.* O. H. Mowrer, Ed. Ronald Press. New York, N.Y.
5. Apteker, H. H. *Jewish Social Service Quart* 27 1953):2.
6. Rose, J. A. *Jewish Social Service Quart* 27 (1953):3.
7. Rogers, C. R. 1942. *Counseling and psychotherapy.* Boston, Mass: Houghton Mifflin.
8. Rogers, C. R. *et al.* 1951. *Client-centered counseling.* Houghton Mifflin. Boston, Mass.
9. Rogers, C. R. and R. F. Dymond. 1954. *Psychotherapy and personality change.* Chicago, Ill: Univ. Chicago Press.
10. Group for Advancement of Psychiatry. *Considerations on Personality Development in College Students.* In press.
11. Hahn, M. E. *Am. Psychologist* 10 (1955):7.

NOTES

1. This paper, presented by Doctor Perry, was written by him in collaboration with the other members of the Commission in Counseling and Guidance.
2. The phrase "dynamic psychology" will be used throughout this paper to refer both to psychoanalytic theory, which has its origins in the study of pathology, and to the developmental and functional formulations drawn from normal behavior by such psychologists as McDougal, Wilhelm Stern, Harold Jones, Caroline Zarachary, Piaget, Wermer, Lewin, Murphy, and others.
3. The paper was constructed for oral delivery. The figures, which are less graphs than "pictures," were intended to convey, when thrown on the screen, the structure of the argument and a rough notion of "how much" difference and "how much" sameness the commission assumes to exist between the activities of representative counselors and psychotherapists.
4. For a review of role theory see R. R. Sarbin, 1954, in *A Handbook of Social Psychology,* G. Lindzey, editor, Addison-Wesley, Cambridge, Mass. The terms "identity" or "self" is used here to refer to the product of the interaction of "personality" and "roles." Compare with R. Linton, 1947, *The Cultural Background of Personality,* Routledge and Kegan Paul, London, England.
5. For an insightful use of role theory in the elucidation of the therapeutic process itself see J. P. Spiegel, 1954, *Psychiatry,* 17:7, 369-76.
6. No effort is made here to distinguish between transference in the extreme psychoanalytical sense and transference in the general sense of the initial assimilations of all perceptions to a prototype. In his work with normals who have learned in infancy the prototype for a workable trust, the counselor is, of course, making use of a kind of "positive transference."
7. We feel that so-called "personal counseling" and "psychological counseling" are not the exceptions they would seem to be to this framework. We look on the words "personal" and "psychological" as distinguishing a form of counseling from "marriage" or "vocational" in a correlate sense. This position can be defended on two grounds: (1) In one set of conditions the word "personal" turns out to mean "social"; that is, the person comes to the counselor in concern about his "personality" in the social sense, rather than as we have used it here at the left end of our dimension. Or (2) he comes in a general dissatisfaction in his function in most of his roles; he is looking out at his roles and wondering why he gets no satisfaction out of them. He is in some sense detached from them or unable to commit himself. Where disturbance is not severe, dynamics will be considered in relation to role areas (as at the right hand end of the dimension) and "personal" and "psychological" counseling still have the characteristics which we have described for counseling. It is, of course, true that the word "psychological counseling" is frequently used, or should we say misused, to cover processes which according to our scheme should frankly be called psychotherapy. We feel that in common usage "psychological counseling" is something of a misnomer when applied to the long-term relationship-treatment of a hospitalized hebephrenic schizophrene.

2. COUNSELING: ITS DUAL FOCUS

Norman A. Sprinthall

Peter Schwarzburg

Counseling and Guidance:
A Problem in Definition

Although no one has yet proposed a specific definition of counseling which is satisfactory to all, there is, more by common consent than anything else, general agreement that counseling is a very significant aspect in any general model of guidance. In fact, some would consider individual or group counseling as the central core of

guidance (Rogers, 1965). This position would stress the importance of in-depth exploration of feelings about self, and the confidential nature of such a private and personal counselor-client relationship. The position emphasizes a separate and distinct guidance role limited quite exclusively to the establishment of an appropriately sensitive and accepting relationship with clients. "We have come to recognize that if we can provide an understanding of the way the client seems to himself at this moment, he can do the rest." (Rogers 1951, p. 30.) In this view, with such a strong emphasis on growth of self toward self-actualization and self-realization, guidance may be synonymous with counseling, and its function circumscribed to highly sensitive listening conveyed through "empathy" and "unconditional positive regard."

Emanating from this single posture, individual counseling as concept and method for guidance swept the field, inducing near total acceptance as the proper focus. Super has noted that guidance theory may reach the stage where it can assimilate useful ideas and modify itself in the light of newly discovered facts, rather than be swept by them as it was by Rogerian theory (Super, 1964, p. 156). When Carl Rogers proposed his ideas, the field of guidance in general showed no such ability to assimilate and modify, but rather accepted the views without an awareness of their implicit limitations. By focusing so exclusively on the emotional and affective component of students or clients, the counselor was creating a role that was almost nontranslatable, or at least quite unintelligible to an emergent profession in education. In fact distinctiveness of function, it could be claimed, was deliberately blurred and obscured so that the client-centered teacher, counselor, or psychotherapist were figuratively joined under the common goals of the actualization of self.[1] In our view, this obfuscation proved a substantial hindrance to guidance theory. The counselor was denied, in principle, the opportunity for an objective assessment of client and process. Client-learning in counseling was limited to actual experiencing based on an implicit dichotomy separating knowledge from experience. While it is possible to continue an analysis of our difficulties with this model of counseling, our chief concern is the resultant

limitation on counselor activity, not only with clients but also with the school as a social system.

Counseling on an individual basis as a means of enhancing more effective personal choice will, of course, assume a significant portion of the guidance professional's role. But we do again want to stress that this is still only one aspect, not the entire role definition. We think that some of the most enduring difficulties in reviewing counseling and guidance literature derive from the lack of acceptance or understanding of this problem. If counseling remains the sole and real core of guidance, then we will continue to witness attempts to wiggle out of the impossible trap created by the sheer numbers of school students involved. Too often the "splendid isolation" of counseling (at least in theory) from the rest of what goes on in an educational setting creates a bind. Solutions are sought which must be temporary at best, such as seeing each student (in a caseload of 400 or 500 students) at least twice each year. The idea that any counselor, no matter how well trained or competent, can provide a significant learning experience (such as promoting more effective individual decisions and personal autonomy) in two 45-minute sessions a year is incredible if it were not ludicrous. There have been other attempts to deal with the number problem through modifications of individual counseling procedures: a more limited number of sessions combined with group guidance, reduction in time for counseling sessions, plus a series of other suggestions which, taken as a whole, really represent little more than administrative juggling and hence an avoidance of the main issues.

Counseling: Its Role in Guidance

We have stressed in this book, a general view for guidance in education as a complementary educational function implying concepts such as normal development, personal autonomy in interdependence, and stage tasks and discontinuities. From this view, it is possible to derive a function for counseling as one aspect of the guidance profession. This means, however, that we are required to discard the limitation of equating individual counseling with guidance. As we noted earlier, guidance as a concept and profession represents an applied behavioral science. Counseling is one aspect of this science, one part of the guidance function. To define and differentiate these concepts is not an easy task, and we will be most candid in admitting that one of the most consistent themes and most remarkable achievements in guidance theory in general has been the ability to confuse through definitional obscurantism. Indeed the ambiguity that usually confronts a reader in guidance is probably a reflection of the uncertainty with which the views on counseling and guidance were elaborated. Lortie captured this uncertainty when he stated as the goal for an article on guidance: "I shall attempt to demonstrate that the current position of the counselor contains diverse, contradictory functions and that members of the occupation will be forced to resolve thorny issues in moving toward the professional model of work organization." (Lortie 1965, p. 128.) Lortie noted in substantiation that McCully, one of the leaders of the profession, could find no consensus on what were the essential and primary services offered by counselors. We would add that if it is hard to find a consensus as to present function, it is very difficult to foresee the emergence of a professionally distinct model for guidance. But let us return to the thesis of this chapter, that counseling may represent one of a series of guidance functions.

There have been a series of developments within the field of counseling theory which have broadened the scope of counseling as an aspect of guidance, and which point to a direction and definition for counseling within the aspects of guidance. As we have noted elsewhere, the acrimony over the rather tiresome dialogue between the so-called directive and nondirective counseling theorists has mercifully subsided. These orthodoxies of the 1950s have apparently run their course. There seems to be a substantial recognition that this forced dichotomy had created a stalemate. Loughary has gently reminded us of the need for understandable articulation: "As our profession became more visible, we were asked with increasing frequency to explain our functions and describe our procedures, and we began to describe what must have appeared to many listeners to be more akin to religion than to a systematic discipline." (Loughary, 1965, p. 46.) The thesis of nondirective counseling and its antithesis, directive counseling, has given way to a synthesis. Through this resolution, a counseling role emerges which not only permits other activities for the guidance counselor, but also implies that the overall guidance function itself can subsume counseling. The resolution has come, we feel, from the recognition that neither position was tenable when viewed from the framework of an educational function. Nondirective counseling theory became too broad. Froehlich noted the increased emphasis on therapy:

. . . the followers of this school of thought have over-emphasized psychotherapy at the expense of counseling. Carl Rogers entitled an early book *Counseling and Psychotherapy*. One of his disciples has written a book entitled *Introduction to Therapeutic Counseling*. More recently Rogers has wisely dropped the pretense of counseling and has called his latest book, *Client-Centered Therapy*. . .[2]

(Froehlich, 1960, p. 373)

As long as distinctions between counseling and therapy were held as irrelevant, so long could nondirective theory hold a place as the model for guidance. In fact as we pointed out in the introduction, by blurring distinctions between counseling as an educative function or as a therapeutic function, client-centered counseling-therapy attempted to become the definition of guidance theory.

Similarly, the assumptions behind the so-called directive counseling models came into question and could be considered inadequate. The directive posture assumed that the counselor possessed information, content, and facts which he then told to the student. An informational deficit was, in effect, the presenting problem and could be quickly and efficiently resolved. In our review, this concept of guidance is superficial, even though, as we indicated in the introduction, the position represents the major rationale for guidance practice. The imparting of information as the major theoretical role for guidance is as disjunctive to the goals of guidance as is the classroom teacher who functions merely as a presenter of content. Both avoid a major educative goal—the process of disciplined inquiry in the case of the classroom, and the process of learning to make one's own personal decisions in the case of counseling. These two aspects of the process of education as the major educative goal, represent for us the point of complement between teaching and guidance. For teaching, as we have noted, this would involve the growth of individual autonomy in the use of ideas, facts, questions, and content in the various subject disciplines, such as English, social studies, science, etc. For guidance this would involve a similar process, but with a shift in focus to the creation of personal autonomy, purposeful action, and effective personal decision-making.

Counseling: A Differentiated Theoretical Basis

The synthesis of ideas for counseling as an aspect of guidance has been recent. While it had been recognized that counseling with individual students would represent a major segment of guidance, in practice, probably by definition if for no other reason, it has never really been clear just what this function would involve. In fact it probably can be demonstrated that while university training centers were engaged in the "directives" vs. "nondirectives" controversy, in practice, the counselors in schools were generally following a nonmodel—eclecticism. There is now available some rather extensive data on this problem. A recent investigation demonstrated forcefully that guidance counselors in general do not involve themselves to any extensive degree in individual counseling. If pressed for a theoretical view, counselors tend to describe what view they don't hold and call what they do an eclectic approach[3] (Armour, 1969). This kind of eclecticism has been called the "smorgasbord approach," or "cafeteria style" counseling. Almost any kind of interaction between a counselor and a student is called counseling. Counseling is represented so broadly that the concepts have almost no meaning at all. The essential superficiality of an eclectic approach is probably more of a symptom than anything else. It is a symptom of an excessively restrictive model for guidance counseling that has been prominent.

The development of ideas and concepts for counseling within the frame of guidance is now becoming insistent. The dissatisfactions with the rigid orthodoxies of the past have produced a trend to a more comprehensive set of concepts. We will draw heavily on the ideas of some theorists in outlining important counseling concepts for a guidance role.

As we noted in chapter 1, there were a cluster of assumptions and concepts descriptive of a guidance model. These assumptions pointed to a direction different from a service or ancillary role. By describing educative, developmental, and proactive concepts as general goals of guidance, we can turn to counseling as a specific case within this framework. A leading theorist, Brayfield, noted an emergent consensus for counseling which includes: (1) a primary focus on counseling with normal people, (2) an emphasis on the personality strengths and assets of clients, and (3) an increased emphasis on cognitive activities, especially those involving choice and decision (Brayfield, 1963). Some of the most important contributors to this consensus, particularly with reference to counseling, have been theorists such as Perry, Bordin, Hummel, and Tyler. There is a strong common theme from these writers which stresses a counseling model that comprehends both rationality (cognitive problem solving) and emotion (the affective determinants of behavior). It is in such a combination that differentiated counseling models are possible. A differentiation helps set counseling apart from other forms of education, such as teaching, and equally from other forms of one to one "treatment," such as psychotherapy. We plan to outline briefly a few of the major ideas developed by the above authors as examples of the consensus.

Perry (1955) identifies two dimensions of counseling: (1) the "direction of regard" by client and counselor and (2) the intensity of involvement. In counseling, the counselor and client often examine the latter's role areas or problems. The term "role" refers to various sectors/areas of the counselee's present social existence. In an educational set-ting, for example, the individual's major role is as a student confronted with certain educational and vocational decisions. For Perry, counseling would focus on the social roles with which the individual is concerned. Counseling is not directed toward broader aspects of personality, or "psychodynamics," i.e., the interplay of instinctual and unconscious forces affecting human behavior.

The intensity of the counseling involvement represents a second parameter. The counselor in the Perry model works with the client on the pertinent role problems. Therefore, the intensity of the counseling relationship will be significantly different from what is typical of psychotherapy. Transference will be at a minimum. Perry also notes that the so-called personal or psychological counseling would still fit the role problem framework:

This position can be defended on two grounds: (1) In one set of conditions the word "personal" turns out to mean "social"; the person comes to the counselor about his personality in a social sense . . . or (2) he comes, in a general dissatisfaction in his function in most of his roles . . . .   (Perry, 1955, p. 404)

Counseling, then, connotes role problem solving. The client can be aided in learning "the skills of choice and management among life's roles" (Perry, p. 401).

Bordin's recent work (1968) is relevant because he also emphasizes a counseling model directed toward a problem solving process. Counseling is focused on the rational elements in this process, rather than on the intensely affective areas. This does not deny the reality of emotional and irrational forces. Bordin suggests a cognitive-conative balance through which the counselor, while acknowledging the latter, works toward enhancing the former. The array of personality variables involved in any such dimension is, of course, infinite. However,

Bordin takes particular note of that segment of personality that is mostly involved with the organization of plans, choice among alternate plans, and what is sometimes called purposive action.

The differentiation between the cognitive and the conative is similar to the distinction in psychoanalytic terms between the ego and id. In a sense, Bordin is revising the more traditional analytic theory of personality to include a greater emphasis on ego functions of thought, planning, and problem solving. This framework of ego processes, then, becomes an acknowledged basis for a viable counseling theory.[4] Bordin notes:

The measure of the effectiveness of our counseling is not how thoroughly or how completely the client's feelings and emotions have been brought into the counseling relationship, but how much flexibility, increased integration of feelings, and better ability to handle life situations (present role reality) for his own satisfaction and productivity been achieved.   (Bordin, 1968, p. 371)

Hummel's work (1965) in developing an ego-counseling model represents another important theoretical contribution to a general definition of counseling. A central distinguishing feature of Hummel's "ego-counseling" is the importance it ascribes, theoretically and methodologically, to "secondary process" (i.e., to the ego functions of impulse control, planning, logical thinking, and problem solving). Ego-counseling, then, is operationally involved with cognition—with analysis and thinking activity. The particular focus is on the personal condition of the individual, i.e., reasoning about, and revision of, one's own (rather than abstract, or others') reality problems, plans, and actions. A concern with cognitive theory follows logically. In short, the special "cognitive-conative balance" characterizing ego-counseling derives support both from ego theory (from Allport, Hartmann, Bron-

fenbrenner) and from the "fruitful promise for counseling theorists in the work of Piaget, Bruner, Rapaport, George Kelly, and of others who have inquired into the nature of thinking." (Hummel, 1965, p. 97.)

Ego-counseling is not a narrow or naive (i.e., pre-Freudian) rationalism. It assumes, however, that ego energy and ego processes can be functionally autonomous within the personality structure; that, in Allport's terms, "the rational functioning of the proprium (i.e., ego) is capable . . . of yielding true solutions, appropriate adjustments, accurate planning, and a relatively faultless solving of the equations of life" (Allport, 1961, p. 46).

Tyler's recent outline (1969) of counseling clearly relates to these notions. She construes counseling as the "appraisal with" the client of the array of alternative "possibility structures." The goal is an enhanced rational understanding by a client, to enable him to choose the most appropriate course of action. Although Tyler's terminology is somewhat distinct because of her orientation toward individual differences as the basis for theory, there is an analogue between her concept of appraisal and the concept of counseling advanced by the contributors already noted. Her term "possibility structure" refers to the long-range strategies for choosing that are possible for an individual. Other theorists identify this concept as ego organization (Hummel), or ego processes (Bordin). Further extensions of counseling theory may be derived from this aspect of personality.

We suggest that the counselor's role and function can be viewed within this comprehensive model we have derived from the literature. For example, the counselor provides special individual assistance to relatively normal clients. As Tyler notes, the client does not necessarily need to have a "presenting problem" since the aim is for increased effectiveness of behavior-choice. However, the nature of our present society confronts the individual with certain discontinuities and therefore requires choice. This is particularly true for the period of adolescent development, and may be equally relevant at the elementary level. In settings such as school or college, the student population is obviously confronted with the realities of choice: educational, vocational, and personal decisions must be made. At any given point, some of these students may not resolve these role area concerns. The complexity inherent in our increasingly technological, corporate, and bureaucratic structures means that decisions become categorical imperatives with attendant "real" anxieties. "No longer can youth contemplate its future under the protection of the great social stabilizers of the past. No longer can one counsel within the framework of Victorian decorum, theological certainties, or the Pax Britannica." (Allport, 1965, p. 377). The simple time lag or prolonged adolescence that our educational system imposes serves to heighten the problem of adequate decision-making and performance by our youth. The extensive "rites of passage," while attempting to confront responsibility, create the ground upon which the counselor and client stand.

Counseling as Method

The model previously described for counseling may appear overly rationalistic because we have deliberately emphasized the goals of the counseling process in terms such as more effective cognitive direction, increased awareness into present role demands/tasks, or an enhanced rational perspective of an immediate "problem" or environmental press. However, in terms of counseling procedures, we do wish to emphasize the importance of the interpersonal relationship, while retaining the cognitively based concepts as goals. By truism, if not by definition, all counseling is centered on the student. Counseling cannot but involve examination and exploration of his "private world," his way of perceiving, thinking, feeling, etc. To this extent, then, all counseling theories are at least partly phenomenological. Also, as a result, all developed counseling theories share this view of a sensitive, understanding, accepting relationship as at least one essential ingredient of the process. We by no means disagree or dispute the relevancy of this aspect of a counseling process.

We hold that a genuine and sensitive concern for the client is a necessary condition for effective counselor-client collaboration. The critical issues in counseling most surely connote parameters which are personal—those of the counselee. Hence, the counselor must be free of a requirement to make objective academic evaluation of the student, or to impose sanctions (grades, discipline, detention, etc.). The relationship must be unencumbered by requirements to teach in a pedagogical sense, in order to permit a stance toward open-ended exploration by both client and counselor. At the same time, we do view the goals of the process in terms other than the experiencing of an accepting interpersonal relationship. In this sense, the relationship becomes part of, but not the exclusive element in counseling. Perhaps we can best illustrate this view by suggesting that the effective counselor is "tuned in" to both the emotions and the content expressed by a client. As a result, the counselor may often "reflect feelings" in the traditional Rogerian sense, not only to clarify possible meaning but also as an indicator that he does, in the best sense of the word, "understand" the client. But, the counselor is not enjoined by theory to go no further in the interaction. In fact we are suggesting just the opposite, that the clients and counselors work effectively through an open-ended dialogue. Perry's phrase "heuristic set" or Bordin's "mutual deliberation" connote similar meanings in this regard. Bordin, in particular, notes the problems created by a narrow counseling model that limits the interaction to subjectivity and affect exclusively. He points out that the counselor who is proceeding exclusively at the affective level may be congratulating himself on having successfully involved the client in the therapeutic process.

However, the counselor is often astonished at the consequences of his failure to help the client arrive at a redefinition of his goal and task. Suddenly the client will pull up short and say something like, "Well, this has been very interesting, now I guess we'd better get down to business and talk about my specific decision. . . ."

(Bordin, 1968, pp. 223-24)

This suggests that the counselor's activity in individual counseling includes respect for both sides of the human condition, ideas and feelings. The counselor can suggest alternatives and clarify consequences. Tyler indicates that in this mode, the counselor should be flexible enough to encourage expression in taciturn clients, present alternatives, and make vague meanings more explicit to the client (a kind of interpretation). The counselor acts to clarify the structure which surrounds the client, to illumine possible encumbrances as an initial step. Bordin denotes this as the clarification of task and goal of the counseling process. The stance of the counselor, then, consists of at least two major elements: genuine interpersonal sensitivity and a flexible response set. The latter implies an active set of responses, a problematic orientation (i.e., questioning, suggesting alternative perceptions, introducing differ-

ent modes of viewing the presenting situation, etc.) to promote an open-ended exploration and examination by the client of his own "self" in the present reality situation.

Some recent research investigations have tended to confirm the importance of flexibility and openness as critical dimensions of counselor effectiveness. Counselors who were able to respond to both the thoughts and feelings of clients were adjudged more effective than counselors who tended to operate more or less exclusively in either the cognitive domain or the affective.

REFERENCES

Allport, G. W. *Pattern and growth in personality.* (1961) New York: Holt, Rinehart and Winston.

Bordin, E. S. *Psychological counseling,* 2nd ed. (1968) New York: Appleton-Century-Crofts.

Brayfield, A. H. "Counseling." *Ann. rev. psychol.,* 15 (1964):319-50.

Froehlich, C. P. "Counseling, Its uses and abuses." In *guidance readings for counselors.* Farwell, G. F. and Peters, H. J. eds. (1960) Chicago: Rand McNally.

Hummel, R. C. "Ego counseling in guidance." In *guidance: an examination.* Mosher, R. L.; Carle, R. D.; and Kehas, C. D. eds. (1965) New York: Harcourt, Brace & World.

Loughary, J. W. *Counseling: a growing profession.* (1965): p. 46 Washington, D. C.: Am. Pers. and Guid. Assoc.

Lortie, D. C. "Administrator, advocate, or W. G. "On the relation of psychotherapy and counseling."*Annals of N. Y. academy of sciences,* 63 (Nov. 1955):396-407.

Rogers, C. R. *Client-centered therapy.* (1951) New York: Houghton Mifflin.

Rogers, C. R. "The interpersonal relationship: the core of guidance." *In guidance: an examination.* Mosher et al.

Super, D. E. "Guidance in American education: Its status and its future."*In guidance in American education.* Landy, E., and Perry, P. eds. (1964) Cambridge, Mass.: Harvard Graduate School of Ed.

Tyler, L.*The work of the counselor.* (1969) New York: Appleton-Century-Crofts.

Wrenn, C. G. *The counselor in a changing world.* (1962) Washington, D. C.: Am. Pers. and Guid. Assoc.

NOTES

1. We do not plan to engage in a long theoretical discussion on the meaning of self-actualization, nor do we question the possibility of "positive forces for growth" or "growth-promoting relationships." We do point out, however, that these views seem too global, too total, and thus too exclusive of other views to provide an adequate framework for guidance in education.

2. Perry (1955) has documented this same point by noting the astonishing decline of references to "counseling" in Rogers' more recent writings when compared to his earlier work and the dramatic expansion of client interviews from short to long term cases; from counseling to psychotherapy.

3. It has always struck us that eclecticism in guidance or education lacks a consistency, originality, and genuineness that is very analogous to eclecticism in art. The artist simply borrows a few of the attributes of great art of an earlier period and completely misses the essence of the ideas and aesthetic Qualities portrayed. So too may the eclectic counselor operate!

4. Bordin is currently involved with the development of personality theory in such a framework. The emphasis is on constructive or adaptive functioning, with theoretical analogues to the work of Erik Erikson and Robert White.

3. THE MISAPPLICATION OF THERAPY MODELS TO SCHOOL COUNSELING

Roger F. Aubrey

Peter Schwarzburg

For the past two decades, counselor educators have borrowed heavily from psychotherapeutic theories in an attempt to discover an adequate framework for counseling in a school context. At the same time, school counselors have significantly departed in practice from psychotherapists. In addition, the school counselor's training program has been less rigorous and demanding than that of the psychotherapist, with an orientation and perspective weighted toward that of the adequately functioning individual, rather than the neurotic and pathological one.

In a critical appraisal of the current situation, Shertzer and Stone (1968) have surveyed the field and concluded that

. . . close examination of the counseling literature reveals that its theoreticians and practitioners have done little to specify the conditions under which techniques should or should not be used, have failed to organize techniques and practices into a meaningful system, and are unable to predict what behavioral results will be produced by certain techniques.

Nevertheless, the attraction of systematized, consistent, and logical psychotherapeutic models have proven too much of a lure for most counselor educators to resist. The secondary school, in particular, has increasingly been a proving ground for theories, methods, and techniques initially devised for a clinical setting. However, client-centered, psychoanalytic, and behavioral models have met with only slight success in the school context, and that evidence which has accumulated (Kehas, 1966; Krumboltz, 1965; Reed and Stefflre, 1963; Thoresen, 1969) is so slight and sparse that it raises more questions than it answers. What the research implies, in part, is that disparate counseling philosophies are vying for ascendancy in the public schools.

Decline of Permissive Counseling

After an initial romance with client-centered philosophy, some school counselors became disenchanted; and in recent years the behavioristic (Krumboltz, 1965, 1966; Thoresen, 1969b) and neo-Adlerian views (Dinkmeyer, 1964; Dreikurs, 1967) have received increased attention in counseling literature. School counselors have quickly attached themselves to theories which require "no necessary and sufficient conditions" in order for counseling to commence. In actuality, it would appear that many school counselors, the majority of whom are former teachers, have long awaited counseling philosophies that would allow them to return to a more comfortable authoritative position similar to that of the classroom teacher. This position was first documented in Waller's The Sociology of Teaching (1932), and in recent years has been described by others (Getzels and Jackson, 1963; Gordon, 1955).

This authoritative posture grants its bearer certain privileges and immunities, and it seems no exaggeration to suggest that the teaching profession has long had an attraction for persons with a strong moralistic bent. Couple that with a captive audience of young, inexperienced pupils, and the adult-child relationship is hardly optimal for counseling. Rarely is the student given an opportunity to terminate his "treatment," and seldom is he presented with viable alternatives in resolving difficulties. Problems are invariably enmeshed with institutional demands and choices are frequently limited to an area circumscribed by institutional norms. In addition, teachers and school counselors are often confronted with two dimensions psychotherapists rarely face: time and the involuntary counselee.

The Tyranny of Time

The first and most important dimension is time. The average school counselor has a yearly load of some 300 to 500 pupils. During the estimated 1,200 hours in a typical school year, he is quite often expected to see each of his counselees once for scheduling purposes, and many times if they require special assistance. This schedule alone exerts tremendous pressure on the average counselor. He values each minute and feels that any time spent building rapport, exchanging information, or actually counseling must pay off in an immediate change in counselee attitude and behavior. In an evaluative sense, it is notable that the press of the school environment seems to make for a special distinction between *counselee attitude* and *counselee behavior*. Counselee attitude is gauged more by student conduct in interpersonal relations, while counselee behavior is reflected more in changes in pupil grades, standardized test performance, and the like. The interpersonal aspect in this sense speaks to the "hidden business" of the school. On the other hand, grades, test scores, classroom performance, etc., reflect the "real curriculum" of the school.

The school counselor also has a difficult time systematizing his working day. Unlike the therapist who conducts business on an hourly or regular schedule, the school counselor must sandwich his counselees between classes, before or after school, during study hall or library period, and on days when there are no assemblies. His schedule, like his role, is of necessity flexible, changeable, and at the whim and caprice of teachers and administrators.

Thus, the counselor's schedule is dictated more by institutional limitations than the personal needs of either his clients or himself. In addition, the counselor's allegiance is constantly challenged and put to the test by the conflict between the needs of students and the institutional demands of the school. This often takes the form of legitimate requests for intervention on behalf of pupils and the expected enforcement of norms and sanctions by school administrators. This conflict is in decided contrast to what occurs in private practice, or even a clinical setting, where the institutional demands are predicated upon, and congruent with, the needs of the counselee.

Reluctant Counselees

The second dimension the therapist rarely faces is a reluctant or involuntary counselee. The therapist outside the school setting usually works with counselees who have either been referred by another agency or who have referred themselves. Even then many therapists utilize the option of interviewing prospective counselees to determine if they wish to work with them.

Quite the reverse occurs in a school setting. Those students needing counseling or presenting serious behavioral difficulties are often given no option by teachers, administrators, or even counselors. They are referred to a specific counselor, not because he presents those skills, techniques, or personality characteristics best suited for this particular student, but merely because he is assigned to a particular grade or alphabetical unit. In many instances, both student and counselor enter an undesirable relationship because of the caprice of a teacher or administrator or the rigidity of the school structure, not because of a thoughtful and considered decision by each party.

Needless to say, involuntary counseling

rarely succeeds when student and counselor are victims of a system based on expedience and tradition. Both parties are exploited although, it should be noted, the counselor is much more aware and responsible for the nature of the exploitation. On the other hand, the student usually acquiesces in the first stages of the counseling process. In time his anxiety is heightened, not only by a confrontation with a school-appointed counselor delving into his personal insecurities but also because he is given little choice or determination regarding direction, termination, or compatibility.

Psychotherapeutic Models

Under these circumstances are any psychotherapeutic models of use to counselor educators? Is the combination of school structure, inadequate counselor preparation, lack of time and facilities, counselor load, and institutional norms too much to overcome? Perhaps, but thousands of school counselors are functioning daily in schools throughout the country, many under the assumption that their particular mode of counseling is backed by a substantial body of research and data. What, then, can be done?

First, counselor educators, psychotherapists, psychologists, and researchers must enter the schools (and stay a while) and examine the situation as it now exists. This means, among other things, that research studies not be limited to the experience of interns and practicum students. Results of counseling must be determined by how on-the-job working counselors actually function and perform. Obviously, this would meet with resistance from school officials and would require tremendous amounts of time and effort. A large number of counselors and students would have to be carefully scrutinized, evaluated, and assessed before some guidelines could be established.

In addition, longitudinal and follow-up studies would be necessary. At present, much of what passes for the effect of various counseling stances on student behavior consists of master's and doctoral dissertations with little commitment to long-term research. Reportable changes in counselee attitude and behavior are often inferred or projected upon a time dimension extending beyond the study itself, and in most instances have not been documented by evidence or follow-up studies.

The need for more research and experimentation extends beyond longitudinal and follow-up studies. If psychotherapeutic models are modified, altered, or "converted" before they are applied in a school context, then both the process and the extent to which the original theorem or method was changed must also be analyzed. Otherwise, we may be drawing conclusions about a method or technique so transformed by its adaptation from a psychotherapeutic to a school setting that it lacks any semblance of its original state.

Therefore, before any meaningful research or experimentation can begin, it is imperative that competing counseling postures be rigorously examined. In particular, it seems essential to investigate the degree of similarity between the original psychotherapeutic model and the manner in which it is carried out in the school context. It would also be desirable to establish procedures to minimize differences in levels of competence among counselors implementing these studies. Hosford and Briskin (1969) have also suggested a need for "new research designs . . . to avoid the confounding effort of selecting subjects from those who volunteer for counseling." This variation between both counselors and their assigned counselees is another crucial but neglected factor. Even when all these factors are taken into account, however, other variables can easily contaminate results. Earlier, two such crucial variables were mentioned: time, and the voluntary nature of much of what passes for school counseling.

Transitoriness of School Counseling

Time, in particular, has often been ignored by investigators. Time, in this sense, refers not only to the length, duration, or number of sessions a counselor and counselee spend together; it also includes the "set" or attitude of the two parties toward this concept. It is one thing for counselor and counselee to form a contract mutually over a stipulated period of time. It is something entirely different, however, when a counselor irregularly calls a counselee to his office or when the counselee hastily asks to meet due to some pressing need.

Certainly these latter instances typify counseling as it occurs in many schools today. School counseling simply does not fit the picture of the typical research model or clinical setting with a nice, neat time sequence, uniform referral procedures, voluntary counselees, administrative support, highly skilled and supervised counselors, etc.

Time, therefore, cannot be separated from the attitude and behavior of both counselor and counselee. The majority of research efforts in school counseling has made little or no effort to control the behavior of the counselor (Wicas & Mahan, 1966). The focus has been on the pre- and post-behavior of the student, rather than on an assessment of the consistency and effectiveness of counselor technique. However, most school counselors are quite aware that their counseling stance often changes in ac-

cordance with the topic, counselee, institutional length of time one has known and press, intensity of the relationship, work with the counselee, and a host of other factors. Therefore, differentiating or categorizing counselor behavior is an extremely tricky business, compounded by the irregularity with which a counselor sees his counselees.

To control time so that meaningful and accurate data is generated, researchers must be aware of the transitory nature of school counseling. The assumption that there is a marked degree of stability in school counseling relationships is both naive and detrimental for research purposes. This does not mean that psychotherapeutic models are inappropriate for a school context, but research designs are certainly called for approximating that which psychotherapeutic models seek to examine and improve.

The involuntary nature of much of what passes for school counseling raises a serious question as to the usefulness of any psychotherapeutic model. The ideal of having the bulk of counselees on a self-referral basis is totally unrealistic in a school context, and, when attempted, places counselors in a competitive popularity contest, vying for student favor. At the very least, counselors are frequently forced to "sell themselves" to wary and cautious students. The alternative to persuading counselees is often even more unpalatable, for it requires that the counselor assume a quasi-administrative posture whereby the client is obliged to enter a "counseling" relationship.

When this compulsory relationship is labeled counseling and results are based primarily on institutional values such as grades or test scores, the entire question of which counseling model or technique is more effective becomes ludicrous. However, this is not to deny counselors the skills and techniques they need in dealing with reluctant and involuntary students as long as school administrators base part of their evaluation of the guidance services on this criterion. Changing administrative attitudes would certainly obviate this problem to a great extent, but at present there seems to be little hope of accomplishing this feat.

What the Schools Need

Models and techniques which speak to the on-going problems of students and counselors must be formulated, and not Pollyanna-like schemes which promise much but deliver little. Researchers and theoreticians alike would be well advised to examine the sociological structure of the school before suggesting counseling frameworks directly antithetical to institutional norms and expectations. The school is simply not a guidance clinic or mental health center, and those counseling models failing to take this into account lull counselors into entanglements beyond their expertise and institutional prerogatives. School counselors certainly are in desperate need of assistance in the area of theory and research. However, the price they now pay for attempting to operationalize impractical and unsuitable designs makes it doubly imperative that theoreticians and researchers closely scrutinize the school structure before exporting models intended for other settings and purposes.

What the schools need are theoretical models congruent with educational purposes, and/or realistic designs which will enable guidance personnel to modify or change existing educational structures and practices. Those psychotherapeutic methods and techniques which fail to take into account the counselor's training and background, the conditions under which he works, the involuntary nature of many counselees in a school setting, the limitations of time and scheduling, the institutional expectations, and the structure of the school setting should be approached with extreme caution.

The lack of theory and research in the field of school counseling has long led guidance practitioners to appropriate designs from other disciplines. Hopefully, the guidance profession and counselor educators are now at a point where they can seize the initiative and evolve corrective measures which speak to the issues with which counselors have been struggling for so many years.

REFERENCES

Dinkmeyer, D. Conceptual foundations of counseling: Adlerian theory and practice. *School Counselor* 11 (1964):174-78.

Dreikurs, R. Guiding, teaching and demonstrating: an Adlerian autobiography. *Journal of Individual Psychology* 23 (1967) 145-57.

Getzels, J. W., and Jackson, P. W. The teacher's personality and characteristics. In N. L. Gage (Ed.), *Handbook of research on teaching.* Chicago: Rand McNally, 1963. Pp. 511-82.

Gordon, C. W. The role of the teacher in the usual structure of the high school. *Journal of Educational Sociology* 29 (1955):22-29.

Hosford, R. E., and Briskin, A. S. Changes through counseling. *Review of Educational Research* 39 (1969):189-207.

Kehas, C. D. Theoretical formulations and related research. *Review of Educational Research* 36 (1966):207-18.

Krumboltz, J. D. Behavioral counseling: rationale and research. *Personnel and Guidance Journal* 44 (1965):383-87.

———, (Ed.) *Revolution in counseling.* Boston: Houghton Mifflin, 1966.

Reed, H., and Stefflre, B. Elementary and secondary programs. *Review of Educational Research* 33(2) (1963):152-62.

Shertzer, B., and Stone, S. C. *Fundamentals of counseling.* Boston: Houghton Mifflin, 1969.

Thoresen, C. E. Relevance and research in counseling. *Review of Educational Research* 39(2) (1969):263-81. (a)

Thoresen, C. E. The counselor as an applied behavioral scientist. *Personnel and Guidance Journal* 46 (1969):841-48. (b)

Waller, W. *The sociology of teaching.* New York: Wiley, 1932.

Wicas, E. A., and Mahan, T. W., Jr. Characteristics of counselors rated effective by supervisors and peers. *Counselor Education and Supervision* 6 (1966):50-56.

PART ONE
COUNTERPOINT

DEFINING COUNSELING

Dear Editor:

"I got the impression as I read these articles that each was trying to say the same thing, and none was quite succeeding at saying what it wanted to. These writers, like so many people in our profession, are trying to find the proper niche for counseling in the vast panorama of mental health services. On the one hand, they are trying to do this by differentiating counseling as a theoretical modality which differs from other modalities: on the other hand, they are striving to find *operational* differences between counseling, guidance, and psychotherapy. . . . I think that if we concentrate more on finding effective methods for helping people overcome (or cope with) their problems, rather than trying to set up distinct categories of treatment, we would fare much better and provide much more useful services to the public."

E. S.

• • •

Dear Editor:

"The three articles made clear to me (I'm a first-year student in the program) how counseling really stands on its own as a discipline. The illustrations in the Perry article prove the old adage, 'a picture is worth a thousand words.' My friends who are not familiar with the true place of counseling argue that it's a form of therapy. But what Dr. Perry demonstrates is that counseling, above all else, deals with the real problems of living, and for a person having difficulties in these areas, this would certainly be the most important thing."

M. M.

• • •

MANY-BRANCHED ROOTS

Dear Editor:

"One thing the three articles in this section did not go into is what I would consider a very important point in distinguishing between guidance, counseling, and psychotherapy. Since the three practices, regardless of their present differences, come from very different roots, at different times in history, it is inevitable that there should be fundamental differences between them. Guidance is a service-oriented profession, derived from the vocational guidance movement of the early 1900s in the United States: counseling combines psychological and psychotherapeutic roots in a comprehensive mental health treatment program: psychotherapy derives from, and is still influenced by, the medical profession (and, therefore, the medical model). Maybe some fourth term can be found to include all of these services under one banner."

                                                                                    C. J. S.

Note. This reader is quite right in pointing out the different roots of the three disciplines. There is a fuller discussion of these differences, and of the histories in "What is Counseling?" Part One of *Practical Counseling in the Schools* (by Gary S. Belkin: Dubuque, Iowa: Wm. C. Brown Company Publishers, 1975).

A REALISTIC APPRAISAL

Dear Editor:

". . . The simplest distinction between a counselor and psychotherapist, in real life anyway, is the price they charge, the education they have, the setting in which they work, and the social esteem each enjoys from colleagues and from the general public. Despite all the seemingly genuine attempts to distinguish one from the other, the reality of the situation is that a psychotherapist is generally better trained than a counselor; a counselor receives less compensation than a psychotherapist; no one working in the school setting dares call himself a psychotherapist. In other words, if you water down psychotherapy, what you have is counseling!"

                                                                                    E. H.

Note. Although this reader's letter reflects a popular position, it is based on misinformation rather than evidence. In fact, there is no evidence to show that psychotherapists are really better trained than counselors, even though the general public may believe this is true. While psychotherapists may charge more and enoy more social prestige, this situation is the result of a misinformed public atttitude rather than a consequence of an objective evaluation of their respective competencies.

STILL LOOKING FOR CONTEXTS

Dear Editor:

"I am reminded of the story of when James Thurber was asked by an acquaintance he met on the street, 'How's your wife?' and he replied, 'Compared to what?' If you really wanted to get at the contexts of counseling in this section, I am afraid you've failed. But if your ambitions were lesser, and if you are satisfied to raise a few engaging issues, without adequately answering them, then you can consider your venture successful."

R. G. K.

• • •

DON'T FORGET THE CLIENT

Dear Editor:

"As a school counselor who works with emotionally disturbed children (in specially-designated classes), I've often asked myself; 'What am I supposed to be doing to help these children?' Over the years, I've resolved this question through the recognition that what these children need is understanding, an opportunity to speak to someone who will listen and who *cares,* a little love and guidance, with some discipline, firmness, and values thrown in. . . . I've always thought of this simply as good teaching, even though I felt it was more than that—it was touching something deep down inside. Now, after reading these papers, I realize that I've been doing counseling all along. . . . What I'm trying to say is that whatever you name the combination of personal ingredients that goes into helping people, and of course this occurs in many different settings, maybe it is these ingredients that really are what you call the *contexts of counseling.*"

D. J.

• • •

Dear Editor:

"There are two ideas I have on what you call the contexts of counseling. First, that these contexts differ so much from client to client (which you imply in your introduction) that it is futile to try to make general guidelines for what constitutes counseling. Counseling, in other words, is different things to different people, and by people I mean both 'clients' and 'counselors'—not to mention the administrators who employ counselors and often dictate, or try to dictate, what the counselor should be doing. Second, I notice that the progression in reasoning from Perry to Sprinthall to Aubrey, and would like to suggest the next logical step; namely, that psychotherapy models be disregarded entirely in working with people, and that some more humanistic attitude (as opposed to model) be put in its place. Someday, I'll write a paper and call it "The misapplication of therapy models to all life situations." Maybe it will find its way into your next book!"

D. H.

Note. Goodluck on your paper. I quite agree with many of your perceptions. You might want to look at Gerard Egan's *The skilled helper: A model for systematic helping and interpersonal relating* (Monterey, Ca.: Brooks/Cole, 1975). This book does some of the things you are speaking about. Also, a couple of the points raised in part three of this anthology, "Models of Helping," may be consistent with your position.

A BEHAVIORAL RESPONSE

Dear Editor:

". . . In Dr. Sprinthall's paper, 'Counseling: its dual focus,' he makes the point that all counseling is involved in an exploration of the client's private world; that is, that counseling is necessarily phenomenological. But might this not be a fault rather than a virtue of counseling? . . . What I am trying to suggest is that if counselors concentrated more on behavioral problems (as behavioral counselors try to do, for example), then counselors would not be wasting their time and the client's in attempting to reconstruct an inner-world which is not only intangible, but which may not exist at all. . . ."

W. G.

Note. Chapter 4 of Dr. Sprinthall's fine book, *Guidance for human growth,* which examines the behavioral counseling position in great detail and with great insight, will answer your objections. In that chapter, he examines the claims of behaviorists and their major arguments, and points out "inconsistencies and pseudoscientific aspects in these claims."

PART TWO

THE COUNSELOR

I've often wondered why most case studies that we find in the literature are case studies of the client rather than of the counselor. Do you think Shakespeare would have succeeded had he written a *Juliet* without a *Romeo*, or would Raskolnikov have been as compelling a character without a Svidrigailov to prod him on? I hardly think so.

Likewise, the client, as he exists *qua* client, extracts and maintains a part of his identity vis-a-vis his relationship with the counselor. In this part of the book we will take a long, deep, intense, and hopefully incisive look at the counselor—that sometimes mysterious, always ineluctable variable of the counseling process. We will begin with Gordon Allport's, "Psychological models for guidance," which sets forth the tone of this part: "However excellent his natural eyesight may be, a counselor looks at his client through professional spectacles. It could not be otherwise." Allport then dissects brilliantly the images through which the counselor sees his client, and discusses the implications for guidance.

The next article further expands the idea of the counselor as a critical, albeit subjective, variable in the counseling process. Arthur W. Comb's trenchant analysis of "self-actualization and the teaching function of counselors," synthesizes the author's work of many years and applies his insights to the counseling situation. Combs, whose *self-as-instrument* approach has enjoyed wide recognition, examines counseling in terms of the counselor's phenomenological perceptions. "Becoming a counselor," he says, "is not a matter of learning how to counsel. It is a question of personal discovery, of learning how to use one's self well." Through his presentation of the counselor's perceptual organization, and its objective meaning, Combs makes clear to the reader the relationship between counseling and personal growth. This brief paper, more than any other discourse on the subject, has made clear to me (at last!) what self-actualization really is, and what relevance the concept has for counseling.

Finally, we conclude this section with David R. Cook's. "The change agent counselor: a conceptual context," which combines psychological, sociological, and philosophical insights in a discussion of the school counselor's role as an agent of change. Many papers on the same subject have been published during the late 60's and early to mid-70's, but Cook's is still, in my mind, the best. It directs itself to those in the field, and succeeds in touching upon a difficult topic with depth, and in making it accessible to many different readers.

SUGGESTED ADDITIONAL READINGS

Blocher, D. N. Can the counselor function as an effective agent of change? *The School Counselor*, 1966, 13 (1966):202-206.

Ivey, A. E. and Robin, S. S. Role theory, role conflict, and counseling: a conceptual framework. *Journal of Counseling Psychology*, 13 (1966):29-37.

Morgan, L. B. The many publics of the counselor: a dialogue. *Personnel and Guidance Journal*, 52 (1974):665-70.

Peterson, J. A. *Counseling and values*. Scranton: International Textbook, 1970.

Robb, W. J. Self-discovery and the role of the counselor. *Personnel and Guidance Journal*, 45 (1967):1008-1011.

Tyler, L. A. *The work of the counselor*, 3rd ed. New York: Appleton-Century-Crofts, 1969.

Vordenberg, W. The impact of personal philosophies on counseling. *Personnel and Guidance Journal*, 31 (1953):439-40.

4. PSYCHOLOGICAL MODELS FOR GUIDANCE

Gordon W. Allport

Peter Schwarzburg

However excellent his natural eyesight may be, a counselor always looks at his client through professional spectacles. It could not be otherwise. After all, he has invested time and money in his psychological training. Of what use is it unless it adds special prisms to his own unaided eyesight?

The lenses we wear are ground to the prescription of our textbooks and teachers. Even while we are undergraduates a certain image of the nature of man is fitted to our eyes. We grow accustomed to the image and when we become practitioners or teachers we may still take it for granted.

But every so often comes a time for optical re-examination. Perhaps the image we have is still the best fit we can get; perhaps it is not. We can tell only by examining alternative lenses. In particular I believe that three are worthy of special scrutiny:

1. *Man seen as a reactive being.* Under this rubric I would include outlooks known as naturalism, positivism, behaviorism, operationism, physicalism; these are also sometimes called—mistakenly, I think—"scientific psychology."

2. *Man seen as a reactive being in depth.* Here I include what is variously called psychoanalysis, psychodynamics, depth psychology.

3. *Man seen as a being-in-process-of-becoming.* This label covers recent trends known as holism, orthopsychology, personalistics, existential psychology.

These three images provide a focus not only for guidance practices, but for all other professional psychological activity whether it be teaching, research, counseling or therapy.

Man: A Reactive Being

One hundred years ago in his *Beitrage* Wilhelm Wundt mapped a program for the newly conceived science of psychology. His own view of the proper development of this science was broad and permissive, especially in the field of social psychology. But what has taken hold in the Anglo-American tradition is the experimental outlook of his *Physiologische Psychologie.* Fusing with Darwinism, Machian positivism, the quantitative outlook of Galton and his successors, as well as with techniques invented by Binet, Pavlov, Hull and others—this experimental outlook prevailed and has ground the lens that is fitted to the eyes of almost all undergraduate students of psychology. Many of us who continue in the profession feel no need for further correction in this image of man.

Seen through this lens man is no different in kind from any other living reactor; and therefore, like the paramecium or pigeon, may be studied biologically, behaviorally, mathematically. To be sure a few special concepts need to be devised to take care of the vast complexity of human behavior, but all these concepts—among them habit hierarchy, secondary reinforcement, input and output of information, and the like—are consistent with the postulates of physicalism and naturalism.

If we ask, "What does it mean to be a human being?" this school of thought replies, "Man is one more creature of nature; his behavior though complex is predictable in principle. His present state is determined by his past state. A man's consciousness is unreliable and must be distrusted, preferably disregarded altogether. We seek the general laws of nature, not personal uniqueness. We study man, not men; objective reality, not subjective."

In principle this broad positive tradition, which we all know so well, puts a desirable end to psychological naivete. It cautions us not to believe every verbal report that comes to our ears; it warns us to be skeptical of our own naked eyesight; and from it we learn to check ourselves for observer reliability. It teaches us to use precise and repeatable methods. Because of its stress on reliable methods this favored tradition in psychology has becone known as "scientific psychology." Its methods are indeed scientific; but its primary postulate—that man is simply a reactive organism—is no more scientific than any other postulate.

It is here that the counselor encounters his first difficulty. Trained in tests, statistics, and experimental design, he may think, quite mistakenly, that to employ these useful aids he must also view his client as a reactive being—an exclusive product of stimulus impact, homeostasis, drive-reduction and reinforcement learning. The term "scientific" has spread like a grease spot from method to theory. Just because most of our methods evolved through the positivistic tradition does not mean that the postulates of this tradition concerning the nature of man are the only acceptable postulates for scientific psychology.

A counselor whose theoretical spectacles disclose a merely reactive being, is likely to think of his client in terms of past conditioning and potential re-conditioning; in terms of reinforcements, in terms of environmental determinism. He will assume that his client's basic motives are drive-reduction or second-order conditionings which in some shadowy way are supposed to account for all his adult interests and vocational ambitions.

The vocabulary emanating from this type of postulate is replete with terms like *reaction, response, reinforce. The reference is backward. What has* been is more important than what *will* be. Terms such as *proaction, progress, program, production, problem-solving,* or *propriate* are characteristically lacking. One would think that the client seated opposite would *protest,* for the

language of response negates the subject's immediate certainty that his life lies in the future.

The positivistic view of man as a reactor has performed a good service, shaking us out of common sense naivete, endowing us with useful methods, and correctly informing us that man is, in *some* aspects of his being, a simple respondent to simple pressures. Its postulates are, however, questionable. It sees reality as ordered but not as personal; it sees consciousness as a nuisance; it looks at man as reactive not proactive.

It is probably true that no counselor fully follows this creed in his daily practice. Indeed he could not do so. It is too impoverished a view of real life. When a convinced positivist attempts to fit his image of man to concrete human situations, as B. F. Skinner has done in *Walden Two,* the result strikes many of us as threadbare, even pitiable.

Probably for this reason many behaviorists (starting even as far back as E. B. Holt in *The Freudian Wish and Its Place in Ethics*) attempt to combine stimulus-response with psychonalysis. Neal Miller and John Dollard in their *Personality and Psychotherapy* offer a good example. Man as a reactive being is combined with man as a reactive being in depth.

Man: A Reactive Being in Depth

So influential is this image of man that we find it everywhere: dominant in literature, in social work, in guidance, in therapeutic practice, and in the market place. There is no need today to describe this image to any educated, or even semi-educated, American adult. Freudianism, like positivism, is our daily dish.

What I should like to do is to make clear that Freudianism (in spite of its less reliable methods) is a close kin of traditional positivism. The only change in the image of man lies in adding the depth dimension. To the long psychological vocabulary of re-compounds, depth psychology adds *repression, regression, resistance, abreaction, reaction formation,* and many others.

Like other simple naturalistic views of man, psychoanalysis puts its chief weight upon the press of pleasure and pain. This pressure produces in the organism a tendency to seek an equilibrium between the force of his drives and the circumstances of reality. The fact that Freud maximizes the role of sex and locates the whole constellation of reactive forces chiefly in the unconscious does not alter the essential similarity.

For Freud causation lies in the past history of the individual just as it does for the conditioned-response theorist. Both have a dismaying disregard for the person's phenomenology of the future, for his sense of personhood and sense of freedom. The ego is a reactive agent, having no energy of its own, but borrowing from the unsocialized Id.

Central to depth psychology, and important for guidance, is the doctrine of *recall* and *recovery* (two more *re-*compounds). Therapy, and presumably guidance, proceeds by disclosing to the client some buried motive, or a troublesome and repressed psychic trauma. The client's salvation, if indeed he has any, lies in this vital recall. A troublesome memory is brought to cognizable form. Presumably the result is helpful to the individual in solving his conflicts. The theory, however, does not allow for any interaction between the person and the recovered memory. Simple re-instatement is itself, as Freud says, the "pure gold" of psychoanalysis. What values a client should live by when once the re-instatement has taken place is not the "pure gold" of psychoanalysis. That all adult values are simply sublimated aim-inhibited wishes, is

the central doctrine. Freud never allows for the individual's capacity to disregard his past or to reshape it freely. Indeed, since the structure of the Id never changes, the future can at best be a redirection, never a transformation, of one's purposes. What one becomes is essentially what one is, and what one was.

Among the valid portions of psychoanalysis of special use to all counselors, is the brilliant account given us by Freud and by his daughter Anna, of the defensive mechanisms of the ego. In dealing with our client we do well to follow the advice of psychoanalysis and watch for rationalizations, denials of reality through repression, and displacements of aggression. All these, and other, ego-defenses belong to the nature of man' and therefore must find a place in any theory of human personality.

But what perplexes me is why so many of the ego-processes described by psychoanalysis should be merely protective strategies. Are there no ego-processes that lead to a transformation of what is recovered? To a creative cognition? To a revised sense of personhood and a new phenomenology of the future? To a Freud the person seems never to be truly proactive, seldom even active. Almost always he is seen as reactive to early fixations—perhaps to some castration threat that occurred years ago, or to some other unsocialized infant complex, especially to Oedipal fantasies. My difficulty with this image of man is summed up most tersely by the late satirist, Max Beerbohm, who said, "They were a tense and peculiar family—those Oedipuses."

There is, I am well aware, a large group of theories that derive from the psychodynamic tradition but at the same time deviate considerably from the orthodox view of reactivity-in-depth. All these theories, in my judgment, move in a desirable direction.

Here I shall mention only some of the relevant authors: Adler, Jung, Hartmann, Horney, Erikson, Fromm. Still more deviant from Freud are Goldstein, Maslow, Rogers, and Robert White. These and other writers offer a type of theory that views man as a being in the process of becoming. Many of them ask the pivotal question differently from the reactivist schools of thought. And it makes a good deal of difference just how a question is asked.

A story is told about two priests. They were arguing whether it was proper to smoke and to pray at the same time. One said "Yes," the other "No." To settle the matter they decided that both should write to the Holy Father for his opinion. Sometime later they met and compared notes. Each claimed that the Holy Father had supported his view. They were perplexed. Finally one asked, "How did you phrase your question?" The other replied: "I asked whether it was proper to smoke while one is praying; and the Pope answered, 'Certainly not, praying is serious business and permits no distractions.' And how did you phrase your question?" "Well," said the other, "I asked if it were proper to pray while smoking, and the Pope answered, 'Certainly, prayer is always in order.'"

Instead of asking Aristotle's question, "What is the place of man in Nature?" many authors today are asking St. Augustine's question, "Who am I?" This question, rephrased in the 20th Century, has opened the floodgates to a new theorizing of the broad type often labeled *existentialist*.

Man: Being in the Progress of Becoming

Seelye Bixler, former president of Colby College, tells of a student who recently remarked, "I can't tell you how much satisfaction I take in my existential despair." In some student circles despair has always been popular. To label it "existentialist" makes it doubly attractive, in fact irresistible.

But overlooking the fashionable flavor of existentialism it is surely necessary for the modern counselor to take seriously the present-day anxieties of the younger generation. No longer can youth contemplate its future under the protection of the great social stabilizers of the past. No longer can one counsel within the framework of Victorian decorum, theological certainties, or the Pax Britannica. It is obvious to us all that some sort of shattering transformation is under way. The comfortable stabilities of culture, caste, the gold standard, and military supremecy are no longer ours.

Nor are the comfortable stabilities of traditional psychology adequate. Of what use is it to invoke an impersonal theory of learning, a biological theory of motivation, and a late Victorian formula for the unconscious, when youth's problems today are acutely conscious, intenssel personal, and propelling him like an unguided astronaut into an unknown future? A counselor is not equipped for his job unless he can share in some degree the apprehensions of modern youth, and sense the swampy underpinning on which youth treads. Over his desk the counselor might well tack the wisdom of the Spanish writer Unamuno, "Suffering is the life blood that runs through us all and binds us together." While not every youth who comes to the counselor is at that moment a sufferer, it is a safe assumption that he comes for guidance that will fortify him for the inevitable suffering that he will encounter in his course of life.

Tentativeness and Commitment

From the existential point of view the ideal counselor will strive to develop two attitudes in his client. Taken separately they seem antithetical; but fused into a world-view they provide strength for the future. One attitude is tentativeness of outlook. Since certainties are no longer certain, let all dogmas be fear-lessly examined, especially those cultural idols that endanger a false sense of security: dogmas of race supremacy, of naive scien-tism, of unlinear evolutionary progress. Let one face the worst in oneslef and in the world around him, so that one may correctly estimate the hazards.

Taken by itself such tentativeness, such in-sightfulness, might well lead to ontological despair. Yet acceptance of the worst does not prevent us from making the best of the worst. Up to now psychologists have not dealt with the remarkable ability of human beings to blend a tentative outlook with firm commitment to chosen values. The poet Tennyson perceived the point.

> There lives more faith in honest doubt,
> Believe me, than in half the creeds.

A commitment is, as Pascal has said, a wager. One may lose it, but one may also win. Cardinal Newman warned us that our religion can never be a matter of certainty. It is at best a subjective condition of certitude which he defined as "probability supported by faith and love." Yet a mature religion, thus defined, can be infinitely sustaining and heroically motivating. Existentialism, whether theistic or atheistic, makes the same point. We have the freedom to commit our-selves to great causes with courage, even though we lack certainty. We can be at one and the same time half-sure and whole-hearted.

William James, probably America's greatest thinker, tried to teach us this lesson, but fifty years ago we were not ready for it. It is surely noteworthy that, writing as he did in a period of social stability, James saw clearly how ultimately uncertain are our foundations of value. Wealth, he saw was a false god, leading us into a national disease that has recently been called "galloping con-sumption." The more we build up our ma-terial resources, the more we fear poverty. In religion, James knew, there was no certain-ty; yet, like Cardinal Newman, he recog-nized the constructive power of a mature religious commitment. Whatever ideal leads to long-range constructive consequences is psychologically sound. It is also prag-matically true. And who is to say that we have a test for truth more absolute than our own commitment in so far as it is validated by fruitful consequences?

Neither positivistic nor psychodynamic schools of thought allow for the fact that our psychological constitution permits both total tentativeness and total commitment. Such a paradox reminds us of the electron that is able to go in two opposite directions at the same time. Taken by itself tentativeness is disintegrative; commitment is integrative. Yet the blend seems to occur in personalities that we admire for their soundness and per-spective. Presumably through teaching and guidance we may develop both attitudes in our youth.

Whenever the two attitudes coexist in a life we find important desirable by-products from the fusion. One is a deep sense of com-passion for the lot of the human race in general and in each separate social encounter that marks our daily life. The other by-prod-uct is likewise graceful; it is the sense of humor. Humor requires the perspective of tentativeness, but also an underlying system of values that prevents laughter from sour-ing into cynicism. As Meredith said, humor is a capacity to laugh at the things you love and still to love them.

Rationalism vs. Irrationalism

The chief criticism made of existentialism is that it leads away from reason and exalts irrationalism. While this charge may apply to certain literary and theological trends in the existential movement I doubt that it jeopardizes the future of scientific psychology. The attitudes of tentativeness and commitment of which I speak are perfectly sound concepts—call them "intervening variables" if you wish. Indeed in so far as they reflect important states in human personality, and thus lead to inprovement in understanding, prediction, and direction of human behavior, they are sounder scientific concepts than many of those we have been using.

And just what is rationalism? We venerate the ancient Greeks for their exaltation of human reason; and as psychologists we venerate Aristotle for asking the question, "What is man's place in nature." But Greek rationalism was broader than the limited, method-centered, scientism into which it has degenerated. The Greeks themselves saw a place for tentativeness and commitment within the scope of reason. The case is beautifully stated in an ancient inscription found somewhere on the coast of Greece:

> A shipwrecked sailor buried on this coast
> Bids you set sail.
> Full many a bark, when we were lost,
> Weathered the gale.

The dead sailor urges us to make the wager, take the risk, although we cannot be sure of coming through to our destination.

Implications for Theory

What does all this mean in terms of psychological theory, and in terms of guidance? First of all it means that in order to achieve a more realistic image of man and his potentialities, we need to revise our current theories of learning and growth, of motivation and personality structure. Elsewhere (in *Pattern and Growth in Personality*, 1961) I have discussed some of the needed changes in detail, and so shall say only a few words about each.

The trouble with our current theories of learning is not so much that they are wrong, but that they are partial. They fit best the learning of animals and young children. The concepts of conditioning, reinforcement, identification, seem a bit hollow when the counselor tries to apply them to his work. They are not very helpful, for example, in explaining how a youth may learn both tentativeness of outlook and firmness of commitment. Supplementary theories in terms of organizational, biographical, and propriate learning are needed.

Except in the sense of physical maturation the concept of *growth* scarcely exists in psychology at all. Nor will it have its proper place until we have agreed upon normative standards for the maturity of personality. Up to now normative problems, except in the sense of statistical norms, are much neglected.

As for motivation and personality structure psychologists are in a state of turmoil and disagreement. That the past stages of a life do not fully explain the motivational "go" of the present, I for one am firmly convinced. Therefore we need a concept (*functional autonomy*, I think will do) to represent that portion of a life that is oriented toward the future and not toward the past. Also we need a theory of personal structure (of *personal dispositions*) to represent the important cleavages and foci of a given, concrete personality. Such theory will, I am convinced, carry us much further than a conception of uniform variables to which every client is forcibly ordered, whether we call these variables factors, needs, dimensions, or common traits.

Most of all we need to surrender the models that would compress human personality into the routine homeostatic situation that we find in quasi-closed systems. Human personality is a wide-open system, responsive to tangible and intangible culture, on the look-out for new ideas, and capable of asking an altogether new type of question—asked by no other creature in nature, viz., "Who am I?"

There are, I am glad to say, many psychologists who feel as strongly as I that these various types of improvement need to be made before the counselor will have a fully fashioned science of psychology to undergird his practice.

Implications for Guidance

Guidance is not a matter of gimmicks, nor of rules of thumb. A guide, like a philosopher and friend, is a person who loves wisdom and loves his fellow men. True, he has skills to mark him off from the professional philosopher or the untrained friend. To some extent the counselor's present-day skills are useful. Standard tests and measurements are helpful; so too achievement records and focused interviews. Most of our devices come from researches conducted under the positivistic outlook, or (in the case of projective techniques) under the psychodynamic. While many of them are serviceable I look forward to the invention of new instruments still better suited to the study of the central or propriate aspects of single personalities.

Most important, of course, are the spectacles the counselor wears. The image should no longer be borrowed from the tradition of simple naive reactivism. Just as centimeters, grams, seconds are outmoded in modern physics so too are simple stimulus-response connections in modern psychology. In psychology, even more than in physics, we need theory capable of dealing with fluid becoming.

The plain fact is that man is more than a reactive being, more even than a reactive be-

ing in depth. If he were comfortably fixed at these levels we could with confidence apply a uniform stencil in studying his nature. But the life process is no less paradoxical than the processes of modern physics. How can one deal with space that is both finite and unbounded, with light that is both wave and particle, with electrons that pass from orbit to orbit without traversing the space between? Similarly, a human person is both structure and process, a being both biological and noetic, a being who changes his identity even while he retains it. Small wonder that at the end of his life, the famous physicist, P. W. Bridgman, said, "The structure of nature may eventually be such that our processes of thought do not correspond to it sufficiently to permit us to think about it at all."

We need not, I think, be quite so pessimistic. Our first duty is to affirm a new and wider rationalism; that is to say, to redouble our efforts to find a more adequate image of man to guide us in fashioning a more suitable science of personality.

And what about our personal attitudes as guidance specialists or teachers? Should we not cultivate the same twin virtues that we recommend to client and student: tentativeness and commitment? We can hold our own present image of man on trial, reviewing our own past psychological training in critical perspective. At the same time we can embrace courageously our task of interpreting the wisdom of the past in such a way as to make it most available to the youthful personality who is facing an uncertain, but not uninviting, future. Tentativeness and commitment are twin ideals for both counselor and client. To my mind they lie at the heart and center of guidance, of teaching, and of living.

5. SELF-ACTUALIZATION AND THE TEACHING FUNCTION OF COUNSELORS

Arthur W. Combs

Peter Schwarzburg

The Teaching Role of the Counselor

Historically, counseling and psychotherapy were developed as methods for *rehabilitation*. The problem was to help people who were sick or "off the track" to return to the stream of life. This called for counselor to be menders, manipulators, repair men; persons who could help the client "return to normal." Later we came to understand the counseling process also as a matter of *prevention*, of helping people avoid illness. This often cast the counselor in the role of protector, defender, supporter or "parent surrogate." Only recently have we begun to appreciate counseling as an instrument for self-actualization, the production of supremely healthy people. It is no longer enough for a client to be "unsick." Counseling must help him *become* the best he is capable of. This calls for a far more creative role for the counselor. It is not enough for him to repair damage or protect the status quo. It is required that he aid his client to transcend the status quo to achieve self-actualization.

The counselor must be a teacher. The notion of the therapist as a teacher, however, is not a happy one in most counseling circles. One reason for this may be the memory of the counselor's own unhappy experiences with teachers. Or, it may be the counselor has absorbed some of the popular stereotypes about teachers which are no more descriptive of what teachers are really like than the "headshrinker" stereotype is descriptive of the psychotherapist. As a matter of fact the teaching profession has gone through the same phases in their branch of the helping relationship over the past thirty years as our thinking has about the relationship of psychotherapy. Education, too, has experienced its rehabilitative and preventive stages and finds itself now as concerned with self-actualization as counselors are. Bad teaching and good psychotherapy are worlds apart. Good teaching and good counseling, however, are both expressions of the helping relationship and remarkably similar in principle. A recognition of these common bases in both professions would go a long way toward making it possible for each to communicate with and learn more effectively from the other.

I see no point in rejecting the idea of the counselor as teacher. I am no passive lump of clay in the counseling hour. My client learns from me whether I am aware of this or not. It seems to me far more desirable that I accept this role and work with it than pretend it does not exist. People learn who they are and what they are as a consequence of their experience with the significant people in their lives. It is the function of the counselor, as it is the function of the teacher, to be a significant person in the life of a client or student.

The counselor is much more than a facilitator. He is an active agent teaching his client by his very existence. What people learn is not a question of what they have been told but of their experience of the process. It is the totality of the counselor's behavior that produces the experience, not simply the limited function of what he says. What he thinks, feels, does or does not, like the old Indian saying, "speaks so loudly I cannot hear what you say!" and teaches his client whether the counselor is aware of his impact or not. It is in this sense that therapy is teaching.

The "Self-as-Instrument" Concept

The effective professional worker is no longer regarded as a technician applying methods in a more or less mechanical fashion. We now see him as an intelligent human being using himself, his knowledge, and the resources at hand to solve the problems for which he is responsible. He is a person who has learned to use himself as an effective instrument. In medicine, this principle finds expression in the "problems approach" to training. In social work, it is found in the concept of supervision. Modern nursing has adopted a human-relations approach to patient care. Counseling and psychotherapy stress the philosophy of the counselor and the importance of his own personal therapy. These professions do not seek the production of automatons. They want creative, thinking human beings able to use themselves as refined and trustworthy instruments for dealing with complex problems.

The good counselor is no carbon copy but possesses something intensely and personally his own. Artists sometimes call this "the discovery of one's personal idom." The good counselor has found ways of using himself, his talents, and his surroundings in a fashion that aids both his clients and himself to achieve satisfactions—their own and society's too.

For the student entering the profession the "self-as-instrument" concept requires that his education be regarded as a problem in becoming. Becoming a counselor is not a matter of learning how to counsel. It is a question of personal discovery, of learning how to use one's self well. No counselors' college can make a counselor. The best it can do is provide students with problems, resources, information, and opportunities to explore what they mean. Beyond that the student is his own pilot and must find his own best ways of working. He must make a commitment to the process of learning. After all, the self is unlikely to change if it is not permitted to "get in the act."

If we adapt this "self-as-instrument" concept of the professional worker to counseling, it means that counselor-education programs must concern themselves with persons rather than competencies. It means individualization of instruction. It calls for the production of creative individuals, capable of shifting and changing to meet the demands and opportunities afforded in daily tasks. Such a counselor will not behave in a set way. His behavior will change from moment to moment, from day to day, adjusting continually and smoothly to the needs of his clients, the situations he is in, the purposes he seeks to fulfill, and the methods and materials at his command.

Counselors teach by who they are and what they are, by the ways they use themselves in the therapeutic process. The teaching role of the counselor will not go away if we ignore it. We do that at our peril. What is necessary is that we acknowledge the function, and use it effectively in the task of contributing to the growth of the client.

Self-Actualization: The Goal of Counseling

The moment we accept the teaching role for the counselor, however, we are faced with the problem—teach what? In their reaction against the advice giving, coercive tactics of former generations, some counselors have gone so far as to protest that they have no goals for their clients. The public has a most difficult time understanding this claim and, of course, it is not true. Counseling *does* have a goal for its clients. That goal, for most modern counselors, is self-actualization. The acceptance of such a goal, however, automatically sets the course and direction of our function. Whatever we believe self-actualizing people are like provides the guidelines for what we do and how we must behave in all of the helping professions, including counseling. The goals we accept have built in demands for action.

Increasingly, I have found the concept of self-actualization serves as a helpful yardstick by which I can measure much of my behavior both as teacher and as therapist. Sometimes the application of these criteria corroborates my practice. Sometimes, I am forced to raise serious questions about what I have been doing. Best of all, the attempt to apply these principles to the practice of counseling has pointed to new and promising directions for further exploration and thought. In this paper I have tried to illustrate only a few of the meanings these concepts have had for me.

Two Ways of Looking at Self-Actualization

Most counselors currently in practice grew up with a concept of human adjustment understood as a function of the normal curve. According to this view the well-adjusted individual is the one in the middle, while maladjusted persons are the "deviants" at either end of the scale. Many people have long been unhappy with the implication of such a view which makes adjustment equivalent to "being average." It is a welcome development, therefore, that recently a number of writers have bypassed the question, "What does it mean to be adjusted?" and have asked, instead, "What can man become?" or "What should an individual be like who was supremely healthy in the highest possible sense?" In the public health field Dunn (1958) has discussed the problem as "High-level wellness." Maslow (1954) has written of "the self-actualizing person," Rogers (1961) of "the fully functioning person," Combs and Snygg (1959) of the "adequate personality," Allport (1955) of "self-fulfillment" and Mead (1934) of "self-realization," among others. By whatever name, however, all are concerned with a conception of human capacities that far transcends the static levels we have been used to.

One way we can look at the problem of self-fulfillment is to examine how self-actualizing people typically behave. This is an objective or *descriptive* approach and provides us with a list of characteristic traits or behaviors. Maslow (1954), for example, finds self-actualizing people show such behaviors as: spontaneity, problem centering, acceptance, autonomy, democratic behavior and an unhostile sense of humor. Rogers (1961), describes such people, among other things, as "trusting their organism" or being "open to experience." Such descriptions of self actualizing people are helpful but provide us with very few clues as to how to produce such people. How, for example, does one go about teaching someone to have an "unhostile sense of humor" or to "trust his organism?" One shudders at the thought of having to live with a person working on his sense of humor!

A second way of looking at self actualization is to approach the question phenomenologically from the point of view of the behaver rather than the outside observer. The problem is examined perceptually in terms of the characteristic ways self-actualizing persons see themselves and the world in which they live. This frame of reference has proven far more useful to me as a counselor and teacher than the objective view as it seems to provide more direct clues to action. From a perceptual orientation self-actualizing people seem characterized by four major characteristics (Combs, Richards, and Richards, 1976, ASCD, 1962):

1. A positive view of self.
2. An open perceptual field.
3. A deep feeling of identification.
4. A rich, extensive and available perceptual field.

These four characteristics seem omnipresent in the perceptual organization of self-actualizing persons and are usually lacking in inadequate ones.

The Positive View of Self

Self-actualizing people see themselves in essentially positive ways. They believe they are basically liked, wanted, acceptable, able, dignified, worthy, etc. Psychologically sick people, on the other hand, see themselves as unliked, unwanted, unacceptable, unable, undignified, unworthy and the like. The positive or negative character of the self-concept seems to be the most outstanding factor determining whether an individual is psychologically well or ill. What a person believes about himself is learned from his experience. It follows then to help a client see himself in more positive ways the counselor must treat him *as though he were*.

Helping an individual to see himself in positive ways goes beyond the "supportive" role we have often discussed in counseling. The supportive concept has usually meant "helping" the client, often in the sense of doing something for him, providing him solace and comfort or cheering him on in his struggles. These are essentially manipulative functions originating in the counselor, not in the client. The net effect of such support often ended with the client deeply dependent upon the counselor. Thus, many of the counselor's attempts to contribute to his client's "ego strength" only served to make him weaker, more dependent upon his counselor. I believe these errors were made because the counselor was intent upon what he was doing rather than upon the experience the client was having.

Contributing to the client's positive views of self goes beyond being supportive. It does more than keep him from falling. It encourages and propels him. A positive view of self is a source of strength and power, a well spring to draw upon for dealing with life. Providing a man with a better boat does more than keep him dry and afloat. It permits him to go adventuring on unknown seas. It is the goal of counseling to produce a more positive self and every act of the counselor, I now believe, must contribute to this end. How does he do it?

The answer, I think, is to be found in the perceptual organization of self-actualizing people. They see themselves as persons who are liked, wanted, worthy, dignified and able among other things. But these are qualities learned from experience and it is here we can look to find clues for the therapist's behavior. The "how to" guides for counseling are to be found in the answers the counselor finds to the questions posed for a positive self:

How can a person feel liked, unless somebody likes him?

How can a person feel acceptable unless somebody accepts him?

How can a person feel able unless somewhere he has some success?

How can a person feel dignity unless somebody treats him so?

How shall a person feel he matters unless someone cares?

In my answers to these simple questions I have increasingly found effective guides to practice. These are not easy answers, however, because the kind of experience which produces such feelings in the client is not a matter of manipulation. The counselor cannot produce them unless he believes them. He contributes to the positive view of self not by what he does *for* his client or *to* his client, but through what he conveys of his feeling and belief about him. I cannot teach my client he is able, unless I *believe* he is. So, the criteria for self-actualization also provides us with clues to the perceptual organization that must characterize the counselor himself.

This observation is borne out by the results of a study of the perceptual organization of effective counselors carried out at the University of Florida (Combs and Sopor, 1963). In this study "good" counselors could be distinguished from "poor" ones, among other things by the ways in which they perceived people. More effective counselors tended to see people as able, dependable, friendly and worthy. Less effective counselors, on the other hand, had serious doubts about people. They tended to see them as unable, undependable, unfriendly and unworthy. These results have been corroborated repeatedly in a whole series of studies on the helping professions at the University of Florida and at Northern Colorado University (Combs et al., 1969).

One hardly needs to point out that such findings have great implications for the training of therapists. The production of "beliefs" or ways of perceiving in the beginning counselor is a quite different matter from teaching him techniques. It means he must be helped to *become* something as well as to *know* something. That is no easy task and suggests a review of some of our time-honored approaches to training. It certainly raises interesting questions about "quickie" programs of training.

A Perceptual Field Open to Experience

Self-actualizing persons seem much more open to their experience. They are able to accept themselves and the world and to confront new experience with a minimum of defensiveness and distortion. Inadequate persons, on the other hand, find it extremely difficult or impossible to be open to their experience. As a consequence; they behave ineffectually for lack of data or because the data they have is distorted. To a very large extent, whether a person can be accepting and open to experience is dependent upon a positive view of self. The inner strength con-

tributed by a positive view makes acceptance and openness possible. On the other hand the failure of acceptance and the inability to be open to experience is in large measure the product of a feeling of personal inadequacy. Whatever contributes to a more positive view of self makes the possibilities of acceptance and openness to experience more likely. What the counselor does to produce a positive view will at the same time contribute to the possibilities of acceptance and openness.

This second criterion of adequacy certainly underscores the importance of a non-threatening atmosphere in the counseling relationship. The effect of threat in producing "tunnel vision" and forcing the defense of self is the antithesis of the kinds of experiences required for the encouragement of openness. Teachers have long been aware of the importance of "readiness" and "pacing" in the learning process. They have learned to confront students with materials as the student is ready for them and to pace consideration to the speed with which students can grasp it. They have learned maximum progress occurs when students are challenged without being threatened. The principles are the same for counseling.

Openness to experience is learned. In part, it is made possible by the security of a positive feeling about self. It is also a function of an attitude which regards the confrontation of life as, not only possible but, even, enjoyable and rewarding. We have talked much in the theory of counseling about the importance of the counselor's remaining unshockable and demonstrating for his client his own willingness to look at events without fear or hesitation. Mostly we have sought these goals because it made it more possible for the client to look at his problems. But the counselor's demonstration of openness to experience is much more than a technique for the facilitation of talking. It is a most important teaching technique which provides the client with an experience that may add considerably to his strength and stature.

Nearly all schools of thought in psychotherapy have stressed the importance of client acceptance. Seen in the light we are discussing it here, however, it has a much more important function. The counselor who demonstrates by his behavior that he can and will walk with his client through the dark and scarey places of life is doing much more. He is teaching his client it is possible. He is teaching his client also that he is an acceptable person. This strikes at the very roots of neurosis.

The acceptance and openness to experience characteristic of the perceptual fields of self-actualizing persons thus has important implications for counseling practice. It provides additional criteria in terms of which the therapist may examine his practice by asking such questions as: Does this technique assist my client to accept himself and the world? Is the atmosphere I am creating truly encouraging my client to be open to his experience? Am I demonstrating by my own behavior that acceptance and openness is possible? Am I teaching my client that he can accept himself and need not fear his experience?

The Feeling of Identification

Self-actualizing people perceive themselves as more deeply and broadly identified with others and the world. They have a feeling of oneness with other people, which, in the case of the saints, may embrace the whole of mankind. Such a feeling makes possible the kinds of behavior currently of great interest to psychologists; commitment,

involvement, encounter, and dialogue. The extremely healthy person has a feeling of oneness and of being in the world. This is quite different from the psychologically sick individual who feels alone, cut-off or alienated. The feeling of identification also has important implications for counseling practice.

The concept of identification not only sets goals for the client, it also calls for a positive contribution on the part of the counselor. People learn to enter into an encounter, to become involved with another from their experience with significant others. It is just this experience which counseling dialogue provides—an experience in involvement. When it occurs, counseling is not just beginning, it is already far along. The commitment to therapy is, itself, an enormous step forward.

In the past we have often described the counselor-client relationship as a method, a technique by which the client could be reached or through which some therapeutic event could be facilitated. The relationship was seen as the vehicle of therapy, not therapeutic in itself. As a requisite of self-actualization, identification is a dynamic of growth. The relationship of counselor and client is more than a preparation for healthy living. It is an experience of health. Among professional educators similar understanding has been growing. Most people regard our public schools as "preparation for life." Modern learning theory recognizes that the child's experience in school is not just preparation; for him it *is* life.

Identification is learned from successful encounter. When a counselor is able to give of himself he does much more than facilitate. He is, himself, a demonstration of commitment, a living invitation to his client to join the human race. Empathy, too, is more than a technique. It is a demonstration of commitment and involvement. It is an invitation, a

holding out of the hand, an indication that—
"You are there!"

I do not believe we have sufficiently understood the importance of the relationship itself as a learning situation. I believe counseling must be seen as more than freeing clients for the satisfaction of need. It must be seen as an experience in need satisfaction itself. From learning theory we know that people learn best when their needs are satisfied *in the process* of learning. Teachers know that intellectual matters can hardly be comprehended when unrelated to the student's need. Persons whose needs are too deeply deprived cannot even hear. The satisfaction of need is important in any learning. Among the most basic of human needs, in our society, is the need for love. Most maladjusted persons are so precisely because they are unable to enter satisfying relationships with other people.

The discussion of love between counselor and client is always a matter which makes us uneasy. We are caught between Scylla and Charybdis. On the one hand we are fearful of romantic love and the dangers of seduction or unethical practice. On the other, we are fearful of the pathology of transference. I once watched Nathaniel Cantor play upon this confusion in the minds of a group of young counselors in a devastating way. The counselors were engaged in a discussion of the counseling relationship when Cantor began to lead them down the primrose path.

"It's an atmosphere free of threat," he said.

"Indeed it is," they replied.

"A warm atmosphere," he continued.

"Oh yes," the counselors agreed.

"A very human, intense relationship."

"That too," the counselors agreed.

"A kind of loving relationship." Again the counselors nodded.

"I see," said Cantor, "the counselor is a kind of panderer of professional love!" At this point the room exploded!

I submit that there is a kind of loving which is neither seductive nor erotic on the one hand or dependency-producing on the other. It is the responsible kind of loving described by Fromm. (1956) It is the biblical sense of loving of persons for persons, a compassionate caring experience of "oneness in the human condition." In the light of our new understandings about self-actualizing people this is an experience prerequisite to health. It is not an artifact of counseling. It is an integral part of the process itself and I believe it needs much more consideration than it has been given so far.

If the encounter of psychotherapy is as important as we have been suggesting, there are important implications also for the training of counselors. Involvement, commitment and encounter are not methods or techniques to be put on demand. They require a capacity on the part of the counselor to give deeply and richly of himself. The essence of counseling is the relationship to be sure but there can be no relationship with a nonentity. The counselor must *be* somebody willing and able to share himself with his client in meaningful fashion. Being somebody, however, is not an easy thing to learn. It, almost certainly, cannot be taught in formal courses or in "one shot" programs of counselor training.

Self-Actualized Persons Are Well-Informed

Self-actualizing persons have perceptual fields that are rich, extensive and available. This is to say, self-actualizing people are informed. These are not stupid people. They are deeply knowledgeable. They possess a fund of information sufficient to live richly and meaningfully in their chosen worlds. In contrast, the mentally retarded, the criminal and the mentally ill possess perceptual fields which are seriously lacking, contain information not relevant to individual needs or, for one reason or another, remain unavailable when action is called for. If being informed is a characteristic of self-actualizing people it follows that counseling must help the client to acquire a rich, extensive and available perceptual field.

The reaction of Carl Rogers and his students against the concept of counseling as a process of "diagnosing and prescribing" thirty years ago was a long step forward for counseling theory. In that first flush of rejection against "telling" clients, some of us become so "nondirective" we wouldn't have given a client the time of day if he asked for it! Like many new ideas it got pushed to absurdity in the process of exploring its meaning. The problem of information we now recognize is not a question of giving or withholding but of understanding the processes of communication so that information contributes maximally to the helping process. In my own practice I have become far more willing to give information than I was years ago.

The openness to experience which I am trying to produce requires an attitude on my part that there is, literally, no information my client ought not have. I will tell my client (a) anything I know, (b) that I am free to tell him, and (c) which seems to me will be helpful to him. If telling him something will help him to get better quicker, it is cruel and inhuman for me to prolong his agony. My responsibility as a counselor is to help my client *the quickest way possible*. If there is a quicker way I must use it. Interestingly enough, this point of view about giving information has tended to make my counseling more client-centered rather than less client-centered.

While I am willing to tell my client anything I know, I find that over the years I am less and less certain about what I know, so there is less and less I can tell him! When a client asks, "What do psychologists think about this?" I can often tell him and I do. When he asks me, "What shall I do about this?" It is a different matter. I don't know the answer to that.

What the counselor believes he knows is even a more important differentiation between beginning counselors and experts. A recurring problem for the beginning counselor is what to do with the client who asks "What shall I do?" His client persistently asks this question in many different forms. Unless some resolution for it is found, counseling may end in a stalemate between the reluctant counselor and the coaxing client. This problem does not exist for the expert counselor who is less certain about what he knows. When the expert tells his client, "I don't know," his client believes him and goes on about the business of searching for an answer himself. The beginner, however, really *believes* he knows. So, when his client asks, "What shall I do?" and he answers, "I don't know, " the client doesn't believe him. Instead he feels his counselor is being cagey and seeks to worm the answers out of him in other ways. Humility is not just a nice idea. It is a practical aid in resolving some of the dilemmas of counseling.

Learning from a perceptual point of view is the discovery of personal meaning. Its basic principle can be stated as follows: "Any information will affect an individual's behavior in the degree to which he has discovered its personal meaning for him." (Combs, Richards, and Richards, 1976). Learning is thus a function of two events: (a) the confrontation of information and (b) the personal discovery of its meaning. The first of these aspects we know very well how to do. People have been telling other people since the beginning of man's history. How to help people explore and discover the personal meaning of information so that it makes a difference in their behavior, however, is a more knotty problem and one we have only begun to understand. This is not only true in counseling. It is currently the largest problem we face in education. Modern educators, like counselors, have been trying to escape from the "show and tell" concepts of behavior change characteristic of past generations. The experiences of counselors have even made important contributions to our understanding of the teaching function in recent years. Working in the intimacy of the one-to-one, face-to-face relationship, counselors have often been able to explore ways of helping clients toward personal discovery of meaning with much greater freedom than classroom teachers working with large numbers of pupils. Out of this experience have come important principles about learning, not only for counseling, but much more broadly to the field of education itself.

Self-actualizing people are informed, knowing people. It follows that counseling must help them to become so. In this sense, counseling is, indeed, a teaching process. This does not mean that counselors must necessarily be tellers any more than modern teachers are. Helping people become informed does not mean we need to give up being counselors. On the contrary, it means we must continue our efforts to find the most effective and efficient ways of helping people become informed in the fullest possible sense.

In this article there has been room to suggest but a few of the directions our new concepts of self-actualization and human adequacy imply for counseling and psychotherapy. I am continually amazed at the way in which many stubborn problems of theory and practice are reduced to simplicity and brought into elegant harmony and order when observed through these new glasses. It has brought changes in my concepts of the counselor's role and forced me to reconsider the concepts I formerly held about the professional training of counselors. (Combs, 1971) As Maslow has suggested, whenever our ideas change about what man can become, great changes are called for everywhere in our thinking about human problems—perhaps nowhere so much as in the helping professions of counseling and teaching.

Note. Studies have been completed to date on good and poor counselors, residence advisors, student teachers, elementary teachers, college professors and episcopal priests. Most exist on unpublished doctoral dissertations. Interested persons may obtain a complete listing by writing:

Dr. Arthur W. Combs
305 Normon Hall
University of Florida
Gainesville, Florida 32601

REFERENCES

Allport, G. W. *Becoming*. New Haven, Connecticut: Yale University Press, 1955.

Association for Supervision and Curriculum Development. "Perceiving, Behaving, Becoming." 1962 Yearbook, Washington, D.C.: National Education Assn. 1962.

Combs, A. W. Some Basic Guidelines for the Training of "Helpers." Proceedings, National Faculty Development Conference, Southern Regional Education Board, Atlanta, Georgia, 22 pages 1971.

Combs, A. W. *et al*. Florida Studies in the Helping Professions. University of Florida Social Science Monograph No. 37, University of Florida Press, Gainesville, Florida. 1969.

Combs, A. W., Richards, A. C. and Richards, F. *Perceptual Psychology: A humanistic Approach to the Study of Persons*. New York City: Harper & Row, 1976.

Combs, A. W., and Snygg, D. *Individual behavior*. New York: Harper & Row, 1959.

Combs, A. W., and Soper, D. W. "The perceptual organization of effective counselors." *Journal of Counseling Psychology*. 10 (1963):222-26.

Dunn, Halbert L. "Positive Wellness in the Human and National Posture." *Development Planning Note*. No. 58-DAP -7. 1958.

Fromm, Erich. The Art of Loving. New York: Harper & Bros. 1956.

Maslow, A. H. *Motivation and personality*. New York: Harper & Row. 1954.

Mead, G. H. *Mind, self and society from the standpoint of a social behaviorist*. Chicago: University of Chicago Press, 1934.

Rogers, C. R. *On becoming a person*. Boston: Houghton-Mifflin, 1961.

6. THE CHANGE AGENT COUNSELOR: A CONCEPTUAL CONTEXT

David R. Cook

Peter Schwarzburg

The notion that a school counselor can, perhaps should, function as an agent of institutional change is now being set forth with greater and greater frequency. Taking into account the history of school counseling and the present inquiry into its effectiveness in schools, there is something almost absurd in the suggestion that the counselor should be a change agent. We have demonstrated so little ability in the past to change student behavior, how can we now presume to change institutional behavior?

The question is a reasonable one. If you are a school counselor presently overloaded with programming, college advisement, intelligence testing, and crisis solving, the idea of tackling the school system probably strikes you as ridiculous. It is ridiculous; but someone needs to do it.

The Conditions that Require Change

Why the counselor? Why not the principal or the superintendent or parents or even teachers? This question probably comes to mind first before considering why it needs to be done at all.

Over the past several years a flood of literature has painted the dismal picture of schools as dreary places for children; as places that stultify rather than stimulate. Schools are accused of teaching how to beat the system rather than how to learn, of dehumanizing youngsters, of promoting organizational conformity that thwarts maturity, and in general of producing antieducational outcomes.

The fact that there is excellence, candidness, innovation, dynamism, creativity, and many other good and exciting things happening in education only throws the negative elements into bold relief. The current economic crisis in education threatens to intensify the negative conditions and remove our attention from needed changes. Our attention automatically shifts to survival because school counseling is threatened more by economic cutbacks than other educational professions. Chicago and other places demonstrate this (American Personnel and Guidance Association, 1972).

When the needed changes are overlooked, inefficient management as well as dysfunctional outcomes are produced. Decisions concerning the allocation of resources or the cutback of resources are rarely made on the basis of clearly articulated goals and objectives along with the evaluation of those goals. Instead, management is often by politics and gamesmanship.

Schools are formal organizations that have the general characteristics of bureaucracies. These characteristics include the tendency toward impersonal behavior on the part of the members—behavior that is directed more to organizational goals rather than individual goals, a structure of hierarchical interpersonal relationships demanding obedience from those at the bottom, and a division of labor resulting in a high degree of specialization. All of these characteristics are somewhat destructive to the goals of individual learning and development. Schools are generally organized to make real learning unlikely. The learning that does take place may be useful for some, but destructive for others and probably irrelevant for most.

These generalizations about most educational systems have proved to be true. The extent to which any of these phenomena are true, however, for a given school system, a given school, classroom, guidance unit, or any other subsystem of the larger system of schooling is a matter to be determined by organizational analysis in the real life setting.

Where Does the Counselor Come In?

The point is that schools as organizations present environments for pupils that can cause problems which they wouldn't have otherwise or make education more difficult for them. Functioning at its best, therefore, a school should be an enabling instrument in the task of educating our youth, not an inhibiting instrument.

Organizations are made up of individuals. It is individuals who act and make decisions not organizations. Organizational theory and research only clarify that the behavior of people in the context of the organization is greatly affected by the organizational climate and structure. The question of whether you change organizations by changing people or change people by changing organizations is one of many questions that is best resolved by asserting that both approaches are necessary. Critical to understanding this position is the realization that the organization, per se, cannot be ignored if you are concerned with changing behavior and improving education.

The question, "why the counselor?" is answered by making it clear that others (ie., administrators, teachers, parents, etc.) also have a stake in institutional change. The concern here is not to place the entire burden for change agentry on the counselor, but to articulate the rationale for the counselor's unique and necessary role in institutional change.

A rationale for the importance and necessity of the counselor assuming the role of change agent in the schools can be summarized in the following series of brief statements:

1. The counselor is a member of the organization and implicity committed to helping the organization attain its publicly stated goals.

2. The counselor's professional commitment, as a member of the school counseling profession, includes a commitment to facilitate the development of the organization's client population.

3. Where organizational goals and individual goals come into conflict, the counselor as an individual must decide which side he will support.

4. The counselor is (or should be) by training and experience an expert in human relations and problem solving. These skills can be placed at the service of the organization and the individual.

5. If the organization functions to facilitate the development of the individuals it serves, there can be no overt conflict between the counselor's professional commitment and his commitment to the organization.

6. If the organization functions in a way that inhibits, blocks, or destroys the client's individual development, there is a conflict between the professional and the organizational commitment of the counselor at that point.

7. If the organization is committed to any publicly stated goal that would inhibit, block, or destroy the individual development of the clients served by the organization then there will be a conflict between the counselor's organizational and professional commitments.

These seven statements are essentially a series of assumptions that need to be examined further. This further examination should include a look at the history of the counseling profession, the present state of affairs in school counseling, and what part these assumptions play in the counselor's potential role as a change agent.

Where We Come From

The history of guidance may be viewed from a number of contexts and many good historical reviews are available. The particular context in which I want to view this history appears in more detail elsewhere (Cook, 1971).

The school counselor was essentially the creation of school administrators (Kehas, 1965). His job was to sort and allocate students within the educational system. As our public schools grew in size and heterogeneity and as the demands of our economic system became more numerous and complex the need to "process" students in our high schools with greater educational efficiency became evident. Curriculum choices multiplied both horizontally in the way of more courses and vertically through ability tracks. The organization was in need of members who could help students make the educational decisions demanded by this increasing complexity. Some of this complexity was generated by the increasing growth of formal work organizations in society that provided the jobs for the graduates of our schools.

Certain classroom teachers were originally tapped to do this job and were called guidance counselors. Since that time, much of the professional development of school counseling has been to make the sorting and allocating function increasingly sophisticated. School counselors today who devote a large portion of their working time to planning programs, grouping ("tracking"), making schedule changes, helping in college selection and even job placement are essentially performing this sorting and allocating function. This has been termed the *administrator* role. That counselors are still spending much of their time in this role testifies to the fact that these functions have become almost

ends in themselves. Have you ever been frustrated by these tasks, yet shrugged your shoulders knowing that it had to be done and that there was no one else to do it?

The influence of Carl Rogers and others plus the increasing pressure for a unique professional identity through which school counseling could become institutionalized, led school counselors to consider counseling as their primary function. This approach had the advantage of moving the counselor's function closer to the needs of individuals, but at the same time gradually isolating him—sometimes even alienating him—from the teaching faculty and the central educational purposes of the school. It was as if the students needs for counseling existed independently of the institution in which both the student and the counselor played their roles. This particular thrust in school counseling has been termed the *therapeutic* role.

Administrator role and the therapeutic role represent two major historical currents that have influenced the present state of affairs in school counseling and guidance (Lortie, 1965).

Present State of Affairs

Neither of these roles is adequate to meet the demands of the assumptions given above for a change agent role. Yet it is probably fair to say that most school counselors today function primarily as either administrators or therapists or a tenuous blend of both, depending on the circumstances.

Regarding the first two assumptions, the administrator counselor is most likely to be aligned with the organization while the therapeutic counselor will more likely be committed to the individual. When conflict arises between organizational and individual goals, as mentioned in assumption three, the administrator counselor will tend to side with the organization and the therapeutic counselor will tend to side with the student. The counselor who is a "blend" will suffer a good deal of ambivalence and often behave erratically depending on "which way the wind is blowing."

The school organization that is functioning with a high level of congruence between its goals and the goals of its student clients will provide a relatively conflict free work setting for both the administrator and the therapeutic counselor. Unfortunately, this situation rarely exists in pure form.

Assumptions five and six state in more detail, the manner in which a conflict situation between organization and individual can come into being. In one case it happens through organizational dysfunctioning. In the other case it is through inappropriate organizational goals. The administrator counselor will tend to be torn one way and the therapeutic counselor the other way. The counselor who wants it both ways will be frustrated.

Thus the present dilemma for school counselors as they presently tend to function can lead to one of these three conditions: (a) Internal stability and reduction of organizational conflict gained at the cost of identifying primarily with the organization at the expense of the student; (b) Internal stability and reduction of conflict with students' demands gained at the cost of identifying primarily with the students and perhaps alienation from the organization; (c) Internal instability, conflict, frustration, and aggravation coming with the price of role ambivalence, which usually results in the dissatisfaction of the students and the organization.

The internal stability mentioned in (a) and (b) above is highly relative. No conscientious counselor of any persuasion can always remain in a state of internal harmony and equilibrium. To do this would require a compartmentalization of existence and the exclusion of reality. This is, of course, possible and some counselors (as well as teachers, principals, etc.) do so.

Out of the Dilemma, but Not the Conflict

The role of the counselor as a change agent is essentially to help bring organizational goals and individual goals into harmony to enhance the learning function. This means playing a strong advocate role for students and a change agent role within the institution. Both roles can enable the counselor to serve both the organization and the student, but not without confronting conflict. In carrying out this role, the counselor may even generate conflict.

The following statements reexamine the six previous assumptions when placed in the context of the change agent's role:

1. The publicly stated goals of our schools, however badly articuated, generally represent educational commitments that can be subscribed to by most counselors concerned for the educational development of students. In that sense, the commitment to the organization is an honest and important one.

2. The commitment to individual development on the part of the school counselor has a long history in guidance. The professional record attests to the primacy of the individual student as the major locus of concern for the counselor. This is as true for the change agent counselor as for any other kind of counselor.

3. Conflict between the organization and the individual inevitably results from the organization's failure to utilize means that will lead to the attainment of public goals or

its failure to allow students to participate in the establishment of the organization's goals. It is at this point that the change agent counselor begins to act out the implications of the change agent role.

4. Dealing with student versus organizational conflicts demands good human relations skills. Such conflicts also demand good skills of organizational analysis, organizational change and problem solving. Counselors should possess these skills as a reasonable expectation of their professional preparation.

5. When the public goals of the organization are being implemented by means that are congruent with those goals, there is less likelihood of conflict between the organization and the students. The change agent counselor will work to maintain harmony by emphasizing the function of feedback to keep the system honest and changing to meet changing needs and problems.

6. When the functions of the organization are out of harmony with the public goals, then it is the task of the change agent counselor to point out the dysfunction and prescribe some remedies.

7. When the publicly stated goals include some to which the student population objects because they consider them irrelevant or lacking in integrity, the change agent counselor has the task of pointing out the problem and working to change the goals. The students should be involved in the goal setting activity.

In these ways the change agent counselor serves the organization by keeping it more open to information that will help bring about change and develop dynamically in keeping with the needs and interests of the student population. The change agent counselor serves the students by acting as their advocate within the organization as well as assisting them as individuals to meet their goals and solve their problems.

What Is Required?

With the groundwork laid for an advocate-change agent role for the school counselor, I want to conclude with a few comments regarding what might be functionally required of the counselor who chooses to move in this direction.

First of all, the role requires that the change agent be strong, gutsy, self-confident, tactful, and knowledgeable. With counseling training you should understand what threatens people and how you can reduce the threats. The aim is to help people do what they do not want to do or are afraid to do.

He must be able to operate in the midst of conflict. It won't be easy to tell a principal that his ways of dealing with students only provoke them and make them want to challenge his authority. Teachers will not want to hear that the curriculum is boring and irrelevant to many students and that the choices available are too narrow and restrictive. When students create conflict, the counselor should be ready and able to find out what the problems are and to help mediate solutions even while tensions are high.

Counselors will need to begin paying attention to the goals of the school, as well as those of the guidance program. Many schools do not have a written set of goals. Many written goal statements were dashed off by the principal to satisfy an evaluation team several years ago. No one has looked at them since. The guidance department probably has never written down its goals, or even discussed them. A change agent counselor must think in terms of goals because they are the only leverage for change. Change for the sake of change is pointless.

Perhaps your school has a goal statement somewhere that goes like this: "The aim of Kennedy High School is to foster independence and teach the democratic way of life"; and ironically perhaps the same school is structured so that students have very little choice of courses, very little freedom of movement around the building, no participation in the decisions of school curriculum, no choice of teachers and no participation in establishing the rules of the school. These students may elect student council representatives, but the student council may function on an insignificant level and only with the advice and consent of a faculty member. The change agent counselor in Kennedy High School ought to be able to analyze this situation and point out that the operations of the school hardly foster independence and democracy.

Is the guidance goal of enhancing the self-worth of the individual met by planning programs, giving information, advising on college choice, filling out record forms, and scoring tests? A typical guidance counselor in the high schools of this nation probably devotes 50 to 75 percent of his time to these functions. The change agent counselor should be looking for a more efficient way to accomplish some of these tasks and getting rid of others entirely. Organizational analysis skills will help in identifying the tasks that are more related to the guidance program goals.

Finally, the change agent counselor understands that change in an organization depends, in part, on the free flow of information to all parts of the system. As one of the best contact people for students, the counselor should gain much important information about student needs that can be fed to other parts of the system. Is it a system where information always seems to go in one direction only—from the top down? (Have you ever tried to send information back up

and found that it was ignored?) Try face to face communication with a request for feedback. This can be very difficult to do, but it is one way to force change, or at least a confrontation with the status quo.

Counselors as a group have tended to shy away from change agentry for a number of reasons. Most counselors feel powerless. Many are frankly "establishment" and committed functionally to the organization, even if rhetorically committed to the students. Many would like to do something, but are afraid of the risks involved to their job, their status, or their image. Many are ready to take action, but lack the theoretical and practical tools to make the right moves. Counselor education programs have generally been of little help in this regard.

Despite all these negative factors, the future is open to school counselors who are willing to take some risks and make some mistakes in helping the organization do a better job of educating students. I have tried in this article to provide a rationale and a few ideas to help counselors develop the will to give serious consideration to including change agent strategies in their role as school counselors. To those who have tried or will try in the future it would behoove us all if you shared some of your successes and your frustrations in this and other journals.

REFERENCES

American Personnel and Guidance Association. *Guideposts*, 1972, 14, 100-200.

Cook, D. The future of guidance as a profession. *Guidance for education in revolution.* Boston: Allyn & Bacon, 1971.

Kehas, C. D. Administration structure and guidance theory. *Counselor Education and Supervision*, 1965. 4(3), 147-53.

Lortie, D. C. *Administrator or, advocate, or therapist? Alternatives for professionalization in school counseling. In Ralph Mosher, Richard Carle and Chris Kehas (Eds.), Guidance: An examination.* New York: Harcourt Brace, 1965.

PART TWO
COUNTERPOINT

AN 'OBJECTIVIST' POSITION

Dear Editor:

". . . I totally disagree with several of the points in the articles you have included in this section, not so much because of what they say, but rather because of what they don't say. As a follower of Ayn Rand's objectivist philosophy, I advocate the position that as the counselor recognizes his or her own self-interests and communicates these, within an appropriate context, to the client, this best serves the interest of the client too, in the long run. Selfishness, Ayn Rand points out, is a virtue—not a vice . . . . When I hear things about the counselor 'giving' of himself it goes directly against the grain of the objectivist psychology and philosophy, which can be studied in a number of books, including Ayn Rand's *The virtue of selfishness* and *For the new intellectual*, both available in inexpensive paperback editions . . . ."

M. H. H.

COMB'S ACHIEVEMENT

Dear Editor:

"As an undergraduate student, I was first introduced to Dr. Comb's ideas about the self and about growth. Since that time, I have read many articles by him and his books. But I think his article in this book represents his best achievement to date: it makes directly relevant for me, *as a person*, how teaching, counseling, and interacting with others are combined. One idea I had after reading the article is that when I do counseling, I will grow as much as the clients I am helping, and this is a very desirable idea."

E. M.

WHO IS THE COUNSELOR?

Dear Editor:

"After reading the last part, I eagerly looked forward to finding out some answers to "Who is this person—the counselor," but instead I only find more questions (which you did warn us about in the preface). Why is it so complicated an issue to define. After all, it's easy to say what a physician is, what a car mechanic is, and so on—what is so complicated about the counselor. This is a rhetorical question, because I know the answer: that counseling is not a smooth, structured, highly predictable process, but something that is full of change and has a spontaneous dimension. Therefore, the counselor is not a single thing, but a combination of ingredients that emerges differently at different times."

L. L.

CAN COUNSELORS MAKE CHANGE?

Dear Editor:

"As a person who has taught in the schools for many years and is now studying to be a counselor, I wonder if it is really possible for the counselor to function as an agent of change in the schools. First of all, the counselor is not usually perceived this way by his constituency, and most of the counselors I've worked with hardly have enough time for their administrative duties. Also, shouldn't the counselor be a noncontroversial, neutral figure rather than someone perceived (even if unfairly) as a rabble-rouser. How is the counselor to know that his judgments about what is to be changed are the same as his colleagues and clients' judgments. Acting as an agent of change is a very risky thing, and I'm not so sure the counselor should be willing to take that risk."

S. H.

PART THREE

MODELS OF HELPING

I feel now, as I look over the articles that precede this section, that we have made some progress. I'm beginning to get a sense of what "counseling" means, as the term is used, and who this person of the "counselor" is. But still, the process of counseling—as the counselor "does it"—remains to be defined and critically examined. Such is the purpose of this part of the book.

If we agree, as I hope we do, that counseling takes place under many different conditions, and that it involves a variety of different types of activities, and that some of these activities are explicit behaviors on the part of the counselor or client—that is, they are thought out and intentional—and that other activities are intuitive and spontaneous . . . if we agree about this, then the logical question is "How can we organize the behaviors that constitute counseling practice so that we can better understand what makes counseling effective or ineffective?" In answering this type of question, we will also be reflecting upon the different variables that affect counseling outcomes, and in so doing will have a better idea of the cause-and-effect links within the counseling process.

Since counseling is, above all else, a helping process, the models we will be examining—models of counselor-client interaction drawn with respect to the processes and goals of the interaction—will be, in the broadest sense, models of helping. What any given model means by "helping" differs in many ways from what another model means, but certain similarities which underlie the different approaches will begin to emerge by the end of this part.

We begin with brief therapy approaches, in which "helping" is characterized through a short-term encounter between client and counselor. The time limitation is an important treatment consideration; one which is not always taken sufficiently into account by theorists and practitioners who strive toward goals that demand many years of treatment; or who advocate treatment over a long period of time which is not feasible in such settings as the school, the social agency, the hospital or clinic, or other settings in which long-term therapy is precluded. Leona Tyler's "Minimum change therapy" is a seminal contribution to the field, particularly applicable to the school counsling milieu. While Tyler offers a number of salient suggestions, such as emphasizing the client's strengths, working toward a small, incremental change, and setting realistic goals, she is not entirely clear as to the counselor's role in carrying these out. Wolberg's "Methodology in short-term therapy," utilizes an eclectic framework to examine the phases of short-term counseling and psychotherapy in some detail. Wolberg is optimistic about the value of short-term treatment, and one of the strong points of his paper is in his contention that short-term therapy will, "as its methodology becomes elaborated, develop into the treatment of choice for a considerable number of patients."

Psychoanalysis, a term which is generally used synonymously with Freudian psychoanalysis, is often viewed as the very antithesis of short-term treatment, and yet in a penetrating approach, William Kirman's "Modern psychoanalytic counseling" demonstrates that this neo-Freudian model of helping is applicable for short-term as well as long-term counseling. Kirman's ideas, which are outside the traditional approaches that generally make their way into such books as this one, may startle some readers, and may cause some contention among educators. But I feel this approach has been sorely neglected in the literature, and as far as I know this paper is the first of its kind to appear in print. Following Kirman's paper is Jacob Kesten's "Learning for Spite," which uses the modern psychoanalytic approach to deal with a school-related situation. The juxtaposition of Kirman's and Kesten's papers illustrates the theory and practice of what may become a major force in counseling during the next decade.

Five basic models of helping—client-centered, existential, Adlerian, Reality Therapy, and Behavioral—are next considered. Roger's paper, "The interpersonal relationship: the core of guidance," is one of several papers he has written which adequately sums up his copious writings on the client-centered approach. It serves as a concise, accurate, inclusive introduction to the "Rogerian" brand of client-centered counseling. Selecting material to represent the existential approach was more difficult, since so many fine articles have covered this area from different perspectives. What I chose to do was select a paper that provides the strongest philosophical orientation and yet relates directly to counseling. C. Gratton Kemp's "Existential counseling," succeeds in clearly explaining the existential stance while outlining the basic philosophical roots of this counseling position.

The Adlerian counseling approach, particularly popular in the schools, is treated in two papers. Garfinkle, Massey, and Mendel's "Adlerian guidelines for counseling" offers a fine introduction to this model, and presents two case studies which demonstrate the validity of the approach in practice. Thomas W. Allen's "Adlerian interview strategies for behavior change," is a particularly important contribution, both in the theoretical and practical sense, since it offers concrete examples of counselor response during the counseling interview. Glasser's paper on "Reality therapy and counseling" sums up his basic ideas and translates them into the counseling setting.

Behavioral counseling is an extremely complex field which encompasses a number of different methodologies. John D. Krumbholtz's "Behavioral goals for counseling," is a good general introduction to what behavioral counseling is all about, in terms of its point of view, general goals, etc. The two other papers, Benoit and Mayer's "Extinction and timeout: guidelines for their selection and use," and Garvey and Hegrenes' "Desensitization techniques in the treatment of school phobia," are practical papers, which illustrate the specific implementation of behavioral techniques. Again, I have tried to select material that has a practical bent, and allows counselors-in-training to get some idea of how to use the things they are reading about.

John Melleker's paper, "Transactional analysis for counselors" may come as a surprise to those familiar with Berne's work on "TA" and with the "I'm O.K.—You're O.K."! spate of books that have glutted the market in recent years. Mellecker's approach is really designed more for the non-TA counselor who wants to integrate some new approaches into his or her practice. It presents a conceptual system that fits into many other modalities, and is therefore a model of helping that can be easily integrated into other models discussed in this part.

Since the late 1960s there has been a trend, led by Robert Carkhuff and his associates (Charles Truax, Bernard G. Berenson, and others) to develop a systematic model of helping based on empirical study rather than *a priori* assumptions which underlie many of the other systems. In his paper, "The development of systematic human resource development models," Carkhuff outlines the development of this approach. Readers who wish to gain a fuller understanding of this approach may want to read Carkhuff's *Helping and human relations* or *The development of human resources* (Both New York: Holt, Rinehart & Winston) or *The art of helping* (Amherst, Mass.: Human Resource Development Press, 1972).

SUGGESTED ADDITIONAL READINGS

Ansbacher, H. L. and Ansbacher, R. R. eds. *The individual psychology of Alfred Adler: A systematic presentation in selections from his writings.* New York: Basic Books, 1956.

Bandura, A. *Principles of behavior modification.* New York: Holt, Rinehart & Winston, 1969.

Belkin, G. S. *Practical counseling in the schools* (Part Three). Dubuque: Wm. C. Brown Company Publishers, 1975.

Berne, E. *Games people play.* New York: Grove Press, 1970.

Carkhuff, R. R. *The art of helping.* Amherst, Mass.: Human Resource Development Press, 1972.

Carkhuff, R. R. and Berenson, B. G. *Beyond counseling and therapy.* New York: Holt, Rinehart & Winston, 1967.

Corsini, R. J. *Current psychotherapies.* Itasca, Ill.: F. E. Peacock, 1973.

Cunningham, L. M. and Peters, H. J. *Counseling theories: a selective examination for school counselors.* Columbus, Ohio: Charles E. Merrill, 1973.

Frankl, V. *Pyschotherapy and existentialism: selected papers on logotherapy.* New York: Simon and Schuster, 1967.

Freud, S. *A general introduction to psychoanalysis.* New York: Pocket Books, 1969.

Glasser, W. *Reality therapy: a new approach to psychiatry.* New York: Harper & Row, 1965.

Krumbholz, J. D. and Thoresen, C. E. *Behavioral counseling: cases and techniques.* New York: Holt, Rinehart & Winston, 1969.

May, R., Ellenberger, H. E. and Angel, E. eds. *Existence.* New York: Basic Books, 1959.

Meyer, J. B. and Meyer, J. K. *Counseling psychology: theories and case studies.* Boston: Allyn & Bacon, 1975.

Rogers, C. R. *Client-centered therapy.* Boston: Houghton Mifflin, 1951.

———. *Carl Rogers on encounter groups.* New York: Harper & Row, 1970.

Spotnitz, H. *The couch and the circle.* New York: Lancer, 1961.

———. *Modern psychoanalysis of the schizophrenic patient.* New York: Grune & Stratton, 1968.

Strean, H. *New approaches in child guidance.* Metuchen, N.J.: Scarecrow Press, 1970.

7. MINIMUM CHANGE THERAPY

Leona E. Tyler

Peter Schwarzburg

I have some misgivings about the problem we are considering today. Any attempt we make to limit the duration of counseling, though we may think of it as a purely quantitative change, may turn out to have large qualitative effects. One of our ground rules, so basic that we seldom even state it explicitly, is that a person is *worth* whatever amount of time and trouble it takes to help him. We do not measure concern and kindness in hours or dollars. It would be as though a mother should say to herself: "Let's see. I can afford to devote ten years of my life primarily to the nurture of these children. That means that the total amount of time that each of them can claim is 10,000 hours." Instead of thinking in this fashion, a mother naturally assumes that she must give whatever the task demands, without rationing it. An increasing mass of evidence is showing that the optimal growth of a human being requires just this kind of unlimited commitment on somebody's part. Under favorable circumstances, a person has had enormous amounts of love and care devoted to him by the time he reaches maturity.

The experience of having someone really care about him is such an indispensable part of what counseling means for a client that we must be especially careful never to jeopardize it. It is for this reason that I am inclined to doubt the wisdom of setting arbitrary time limits. If what the client understands by the arrangements we make is: "You are worth spending 10 hours on, but no more," an experience he might otherwise have had simply will not occur. It has always seemed to me that there is a big difference psychologically, between limits that are inevitable and obviously necessary, such as those resulting from the end of a school term or the illness of the therapist and those that are arbitrary or unexplained.

However, after all this has been said, the fact remains that to prolong counseling con-

tacts unnecessarily does not do a client any good and may even hamper his further development. And our own full schedules make it imperative that we try to avoid this type of error. Thus we do need to give some thought to the matter of how this can best be done.

Change or Utilization

My own approach to this and other counseling problems has been to attempt to clarify the nature of the task itself. Elsewhere during the last year I have tried to distinguish between two kinds of helping process. Therapy generally has as its goal personality *change;* counseling attempts to bring about the best possible *utilization* of what the person already has. It is a distinction similar to the one Tolman years ago introduced into learning theory, the difference between learning and performance.

The only trouble with simple, clear-cut classifications like this is that they don't seem to fit a lot of the tasks and situations with which we are confronted. Certainly most of the work we do in facilitating occupational choices and educational decisions can be classified as *utilization* rather than as *change*. But what of the client with major or minor personality problems? Is the treatment we offer in such cases therapy or counseling? Is it perhaps really therapy, but called counseling in order to make it more palatable to him or to the community? It would not be so important what label we used, except that the ambiguity spreads out over our own thinking about what we call therapeutic counseling. And because we are not at all sure what we are trying to accomplish, we never know just when we are through.

What I have been questioning in my own mind more and more is the assumption that therapy should attempt to bring about as much personality change as possible. Could it be largely because of the enormous prestige psychoanalysis has acquired that we tend to assume that personality reorganization is the goal toward which we should strive? Is it really true that the therapy that produces the most changes is the best therapy? Would it not be possible to make the opposite assumption and deliberately set as our goal "minimum-change" therapy? This would be a kind of undertaking that would fit in well with the rest of the activities that go on under the name of counseling. We would try in each case to help the person discover some unblocked path in which he could move forward, develop his unique personality, and thus transcend rather than delve into the anxieties and conflicts in which he is now enmeshed.

I picture this process in terms of a change of *direction* rather than in terms of distances or amounts. The difficulties a client is experiencing can be thought of as indications that he is headed in a direction that is wrong for him or that he has at some former time made a wrong turn into a blind alley. All of this may have occurred without conscious awareness of course. Counseling can create a situation in which a person may become aware of the directional shifts that are possible for him and in which he can be sure someone will see him through what may be a difficult "rotation of his axis." In pursuing the implications of this geometric analogy a little further I calculated that a directional shift of only ten degrees makes a difference of 170 miles in where one comes out if his journey is 1,000 miles long—enough to make a considerable difference in terrain and landscape. Similarly, a relatively minor shift in the psychological direction in which a person is moving may well change his life considerably over a long period of years.

This is what I mean by *minimum-change* therapy. It has made it possible for me to see

how in principle therapeutic counseling could be shortened considerably without making it any less valuable. It involves no great change in the procedures we use, but some aspects of the complex counseling situation need to be empahsized or even modified to some extent.

Emphasis on Strength

In the first place, it implies that more emphasis than one ordinarily finds be placed on *positive* diagnosis. By and large, our diagnostic thinking rests on concepts taken over from psychopathology. We try to ascertain where a person's weak spots are. Many psychologists, especially in recent years, have criticized this approach and advocated the diagnosis of strengths. In minimum-change therapy we pay no attention to personality weaknesses that are adequately controlled or neutralized. We all have areas like this. It is only the difficulties that are actually blocking the person's forward movement that we must attempt to deal with. And as suggested in the previous section, it is quite possible that these may be by-passed rather than attacked. A person who knows his real strengths and is clear about his basic values may be able to turn away from anxieties about aspects of his life that would be very difficult to change.

Though there is a widespread current interest in ego processes and positive personality traits, we do not as yet have tests we can count on for this sort of diagnostic task. We are more likely to become aware of a person's strengths by observing things he does than by asking him questions. Some of this meaningful behavior occurs in the interview situation itself. For example, when Mary Hart flashes a sudden smile as she is struck with the amusing aspects of a particularly humiliating social experience she is recounting, we know that she possesses an asset that may be of considerable use to her. Call it a defense if you will, but in social situations and in personal emotional adaptation to the vicissitudes of life her ability to laugh at her own predicament will be a valuable asset. Other assets frequently showing up even in interviews where hostility, doubt, guilt, and anxiety are the main themes include moral principles of which the person is absolutely certain, demonstrated courage in the face of adversities, loyalty to those he loves. Whether or not it is advisable for the counselor to reflect or interpret such expressions at the time they occur is another question. But he can make a mental note of them.

We are more likely to become aware of a client's personality assets if we have some knowledge of his life outside the counseling room. In small or moderate-sized colleges, the counselor is likely to encounter his clients here or there—on the street, in the student union, at concerts, plays, or games. The growing practice of placing psychologists on the wards in mental hospitals serves the same purpose of permitting the kind of observation that positive diagnosis is based on. Conversations with a client's family or friends is another resource, but I am strongly of the opinion that it should not be used without the person's knowledge or permission. It is the characteristics he *knows* you have had a chance to observe—the things you can talk over together—that are grist for counseling's mill. In the last analysis, it is the client himself who must make the positive diagnosis we have been talking about if it is to be effective in his life.

Counseling Structure

A second point of emphasis in minimum-change therapy is the way in which the situation is structured for the client. We must take into account *his* expectations and goals

as well as our own. To a person profoundly dissatisfied with the way his life has been going, the only thing that really looks good is change—complete change. What he may have read about psychotherapy in popular magazines or seen in movies leads him to expect or at least hope that some fundamental change will occur. True, the experience of countless therapists has shown that such a person will hang on to his unconscious defenses and fight every sort of change at every step of the way. But if anyone *tells* him at the beginning that small shifts of direction rather than larger changes in total pattern are to be expected he is likely to reject the whole undertaking. He thinks he wants to be made over.

It is in this connection that some explicit verbal distinction between counseling and therapy may be useful. Instead of trying to fight the person's wishful dreams about miraculous effects of therapy, I can simply explain that I am a counselor rather than a psycholanalyst and that my job is to help a person find out what his personality is like and decide how he can use the assets he has and get rid of the obstacles that are blocking his progress. If he accepts the situation on these terms, therapeutic counseling can proceed within the framework of the very broad general question "What kind of person are you?" Anything the person wishes to bring up can be considered but we have not committed ourselves to an analysis of all his problems and innumerable childhood experiences out of which they may have arisen.

Necessary Support

A third essential feature of minimum-change therapy is the use of the counseling relationship to reduce the client's anxiety enough to allow him freedom to consider new possibilities. This, of course, is nothing new or at all peculiar to therapy of this type.

It seems to be the one common denominator linking together all sorts of diverse procedures. I suppose many workers in the psychotherapeutic vineyard would classify the approach I have been presenting as just another variety of *supportive* therapy. I would have no quarrel at all with that idea were it not that we are so prone to discredit support and to think of it as a superficial palliative measure to be used when more powerful methods are impractical. The idea of support should not be devalued in this way. Obviously by support I do not mean inspirational pep talks, shallow reassurance, or the encouragement of dependence. What I do mean is the act of lending one's own strength to the client for the period during which he needs it, so that he can be certain that his world is not going to fall apart if he moves. I have an idea that this is by far the most important thing we do for our clients, whatever our special theoretical predilections are. It is the crucial factor that enables his own development processes to operate.

I suspect that it would be possible in many cases to furnish this firm support much more economically than we now do if we are willing to use it without working for insight or drastic restructuring of self-concepts. Once a client has established a new direction for himself, it may well be that regularly scheduled interview hours a month apart may be enough to maintain his courage and confidence. It is the quality of the relationship rather than the amount of time spent in the counselor's presence that constitutes support.

The Closing Phase

This brings us to the last point I wish to make about minimum-change therapy. Its intensive phase is brought to a close as soon as a clear direction has been established in the client's life, even though there are many emotional complexes still unexplored, many interpersonal problems still unsolved. Here again, as in the preliminary diagnosis, evidence from outside the interview room can be combined with what comes up during therapy sessions in judging whether a change of direction has been stabilized. A client may mention casually, without apparently attaching any importance to the remark, something that marks such a significant movement. Mr. Elridge, for example, may speak of having had a long talk with his wife the night before, an action unprecedented in his previous experience. Gwen Riley, who has always been an anxious, perfectionistic procrastinator, may say that she has handed in, on time, an assigned paper for a course she is taking. Or the counselor may note the change in the incidental observation we discussed earlier. When he sees Bill Laraway having a coke with a girl, he knows that Bill has taken the first step toward overcoming the paralyzing shyness of which he has been complaining. A newspaper item stating that Mr. Bellingham has given a talk before the Active Club indicates to the counselor that this client's inferiority feelings are being surmounted. I know that, taken alone, such examples sound trivial. But remember, it is these ten-degree or even five-degree changes in direction that we are trying to facilitate. A small change in the direction of closer emotional ties with one's family or greater willingness to assume responsibility is the kind of shift that has a profound effect on later development. When it is clear that this shift has occurred it is time to think about the termination of formal therapy interviews.

One way of characterizing this kind of therapeutic counseling is to say that its basic premises come from the psychology of development and individual differences rather than from the psychology of adjustment. Its most fundamental assumption is that there

are many different ways of living an individual life richly and well, and that it is
natural for a person to continue to develop
throughout his life in his own unique way.
We work with nature instead of fighting or
ignoring it.

I have often been struck by the fact that
almost any personality trait one can think of
may be either an asset or a liability, depending on how it is used. Touchy oversensitive-
ness to slights and insults is not really
basically different from tact and social
awareness. Agression can lead to high
achievement as well as murderous rage.
Timidity and reasonable caution, compul-
siveness and constructive orderliness are opposite sides of the same coins. Instead of
bewailing our heredity and the mistakes that
were made in bringing us up, perhaps we can
learn to turn what we have to good account.

I have been thinking a good deal about the
way in which therapeutic counseling of this
sort might be evaluated. It is an intriguing
thought that the very failure to obtain clear
evidence for personality change as a result of
therapy may be construed as success rather
than failure if we reverse our basic assumption—namely, that maximum change is

what we are after. It may even be that Eysenck is right and that no kind of therapy
produces change that is greater than that
which time and the processes of nature
would ultimately have brought about by
themselves. The therapist may make a contribution only to the extent that he facilitates
or speeds up this natural process. The kind
of evaluation I should like to see would be
designed to show whether our therapeutic efforts do in fact accomplish this facilitation,
so that individuals find their way with less
suffering and wasted time with therapy than
without. And if so, we need to know what
aspects of the help we give contribute most
toward this end.

To come back at the end to the topic of
this symposium, the point I have been trying
to make is that we can best control the duration of counseling contacts by adopting consistently an attitude of respect for what each
individual client now is and lending him support and understanding while he comes to
terms with this unique self of his. Whether it
takes him two hours or two hundred, if he
succeeds the effort will have been very much
worth while.

8. METHODOLOGY IN SHORT-TERM THERAPY

Lewis R. Wolberg

Peter Schwarzburg

The advantages of short-term therapy may be debated on various grounds. Financial savings, more efficient employment of psychotherapeutic resources, opportunities to reduce waiting lists—these and other expediencies are often presented as justification for short-term programs. Admitting that there may be pragmatic reasons for abbreviating treatment, we may ask a crucial question: "How truly effective are short-term approaches in modifying disturbed neurotic patterns?"

In a study of the results of patients treated by a team of psychoanalytically trained therapists from the Tavistock Clinic and Cassel Hospital, Malan(1) concludes that long-lasting "depth" changes are possible even in severely ill patients treated on a short-term basis. The findings in this study are similar in some respects to those I have observed among a large group of patients with whom I have worked briefly over the past twenty-five years. Follow-up visits persuade that not only have symptoms been controlled, but in a considerable number of patients reconstructive personality changes have been brought about. The rationale for short-term therapy and a detailed delineation of techniques have been elaborated elsewhere(2). In this paper some stratagems found helpful will be outlined that may possibly be adaptable to the style of other therapists.

The psychotherapeutic process in short-term treatment may descriptively be broken down into four phases: a supportive phase, an apperceptive phase, an action phase and an integrative phase.

The Supportive Phase of Therapy

Turning to another human being for help is an inevitable consequence of feelings of helplessness, bewilderment and anxiety. It represents a final acknowledgement by the individual that he is unable to cope with his difficulty through his own resources. More or less every emotionally ill patient overtly or covertly regards the helping authority as a source of inspiration from whom infusions of wisdom must flow that will heal his wounds and lead him to health and self-fulfillment. Such credences are powered by the helplessness that inevitably accompanies a shattering of the sense of mastery. Because his habitual coping mechanisms have failed him, the patient believes himself incapable of independent judgments and he delivers himself body and soul to the powerful therapeutic agent whose education and experience promises to take over the direction of his life.

This design is obviously unwholesome if it is permitted to continue, for elements will be released that undermine the patient's independence, inspire infantility and mobilize anachronistic hopes and demands that superimpose themselves on the patient's other troubles, further complicating his existence.

Knowing that the patient covets a scheme to enmesh himself in a passive role with an omniscient deity, beneficent protector and idealized parent, the therapist may plan his strategy.

First, it is essential to establish as rapidly as possible a working relationship with the patient. This can often be done by a skilled therapist in the initial interview. It is difficult, however, to designate any unalterable rules for the establishing of contact with a patient. Variable factors apply in one case that are not applicable in a second. However, there are certain general principles that are useful to observe within the bounds of which one may operate flexibly. For instance, the expression on meeting the patient of a sympathetic and friendly attitude is remarkably helpful in relaxing him sufficiently to tell his story. As obvious as this may seem, many therapists greet a new patient with a detached and passive attitude in the effort to be objective and nondirective. This can freeze the patient in a resistive bind from which he may not recover during the span of his contact with the therapist.

Second, it is important to treat the patient no matter how upset he seems as a worthwhile individual who has somehow blundered into a neurotic impasse from which he will be able to extricate himself. Neurotic difficulties influence feelings in the direction of being unloved and unlovable. The patient may harbor doubts that he can be accepted or understood. Irrespective of denial mechanisms, he will crave extra-ordinary reassurance that the therapist is interested in him and cares about what happens to him. This obviously cannot be communicated verbally, but it may be expressed through a manner of respect, considerateness, tact, solicitude and compassion.

Third, the patient must be inspired to verbalize as much as possible, while the therapist attends to what he is saying, encouraging him by facial expressions, gestures, utterances and comments that reflect an interest in the patient and an understanding of what he is trying to say. The patient is constantly drawn out to express his problems, pointed questions being phrased to facilitate the flow of ideas and feelings.

Fourth, it is vital to avoid arguing or quarreling with the patient no matter how provocative he may be. The available time for therapy is so limited that one cannot indulge in the challenges and confrontations possible in long-term therapy. The therapist may not agree with what the patient says, but he should convey a respect for the patient's right to express his irritations and misconceptions.

Fifth, empathy is the keynote in establishing contact. Understandably one may not be able to sympathize with some of the attitudes, feelings and behavior of the patient. It may also be difficult to put oneself in his place. Yet the therapist may be able to detect an essential dignity in the patient, considering that his problems, destructive to him and to other people, have deviated him away from creative and humanistic aims. While it is inexpedient therapeutically to reassure too readily or to praise, it is essential in the early stages of treatment not to underestimate the patient's constructive qualities. In concentrating his attention on his bad points, the patient will tend to minimize his worthwhile characteristics which may lend themselves to a recounting by the therapist after he has gathered sufficient data.

Sixth, the therapist may by his verbal and nonverbal behavior signal confidence in his ability to help the patient without promising him a cure. This presupposes that the therapist has faith in what he is doing and a conviction that all people, given even a minimal chance, have the capacity to develop.

Seventh, even in the first interview the patient may be told that the rapidity of his recovery will depend on his willingness to cooperate in working on his problems. The therapist will show him how he can do this and will help him to help himself.

The Apperceptive Phase

If we are to proceed beyond the supportive phase toward an attempt at reconstruction of personality, we must strive to bring the individual to some recognition of what is behind his disorder. The power of "insight" has, of course, been greatly exaggerated, but irrespective of how valid or invalid an "insight" may be, it constitutes, when it is accepted, a significant means of alleviating tension and of restoring to the individual his habitual sense of mastery. The fact that we couch our "insights" in scientific terminology, being assured that they validate our theoretical preconceptions, does not make them accurate, even though the patient responds to them with relief, hope and abatement of his complaints.

Yet the principle is a correct one. Some explanation for his trouble is essential and we must give our patient one that is as close to our current scientific understanding of human nature as possible, always mindful of the fact that as behavioral scientists we are balanced precariously on the pinnacle of profound ambiguities. What seems like the truth of today may be the exploded myth of tomorrow.

But myth though it be, we have no other more tenable explanation; so we make it, hopeful that it will find its mark. The most effective vehicle that we have for this is the unique relationship that is set up between the patient and therapist which acts as a corrective experience for the patient. The patient may project into the relationship the same kinds of irrational demands, hopes and fears such as have shadowed his attitudes toward early authorities and other significant people in his past. But instead of meeting indignation, rejection, ridicule or hostility—the usual and expected rebuttals—the therapist interprets the patient's reactions with sympathy and understanding. Bringing these, if they are apparent, to his attention in a noncondemning manner helps the patient to arrive at an understanding of the meaning and possible origin of his drives while actually reexperiencing them in the protective relationship with the therapist. Under these circumstances the patient may come to realize that his responses toward the therapist are the product, not of any realistic situation that exists, but rather of what he anticipates or imagines must be as a result of past rela-

tionships. He may then appreciate that what is happening with the therapist also happens under some circumstances with other people. Thus varied defensive reactions become apparent to the patient, not as theories, but as real experiences.

In short-term therapy, time prevents the employment of the conventional tools of free association, extensive dream interpretation and the building up of a transference neurosis. However, an experienced therapist will be able, perhaps even in the first session, to gain knowledge of the operative dynamics from the history given by the patient, particularly the quality of his relationship with his parents and siblings, from one or two dreams, from the nature of the symptomatology, and from the patient's behavior with the therapist during the interview. He may then present at a propitious moment a cautious but firm explanation to the patient of the impact on him and his personality of some of the experiences and deprivations in his childhood, of the defenses he has developed, of how environmental precipitating factors have operated to bring his conflicts to a head and how these are registered in his immediate symptoms and sufferings. Only a fragment of the existing conflicts may lend itself to such exploration and interpretation in short-term therapy, but this can be like a biopsy of the total psychodynamic picture. If the patient grasps the significance of an interpretation and sees the continuity between problems in his development, their crystallizations in his general personality structure and their relation to the current complaint factor, a deep penetration will have been achieved. By concerted self-examination, the patient may thereafter progressively widen his own insights. In any equation the shifting of one factor will bring other elements into realignment.

Obviously, interpretations will have to be

made that coordinate with the patient's capacities for understanding. The therapist will need to employ language comprehensible to the patient, encouraging the patient to restate what has been expressed to test his comprehension. It is surprising how patients, even those without an extensive education, can grasp the meaning of relatively complex psychological concepts if these are presented in terms of the patient's own experience. When a good relationship exists between the therapist and patient, even unconscious repudiated aspects may be explored without provoking too severe reactions of resistance. If the patient is unable to acknowledge the accuracy of an interpretation, the therapist may ask him to consider it nevertheless before discarding it entirely. The patient may also be encouraged to alert himself to factors that stir up his tensions, to work on connections between these provocative factors and what is being mobilized inside himself. Are his reactions habitual ones and if so how far back do they go? Are they related to important experiences in his childhood? Some patients may be able to get considerable understanding through the discipline of searching within themselves. Some may even learn to interpret their dreams in line with such percipience.

Sometimes the patient will, due to resistance or the lack of time, fail to arrive at any basic realizations in the course of short-term therapy. This need not deter the therapist from encouraging the patient to work on himself toward self-understanding after the treatment period is over. It is quite rewarding to observe how many patients, some months and even years later, arrive at insights which strike them with a dramatic force and which they can utilize constructively. Examining these one may recognize them as patterned after some of the therapist's original interpretations, which could

not be accepted during the short treatment phase, but which were subjected to spontaneous "working-through" following treatment.

The Action Phase

The acid test of therapy lies in the patient's capacity to put his acquired new comprehensions into definitive action. This means that he must challenge conceptions that have up to this time ruled his life. A symptom may rapidly be overcome in the supportive phase of therapy; but a personality pattern, one that disorganizes relationships with other human beings, will scarcely be altered except after a period of resistance.

In short-term therapy even the tiniest action opposing neurotic misconceptions can be scored as a gain. The therapist may actively invite the patient to challenge his fears and engage in actions that hold promise of rewards. Discussion of the consequences of his movements may then prove fruitful. I have found several tactics of importance here. First, I actively outline specific courses of action hoping that the patient, prompted to act on my suggestion, will achieve a small success which will reinforce his determination to try again. Even after a signal success, patients will need further urging. Having escaped hurt by the skin of their teeth, they may feel that their luck will collapse the next time they engage in an experience that threatens to set off anxiety. Second, a tranquilizer or a barbiturate taken prior to a challenge may reduce anxiety sufficiently so that the patient may allow himself to enter into a fearsome situation and see it through. As soon as possible, a repetition of this action with reduced and finally no drug will be indicated. In borderline patients, a phenothiazine derivative like trifluoperazine appears to work better than the tranquilizing drugs. Third, I sometimes teach the patient self-hypnosis(3). In the trance the patient is trained to visualize himself successfully mastering situations that upset him. The patient may phantasy an overcoming of progressively challenging difficulties, gradually working himself up to more fearsome ones. Suggestions made to himself in the trance that he will have the desire to tackle his problems may enable him to handle these with greater and greater ease.

The Integrative Phase

Consolidating therapeutic gains will require practice the remainder of the individual's life. The chinks in the patient's defensive armor must be widened by constant challenges and repetitive salutary actions. Complacency, riding on the notion that one feels better and hence can remain at a standstill, invites a recrudescence of symptoms once stress exceeds existent coping capacities. Constant alertness to what is happening within oneself, and a resisting of subversive neurotic temptations are mandatory.

In short-term therapy one must depend on the posttherapeutic period to harden what has been molded during the active treatment phases, and to restructure into new patterns aspects that were only casually perceived before. Encouraging is the fact that once the old way of life has been unbalanced in one dimension, new zones of activity and more wholesome modes of being and feeling may present themselves.

Before therapy is terminated, the patient may realize that it is possible to control tension and anxiety once it starts by making connections between symptomatic upsets, precipitating factors in his environment, and his operative personality forces; and by recognizing that he is capable of developing a different philosophy that can lend to his life a salutary meaning.

In some cases I encourage the patient to employ the technique of self-hypnosis or self-relaxation periodically when he is upset, both to resolve his tensions and to explore reasons for the revival of his symptoms(3). Patients can easily learn to apply this two-fold tactic by giving themselves the assignment to figure out the aspects within their environment and within themselves that have precipitated their anxiety. This may result in direct understanding, or stimulated phantasies and dreams may yeild some leads. A helpful course of action may then spontaneously be evolved. No more than a few sessions are usually required to restore equilibrium.

The patient may also be counseled temporarily to employ a mild tranquilizing drug if his tensions do not resolve after a while. He must be cautioned, however, that drugs, while provisionally useful, cannot constitute a way of life. The basic therapeutic factor at all times is greater self-understanding. Drugs cannot and must not replace such self-directed efforts.

Finally, the patient is exhorted to adopt a few basic philosophical principles. Superficial as they sound they sometimes make a profound impact on him. In long-term therapy the patient is expected to develop new values through his own spontaneous efforts. In short-term therapy a different way of looking at things may be presented in an active educational effort. For example, the following principle may be proferred: "It is useful to remember at all times that while you are not responsible for what happened to you in your childhood, and the faulty ideas and fears you learned in your past, you are responsible for carrying them over into your adult life." This principle, if accepted, may block the patient from making a career out of blaming his parents and crediting to past unfortunate episodes all of his current problems, justifying his neurotic carryings-on by the terrible things done to him as a child over which he had no control.

Another principle is: "No matter what troubles or terrible scrapes you have gotten yourself into in the past, you can rise above these in the future with the knowledge you now have. You need not indulge in patterns which you know you should be able to control, and really want to control." This precept, if incorporated, may help some patients control certain neurotic patterns, realizing that they have powers to inhibit them. The putting together of certain persuasive formulations in this way can be useful to patients who are unable to structure a philosophic formula by themselves. This may help consolidate the gains they have made in therapy.

Within this broad framework, then, the therapist may apply himself flexibly to the problems of his patients, utilizing techniques from various fields, blended in an eclectic approach. Hopefully out of the experiences of workers from the various fields of human relationships there will eventually emerge a more scientific methodology in short-term psychotherapy that will enable us to help the greatest numbers of patients in the shortest possible time.

Summary

Short-term therapy has more than utilitarian value. There are indications that it will, as its methodology becomes elaborated, develop into the treatment of choice for a considerable number of patients. This conviction is supported by observations from a variety of sources to the effect that patients suffering from a wide spectrum of emotional problems, treated over a short period of time, may obtain not only sustained relief, but also, in some cases, personality changes of a reconstructive nature that would have been considered significant had long-term treatment been employed. Four stages in the course of short-term therapy seem apparent: (1) a supportive phase during which homeostasis is brought about through the healing influences of the relationship with the therapist, the placebo effect of the therapeutic process, and the decompressive impact of emotional catharsis; (2) an apperceptive phase, characterized by the ability to understand, even minimally, the meaning of the complaint factor in terms of some of the operative conflicts and basic personality needs and defenses; (3) an action phase distinguished by a challenging of certain habitual neurotic patterns, facing them from a somewhat different perspective; and (4) an integrative relearning and reconditioning phase which continues after termination on the basis of the chain reaction started during the brief treatment period.

The specific techniques that are outlined in the paper are contingent, first, on the acceptance of eclecticism, adopting procedures from every field of psychiatry, psychology, sociology, education and even philosophy, that may be of help in the total treatment effort; second, on the existence of flexibility in the therapist that enables him to adjust his stratagems to the immediate needs of the patient and therapeutic situation; and third, on the studied employment of activity in the relationship. All modalities are employed in those combinations that may be of value, including psychoanalytic techniques, interviewing procedures, drugs, hypnosis, reconditioning and group therapy.

Among the procedures that may expedite treatment are the following: (1) establishing a rapid working relationship (rapport); (2) circumscribing the problem area as a focus for exploration; (3) evolving with the patient a working hypothesis of the psychodynamics of his difficulty; (4) employing dream interpretation where the therapist is analytically trained; (5) alerting oneself to resistances and resolving these as rapidly as possible; (6) dealing with target symptoms like excessive tension, anxiety and depression, through the careful use of drugs; phobic phenomena by conditioning techniques; obsessive-compulsive manifestations by persuasive tactics, etc; (7) teaching the patient how to employ insight as a corrective force; (8) outlining with the patient a definite plan of action by which he can use his understanding in the direction of change;

(9) searching for transference elements and resolving these quickly before they build up to destroy the relationship; (10) encouraging the development of a proper life philosophy.

REFERENCES

1. Malan, D. H.: *A Study of Brief Psychotherapy.* Springfield, Ill.: Thomas, 1963.
2. Wolberg, L. R.: "The Technique of Short-Term Psychotherapy," In Wolberg, L. R., ed.: *Short-Term Psychotherapy.* New York: Grune & Stratton, 1965.
3. Wolberg, L. R.: "Hypnosis in Short-Term Psychotherapy," in Wolberg, L. R., ed.: *Short-Term Psychotherapy.* New York: Grune & Stratton, 1965.

9. MODERN PSYCHOANALYTIC COUNSELING

William J. Kirman

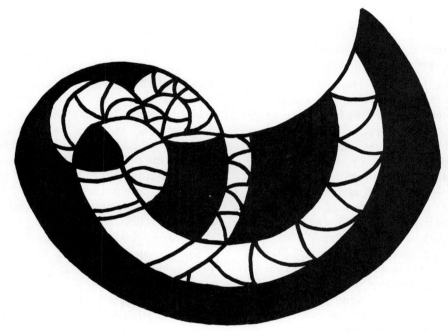

Vasilije Knezevic

It is time that the basic principles of modern psychoanalysis were applied to the counseling setting and that our schools, colleges and community agencies were able to profit from these new understandings. While almost all counseling approaches work with some people some of the time, it is our thesis that a modern pyschoanalytically trained counselor can work more effectively with more people more of the time.

Although a number of writers have suggested that the principles of psychotherapy are not applicable to school counseling or to counseling in general (Aubrey, 1967, Tyler, 1960), we take issue with this point of view. While they state that the goals of short-term counseling differ markedly from the goals of psychotherapy and that the expectations of the client and kinds of problems presented are different in the school setting, we do not agree that this necessitates a more superficial theoretical model.

In this paper we will discuss these concepts in terms of a counseling model based on the principles of modern psychoanalysis. At the same time we will attempt to show that the basic principles which underlie long-term modern psychoanalytic treatment are directly applicable to school counseling, vocational counseling, pastoral counseling, and other short-term counseling experiences. Illustrations will be used to demonstrate how these principles may be applied in context.

What Is Modern Psychoanalysis: Basic Concepts

When we think of psychoanalysis, our attention turns to the writings of Sigmund Freud, which are indeed the foundation of all psychoanalytic thought. Freud's contributions regarding the importance of the unconscious mind, the relevance of dreams, the psychosexual stages of personality development, the significance of early childhood, as well as the concepts of free association and interpretation, are indeed crucial to our understanding of the individual.

Psychoanalysis in its classical form, however, has not been sufficiently flexible to make the contribution it deserves to the counseling movement. Some of the philosophically appealing and more simplistic concepts present in Rogers, Tyler and Glasser are absent in psychoanalysis. More intensive training is required including that all important personal therapeutic experience in order to fully understand the system. Freud's brilliant discovery that the unconscious mind wields a powerful and often decisive influence in our lives has not been sufficiently understood nor appreciated in all its implications.

As psychoanalytic research has proceeded, many dark corners of the mind have been illuminated and more sophisticated techniques have followed recent theoretical understandings. The field of modern psychoanalysis has extended classical psychoanalysis in two basic ways: (1) it has made help available to kinds of people and types of problems not considered for traditional psychoanalysis, and, (2) it has extended and adapted the medium of psychoanalysis to situations and settings (i.e., group, classroom, industry, etc.) that have traditionally been excluded. It is this second application that is relevant to the counseling movement.

Modern psychoanalysis, which was developed from the early 1950s to the present, most notably by Dr. Hyman Spotnitz and his students, was originally designed to overcome some of the limitations inherent in the classical psychoanalytic model in dealing with seriously disturbed individuals. Problems which had their origins in the first two years of life (the pre-Oedipal stages) did not respond adequately to the classical Freudian method of interpretation, nor did classical theory fully understand these people.

Interpretation, the major tool of classical psychoanalysis, has little impact on a client whose problem originated at a preverbal time in life, when explanations were not relevant—indeed, not even understood. In fact, most people will respond negatively when told what is wrong with them. An explanation is often experienced as an attack regardless of its truthfulness or relevance. Relatively few people are able to improve as a result of causative explanation.

The classical analytic emphasis on libido or sexuality, while perfectly valid for certain problems, seems irrelevant when a person is emotionally conflicted in a different area. Accordingly, modern psychoanalysts place a greater emphasis on the role of aggression and its appropriate expression which is seen as a major problem in many personalities.

In modern psychoanalysis, the traditional concept of object transference where the patient sees the analyst as a significant person from the past is accepted but emphasis is placed on the narcissistic transference, i.e., those feeling states in the patient where he interchanges his own feelings with those of the analyst (Spotnitz, 1969). The analyst is here seen as an extension of the patient and not as a significant person from the past. This kind of transference is necessary when an individual's ego development did not proceed satisfactorily during the early years and he is initially unable to form an object transference. Modern psychoanalysis, in understanding the meaning and need for a narcissistic transference, makes help available to people who function at a more primitive emotional level.

In addition, the study of narcissistic transference phenomena has demonstrated many useful applications to the more normal and less disturbed individual. Indeed, one study has illustrated the therapeutic use of the narcissistic transference in a normal classroom setting. Since most individuals have some component in their personalities relating to difficulties during the first two years of life, these unresolved problems can be most effectively dealt with in the context of a narcissistic transference. These include problem areas centering around negativism, stubbornness, giving and receiving, separation, self-blame, etc. The various modern psychoanalytic techniques used to establish the narcissistic transference help solidify rapport with the patient (i.e., help him feel understood) and relieve his sense of aloneness and isolation.

The classical analytic concept of resolving resistance as a prime goal of treatment is maintained in modern psychoanalysis. A resistance is defined as any factor in the office that impedes growth toward emotional maturity and any behavior or attitude on the part of the patient that impedes progressive communication (i.e., talking about different

psychologically meaningful topics). The latter is called the *transference resistance* and becomes the major focus of the therapeutic relationship. What the patient does with the analyst in the office, what he says, fails to say, his verbal and nonverbal means of making and avoiding contact, etc., take precedence over any outside topic he may discuss. This emphasis on the here and now—what is going on in the office this moment between two people—is crucial in resolving the transference resistance. And it is precisely in the resolution of resistance that the modern analyst brings new and more effective tools to his work.

Another concept of importance for modern psychoanalysis is that of maturational need and maturational communication. In the course of growing up, we all have certain needs that must be met in order for us to mature and grow. These are called maturational needs. (Havighurst's concept of "developmental task" is somewhat related.) The child needs a sense of basic trust in the first year of life (Erikson), a feeling that he can count on the mother. Later, he needs to feel that the products of his body are desirable and worthwhile. He needs to learn not to hurt himself, not to hurt others; he has to experience his sense of independence, his ability to control impulses and delay gratification: he needs a sense of awareness of other people and of other people's needs; he needs the opportunity to be selfish and inconsiderate, as well as the opportunity to share and be involved with others; he needs the experience of feeling the full force of his rage and to recognize that these feelings in themselves will do no harm.

Invariably, some of these needs go unmet. No one has perfect parents, and it is inevitable that there will be some deficiencies in one's development. If these deficiencies in learning and feeling are not corrected by later life experiences, emotional problems develop which require professional help.

It is precisely the understanding of which maturational needs in the client have gone unmet that enables the counselor to intervene effectively. It is, of course, impossible for the counselor to meet all of the client's maturational needs in the offfice. The counselor's goal is rather to help resolve resistances whose resolution will enable the client to get his unmet maturational needs met in a satisfactory and productive way.

A third important contribution of modern psychoanalysis is the understanding that emotional growth precedes insight. The client does not generally gain insight through interpretations of his unconscious or his behavior and then change. Rather, he can appreciate such interpretations or explanations *after* he has grown sufficiently. Thus, the Freudian method of interpretation is used cautiously by the modern psychoanalyst. With these three basic principles in mind, let us examine how modern psychoanalysis can be used in the counseling setting, and at the same time address ourselves to that perennially troublesome question, "Does counseling differ operationally from psychotherapy?"

Modern Psychoanalysis: Applications

The attempts over the years to differentiate between counseling and psychotherapy have been varied. Writers usually address themselves to the level of skill of the practioner, the frequency of contact, the goals of the treatment and the treatment setting. Many writers have viewed counseling and psychotherapy as qualitatively different from one another which implies that personality is compartmentalized or layered and that the outer layers may be helped more easily than the inner ones. The appreciation of the totality of a human being is temporarily dropped in one's eagerness to differentiate degrees of competence relevant to different settings and frequencies.

The modern psychoanalytic point of view sees counseling as a specialized application of modern psychoanalytic psychotherapy somewhat modified in relation to a particular setting. The basic theory and techniques, however, remain essentially the same. Since many patients in modern psychoanalysis are seen only once every other week or only weekly in a group setting, the potentially reduced contact in a school or college setting is not seen as altering the therapeutic relationship or theoretical model in any significant way. In modern psychoanalysis there is no evidence that greater frequency of contact necessarily leads to quicker or better results. Greater contact simply makes the therapist's and client's jobs easier. Thus, the role of the modern psychoanalytic counselor is seen as a more difficult one than that of the psychotherapist. He uses the same theoretical model, very similar techniques and yet has less opportunity to study his client because of reduced frequency of contacts. Therefore, we must conclude that effective counseling that is clearly conceptualized and firmly anchored to theory that can be generalized and where the counselor proceeds basically by design rather than intuition— this kind of counseling is *more* difficult than psychotherapy. Seeing clients less often in specialized settings makes the task more difficult—not less. But it does not make it qualitatively different. Of course, as in psychotherapy, the counselor's personality, self-awareness and technical skill define the nature, kind and degree of help he is able to provide. Thus any limitations in the help that a client may receive in counseling is a function of what assets the counselor brings to the session—not of the limiting nature of counseling.

Viewed another way, the person who comes for help is basically not concerned about how the counselor defines his role. He is not concerned about the skills, the abilities, the perceptions, and the expectations of the counselor; but rather, the counselee is concerned about his own needs and problems, his own life difficulties that have brought him into treatment and is concerned only whether his counselor can help.

In other words, when we perceive the helping process from the point of view of the counselee, the differentiation between counseling and psychotherapy becomes meaningless. We take from each helping relationship what it has to offer though we may have hoped for more. We give in each helping relationship what we are able regardless of the definition of role.

The client comes into the counseling setting with various perceptions, unmet maturational needs and resistances. In the modern psychoanalytic model people are not able to solve their problems because of resistances which impede healthy functioning and in the counseling relationship interfere with progressive communication. The client may be having difficulty making an occupational choice, getting along with friends, finding an appropriate college, etc., because his resistances are in that particular area. Simple difficulties are attended by simple resistances, complex difficulties by complex resistances. Anything that interferes with sound functioning, which blocks growth and life progress, is considered a resistance. Within the counseling context, a resistance is anything that interferes with the free flow of communication between client and counselor. It is the job of the modern pyschoanalytic counselor to help resolve these resistances by verbal interventions.

This helps the client to say "everything" to the counselor and thereby enables him to function more effectively.

The major task of the modern psychoanalytic counselor, therefore, whether he is working in long-term or in short-term counseling, is to help resolve resistances. One of the most effective ways of doing this involves understanding maturational needs and how to intervene in terms of this understanding.

By meeting the client's maturational needs symbolically in the office, the counselor helps the client resolve his resistances to further communication and to function better in the office and outside. Until these resistive forces are resolved, the client will not be able to engage in productive communication or be able to solidify his gains on a long-term basis.

This does not mean that the goal of counseling is necessarily "deep personality change" (whatever one can agree that is), which is generally considered outside the purview of counseling. The distinction between "maximum" change and "minimum" change, cited by Tyler, is a concept that rests in the mind of the practitioner, not in the mind of the client, who is there to be helped. The client who comes to a counseling interview is not asking himself, "Do I need minimal change or maximal change?" or "Do I have to come forever or just once?"

In fact, the whole concept of degree of change is a decision made by the client, not the counselor, and then only on an unconscious level. When the client's ego strength has matured sufficiently and he is ready to assume the risks of altering the emotional status quo—of giving up the familiar to try the unknown—then and only then does change take place. Whether this change is "minimal" or "maximal" is a function of the new homeostatis that is practicable for the personality. It is not for the counselor to determine the degree of change—unless his lack of sophistication leads him to latch onto the superficial uncharged communications of the client. In this case what we have is not "minimal" change but no change, or even damage. Under these circumstances, the client may come away with the feeling that he has not been understood, that his more important and meaningful feelings have been brushed aside or ignored. It is often this kind of implicit communication from the counselor which the client responds to.

Of course, the client will often respond to the underlying goodwill or nurturance of even the most blundering counselor, and these therapeutic feelings of the counselor often meet a maturational need of an emotionally deprived client. But then goodwill and nurturance is responded to in the school custodian, the policeman or the grocery clerk. A professional counselor should have more sophisticated tools than untrained people, even though they also help. What is viewed as successful "minimal" change counseling can occur when the counselor chances to resolve a resistance by meeting a maturational need and this intervention is felt to be "easy" for the counselor.

For some clients a suggestion of how to study for an exam may be all that is required. If this simple intervention succeeds with a failing student and he then gains excellent grades and is admitted to a fine university, can this change be considered minimal since it has changed his entire life? If, on the other hand, a client needs to understand his underlying contempt for the counselor as a mask for the contempt he feels for himself—and this understanding necessitates first solidifying the narcissistic transference where the client can examine his projection in the counselor's ego and then reconstructing the parental patterns of interaction to help the client recall painful memories—and if the result of all this is simply for the client to diminish his contemptuous attitude toward authority figures, is this then maximal change? It depends on how the client views it. Besides, as has been stated, the skilled counselor has *no* choice—he is there to supply what the client needs.

When we look at the process from the client's point of view, we find that different clients have different needs and perceptions. In order to seek help at all, some clients have to feel that they need only come once, and this feeling itself may help them continue in treatment. One counselor had a client whom he had to tell every single session that this might be the last time he would see him. He did this for three years, and each time the client came, he reminded him this might be his last session. This enabled the client to feel sufficiently free and untrapped to go on with counseling and resolve many serious problems. Another client who was terrified of abandonment asked a counselor, "Dr. Smith, how long can I come to you?" Knowing this client well, the counselor responded, "As long as I'm alive, you can come to see me, and if I die before you, I have named someone in my will who will continue to see you." This client laughed with delight; the counselor's maturational communication helped him resolve his resistance to expressing what a clutching, clinging baby he really felt himself to be. These two opposite communications illustrate that the counselor's words are intended to affect unconscious feelings in the client and are not intended to be taken at face value. After all, one needn't see a counselor for ordinary, simple conversation; one has undoubtedly already tried that and it hasn't worked. In both these examples, the counselor was meeting the client's maturational needs by joining their resistances.

A client whose presenting problem is a

sense of unworthiness, who feels he deserves nothing and is unable to ask for what he needs, can be helped to deal with these feelings by exploring them in terms of a specific interaction between himself and the counselor. This maximizes the transference, and when the counselor symbolically meets the client's maturational needs and the resistance is resolved, the unsayable will become verbalized. If, for example, in a session with a client the discussion focuses on food, the counselor can help resolve the above resistance by pursuing the topic as follows: He can discuss with the client what foods he would like served in the office, how he would like them served, what should be served first, and so on. The client's protests are met by reassurances that this is indeed a legitimate topic to discuss. All of these questions symbolically deal with the underlying problem that has brought the client there in the first place.

If the presenting problem is an educational or vocational one (with the same underlying dynamics, as is often the case), the counselor may intervene with the same treatment plan vocationally focused: ask what prestigious occupations the client would like to consider entering, what locale would make him happiest to work in, which of the several excellent universities he would like to attend, how should you, the counselor, help him to achieve this? The client's reluctance to discuss these "silly" questions must be brushed aside as in the discussion about food and he will come to respond to the counselor's genuine feeling that he can, indeed, think more positively about himself. Whether the client will realistically achieve those things is not important—the counselor is, in this stage of counseling, focusing only on resolving the feelings of unworthiness. Reality considerations represent an essential but later part of the counseling with this client. In discussing this with the client, you, the counselor, are showing him via the transference relationship that he has a right to receive, and that you are pleased that he is considering receiving. You are showing him your willingness to help him with his problems, and at the same time encouraging him to dare feel and ask for what he wants, not only with food but in life in general. The benefit of such a discussion with a client in the context of a strong transference will generalize to a number of outside situations.

The kinds of transference that develop in counseling follow the level of ego development of the individual client. Clients whose emotional lives have been relatively satisfying demonstrate *object transference* from the start of counseling and perceive the counselor as mother, father, or other significant person from childhood. This proclivity for predominantly object transference is limited to the more emotionally mature clients and has been fully dealt with in classical analytic writings (cf. Freud, Greenson). The majority of clients, however, evidence the kind of transference that modern psychoanalysis has carefully investigated in its research; namely, narcissistic transference. These clients, because of their inability emotionally to clearly differentiate ego and object (a quality of all early resistance patterns) attribute their own feelings about themselves to the counselor (see Spotnitz references). Since the origin of these resistances is during the first two years of life (the pre-Oedipal stage), the techniques of modern psychoanalysis are particularly well suited to deal with them effectively. Very frequently the counselor (who must reveal much more of himself than the analyst) comes to represent an aspect of the despised and idealized self for the student and is detested and worshipped accordingly. This *negative narcissistic transference* is handled as in modern analysis; namely, helping the client to accept his despised self in the counselor which in turn leads to self-acceptance. The *idealizing narcissistic transference*, however, is not analyzed; instead, the client is helped to become the kind of person he admires in the counselor and the cathexis is encouraged to generalize from the counselor to healthful activities and studies in school. This idealizing narcissistic transference, if properly utilized by the counselor, can effect great influence on the student's life. It entails the most basic type of learning—learning by identification—a situation where the counselor's character, values, goals, and knowledge exert a significant influence on the student. Contrary to the suggested dictum, the student emulates the counselor on the basis of "do as I do—not as I say." Students identify with what they experience—not with what they are told.

One objection that has been lodged by Tyler, among others, is that the client is not always there voluntarily. According to the psychoanalytic model, whether or not he is there voluntarily is many times irrelevant to the task at hand. Many clients who come to a private practioner are there because the mother, or spouse, or employer, or teacher, or some other person has overtly or covertly insisted. In addition, effective counseling takes place in penal institutions, in mental hospitals, and in other settings where the patient has no choice. This reluctance does not necessarily directly affect the therapeutic gain. Freud himself has stressed that success in psychoanalysis depends ultimately on resolving the unconscious resistance; the immediate and often temporary conscious resistances can be less important and are often quickly given up. Prison psychologists report that reluctant clients who come for appointments only to relieve the monotony of cell life can sometimes make startling gains well beyond the average client who walks "voluntarily" into the counselor's office. Again, the focus is on unconscious motivation.

The concept of "joining the resistance," a modern psychoanalytic technique, can often be employed effectively with a reluctant client. A woman whom a counselor had been seeing for a while wanted very much for him to work with her husband as well in order to improve their marriage. He agreed to see the husband for a consultation. When the husband appeared, he made it very clear to the counselor that he was not in need of therapy or counseling—that there was nothing "wrong" with him and that in fact his wife was the cause of all problems between them. The counselor assured him that he was not planning to analyze him or to discover what was "wrong" with him. Instead the counselor expressed sympathy for him in having to live with so difficult a woman as his wife. After all, the counselor knew how difficult she could be, etc. The man seemed relieved and proceeded to enumerate all of the problems involved in living with such a difficult woman. At the end of the session the counselor thanked him for helping him to understand his wife better and asked whether he would like to come to see him from time to time to be of help with his wife's case. The man eagerly agreed to be his "consultant" and a time was set for his next appointment. After a number of sessions similar to the one I have described, this man stated, "Look here, Dr. Smith, my wife can't be to blame for everything—I must be contributing a little something to the problem. Can't we discuss that?" And so he became a client motivated to learn about himself. Obviously this client was more motivated for help than his conscious intentions would lead a counselor to guess. Had this not been the case, the technique of "joining the resistance" would not have changed his motivation toward increased self-knowledge.

Modern Psychoanalysis in the Schools

While techniques have been discussed only briefly in this paper, the following list of suggestions may be helpful in applying modern psychoanalytic principles in a school setting.

1. The student who has a history of always being "wrong" and stupid is encouraged to relate to the counselor so that he can be "right" in the office. Only after he has experienced a period of being right, and he knows he can be right as well as wrong, should the counselor explore his resistances to being right and his reasons for feeling inadequate.

2. The pampered student who demands instant gratification should be helped to wait and tolerate frustration.

3. The insecure student may be told that the counselor, too, feels inadequate and stupid. This technique of emotional mirroring helps build the narcissistic transference.

4. The opinionated student is encouraged to give facts and not opinions. This helps explore an alternative mode of interaction and uses the transference to broaden the student's repertoire of responses.

5. The compliant student is encouraged to question and doubt. The suspicious student is encouraged to accept things simply on faith. Only later, after an alternative response has been established should the original inadequacy be analyzed, if at all.

6. The student fearful of having missed some important explanation is told not to worry since the counselor can repeat these ideas any time he likes. In fact, the counselor

enjoys repeating things. This reassurance often allays anxiety.

7. The detached but self-blaming student is "joined" in his intellectual defenses and encouraged not to feel anything since the counselor already hears so much emotion during the day. In fact, the counselor can say he thinks it is a refreshing change to work with a real intellectual.

8. The negative, challenging student is joined in believing that the counselor may indeed be wrong while it is made clear that the counselor is immune to his negativism.

9. A disbelieving student is encouraged to doubt and still perform properly. This makes the necessary distinction between feeling and doing and at the same time avoids a nonproductive argument. Much counselor energy is wasted in trying to convince doubting students. A comment such as, "You are not required to believe anything I say—just be sure to remember I said it," effectively nullifies the secondary gain of the negative student.

10. A student bemoaning the separation that must follow graduation is encouraged to continue contact with the counselor and helped to understand that absence need not mean loss.

11. The clinging student at the end of the course is helped to relate to a new teacher. His security in the old relationship is preserved while he is nudged ahead toward new horizons.

Conclusions

School and vocational problems are seen as occurring in the context of a total and integrated personality. This personality is seen as possessing unconscious as well as conscious thought processes and any meaningful communication from the counselor must directly or indirectly address itself to these processes. Let no one think this is an attempt to make the simple complicated or to encourage reductionism—like Ogden Nash's "Mrs. Marmaduke Moore who traveled the world in search of panaceas and went 'to Vienna to see St. Sigmund the Freud' to return to 'preach his doctrines to the unemployed.' " A simple request for occupational information should, of course, not be met with ridiculous questions but should be freely given. A need for information based on the counselor's maturity and experience can, of course, be offered without analysis. Advice, encouragement, warmth, appreciation or an appropriate scolding all have their place in the context of a human relationship. The problem does not lie in making a simple task complicated; rather we must gain the courage to face the complexity of many of the communications of our clients—to recognize that the limitations of theoretical models and our personalities deter us from maximizing our effectiveness as counselors. The role of the counselor must not be watered down; the sophistication of his training must be built up.

In the course of our lives much help is given by dint of intuition, common sense and experience. If modern counseling is to be more than this, it is not enough to light the candle rather than curse the darkness; we must look closely at the "emperor's clothes" of simplistic counseling models and their results. Modern psychoanalysis which is only one meaningful and effective model (and in my view the most effective) should be seriously viewed as a viable alternative to traditional methods of school and college counseling. Even limited exposure to a stimulating and comprehensive counseling model, though it will leave many gaps in the training, is preferable and more helpful for the student counselor than giving him a greater sense of mastery and accomplishment of simpler models that only pretend to help or help in a willy-nilly manner.

REFERENCES

Aubrey, R. F. The misapplication of therapy models to school counseling. See pages 23-29 of this text.

Freud, S. The dynamics of the transference. *Collected Papers of Sigmund Freud,* vol. II. New York: Basic Books. (Originally published, 1912.)

Greenson, R. R. *Technique and Practice of Psychoanalysis,)* vol. I. New York: International Universities Press, 1967.

Spotnitz, H. The narcissistic defense in schizophrenia. *Psychoanalysis and the Psychoanalytic Review,* 1961 48(4), 24-42.

———. The toxoid response. *The Psychoanalytic Review,* 1963, 50(4), 81-94.

———. *Modern Psychoanalysis of the Schizophrenic Patient.* New York: Grune & Stratton, 1968.

Tyler, L. E. Minimum change therapy. See pages 67-72 of this text.

LEARNING FOR SPITE

Jacob Kesten

Peter Schwarzburg

Increased understanding of ego development within the last decade has led to new ideas and methods of treating people with emotional disorders. This paper will concern itself with an account of the treatment of a ten year old boy who presented learning difficulties. Particular reference is made to understanding the unconscious ego of this boy and the use of one of the newer techniques in treatment.

Introductory Remarks

We know that a child frequently reacts to an unfavorable environment with negative attitudes, such as resentment, anger, rage, revenge and hate. Because these attitudes are often unacceptable to the child's conscious ego as well as to his environment, they are repressed into the unconscious part of the ego. There, unbeknown to the child, they exert a destructive influence upon whatever the conscious and realistic portion of the ego constructively attempts to do. Much has been written about successful treatment of children by the standard proven methods of psychotherapy such as interpretation, abreaction, play therapy, suggestion, environmental changes, and the use of a good relationship. The therapeutic method described in this paper consists of the reflection of the unconscious negativistic portion of the ego by the therapist. The rationale for this technique is based upon the idea that the child can better deal with his own repressed oppositional negative attitudes when they are presented to him as an external adversary. It is hoped that this technique would enable the child to observe an enemy hitherto unseen, to study its strategy, to make self-preservative counter strategic moves, to understand and control it, to redirect it, and thus be enabled to pursue his conscious desire for psychic progress and social growth.

Background and Explanation of Symptom

Patient, a ten year old boy, was retarded two years in reading ability despite an IQ of 135. He complained that disturbances of thinking and concentration were forces that interfered with his conscious desire to overcome his reading handicap. Unable to explain the reasons for his difficulty, he resorted to the explanation that was given to him by his parents, namely, that he was emotionally blocked and in need of a tutor who would employ some kind of psychological magic to rid him of this block.

A study of the family dynamics produced the following: The parents were emotionally unable to love the patient unless he brought them academic success. The patient was emotionally unable to comply, although he consciously wished this, unless his parents first gave him unconditional love. The more the parents pressured patient to be successful, the more devastating were his failures.

Dr. Nathan Ackerman in his paper, "Interpersonal Disturbances in the Family"[1] states, "If we aspire to specificity in family therapy' we would hope, if possible, to reduce the definition of disturbance to a single formulation of the interaction pattern of the family, which encompasses within it the dynamics of intra-personality processes. To achieve such formulation, it seems necessary to view the functioning of individual personality in the context of the dynamics of family role."

Dynamically, patient identified his parents with his unconscious ego, and by defeating them, he defeated himself. This unconscious central theme which originated within the family found its way into the social sphere. Unbeknown to the patient, his mode of relating to parentlike figures may be formulated as follows: "The only pleasure that I get out of life is to find out what the teacher or any parentlike figure wants of me, then to defeat him in his purpose regardless of what it is, even though I too am crushed in the process."

Description of Technique

In the first interview, patient initiated contact by an enthusiastic handshake. He spoke freely and easily without help; seemed outgoing, bright, and delightfully pleasant. He dwelled at some length upon his former tutors who were unable to help him because they were not "psychologically trained." The emotional overtones in connection with statements about his former tutors clearly indicated the patient's delight in their failures with him. A slight feeling of remorse accompanied his statement that both he and his parents felt badly about his reading difficulty. When asked how he thought he could best learn to read, he produced two books that he had brought with him and spoke in detail about the way in which his former tutor worked with him. When it was pointed out to him that the very method that he described had failed with him, he reacted to this with the statement that the injection of some kind of psychology would surely produce success. His parents had assured him of this. He pressured that work start immediately because time was being wasted by merely talking.

In the second interview, patient again brought the two books and again pressured that the job of tutoring begin without delay. He submitted to a series of brief reading tests with the understanding that a retest would be done three months hence for the purpose of evaluating the treatment. The grading was done in his presence. He seemed pleased with the few correct responses, and groaned at his mistakes.

From the third session on, the therapist adopted a deliberate therapeutic attitude that conveyed to the patient that the therapist was not interested in helping him to read. The therapist employed stalling tactics by telling stories, engaging in discussions with the patient and encouraging him to draw, use clay or play. The patient perceived this and confronted the therapist with his diversionary tactics. It was discussed with the patient that the therapist had nothing to gain and everything to lose by helping the patient to read. The therapist realized that the patient was very bright and with the therapist using his magic psychology, the patient would learn to read ever too quickly and then the therapist would be out of a fee. The patient reacted to this with amazement. The therapist explained that money was very important in life and was amazed that the patient could not see this. The patient threatened to stop coming. The therapist stated that he had anticipated such a possibility and realized that he would have to take this chance because surely he would lose out if he tutored the patient. The patient tried a moral appeal, referring to the therapist's devotion to his work. The patient also threatened to expose the therapist to his parents. The therapist insisted that his desire

for fees transcended all of the patient's arguments. The therapist recognized the patient's right to be angry, gave him a great deal of sympathy for the unfortunate position in which he found himself. However, the therapist did not wish to be a failure either and why could not the patient understand his point of view. The patient laughed and stated that the therapist was using psychology with him. He tested out his idea by reading aloud. Stumped by a word, he pressured for a correct response. The therapist yawned, looked out the window, and pretended not to hear. The patient jumped out of his chair, held the book close to the face of the therapist, pointed to the word in question, and prodded for an immediate response. The therapist volunteered a word obviously incorrect from both syllabic and phonetic aspects.

The patient's hope that the therapist was using psychology perished. In an angry outburst, the patient expressed disapproval of the therapist and praised his former tutors. The therapist was quite sympathetic with the patient's feelings, recognized them as completely justified, and told several stories of people who also found themselves in similar unfortunate situations.

The patient came regularly twice a week and was never late. He found himself caught in a web. He enjoyed the sessions; his feelings were recognized; he felt understood; received sympathy, enjoyed the relationship and the stories he heard; felt respected and accepted. He was not pressured to learn. In fact, pressure was placed upon failure. Whenever appropriate, the therapist (tongue in check) lectured him upon the dangers of reading offering incredible examples. For instance, when patient mentioned a movie that he had seen, the therapist hoped it was a talking movie. Silent films required reading of lines and should he learn to read in a movie, the chances of reading elsewhere would be severely impaired. The therapist drew fake diagrams and eyesight tables to further his contention.

The patient argued that he did not receive notes from other children because they knew that he read poorly. The therapist spoke of the value of illiteracy, citing examples that notes are frequently intercepted by teachers who might humiliate him or grade him poorly in conduct. Moreover this might foster in patient sneaky character traits. The patient reacted to the therapist's remarks with mirth and laughter and took delight in discrediting the therapist's statements. At times the therapist expressed the hope that when the time for the retest arrived, the therapist would have succeeded in keeping the patient a failure.

Subsequently the patient brought numerous test papers into the interviews showing that he was improving in reading. He was very confident that the retest would show that he had improved. Moreover his teacher had complimented him upon him improvement. The therapist pretended to be defeated by these signs of success and attempted to learn the patient's secret plan. The patient would not reveal "his" magic psychology. Pretended attempts to trick him into revealing it were met with giggles.

The patient had been reading one book after each session from a list given to the parents. At home he asked his parents to help him and they eagerly complied. The impetus to read appeared motivated by spite and stemmed from the patient and not from parental pressure.

After three months had elapsed the patient was eager to be retested. He seemed to be living for this moment. The therapist expressed the hope that the patient would show no progress. The patient confidently announced that he *knew* that he had improved. The grading was again done in his presence. Each time a response was checked as correct, the therapist groaned and the patient clapped his hands. The patient had gained nine months in reading ability during the three months of treatment. The patient then announced triumphantly that he had won over the therapist. His long suppressed negative feelings rose to the surface, and for the first time he felt his true feelings. He expressed direct hostility in an angry outburst, called the therapist names, and vowed never to return again for a session. He could get by now without the therapist; could study by himself and he no longer had need for the therapist. He had continued coming in order to have this day of triumph. Now there would be no future fees for the therapist.

It was at this point that the therapeutic plan was revealed to him. His negative suggestibility was clearly shown to him and how it was used for his advantage. He had been put in a position of defeating the therapist in only one way, that was by learning. The patient's reactions were dramatic. He burst forth with laughter, walked around the office shaking the chairs and table as if he wanted every piece of furniture to laugh with him. The patient was enabled to utilize his new insight toward further growth in treatment.

Conclusions

Herein is described a plan of treatment, differentiated, to suit the personality of one child. An understanding of adaptive and intra-psychic factors were essential for this highly focussed therapy. The therapeutic attitude on the part of the therapist had psychic repercussions in this boy. For the first time in his life, he was with a person who did not pressure him to achieve. In fact, pressure seemed to be placed on failure. The challenge to defeat the therapist was invoked for the advantage of the patient. He seemingly defeated a parentlike figure, not to his detriment, but to his advantage. Since the therapist's behavior seemed designed for his own personal gain (interest only in fee), the patient was invited by example to think and behave for his own advantage. Hostile energy that had been used to defeat his parents by failure became redirected toward constructive goals. He became more interested in defeating the therapist by learning than in defeating his parents by not learning.

There was less of a need to fight pathologically for unconditional acceptance. The patient had the therapist as a new model for identification.

This procedure may be attempted with patients whose learning difficulties stem from unconscious resentment, and present strong involuntary characterological negativism. Also this method is offered not as a demonstration but rather as a suggestion for further investigation of the structuring of a relationship for therapeutic gain.

10. THE INTERPERSONAL RELATIONSHIP: THE CORE OF GUIDANCE

Carl R. Rogers

Peter Schwarzburg

I would like to share with you in this paper a conclusion, a conviction, which has grown out of years of experience in dealing with individuals, a conclusion which finds some confirmation in a steadily growing body of empirical evidence. It is simply that in a wide variety of professional work involving relationships with people—whether as a psychotherapist, teacher, religious worker, guidance counselor, social worker, clinical psychologist—it is the *quality* of the interpersonal encounter with the client which is the most significant element in determining effectiveness.

Let me spell out a little more fully the basis of this statement in my personal experience. I have been primarily a counselor and psychotherapist. In the course of my professional life I have worked with troubled college students, with adults in difficulty, with "normal" individuals such as business executives, and more recently with hospitalized psychotic persons. I have endeavored to make use of the learnings from my therapeutic expience in my interactions with classes and seminars, in the training of teachers, in the administration of staff groups, in the clinical supervision of psychologists, psychiatrists, and guidance workers as they work with their clients or patients. Some of these relationships are long-continued and intensive, as in individual psychotherapy. Some are brief, as in experiences with workshop participants or in contacts with students who come for practical advice. They cover a wide range of depth. Gradually I have come to the conclusion that one learning which applies to all of these experiences is that it is the quality of the personal relationship which matters most. With some of these individuals I am in touch only briefly, with others I have the opportunity of knowing them intimately, but in either case the quality of the personal encounter is probably, in the long run, the element which determines the extent to which this is an experience which releases or promotes development and growth. I believe the quality of my encounter is more important in the long run than is my scholarly knowledge, my professional training, my counseling orientation, the techniques I use in the interview. In keeping with this line of thought, I suspect that for a guidance worker also the relationship he forms with each student—brief or continuing—is more important than his knowledge of tests and measurements, the adequacy of his record keeping, the theories he holds, the accuracy with which he is able to predict academic success, or the school in which he received his training.

In recent years I have thought a great deal about this issue. I have tried to observe counselors and therapists whose orientations are very different from mine, in order to understand the basis of their effectiveness as well as my own. I have listened to recorded interviews from many different sources. Gradually I have developed some theoretical formulations (4, 5), some hypotheses as to the basis of effectiveness in relationships. As I have asked myself how individuals sharply different in personality, orientation and procedure can all be effective in a helping relationship, can each be successful in facilitating constructive change or development, I have concluded that it is because they bring to the helping relationship certain attitudinal ingredients. It is these that I hypothesize as making for effectiveness, whether we are speaking of a guidance counselor, a clinical psychologist, or a psychiatrist.

What are these attitudinal or experiential elements in the counselor which make a relationship a growth-promoting climate? I would like to descirbe them as carefully and accurately as I can, though I am well aware that words rarely capture or communicate the qualities of a personal encounter.

Congruence

In the first place, I hypothesize that personal growth is facilitated when the counselor is what he *is*, when in the relationship with his client he is genuine and without "front" or facade, openly being the feelings and attitudes which at that moment are flowing in him. We have used the term "congruence" to try to describe this condition. By this we mean that the feelings the counselor is experiencing are available to him, available to his awareness, that he is able to live these feelings, be them in the relationship, and able to communicate them if appropriate. It means that he comes into a direct personal encounter with his client, meeting him on a person-to-person basis. It means that he is *being* himself, not denying himself. No one fully achieves this condition, yet the more the therapist is able to listen acceptantly to what is going on within himself, and the more he is able to *be* the complexity of his feelings without fear, the higher the degree of his congruence.

I think that we readily sense this quality in our everyday life. We could each of us name persons whom we know who always seem to be operating from behind a front, who are playing a role, who tend to say things they do not feel. They are exhibiting incongruence. We do not reveal ourselves too deeply to such people. On the other hand each of us knows individuals whom we somehow trust, because we sense that they are being what they *are*, that we are dealing with the person himself, and not with a polite or professional facade. This is the quality of which we are speaking, and it is hypothesized that the more genuine and congruent the therapist in the relationship, the more probability there is that change in personality in the client will occur.

I have received much clinical confirmation for this hypothesis in recent years in our work with randomly selected hospitalized schizophrenic patients. The individual therapists in our research program who seem to be most successful in dealing with these unmotivated, poorly educated, resistant, chronically hospitalized individuals, are those who are first of all real, who react in a genuine, human way as persons, and who exhibit their genuineness in the relationship.

But is it always helpful to be genuine? What about negative feelings? What about the times when the counselor's real feeling toward his client is one of annoyance, or boredom, or dislike? My tentative answer is that even with such feelings as these, which we all have from time to time, it is preferable for the counselor to be real than to put up a facade of interest and concern and liking which he does not feel.

But it is not a simple thing to achieve such reality. I am not saying that it is helpful to blurt out impulsively every passing feeling and accusation under the comfortable impression that one is being genuine. Being real involves the difficult task of being acquainted with the flow of experiencing going on within oneself, a flow marked especially by complexity and continuous change. So if I sense that I am feeling bored by my contacts with this student, and this feeling persists, I think I owe it to him and to our relationship to share this feeling with him. But here again I will want to be constantly in touch with what is going on in me. If I am, I will recognize that it is *my* feeling of being bored which I am expressing, and not some supposed fact about him as a boring person. If I voice it as my *own* reaction, it has the potentiality of leading to a deeper relationship. But this feeling exists in the context of a complex and changing flow, and this needs to be communicated too. I would like to share with him my distress at feeling bored, and the discomfort I feel in expressing this aspect of me. As I share these attitudes I find that my feeling of boredom arises from my sense of remoteness from him, and that I would like to be more in touch with him. And even as I try to express these feelings, they change. I am certainly not bored as I try to communicate myself to him in this way, and I am far from bored as I wait with eagerness and perhaps a bit of apprehension for his response. I also feel a new sensitivity to him, now that I have shared this feeling which has been a barrier between us. So I am very much more able to hear the surprise or perhaps the hurt in his voice as he now finds *himself* speaking more genuinely because I have dared to be real with him. I have let myself be a person—real, imperfect—in my relationship with him.

I have tried to describe this first element at some length because I regard it as highly important, perhaps the most crucial of the conditions I will describe, and because it is neither easy to grasp nor to achieve. Gendlin (2) has done an excellent job of explaining the significance of the concept of experiencing and its relationship to counseling and therapy, and his presentation may supplement what I have tried to say.

I hope it is clear that I am talking about a realness in the counselor which is deep and true, not superficial. I have sometimes thought that the word transparency helps to describe this element of personal congruence. If everything going on in me which is relevant to the relationship can be seen by my client, if he can see "clear through me," and if I am *willing* for this realness to show through in the relationship, then I can be almost certain that this will be a meaningful encounter in which we both learn and develop.

I have sometimes wondered if this is the only quality which matters in a counseling relationship. The evidence seems to show that other qualities also make a profound difference and are perhaps easier to achieve. So I am going to describe these others. But I would stress that if, in a given moment of relationship, they are not genuinely a part of the experience of the counselor, then it is, I believe, better to be genuinely what one is, than to pretend to be feeling these other qualitites.

Empathy

The second essential condition in the relationship, as I see it, is that the counselor is experiencing an accurate empathic understanding of his client's private world, and is able to communicate some of the significant fragments of that understanding. To sense the client's inner world of private personal meanings as if it were your own, but without ever losing the "as if" quality, this is empathy, and this seems essential to a growth-promoting relationship. To sense his confusion or his timidity or his anger or his feeling of being treated unfairly as if it were your own, yet without your own uncertainty or fear or anger or suspicion getting bound up in it, this is the condition I am endeavoring to describe. When the client's world is clear to the counselor and he can move about in it freely, then he can both communicate his understanding of what is vaguely known to the client, and he can also voice meanings in the client's experience of which the client is scarcely aware. It is this kind of highly sensitive empathy which seems important in making it possible for a person to get close to himself and to learn, to change and develop.

I suspect that each of us has discovered that this kind of understanding is extremely rare. We neither receive it nor offer it with any great frequency. Instead we offer another type of understanding which is very different, such as "I understand what is wrong with you" or "I understand what makes you act that way." These are the types of understanding which we usually offer and receive—an evaluative understanding from the outside. It is not surprising that we shy away from true understanding. If I am truly open to the way life is experienced by another person—if I can take his world into mine—then I run the risk of seeing life in his way, of being changed myself, and we all resist change. So we tend to view this other person's world only in our terms, not in his. We analyze and evaluate it. We do not understand it. But when someone understands how it feels and seems to be me, without wanting to analyze me or judge me, then I can blossom and grow in that climate. I am sure I am not alone in that feeling. I believe that when the counselor can grasp the moment-to-moment experiencing occurring in the inner world of the client, as the client sees it and feels it, without losing the separateness of his own identity in this empathic process, then change is likely to occur.

Though the accuracy of such understanding is highly important, the communication of intent to understand is also helpful. Even in dealing with the confused or inarticulate or bizarre individual, if he perceives that I am *trying* to understand his meanings, this is helpful. It communicates the value I place on him as an individual. It gets across the fact that I perceive his feelings and meaning as being *worth* understanding.

None of us steadily achieves such a complete empathy as I have been trying to describe, any more than we achieve complete congruence, but there is no doubt that individuals can develop along this line. Suitable training experiences have been utilized in the training of counselors, and also in the "sensitivity training" of industrial management personnel. Such experiences

enable the person to listen more sensitively, to receive more of the subtle meanings the other person is expressing in words, gesture, and posture, to resonate more deeply and freely within himself to the significance of those expressions.*

Positive Regard

Now the third condition. I hypothesize that growth and change are more likely to occur the more that the counselor is experiencing a warm, positive, acceptant attitude toward what *is* in the client. It means that he prizes his client, as a person, with somewhat the same quality of feeling that a parent feels for his child, prizing him as a person regardless of his particular behavior at the moment. It means that he cares for his client in a nonpossessive way, as a person with potentialities. It involves an open willingness for the client to be whatever feelings are real in him at the moment—hostility or tenderness, rebellion or submissiveness, assurance or self-depreciation. It means a kind of love for the client as he is, providing we understand the word love as equivalent to the theologian's term "agape," and not in its usual romantic and possessive meanings. What I am describing is a feeling which is not paternalistic, nor sentimental, nor superficially social and agreeable. It respects the other person as a separate individual, and does not possess him. It is a kind of liking which has strength, and which is not demanding. We have termed it positive regard.

---

*I hope the above account of an empathic attitude will make it abundantly clear that I am not advocating a wooden technique of pseudo-understanding in which the counselor "reflects back what the client has just said." I have been more than a little horrified at the interpretation of my approach which has sometimes crept into the teaching and training of counselors.

Unconditionality of Regard

There is one aspect of this attitude of which I am somewhat less sure. I advance tentatively the hypothesis that the relationship will be more effective the more the positive regard is unconditional. By this I mean that the counselor prizes the client in a total, rather than a conditional way. He does not accept feelings in the client and disapprove others. He feels an *unconditional* positive regard for this person. This is an outgoing, positive feeling without reservations and without evaluations. It means *not* making judgments. I believe that when this nonevaluative prizing is present in the encounter between the counselor and his client, constructive change and development in the client is more likely to occur.

Certainly one does not need to be a professional to experience this attitude. The best of parents show this in abundance, while others do not. A friend of mine, a therapist in private practice on the east coast, illustrates this very well in a letter in which he tells me what he is learning about parents. He says:

I am beginning to feel that the key to the human being is the attitudes with which the parents have regarded him. If the child was lucky enough to have parents who have felt proud of him, wanted him, wanted him just as he was, exactly as he was, this child grows into adulthood with self-confidence, self-esteem; he goes forth in life feeling sure of himself, strong, able to lick what confronts him. Franklin Delano Roosevelt is an example . . . "my friends . . . ." He couldn't imagine anyone thinking otherwise. He had two adoring parents. He was like the pampered dog who runs up at you, frisking his tail, eager to love you, for this dog has never known rejection or harshness. Even if you should kick him, he'll come right back to you, his tail friskier than ever, thinking you're playing a game with him and wanting more. This animal cannot imagine anyone disapproving or disliking him. Just as unconditional regard and love was poured into him,

he has it now to give out. If a child is lucky enough to grow up in this unconditionally accepting atmosphere, he emerges as strong and sure and he can approach life and its vicissitudes with courage and confidence, with zest and joy of expectation.

But the parents who like their children—if. They would like them if they were changed, altered, different; if they were smarter or if they were better, or if, if, if. The offspring of these parents have trouble because they never had the feeling of acceptance. These parents don't really like these children; they would like them if they were like someone else. When you come down to the basic fundamental, the parents feels: "I don't like *this* child, this child before me." They don't say that. I am beginning to believe that it would be better for all concerned if parents did. It wouldn't leave such horrible ravages on these unaccepted children. It's never done that crudely. "If you were a nice boy and did this, that and the other thing, then we would all love you."

I am coming to believe that children brought up by parents who would like them "if" are never quite right. They grow up assuming that their parents are right and that they are wrong; that somehow or other they are at fault; and even worse, very frequently they feel they are stupid, inadequate, inferior.

This is an excellent contrast between an unconditional positive regard and a conditional regard. I believe it holds as true for counselors as for parents.

The Client's Perception

Thus far all my hypotheses regarding the possibility of constructive growth have rested upon the experiencing of these elements by the counselor. There is, however, one condition which must exist in the client. Unless the attitudes I have been describing have been to some degree communicated to the client, and perceived by him, they do not exist in his perceptual world and thus cannot be effective. Consequently it is necessary to add one more condition to the equation which I have been building up regarding personal growth through counseling. It is that when the client perceives, to a minimal degree, the genuineness of the counselor and the acceptance and empathy which the counselor experiences for him then development in personality and change in behavior are predicted.

This has implications for me as a counselor. I need to be sensitive not only to what is going on in me, and sensitive to the flow of feelings in my client. I must also be sensitive to the way he is receiving my communications. I have learned, especially in working with more disturbed persons, that empathy can be perceived as lack of involvement; that an unconditional regard on my part can be perceived as indifference; that warmth can be perceived as a threatening closeness, that real feelings of mine can be perceived as false. I would like to behave in ways, and communicate in ways which have clarity for this specific person, so that what I am experiencing in relationship to him would be perceived unambiguously by him. Like the other conditions I have proposed the principle is easy to grasp; the achievement of it is difficult and complex.

The Essential Hypothesis

Let me restate very briefly the essentially simple but somewhat radical hypothesis I have set forth. I have said that constructive personality growth and changes comes about only when the client perceives and experiences a certain psychological climate in the relationship. The conditions which constitute this climate do not consist of knowledge, intellectual training, orientation in some school of thought, or techniques. They are feelings or attitudes which must be experienced by the counselor and perceived by the client if they are to be effective. Those

I have singled out as being essential are: a realness, genuineness, or congruence in the therapist; a sensitive, empathic understanding of the client's feelings and personal meanings; a warm, acceptant prizing of the client; and an unconditionality in this positive regard.

Some Limitations

I would like to stress that these are hypotheses. In a later section I will comment on the way these hypotheses are faring when put to empirical test. But they are beginning hypotheses, not the final word.

I regard it as entirely possible that there are other conditions which I have not described, which are also essential. Recently I had occasion to listen to some recorded interviews by a young counselor of elementary school children. She was very warm and positive in her attitude toward her clients, yet she was definitely ineffective. She seemed to be responding warmly only to the superficial aspects of each child and so the contacts were chatty, social and friendly, but it was clear she was not reaching the real person of the child. Yet in a number of ways she rated reasonably high on each of the conditions I have described. So perhaps there are still elements missing which I have not captured in my formulation.

I am also aware of the possibility that different kinds of helping relationships may be effective with different kinds of people. Some of our therapists working with schizophrenics are effective when they appear to be highly conditional, when they do *not* accept some of the bizarre behavior of the psychotic. This can be interpreted in two ways. Perhaps a conditional set is more helpful with these individuals. Or perhaps—and this seems to me to fit the facts better—these psychotic individuals perceive a conditional attitude as meaning that the therapist *really* cares, where an unconditional attitudes may be interpreted as apathetic non-caring. In any event, I do want to make it clear that what I have given are beginning formulations which surely will be modified and corrected from futher learnings.

The Philosophy Which Is Implicit

It is evident that the kind of attitudes I have described are not likely to be experienced by a counselor unless he holds a philosophy regarding people in which such attitudes are congenial. The attitudes pictured make no sense except in a context of greater respect for the person and his potentialities. Unless the primary element in the counselor's value system is the worth of the individual, he is not apt to find himself experiencing a real caring, or a desire to understand, and perhaps he will not respect himself enough to be real. Certainly the professional person who holds the view that individuals are essentially objects to be manipulated for the welfare of the state, or the good of the educational institution, or "for their own good," or to satisfy his own need for power and control, would not experience the attitudinal elements I have described as constituting growth-promoting relationships. So these conditions are congenial and natural in certain philosophical contexts but not in others.

Empirical Studies

This raises some questions which I have asked myself, and which you too must be asking. Are these characteristics which I have described as essential to a helping relationship simply my personal opinion, preference, and bias? Or do they represent simply a bias growing out of a generally democratic philosophy? Or do they in *fact* promote constructive change and development?

Five years ago I could not have answered these questions. Now there are at least a dozen well-designed research investigations which, approaching the matter in a variety of ways, throw light on the issues (1, 3, 6a through 6j). To report each of these studies would be confusing rather than helpful. Let me try to describe their methods in general terms and then report on the findings.

The studies deal with two rather different classes of clients: students and community members who voluntarily come to counselors for help; and on the other hand, schizophrenic individuals in a state hospital who have been there for periods ranging from a few months to many years. The first group is above the socio-educational average, the second below. The first group is motivated to gain help, the second is not only unmotivated but resistant. The over-all range in adjustment is from well-functioning individuals through varying degrees of maladjustment and disturbance, to those who are completely unable to cope with life, and who are out of contact with reality.

In the different studies there have been three ways of measuring the attitudinal elements I have described. The first method is based on brief segments, usually four minutes in length, taken in a randomized way from the tape-recorded interviews. Raters, listening to these segments, judge the degree to which the counselor is, for example, being accurately empathic, and make a rating on a carefully defined scale. The raters have no knowledge of whether the segment is from an early or late interview, or whether it is a more or less successful case. In most of the studies several raters have made ratings on each of the qualities involved.

A second method of measurement is

through the use of the Relationship Inventory (1), filled out by the client at different points in time. The inventory contains statements regarding the degree to which the counselor is acceptant, empathic, and congruent, and the client responds by evaluating the statement on a six point scale from "strongly true" to "definitely untrue." Examples concerning empathy are: "He generally senses or realizes how I am feeling"; "He understands my words but does not realize how I feel." In relationship to congruence some items are: "He behaves just the way he is in our relationship"; "He pretends that he likes me or understands me more than he really does." The Inventory is scored for each of the four attitudinal elements, and there is also a total score.

The third method is also based on the Relationship Inventory, but this time filled out by the therapist or counselor. The items are identical except for a suitable change in pronouns.

In the various studies different criteria are used for assessing the degree of constructive personality change which has taken place over the course of the interviews. In all cases the criteria of change are independent of the measurement of attitudinal conditions in the relationship. Some of the measures of change are: changes in various Minnesota Multiphasic Personality Inventory scales and indices; changes in projective tests as analyzed "blind" by clinicians having no knowledge of the research; changes in Q-sort adjustment score; changes on a measure of anxiety; therapist's ratings of change in personality and in adjustment.

The Findings

Let me now give some of the general findings from these studies:

The counselor is the most significant fac-

tor in setting the level of conditions in the relationship, though the client, too, has some influence on the quality of the relationship.

Clients who will later show more change perceive more of these attitudinal conditions early in the relationship with their counselor or therapist.

The more disturbed the client the less he is likely to (or able to?) perceive these attitudes in the counselor.

Counselors or therapists tend to be quite consistent in the level of the attitudinal conditions which they offer to each client.

The major finding from all of the studies is that those clients in relationships marked by a high level of counselor congruence, empathy and unconditional positive regard, show constructive personality change and development. These high levels of conditions are associated with: positive change on MMPI scales and indices, including ego-strength; positive change from the pre- to post-test battery as rated by clinicians working "blind"; decrease in anxiety scores and in a self-consciousness score; a higher level on Process Scales designed to measure process in therapy; and positive change in counselor's ratings.

Clients in relationships characterized by a low level of these attitudinal conditions show significantly less positive change on these same indices.

In studies of clinic clients the correlation between the client's perception of the conditions offered early in the relationship and the degree of change at the conclusion of the interviews is somewhat higher than that between the counselor's perception of the conditions offered and the degree of change. The client's perception is, in other words, the better predictor of change.

This finding does not hold for the schizophrenic client, whose inner disturbance makes it difficult for him accurately to perceive the conditions offered by the therapist. With our schizophrenics, the rating of the conditions made by unbiased raters is the best predictor of change.

An unexpected finding with the schizophrenic clients is that low conditions in the relationship are associated with *negative* change in several respects. The clients not only fail to show constructive change but become worse in the judgment of clinicians rating their pre- and post-test batteries; show an increase in anxiety; are worse off than their matched no-therapy controls. Whether this finding holds for clinic clients who come for help has not yet been determined.

A finding which seems to lend validity to the studies is that, as might be expected, more experienced counselors, when compared with inexperienced counselors, offer a higher level of these conditions, and are more successful in communicating these to their clients. Thus they are perceived as offering higher conditions, and their clients show more change over the course of the interviews.

Implications

What are some of the implications of these hypotheses and of these findings for the field of counseling psychology and quidance? I would like to mention four which occur to me.

In the first place, these studies indicate that perhaps it is possible to study cause and effect in counseling and psychotherapy. They are actually, so far as I know, the first studies to endeavor to isolate and measure the primary change-producing influences in counseling. Whether they are still further confirmed by later research, or whether they

are contradicted or modified by future studies, they represent pioneering investigations of the question, "What really makes the difference in counseling and psychotherapy?" And the answer they give is that it is the attitudes provided by the counselor, the psychological climate largely created by him, which *really* makes the difference, which really induces change.

There is another highly practical significance to these studies. They indicate quite clearly that, by assessing a relationship early in its existence, we can to some degree predict the probability of its being a relationship which makes for growth. It seems to be quite within the range of possibility that in the not too distant future we will acquire an increasingly accurate knowledge of the elements which make for constructive psychological development, just as we have in the realm of nutrition acquired an increasingly accurate knowledge of the elements which promote physical growth. As this knowledge accumulates, and as our instruments grow sharper, then there is the exciting possibility that we may be able, relatively early in the game, to predict whether a given relationship will actually promote or inhibit individual psychological growth and development, just as we can assess the diet of a child and predict the extent to which this diet will promote or inhibit physical growth.

In this connection the disturbing finding that an inadequate interpersonal relationship can have a negative effect on personal development, at least in the case of highly disturbed individuals, makes such early assessment of a relationship an even more challenging possibility and responsibility.

Another significant meaning for the counseling field is that we now have the beginnings of a theory, and some empirical facts supporting the theory, as to the specific elements in an interpersonal relationship which facilitate positive change. Thus we can now say with some assurance and factual backing that a relationship characterized by a high degree of congruence or genuineness in the counselor, by sensitive and accurate empathy on the part of the counselor, by a high degree of regard, respect and liking for the client by the counselor, and by an absence of conditionality in this regard, will have a high probability of being an effective, growth-promoting relationship. This statement holds, whether we are speaking of maladjusted individuals who come of their own initiative seeking help, or whether we are speaking of chronically schizophrenic persons, with no conscious desire for help. This statement also holds whether these attitudinal elements are rated by impartial observers who listen to samples of the recorded interviews, or whether they are measured in terms of the counselor's perception of the qualities he has offered in the relationship, or whether they are measured by the client's perception of the relationship, at least in the case of the nonhospitalized client. To me it seems to be quite a forward stride to be able to make statements such as these in an area as complex and subtle as the field of helping relationships.

Finally, these studies would, if confirmed by further work, have significant implications for the training of counselors and therapists. To the extent that the counselor is seen as being involved in interpersonal relationships, and to the extent that the goal of those relationships is to promote healthy development, then certain conclusions would seem to follow. It would mean that we would endeavor to select individuals for such training who already possess, in their ordinary relationships with other people, a high degree of the qualities I have described.

We would want people who were warm, spontaneous, real, understanding, and nonjudgmental. We would also endeavor so to plan the educational program for these individuals that they would come increasingly to *experience* empathy and liking for others, and that they would find it increasingly easier to be themselves, to be real. By feeling understood and accepted in their training experiences, by being in contact with genuineness and absence of facade in their instructors, they would grow into more and more competent counselors. There would be as much focus in such training on the interpersonal experience as on the intellectual learning. It would be recognized that no amount of knowledge of tests and measures, or of counseling theories, or of diagnostic procedures could make the trainee more effective in his personal encounter with his clients. There would be a heavy stress upon the actual experience of working with clients, and the thoughtful and self-critical assessment of the relationships formed.

When I ask myself whether the training programs I know, in guidance, in clinical psychology, in psychiatry, approach this goal, I come up with a strong negative. It seems to me that most of our professional training programs make it *more* difficult for the individual to be himself, and more likely that he will play a professional role. Often he becomes so burdened with theoretical and diagnostic baggage that he becomes *less* able to understand the inner world of another person as it seems to that person. Also, as his professional training continues, it all too often occurs that his initial warm liking for other persons is submerged in a sea of diagnostic and psycho-dynamic evaluation.

Thus to take the findings of these studies seriously would mean some sharp changes in the very nature of professional training, as well as in its curriculum.

Conclusion

Let me conclude with a series of statements which for me follow logically one upon the other.

The purpose of most of the helping professions, including guidance counseling, is to enhance the personal development, the psychological growth toward a socialized maturity, of its clients.

The effectiveness of any member of the profession is most adequately measured in terms of the degree to which, in this work with his clients, he achieves this goal.

Our knowledge of the elements which bring about constructive change in personal growth is in its infant stages.

Such factual knowledge as we currently possess indicates that a primary change-producing influence is the degree to which the client experiences certain qualities in his relationship with his counselor.

In a variety of clients—normal, maladjusted, and psychotic—with many different counselors and therapists, and studying the relationship from the vantage point of the client, the therapist, or the uninvolved observer, certain qualities in the relationship are quite uniformly found to be associated with personal growth and change.

These elements are not constituted of technical knowledge or ideological sophistication. They are personal human qualities—something the counselor *experiences,* not something he *knows.* Constructive personal growth is associated with the counselor's realness, with his genuine and unconditional liking for his client, with his sensitive understanding of his client's private world, and with his ability to communicate these qualities in himself to his client.

These findings have some far-reaching implications for the theory and practice of guidance counseling and psychotherapy, and for the training of workers in these fields.

REFERENCES

1. Barrett-Lennard, G. T. Demensions of therapist response as causal factors in therapeutic change. *Psychol. Monogr.* (In press)
2. Gendlin, E. T. Experiencing: A variable in the process of therapeutic change. *Am. Jour. Psychother* 15 (1961):233-45.
3. Halkides, G. An experimental study of four conditions necessary for therapeutic change. Unpublished doctoral dissertation, University of Chicago,1958.
4. Rogers, C. R. The necessary and sufficient conditions of therapeutic personality change. *Jour. Cons. Psych.* 21 (1975):95-103.
5. ———. A theory of therapy, personality, and interpersonal relationships as developed in the client-centered framework. In S. Koch ed. *Psychology: a study of a science, vol. III.* New York: McGraw-Hill, 1959, 184-256.
6. Wisconsin Psychiatric Institute: Research Reports (unpublished)

   a. Spotts, J. E. The perception of positive regard by relatively successful and relatively unsuccessful clients.
   b. Traux, C. B. Comparison between high conditions therapy, low conditions therapy, and control conditions in the outcome measure of change in anxiety levels.
   c. ———. Constructive personality change in schizophrenic patients receiving high-conditions therapy, low-conditions therapy, and notherapy.
   d. ———. Effects of therapists and effects of patients upon the amount of accurate empathy occuring in the psychotherapeutic interaction.
   e. ———. Effects of therapists and effects of patients upon the level of problem expression and experiencing occurring in the therapeutic interaction.
   f. ———.The relationship between the patient's perception of the level of therapeutic conditions offered in psychotherapy and constructive personality change.

g. ———. Liccione, J., and Rosenberg, M. Psychological test evaluations of personality change in high conditions therapy, low conditions therapy, and control patients.

h. ven der Veen, F. The effects of the therapist and the patient on each other's therapeutic behavior early in therapy: A study of the beginning interviews of three patients with each of five therapists.

i. ———. Perceived therapist conditions and degree of disturbance: A comparsion of conditions perceived by hospitalized schizophrenic patients and counseling center clients.

j. Wargo, D. G. The Barron Ego Strength and LH4 Scales as predictors and indicators of change in psychotherapy.

11. EXISTENTIAL COUNSELING

C. Gratton Kemp

Peter Schwarzburg

Existentialism: The Basis
For Existential Counseling

Existentialism is an endeavor to understand man as he really is. It takes issue with the assumption of science that to know the essence of man means that we have grasped the reality of man. Existentialism is also critical of the methods of knowing man which are the products of the rational approach since this approach may clarify the essence of man but offers little help in understanding the reality of man.

Reality is not identified with "objective being" but neither is it identified with "subjective being," that is with "consciousness" or feeling. Existentialism is not engaged in contrasting the objective and subjective. Instead it emphasizes the possibility of grasping oneself at a level which makes the subject-object dichotomy irrelevant. Our difficulty in trying to know ourselves is that we think of ourselves in "spatialized" terms approximate to objective things. "The moments in which we grasp ourselves are rare and consequently we are seldom free. Our existence is more in space than in time." (1) Our immediate experience so often has to be screened or put through the sieve of some objective or subjective necessity. True freedom is experienced in moments when we grasp ourselves as we really are. "When he came to himself" is as infrequent for us as it was for the Prodigal Son.

Kierkegaard and other existentialist thinkers engaged in a desperate refusal to identify Reality with the world of objects. Neitzche wrote: "When we have reached the inevitable economic administration of the earth, then mankind as a machine can find its meaning in the service of this monstrous mechanism of small and smaller cogs adapted to the whole."(2)

Existentialism is a reaction against the steady encroachment of technology in which existentialist thinkers see man fast becoming like the machines he operates, losing both his claim on human freedom and his ability for self-transcendence. Each thinker in his own way is trying to help man in his search for meaning. Each assists him to reclaim his dignity to heal the split within him in which the essence of objectivity can be found in the depth of subjectivity. No means of empirical measurement can (as Allport (3) emphasizes) help us to understand the "Johnian in John." It is this kind of understanding with which existentialism is concerned. The expressions of existential thinking in literature, psychology and philosophy analyze and portray man at a level below that of the principles of both materialism and idealism. The one-dimensional man engrossed in the transient objects of his environment is delivering up his true Being for "a mess of pottage."

Why the Existential Attitude
Developed in Europe

The existential attitude was a response to the critical conditions of the mid-nineteenth century. It arose through the independent thinking of many minds in a spontaneous answer to the loss of a personal center. It emerged in art, literature and philosophy.

Its beginnings in Europe and especially in Germany go back over a century to the decade of the 1840's when its main contentions were formulated by such thinkers as Schelling, Kierkegaard and Marx. They were sharply critical of the reigning "rationalism" of the Hegelians. They were followed in the next generation by Nietzsche and Dilthey.

The basic critical drive of the Existential philosophy is a part of a more general philosophical movement which counts its representatives not only in Germany but in

France, Switzerland, Holland, England and America.

This drive expresses itself in calling men back to "Existence." Especially among the German thinkers there was criticism of the identification of Reality or Being with Reality-as-known, as the object of Reason. They began by distinguishing essence from existence and insisting that Reality or Being in its fullness is not essence, not the object of cognitive experience, but is in fact existence. It is Reality as immediately experienced, with the accent on the person and personal character of man's immediate experience.(4)

Ibsen's *A Doll's House* vividly illustrates what was happening in Europe in the last half of the nineteenth century. It is an attack against the fragmentation and compartmentalization of life in all of its aspects. The play emphasizes the folly of the man who keeps his wife and family in one compartment, his work in another, and his friends in a third. Compartmentalization became the distinguishing characteristic of all areas of life. In all its forms it symbolized an escape from the realities of life, from both existence and nature. Ethics was divorced from business, and religion from daily life.

Even more serious was the compartmentalization within the person himself. Reason, it was thought, told him what to do; his will put it into effect, and if his emotions got in the way, they were suppressed or channeled into compulsive drives and forced rigidly into currently acceptable mores. There was great emphasis on the rational; the "irrational" was consigned to the fairly regular events planned as emotional outlets.

Such compartmentalized individuals conformed well to the demands of a developing industrial society. They were able to manipulate themselves in the same way as they manipulated the machines they operated. Rewards such as the paycheck were the

validation of personal worth. Employees' chief and often only significance was reckoned in terms of what they produced. Such indivicuals are described so well by Erich Fromm in his emphasis on the "marketplace orientation." He writes: "As with any other commodity, it is the market which decides the value of these human qualities, yes, even their very existence. If there is no use for the qualities a person offers, he has none, just as an unsaleable commodity is valueless though it might have its use value."(5)

Men surrendered their self-awareness as a protection against reality and paid the price in anxiety, compulsions for self-negation and despair. But the great analysts of the era, Kierkegaard and Nietzsche, concluded that the sickness of Western man was only partially explained by the specific individual or social problem. Industrialization and technological development nudged him into this condition, but as Nietzsche declared: "This is Europe's true predicament, . . . together with the fear of man we have lost the love of man, confidence in man, indeed, the will to man."(6)

In the fast developing industrial society, increasing importance was placed on the "rational" system of thought. But the interpretation of reason itself changed from "the power of truth and justice embodied in man as man," (7) to technical reason applied in the making of machines which ushered in a world-wide mechanism and with it a mechanized way of looking at man.(8) This system of thought and life developed by the industrial society and philosophic writings such as those of Hegel was opposed by the philosophers of Existence Poets, artists, and philosophers in every European country tried to stem the encroachment of the self-estranged form of life which was fast losing contact with the Eigenwelt world of being.

Such artists as Van Gogh, Cezanne and Picasso indicate in their works the desperate attempt to express the immediate underlying meaning of the modern human situation, even though this means portraying despair and emptiness. Indeed, Tillich holds that Picasso's painting "Guernica" gives a most gripping and revealing portrayal of the atomistic, fragmentized condition of European society which preceded World War II.

In light of what has happened in the last hundred years, their opposition is more than justified. As Tillich describes it, the implications of this system have become increasingly clear: "A logical or naturalistic mechanism which seemed to destroy individual freedom, personal decision and organic community; an analytic rationalism which saps the vital forces of life and transforms everything, including man himsef, ito an object of calculation and control; a secularized humanism which cuts man and the world off from the creative Source and the ultimate mystery of existence."(9)

The focus of the transition was the changing attitude toward religion and religious values. All groups faced the problem created by the breakdown of the religious tradition under the impact of the social revolution, bourgeois liberalism and the ideas of the enlightenment. Religion moved to the periphery of life. It lost its relevance for all groups—the educated and the great numbers of industrial workers. It was no longer a present and immediate resource and it offered no unquestioned sense of direction.

There were efforts to try to return religion to its former regency. Hegel attempted to do this by conscious reinterpretation, but he did not succeed. His approach was attacked by a revived theology on the one hand and by philosophical positivism on the other.

It was in this matrix of change that existential philosophers endeavored to find the ultimate meaning of life. For them it could not be found in the "estranged" objective world. It was beyond the reach of reinterpretation, revived theologies and philosophical positivism. They sought it in the inward experience, in reality as immediately experienced in actual living. So they turned to man's immediate experience, toward "subjectivity" as the living experience in which both objectivity and subjectivity are rooted. Such an undertaking had strong mystical overtones but there was no intention of a mystical union with the transcendent absolute. Instead it was an expression of faith toward union with the depths of life whether ventured upon by individuals or groups.

An examination of what was taking place at that period in England reveals a remarkable contrast. England was the only European country in which the existential problem of finding a new meaning for life had no significance. Here positivism and the religious tradition were on friendly terms. This existed partly because social conformism prevented radical questions from gaining the floor of consciousness. During the time of upheaval (1830 to 1930), religion retained its central and unique place in the thinking of the people. This condition suggests that the existential attitude and philosophy arose on the mainland out of the problems created by the breakdown in the religious tradition.

The Slow Acceptance of Existential Thought in America

1. *European philosophy and psychology has made slow progress in America.* It has clearly been eclipsed by the ideas imported from Britain. Allport has compared the influence of the two streams, the philosophy and especially the psychology of the

Lockean or British emphasis and the Leibnitzian or European emphasis. In his comparison he writes that the Leibnitzian tradition maintains that the person is not a collection of acts, or simply the locus of acts; the person is the source of acts. (10) Gestalt theory imported from Europe has become the most influential version of the original meaning in adjusting to Anglo-Saxon empiricism. The idea of intention gave way to the passive concept of expectancy. Planning, foresight and purpose bowed to the cognitive theories of "maps" or "sets."

Even these distorted and weakened versions of the active intellect are challenged by those American positivists who emphasize stimulus response and associationism. Thus positivism, including not only behaviorism and operationism but also associationism, became the right wing of contemporary American psychology. Cognitive theory became the left wing which has remained Lockean. It has little to do with a truly active intellect intrinsic to the personal self which was the insight of Leibnitz and his successors.

Generally speaking there is little enthusiasm for the concept of being or existence when it is differentiated from essence which is the result only of cognition or rational thought. However there are some trends in the direction of making room for the existential point of view. There are those whose central theories parallel Spinoza's doctrine of conatus. The writings of Angyal, Cantril, Lecky, Rogers and Goldstein emphasize self-actualization to varying degrees. Although these authors are not existential thinkers, they do postulate one basic motive in life—the maintaining and actualizing of the organism.

2. *There appears to be at times an almost irrational fear of an encroachment of philosophy into science.* Such a fear or suspicion has several roots. This encroachment is in part a continuance of nineteenth century attitudes when psychological science won its freedom from metaphysics. It is sometimes forgotten that the existential movement resulted from an intense concern to be more rather than less empirical. This movement is in part a reaction to the tendency of seeing the counselee in forms fashioned to the counselor's own preconceptions or to make him over into his own predilection. Counselors have been and still are guilty of the "Procrustean bed" approach. In this respect existentialism is within the household of the scientific tradition.

On the other hand, it is a threat to the purely scientific approach (narrowly conceived) in its acceptance and use of the facts which human beings reveal in art, literature, and philosophy, and in its study of cultural changes which provides insights into the anxiety and conflicts of contemporary man. In the existentialists' search to understand they unite science and humanism.

The aversion to the use of philosophical insights is short-sighted. Counselors need to recognize that every scientific method rests upon philosophical presuppositions. The reality which the counselor sees is determined by his knowledge and use of philosophical undergirding. By examining the philosophical bases of what he is doing and plans to do the counselor must recognize whether or not it agrees with what he believes about human nature and is relevant to real problems.

It is a common but naive and erroneous premise that the counselor is better able to observe facts if he avoids having anything to do with philosophical assumptions. This premise results in his identification with methods of isolating factors and observing them from an allegedly detached base, a method resulting from the split between subject and object made in the seventeenth century in Western culture and developed in its present form in the last hundred years. (11) It is accepted that science should question its own presuppositions. This means that the counselor should analyze his philosophical assumptions, and many counselors find this difficult to do.

3. *Counselors are preoccupied with technique.* They are also action oriented. These two characteristics may explain in part their lack of interest and knowledge of the theories upon which the various methods of counseling are based. One explanation may be found in our pragmatic approach to almost every kind of problem, and our optimistic, activistic concern for helping and changing people. This is demonstrated by our progress in the behavioristic, clinical and applied areas.

Our concern with technique is a worthy one, but what shall be the source of our rationale? It must be apparent that if technique only is emphasized, it will finally become self-defeating. Can we be sure that the environment and our interpersonal relationships will supply the most comprehensive insights for progress?

Why Existential Counseling Has Meaning for Us

Some individuals today are homeless and lost, giving up awareness and sinking into dogmatism and conformism. Others are striving for a heightened self-consciousness by which to become aware of their existence with new convictions. At this time of crisis in history, existentialism and existential counseling become especially relevant.

Counselors are becoming more introspective. They realize that they may be far removed from the reality of those they wish to help. Is the counselee or group member only an object and perceived as the projection of our particular theory of behavioral change? Do we expect him to fit the conceptual system in which we have been trained (this is not to minimize the importance of knowledge and training, but only to suggest that it may be inadequate, biased, and even irrelevant in certain specific situations)?

May Smith, sitting across from us, may not be capable of being understood through the use of any of our conceptual systems. It is difficult for us to accept that she does not have to be logical or consistent, and that she has human freedom. How can we know whether or not we see May Smith as she really is, in the world in which she "lives, moves, and has her being?"

This was the concern of those in Europe who have become known as members of the Daseinanalyze or existential-analytic movement. The movement, as described by its chief spokesman, Binswanger, "arose from dissatisfaction with the prevailing efforts to gain scientific understanding in psychiatry . . . . Psychology and psychotherapy as sciences are admittedly concerned with 'man,' but not at all primarily mentally ill man but with man as such. The new understanding of man, which we owe to Heidegger's analysis of existence, has its basis in the new conception that man is no longer understood in terms of some theory—be it a mechanistic, a biological or a psychological one . . . ." (12) In a time of radical upheaval in the period of transition from Medievalism to Renaissance, Pascal courageously probes the meaning of our existence. He writes: "When I consider the brief span of my life, swallowed up in the eternity before and behind it, the small space that I fill, or even see, engulfed in the infinite immensity of spaces which I know not, and which knows not me, I am afraid, and wonder to see myself here rather than there, now rather than then . . . ."(13)

Pascal could have written this today, to you and me. Many of us also are aware of the contingency of life, its "throwness." Too many of us have wondered why we are here, not there; why it was a friend, a wife or husband and not ourselves. We would like to have a satisfying understanding but find none, and sometimes, to still our disquietude, we take refuge in some superficial explanation of time and space.

It is little comfort that we in the Western world seem to have gained power over and conquered nature. Deep in man's being the result has been not only his estrangement from nature but also his estrangement from himself. Existentialism seeks to overcome the resulting split between subject and object and to grasp reality at a level which is below such cleavages. Oriental thought speaks to our search although it is on a different level and from a very different perspective. In quotations from Laotzu's *The Way of Life*, we read: "Existence is beyond the power of words to define: terms may be used but none of them is absolute. "Existence is infinite, not to be defined and though it seem but a bit of wood in your hand, to carve as you please, it is not to be lightly played with and laid down." "The way to do is to be." "Rather abide at the center of your being, for the more you leave it, the less you learn."(14)

Many conditions in America now parallel those in Europe during the period of the development of existential philosophy. There is a breakdown here of the religious and humanistic traditions. The church is uncertain and pragmatic expediency is in the saddle. For many, the religious tradition is irrelevant to the problems of the times; to others it is an afterthought. Freedom and responsibility are little understood and less

respected. Rebellion and force are accepted by many as the means of securing change.

There is a lack of direction which causes deep concern in all levels of society. The trained and educated place much hope in sophisticated systems of analysis and the best insights of the behavioral sciences. There is a hidden assumption that technical reason, successful in other realms, will succeed here too, given a little time and encouragement. In other words, the problems are located in environment and interpersonal relationships. Lofty symbols and productive imagination are reduced to signs, which make creative imagination seem unnecessary. We ask the wrong questions therefore, and seek meaning in the advancements of the technological society. Many assume that man lives by bread alone, and those who wonder seemingly cannot extricate themselves from searching only in the empirical world.

The Counselee's World from the Existential Viewpoint

Each one of us has three simultaneous aspects of world which characterize our existence as being-in-the-world. We live in the natural world, the world of objects around us, generally called the environment and known as Umwelt, meaning "world around." We live at the same time in the world of interpersonal relationships, the world of one's fellow men, and known as Mitwelt, literally the "with-world." Eigenwelt, the third world in which we live, is generally ignored. It is not adequately discussed in modern psychology or depth-psychology. It presupposes self-awareness, self-relatedness, self-transcendence and is possessed only by human beings. It is the potential for grasping what something, such as a snow-topped mountain, a ballet, or a personal relationship means to us. It is the basis on which we see the real world in its true perspective. But whereas we are impelled toward the first two relationships, i.e., to the natural world and to relationships with others, the Eigenwelt aspect of world may remain underdeveloped. We tend to objectify this potential for development known as Eigenwelt, or "own-world." We say "that is a beautiful sunset," but we leave out the "for-me-ness" of the experience. Our dichotomy between subject and object has conditioned us to believe that more is said when we state that it is beautiful—separated from ourselves. In our false attempt to be more scientific, more "truthful," we lose the sense of reality in our experiences.

We live in all three modes of world— Umwelt, Mitwelt and Eigenwelt. They are always interrelated and therefore influence one another. Each of these three worlds has its own host of special meanings.

Umwelt, the first mentioned, is the world common to all organisms. For animals and ourselves, it includes biological drives, needs and instincts. It is the world of natural cycles of sleep and wakefulness, of desire and relief. It is the world of biological determinism. It is appreciated, accepted, and honored by the existentialists. As Kierkegaard wrote, ". . . natural law is as valid as ever." On the other hand, it is to be expected that the existentialists place it in more proper perspective than the essentialists, who emphasize "drives" and "substances" and ignore or place little emphasis on the other modes of world.

Mitwelt, the second mentioned world of interpersonal relationships, does not mean any form of "social determinism" or "collective mind." It refers to a much more complex interaction in which the meaning of others in the group is partly determined by one's own

relationship to each of them. Such a relationship carries with it a sense of responsibility, of caring, of commitment and communion. It is a true organic group as opposed to an aggregate group or collection of individuals. The implications of the relationship which exists in Mitwelt have been developed by Martin Buber in his "I and Thou" philosophy.(15) In the description of Umwelt, the categories of "adjustment" and "adaption" are accurate, whereas in Mitwelt the term "relationship" describes the interaction. If the counselor induces the counselee to adjust to test results or his analysis of a set of conditions, the counselee loses his personhood and is only an instrumentality, an object. Relationship implies a readiness on the part of both counselor and counselee to change.

The understanding of Eigenwelt is more difficult. For many who are preparing to counsel it is strictly foreign to their way of thinking. Some verbally refute it; others ignore it; still others distort its meaning. It poses a difficult problem for a sizeable proportion of this group. This is unfortunate, but it should not be altogether surprising. Eigenwelt is an unexplored territory of psychotherapeutic theory. What do such terms as "the inner choice" and "a personal center" mean? Or what does it mean to say "the self in relation to itself," or the "self knowing itself?"

This understanding of the self in relation to itself was not dealt with by Freud. Nor have the interpersonal schools dealt with it. Sullivan's approach tends to make the self a mirror of the group around one. This empties the self of vitality and originality and reduces the interpersonal world to one of "social relations." The schools who see relationships within the boundaries of Mitwelt deal inadequately with love as might be expected. Sullivan uses his concept of the meaning of "chum" which leaves it without depth or symbolic meaning. Love cannot be understood if Eigenwelt is omitted. Omit it and love lacks power and the capacity for development. Nietzsche and Kierkegaard insisted that to love one must have become the "true individual."

Kierkegaard insisted that to love presupposes that one "has comprehended the deep secret that also in loving another person one must be sufficient unto himself." (16) Marriage counselors sometimes rephrase this in words such as "the one who makes the best marriage partner is the one who does not need to marry." Such a statement in general proves to be a conundrum to many college students since they are steeped in the Umwelt and Mitwelt modes of being.

Basic Concepts in Existential Counseling

1. *To know the counselee is to relate to him in his totality, to grasp his being.* This is different from knowing *about* him. Valuable as definitive and comprehensive data may be, we do not learn *of* him, only *about* him. This is not really seeing the other as a person. In fact it may be a means of defending oneself from the anxiety of involvement of being with him. To encounter the being of the counselee with the readiness to love him is to open oneself to a profound experience and this involves a creative risk. Sartre wrote: "But what each of us requires in this very effort to comprehend another is that he should never resort to this idea of substance, which is inhuman because it is well this side of the human. If we admit that the person is a totality, we cannot hope to reconstruct him by an addition or by an organization of the diverse tendencies which we have empirically discovered in him."(17)

2. *The sense of being is real.* It is said, generally speaking, in our Western culture the real is only what is measurable. A thing or experience is not real if we cannot reduce it to numbers. It is quite difficult for us to accept our realization that "being" belongs to such realities as love, will and conscience. We cannot be measured or counted or fully explained in terms of relationships. If we segmentize or abstract we lose ourselves, we get nowhere.

It becomes clearly evident to any discussant of being that the psychological need to avoid or suppress the whole idea of "being" permeates our culture. In this matter we are contrastingly different from the Indian and Oriental cultures. Some explain our condition as the result of emphasizing our function (what we do, or what we are, clerk, grocer, teacher), and to the widespread conformist tendencies in our culture. When the counselor has diaries, biographies, inventory results and test results before him, he may conclude he knows everything about the counselee, and he does know everything except the "Johnian in John."

Being is not comprehended in his attributes. Being is the counselee's ability despite his environment and relationships to become aware of the forces acting upon him, of his condition. With such awareness he has freedom to decide in favor of this rather than of that.

Existential therapists Binswanger, Kuhn and others describe man as the being who is *there*. Each man has his particular *there*, his own place in time and space of which he is conscious and for which he is therefore responsible. Binswanger describes him as "The person—who—is—responsible—for—his—existence—choosing."

We fall prey to thinking of "being" as static rather than as a continuous state of becoming. Each of us can best be understood in terms of what we are becoming. We come to grips with ourselves as we project our possibilities in action. The past and present can best be viewed in terms of the future, or what the individual's aims may be.

Man can be and is aware of himself and responsible for himself. But also he is aware of the fact that some time in the future he will not be. Within him dwells being and nonbeing. His choices determine what will live (have being) and what will die (lose being) within him. Continuously he makes choices "to be and not to be." This dialectical relation is the means of his becoming.

Each time he so chooses he affirms the "I am" of his existence. It is possible to grasp the "I am" experience at anytime. It is most likely to be grasped in times of great change in the life of the individual: success, failure, tragedy, heightened joy.

In the counseling relationship, individual or group, the counselor may help create the conditions in which another feels accepted. This feeling of acceptance and of being able to trust one or more others may be a helpful and necessary condition for the "I am" experience but that is all. This is an experience of Dasein. It is realized in the Eigenwelt, one's own-world, but not in the Mitwelt, the world of social categories. If acceptance is unconditional, it frees the person to experience his own being. The crucial and unpredictable situation is what the individual does with the fact that he is accepted in his own awareness and sense of responsibility for himself. Counselors are prone to assume that love and acceptance are all that are necessary. They may be generally helpful, but are not of themselves sufficient.

It follows then that authentic being is not the result of the introjection of social and ethical norms. Being is not the product of conditioning. If my existence is authentic, it is what I have come to understand and believe is me. The result is likely to bear some resemblance to what others have told me or have not told me; it is not necessarily *because of* or *in spite of* incoming experience but rather what I have done with it. It is from this personal center, "own-world" that I can and should decide upon my future.

3. *Being-in-the-world.* Existential thinkers emphasize that to understand a person is to understand his world. Being together then means being together in the same world. To know the counselee is to know him in the context of his own world. Binswanger, a leading existentialist, emphasizes that too much importance has been placed on the way in which our counselees have deviated from what we call the norm instead of trying to understand them in their own or private world.

But we don't understand the counselee's world through the results of tests or the accumulation of data concerning him. Neither do we understand him by some sentimental identification. We need to go deeper than the subject-object dichotomy. Difficult as this is, it is of the first importance. It meets the counselee at the point of his greatest need. Counselees like many others suffer because they have lost their world, they have no community. They have lost not only the meaningful relationship with the human world, but are strangers on probation in the natural world itself. Many persons who are to a large degree detached, unrelated and lacking affect, tend toward depersonalization. Frequently they hide their condition by means of intellectualism.

People say the play was well done, or the game was well played instead of saying, "I liked the play," or "I liked the game." Many have written of this condition of personal isolation and alienation, such as Fromm in *Escape From Freedom* with respect to sociopolitical considerations, and Tillich who writes from the spiritual viewpoint.

This isolation affects man at all levels of life including his alienation from the natural world itself. It is the result of centuries of the separation of man as subject from the objective world. David Bakan describes this separation of man from his world as "epistemological loneliness." He concludes that it results in part from the inherited skepticism of the British empiricists, Locke, Berkeley and Hume. The alienation arose by thinking of man "as essentially alone rather than as a member and participant of a thinking community."(18)

There was a time when this loneliness was almost nonexistent. In the Middle Ages, man in the depth of his being was considered to be related to the real world. The world was experienced as directly real (vide Giotto) and the body as immediate and real (vide St. Francis). Since Descartes there has been a separation; soul and nature have nothing to do with each other. Nature belongs to a different realm and is to be understood mathematically.

In modern times, man's alienation from nature and from himself was deepened. Tillich writes, "The picture of western Europe from Great Britian to Italy as I saw it in the years 1936 and 1937 was the picture of a complete cultural disintegration, especially in the younger generation." He views this disintegration to be characterized by four feelings: fear, uncertainty, loneliness and meaninglessness. At that time, two decades ago; he saw America as living "in a happy backwardness." Today there is hardly a doubt that he would have seen it to be in the midst of a thorough disintegration, similar in degree but otherwise different from what had then already taken place in Europe.

Existentialism is interested in trying to reestablish the possibility of meaning. Existentialists undertake this by showing that man is interrelated with his world. They maintain that the person and his world must be understood as one. Self implies world, and world implies self; one cannot be understood without the other. When we think of a man in his home, in the office, or in a meeting, we frequently think of a spatial relationship, but much more than this is implied.

Ignoring the integral relationship between man and his world leads to oversimplification. Counselors often assume that they can arrive at understanding the counselee's behavior from a study of his environment. We miss the fact that each one of us lives in his own world which in some ways is different from the world of all others, or that persons living in what seems to be an identical environment are really living in different worlds. Binswanger explains that "there is not one space and time only but as many spaces and times as there are subjects."(20)

World and being-in-the-world have a unique meaning for the existentialists. World is that person's unique structure of meaningful relationships and the design in which he participates. It is necessary for the counselor to know the counselee's environment, but the important challenge is to know the *meaning* of this environment to the counselee. The counselee's world consists of past events and the variety of conditioning influences, but their meaning derives from how he relates to them, what he selects from them to build his future. The counselee is continuously using what he selects, molding, forming, and building it into every minute of his relating. Self-awareness and designing is an ongoing process.

This ongoing process is openness to all experiences, it is the "openness of world." The counselee's world—this openness—is not identifiable with culture. Even if man could know all the languages and cultures and experience them, he would know only the historically knowable world; he would not know the infinity of future possibilities. Regardless of his finitude and the limitations of every kind which affect him, the counselee designs his own-world. These future possibilities are the significant aspects of the world of each of us. The counselor ignores or discredits the potentialities of the counselee when he perceives him only in the framework of accepting, adjusting, or fighting. The counselee has many possible ways of behaving but all of these are rooted in this manifold potentiality of being.

4. *"Ego" and "being" are different.* Counselors readily confuse the functioning of the ego with authentic "being." This is understandable because of the current emphasis on ego and the fact that the subject-object dichotomy has become so acceptable in much of counseling therapy.

Since its inception the ego has been considered only a part of the personality and a relatively weak part. Traditionally it was conceived as a passive and derived agent. It is "derived from the aid by modifications imposed upon it from the external world" and "is representative of the external world."(21)

The ego is a reflection of the outside world. Its strength or weakness depends upon the approval or disapproval of people and forces outside the person. The sense of being or "being" itself is not the agent of world awareness. It is firmly grounded in one's own experience of existence. It is not the capacity to evaluate events in the world but the capacity to be conscious of oneself as one in the world, as the being who can do these things. In the subject-object dichotomy, ego is the subject, but "being" is prior to this dichotomy. The sense of being is the knowing that I am the one who initiates what is occurring. In my being I am not against the outside world necessarily but my

knowing includes my capacity to be so. If I choose I can confront nonbeing if it seems necessary.

The neglect of recognition and the understanding of "being" has led counselors to settle for adjustment as the goal of counseling. In so doing they assume that the ego is primary, and the socially acceptable satisfaction of ego demands the end result. Such a viewpoint is the handed-down assumption of viewing the individual as the passive recipient of forces acting upon him, and the product of conditioning influences. These influences today are strong and varied but not necessarily all-powerful.

5. *The fact of nonbeing.* It is common to think of life in terms of being or becoming but to avoid thinking of one's demise in any form. We discuss our "beings," our first days of becoming, but avoid talking about the endings whether they be job, health, friendship, marriage or life itself. Yet we know that all things come to an end; nonbeing is not popular but it is real. We know too that "being" in any sphere or activity of our lives is not automatic and should not be taken for granted. Every new experience threatens our being. We can choose escape, or denial, or rationalization and thus deny being within us, and allow nonbeing to become a reality. We do not consciously create being; it takes place incidentally as we dedicate ourselves to an ideal in the future. We cannot overcome the appearances of nonbeing by an act of will alone. When we try, we are like the man who cleaned his house of one demon only to find that seven others came in to take up their abode.

Being and nonbeing are the opposite poles of existence. One cannot and does not have meaning without the other. It is when nonbeing threatens us that we are most aware of being. The degree of our awareness bears a direct relation to our courage to accept and take into ourselves the evidence of nonbeing. Nonbeing becomes actual only in its negation of being. Even in our strong affirmation of being we know that nonbeing is in the wings ready to come down-stage. The vividness of our being is dependent upon our affirmation of it in the face of nonbeing.

Of course death is the undeniable fact of nonbeing. But the problem of nonbeing is ever with us. It is evident in our failure to confront it in the daily pressures to conform. It is in the tendency of each of us to let himself be absorbed in the multitude of superficial collective responses and attitudes. Such absorption robs us of our self-awareness, our potentialities, and the ways in which we are in touch with our uniqueness. Such absorption often serves as a means of escape from the anxiety of nonbeing (uselessness, emptiness) but at a cost of forfeiting our sense of existence and the development of our potentiality.

But nonbeing confronted can result in growth, in the experience of being, in aliveness. We confront nonbeing when we have the courage to accept it or take it into ourselves without suppression, repression, anxiety, hostility or aggression.

It is a mistake to try to preserve our being by running away from situations which could be expected to produce anxiety or from those of potential hostility and aggression. At such times we are left with a weak, unreal sense of being. Nietzsche wrote of the "important people" who escape aggression by repressing it and as a result experience a "drugged tranquility." These situations are not the unusual or infrequent ones which may come to mind, but rather the usual, almost day-to-day kind with which any person has to cope. The person who does succeed in accepting and dealing with the normal forms of these states develops his sense of being, his at homeness with and in his in-

ner self. The counselor who has not developed his own sense of being may be less helpful in recognizing and helping the counselee whose problem is rooted in this kind of struggle.

6. *The ontological perspective on anxiety.* The majority of counselors consider anxiety to consist of two types: neurotic and normal. Few consider existential anxiety of being. May lists three characteristics which differentiate neurotic anxiety from normal anxiety: (1) Neurotic anxiety is disproportionate to the objective threat whereas normal anxiety is proportionate to the objective threat. (2) Neurotic anxiety involves repression and other forms of intrapsychic conflict whereas normal anxiety does not. (3) Neurotic anxiety is managed by means of various forms of retrenchment of anxiety and awareness, such as inhibitions, the development of symptoms, and the various neurotic defense mechanisms, but normal anxiety can be confronted constructively on the level of conscious awareness or can be relieved if the objective situation is altered.(22)

If anxiety has its roots in the culture, which is the position taken by Freud, Harvey, Kardiner and others, the counselor need only be concerned with its psychological and sociological bases. He may hope to relieve the counselee of his neurotic anxiety when he counsels with him in terms of these understandings.

Counselors are aware that our society is faced with a radical change of structure. Threats felt today by both counselor and counselee are significantly different from any they have ever before experienced. The threats now are those related to "ends" rather than "means," and cannot be removed on the basis of cultural assumptions. (23) The threat today in the Western world is not to subsistence or prestige. Rather the culture is seen as a threat to basic assumptions which have been identified with the existence of the culture. The individual, as a participant in the culture, identifies the threat with his own existence.

Sociological theories of anxiety do not explain some of the anxiety we experience. We suffer from another anxiety: the knowledge that our days are numbered. Our finitude, which impresses itself upon us in many ways, we know as anxiety of a very different kind. Fromm, May, Mowrer, Harvey, Tillich and others recognize this form of anxiety. They have named it Urangst, a name for the existential anxiety of knowing that we are finite, that someday we shall die.

Harvey carefully distinguishes between existential anxiety and neurotic anxiety. Urangst does not connote hostility or provoke inner conflict leading to neurotic defense measures. May emphasizes that existential anxiety should not be identified with fear or termed neurotic.

Tillich has gone further. He believes that existential anxiety is basic to all anxiety. He wrote, "A more exact analysis shows that in the anxiety about any special situation, anxiety about the human situation as such is implied. It is the anxiety of not being able to preserve one's own being which underlies every fear and is the frightening element in it." He distinguishes three types of anxiety, "according to the three directions in which nonbeing threatens being: (1) Nonbeing threatens man's ontic self-affirmation (his affirmation of his own being), relatively in terms of fate, absolutely in terms of death; (2) It threatens man's spiritual self-affirmation, relatively in terms of emptiness, absolutely in terms of meaninglessness; (3) It threatens man's moral self-affirmation, relatively in terms of guilt, absolutely in terms of condemnation."(24)

Tillich sees the anxiety of our time as one in which we experience the threat of spiritual nonbeing. We escape this anxiety by detachment and conformity. We detach ourselves from meaningful relationships with others and with ourselves. We evade any deep search within ourselves concerning the meaning of existence by conformism. We indulge in activity which we hope will assuage the yearning for exhilarating creativity with meaning, frequently with little success.

The counselor in this environment does not escape the threat of anxiety and emptiness either in himself or in the counselee. If he views the anxiety and the behavior which ensues as a result only of environmental conditions, he is at a loss to understand his own uneasiness and the ennui or irresponsibility of the counselees. If our anxiety is basically ontological concern for our own being, then recognition of this fact is the starting place. At present we may be confusing "means" and "ends." In fact, a balanced approach requires the inclusion of the centrality of the existential ground of all anxiety. May writes, "In my judgment, our psychological and psychiatric dealings with anxiety phenomena of all sorts will be greatly helped by shifting the concept to its ontological base." (25)

The ontological approach recognizes that anxiety is a conflict between being and nonbeing. From this point of view, anxiety occurs precisely at the point where some emerging potentiality or possibility faces the individual! He knows that something must die in order that something is born. The very possibility of the new involves the destroying of present security. Herein lies the anxiety. Although we do not we come and often evade anxiety, it is prerequisite to the possibility of becoming, of developing the new. It also means that we possess some freedom to change; otherwise there would be no anxiety. To Kierkegaard, anxiety was "the dizziness of freedom"; he explained that "anxiety is the reality of freedom as a potentiality before this freedom has materialized." Unwelcome as it is anxiety has its constructive aspects.

It is clear that to understand anxiety correctly and fully, those concerned must recognize and accept the fact that each person has a depth dimension. This dimension must be honored and respected, for it is at this level of experience that anxiety should be dealt with.

The counselor is not engaged in trying to free the counselee from anxiety. He recognizes that anxiety is to be valued as an opportunity for growth. Therefore he is interested in helping the counselee to accept anxiety as a constituent of life. He hopes to be successful in helping him to discover and to take issue with his anxiety, accepting what cannot be changed and changing what can and needs to be changed, both within himself and in the external world.

7. *Ontological perceptions of guilt.* Odier (26) and Tournier (27) describe two forms of guilt: functional or societal guilt, and true or ontological guilt. The first is the guilt one feels when he behaves in a manner generally unacceptable to society. What he does which results in guilt feelings varies with the immediate subculture which has provided the values. A boy in one subculture may feel guilty if he "lifts" small articles in a department store, but a different boy in a different subculture may feel guilty if he does not.

True or ontological guilt has its source in one's "own-world." Each person has potentialities or values, and when he denies them or fails to fulfill them his condition is guilt. Each of us has potentialities given in his "core." One is indebted to actualize these, and failure results in guilt feelings in a thousand forms.

The existentialist does not say in the common manner that one has guilt feelings. It may be that the counselor's reduction of guilt to guilt feelings has contributed to the sense of illusion in counseling. Instead the existentialist's approach to guilt is direct: the counselee is guilty.

This guilt is not necessarily linked to the religious. A person is just as guilty in refusing to accept the corporeal aspects of life as the intellectual or spiritual aspects. For the counselor it means accepting the counselee's life and experience seriously and respectfully.

There are other forms of ontological guilt besides the refusal to accept and develop one's potentialities. Another is our failure to perceive another person as he really is. We are prone to see one another through our own limited and biased views. The result is that we misunderstand, we are unfair and fail to meet the other's needs. This should not be confused with moral slackness, although the guilt may be increased by lack of moral sensitivity. The fact is simply that try as we may, we are unable fully to see the world through another's eyes.

A less frequently discussed but more comprehensive form of ontological guilt is our separation from nature as a whole. This means separation from the source of our being. There is a depth of meaning in the phrase, "from dust we come and to dust we shall return." In some lost sense, nature is our home. Nature, whether beautiful, dramatic or terrifying, has a way of calling us back to ourselves. It disturbs us when we realize that nature has little or no meaning for us.

Ontological guilt differs from other forms of guilt. Its source is not in the culture or in any introjection of authority figures. It is not that one is guilty because he broke the law or because he did not live up to someone's expectations. Rather, it is rooted in his knowledge of himself, his self-awareness, the fact that he can see himself as the one who makes his own choices.

This kind of guilt is different from neurotic guilt. If one does not recognize this guilt, or recognizing it, represses it, it turns into neurotic guilt. If one does accept it, it usually has constructive results on his personality. One who accepts his ontological guilt is likely to become more humble, more sensitive in his interpersonal relationships, and better able to use his potentialities more creatively.

The Meaning of Time

Existential analysts have a distinctive approach to time. Their thesis is that the profound experiences of life, joy, tragedy and anxiety, occur more in the dimension of time than of space. They therefore place time in the center of the psychological understanding of the counselee. In this context, how one relates to the future is of signal importance.

One's capacity to relate to the past, present, and long-term future is the unique characteristic of human existence. The fact that we can look back and see ourselves as we were in the past and project ourselves in self-conscious imagination into the future for weeks, months or years makes intelligent growth and change possible. This is considered to be the distinctive dimension of human personality. Mowrer describes us as "Time-binding—that is, the capacity to bring the past into the present as part of the total causal nexus in which living organisms act and react together with the capacity to act in the light of the long-term future—is the essence of mind and personality alike." (28)

Existential and thinkers culminate their analysis of finitude in the analysis of time. They distinguish "Existential" or immediate-ly experienced time from dialectical timelessness on the one hand, and from the infinite, quantitative, measured time of the objective world on the other. Qualitative time, as opposed to the Aristotelian and common Western idea of quantitative measured time is characteristic of Personal Experience.

Each existentialist has his own explanation of time as qualitatively and immediately experienced. Kierkegaard writes of the pregnant moment in which eternity touches time and demands a personal decision. Nietzsche uses his doctrine of "external recurrence," which gives to every moment the weight of eternity. Heidegger the most radical), in his analysis of Kant, indicates that for him time is defined by "self-affection," grasping oneself or one's Personal Existence. In this sense temporality is existentiality.

The meaning the counselor places on time bears a direct relation to his view of being-in-the world. If time is viewed only in "clock time," it is understood as an analogy from space; that is, it is perceived much like regularly spaced points on a clock or a calendar. This approach fits the Umwelt view where the individual is an object, an entity moving among the various conditioning and determining forces of the natural, quantitative world.

But the counselor is interested in the world of interpersonal relations, the world of caring and love. This is the Mitwelt world, in which we realize that time has little to do with the significance of the experience. The degree of affection between two persons is not a measurement of the length of time they have known each other. The remembered moments are those which break through the steady progression of time. Hence the expression, "Time stood still." Strauss quotes the German proverb, "No clock strikes for the happy one."

These two levels of experience require a third level or world for completeness. To varying degrees, we have developed our potential for seeing the meaning of an event for ourselves. This is our own-world, the world of self-relatedness and self-awareness.

The insight into the meaning of an event for ourselves is instantaneous, and the moment of awareness has significance for all time. This insight is not arrived at through critical examination. It arrives, unannounced, in its entirety, complete. Other meanings may attach themselves, but the core of meaning remains as it was when born: whole!. When this insight or "breakthrough" is traumatic, the person may be unable to "have" a future. He may be unable to get beyond the traumatic experience, to think or imagine forward. Repression and related neurotic symptoms are a means of making sure that the usual relation of past and present will not obtain.

Not only is time placed in the psychological center, but the future in contrast to the past or present is the significant mode of time. This is in accord with the view that man is always emerging, always becoming. Kierkegaard wrote, "the self is only that which is to become." The future which is assumed is not the distant future, not an escape in phantasy, but the immediate future. The individual is in a dynamic self-actualizing process only to the degree that he has developed self-awareness. He explores, tests reality and moves into the immediate future.

If the person is always becoming, always emerging, then personality can only be understood as we perceive it on a trajectory toward the future. This does not mean we can neglect the past, but rather that to understand the personality, we must look at the Umwelt world of the contingent, of the natural historical, and of those forces acting upon us. We do not live entirely in this world; neither are we necessarily the victims of pressures from the past.

However, the past is not a collection of unrelated events or a reservoir of memories. The past is the dynamic contingency in which we accept what has occurred. Also, from the past we select what we perceive will give us satisfaction and security in the immediate future and that which will help us to fulfill our potentialities.

It is common knowledge that we select from the past a particular and special event, a critical incident so to speak, and not the thousand and one things we do every day. Alfred Adler considered the form of memory a mirror of the individual's style of life: what the individual seeks to become determines what he remembers of the past. What he seeks to become may be at the level of intentionality and not necessarily part of his conscious awareness. In this manner of thought, the future determines the past in a dynamic sense, and what the counselee is able to recall depends upon his decision or commitment with regard to the future.

We are prone to conclude mistakenly that it is the impoverished past of the counselee which accounts for his indecision. Although the past does have an influence, the counselee's condition is primarily the result of his lack of commitment to the present and future. He does not relate or definitely select from the past because he perceives a future in which nothing matters to him. Unless there is a commitment to work toward changing something in the immediate future, uncovering the past will have no reality.

Counselors slip easily into thinking that given time, matters will work out satisfactorily. It is understandable that counselors may desire to take refuge in some automatic doctrine of historical progress. However, belief in progress is unacceptable to existential thinking. This is true whether it be concerned with historical materialism, technical progress, psychological doctrines of determinism or religious beliefs in predestination or providence. We do not progress in the things that are genuinely human, for example, love. Each generation starts from scratch. Kierkegaard wrote, "Every generation begins primitively, has no different task from that of every previous generation." (29) Of course we make so-called progress in technical areas, and we may even improve conditions conducive to what is genuinely human, but no more.

The usual use of data from the past is in disagreement with the existential point of view. Counselors assume that present behavior bears a significant direct relation to past experience. This use of data is based on the concepts of the Umwelt world and ignores the Eigenwelt or own-world. Existential counselors place primary and first importance on the counselee commitment in the future. The past which enters into the counseling experience is that which is selected by the counselee. The procedure in the use of data is the reverse of the customary method. Usually the counselor decides which data is useful in understanding the counselee. In existential counseling, the counselee decides which has ongoing meaning. He makes the choice not according to the expectancy of the counselor, but rather in terms of what the experience means to him.

Often counselors assume that if the proper conditions for love are developed, the participants will love one another. This is the critical dilemma of T-groups and basic encounter groups. The pressure engendered may only result in pseudo forms of love. The conducive conditions carry no assurance that members will take the creative risk of truly loving.

There is another prevalent assumption among counselors that insight results from an intellectual act. Of course the intellect is necessary and to some degree prepares the conditions for the insight to occur. However, that which Kierkegaard calls the Augenblick, or "the pregnant moment," (generally referred to as the "aha" experience), is more than a cognitive act. For Paul Tillich, it is the moment when "eternity touches time." This is his concept of Kairos, "time fulfilled."

The counselor frequently sees the counselee as static, predictable and somewhat set or "fixed" in his attitudes. Thus he is unlikely to see what is "crying to be born"; the emergent becoming of the counselor escapes him. This is due in part to the counselor's perception of his function. Counselors take over the burden of learning to love for the counselees. Instead they should help the counselees to remove the blocks which keep them from being; the counselors cannot love for them, and in trying to do so run the risk of dulling the counselees' own consciousness.

The Meaning of Self-Consciousness

Frequently self-awareness and self-consciousness are mistakenly identified. Self-awareness is present in forms of life other than human, but only human life has self-consciousness or the capacity for self-transcendence. The dog is aware that his owner putting on a coat means he is going outdoors. He is also aware that he is hungry, but he does not have the capacity to know himself as the one who is hungry. This capacity of self-consciousness is unique to man. He knows himself as the one who feels joy or fear; he experiences himself as the subject who has a world. This capacity for self-consciousness is the basis of his capacity to use abstractions and symbols.

Self-consciousness or self-transcendence is the most unacceptable concept to the non-existentialist. It is the foundation of Existentialism and therefore most crucial to the understanding and acceptance of existential counseling.

Objections stem from several sources. hey arise from the suggestion that self-consciousness refers to the unempirical and is unrelated to actual experience. It is rejected by those who retain the traditional way of describing human beings in terms of static substances. Self-consciousness is also rejected by those who view the differences in degree and not differences in kind. Some handle the distressing idea of self-consciousness by means of distortion. For these, it exists only as the capacity to ask the res extensa questions of the horizontal dimension (Tillich), or of the Umwelt and Mitwelt worlds. The general objection is clearly described by Murphy. He asks, "Should the student of personality, at the present stage of research, posit a nonempirical entity, distinct from both organism and its perceptual response to forms and symbols, which is called a 'self?' " His decision is that "a tentative negative answer to this question seems advisable." However, he suggests that another answer may be given when "the present stage of inquiry is more advanced." The dilemma of those who hold to empirical explanations is expressed by Immergluck. He writes: "There is, on the one hand, modern psychology's commitment to the scientific method. . .while on the other hand, there remains the nagging conviction that somehow man must be personally free. How to resolve this antimony?"

The existentialists do not have this dilemma. For them, the capacity of the normal person to transcend the present situation reveals itself in all kinds of behavior. They see this capacity in man's ability to bring the distant past and the long-term future into one's immediate existence. It is demonstrated also in our unique capacity to think and to talk in symbols. It is evident in our attempts to understand ourselves. We think of ourselves as evil, but then we are confronted with the question that if we were truly evil, would we be able to recognize this? At other times we view ourselves as essentially good, but find it difficult to account for evil. We ask if life is worth living and recognize that the ability to ask such a question implies a capacity beyond our rationality.

Communication and communion in human relations presuppose that each of us knows he is the one who is in communion with another. The whole scope of trust and responsibility presuppose that we are able to some degree to understand how others see us. Nietzsche has described man as "the animal who can make promises." The capacity to make promises is not the result of conditional "social behavior." It implies a conscious self-relatedness, the ability for self-transcendence. For Sartre, dishonesty was a uniquely human form of behavior: "the lie is a behavior of transcendence."

Counselors regularly assume that "introjection," "identification," etc., describe the dynamics of social adjustment. This is an oversimplification which is also inadequate. It omits the profound and central fact that the person is aware at the time that he is the one who is responding; that is, he is choosing or not choosing to accept and use a certain model. This supplies the needed explanation of the difference between unexamined social conformity on the one hand and the creativity and freedom of genuine social response on the other.

For existentialists, the significant world is not Umwelt or Mitwelt but Eigenwelt. Eigenwelt is the mode of behavior in which a person sees himself as subject and object. In fact, the term "exist," that is, "to stand out from," assumes this capacity. Existing is the continual emerging, a transcending of one's past and present in terms of the future. This capacity to transcend the situation implies that one is able to stand apart and look at one's self and the situation, to consider the several alternatives and reach a decision. To ignore or discount this capacity is to settle for a partial view of man and to limit his possibilities for helping and being helped.

This capacity for transcendence of the immediate situation is not another attribute or faculty; it is a given in the ontological nature of man. Some persons develop or make use of this potential much more than others. Persons vary in their perceived need to make use of this capacity. Many relate to life and generally make decisions only on the basis of pragmatic expediency.

Self-transcendence requires imagination in order that alternatives may be considered and decisions made. Kierkegaard views imagination as of signal importance. He wrote, "What feeling, knowledge or will a man has depends in the last resort upon what imagination he has, that is to say, upon how these things are reflected. . . . Imagination is the possibility of all reflection, and the intensity of this medium is the possibility of the intensity of the self." (32) A modern philosopher writes, "Our inner life is determined by images, produced by practical imagination." (33) But the person may use a form of imagination which focuses upon the past and the manifest content. This leads to a method of interpretation which Jung has called reproductive. (34) Such a method is immediately visible, thoroughly intelligible and may obviate the need for deeper understanding. This is imagination at work in the Umwelt and Mitwelt modes. The imagina-

tion of the Eigenwelt mode is productive imagination. Such imagination leads to a method of interpretation that is purposive. This does not ignore either the past or manifest content, but transcends these in a manner that permits them to point to other meanings in which both the past and manifest content participate—i.e., permits symbolic meanings to arise.

The interaction of imagination and sign or symbolic thinking influences change in behavior. When the counselee thinks with the use of signs he makes use of productive imagination. He engages his imagination to visualize what has been the outcome of his thinking. This kind of thinking is unlikely to initiate the new, except perhaps incidentally. The power lawnmower stops. The operator knows that the motor uses gas. His imagination proposes to him that the gas tank is empty. This is reproductive imagination. It is a kind of imagination which finds wide and useful application. However, used by itself it lacks adequacy and comprehensiveness in the counseling relationship.

A counselor complained about the unrealistic attitude of some of his counselees. "Imagine," he said, "John with an I.Q. of 120 and in his circumstances (father in lower income bracket) wanting to become a medical doctor." This may have been a situation in which the counselor was using reproductive imagination and "old sets." To John, being a medical doctor could have been a symbol—a symbol of doing his part to reduce the misery of the world, concerning which he already has some understanding.

Implicity in the capacity of self-transcendence and the use of one's imagination is the basis of human freedom. It is difficult to accept this freedom, and as a result, many do not energize the depth dimension of the Eigenwelt world. "Some counselees do not get beyond the pseudo-freedom of rebellion. Rebellion easily becomes confused with freedom because it is a normal interim move toward freedom. Rebellion acts as a substitute for the more difficult process of struggling through to one's own autonomy, to new beliefs, to the state where one can lay new foundations on which to build." (35)

The counselor who is aware of this potential for human freedom remains alert to the ways in which the counselee proceeds to use his freedom. He may use it to move forward, to have the "courage to be," or he may relinquish his freedom, thus having only the "courage to be as a part." One psychologist writes, "the urge to grow, pursue meaning, seek unity is also a 'given.'. . . Growth toward this end is a law to which most personal ties seem to conform. The promise I see for myself is the essence of my freedom. When a critical situation challenges me I call forth this promise—it becomes a major factor in the solution of the problem in hand."(36)

The counselor should be sensitive to the counselee's use of his freedom to decrease his self-awareness, to withdraw from life. A very common and almost unconscious method of the counselee in relinquishing his freedom is the submergence of himself in a group, society or cult. He becomes very adaptable, meeting each situation without effort. He fulfills the expectations of others. The risk is that he relinquishes contact with himself gradually genuine individuality and spontaneity disappear.

"The counselee may also relinquish his freedom by rejecting the poignant feelings of doubt concerning the meaning of existence. He discontinues the question, 'Why?' The counselor assumes routine duties, working on a 'horizontal' level that makes real confrontation with life unnecessary. Thus we escape from our freedom by asking only the questions that can be answered and by ac-

cepting answers imposed upon us authoritatively. Such retrenchment unfortunately provides a false sense of being in command of life, a feeling of belonging. Doubt is rarely present." (37) "Meaning is saved but the self is sacrificed. And since the conquest of doubt was a matter of sacrifice—the sacrifice of freedom of the self—it leaves a mark on the regained certitude; a fanatical self-assertiveness."(38)

Not all counselors recognize and accept this potential of human freedom. Carl Rogers characterizes assumptions that man has potential freedom as simply speculations. His lack of acceptance of this potential of human freedom becomes apparent in his contention that freedom can be researched. He thus removes human freedom from the Eigenwelt to the Mitwelt world. Such counselors may have no basis for hearing and understanding the Eigenwelt concerns of counselees. Such concerns, if and when expressed, are perceived as having their roots in the Mitwelt world of interpersonal relationships. Counselees soon become aware of those counselors for whom the Eigenwelt world is foreign or out-of-bounds and therefore do not express these concerns. In any case, when these concerns are expressed they are apparently carefully disguised, often appearing only as a prefix or suffix in the expression of an idea.

Basic Assumptions in Existential Counseling

Existential counseling is a radically different approach to the counselee and counseling. A review of the foregoing concepts reveals that it differs from other approaches in at least the following significant ways:

1. *Technique follows understanding.* The simple can be understood only in terms of the complex. This principle differs from the

usual counselor assumptions. Counselors generally assume that the simple, the Umwelt and Mitwelt modes of relationship can be understood by direct study. Pierre Teilhard de Chardin in his book, *The Phenomenon of Man*, takes the position that when a new function emerges such as self-consciousness in man, the whole gestalt shifts; and the organism can not be understood only in terms of the new function. The potential of self-consciousness introduces a new complexity which significantly affects all the simpler elements and their resultant relationships.

This is the direct opposite of much of the current national emphasis. Customarily it is assumed that if the right technique is used, we can then understand the uniqueness of the counselee. The existential counselor's primary goal is to understand the counselee as a person, a being and as being-in-the-world. This does not mean that he has a low respect for technique but rather that technique takes its legitimate place in a new perspective. The new perspective is to help the counselee recognize and experience his own experience.

This approach places emphasis on the context in which counseling occurs. The usual context of viewing the counselee as an object, the product of psychic dynamisms or mechanisms does not obtain. The context in existential counseling is one of seeing the counselee as a person who is choosing, committing and orienting himself toward something emerging in the present.

2. *Existential counselors ask different questions.* Ordinarily the counselor begins with the manifestations of the problem and moves toward treatment of the conditions which are presumed to have caused the problem. He asks questions which may help him to relate the manifestation to the condition and to the cause. He is working within the Umwelt and Mitwelt modes. The existential counselor asks, "What will help me understand the counselee's existence at this moment in his history? What will help me understand his being-in-the-world, his ontological viewpoint as a person?" He is working primarily in the Eigenwelt mode. For example, the college student complains of his inability to speak before a large class of students but feels that he does quite well in small groups. Counselors working only in the Mitwelt world might view this as the counselee's need to overcome his fear and hesitancy. He might even plan steps of how this could be accomplished. He also might set up means whereby his performance with increasing numbers of students could be positively reinforced. The existential counselor working chiefly in the Eigenwelt world would view the fear and reticence of speaking before the large group as a holding back of potentia of the existence of this person. He may or may not deal immediately with the problem, but more important, he would see it not only as a mechanism of inhibition, but as a limitation of the counselee's being-in-the world.

3. *In existential counseling problems take their meaning from the counselee's own immediate ontological existence.* This concept has three aspects: (1) It is not the counselee's past per se that throws light on the present, but rather his perception of it. (2) His present behavior is indicative of what he has learned or not learned to date. (3) Each significant sample of behavior (normal or deviant) is looked at on an ontological basis.

This approach places traditional theories and concepts on an existential basis. Repression in other approaches is viewed as the counselee's need to present an acceptable picture of himself which leads to the inhibition of thoughts, desires and actions unacceptable to the cultural moral codes and religious beliefs. The existential approach views this within the framework of the counselee freely accepting his potentialities. When he represses, he becomes unaware of his freedom. Aware of it, he can decide what to do with it. The chief concern here is how the counselee relates to his freedom to express his potentialities in the first place, repression being one way of relating it.

Instead of treating resistance in the traditional way, the existential counselor is interested in what makes such a phenomenon possible. Looking at it ontologically, he may conclude that it was this person's way of avoiding the development of an original potential. The counselee avoids the recognition of a potential to be developed by becoming absorbed in the Mitwelt world, in the anonymous mass of humanity.

Emphasis, then, is not placed on understanding the phenomena through recognition of the interplay of forces or drives behind them. These forces or drives are not denied; nor are they understood on the basis of energy transformation. They are viewed, rather, as the person's potentia of existence.

One advantage of this approach is that there can be direct and immediate entering into the counselee's framework instead of screening or putting through a sieve the counselee's communication in order to determine the source of its initiation. The counselor is open to the counselee as a being and takes seriously any indication from the counselee of the nature of his being-in-the-world. To the degree that the counselor achieves this, he increases his "translucency," becoming a vehicle and medium through which the counselee sees himself.

4. *Existential counseling requires a unique relationship.* The counselee may be an object to be diagnosed or a person to be understood. To the existential counselor, the relationship is one in which he is concerned in understanding and in experiencing the being of the counselee. The existential counselor disagrees with the traditional position that "the less we are involved in a given situation, the more clearly we can observe the truth."

The counselee may be telling the truth although from the objective standpoint what he is saying may be false. The counselor is prepared to abide by the realization that there is a kind of truth which may be false for everyone except for the counselee who expresses it. The counselor directs his reflection to the relationship between the counselee and his belief. If what he says follows logically from his perception of the matter, then it is considered true for the counselee, even if his criteria and referents are objectively false.

The counselor is assumed to be an expert, but if he remains completely one and proceeds as such, the counselee soon feels he is an object to be done something with or to, in this case, a professional distance exists which severly limits the possibility of the counselee being helped. The existential counselor accepts the need for training and skill, but first and last he is a person. For the time being he is working to understand the problems of someone else rather than his own. The existential approach is distinctive in that the training and discipline necessary for understanding another is not left up to chance or intuition but becomes a significant undertaking.

Such an approach means that two persons are directly relating to each other in a real, basic relationship. The counselor is not escaping or hiding behind some diagnosis he is making to himself of what is taking place. The counselor's direct involvement helps to make clear to the counselee that he is relating, doing something to one who is involved with him. It is assumed that new insights emerge for the counselee when what he is really doing and saying grasps him or "gets to him." This is a different kind of happening than if the counselor told the counselee what the counselee finally understands for himself.

This points to an important aspect of the counselor's functioning: the counselor does not impose himself, his ideas or feelings on the counselee. Instead he follows the affect and leads of the counselee. The counselor is alive and aware; he sticks to his function of helping the other person to bring to birth something from within himself. He does not allow his own involvement to become a means for the counselee to escape his own problem.

The counselor who is too conscious of the technique which he uses is limiting his availability to the counselee. He is blocking presence; he is not coming through. He is in this matter much like the actor. The actor uses technique, but it has become so much a part of him that he is not conscious of it. This is a necessity if he is to be able to be creative, that is, to create an authentic role. The counselor completely gives himself over to understanding the counselee.

5. *Existential counseling requires a unique purpose.* Karl Jaspers contends that we are now in the process of losing self-consciousness, and that this may usher in the last age of historical man. William Whyte is concerned that our emphasis on conforming behavior and adjustment is tending towards the destruction of individuality. In his book *Organization Man,* he concludes that therapists may turn out to be our enemies in their counseling for adjustment. He characterizes them as a "mild-looking group of therapists, who. . .would be doing what they did to help you." Rollo May suggests in *Existential Psychology* that we may be engaged in helping the individual adjust and be happy at the price of loss of his being.

Adjustment may be a last-ditch attempt to preserve one's centeredness by accepting nonbeing. When counselors promote adjustment they frequently are encouraging the counselee to live in a smaller world. Instead of neurosis being viewed as a failure of adjustment, it may be more correctly viewed as an indication that the person had adjusted and that this is his trouble.

Counseling for adjustment comes under criticism in existential counseling. Counseling for adjustment means that the counselee comes to accept a narrowed, distorted world. Without conflict, he makes his world identical with the culture. In this manner he reduces his anxiety and is relieved of his symptoms, since he surrenders the possibilities which caused his anxiety. He has accepted living with only the "courage to be as a part." In this manner, counselors become agents of the culture whose task is to adjust people to it. Counseling becomes an expression of the fragmentation of the culture, not a means of freeing counselees to transcend it. Many schools of counseling are described by the above method. In due time we can expect to reap the results of the resentment and despair of those who have been deluded into using one's self as a machine.

The existential counselor considers himself engaged in an undertaking much more fundamental than releasing the counselee from symptoms and helping him to adjust. He is engaged in helping persons to experience their existence. This is a difficult undertaking, for counselees do not come to be helped to experience their existence; this is about the last thing they want to do. They come instead to find a better, more acceptable way of operating themselves as a mechanism much as they would operate a machine. Many counselees talk of themselves as mechanisms. It is a Western, twentieth century, cultivated escape. Infused with the idea of being scientific and objective, they talk *about* themselves. It is a culturally acceptable way of rationalizing their detachment from themselves and others. Such a procedure has helped them to hide from ontological awareness. Talking *about* rather than *of* themselves saves them from seeing existence as it really is and themselves as they really are.

6. *Commitment is primary*. To the degree that the counselee succeeds in escaping his ontological consciousness he has his being in the Mitwelt world. But the purpose of existential counseling is to have the counselee experience his own-world, the Eigenwelt world. However in order to explore his being-in-the-world, he must be committed to doing so. The usual assumption in counseling has been that after the counselee possesses more knowledge about himself and gets more insight he will make the appropriate decision. The existential position is the reverse; commitment is primary.

There is another significant difference, namely, that the counselee does not see the truth until after he has committed himself. The counselee cannot permit himself to receive knowledge or to allow an insight to come into being until he is ready to decide and has moved to give his decision expression. But this decision is neither a sudden or "conversion" experience. The possibility or readiness to take such action is a necessary condition, but is based upon many small decisions along the way. Decision indicates a decisive attitude toward existence, an attitude of commitment. This is not a pseudo-commitment. It is not the counselee doing what is expected. Nor is it because the counselee sees no alternative or is making a commitment which he does not intend to keep. These kinds of commitments are escape mechanisms to allay anxiety. They are in the Umwelt and Mitwelt mode. This is the situation in which the self-conscious person it taking himself seriously. It is in the Eigenwelt mode.

7. *Attitude toward anxiety*. The counselee finds it difficult to relate to what is troubling him. He talks about it at length but the experience or situation doesn't become real to him. Not until some inner suffering or outer threat unsettles him has he the incentive necessary for revealing his illusions of inner change. At this time, silence is important in helping the counselee gain insight.

Since a certain degree of anxiety and uneasiness is necessary in order that the counselee confront himself directly, questions arise as to how his condition can be facilitated. On the one hand, for the counselor to arouse anxiety is considered a questionable procedure (it is interesting to compare this conclusion with the usual practice in the T-group and basic encounter groups). On the other hand, any attempt to quiet the anxiety of the counselee may hinder the counselee's seeking further help.

The existential counselor asks himself what is keeping the counselee from committing himself unconditionally in some area of his existence. The counselor needs to be able to enter into this existential anxiety. He needs He needs to be able to permit the counselee to recognize that there is the possibility that he may forfeit or lose what is possible in the present. In so many ways and from many sources, counselees have the unarticulated assumption that something will save them, that the counselor or someone will see that nothing harmful happens to them, that somebody "will soften the blow."

The concern that we need to engender anxiety in order for learning to take place is a direct outcome of the degree to which we have watered down anxiety. Life provides enough anxiety, real crises, and the existential emphasis is to help the counselee to confront both joy and tragedy directly. The counselee finds it difficult to accept the fact that if he chooses he can indeed destroy himself. The counselor accepts this fact and its importance is not disregarded. The counselor takes existence seriously and hopes to help the counselee to do likewise.

Functioning of the Existential Counselor

The counselor with existential leanings is no less scientific in his outlook and practices, but he does not assume that the scientific encompasses all the insights and understandings he needs. He takes seriously joy, triumph, despair and tragedy as they occur in living and in his own life. He focuses on the meaning of an experience and secondarily on the experience itself. He does not protect himself or others from the impact of situations and circumstances. He has respect for the carefully conceived and well-supported logical conclusion and also for the penetrating immediate grasp of experience of one's own world. He stands apart from himself and his environment and examines both within the context of the future and his state of becomingness. He is acquainted with doubt and fear, but is capable of hearing that without courage, without concern, without commitment life is hollow. He doesn't aim or set out to be an existentialist. He just tries to be an honest man.

Not only does the existential counselor place importance on all three modes of being, but he himself lives in these three modes. Since he has developed the potential of self-transcendence, he is in touch with his own being and nonbeing-in-the-world. Since he does not ignore or repress his ontological

anxiety or his "functional" guilt, he is more able to allow others to experience themselves in depth.

He views himself as a person and accepts the "mystical" in his life and others. His acceptance of the "mystical" signifies a venture of faith toward union with depths of life. He sees himself as a person, in the words of Jaspers, as "completely irreplaceable." He also accepts the fact that he cannot completely know himself. He does not treat himself as an object nor does he treat others as objects. He dissociates what a person does from what he is. A person remains a person regardless of his behavior.

Because he lives in each of the three worlds and has developed his potential for self-consciousness and self-evaluation, happenings in the Umwelt and Mitwelt worlds are viewed from the Eigenwelt perspective. It follows then that he looks at interpersonal relationships (including counseling) from a different viewpoint, and with different concerns and different questions. Insights gleaned from understanding the counselee's Umwelt and Mitwelt worlds are the basic data used by counselors in general. For the existential counselor, these are useful but not basic. The basic data is that obtained from knowing the meaning of this data to the counselee and the potential of the counselee's Eigenwelt world for designing his own world.

Many counselors are satisfied when the counselee makes adjustments leading to constructive outcomes. The existential counselor considers these worthwhile but less than adequate. He does not counsel for adjustment or for self-actualization. For him, the chief value lies in the degree to which the counselee comes to understand his being in the world and the meaning of personal events in relation to it. This does not mean that the existential counselor is unrealistic, that he does not realize that the counselee has to make adjustments. But the existential counselor believes the counselee's becoming bears a direct relation to his own world, his world of self-consciousness, to conscience and productive imagination.

When the existential counselor grasps the world he does so in terms of his own being, his own world. He has developed to some degree his potential for making judgments. Heidegger has called this capacity "the call of conscience," and Gordon Allport has described it as "the arbitrer of adult values." (39) The kind of decisions or judgments a counselor makes is a function of the modes which describe his existence. If he lives in the Umwelt and Mitwelt modes, his judgments are based on societal norms. In this situation, conscience is the emotional reaction to the harmony between self-relatedness and relatedness to others. The questions or ideas which the counselor considers necessary are directly related to his own existence. If, in dealing with matters calling for moral decisions, he has not developed the Eigenwelt mode of being, he is unlikely to expect the counselee to look at concerns from this perspective. The counselor who lives in all three modes has a broader perspective for understanding the counselee whose behavior some authority has judged unacceptable or heroic.

Customarily the counselor's orientation focuses on doing something with and for the counselee. He hopes that the counselee's release of ideas and feelings regarding the Umwelt and Mitwelt worlds will make it possible for him to acquire information for making an analysis which will aid his future planning. He hopes that this experience will help the counselee to become more amenable to a consideration of the necessary changes to be made. He may use various methods of positive reinforcement to ensure that the counselee will accept and act upon constructive plans for the future.

The existential counselor is engaged in trying to understand what life means to the counselee. He wants to know the nature of his being in the world. He is interested in information about the counselee not for itself or as a means for making judgments and plans, but rather he hopes to understand what the experiences mean to the counselee. Likewise, he is not only interested in test results and other data because they give indications of the counselee's ability and interests, but chiefly in what they mean to the counselee.

The counselor is interested in how the counselee views significant events and problems in hiw own life. He is not so much interested in these because they throw light on the counselee's flexibility and critical thinking efforts, but rather because they help the counselor to understand the depth at which the counselee meets life—whether he has existential understanding and concerns, or if he moves only in the Umwelt and Mitwelt modes of being.

He is interested in the counselee's past as a means of being with the counselee, but not as a means of making prognostications regarding what is possible and best for the counselee in the future. Rather, he is more interested in the counselee's grasp of the future, what the counselee decides regarding his future. He feels he can better understand the counselee's own world from knowing what he sees for himself in the future than by studying the counselee's past in order to predict his future. He is also interested in the counselee's past, since what the counselee selects from the past as being meaningful to the future provides the counselor with another source of understanding.

He does not discount the importance and usefulness of technical and diagnostic concerns, but he recognizes that they are on a different level from the phenomenological grasp of what is immediately occurring in the interview.

He avoids confusing these two methods and levels of understanding or of absorbing or of subsuming one under another. He uses constructs and does not assume that he counsels in some atmosphere of diagnostic purity unrelated to all else.

He is just as much aware, however, of the temptation counselors experience in becoming preoccupied with techniques. He knows that such techniques allay anxiety and save one from the turmoil that comes from being with the counselee. He also knows that they can effectively block him off from the full presence in the encounter which is essential to understanding what is taking place. He is convinced that understanding does not follow from a knowledge of dynamics.

He tries to facilitate the counselee's connection with his own world. He places some importance on motivation, but is more concerned in understanding the will and intentionality of the counselee. He views will and decision as central to therapy. He holds that in the exploration of the counselee's life, the counselee is exerting his will as evident in the direction of his choices. They may sometimes seem insignificant, but even then the counselee is using his freedom and willing a future moving toward being or nonbeing. Such an assumption on the part of the counselor enables him to avoid the subtle pushing of the counselee in one direction or another. The counselor is also interested in the social (and other interpersonal) relationships of the counselee, but more interested in the counselee's perception of his being in relation to them; the significance these relations have for him. He is interested in the traumatic episodes of the counselee's life not only as a means of judging his ego strength, but also in the context of enabling the coun-

selee to see life and situations as they really are, not to hide, distort or camouflage them, but to face them and relate to them.

Rather than strengthen the impression which the counselee may have that the counselor will save him from the impact of the folly of his ways, the existential counselor is interested in having the counselee confront his existence seriously. He hopes that the counselee recognizes that he is free to deny his possibilities and opportunities if he so chooses. Unlike many counseling relationships in which the tendency is to water down or even avoid anxiety, despair and the tragic aspects of life, this counselor is interested in having the counselee see them for what they are.

The result of the practice of dodging or minimizing the realities of life is often a passive withdrawal from much of what needs to be faced if the counselee is to develop his own world. Some methods of counseling, such as T-group or basic encounter, engender anxiety. If such is necessary, it is because the real anxieties of life have been circumvented. The existential counselor assumes that life itself produces enough of such anxieties, and the only real crises and emphasis is placed on confronting these directly.

Counselors are aware of the importance of motivation in counseling. Techniques have been developed to initiate, maintain and enhance motivation. They depend on motivation for change to take place. The general assumption is that if the counselee sees the wisdom of the alternative he chooses, he will carry it out. The counselor is interested in having the counselee make an intelligent and constructive choice. Despite their best efforts, counselees sometimes do not carry out a choice which they seemingly enthusiastically choose.

When this occurs, counselors may become critical of their methods. They then consider ways in which it might be possible to increase motivation. One of the most comprehensive summaries of the conditions most likely to induce desired behavioral outcomes is that provided by McClelland in his article, "Toward a Theory of Motive Acquisition." He lists in table form the "variables conceived as entering into the motive change process."(40)

A second and very different approach for enhancing motivation is that developed by Self Theory. The assumption is that the person who is not motivated does not need reward or punishment, but rather assistance in understanding, accepting and working through the psychological problems that prevent him from knowing what he desires. As he understands, clarifies and accepts for himself, he becomes motivated from within toward a constructive direction.

These kinds of approaches commend themselves to many counselors who develop a great skill in incorporating either of these principles for increasing motivation in their counseling. Methods which are built on the percepts and understanding of the Umwelt and Mitwelt worlds appear generally satisfactory to counselors who themselves experience life in these modes.

These methods do not encompass the means for fully understanding why the counselee behaves as he does. Reinforcement and unconditional acceptance are useful but do not help to the degree we assume they do in explaining the behavior of counselees. They lack comprehensiveness since from the existential viewpoint they omit insights from the Eigenwelt mode, or the world of self-consciousness.

However, Allport in *Existential Psychology* edited by Rollo May, cautions against the conclusion that all counselee problems have existential roots. He suggests that "sometimes at least" an acquired world outlook may constitute the central motive of a life. Those who have not developed the potential of self-consciousness or who rarely consider meaning in depth may have different counseling needs from those who do. Allport concludes that psychology urgently needs to distinguish between lives in which "the existential layer is, in effect, the whole of the personality, and other lives in which it is a mere mask for the rumblings of the unconscious."

One psychologist is foremost in directing our attention to other considerations: Otto Rank gave the will a central place in his counseling theory. He wrote, "Whence comes the will and why psychologically must we interpret this will, not understood in its origin, now as will to power (Adler) and again as sex drive (Freud) and more than that, why must we interpret it at all, instead of being able to recognize is true psychological nature?"(41)

The will has been a controversial subject through the centuries. Whether the will is free to act or is in bondage to the self has been an issue of long standing. These two positions were the subject of the debate between Erasmus and Luther. Erasmus conceived the freedom of the self over its impulses. This point of view originating in the Renaissance has had great influence even to the present time. Luther, a representative of the Reformation viewpoint, considered the will to be in bondage. That is, he believed the will as part of the self was subject to the internal change in the self in exercising its influences. From the Renaissance point of view, the will located in the Umwelt and Mitwelt modes may be influenced by forms of conditioning. In the Reformation point of view, the will functions in relation to the awareness and decision of the self and is thus located in the Eigenwelt mode.

Rollo May places the will and decision in

the center of counseling. Will and decision does not refer only to the life-shaping decisions. These words have a broader and more subtle meaning than we customarily ascribe them. Decision even in small things involes a leap. There are always some elements not determined in the outside situation, but even when they become known, one is unable to predict his reactions to them. In this sense, decision requires the movement of one's self in a direction not completely predictable or known.

Thus the existential counselor considers the will seriously. This does not mean that he is not interested in motivation or what increases it. He is concerned when reinforcement is used to motivate a counselee to do something which does not concur with what the counselee intends and wills. On the other hand, if the counselee intends and wills something, the existential counselor would see inducement via some method of motivation to be useful but only secondary, and in many situations unnecessary.

The existential counselor is interested in understanding the various forms of conditioning and the development of a permissive climate and unconditional acceptance. But he is more interested in and places more importance upon the intentionality and will.

Rollo May defines intentionality thus: "By intentionality I mean the structure which gives meaning to experience."(42) He considers intentionality to be the heart of consciousness and the key to the problem of wish and will. Intentions are decisive with respect to how we perceive the world. May illustrates this by his reference to a house in the mountains. He makes the point by bringing to our attention that if the visitor is a real estate man, he will look at it in terms of its saleability, the profit potential. If the visitor is an artist, he will notice its pattern of lines, how it fits into the landscape, and its ram-shackle condition will heighten the artistic possibilities. In each of the situations, the visitor may be the same man responding to what he sees; it is the same house but his intentions differ.

One side of intentionality originates with the perceiver. The other side is that the object itself influences the perception. May sees it is the bridge between these two. He considers it to be the structure which makes it possible for us to see and understand the outside world. In intentionality the dichotomy between subject and object is partially overcome.

The explanation of why the counselee does not act or why he acts differently from the counselor's expectations lies with the intentionality. Consciously or unconsciously he intended something which was different and which in turn resulted in a different perception and outcome. The counselor who uses reinforcement, or attempts to increase motivation by some other means, may be working at cross-purposes. And when he succeeds with some result in the Umwelt or Mitwelt world, he may only be increasing the counselee's problems.

The degree of willing is seen in the vitality with which an action is carried out. Tillich relates vitality to intentionality in these words: "man's vitality is as great as his intentionality: they are interdependent. . . Only man has complete vitality because he alone has complete intentionality. . . If the correlation between vitality and intentionality is rightly understood one can accept the biological interpretation of courage within the limits of its validity."(43) Tillich insists that being in man is never given automatically as in plants and animals. Being in man depends upon his courage, and without courage he loses his being.

Intentionality and willing go hand in hand; one cannot be understood without the other. The counselor who describes the counselee as lacking in motivation is describing appearances, not the basic cause. The cause is a lack of intentionality. Intentionality and vitality show themselves not simply as a biological force, but as a reaching out, a forming and re-forming of the world in various creative activities. Nevertheless, as counselors we are unable to supply intentionality or directly modify it; we can only encourage the conditions within the counselee which make it possible.

Preparation for Existential Counseling

If existential counseling becomes a perspective which is perceived as useful and necessary for counseling, what changes in the preparation of counselors should be considered?

Currently it is assumed that studies in the behavioral sciences with appropriate emphases on theory and practice, followed by an internship and periodic in-service training are adequate. Such preparation is occasionally embellished by a course or two in sociology, anthropology or political science.

Plainly this type of preparation focuses on counseling using insights from those disciplines whose chief concerns are within the Umwelt and Mitwelt modes of being. This type of preparation is necessary, but it provides no formal basis for thinking and experiencing in the Eigenwelt mode. In fact, this preparation grounded in the behavioral sciences may direct the counselor-in-training away from an appreciation of, and interest in, sources of information in other disciplines.

Granting the necessity of this further perspective, what emphasis and what means could be expected to facilitate the existentialist approach for the counselor? It is not expected that all counselors would be interested or able to engage in existential counseling. This is true not so much because of lack of skill or knowledge as from an inability to be at home with looking at life and living it from within the Eigenwelt mode. In fact, the chief problem may be in a scarcity of those who now look at life and themselves from this depth dimension or are interested and ready to commit themselves to becoming able to do so.

Although all of us as humans possess this potential for self-transcendence and freedom, we do not develop it. It remains undeveloped until we choose to look at life from this perspective or until circumstances force us to do so. We are unlikely to embrace our existence until we are willing to accept the fact that there are understandings which are not necessarily or completely the product of rational thought. We deal then with ourselves and others as essences, measurable quantities and qualities.

This potential for self-transcendence cannot be taught or imposed. But the following thoughts and beliefs may indicate a minimal readiness:

1. The recognition that no person can be completely understood by the use of rational thought and its products.
2. An awareness that information about John, however well organized and sophisticated, does not assist us in understanding "the Johnian in John."(44)
3. The recognition and growing acceptance that there is a kind of truth which may be false for everyone except him who expresses it. Although the counselee's criteria and referents seem objectively false, it is considered true if what he says follows logically from his perception of the matter.(45)
4. An inquiring attitude regarding the significance of productive imagination and the function of symbols.
5. The ability to accept ambiguity. "Instead of accepting change as an academic concept, he must be willing and able to recognize and work with change in its

serious dimensions and bewildering un-predictability."(46)

It is not possible to plan with any degree of certainty the experiences necessary and helpful in the preparation of a counselor to do existential counseling. It is logical to assume that he will need the background of knowledge currently obtained in his studies of the behavioral sciences. However, the content may be viewed from a different orientation and subjected to questions arising from experiences planned to aid in the development of his existential potential. The following are suggestions as to the direction these needed experiences might take.(47)

Experiences in the study and interpretation of history. A foundation for understanding existential counseling could be developed through the study of (1) the roots of existentialism in the biblical and Greek worlds; and (2) the historical changes in Europe which encouraged and led to the development of existential thought in Germany, France, Holland, Russia and other countries.

The meaning of these historical changes and changes in thought patterns should be sought through a study of the interpretation of history, especially European history during the time when Existentialism was developed, approximately 1830-1930. Such an interpretation should focus on political, philosophical and religious elements.

In order to understand the thought patterns and attitudes of our own people toward Existentialism and existential counseling, the influence of pragmatism and of British empiricism should be studied and interpreted from the three foci mentioned above.

Experiences in literature and drama. The study of noble characters in literature encourages the counselor to consider joy, tragedy and ambiguity in depth, to relate to myths and symbols, and to be open to the in-

tuitive searching of the artist concerning the meaning of life. He might wish to read, study and discuss in small groups great prose and poetry in Greek, Shakespearean and modern plays. The discussion might well focus on what the characters experienced, possible reasons for their reactions, and how each counselor's perception of these situations would affect him and his counseling effort. Consider the possibilities for the grasping of existence in a small group discussion of such symbols as Hamlet's "To be or not to be. . ."

Experiences in philosophical and religious thinking. These could provide the counselor with the opportunity to grasp the significance of what the various existential thinkers, such as Schelling, Kierkegaard, Marx, Nietzsche, Dilthey, Bergson, Heidegger and others are saying. Through this study and that of religious literature chosen both from Eastern and Western thought, he could come to understand the meaning of being and the centrality of time in the existential approach.

A second kind of study and understanding would focus on imagination and symbols. Through reading and discussion, the counselor could come to recognize the signal importance of imagination in that (1) it submits the material of sense perception to our understanding and is an important element in the attempt to understand another from his frame of reference; (2) it encompasses the counselee's goals and represents the concrete life of his convictions. The counselee's desired accomplishment is the language of the imagination; and (3) it unifies sensation and reason, and through imagination each counselee views the future goal.(48) Not only should the counselor know the significance of productive imagination, but he should become aware of its use in his own problem-solving endeavors.

A third kind of study is that concerned

with symbolic thinking. Our horizontal living, marketplace orientation, pragmatic thinking, emphasis on the tangible and other subtle, pressing influences have caused us to evade consideration of the symbolic. Yet without the symbolic, which, as Martin Buber states, is a convenant "between the absolute and the concrete," (49) we cannot reach the depth of meaning for which we yearn in our human relationships. It is not that we do not sense this, for we sprinkle the description of counseling with an abundance of symbols, such as freedom, love, sense of responsibility, and personal center. In our attempts to explain them, we treat them as signs, and in so doing we remove them to Umwelt and Mitwelt worlds.

When symbolic meanings are ignored or treated as signs, counseling is forced to become counseling for adjustment. Signs suffice when only adjustment to the world of signs is desired. However, without the probing use of the symbolic, existential meanings are unlikely to be found, and personality changes are unlikely to take place.

To interpret life in terms of signs is to remove the meaning and significance of depth from our experience. Conceivably, then, freedom would mean the license to do what we can get away with; peace, the absence of conflict; and justice, penalty in proportion to the infraction. The true symbol has the following characteristics: (1) it points beyond itself to something else; (2) it participates in that to which it points; (3) it opens up levels of reality which are otherwise closed; (4) it opens up hidden depths of our being; (5) it cannot be produced intentionally; and (6) it dies when it no longer produces a response in the group in which it originally found expression.(50)

In his becoming, the existential counselor will resist his nominalistic tendencies. He will tolerate the ambiguity that accompanies symbolic thinking. He will refuse to try to define the symbol or make it concrete, knowable, and attainable. Not only will he discipline himself in this manner, but he will cultivate symbolic thinking in his own approach to reality. He will build an appreciation of the symbol and its meaning through study and discussion. and will endeavour to realize its significance for interpersonal growth and community self-renewal.

Experiences through art. The basic constituent of counseling cannot be taught. The conditions conducive to its development grow out of experiences which are meaningful and understood. They are the experiences of joy, tragedy, doubt and despair which the counselor shared with all men. Art quickens his perception and understanding of others and opens doors to awareness of self. It can do this since it makes accessible to him both the feelings experienced by predecessors and those expressed by contemporaries.

Not all art enhances the possibility of communion of the counselor with his inner self and with others, but only that art which calls forth his productive imagination, causes him to feel, and to become aware. Whatever form the art may take, the degree to which it intensifies these qualities determines its usefulness. No two counselors can be expected to be equally and similarly helped by any art form.

The degree to which the counselor experiences his own world depends in large measure on the depth to which he is accustomed to examine and experience being in the world. For the counselor who dwells in the Umwelt and Mitwelt worlds, art in any mode is less likely to deepen his sensibilities or attune his understanding to the mystery of life. For the counselor who deeply reflects upon his existence, art in some form can engender understanding of his own world, a prerequisite for participation with others in the same quest. Counselors can benefit from the confrontation which good art, regardless of subject matter, makes possible. Such an experience deepens the counselor's self-consciousness, preparing him to participate in the counselee's search for meaning, confidence, and hope.

Issues

1. Can we as counselors become able to distinguish a problem of the counselee which is centered in the Umwelt (environment) or Mitwelt (interpersonal relationships) from one which is centered in the Eigenwelt, or the counselee's self-consciousness, his being in the world?

2. Can we as counselors keep the proper perspective between essence which indicates the use of techniques, and existence which indicates direct understanding and communication with the counselee? Can we further avoid confusing them or permitting one to be absorbed in the other?

3. Can we posit self-consciousness as an entity in and of itself and use existential concepts as such, or shall we interpret them in the Mitwelt or Umwelt modes and then try to research them?

4. Can we accept human freedom, that is, the capacity of the individual to decide against any odds between being and nonbeing, and therefore understand the meaning of Existentialism and existential counseling without distortion?

5. Can we accept the fact that there may be something about man which is not now or ever will be understood completely within the framework of scientific research and thus value and use existential insights without reducing them to the terms of the Mitwelt mode?

Conclusions

Existential counseling adds a perspective and depth which is especially relevant today.

A high school counselor interested in the fears of students asked three hundred high school students from five different urban schools to write the name of the first fear they thought of. When the results were examined, forty-five percent had fears which may have been expressions of existential anxiety. About twelve percent wrote fear of death, five percent feared the death of parents, five percent wrote fear of failure, five percent fear of the future, eight percent fear of car accidents, five percent fear of war, and five percent fear of loneliness.

This may be indicative of an increase of existential concerns. If such is the case, there is a need for counselors who, because of their own self-consciousness and depth of their life experiencing, appreciate and to some degree understand the existential concerns of others. If such counselors will continually prepare themselves through study, reflection and practice, many more students may be helped.

These counselors will use those techniques and skills which accord in principle with their beliefs about men. Their use of them will be in the manner and to the degree that these are viewed as helping them to help the counselee understand his own being in the world. They will assume that if the counselee can be helped to discover who he is, whom he desires to be, and what has true meaning for him, then the means and information will be used in proper congruence with the counselee's own becoming.

Existential assumptions are controversial. To some they may seem "foolishness." To others they may be a "stumbling block." But to still others they are a call to have "the courage to be."

REFERENCES

1. Henry Bergson. *Essai Sur Les Donnees Immediates De La Conscience.* German tr., Jena: 182 (1922).

2. Walter A. Kaufman. *Neitzsche, Philosopher, Psychologist, AntiChrist.* Princeton: Princeton University Press (1950), 140 ff.

3. Gordon W. Allport. *Becoming: Basic Considerations for a Psychology of Personality.* New Haven: Yale University Press (1959), 18.

4. Paul Tillich. Existential philosophy. *Journal of the History of Ideas* (1944), vol. 5: 1, 44-70.

5. Erich Fromm. *Escape from Freedom.* New York: Holt, Rinehart and Winston Inc., (1941), 19.

6. *Ibid.,* Kaufmann. *Nietzsche, Philosophy, Psychologist, AntiChrist.*

7. Paul Tillich. The world situation. *The Christian Answer,* ed. Henry P. Van Dusen, New York: Charles Scribner's Sons (1945), 2.

8. C. Gratton Kemp. *Intangibles in Counseling.* Boston: The Houghton Mifflin Company (1967), 66.

9. *Ibid.,* Tillich. Existential philosophy.

10. *Ibid.,* Allport. *Becoming: Basic Considerations for a Psychology of Personality,* 7-16.

11. Nietzsche. *Wille Zur Macht X.*

12. L. Binswanger. Existential analysis and psychotherapy, in *Progress in Psychotherapy,* ed. by Fromm-Reichmann and Moreno. New York: Grune and Stratton (1956), 144.

13. Blaise Pascal. *Pensees of Pascal.* New York: Peter Pauper Press (1946), 36.

14. Witter Bynner. *The Way of Life According to Laotzu, an American Version.* New York: John Day Company (1946).

15. Martin Buber. Distance and relation. *Psychiatry,* (1957), vol. 20, no. 2.

16. Soren Kierkegaard. *Fear and Trembling.* Trans. by Walter Lowrie. New York: Doubleday and Company (1954), 55.

17. Jean Paul Sartre. *Being and Nothingness, An Essay on Phenomenological Ontology* by Hazel Barnes. New York: The Philosophical Library (1956), 52, 58.

18. David Bakan. Clinical psychology and logic, *The American Psychologist,* December (1956), 656.

19. Ernest Cassirer. *An Essay on Man.* New Haven: Yale University Press (1944), 22.

20. *Ibid.,* Binswanger. Existential analysis and psychotherapy, 196.

21. William Healy, August F. Bronner and Anna Mae Bowers. *The Meaning and Structure of Psychoanalysis as Related to Personality and Behavior.* New York: A. A. Knopf (1930), 38.

22. Rollo May. *The Meaning of Anxiety.* New York: Ronald Press (1950), 194, 197.

23. *Ibid.,* Kemp. *Intangibles in Counseling,* 93.

24. Paul Tillich. *The Courage to Be.* New Haven: Yale University Press (1952), 41.

25. Rollo May et al. *Existence: A New Dimension in Psychiatry and Psychology.* New York: Basic Books Inc. Publishers (1961), 52.

26. Charles Odier. *Les Deux Sources, Consciente et Inconsciente De La Vie Morale.* Neuchatel: La Baconniere (1943).

27. Paul Tournier. *Guilt and Grace.* New York: Harper and Row Publishers Inc. (1962), 66, 67.

28. O. Hobart Mowrer. Time as a determinant in integrative learning, in *Learning Theory and Personality.* New York: Ronald Press (1950).

29. Soren Kierkegaard. *Sickness Unto Death.* N. J.: Princeton University Press, 163.

30. Gardner Murphy. *Personality, A Biosocial Approach.* New York: Harper and Row Publishers, Inc. (1947), 490.

31. Ludwig Immergluck. Determinism—freedom in contemporary psychology, *American Psychologist* (1961), vol. 19, 270-81.

32. Soren Kierkegaard. Concluding unscientific postscript, in *A Kierkegaard Anthology,* edited by Robert Bretall. Princeton: Princeton University Press (1951), 210-11.

33. Richard Kroner. *The Religious Function of the Imagination.* New Haven: Yale University Press (1941), 9.

34. Carl Jung. *Psychological Types.* New York: Harcourt, Brace and World, Inc. (1923), 577.

35. Rollo May. *Man's Search for Himself.* New York: W. W. Norton and Company, Inc. (1953), 154.

36. Gordon W. Allport. *Pattern and Growth in Personality.* New York: Holt, Rinehart and Winston, Inc. (1961), 563.

37. *Ibid.* Kemp. *Intangibles in Counseling,* 105.

38. *Ibid.* Tillich. *The Courage to Be,* 49.

39. Gordon W. Allport. *The Individual and His Religion.* New York: The Macmillan Company (1950), 87.

40. David C. McClelland. Toward a theory of motive acquisition, *American Psychologist* (1965), vol. 20, 321-33.
41. Otto Rank. *Will Therapy.* New York: W. W. Norton and Company, Inc. (1936), 12.
42. Rollo May. *Love and Will.* New York: W. W. Norton and Company, Inc. (1969), 223.
43. *Ibid.,* Tillich. *The Courage to Be,* 81-82.
44. *Ibid.,* Allport. *Becoming: Basic Considerations for a Psychology of Personality,* 18.
45. *Ibid.,* Kierkegaard. *Concluding Unscientific Postscript.*
46. C. Gratton Kemp. *Foundations of Group Counseling.* New York: McGraw-Hill Book Company (1970), 229.
47. Kemp. *Foundations of Group Counseling,* based upon 230-35.
48. C. Gratton Kemp. *Perspective on the Group Process.* Boston: Houghton Mifflin Company (1964), 15.
49. Maurice S. Friedman and Martin Buber. *The Life of Dialogue.* New York: Harper and Brothers (1960), 320.
50. Paul Tillich. *Dynamics of Faith* New York: Harper and Brothers (1958), 42-43.

12. ADLERIAN GUIDELINES FOR COUNSELING

Martin I. Garfinkle,
Robert F. Massey,
and Ellen Mendel

Peter Schwarzburg

The central concepts in Alfred Adler's writings are social interest, inferiority feelings, and the striving for superiority. Adler developed a more holistic and comprehensive theory than the followers of Freud. The great bulk of his writings deal with the biological, social and psychological aspects of the individual's personality.

Adlerian counseling can be seen as a learning process through which the individual comes to understand himself and his interpersonal relationships. Rudolph Dreikurs, a noted commentator on Adler, describes the counseling process as consisting of four phases. These include forming a relationship, exploration, interpretation, and re-orientation (Dreikurs, 1956).

From Adler's viewpoint, the totality of the client's behavior is both purposive and goal-directed. Past and present information that is offered by the client can be significant in tracing inferiority feelings that continue into the present and in helping to uncover lifestyle patterns. When the goal of the individual's present striving becomes clear to both counselor and client, it is their task to evaluate whether the present behavior is conducive to cooperation and is beneficial to the client and others. If they are in agreement that the present behavior, which is in actuality the way the client is achieving his goal of superiority, is not useful, the counselor may offer alternate solutions to help him develop goals that are more beneficial. It is the need for cooperation between people that pervades throughout all of Adler's thinking. It is the counselor's function to assist in developing the life-style, so that the client will be able to direct a socially useless style of life toward a goal that is more productive.

Adlerian Counseling Techniques

In gaining an understanding of the client and facilitating the solution of his problem,

Adler recommended the use of five diagnostic approaches: (1) the earliest childhood recollections, (2) the position of the child in the birth order—family constellation, (3) childhood behavior disorders, (4) day and night dreams, and (5) the nature of the exogenous factor that causes the illness (Ansbacher and Ansbacher, 1964, p. 328). Each of the above techniques will be briefly dealt with in the following paragraphs.

Adler would begin his exploration of the individual by delving into one's earliest recollections. Through this approach, a lucid view of the person's present life-style can be perceived. A case study will illustrate this in a section to be presented later. Earliest recollections are usually selected from a client's early childhood. However, when these cannot be recalled, any occurrence remembered from the past can be used by the counselor. Early recollections, although not verifiable and perhaps fictitious, allude to significant factors in the client's style of life.

Adler discovered that the position a person occupies in the family often plays an influential part in the formation of his perceptions and behavior towards others. The oldest child becomes accustomed to interacting with persons of authority by receiving the undivided attention of his parents until the birth of another child takes the center of attention away from him. The oldest child may then gain recognition by acting as the leader for the younger sibling(s). A healthy way for the oldest child to adjust to his new position is to share in the responsibility of caring for the other children without attempting to dominate them. If one is a second or middle child, he may resist the authority asserted by the older child and develop a rebellious nature. This reaction may retard future adjustment to group life. The youngest child has never experienced being replaced by another sibling and may show an overdependence on others because of a prolonged close tie with his mother. The youngest child sometimes acts "as if he were cast from a different mold" and feels that he must be exalted above others (Alexandra Adler, 1973, p. 13). This behavior is similar to the biblical character of Joseph.

The birth order position is not an inevitably determining influence, but it does provide a structure within which a person learns to perceive the world and to form a style of life. So attention to the birth order position with its individual nuances for each person may, in conjunction with early memories, offer insight into a person's goals and life-style.

Childhood behavior disorders can be significant in the preschool years since behavior exhibited in this period can be carried over into one's future life-style. Ansbacher (1964) relates this as follows:

Once difficulties in the childhood of the adult patient have been established, this information, in addition to its diagnositc value, can be used to widen his understanding of himself. It helps the therapist to convince the (client) that his present difficulty is not due to any "cause," but that both the present and past difficulty have their common origin in the early established (mistaken) disposition, which is based on an early, mistake in judgment (p. 387).

The specific behavior disorders that were identified by Adler are habit disorders, fears, stuttering, overt aggression, daydreaming and isolation, laziness, and lying and stealing (Ansbacher and Ansbacher, 1964, pp. 187-392). For a more detailed description of each of these disorders, it would be helpful to refer to the reference cited above.

Adler accepted Freud's theory as to the manifest and latent content of dreams. However, he rejected the exclusively sexual significance of dreams. According to Adler, dreams were the result of unsolved diurnal problems and life stresses. Recurrent dream themes and the affective emotional feelings that the person retains upon awakening generally point to consistencies in the person's life-style. A dream and its resulting feelings may serve to evoke an experience that the person is attempting to avoid or to prepare one for an upcoming situation. A case illustrating this point was presented by Adler (1958):

A student is faced with an examination. The problem is straightforward and he should approach it with courage and common sense. But if it is his style of life that he wants to run away, he may dream that he is fighting in a war. He pictures this straightforward problem in a heightened metaphor and now he is far more justified in being afraid. Or he dreams that he is standing before an abyss and that he must run back to avoid falling in. He must create feelings to help him to avoid the examination, to escape from it; and he fools himself by identifying the examination with the abyss (pp. 103-4).

In order to fully appreciate the circumstances of the individual's problem, Adler thought it important for the counselor to gain a clear picture of the external factors surrounding a client's situation. It is important to understand how the individual will handle his environment in order "to know in what way he moves in the face of his external problem" (Adler, 1964, p. 188).

Case Studies

The following two cases exemplify the Adlerian approach to school counseling.

Case 1

Pablo R was referred for counseling at nine years of age. He was a middle child having an older sister and a younger brother. His brother was very bright and earned good marks in school, and his sister was a well-behaved child, both in school and at home. Mr. and Mrs. R were separated, and Mrs. R. bore Pablo's father much resentment. She saw in Pablo many aspects of her estranged husband, so her behavior toward Pablo was quite ambivalent, sometimes provocatively loving while at other times very punitive.

As stated earlier, one of the basic Adlerian principles is that each child will strive for belonging in his family in his own unique way. Pablo's style was to reinforce the identification with his father since he could not compete with his sister's good behavior or his brother's academic excellence. He tried to find his place by continuously misbehaving at home and in school. He also tried to gain recognition by having headaches, through fears of being alone at night, and by crying frequently. He had no friends because he teased the other children, yet he often felt that they had wronged him (a similar feeling to that which he had at home).

Here we see the life-style of a child who seems discouraged about belonging in a socially useful way, so he drifts toward the useless side of life. His basic mistaken conviction is: "Only if I misbehave or am sick will I be noticed and can find my place."

In the exploration and interpretation phases of counseling, Pablo's behavior and his mother's reaction to it were examined. The purpose behind his behavior was explored in the following manner. The counselor formed several hypotheses about the reason for Pablo's behavior and presented them to him.

"Could it be that you like the extra attention when you have headaches?"

(Little reaction.)

Then she checked out another hypothesis:

"Could it be that you get your headaches when you think the work is hard and you're not sure if you can do it?"

(Strong reaction—smile of recognition.)

The counselor has to be aware of nonverbal communication since it often happens that the client answers "No," but there is a smile or some other form of recognition in his facial expression. Recognition of nonverbal cues will give the counselor some tentative ideas about the client's private logic. Each hypothesis will be presented and checked out with the client until a clear picture begins to emerge. It must be pointed out that before counseling the client may not be consciously aware of the purpose behind his behavior.

In the final stage of counseling, the reorientation stage, the counselor suggested that Pablo's mother focus on her son's strengths and assets rather than berate him for his misbehavior. It was reemphasized that Pablo was a discouraged child who needed encouragement to overcome his feelings of inadequacy, and instead of punishing Pablo, she should allow the natural logical consequences of his behavior to follow. For example, if he deliberately sprayed her perfume over the room and spilled her cosmetic lotion, instead of beating him for it, she should teach him how to clean it up and encourage him to replace what had been broken. She could thereby teach Pablo social interest and consideration for others.

A great deal of time was spent discussing alternatives to his having headaches in order to avoid difficult matters. Together with his teacher, the counselor worked out a mutual tutoring program in which he would receive help in reading (his weak subject) from a child who would in turn get help from him in math (his strong subject). The teacher also agreed not to call Pablo's mother when he ran out of the room since that would give him extra attention and would reinforce his attention-getting behavior. As an alternative, she would try to encourage him to cope with his difficulties within the classroom. Pablo was encouraged to stop teasing his classmates and to make new friends. This was illustrated to him through role playing with the counselor. The focus in the counseling session was on helping Pablo to belong to a peer group through improved social interactions and concern for others.

Case 2

Charles S was the older of two boys and was eight years old when he came to the attention of the counselor. What makes this an unusual case is that his younger brother had died at a very early age, and then Charles became an "only child." In such a situation, it is common for the parents to become overprotective and overconcerned about the remaining child. As a result, the child gets much more attention than he would under ordinary circumstances, which was true in Charles' case. At the time of counseling his parents were separated, and he was living with his mother.

As a reaction to his home environment Charles had drawn the following faulty conclusions: "I must get attention at all times, and if I don't, there must be something wrong with me. I must do all I can to get attention." In school he tried to get extra attention by calling out, getting out of his seat to walk around the classroom, showing disrespect for the teacher, and by being antagonistic toward the other children. Moreover, he would get angry when he was not called upon to recite and would be surprised or hurt when he was told that he was doing something wrong. Last but not least, he always thought that he was not being treated fairly.

The effectiveness of using early recollections to gain an understanding of the individual's phenomenological view of life can be seen through the following illustrations. Charles' first recollection is as follows: "My mother and I were going downtown by bus to get a haircut. I had a little watch on my arm which I lost on the bus. My mother got

angry with me, and she smacked me on my arm." When the counselor analyzed Charles' recollection, it was discovered he had an attitude which might be stated as, "Things often happen which make me get into trouble." The counselor realized that Charles' relationship with his mother was an important one.

The counselor looked at Charles' next recollection to see if the same themes were present. Charles related the following: "My mother took a picture of me, and I asked her why she took it, since I had my mouth open." The two recurring themes expressed in the first and second recollections are that things seem to happen to Charles and that he is concerned about his physical appearance (haircut, photograph).

A third recollection is helpful to get a more complete understanding of Charles' life-style.

I remember me and my brother used to play, and he always used to beat me even though he was younger. Once he threw a box over my head. I couldn't do nothing. He put the box right over my head and sat on it. I couldn't get out. My mother took him off the box, so I could get out.

We begin to see the importance of Charles' relationship with his mother and the emergence of a new and important figure, his younger brother. Instead of Charles being the more powerful sibling, he sees his younger brother as always being able to overpower him. It is important for the counselor to understand that Charles is saying, "Everybody beats me, young (brother) and old (mother), and I cannot do anything about it. Everything happens to me, so I need help from someone stronger."

During the counseling sessions, it became evident that Charles still held these same mistaken convictions of himself. It is interesting to note that at school when he gets into trouble, he never feels that he is at fault and often runs to the teacher for help in dealing with his peers. The teacher often hears him say in a whining voice: "Poor me, everything happens to me."

The primary focus in counseling with Charles was to arouse and build his feelings of social interest. This was done by encouraging Charles to make friends as well as by helping him to build up greater confidence in himself. In order to do this, many sessions were spent in focusing on Charles' strengths and positive attributes.

Conclusion

In summary, we can see that Alfred Adler's insights have practical applications for the client and that Adlerian techniques can be used effectively in both short-range and long-term counseling. The counseling situation sets up an interpersonal relationship in which the client's life-style can become apparent. The counselee can become aware of whether he has or lacks social interest and can learn from the counselor how to be more cooperative. As a result his self-esteem will be based not on a neurotic striving for superiority over others, but on co-operation with others.

Adlerian counseling deals with the whole person, one's physical, emotional-interpersonal, intellectual, and spiritual aspects as they interact within the unity of the self. Adlerian counselors use several techniques to improve the total functioning of the troubled or non-self-actualizing client. The ordinal position of the person within the family constellation frequently provides valuable information about how one relates to other people. Early memories generally capsulize a person's life-style in an abbreviated form. Adler discovered that a person can always interpret events to fit into his own life-style. But hopefully through Adlerian counseling the individual learns to interpret life in a way that enhances his own self-esteem as well as enables him to live a socially useful style of life.

REFERENCES

Adler, Alexandra. *Guiding human misfits* (1938). New York: Kraus Reprints Co., 1973.

Adler, Alfred. *Understanding human nature* (1927). Greenwich, Conn.: Fawcett, 1969.

———. *The science of human living* (1929). Garden City, N. Y.: Anchor Books, 1969.

———. *The education of children* (1930). Chicago: Henry Regnery Co., 1970.

———. *The problem child* (1930). New York: Capricorn Books, 1963.

———. *What life should mean to you* (1931). New York: Capricorn Books, 1958.

———. *Social interest* (1938). New York: Capricorn Books, 1964.

Ansbacher, H. L., and Ansbacher, Rowena, R. *The individual psychology of Alfred Adler: a systematic presentation in selections from his writings.* New York: Harper Torchbooks, 1964.

Ansbacher, Heinz L., and Ansbacher, Rowena R. *Superiority and social interest: a collection of later writings of Alfred Adler.* New York: Viking Press, 1973.

Dinkmeyer, Don. Conceptual foundations of counseling: Adlerian theory and practice. *The School Counselor,* 11 (1964):174-78.

Dreikurs, Rudolf. *Fundamentals of Adlerian psychology.* New York: Greenberg, 1950.

———. *Progress in psychotherapy.* New York: Grune & Stratton, 1956.

———. *Psychology in the classroom.* New York: Harper & Row, 1968.

Dreikurs, Rudolf; Grunwald, Bernice Bronia; and Pepper, Floy C. *Maintaining sanity in the classroom: illustrated teaching techniques.* New York: Harper & Row, 1971.

Nikelly, Arthur G. *Techniques for behavior change: applications of Adlerian theory.* Springfield, Ill.: C. C. Thomas, 1971.

Platt, John M. Efficacy of the Adlerian model in elementary school counseling. *Elementary school guidance and counseling.* 6 (1971): 86-96.

Scarth, Peter. *Implications of individual psychology for the school psychologist. Journal of Individual Psychology.* 25 (1969):146-54.

ADLERIAN INTERVIEW STRATEGIES FOR BEHAVIOR CHANGE
Thomas W. Allen

Vasilije Knezevic

The Adlerian view is that behavior springs *not* from what the person "actually" is but from what he *believes* himself to be; not from the stimuli which the world thrusts upon him nor from his biological substratum but from how he *construes* those events. In other words, a person's behavior rests heavily upon his *expectations*, and after the manner of "self-fulfilling prophesies," these anticipations often contain the seeds of their own confirmation.

For example, if a person concludes that the world is a hostile place and that one is consequently well-advised to "do unto others before they do it unto him," he may well behave in a manner which others perceive as exploitative or hostile. They are then likely to respond to him in kind. These responses naturally serve to confirm his basic premises about life and entitle him to greater belligerence toward the world. Or consider the person who believes that he is but a helpless pawn of all manner of forces, both internal and external, unable to make any impact of consequence on his world. Such a person quite "logically" shrinks from life and, of course, behavior of this stripe not infrequently results in one having things done to him to a rather extraordinary extent.

The principal therapeutic objective of the

Adlerian is then to alter such self-defeating, asocial beliefs, to convert a vicious cycle (self-defeating convictions which lead to behavior of a variety which generates more evidence for the original conviction) to a more benign spiral. The interview, although perhaps overvalued in some corners as the *sine qua non* of counseling practice, remains a useful tool in this attempt.

Disappointing Dysfunctional Expectations

The counselor's initial objective may be that of modifying the client's behavior in a way which is most likely to evoke immediate responses from his environment, responses which are at odds with his troublesome expectations. For example, one young man staunchly maintained that virtually everyone he met took an instant dislike to him and was, moreover, eager to "do him dirt." The counselor noted that his client characteristically went about with a dour expression on his face that could well be supposed to provoke defensive maneuvers on the part of others. Consequently, the client was directed to smile at others even though he didn't feel like smiling. In a week of such "hypocrisy" he found that others would respond more positively to him, given this change in his behavior. This discovery occasioned both surprise and chagrin since it tended to undermine his continuous assertions that others instinctively responded to him with hostility. Other examples of this tactic are to be found in Adler's writings and in the work of a number of contemporary writers, Milton H. Erickson's (1954) discussion of hypnotherapy and Joseph Wolpe's (1969) description of "assertive training."

In other cases, the counselor may "spit in the client's soup." "Spitting in the soup" (which Adler also termed "besmirching a clean conscience") is ostensibly derived from the boarding school technique of wresting another's rations from him by "contaminating" it with spittle. It is then but another version of the central Adlerian strategy of modifying behavior by changing its *meaning* to the person who emits it.[1] In this instance, the counselor is concerned with divining what it is that the client is up to when he behaves "systematically" and with acting in a way which will spoil this self-defeating game for him. (Remember that so-called "symptoms" are not perceived as "eruptions" but as tools which to the individual seem to be the most promising devices at his disposal to deal with life. To be sure, their disadvantages are frequently well-recognized, even publicized by the client himself, but he still maintains the behaviors as long as he perceives a slim margin of advantage to be derived from them. Of course the recognition of this advantage is frequently tantamount to its forfeiture. Thus, the right hand studiously avoids learning what the left hand is about.)

"Spitting in the soup" is an attempt to reduce a problem by undermining its utility in the eyes of the client. Consider the following instance of the maneuver:

The counselor had noted that the client, the oldest child in his family, had been born when his father was 50 years of age. When the counselor observed that he must have been really "special" to his parents the young man replied that when he was born, there had even been a special Christmas card devised in his honor. The way in which he reported this fact left little doubt that he had been the "Christ Child", in his family.

At the following session, the client said, "Guess you really hit it. . . Guess I should give up trying to be special. Is that what you are telling me?"

Counselor: Well, it's just that I'm against slavery.

Client: ?!

Counselor: You have to look so carefully at what others do in order to find out what you can permit yourself to do. You're tied to their movements. If they do something or want you to do something, then of course you *can't* do it even if you'd really like to.

By this means, the behavior which the client had previously employed to be *somebody,* bsomebody important, flaunting a rave banner of independence, proclaiming his dignity as someone who did what he pleased, plainly lost some of its savor to him. Now despite himself, his pleasure in it was seriously impaired since his actions had been reconstrued and might well have the opposite meaning.

"Spitting in the soup" may also involve "encouraging" a client to emphasize his symptoms even more. Adler sometimes called this ploy "antisuggestion."[2] He tells of an eleven-year old child who literally controlled her family with her refusal to go to school. Adler suggested "spitting in her soup," saying in a very friendly manner, "School is the most important thing in the world, and if I were you, I would make even a greater fuss about it (Adler, 1956, p. 398)."

Similarly Israel Goldiamond, an avowed behaviorist who is in many ways a "crypto-Adlerian," presents an excellent example of this technique:

An "autistic" child was terrorizing his parents in Goldiamond's office with mutilation. He dug away at his finger with a paperclip, elaborating a small lesion and smearing the blood about. Goldiamond then took a huge novelty paperclip from his desk, straightened it into a formidable weapon, and simply handed it to the boy as if to say, "Here, do a really good job." At this point the boy stopped his self-mutilation and burst into tears.

Rudolf Dreikurs was once leading a classroom discussion when a boy began pulling the hair of the girl in front of him. Dr. Dreikurs turned to the girl and said, "Do you want me to tell you why Johnny is pulling your hair?. . . Because he likes you." At that juncture, of course, you couldn't have

paid Johnny enough to persuade him to pull her hair. "Show that he liked a girl. Are you kidding? No, Sir!"

In the same vein the counselor can sometimes be helpful to "rebellious" clients by pointing out that they seldom have a chance to do what *they* want since they have to be constantly concerned with driving others up the wall. Similarly the counselor may comment on how strangely but nonetheless faithfully the revengeful client is devoted to the object of his vengeance, noting how he has greatly magnified the importance of his enemy by his "dedication" which has made him "someone."

A high school student had a vendetta going with a male teacher. The student maintained that he was innocent of any wrong-doing and that the teacher was constantly trying to provoke him. The counselor asked what it was that the teacher seemed to have in mind and the student replied that the teacher obviously wanted him to get into trouble.

The counselor looked at the student with astonishment. "How can you cooperate with such a guy?" he asked. "Cooperate with him?! I don't!" the student replied vehemently. "Ah, but you do. He wants you to get into trouble, to rise to the bait and you are careful not to disappoint him. You jump happily into his trap," the counselor said. "Obviously," he continued, "the teacher has your number, has you just where he wants you in his power." Imagine how disappointed "Teach" would be if the student didn't fall for his line. The student's behavior changed immediately and unmistakably.

On other occasions the counselor may want to insert a new bit of behavior in the client's repertoire, knowing that it is likely to be rewarded by the environment and retained if only the client can be induced to emit it in the first place. A technique closely related to those presented above can be of considerabe utility in such a situation. I call it "sweetening the pot." In employing this maneuver the counselor sets out to imbue the behavior in question with a meaning which makes it extremely difficult for the client to eschew it without experiencing considerable discomfort.

A young man was seething in his social isolation. He was estranged from his mother who frowned on any ties which he might have with any female other than herself. After long training, he could not bring himself to initiate friendships, particularly with girls though he came in contact with a number who interested him a good deal. Inevitably he would get cold feet just at the last moment before introducing himself or asking for a date. The counselor said in as colorful a manner as possible that whenever the young man succumbed to such fears, he might as well post a victory for his mother. He could justifiably visualize a giant smile of pleasure on his mother's face.

With this image before him, the client immediately went out and secured a date.

Avoiding the Tar Baby

If the foregoing approaches might be subsumed under the rubric, "Bre'r Rabbit's ploy" (you know, "Do anything to me, Bre'r Fox, just please, oh, please, don't throw me in the briar patch"), then another important tactic in counseling might be deemed "avoiding the client's Tar Baby," after another Uncle Remus tale. The Adlerian recognizes all too well that as self-defeating and incommodious as a particular *modus vivendi* or "identify" may be, it remains, in the eyes of the client, his best bet—and accordingly, he will defend it. As dismal as his set of expectations for himself in this world may be, they at least enable him to make sense out of the "blooming, buzzing confusion" and perhaps even entitle him to certain concessions. So, he will struggle to maintain their claim to validity.

Therefore, the client is continuously at work in an attempt to fit the counselor (along with everyone else) into his schema. It is, however, crucial that the counselor elude

the traps set for him and in so doing avoid confirming certain of the client's most cherished anticipations. Often the client will, like Bre'r Fox, provide the counselor with excellent opportunities to entrap himself while the client, in the mode of the fictional fox, "lays low." For example, some clients attempt to annoy the counselor in order to establish the validity of his thesis that he is an unlikable person ("See, even my counselor whose job it is to like all sorts of people, dislikes me."). Other clients will try to discourage the counselor in order to validate the hopelessness of their position or the wisdom of their decision to do nothing about it. In effect the counselor's sense of discouragement is used by such clients as license to curse the darkness and to avoid the unpleasantness involved in the attempt to generate any light by their own efforts. Yet other clients set others up to make decisions for them and then having botched them, promptly put the blame on their advisors.[3]

A high school drop-out who had been subjected to a good deal of counseling and therapy without result came to a new counselor. He said quite casually at the outset, "I suppose you want to ask me a bunch of questions about me?" The counselor who, in fact, had had some diagnostic procedures in mind demurred, "No, I don't want to pry. After all, you don't know me yet. So I don't feel it's right for me to do so. Let's get to know each other first." The counselor noticed that the client was carrying several books concerned with animal behavior. So, instead of launching into a psychological discourse of one sort or another for which the client was fully prepared, he engaged him in a spirited discussion of animal behavior, a topic which occupied portions of several more sessions and led gradually into a confrontation of a number of issues in the client's life.

The client was surprised at not being "psychologized." He had been forced to come to the counselor, but had expected to make short work of him by playing "psychiatrist" (as in Berne's games) after the fashion which had been so successful with his other "shrinks." The counselor's failure to play his "assigned" or "expected" role in the game left matters up for grabs. Unable to put the counselor in the pigeonhole which he had so carefully prepared for him, the client was left open for a productive relationship by means of which he returned to school, ultimately to graduate and go on to college.

Consider also the student who is at war with parents, with teachers, with the school and with society. He may well be eager to confirm his view of others as untrustworthy, predatory, and self-serving.[4] Thus, he may attempt to lure others, including the counselor, into some indiscretion. It is crucial for the counselor to disappoint these attempts, remaining, like Caesar's wife, "above reproach." But this assignment is by no means an easy one.[5]

A young man whose unhappiness clearly resulted from the fact that he had not been trained for cooperation, for social living, turned in upon himself and reaped the misery of isolation for his reward.

He handled his feelings of worthlessness by keeping a keen eye out for the foibles and failures of others. He argued that others were invariably hostile to him, that no matter how good he was to them, he garnered only distrust and maltreatment for his pains. As a result, he was clearly justified in shunning the world and in committing desultory small thefts.

The important task for the counselor was to *document* concretely how the young man provoked others into the responces which he expected, how he systematically discounted those experienced which contradicted his dismal model of human relations, labeling them "exceptions." At the same time, the counselor had to be wary lest he be considered yet another example of human perfidy.

Similarly, with the attention-seeker, the wise counselor is careful to attend only to those behaviors which are useful in character, declining the client's invitations to reward his "mischief" by attending assiduously to it. He will generally refuse to do battle with the discouraged client who seeks to gain a sense of self-worth by demon-

strating that he can overpower the counselor. He will be likewise wary of showing hurt to the client who wishes to revenge himself upon the world.[6] Neither will he be readily trapped into expressing disheartenment in regard to his attempts to help the client who has given up and seeks confirmation of his assertions that he is a "hopeless case."[7]

William Glasser (1965) provides an excellent example of this technique:

Glasser was treating a businessman who came to therapy in order to deal with the temptation which he felt to leave his family, abandon his career, and devote himself to the homosexual life. In his attempt to legitimize a homosexual resolution of his conflict, Fred (as Glasser calls him) would argue that he was basically homosexual. If indeed he had not been born that way, the traumas which earlier uncovering therapy had identified had created him in this manner. When Glasser refused to "certify" his "basic" homosexuality, Fred played one of his trump cards. He told Glasser that when he was 17 he had had sexual intercourse with his mother. But Glasser did not fall for this "tar baby." He did not cooperate by being shocked. Fred's intention seemed to be that of making an impact on the therapist in such a way as to convince him once and for all that his past was so distorted that normality was plainly out of the question for him, that he was entitled to succumb to the temptations of a life with fewer responsibilities.

Glasser, however, got therapy seriously underway by responding calmly, "So what? Is that what makes you queer today?" (pp. 151ff.)

The foregoing techniques are intended to interrupt the client's dismal cycle of discouragement. The aim is, on one hand, to interfere with behavior which contains the seeds of further disillusionment or, by altering its meaning to the client, to induce behavior with greater adaptive potential. On the other hand, the intent is to abort the client's self-defeating expectation-behavior-system by responding toin ways contrary to his expectations or script (Berne, 1969).

The Prime Mover: Encouragement

Since the client's underlying *discouragement* remains the principal villain in the piece as far as the Adlerian counselor is concerned, he quite naturally sees the counselor's principal task to be *encouragement.* Now encouragement does not mean reassurance, e.g., the insistence that one can certainly do whatever it is that needs doing, that everything will work out just fine in the long run, that there is nothing to be feared, that "God's in His Heaven and all's right with the world." Encouragement involves rather a convincing *demonstration* that the client has resources and options which he can bring to bear on significant issues in life.[8]

Indeed, the success of behavioral counseling and behavior modification may well lie in the fact that the "behaviorists" have concentrated on bringing powerful techniques for encouragement to bear on human difficulties. Consider, for example, Skinner's emphasis on "successive or progressive approximations." According to this strategy a person is brought along in a series of very small, easily-negotiable steps to the criterion performance. Since the steps are so readily surmounted, the person has a virtually continuous sense of success, of progress, which serves to propel him further.

Neither should one underestimate the encouraging properties of the behaviorist's own psychological "set." Typically he assumes that the client's difficulties arise from inappropriate bits of training and that these difficulties will be dissolved when the appropriate retraining has taken place. It is not the essential person which is deficient nor some malignancy at the core of his being which is culpable. It is not a deficiency in that nebulous and impalpable, yet pervasive entity, "the personality," which deserves attention, but rather a relatively circumscribed piece of behavior. Thus, the client need not conclude, "There is something wrong with me, with the person I am in the deepest recesses of my being." He can instead say to himself, "Some of the behavior which I picked up somewhere along the way has some real disadvantages. Consequently, it would be advantageous for me to replace it with some other behavior which has a more auspicious set of results."

What is more, many behavioral counselors conduct themselves in a manner which is most "encouraging" since it serves to disabuse the client of the belief that he is nothing but a victim or pawn of forces beyond his control. Far from confirming a narrow conception of man, so-called "operant conditioning with human beings often leads the individual to affirm his potentialities, his strengths, his responsibility for himself.[9] For the Adlerian this state of mind is a necessary ingredient of any attempt to solve personal problems. It is the very antithesis of discouragement.

The Relationship of Encouragement

Unlike Freud who saw the human relationship between client and counselor as a source of "contamination," Adler saw it as a crucial therapeutic tool. He spoke of the counselor's "material function." In his view, in the normal socialization process, the child's mother first wins the child's interest in herself. Subsequently this interest is transferred by the mother (or in Sullivan's terms, "the mothering one") to wider and wider segments of society. In cases of psychopathology, Adler maintained, this process has malfunctioned in one way or another. Consequently, the person possesses too little "social interest" to meet the various challenges and crises posed by life in a straightforward fashion and resorts to dubious maneuvers ("symptoms") to deal with them. The counselor's task then becomes that of establishing a viable connection between the client and society. In other words, the counselor must do belatedly what the client's "mothering one" accomplished to imperfectly.

The relationship is obviously an important tool in this attempt. By establishing a positive relationship with the client the counselor often quickens the client's natural but undeveloped interest in others. The relationship with the counselor may afford the client his first meaningful glimpse of the possibility of establishing cooperative relations with others and of the rewards which such arrangements can produce. In addition, the counselor's interest as a graphic suggestion to the client that he is is indeed someone of significance rather that the negative entity he fears himself to be.

The validity of Adler's observation is richly testified to by the research conducted by Carl R. Rogers, his colleagues, and students (cf. Truax and Carkhuff, 1965). This impressive body of findings between a good personal relationship of counselor and client and constructive change on the part of the latter.

At the same time, the data seem to support Adler's notion that the encouragement process requires something more than a good relationship. On the whole, the relationship variables (empathy, genuineness, and warmth) employed in these many studies account for less than half of the therapeutic effect noted (Truax and Carkhuff, 1965, p. 114; Allen and Whiteley, 1968, pp. 117-125). Clearly additional strategies of encouragement are required. The following case examples are intended to illustrate some of these strategies.

1. A small eight-year-old boy had found the transfer to a new school unappealing and had been (unwisely) allowed to do his work at home with the aid of a tutor. As time went on, he acted more, rather than less, "fearful of school." Indeed he resisted any attempt to induce him to conform with uncontainable fury.

His "fearfulness," or at least his resistance, extended to all manner of health care. So a crisis arose when an abcess in his tooth became a substantial threat to his well-being. Under the influence of the pain which the infection generated, he agreed to go to the dentist with his counselor. But when the moment to depart for the appointment arrived, he demurred.

The counselor's attempt at encouragement was not that of minimizing the event nor of issuing assurances (a specious form of "encouragement"). Neither did he attempt to cajole him with references to being a "big boy" and to the "fact" that big boys marched right into dentists' offices without hesitation (a not-too-subtle variety of condescension).

The counselor simply expressed his understanding of how the situation must look and feel to his dimunuitive client. He articulated as well as could his sense of the magnitude of the challenge the boy perceived.

There was no reply. Then the boy left the room with an air that suggested that his decision was irrevocable. But moments later he returned fully dressed and ready to go. The surgery turned out to be quite an ordeal. Nevertheless this volatile youngster who had not long before kicked a pediatrician in the shins and run from the building in the course of a routine physical examination bore it all with an unmistakable dignity.

The pride which he took in himself for having negotiated this gauntlet subsequently provided momentum for tackling other problems, such as returning to school.

2. A sixteen-year-old girl came into counseling as a runaway, a truant, and a desultory experimenter with a wide range of chemical substances. She had in fact made a trip to the emergency room of a general hospital as the result of an infelicitous melange of pharmaceuticals which she had injected and ingested.

Mother's attempt to help was, in the main, moralistic. She was indignant over the disgrace and difficulty which such behavior brought her. But Mother's main "contribution" was her extensive and vociferous worry. She waxed eloquent with doomsday prophesies in her effort to help. Such rantings were periodically punctuated with, on one hand, "hand washings" ("I give up. . . etc.") and, on the other, wistful odes to the virtues and accomplishments which would be her daughter's if only she would but turn her back on her evil ways.

It was, then, not surprising for the counselor to find himself confronted with a cynical girl thoroughly convinced of her own lack of worth. Indeed, her conviction was that she was so worthless that a fatal error in the use of drugs would be of little moment. She was, she insisted, well-advised to grab whatever excitement and pleasure was readily at hand since a person of her stripe could not expect very much of life in the long run.

In counseling interviews she was unable to come up with anything about herself which was positive in character. At last by listening carefully the counselor discerned that other kids tended to confide in her. She admitted that others seemed to find loyalty and circumspection in her, qualities which they themselves generally lacked. Mother, of course, saw these virtues as perversity, as collusion with a host of thoroughly depraved and marginly human beasts in a conspiracy against all that which was good in life. Encouragement consisted of a series of attempts to induce recognition of these characteristics as strengths, to help her see that mother's fulminations were in fact more a function of mother's feelings and foibles than of the client's basic depravity and to provide her with a relationship in which trust could flourish. Work with mother focused on her (mother's) feelings. The counselor expressed his understanding of her feelings and acknowledged her right to them while simultaneously attempting to help her see that their unmitigated expression tended only to lead to more difficulty for *her* since they merely served to provoke her daughter. These efforts yielded some appreciable positive consequences although the situation proved to be exceedingly difficult to resolve.

3. A late adolescent was quite depressed and having difficulty attending to her school work although she possessed considerable aptitude for it. She seemed to be hopelessly obsessed with all manner of trivial things. She pictured herself as being helpless, locked in the grip of titanic forces (traumas, drives, etc.) beyond her control.

Finally, the counselor commented on how adroitly the girl had maneuvered others—particularly her parents and various professionals—by being weak and defeated. The counselor marveled, quite honestly, at her skill in manipulating others and at the social skill implicit in this manipulation.

At first, she was thunderstruck, then, defensive, but literally minutes later she was struck by the discovery of unrecognized resources and the possibilities they offered. No longer need she wheedle others by being the helpless, bedeviled child. Anyone who was able to accomplish what she had, had resources to deal with people directly. Quite radical changes in her behavior were rapidly forthcoming.

4. A 13-year old boy was in constant trouble with school authorities and with civil authorities as well. On one occasion, after a family fight, he ran away from home. But the counselor learned from him that he had sneaked back that night in order to feed and care for his pet chickens. The counselor responded to this fact and to the positive response which he generally got from animals. The counselor further arranged situations where he could interact with animals and thereby provided effective opportunities for him to begin to construe himself in more positive terms—which had appreciable, i.e., beneficial, effects on his relations with other people.

5. A seventh grader made an obvious display of his failure to do his work in class and was ostentatiously slow in complying with the teacher's requests. For example,

Teacher: Please put that magazine away. It's time to get some of this work done.
Bill: OOO—KAY. (Making no move to do so.)
Teacher: Well. . .
Bill: OOO—KAY
Teacher: Please don't say that.
Bill: OOO—KAY
Teacher: I,m afraid I,m going to have to keep you for detention.

But days passed and Bill did not appear to serve his sentence. Since Bill's parents cared little or nothing about school or learning, they were no source of help. Finally, for some unfathomable reason Bill appeared for detention. But instead of working, he began to read an automobile magazine. Resisting the urge to respond to his provocation, the teacher expressed interest in the magazine. Bill then began to explain some of the technical aspects of automobiles in some details.

The teacher expressed genuine admiration for his knowledge which so dwarfed hers.

There was an immediate change in his behavior—for the better. Bill became much more pleasant in his classroom and much more cooperative. What is more, he beqan supporting the teacher's efforts at classroom management instead of exerting his influence in the opposite direction.

It should, perhaps, be emphasized in closing that the foregoing examples and some demonstrations to the contrary, "encouragement" is not always the result of a *tour de force* or *bon mot*, but of a continuous process of some duration. Nonetheless, "encouragement" is an extremely potent tool in human relations. Correctly understood and imaginatively implemented it can have far-reaching effects in a relatively short period of time.

This paper has not attempted to present an exhaustive account of "specific" techniques which Adlerians have found to be of considerable utility in counseling.[10] Its intent has been rather to introduce the reader to a mode of approaches to the problems which counselors confront. The key notion of Individual Psychology, socioteleoanalytic emphasis, which underscores the pivotal position of expectations in human behavior, will hopefully suggest a number of therapeutic possibilities to the counselor as he works with his own clients.

NOTES

1. Mark Twain clearly recognized the extent to which behavior could be modified by changing the meaning it has to the behaver. He illustrates the point graphically in the fence white-washing eipisode in *The Adventures of Tom Sawyer*. In another context, Twain wryly asserts that had God only bidden Adam and Eve to pursue Truth, it is likely that they would have eaten the snake rather than the apple.
2. Cf. Viktor Frankl's (1960) exposition of "paradoxical intention" and Jay Hayley's (1963) treatment of "therapeutic paradoxes."
3. Remember the definition of an expert which had been about for many years, "An expert is a guy who is called in when it is too late to share the blame."
4. Anyone who has worked with delinquents or adult offenders rapidly becomes aware of the eagerness with which they pursue evidence of malfeasance on the part of society.
5. The point is well made in a story which Dr. Bernard H. Shulman of Chicago tells,
   Two strangers were rooming together at a convention.
   First: Darn, I forgot my pajamas.
   Second: Don't worry. Here, I have an extra pair.
   First: Rats, I forgot my towel.
   Second: It's O.K. You can use mine.
   First: Now doesn't that beat all! I forgot my toothpaste.
   Second: You are welcome to use mine.
   First: I don't even have my toothbrush.
   Second: Well, it doesn't seem to be a very good idea for us to use the same toothbrush.
   First: See, I knew you had something against me!
6. Adler's principal biographer, Phyllis Bottome (1939), relates an incident concerning a demanding, spiteful patient who had taken to calling Adler at odd hours with trivial questions. Finally, she called at 3:00 a.m. to ask if oranges were good for her. Of course, she was simultaneously full of apologies, "I see it's very late; I'm afraid I must have disturbed you." Adler, who well knew that her chief aim was to disturb others, simply replied, "Oh, no! Why should you think that? I was expecting you to ring and have been sitting up for the last half hour close to the telephone!" This was the last time the lady resorted to the trick (Bottome, 1939, p. 92).
7. It must be recognized that the old saw, "Can't can't do anything," is in serious error. Adler observed that, in fact, many human beings conclude that they can do a good deal better in life once their incompetence has been duly certified. This conclusion is after all not without some basis. In many situations people are able to exert a substantial influence and control by means of their incompetence.
8. Rotter, whose "social learning theory" shares a good deal with Individual Psychology, puts a similar point in somewhat different language: ". . . one of the most important aspects of treatment . . . is to reinforce in the patient the expectancy that problems are solvable by looking for alternative solutions (1956, p. 342)."
9. In "behavior modification," the consequences of selecting among the various options open to the person are made a great deal clearer to the individual than is usually the case in life. Thus, such therapy may well be less a matter of "conditioning" than one of providing unambiguous choices in which the positive consequences are unequivocally weighted on the side of the alternative favored by the therapist.

Operant conditioning is not then to be considered a

mechanical process. Rather, it assumes the existence of such unmechanistic phenomena as *choice* and *anticipation*. The "behavior modifier" generally arranges the circumstances in such a manner as to provide the subject with an effective *enticement* to behave "more constructively." Unsurprisingly the subject tends to elect to behave in this fashion with the expectation of securing the relatively more congenial consequences as a result.

Thus, the behavior modifier—like the Adlerian—implicitly assumes that the individual can *choose* to pursue a different course of action, regardless of his present level of functioning. For example, Wagner and Paul (1970) present a typical example of behavior modification. These workers had appreciable success in bringing about a substantial decrease in the incontinence of chronic mental patients. They simply made the receipt of certain positively-valued objects and events contingent upon continent behavior across fixed time periods. In the face of such an arrangement, the patients altered their behavior in the desired direction.

Obviously in this experiment there was no retraining of the nervous system, no alteration of habit strengths, etc. The patients were simply provided with an effective *incentive* to behave differently. Although it had previously been assumed that they were too sick, too deteriorated, too "regressed" to control their excretory functions, when an appealing and readily attainable "pay off" was proffered they elected to employ their neglected ability to control themselves.

Pratt and Tooley (1970) make a similar point. They conceptualize operant behavior therapy as a "contractual negotiation and exchange process, including specification of conditions, choice, and reciprocal action- consequence sequences" (p. 367). These authors make reference to the use of operant "conditioning" with "autistic children." Such work involves a "structured series of contractual exchange events." It is a matter of "You give me that and I'll give you this; if you do that, I'll do this." Reciprocal expectancies are generated for child and 'therapist'—when the child gives or does (contingency behavior) he finds that he has a right to expect to get, or to get to do (reinforcing behavior or event). Both parties are reinforced—the child gets to play his game and to believe in his hypotheses through action confirmation."

10. Cf. also Adler (1964), Dreikurs (1967), Dreikurs *et al.* (1959), Mosak and Shulman (1963), Shulman (1968), Allen (1972).

REFERENCES

Adler, A. *The individual psychology of Alfred Adler.* Edited by H. L. and R. R. Ansbacher. New York: Basic Books; 1956.

———. *Superiority and social interest.* Edited by H. L. and R. R. Ansbacher. Evanston, Illinois: Northwestern University Press, 1964.

Allen, T. W. Commentaries In Calia, V. and Corsini, R. eds. *Critical incidents in school counseling.* 1972.

Allen, T. W. and Whiteley, J. M. *Dimensions of effective counseling.* Columbus, Ohio: Charles E. Merrill, 1968.

Berne, Eric. *Games people play.* New York: Grove Press, 1969.

Bottome, P. *Private worlds.* Boston: Houghton-Mifflin, 1939.

Dreikurs, R. Psychodynamics, psychotherapy, and counseling. Chicago: Alfred Adler Institute, 1967.

Dreikurs, R.; Corsini, R.; Lowe, R.; and Sonstegard, M. eds. Adlerian family counseling: A manual for counseling centers. Eugene, Oregon: University of Oregon, 1959.

Erickson, M. H. Special techniques of brief hypnotherapy. *Journal of Clinical and Experimental Hypnosis* 2 (1954):109-29.

Frankl, V. Paradoxical intention. *American Journal of Psychotherapy* 14 (1960):520-25.

Glasser, W. *Reality therapy.* New York: Harper & Row, 1965.

Hayley, J. *Strategies of psychotherapy.* New York: Grunee & Stratton, 1963.

Mosak, H. H. and Shulman, B. H. *Individual psychotherapy: A syllabus.* Chicago: Alfred Adler Institute, 1963.

Pratt, S. and Tooley, J. Toward a metataxonomy of human systems actualization the perspective of contract psychology. In A. R. Mahrer ed. *New approaches to personality classification.* New York: Columbia University, 1970, 349-80.

Rotter, J. *Social learning theory and clinical psychology.* Englewood Cliffs, N.J.: Prentice-Hall, 1956.

Shulman, B. H. *Essays in schizophrenia.* Baltimore: Williams & Wilkins, 1968.

Truax, C. and Carkhuff, R. *Toward Effective counseling and psychotherapy.* Chicago: Aldine, 1965.

Wagner, B. R. and Paul, G. L. Reduction of incontinence in chronic mental patients: A pilot project. *Journal of Behavior Therapy and Experimental Psychiatry* 1 (1970):29-38.

Wolpe, J. *The practice of behavior therapy.* New York: Pergamon Press, 1969.

13. REALITY THERAPY AND COUNSELING

William Glasser

Peter Schwarzburg

Reality Therapy is an effective method of psychiatric treatment for people's psychological problems. Although to date its principal applications have been in the treatment of office patients, mental hospital patients, and adult and juvenile lawbreakers, it has been practiced with some success in California schools, especially in the Sacramento area. It has the advantage that it can be taught in a relatively short period of time to teachers, administrators, school nurses, guidance counselors, and psychologists, whether or not they have any previous training in psychology. All that will be possible in this brief account will be a general description of the theory and practice but a book[1] is now available for those who wish to pursue this subject further.

The Theory

In order to understand the underlying theory we must assume that everyone has two constant psychological needs. First there is the need to love and to be loved, second there is the need for achievement or self-worth, the feeling that you are worthwhile as a person both to yourself and to others. In each instance these are two-way needs. It is not enough only to feel worthwhile to oneself or to feel worthwhile to other people; both aspects of worth must be satisfied. Similarly, to fulfill the need for love we need not only love others but also to have others love us. In order to satisfy the need to love, therefore, there must be at least one other person in this world we love and he or someone else must love us. Ordinarily, there are several people who love us and whom we love and, in the case of self-worth, the feeling that we are worthwhile to at least a few people, hopefully many.

With this in mind, what happens if we do not satisfactorily fulfill these two basic needs? Under these conditions we will suffer and our suffering will be manifested either directly, by causing others to suffer, or most often by a combination of these two common conditions. From a treatment standpoint, and Reality Therapy is treatment, it should be emphasized that the way we suffer when we are unable to fulfill our needs is relatively unimportant. In psychological or psychiatric terms, this suffering is manifested as the "symptoms" from which "diagnosis" of the person who has the problem is derived. For example, a person who is unable to fulfill his needs might become psychotic, that is he might withdraw from the real world and try to establish a world of his own, hoping that in his self-created world he might better fulfill his needs. All psychoses, which include schizophrenia, autism, dementia praecox, and other common, but meaningless, psychiatric terms, can be understood as the behavior and thought processes that reflect the suffering of a person unable to fulfill his needs. Why he becomes psychotic is yet unknown but it is a common and not illogical choice for people who are unable to fulfill their needs. In the elementary, junior and senior high schools and in college, we see many evidences of psychotic behavior but we must not be misled by the extremeness of this particular expression of the inability to fulfill one's needs. With this, as well as all other psychological problems, we must understand that psychosis was, or is, the best the person is able to do at the time, but that if we can help him to fulfill his needs, the psychotic behavior will disappear. Psychosis is only one of the many psychological results of inability to fulfill needs. Far more common than psychosis in the school situation are the acting out problems or character problems, exemplified by students who seem to have no regard for the rights and feelings of others or normal social values. They behave irrationally, erratically, and with hostility for seemingly unexplainable reasons. If we examine this behavior in terms of need fulfillment, however, we can discover that the purpose of their behavior is either to gain recognition or attention or is an angry reaction to their inability to gain recognition through socially acceptable pathways. Most often it is a combination of these conditions. Rather than withdraw into a psychosis, the child with character problems fights the world in an attempt to wrest his need fulfillment from it forcibly. The fact that his antisocial methods fail only causes him to increase his unsuccessful struggles; character and behavior problems therefore tend to intensify as the needs are more and more unsatisfied.

In addition to these two main psychiatric categories or ways in which people suffer, there are many neurotics, people who, unable to fulfill their needs, develop extreme anxiety about this inability. In an effort to free themselves from the anxiety they develop neurotic patterns of behavior—phobias, hysteria, obsessions, compulsions, hypochondriases—all examples of major neuroses. The last major group of people who suffer because they cannot fulfill their needs are those who either become severely depressed or have psychosomatic problems such as stomach ulcers, asthma, migraine headaches, or eczema. Although these kinds of suffering are indirect and difficult to understand, the depressed and psychosomatic sufferer uses these expressions to get attention, recognition and care, as well as to express hostility to the world because he is unable to fulfill his needs. Why one person chooses depression and psychosomatic illness, another psychosis, a third a behavior disorder, and a fourth neurotic behavior is not well known at present and, from the standpoint of Reality Therapy, is unimportant. What is important is to understand that none of these people is able to fulfill his needs. The form of suffering they exhibit,

whatever their symptom or diagnostic category, will disappear once we can help them fulfill their needs

Reality Therapy is a psychiatric treatment which attempts to solve this basic lack for those who are unsuccessful in fulfilling their needs, but it has been derived from careful observation of people who are essentially successful in fulfilling their needs. From this observation one important element has been found which is essential to need fulfillment—people. In order to fulfill our needs we always need someone whom we feel cares about us and thinks we are worthwhile. It is through this person and persons that we gain human involvement, closeness, psychological warmth and emotional ties which are necessary to fulfilling our needs. We assume, therefore, and this may seem to be a drastic assumption to some, that when the person is unable to fulfill his needs, when he is suffering in his own particular way, he does not have anyone close enough to him or involved enough with him emotionally so that he can fulfill his needs. Unless we, whatever our capacity may be, school teacher or psychiatrist, can provide this person, there will be no therapy.

It therefore follows that people who are unable to fulfill their needs and suffer psychologically are isolated, alienated, or separated from people at the time we become aware of their suffering. Further, we may assume that in the majority of cases this isolation from people has been going on for a long time. We will find in using Reality Therapy that intensive review of this misery, commonly referred to as the case history, is unnecessary. No matter how long the isolation has been, what is important to us as therapists is that the individual is isolated now. To help him fulfill his needs we must get enough peronally involved with him to break down his isolation. Whether the therapist is a **psychiatrist**, psychologist, social worker, school teacher, school psychologist, or administrator, he therefore must, fundamental to Reality Therapy as soon as possible get humanly involved with this suffering person. As limited as the therapist's time may be, he must develop a warm emotional involvement through which the person who is suffering can begin to feel "here is someone who cares enough about me so that I can begin to work toward the fulfillment of my needs, first through him and then through others."

Axiomatic to this process is the concept that the behavior which the suffering person exhibits is always unrealistic. He never engages reality in an adequate way but always distorts it, runs from it, escapes from a portion of it, or suffers at the hands of reality in a way which is always unrealistic. The job of the therapist therefore is not only to get involved with the person but to get involved with him in a way that he is able to present reality to the patient; only if the patient can learn to fulfill his needs within the bounds of reality will he successfully surmount his suffering. What we do is called Reality Therapy because the therapist's primary task, together with his involvement, is to be completely honest in every aspect of his relationship to the patient. Only through behaving within realistic social standards can the patient learn to fulfill his needs, and only after he fulfills his needs will he be able to be relieved of his suffering.

This brief discussion of the theory outlines the therapist's approach which we call Reality Therapy. Theory, however, is worthless unless it can be applied in a reproducible way to various problems. So far this theory has been used successfully in the treatment of adolescent delinquents in institutions, psychotic persons in mental hospitals, patients who come to a psychiatrist in private practice, and children in school situations by teachers, administrators, school nurses, and psychologists. As this theory becomes more well known it will be applicable to other problems, but its application has been successful enough so there is reason to believe it can be applied more widely in schools as one way to cope with the increasing number of school children who present serious problems.

Before explaining the specific application of this theory, I must emphasize that no theory will solve many specific and serious school problems. Children will continue to behave in ways which will baffle the best psychologists and psychiatrists and defy the most intensive work by classroom teachers and administrators. What needs to be established first, and has proven successful in institutions for delinquents and mental patients is a set of principles for working with pupils, principles which if applied through a school system will substantially reduce the number of children who manifest serious psychological problems. The writer therefore emphasizes Reality Therapy as a total approach to the whole school system as much or more than as a specific approach for problem children. If this is utilized, fewer requests will be made of the guidance counselor for individual help, freeing him to assist the classroom teacher in working out solutions for those children who require a more specific application of Reality Therapy to help them to fulfill their needs.

The Application of Reality Therapy—the Process

First and most important the teacher must attempt to get involved with his pupils so that they feel he genuinely cares about them. So that the child understands that his teacher cares, his principal cares, his nurse cares and others in the school really care about him, these people must be personal in their approach to him. This means that in their everyday dealings with children the personal "I" must be substituted for the impersonal "we," "they," "the school," or "It is good for you." As much as possible these impersonal phrases, should be eliminated from the school vocabulary. The teacher's approach should be, "I am interested in you," "I want to teach you," "I want to explain to you what you are doing," "I want to point out to you the things that you might do that are better," "I would like you to behave better for me," "I would like you to do your homework for me," "It is important to me that you are here every day." These phrases emphasize the personal; they lead to involvement with the child not only as a teacher but as a person who cares about him, who teaches him important things which he needs to know. With this personal approach there is the obvious danger that the teacher, who becomes personally involved as the writer has advocated here, can also be hurt much more than the teacher who remains objective and from the child's point of view, detached. Objectivity, a poor approach to any child, is useless with problem children. They have had too much objectivity. They need personal interest, an immediate involvement with someone so that they can begin to fulfill their needs. Without this, they are helpless to change their behavior.

Although subjectivity is essential in the process of relating to the child, the teacher must take an objective and realistic approach to the child's behavior. Without neglecting his personal interest in the child, the teacher must stress that he cares about what the child does, his school work and his conduct. The behavior of the child must be emphasized more than the child's feelings; the completion of homework, for example, is more important than the fact the child

may be upset. Reality Therapy emphasizes behavior and deemphasizes the feelings or emotions that accompany deviant behavior. Teachers should learn that they can do nothing directly to make a child happy unless they condone bad behavior which is unrealistic—short-lived at best. If the teacher believes that the child behaves badly because he is emotionally disturbed, and that first he must work with the child's feelings, he will fail. Instead he must show little interest in the child's emotional upset and guide his counseling toward behavior by saying, "What is important to me is what you do; if you feel badly, I can't help you but I do know that if you do better you will feel better." This statement, stressing the personal interest of the teacher and the reality of the child's behavior, is the backbone of Reality Therapy. We believe very firmly that bad behavior leads to bad feelings, and that bad feelings can best be corrected by better behavior. We have been unable to correct bad behavior by changing bad feelings into good feelings because we have never been able to do this even though it is a part of the psychiatry we learned. It just can't be done. Even if it could be done or if, as some may assume, this were a "chicken-and-egg" situation, we have been unable to help children unless the behavioral approach is used.

A further factor in the application of Reality Therapy (in practice these are all interwoven) is the necessity to accept the child as he is now, regardless of his past. In contrast to the teaching of most courses in guidance and counseling, as well as what is ordinarily taught in psychology and psychiatry, we believe that the patient's history, what has happened to him prior to our seeing him, is unimportant for therapy. The statement that our job is to help him, not to understand why he became the way he is, is not facetious. Why he becomes the way he is is important to sociologists and research psychologists who wish to change social patterns, but to help individuals fulfill their needs, the less we know about their history the better. If we can accept that he is doing the best he can do, regardless of how badly he is behaving, then we must accept him as he is. Reality Therapy therefore accepts the child as he is with the understanding that we believe that he can do better. Our emphasis is on what he is doing, on his behavior, and that better behavior will lead to better feelings and further better behavior.

Further, our acceptance of him does not mean we accept any excuse for present bad behavior. The child must understand that no one in the school, above all his teacher, will excuse him for doing something that is wrong. There must be no excuses for the child who disrupts the class, who doesn't do his homework, who doesn't come to school on time, who cuts school classes—any of the common behavior problems. With this approach consistently applied the child will learn that he can do better, that we are interested enough in him personally not to excuse or condone behavior which does not lead to need fulfillment. We never encourage him to look for the reason that he behaves the way he does. We are uninterested in discussing why he has not done his homework, why he disrupts the other children, why he fights, steals, lies, cheats or cuts school. On the other hand, we are extremely interested that we know and he knows what he is doing that is unsatisfactory. All of our discussions with him, brief as they may be, must point out to him what he is doing and ask, "How can this help you?" and "Do you feel that what you are doing is right?" Our job is not to look for excuses but to point out the reality of his behavior and further (this is essential to Reality Therapy) ask him to make a value judgment of his behavior in terms of right or wrong or good and bad.

In our work with patients, school children included, we emphasize the importance of right and wrong. In order to avoid confusion, however, we are careful to derive the definition of right and wrong from the basic needs. By this we mean that any behavior which leads to the fulfillment of the two basic needs, love and self-worth, is right, good, moral, or correct behavior. Any behavior which does not lead to the fulfillment of these basic needs—which necessarily must lead to separation from people, to lack of self-worth or self-demeaning behavior—we classify under the category of wrong behavior. The child must be helped to make this judgment himself (and we find he almost always can), to understand that when he does something right it benefits him because he fulfills his needs and he feels better. As we work with him, therefore, the child quickly discovers that we genuinely care about him and that our care is strong enough that we will not accept excuses for bad behavior. We care because we emphasize what he is doing now, that there are better courses open to him, that the behavior which is disrupting the class is irresponsible, unrealistic and, above all, that it is wrong. Further, he learns that we want to help him find better ways than he has been able to up to now.

Therefore, the last and the most important part of Reality Therapy is to make a plan through which the child can improve his behavior. This plan may take only a few seconds to evoke or it may take up to an hour (more than that is very unusual). The plan must always lead to behavior which will allow the pupil to get some recognition, to gain some satisfaction and to move toward a position where he is able to give and receive more love than before. A hypothetical plan for an elementary school child who is disrupting the class with bad behavior is to talk with him briefly, say that his behavior is not good and that he could do better, and then ask him to do something through which he gains an added sense of self-worth. For instance, he could become a playground monitor, take care of the classroom animals, wash off the blackboards or do any one of innumerable jobs around the school. More than this, to fulfill his need for love he might be asked to help direct other children to do these jobs. A simple plan carried out consistently over a period of time always succeeds in alleviating the less serious behavior disturbances. A more complex plan is necessary for more serious problems, but it usually can be worked out. The plan demonstrates that the teacher cares about him, doesn't accept the bad behavior, but is willing to help him toward doing something definite which will lead in the direction of the fulfillment of his needs.

For each child who fails to adjust, the teacher or the teacher and the administrator together must make some plan and then adhere rigidly to it. The plan always involves the nonacceptance of excuses and much positive reinforcement for what the person can do which is good. As emphasized in the beginning of this section, planning for children who are in serious difficulty in school is always difficult, and the best plan may not work as well once the child is in serious trouble as it might have earlier. We therefore feel it is important to apply these principles to the class situation from kindergarten to prevent serious problems later. Few plans are complex but putting them into action requires strength and a working knowledge of these principles. One public school, the Pershing Elementary School of the San Juan Unified District of suburban Sacramento, has attempted to utilize these concepts as part of a total school program. The following excerpt is contributed by Richard Hawes, Psychologist for the District.

Donald O'Donnell, Principal of the Pershing Elementary School and I were first introduced to Reality Theory during the early part of the 1963-64 school year. After consulting the school staff, we decided to try to apply the concepts to the Pershing Elementary School, and I also attempted to use these ideas in secondary school counseling. We wondered if the first phase of this therapeutic process, establishing personal relationships, would be possible in a classroom with thirty-five or more pupils and if the achievement of the first phase would actually minimize irresponsible behavior. We wondered whether we could develop specific techniques from these general principles which could be effectively applied in the typical school environment. We hoped to affect the classroom environment so that the pupils' ego development would be enhanced without distracting from the academic responsibilities of the school.

At this time (early 1965) the entire Pershing Staff is engaged in an experimental effort to improve their understanding of the concepts and to develop specific techniques within the classroom. Aside from encouraging an exciting experimental mood throughout the school, and of course, helping individual pupils, the most significant observation so far is the confidence and strength the individual teachers seem to be gaining as their ability to handle classroom behavior problems (which heretofore seemed impossible with the pupil's only hope lying in that elusive phantom—"outside professional help") improves.

Reality Therapy seems to offer a set of psychological concepts relatively conducive to application in the typical school situation by psychologically untrained people. It offers a way to operate with behavior problems immediately in the classroom or school situation. The process of establishing a personal relationship, not allowing irresponsible behavior, and learning new ways to operate or behave is designed to strengthen the function of the ego. As this process is applied by the teacher, it not only affects the pupil but also seems to strengthen the teacher's ego functioning significantly. Herein lies some of its greatest strength and potential. One of the Pershing teachers explained it this way when asked to comment on Reality Therapy: "It is hard to pin down isolated cases because the methods really changed my entire attitude and approach to discipline. It's impossible to isolate one event because one leads to another."

The first case concerns a ten-year-old fifth grade pupil who was originally referred to me as a candidate for the special education program for mentally retarded pupils because of consistently poor grades and his lack of production and participation in school. Surprisingly, individual testing showed that this healthy, well-built boy not only had bright-normal intelligence but had mastered the basic academic skills (reading, arithmetic, writing, etc.). His referral to the school psychologist was due to his attitude toward class assignments and almost total lack of achievement. He always seemed to find something else to do instead of the assigned class activity. The teacher's problem was to somehow get this reluctant pupil to experience that feeling of worthwhileness that comes with responsible achievement. This is how she did it: One day during class, Joe (as we will call him) was sitting sprawled at his desk tossing a paper clip into the air when he was supposed to be writing ten spelling words for his homework assignment. Mrs. B. approached Joe at his desk, placed her hand on his shoulder (the personal touch), and gently but with just the right amount of curiosity asked, "What are you doing?" Joe's reaction, and one we've experienced many times with this particular classroom technique, was bewilderment, mainly because teachers frequently say, "Stop doing that," or "Get going on your assignment," or "You'd better go to the principal, young man."[2] He did not know how to respond or what to say. At this time Mrs. B. encouraged him by saying something like: "Joe, tell me what you're doing? Describe it. Tell me and show me what you're doing—put it into words." To this Joe remarked, as he demonstrated tossing the paper clip, "Well, I'm throwing up the paper clip." To which Mrs. B. responded with an enthusiastic smile, "That's right, you are." Joe smiled spontaneously, and at this moment is demonstrated a very solid interpersonal experience which took no more time to transpire than some of the more typical procedures and remarks mentioned above which tend to discourage positive personal relationships and rob the pupil of the opportunity to accept and demonstrate individual responsibility.

At this point Mrs. B. simply asked: "Does it help you do the homework assignment?" Which was followed by Joe's equally simple response, "No." With that, Mrs. B. smiled knowingly at Joe, turned, and went on to another classroom activity leaving Joe with the decision to continue his paper clip tossing or to copy the list of ten words for his homework assignment. In Joe's case, as in many others where we have tried this particular technique, the results were encouraging. As the personal relationship between Joe and Mrs. B. became stronger through similar experiences, his irresponsible behavior began to disappear.

Throughout this episode, Joe was treated with dignity and respect as any person should be. The teacher felt he was worthwhile, and she expressed it by her actions. This not only fulfilled part of one of her basic psychological needs but also helped Joe fill his. A curious thing about this whole process is when one becomes more personally involved and consciously tries to make another feel worthwhile, it's very difficult not to feel more fulfilled yourself. This led another teacher to exclaim, as he became more involved in trying to apply these concepts to the classroom situation, "I don't know if these things I'm trying are doing the kids any good. . . (pause). . .Yes! I know it's helping them, but man, is it helping me!" This statement reflects the significant insight we have discovered through the application of reality concepts: One important way to help another is to help yourself in terms of ego fulfillment. Feeling worthwhile as a result of engaging in activities which encourage the development of one's own ego in turn puts you in a better position to help another less fortunate with a significantly weaker ego.

Another illustration comes from a high school in the San Juan District and deals with the typical situation of an extremely angry teacher who has had considerable trouble with the student he sent to the administrator. Jane, the student, has had a long-term problem of disrupting classes—usually talking—and not producing in class commensurate with her ability. Her parents are quite upset because she has received several failing notices, and they are pressing her to do better. She is not too happy with school and threatens to drop out when she gets old enough.

Instead of holding a counseling or lecture session to point out why the pupil shouldn't behave as she has (she has been told this a hundred times), Mr. T., the dean, asks, "What happened?" To which Jane replies vaguely. "Oh we just don't get along well." "I know that," Mr. T. says, "but what I want you to tell me now is exactly what happened this period. I want you to tell me what you did, and what you said, and what he did and said." Again, Jane answered vaguely. "Well, I made a little noise and he blew his top. . . "At this point, Mr. T. interrupted, "Hold it, Jane, that's not what I want. I want you to tell me exactly what you did and said, and exactly what R. (the teacher) did and said."

"Oh, you mean exactly?" Jane queried.

"Yes, exactly," was the reply from Mr. T.

Jane began, "Well, Mary and I were talking in class, making plans for a date when he (Mr. R.) yelled clear across the room to shut up." "What were his words, Jane?" Mr. T. interrupted. To which Jane mimicking Mr. R., replied: "All right you two, knock it off and get busy."

"What did you say?" asked Mr. T.

"O.K., already," Jane said with a rather sarcastic inflection and loud voice.

"And what did he say to that?"

"He said, 'all right, young lady, that's it for you. We're going to the dean!' "

At this point, Mr. T. (the dean) asks in a low-keyed and nonjudgmental way: "How do you feel it worked out?" (The manner in which this is said is critical. It must be said in a nonjudgmental or nonpunitive way. The main point is that you want the pupil to think critically about what happened.) To which Jane hesitates, then rather indignantly said, "O.K!" Mr. T. responds, "O.K. Have a seat in the outer office and I'll see you a little later." (It is important at this point that the dean does not argue with the pupil. This approach would tend to defeat the build-up of a personal relationship. Isolating Jane at this time gives her a chance to work it over in her own mind without outside interference. The previous short discussion should encourage her to think about the recent class episode.)

At the end of the period she is sent to her next class with the comment, "I enjoyed talking with you, Jane, and I want to talk with you again. I'll call you in a couple of days." In the meantime, the dean meets with the teacher in order to give him a chance to express himself about the pupil which, hopefully, will somewhat relieve the teacher's anxiety. The dean then calls Jane to his office and encourages discussion about anything except the situation which just occurred. The sole purpose is to establish a solid personal relationship and not to focus on the irresponsible act. This is sometimes very difficult for school people to do, especially administrators, counselors and teachers, who feel they need to express their power rather than allow the student to express his feelings. The assumption is, if we are able to successfully develop a personal relationship, the ir-

responsible behavior which caused the classroom disturbances will tend to disappear. (Assuming, of course, that the pupil has been the irresponsible one and not the teacher.) The sessions are kept brief (between 5 and 15 minutes) because time is a factor in our district when a counselor, for example, is responsible for 500 or more pupils. It is becoming our opinion that if one has an hour to spend with one pupil during one month in order to establish a personal relationship, it is usually better to spend it in six 10-minute or four 15-minute sessions over a period of time rather than one 1-hour session once a month.

We're particularly encouraged at Pershing School, where Daniel O'Donnell and his staff are attempting to learn and apply reality concepts throughout the school's entire environment. We're learning that it is not easy to do this, and that one successful application of the reality procedure does not necessarily guarantee general responsible behavior thereafter by a pupil. However, we are beginning to realize that each situation where these concepts are applied encourages later positive behavior better than the more traditional ways of handling these problems. Mr. O'Donnell put it well when he said, ". . . The process of establishing a personal relationship tends to eliminate the irresponsible behavior and, in the interim, seems to reinforce the teacher's ability to deal with the specific situation and help set the tone for the entire class. Our experiences to date show that teachers can deal effectively with individual pupils with these concepts if the teachers can withstand temporary setbacks of individual unresponsible behavior."

It remains a question of taking the time and effort to think of new techniques and the strength to put them into practice, even though immediate results are at times discouraging. We welcome inquiries from interested school personnel and would be glad to share our experiences was we learn more about this approach to working with people.

(For further explanation of applied Reality Therapy, see "Reality Therapy: A Realistic Approach to the Young Offender" in *Crime and Delinquency*, April, 1964.)

NOTES

1. *Reality Therapy—A New Approach to Psychiatry,* William Glasser, M.D.;

2. These responses by the teacher suggest that she has decided to exercise responsibility over the pupil rather than having the pupil accept and demonstrate responsibility for himself. The statements also do not encourage a positive personal relationship.

14. BEHAVIORAL GOALS FOR COUNSELING

John D. Krumboltz[1]

Peter Schwarzburg

I shall argue that stating the goals of counseling in terms of observable behavior will prove more useful than stating goals in terms of such inferred mental states as "self-understanding" and "self-acceptance." Self-understanding and self-acceptance are frequently listed among the goals of counseling although definitions of these terms lack precision. Let me make perfectly clear that I am not opposed to people having self-understanding and being self-accepting. Counselors who use these terms probably want the same kind of outcomes which I would want. But with terms as abstract as these, it is impossible to tell whether agreement exists and whether the goals are ever attained.

It is my contention that it would be far more useful to state the goals of counseling in terms of overt behavior changes. Ultimately counselors of all persuasions look to client behavior changes as justification for their procedures. Self-understanding and self-acceptance constitute intermediate mental states which some people assume make possible these ultimate modifications in behavior patterns. It is assumed that if clients can attain some degree of self-understanding and/or self-acceptance, they will be "freed" to change their overt behavior. Whether or not this assumption is justified is an empirical question, the evidence on which is discussed in Krumboltz (1966).

Disavowal of subjective states as goals of counseling is not new. Recently Brayfield (1962) argued that counseling psychologists had placed undue emphasis on egocentric self-regarding internal states and should instead use a performance criterion which would stress dependability, accountability, obligation and responsibility. Similarly, Samler (1962) cited three instances in which problems of prejudice, self-pity and poor workmanship were brought to the counselor. In each case, Samler argued, the important objective was that the client change his behavior in relevant ways whether or not his subjective feelings changed. Such logic finds a foundation in the concept of efficiency as advocated by Wishner (1955) and the concept of competence which was brilliantly developed by White (1959).

Why have objective statements of behavior change not already replaced subjective states as counseling objectives if they are superior? Subjective states are appealing because their very abstractness enables them to be interpreted to suit individual preferences. "Self-fulfillment" commands the same instant acceptance from some counselors as "patriotism" does from some politicians. It is only when attempts are made to specify concrete actions that dissension occurs. With abstract goals real differences between people may still exist but may not be discovered. The resulting harmony is reinforcing to many.

The fundamental obstacle to formulating behavioral objectives has been the assumption that we must write one list of objectives which applies to all counselees. It has been hoped that once we discover exactly what constitutes the "good life" we could analyze and list its elements as counseling objectives. Such attempts quickly bog down when it becomes apparent that what's good for GM is not good for MG. Hence, any list of behavioral objectives, if taken as desirable behavior for all clients, is justifiably vulnerable to criticism.

Criteria for Counseling Goals

Any set of goals for counseling should meet each of the following criteria:

1. *The goals of counseling should be capable of being stated differently for each*

individual client. One set of statements cannot apply to all clients. The unique feature of counseling is the individualization it provides. If we take seriously the assertion that each client is entitled to our respect as an individual, then we should be willing to work toward different goals with each of our clients. The common goals that our society holds for all individuals are partially met by the regular instructional program in our schools and colleges. Helping different individuals attain their different goals provides a unique opportunity for counselors to be of service. If this is true, there may be a virtually unlimited number of goals toward which counselors might help their clients strive. The goals of one client might be in direct contradiction to the goals of another client. For example, one client might wish to learn how to become more assertive in his social responses, while another might wish to learn how to become less assertive. A counselor could legitimately work with both of these clients, helping each one to achieve the particular type of behavior he desired.

2. *The goals of counseling for each client should be compatible with, though not necessarily identical to, the values of his counselor.* To use an extreme example, a boy who wanted help in becoming a more effective bank robber would find few counselors willing to help him attain that particular goal. However, if the boy indicated a desire to consider the possible consequences of a bank robbing career in relation to other career possibilities, then probably many more counselors would be willing to help him think through the alternatives.

This second criterion implies that each counselor has some responsibility for evaluating the particular goals of his clients. This is not to say that he would necessarily attempt to change the goals of his clients, but he must make a judgment of whether or not

he would be willing to help a client attain his particular goal. There might be goals acceptable to some counselors but not to others. For example, a client might ask a counselor for help in strengthening (or abandoning) his religious practices. It is quite conceivable that some counselors working in certain settings would be willing to help attain this goal while other counselors in different settings would not accept the assignment. The counselor's own interests, competencies and ethical standards should place limitations on what he is, and is not, willing to help his client accomplish (Krumboltz, 1965b).

3. *The degree to which the goals of counseling are attained by each client should be observable.* Some means must be available so that competent judges, regardless of their theoretical preferences, can agree that a particular goal has or has not been attained. This means that some overt indication of the client's behavior provides the basis for the judgment. Behavior, of course, is interpreted broadly to include any verbal or written statement, any responses that can be seen or heard, and any other responses that can be assessed reliably through some type of instrumentation.

Three Types of Behavioral Goals

There are three types of goals which meet the criteria listed above and which clearly fall within the scope of counselors' responsibilities. The three categories are not intended to be mutually exclusive or even all inclusive but may provide a convenient framework for organizing the tasks a counselor may accomplish.

Under each category illustrative examples of goals are listed. Clearly all possible goals of counseling can never be listed if we use the above criteria. Any type of behavior change desired by a client and agreed to by his counselor could be listed as an illustrative counseling goal.

1. *Altering Maladaptive Behavior.* Many clients are unhappy because they are engaging in a pattern of behavior which does not lead to the satisfactions they desire. Of course, many are not able to identify the maladaptive behavior pattern to the counselor, especially at first, but instead report their subjective feelings which result from the inappropriate behavior. For example, a client may report "I am lonely" while his typical behavior pattern is to spend all his spare time alone in his own room. Or if he spends time with other people, he may not have learned how to interact with them in a meaningful way.

In any event it is the counselor's job to help the client translate his problem into a behavioral goal that the client wants to attain and that the counselor believes will contribute to the welfare of his client. Considerable skill on the part of the counselor is required to make this translation. Listed below are some illustrative behavioral goals concerned with altering maladaptive behavior.

- Increasing socially assertive responses
- Decreasing socially assertive responses
- Increasing social skills necessary in meeting new people
- Decreasing fear repsonses to examinations
- Increasing ability to concentrate for longer periods of time on school work
- Decreasing the frequency of stealing
- Increasing participation in school activities
- Learning how to initiate social contacts with members of the opposite sex
- Learning to assume responsibility for a task and carry it through to completion
- Decreasing aggressive responses to smaller children
- Increasing aggressive responses to abusive peers
- Learning to respond calmly to hostile remarks

- Decreasing quarreling behavior with other members of the family
- Increasing ability to complete work on time
- Decreasing the frequency of reckless and fast driving
- Increasing the sharing of possessions with friends
- Decreasing excessive sharing with friends and acquaintances
- Increasing ability to say "no" to salesmen
- Increasing ability to return unsatisfactory articles to stores
- Decreasing threatening or violent behavior
- Learning to discriminate between insults and friendly teasing
- Decreasing weeping behavior in social situations
- Increasing ability to communicate with friends and acquaintances

2. *Learning the Decision Making Process.* Another major category of problems concerns decision making. Again the client may not present his problem as a behavioral goal in decision making but instead may simply indicate that a decision must be made, e.g., "What shall I do next year?" "Give me some tests that tell me what I'm good at." "I can't make up my mind between law and engineering." "I don't have the slightest idea of what I want to be." "Shall I get married now or wait until after graduation?"

Counselors seem universally agreed that they cannot provide ready-made solutions for such problems. Instead the counselor must help launch the client on a course of action that will increase the probability that the client will ultimately be satisfied with his own decision. His decision will probably be more satisfactory if he engages in some or all of the illustrative counseling goals listed below.

- Generating a list of all possible courses of action
- Gathering relevant information about each feasible alternative course of action

- Estimating the probability of success in each alternative on the basis of the experience of others and projections of current trends
- Considering the personal values which may be enhanced or diminished under each course of action
- Deliberating and weighing the facts, probable outcomes and values for each alternative
- Eliminating from consideration the least favorable courses of action
- Formulating a tentative plan of action subject to new developments and opportunities
- Generalizing the decision making process to future problems

3. *Preventing Problems.* The highest priority in the counseling profession should involve the prevention of problems. The development of a polio vaccine was far more beneficial than the treatment of persons who had already become victims of the disease. Similarly, developing educational programs that will prevent certain kinds of maladaptive behavior and inadequate decision making should deserve high priority. It is far easier to prevent a problem than to remedy it after it has occurred. Many of the problems that come to counselors need never have arisen if teachers had been more skillful, if parents had been wiser, and if administrators had established more effective programs. It is not necessary, desirable or helpful, however, to blame others for the problems that come to counselors. Instead counselors need to ask what they can do to prevent such problems from arising in the future.

The most valuable and ethical behavior of professional persons consists of eliminating the need for their own services. At the present time we do not know just what programs and systems would prove effective in reducing the incidence of misery, discouragement and waste. Research designed to explore new

possibilities should be encouraged. A few general examples may indicate the the direction these efforts might take.

- Developing a school marking system so that even the poorest student in each class can be encouraged by seeing the extent of his own progress
- Implementing a system of helping young men and women select compatible marriage partners
- Planning an educational program in child rearing techniques for parents
- Helping to construct a curriculum more useful and effective for the students in it
- Evaluating the effectiveness of preventive and remedial programs.

Consequences of Behavioral Statements of Counseling Goals

Why should stating goals behaviorally in this manner be more useful than stating internal mental states as goals? The consequences of shifting to a more behavioral orientation would be the following in my judgment.

1. *Counselors, clients and citizens could more clearly anticipate what the counseling process could, and could not, accomplish.* Counselors and clients would formulate tentative statements of desired behavior changes early in the counseling process. The very process of stating the goals in unambiguous language might have therapeutic effects. The clarification of goals would result in better public relations and public support. In the long run I can see no benefits from having a mystified clientele.

2. *Counseling psychology would become more integrated with the mainstream of psychological theory and research.* By conceiving of their professional problems as problems in behavior, counseling psychologists would be in a position to generate testable hypotheses from the research and theory in learning, perception, developmental and

social psychology. The testing of such extrapolations in counseling settings would have important implications for all of psychology.

3. *The search for new and more effective techniques of helping clients would be facilitated.* With a variety of possible counseling goals, it seems safe to assume that no one counseling procedure would be universally applicable. Work is just beginning on alternative approaches. I have discussed elsewhere some of the philosophic objections to certain experimental guidance procedures (Krumboltz, 1964). It would seem to me that the professional responsibility of each counselor is to seek whatever ethical methods most effectively and efficiently bring about the desired behavior changes. When we are clear on the behavioral goals we are trying to attain, when we have developed adequate procedures for assessing each goal, when our ingenuity has generated a number of alternative procedures which seem likely to attain each goal, then we can test and evaluate the effectiveness of each procedure and determine experimentally what methods produce which results best with what type of clients (Krumboltz, 1965a).

4. *Different criteria would have to be applied to different clients in assessing the success of counseling.* Outcomes would be evaluated in terms of the extent to which each individual had changed his own behavior in the desired direction. Investigators of counseling outcomes would not be able to state one single criterion (e.g., grade point average) which every client would be expected to increase. The reason that some evaluations of counseling have not produced more significant results may be that the criteria chosen were not equally appropriate for all members of the sample. For example, half the counseled students might have

wished to increase their assertive responses while the other half wished to become less assertive. Even if counseling were successful in every single case, the average "assertiveness score" of the experimental group would still be equal to the average "assertiveness score" of the control group. Unless some provision is made for taking into account the different goals of different clients, evaluations of counseling are likely to continue to produce negative results.

A precedent for considering the individual goals of clients has been provided by Pascal and Zax (1956). Although their study may be questioned on certain methodological grounds, it nevertheless makes an important contribution by showing how each subject's own goals and prior behavior can be the baseline for evaluating whether or not changes in the desired direction occur. Bijou (in press) has shown how this can be done by counting the frequency of responses in certain categories. Brayfield (1963) also stressed this point when, in anticipating the present article, he stated, ". . . it remains now for someone to suggest that the counselee set the goals and that evaluation be undertaken in that context" (p. 341).

Discussion

In discussing these ideas informally with groups of counselors, pychologists and counselor educators, a number of questions have arisen. I shall attempt to restate some of the most frequent questions and try to answer them.

I do not regard the views I have expressed here as any final commitment. Questions and comments from my colleagues have been most helpful to me in clarifying my own views, and I hope that continued questioning and discussing will lead us all to a progressive refinement of our notions as to what counselors should accomplish.

Question: Are you saying that counselors have been wrong all these years in stating goals of counseling like self-actualization, self-fulfillment, self-understanding and self-acceptance?

Answer: Not at all. These would be fine goals if each were accompanied by a list of illustrative behaviors to define what it might mean for different clients. These abstract goals are not wrong; they are just not as useful as more specific statements would be

Question: Don't people have feelings and isn't it important for counselors to be sensitive to these feelings?

Answer: Without doubt, people have feelings, and many have learned an extensive vocabulary for describing such feelings. I am not against people feeling they understand and accept themselves; I favor such feelings just as I favor people loving justice, truth and beauty. My point is that, stated as goals of counseling, such subjective feelings will not prove as useful as more objective statements of behavior. Being sensitive to the feelings of a client is certainly a necessary attribute for any counselor. That it is sufficient is questionable (Krumboltz, in press).

Question: But don't people act the way they do because of their feelings, insights and self-perceptions?

Answer: It seems more plausible that positive feelings are the by-product, not the cause, of competent behavior and the rewards it brings. As Hobbs (1962, p. 742) puts it,

> It seems to me that the traditional formulation of the relationship between self-understanding and effective behavior may be backwards. I suggest that insight is not a cause of change but a possible result of change. It is not a source of therapeutic gain but one among a number of possible consequences of gain.

Hense, if we succeed in helping people to act more competently, they will receive more positive feedback from their friends, relatives and employers; then their feelings about themselves will improve as a matter of course.

Question: What would be done about the large number of clients who come to the counselor reporting feelings of dissatisfaction and unhappiness but having no idea about what behavior they could change?

Answer: The possible causes of unhappiness are infinite. An understanding listener is all some people require. Others need help in formulating and implementing plans. The counselor's job is to help the client formulate more concrete goals and take appropriate action.

Question: Aren't behavioral goals pretty superficial? Don't they imply habitual action without comprehension? Wouldn't we be overlooking permanent personality changes? Aren't there some things we can't observe or measure that are nevertheless very important? Don't "self-understanding" and "self-acceptance" really imply much more than can be expressed in words?

Answer: These questions deserve more of an answer than space permits. Undoubtedly, many complicated behavior patterns have not yet been categorized and described, but an affirmative reply to these questions would imply that we should give up without trying.

To those who say there is "something more" than behavior (defined broadly) I would ask these questions: (a) Can you point to any individual who exhibits the "something more" trait? (b) Can you point to any individual who fails to exhibit this trait? (c) What does the first individual do or say differently than the second individual under what circumstances that leads you to conclude that he possesses the "something more" trait? (d) Why don't we list what he does or says under which circumstances as another possible behavior goal?

The task of stating behavioral goals is hard work and the job has scarcely begun. But only when our goals are clearly stated and communicated will we be able to engage in the service and experimentation which will ultimately benefit clients, counselors and citizens alike.

Received August 17, 1965.

REFERENCES

Bijou, S. W. Implications of behavioral science for counseling and guidance. In J. D. Krumboltz ed. *Revolution in counseling: implications of behavioral science.* Boston: Houghton Mifflin, in press.

Brayfield, A. H. Counseling psychology. In P. R. Farnsworth, Olga McNemar, and Q.

McNemar eds. *Annual review of psychology.*
Vol. 14. Palo Alto, Calif.: Annual Reviews,
1963. Pp. 319-50.

———. Performance is the thing. *J. counsel.
Psychol.,* 9 (1962):3

Hobbs, N. Sources of gain in psychotherapy.
Amer. Psychologist, 17 (1962):741-47.

Krumboltz, J. D. The agenda for counseling. *J.
counsel. Psychol.,* 12 (1965):226. (a)

———. Behavioral counseling: rationale and
research. *Personnel guid. J.,* 44 (1965):383-87.
(b)

———. Parable of the good counselor. *Personnel
guid. J.,,* 43 (1964):118-24

———. Promoting adaptive behavior: new
answers to familiar questions. In J. D. Krumboltz ed. *Revolution in counseling: implications of behavioral science.* Boston: Houghton
Mifflin, in press.

———. *Stating the goals of counseling.*
Monograph published by the California
Counseling and Guidance Association, 1966.

Pascal, G. R., and Zax, M. Psychotherapeutics:
success or failure. *J. consult. Psychol.,* 23
(1956):325-31.

Samler, J. An examination of client strength and
counselor responsibility. *J. counsel. Psychol.,* 9
(1962):5-ll.

White, R. W. Motivation reconsidered: the concept of competence. *Psychol. Rev.,* 66
(1959):297-333.

Wishner, J. A concept of efficiency in
psychological health and in psychopathology,
Psychol. Rev. 62 (1955):69-80.

NOTES

1. For helpful comments and suggestions on a
   preliminary draft of this manuscript, I am indebted
   to W. H. Cowley, Helen B. Krumboltz, Eleanore B.
   Luckey, H. B. McDaniel, David V. Tiedeman, D.
   Gilbert Wrenn and the graduate students in counseling. at Stanford University. The views expressed
   are, of course, my own and do not necessarily reflect the views of those named here.

EXTINCTION AND TIMEOUT: GUIDELINES FOR THEIR SELECTION AND USE

Robert B. Benoit
G. Roy Mayer

Peter Schwarzburg

This paper focuses on the use of extinction and "timeout" as classroom behavior modification techniques, examining whether or not the counselor should suggest the use of one of them in a given situation and how to insure its maximal effectiveness once one has been chosen as an appropriate procedure. The authors present some questions to be considered when deciding whether or not to use extinction or timeout and give guidelines for their best use. The questions and guidelines are presented in a flow chart in order to facilitate easy and quick use by practitioners.

This paper is an expansion of two articles: Benoit, R. B. and Mayer, G. R. Extinction: Guidelines for its selection and use. *Personnel and Guidance Journal,* 52 (1974):290-95.

There are a number of "reductive" techniques which counselor-counsultants can recommend to teachers for dealing with student behavior problems. We will explore the differential use such behavioral techniques: extinction and timeout. Too often, these procedures have been recommended without due regard to the conditions and circumstances which ultimately determine their functional appropriateness.

This article attempts to (a) give counselors who consult with teachers a guide for determining the appropriateness of using either extinction or timeout in a given classroom situation and (b) discuss how extinction and timeout can be applied with maximal effectiveness. Flow charts are presented, along with an explanatory text, which should serve as a rapid, systematic guide for counselors who recommend the use of these procedures as an approach to changing behavior.

Extinction Defined

Extinction is a procedure that involves the withholding of reinforcement following the occurrence of a specific behavior. Behavior that has been "put on extinction" gradually becomes weakened over time. If extinction is used with maximal effectiveness, the behavior virtually disappears from an individual's repertoire.

Considerations in Selecting Extinction

Let's take the following hypothetical case. Mrs. Jones, a third grade classroom teacher, has begun working with Bernie in a program designed to strengthen his "good" behavior of increasing the number of arithmetic papers he completes. She decided to attempt this project because of the success she has had in using a behavioral approach with Erica. In Erica's case, the goal had been to decrease the number of times she talked out during class without raising her hand. The counselor had advised Mrs. Jones to ignore Erica's outbursts and attend to her only when she had her hand up. It was a little trying at first, but now, after a couple of weeks of consistently following the counselor's advice, Mrs. Jones is observing that Erica only occasionally blurts out without waiting her turn. Flushed with the success of such an effective procedure, Mrs. Jones has decided to take on the big one: "Bad-News Bernie."

Bernie, while having a history of being a "disruptive" child has nevertheless reported that he likes school. His assignment completion program has been showing favorable results during this first day of the program. However, as Mrs. Jones turns to help another child, the sound of a wet paper ball whisking through the air tells her that Bernie is up to his old tricks.

Emphasize the positive, ignore the negative, the counselor had advised. It worked before, let's try it again.

There goes another wet one. Harry is returning Bernie's fire. The other children are giggling with glee. Johnny just threw one at Norma—Johnny? He hardly ever does anything like that! Mrs. Jones is choking with embarrassment and anger but is determined to follow the rules and "rise above" this chaotic scene. But not only is Bernie becoming more and more obstreperous, other children are starting to act up too. It worked with Erica, why hasn't it worked with Bernie? Something has gone wrong. What?

The flowchart in figure 1 is designed to help answer these questions and provide guidance as to alternative measures that might have been taken. It is assumed that all professionals involved will proceed in the use of this flowchart in accordance with established codes of ethics.

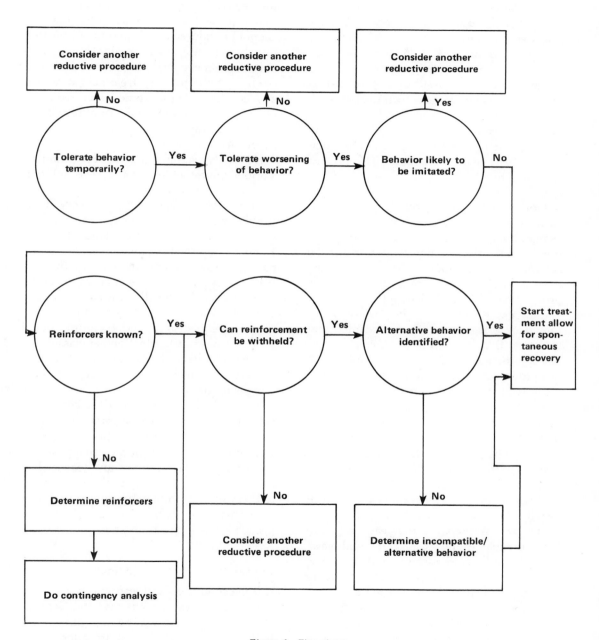

Figure 1. Flowchart.

Can the behavior be tolerated temporarily? Anyone using extinction must be prepared to put up with the identified behavior awhile longer. One must ask, "Can this behavior be tolerated temporarily?"

To answer this question it is helpful to know the present rate at which the behavior is actually occurring, unless, of course, the behavior is so objectionable—Mike is hitting Joe over the head with a baseball bat—that any occurrence is intolerable. The present rate can be determined by recording the specific instances or duration of the behavior's occurrence over prespecified periods of time (Patterson, 1971; Sulzer and Mayer, 1972). These data provide an objective basis for determining wheer or not the behavior can be endured for at least a few more days. If it cannot, some other reductive procedure should be considered.

Can an increase in the behavior be tolerated? It has been well documented that behavior that has been reinforced in the past, particularly on certain schedules, will tend to occur with even greater frequency when reinforcement is abruptly withdrawn. The use of extinction may result in the behavior actually getting worse before it gets better.

Erica, who is on extinction for talking out, may temporarily go so far as to yell a few times in order to gain attention. The shock of such a temporary "getting worse" can usually be borne, particularly when the counselor has prepared the teacher to anticipate such an increase. But "Bad-News Bernie" and his spitballs are another matter. An increase in such behavior probably couldn't be tolerated by most teachers.

Frequently, when teachers are advised to "reward good" behavior and "ignore bad" behavior, they do not realize that they may be asking for trouble when they attempt to ignore a blatantly "disruptive" behavior. If

the behavior in question is of such a nature that its present rate or an increase in that rate cannot be endured over a period of time (hitting, biting, etc.), the counselor should probably recommend that the teacher reject extinction as the primary treatment of choice and consider instead some other reductive technique (Krumboltz and Krumboltz, 1972; Sulzer and Mayer, 1972), as indicated on the flowchart.

Is the behavior likely to be imitated? Various investigations have revealed that certain behaviors, particularly those commonly labeled "aggressive," are very likely to be imitated by students who observe them—particularly male students—even when an observed behavior receives no apparent reward. If the students see that the behavior is rewarded, the chances for imitation are even greater (Bandura and Walters, 1963). Erica's behavior does not fall into the "aggressive" category and therefore would probably have little effect on her classmates. On the other hand, imitation is what appears to have happened in Bernie's case, with bedlam the result.

The problem lies not with the technique of extinction but in its inappropriate use. Mrs. Jones' attempt to overlook Bernie's actions was simply an inappropriate attempt to use extinction. If the counselor and teacher had followed the flowchart up to this point, surely their answers to the questions posed on it would have led them to use a different approach in working with Bernie.

Considerations in Using Extinction

If the conditions and restrictions described above have been met, the next step is to assure that extinction will be used effectively. If the following guidelines are adhered to, the effectiveness of the extinction procedure will be enhanced.

Are the reinforcers known? Extinction's apparent simplicity has led to its being inaccurately interpreted as "ignoring" a given response. This easy interpretation overlooks the fact that frequently adult attention is only one of several sources of reinforcement—particularly in the case of "disruptive" behavior. Some of the most common reinforcers for "disruptive" behavior reported in the literature are: teacher's attention, teacher's critical comments (Becker, 1971), attention of classmates, and avoidance or escape from a boring assignment (Reynolds, 1968).

Before extinction can be effectively applied, all possible reinforcers must be identified. Ignoring behavior, while perhaps effective in individual counseling, will not be very effective in the classroom if the behavior is being simultaneously reinforced by other students.

How does one identify reinforcers? Procedures for identifying both reinforcers and behavioral antecedents are described in detail elsewhere (Goodwin, 1969; Sulzer and Mayer, 1972). Briefly, a common approach is contingency analysis. (A form for this purpose is available from the authors.) This method usually entails analysis of (a) the prior events and conditions under which the behavior of concern and the goal behavior occur and (b) the consequences that ensue for each. It is therefore helpful for the counselor and teacher to hypothesize just what environmental antecedents and consequences are contributing to the occurrence or nonoccurrence of an individual's behavior. Reinforcers for Erica might include getting teacher attention, getting teacher approval, and giving correct answers. For Bernie, reinforcers might include getting teacher attention, getting peer attention, and escaping from undesirable schoolwork.

Can reinforcement be withheld? Iden-

tification of all possible reinforcers of a behavior is a necessary but not a sufficient step in using extinction effectively. Often through a contingency analysis it is discovered that the attention of classmates (giggles, looks, smiles—even disapproval) is a reinforcing event for a particular student. Is the teacher in a position to withhold this reinforcer of peer attention? Perhaps. Perhaps not. In any event, it may not be feasible to attempt to use extinction unless control of the reinforcers has been established. It may be necessary to develop novel and creative ways to withhold reinforcement if the reinforcement is not routinely under the control of the teacher.

There are studies in the literature (Barrish, Saunders and Wolf, 1969; Coleman, 1970) that describe attempts to solve this particular sort of problem. In the case of classmate attention as a reinforcer, arrangements may be made to reinforce peers for ignoring the behavior that is being extinguished. Another method reported is that of rewarding the entire group when the student acts in a manner that is incompatible with the way he or she has previously been acting. In any case, if extinction is to be used with maximal effectiveness, all reinforcers must be identified and consistently withheld.

Have alternative behaviors been identified? If all the questions posed on the flowchart up to this point have been satisfactorily resolved, extinction can be considered a feasible approach. However, it is unwise to use extinction—or any other reductive technique—without also making provision for positively reinforcing behavior that is incompatible with or alternative to the behavior to be weakened. There are two basic reasons for this important step.

First, extinction, while not necessarily negative, is definitely not positive. Identifying alternative behaviors or behaviors incompatible with the undesired behavior generally indicates that a positive component has been added to the treatment program. This strengthens behavior that will bring Erica or Bernie positive feedback from the environment. If adult attention is a reinforcing event, a restructuring of the individuals' environment provides this attention as a consequence of self-enhancing rather than self-defeating behavior. Calling on Erica only when she raises her hand makes her a contributing member of the group and teaches her the social skill of giving others an equal chance to be heard.

Second, reinforcing competing behaviors speeds up the slow process of extinction. Erica cannot be interrupting and at the same time waiting her turn. The competing response tends to interfere with, weaken, and replace the undesired one, thereby hastening extinction.

Institute treatment procedure. The last step on the flowchart is to institute the treatment procedure. Before suggesting that the teacher do so, however, the counselor must make sure that the teacher is aware of each of the questions posed on the flowchart. The teacher must be informed that the effects of this procedure will be gradual and that the youngster may "get worse" before "getting better." The teacher must also be made aware of the fact that not all behaviors should be put on extinction: Aggressive behavior tends to be imitated by classmates when placed on extinction. If such information had been communicated to Mrs. Jones, she probably would not have misused the approach.

Once extinction has been selected, the teacher must be encouraged to present many different reinforcers following a demonstration of the behavior to be strengthened and to withhold all reinforcers following a demonstration of the behavior to be weakened. Even with all the prior preparation,

this may be difficult to do at first, since old habits are sometimes difficult to break. If, however, the counselor and teacher have carefully chosen the behavior to be reduced, have identified the reinforcers and brought them under control, and have arranged for positive reinforcement of competing behaviors, the program should be successful.

The teacher should also be informed of one additional factor: the possibility of spontaneous recovery. After a behavior has apparently been extinguished, it may suddenly reappear. The counselor must tell the teacher this and encourage the teacher to maintain the extinction treatment throughout this brief reappearance phase if eventual success is to be assured.

Once the extinction program has been implemented, the counselor should reinforce the teacher's use of the approach by checking back with the teacher and informing him or her of the progress being made (Mayer, 1972). It is often helpful to monitor and graph the student's behavior. For, as Mayer, (1973) has noted, "When the teacher . . . can see from a graph that the procedure is bringing about the desired change, (the teacher is), in essence, reinforced (p. 165)." Such an approach is usually helpful, since often during the early phases of a behavior change program a small change may be overlooked and the treatment program dropped prematurely. Never, then, should counselors tell a teacher simply to "ignore" the undesired behavior of a student.

The counselor-consultant, realizing he should have communicated a great deal more information to Mrs. Jones, wisely decides to develop a flow chart for an alternate reductive procedure: time-out.

Time-out Defined

Time-out involves *removing access* to the sources of reinforcement for a limited time period contingent on a particular action. Detailed explanations of time-out are available in several publications (Krumboltz and Krumboltz, 1972; Sulzer and Mayer, 1972). The chief difference between extinction and time-out is that in extinction reinforcement is withheld for a particular behavior, while in time-out the student is denied access to all sources of reinforcement through either transferring the student to a nonreinforcing situation or removing the source of reinforcement from the present situation.

Considerations in Selecting and Using Time-out

Let us return to Bernie, his teacher (T), and the counselor-consultant (C-C). The counselor has explained to Mrs. Jones why extinction was not effective in reducing spit-ball throwing (which was imitated by classmates) and has developed a time-out flow chart which he has in his possession.

C-C: Mrs. Jones, Bernie will be better served if we can use an approach that will immediately stop his disruption of the class. We can do this by removing him temporarily.

T: Oh, you mean send him to the office. I've tried that. It doesn't work.

C-C: I know, and I think I can tell you why. I happened to see Bernie on a day you sent him to the office. Let's look at the second question on our flowhart.

Is a nonreinforcing place available? C-C: When I witnessed Bernie's ejection, I decided to watch what he would do. As he headed for the office, the friendly custodian stopped him and joked with him about going to the office so often. Then Bernie met Ziggy, who was just returning from banishment to the office, and they exchanged bubble gum cards. Then Ms. Shortskirt, the secretary, gave him a warm welcome and sat him down

right by her chair. Need I mention the heart-to-heart chat with the principal? Mrs. Jones, all the other kids were working while Bernie was having a ball!

T: So?

C-C: So we need a nonreinforcing place—a quiet spot that doesn't serve as an inadvertent "reward" for disrupting the class. You might say we need a blah place where Bernie will be, shall we say, temporarily neutralized. It isn't punishing, but it isn't fun either. It serves the function of removing Bernie from the reinforcing consequences of his behavior. It gives him a chance to cool off.

T: Oh, I see. Sending him to the office could be fun for him and act as an incentive to misbehave.

C-C: Very possible. Do you have a quiet place available?

T: Yes, in one corner of the room. I can remove several posters and some play materials and convert it into a very bland cool-off place.

C-C: Great, Mrs. Jones! Any place will be fine, as long as it effectively serves to remove Bernie from the source of the reinforcing consequences of his disrupting the class. For example, some teachers use the cloakroom area, others partition off a section in the rear of the room. In some cases it's enough to have the youngster simply put his or her head down on the desk. With other children it has been necessary to find a small, empty room. For Bernie, your idea should work very well.

T: Sounds easy and simple. But so did ignoring. Is there anything else on that flow chart I should know about?

C-C: Very much so. Tell me, Mrs. Jones, does Bernie enjoy being in your class?

T: Yes. He likes school, by and large. Seldom misses a day. He seems to enjoy his assignments, and he has many friends in class.

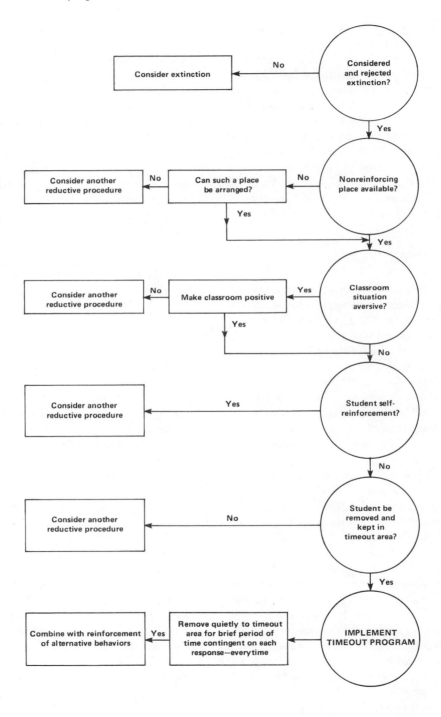

C-C: Good. Look at the next question on the flow chart.

Is the classroom situation aversive? C-C: It's important that Bernie likes being in your class. What do you think might happen if he disliked your class and got sent out of it when he was disruptive?

T: He might continue to be disruptive in order to escape. I could be playing into his hands without being aware of it.

C-C: That's right. Behavior that produces escape from something unpleasant is likely to occur again, even though it may be a self-defeating kind of thing to do in the long run.

T: Now that you point these things out, I can think of any number of children I have seen who have been repeatedly sent out—to the office, outside in the hall, and so on. The more they were sent out, the worse they became. None of us could figure it out. It didn't seem logical. I can see now, though, that these children may have had fun where they went or may have gotten out of a situation they found to be distressing. Maybe some of us need to take a look at how interesting it is to be in our classes.

C-C: Could be. Why do you think the teachers kept doing it even though the youngsters got worse?

T: Good question! Aha—because removing those children permitted the teachers to escape temporarily from the situation, or get rid of the irritating behaviors.

C-C: Wouldn't be surprised. But back to Bernie. How would you describe his personality in general terms?

T: Oh gregarious, extroverted, active, realistic.

C-C: Does he sit and stare out the window? Daydream, things like that?

T: Very seldom, if ever, he's too busy shooting paper wads.

C-C: Good. Let's look at the flow chart again.

Does the student engage in self-reinforcement? C-C: Some children tend to seek out opportunities to engage in self-stimulation, by doing such things as daydreaming, masturbating, and so on. The "in" terminology now is "self-stim." Were Bernie to be this type of youngster, we again might be providing reinforcement rather than nonreinforcement if we were to use time-out.

T: I think we're okay on that count. How do I go about this? What's the best way to signal time-out to Bernie?

C-C: Before we get to how you actually go about signaling time-out, let me ask one more question. Is there any chance Bernie will openly resist leaving for the time-out area?

Can the student be removed and kept in time-out area? T: Do you mean by saying, "I won't go?" or just refusing to get out of his seat?

C-C: Exactly. Because if he is likely to act that way, time-out becomes a very questionable intervention strategy.

T: I can't completely rule that out, but I really doubt that Bernie would go that far. In looking at the flow chart, I notice it also asks whether or not he'll stay there. While Bernie is a spirited youngster, he is not an angry child or a child who is completely out of control. He won't be too thrilled, but I'm sure he will do as I request and remain there until I signal him to come back.

C-C: Okay, but Bernie's a pretty big boy for his age. If you think he might resist you physically, better forget time-out.

T: He's large all right, but in the past when I've sent him out or given him other directions, he's gone along. He isn't happy to do so, but he goes along.

Implement time-out program. C-C: Good. We're ready, then, to discuss how you actually go about using time-out. First of all, be sure to sit down with Bernie in advance and calmly explain to him that his present behavior isn't doing him, you, or the class any good and that from now on you will simply give him the chance to wind down when he seems to be wound up. Explain that you will ask him to leave the area for a time and sit quietly in the time-out area.

T: Should I say anything to him?

C-C: Say as little as possible. Don't jaw at him, whatever you do. Your talking could be reinforcing, as you probably already suspect.

T: Indeed. Anything else?

C-C: Yes. Be sure to remove him every time the behavior occurs, and keep the time-out period short.

T: How short?

C-C: Generally five to fifteen minutes is about right if he hasn't experienced a longer time-out duration in the past. If time-out is to work, you must keep him in time-out at least as long as his recent average previous experiences.

T: No problem. All I've ever done is send him to the office, which I now realize wasn't really time-out.

C-C: Be sure you don't forget about him and leave him for too long a time.

T: Okay.

C-C: One last but very important matter. Any so-called reductive technique carries with it the possibility, if not probability, of negative emotional side effects, such as aggressive acts and attempts to escape. Also, time-out may communicate what Bernie shouldn't do, but in itself it doesn't communicate what he should do. In connection with learning not to disrupt, Bernie needs to learn alternative, constructive ways to deal with others and meet his needs. We need a program to strengthen constructive ways of living as well. The technical term is "reinforcing incompatible behavior." Since Bernie does have friends and likes school, he must act effectively at times.

T: To be sure. He does complete a certain number of assignments, and he enjoys sharing time in the morning.

C-C: Good! Try to be aware of and keep track of when Bernie is getting along, and reward him in some way. I've noticed that he really responds well to your attention. A glance, a gesture, or a friendly word works wonders for him. Attend to him when he is working whenever you can.

T: I will be sure to do that. When you and I meet again, perhaps you could help me with that aspect. For now this seems clear, and I believe it will be helpful. Thank you for your time.

C-C: Thank you for your interest in Bernie's welfare and your willingness to try various ways to help. And thanks for not giving up on me when you found that extinction didn't work for Bernie.

Discussion and Conclusions

Unlike extinction, time-out brings about rapid results, and thus the teacher is quickly reinforced for using it. This can be both an advantage and a disadvantage. It is an advantage because the counselor does not have to reinforce the teacher frequently for continuing to use the approach, as the counselor does in extinction. It is a disadvantage because some teachers find it so reinforcing that they begin using time-out for very minor infractions for which extinction would be a much better treatment procedure. Thus, the counselor must help teachers to understand and change this phenomenon, as the counselor did in our illustration.

Time-out is a more aversive contingency then extinction. It also involves placing the student in an environment away from the classroom teacher and therefore possibly causing the student to miss out on important classroom instruction. This is not a problem with extinction. Time-out is thus a procedure that should be considered only after extinction has been determined to be unsatisfactory.

Many approaches, techniques, and materials are available for the counselor. To be effective, the counselor must use a variety of these. Time-out and extinction are drawn from the behavioral technology. They are but two of many available behavioral procedures that can be used to reduce undesired behavior (Sulzer and Mayer, 1972). The guidelines set forth here have been presented for the counselor to use in determining whether extinction or time-out is appropriate for reducing a classroom behavioral problem and, if so, how to insure its respective maximal effectiveness.

REFERENCES

Benoit, R. B. and Mayer, G. R. Extinction: guidelines for its selection and use. *The Personnel and Guidance Journal* 52 (1974):290-95.

Briskin, A. S. and Anderson, D. M. Students as contingency managers. *Elementary School Guidance and Counseling* 7 (1973):262-68.

Krumboltz, J. D. and Krumboltz, H. B. *Changing children's behavior* Englewood Cliffs, New Jersey: Prentice-Hall, Inc., 1972.

Mayer, G. R. Behavioral consulting: using behavior modification procedures in the consulting relationship. *Elementary School Guidance and Counseling* 7 (1972):114-19.

Sulzer, B. and Mayer, G. R. *Behavior modification procedures for school personnel.* Hinsdale, Illinois: Dryden Press, 1972.

Sulzer, B.; Mayer, G. R.; Cody, J. J. Assisting teachers with managing classroom behavioral problems. *Elementary School Guidance and Counseling* 3 (1968):40-48.

DESENSITIZATION TECHNIQUES IN THE TREATMENT OF SCHOOL PHOBIA *

William P. Garvey and Jack R. Hegrenes

Peter Schwarzburg

A child's fear of school was eliminated by having him approach the school accompanied by the therapist and by proceeding in a series of graded steps from the least anxiety-evoking stimulus situation to the most powerful fear stimulus. After 20 consecutive treatments the child resumed a normal school routine with no return of the symptoms noted during a two-year follow-up period.

*The authors wish to express their appreciation to Dr. Frederick H. Kanfer for reading the manuscript and offering valuable suggestions.

190

A learning theory approach to psychopathology postulates that neurotic symptoms are learned maladaptive patterns of behavior, and that treatment consists of eliminating the maladaptive response (symptom). Eysenck[4] emphatically states:

> Get rid of the symptoms and you have eliminated the neurosis.

Indeed, many articles have reported success with methods using inhibition and extinction for removal of a variety of neurotic symptoms.[4][12] Phobias have been particularly amenable to this kind of treatment. Recently, Patterson[8] has described the successful treatment of a case of school phobia by operant conditioning techniques in a clinic setting. After 23 twenty-minute conditioning sessions over a six-week period, a seven-year-old boy was able to return to school.

The present article deals with a case of school phobia that first was treated for six months in a traditional psychotherapeutic situation. After a summer vacation, however, the child was still unable to return to school. At this point, a desensitization procedure, based on learning theory principles, was introduced and proved successful in removing the phobia. This paper will consider how the child acquired the phobia, based on the interview material during the six-month traditional treatment and how the phobia was eliminated, within the framework of learning theory.

Case History

Jimmy, 10, was referred to the child guidance clinic because he was unable to go to school. A month prior to the referral he had suffered a bronchial infection, following which the Christmas holiday season occurred. After that, the youngster refused to return to school, in spite of efforts by the parents, the teacher and the principal. The patient stated that when he thought about going to school in the morning he became frightened and often vomited. His previous school attendance record was excellent, as was his school work performance. Jimmy was described as being high strung, sensitive and preoccupied with high level performance. As therapy progressed, secondary problems began to arise, consisting of avoidance of friends and peers. Apparently, Jimmy could not find adequate excuses for being out of school, and as his friends telephoned or visited the home, he became quite anxious and finally refused any contact with peers at all. The patient indicated that he did not feel that he could assert himself and that he did not feel as worthwhile as his brother or sister.

The patient described many arguments at home involving everyone in the family. He indicated that he would not be overly concerned if his father moved out of the house, but if his mother left, it would be quite different. "If she goes, the whole family would fade away. We would have to go to another home. . . If it did happen, it would be horrible. I wouldn't know what would happen to myself or anyone else. The family would be just all messed up, and I'd go crazy." This concern about losing his mother was evidenced at other times; for example, the patient also stated that if his mother went to the store, he often imagined that she might get hit by a car. Or even when mother took him to the store with her, Jimmy would stay in the car and begin to think that there might be a robbery and that she might get shot. Other factors that seemed related to his concerns were: (1) Jimmy got lost as a small child and remembered how terribly frightened he was; (2) five years previously when his mother was working he had worried a good deal about her; (3) his mother often used the phrase: "Some day I'll be dead, and you'll wish you had me. You'll want help, and I won't be there." And, in referring to school, she often said, "One of these days when you get home, I won't be here."

After approximately six months of therapy, shortly before school was to start, the patient indicated that he was nervous about trying to go back to school but indicated that he felt "bigger" than he had felt six months previously. He also stated that he felt he knew himself better and felt more confident. There appeared to be a good relationship between Jimmy and the therapist. On the day he was to return to school, the patient could not take the step out of the home, and again he panicked.

Description of the Desensitization Procedure

The desensitization procedure in this case was carried out in the school environment. The school officials were informed of the procedure, and they cooperated fully with the therapist. Jimmy was told that each day the therapist would accompany him to school and that together they would approach the school gradually. Since it was known that he could tolerate going by the school in a car, the first step consisted of Jimmy and the therapist sitting in the car in front of the school. The other steps were as follows: (2) getting out of the car and aproaching the curb; (3) going to the sidewalk; (4) going to the bottom of the steps of the school; (5) going to the top of the steps; (6) going to the door; (7) entering the school; (8) approaching the classroom a certain distance each day down the hall; (9) entering the classroom; (10) being present in the classroom with the teacher; (11) being present in the classroom with the teacher and one or two classmates; (12) being present in the classroom with a full class. This procedure was carried out over 20 consecutive days, including Saturdays and Sundays. The amount of time spent each day ranged between 20 and 40 minutes and involved about 10 to 12 hours of the therapist's time.

The therapist and Jimmy began by coming to school early in the morning when no one else was present. Jimmy was told to report any uncomfortable feelings he was experiencing, and when he reported that he was feeling afraid, the therapist immediately indicated that it was time to return to the car and generously praised Jimmy for what he had accomplished. On several days the patient did not go beyond the previous day's achievement and was asked to remain at that point for a longer period of time. When Jimmy finally entered the classroom, he reported that he was very anxious when the children began to come into the schoolyard. On the following days, the teacher and one or two students came into the classroom while Jimmy was there (deliberately arranged), but when it came time for school to start officially, he reported that he felt more anxious so that it was necessary to leave before the children came to the classroom. On the nineteenth day, after Jimmy had been in the classroom with the teacher and two students for several days, the therapist pointed out to Jimmy that he was no longer afraid of school, since he was now able to immerse himself completely in the school environment. The therapist added that he was going to withdraw from the situation. On the next day, the twentieth in the desensitization procedure, it was arranged for the father to take the patient to school and talk with the principal. This was done with ease, and the principal decided that it would be sufficient for Jimmy to do his schoolwork in the principal's office. Later that same day, mistakenly thinking that the patient's classroom was empty, the principal brought him to the classroom. Through the glass window Jimmy could see that the students were in the room. Very unexpectedly, he opened the door and walked into the room. When he saw that another youngster was occupying the desk to which he had been assigned, the patient politely told the youngster that he was in his seat. Since that time Jimmy has remained in school, and a two-year follow-up has indicated that there have been no subsequent manifestations of the phobia.

Discussion

Acquisition of the Phobia. It is of interest to speculate briefly in learning theory terms about how Jimmy acquired his fear of school, although this analysis is *post hoc* and based only on clues gathered during the interviews with the patient. There is evidence that Jimmy had an intense fear of losing his mother, illustrated by his fantasies about the various kinds of harms that could happen to her and by his fantasies about what would happen to the family if his mother were to leave. In addition, Jimmy's mother, who was herself disturbed, frequently reinforced these fears by telling him:

Some day I'll be dead, and you'll wish you had me. You'll want help, and I won't be there.

Thus, "losing mother," which can be conveyed verbally in various ways, was a danger signal eliciting a fear response. (More precisely, a danger signal elicits certain responses from which the presence of fear may be inferred. These responses, which were not directly observed in this study, are usually thought to be physiological, for example, changes in heart rate, galvanic skin response, etc.) When this danger signal was repeatedly paired with a neutral stimulus such as school (as the mother often did by telling Jimmy that, "One of these days when you come home from school I won't be here"), "school" eventually became a conditioned stimulus capable of eliciting conditioned responses, namely, the physiological responses associated with "loss of mother" and consequently fear. Finally, when this fear became too intense, Jimmy refused to go to school. Two immediate consequences probably followed. First, by staying home his fears were diminished, and since fear reduction is thought to be reinforcing, the avoidance response (not going to school) was strengthened. Second, there were probably many positive reinforcements in the home environment (such as toys to play with, more freedom than in school) that also strengthened the school avoidance response. In this way Jimmy remained fearful of school and continued to refuse to leave home in the morning.

Elimination of the Phobia. The desensitization process employed in removing the patient's phobia is based on the principle of counterconditioning; namely, if a strong response which is incompatible with an anxiety reaction can be made to occur in the presence of anxiety-evoking cues, the incompatible response will become attached to these cues, so that the anxiety response will become weakened or eliminated. This method first was employed by Jones,(6) who extinguished the fear of rabbits in a small child by using feeding responses in the presence of the feared animal. Wolpe(12) makes use of relaxation responses which are inhibitory of anxiety. An anxiety hierarchy is constructed, and the patient, having been hypnotized and given relaxation suggestions, begins imagining weak anxiety-evoking stimuli. Gradually, the patient imagines stronger stimulus situations eliciting anxiety so that eventually relaxation responses become attached to all of the anxiety-evoking stimuli in the hierarchy, and extinction occurs. The method carried out by the authors is similar to that carried out by Wolpe, except that the procedure was carried out in the presence of the anxiety-provoking situation. In the case of Jimmy two responses were inhibitory of anxiety. First, since Jimmy and the therapist had a good relationship, the presence of the therapist may be considered as a relatively strong stimulus evoking a positive affective response in the patient (Shoben(9)). As a consequence, because there was reduced anxiety in the presence of the fear stimulus, instead of an avoidance response, Jimmy was able to make an approach response which was reinforced by the therapist with strong praise.

As described in a previous section, the desensitization process initiated with weak anxiety-provoking cues, proceeding to stronger ones. This is based on the principle of stimulus generalization which states that the conditioned response is evoked by other stimuli that are similar to the original stimulus, but that as these stimuli become less similar or further removed from the original stimuli, the response becomes weaker. Thus, the curb in front of the school, a cue which evoked mild fear in the patient, was presented in the presence of the therapist. The stimulus value of the therapist in evoking positive affective responses was stronger than the stimulus value of the curb in producing mild anxiety responses. Therefore, the stimulus "curb" became attached to the positive affective responses evoked by the stimulus "therapist" so that the anxiety response became inhibited and eventually extinguished. When this occurred it became possible to proceed to the next stronger cue. Twenty treatments based on this desensitization procedure were able to rid the patient of his neurotic symptoms, whereas traditional psychotherapy for several months was unsuccessful in this regard.

One of the crucial aspects to be considered in this analysis is the relative strength of the anxiety-provoking situation and the stimulus situation which produces incompatible responses with that anxiety. Thus, in the present case, just how strong a positive stimulus the therapist was in comparison to the cues in the school situation that evoked anxiety was unknown. It was felt, however, that it would have been impossible for the therapist to bring the patient directly into the classroom. If the child had been forced, it seems likely that a reverse kind of conditioning would have occurred, that is, the fear response would have become attached to the therapist. Solomon and Wynne(10) point out that Jones ran the risk of producing neurotic inhibition of eating in her procedure; actually this is probably what often happens when a child is forced to go to school. He reacts negatively, and the people

who try to get him into the school become anxiety-producing cues through a classical conditioning process. Therefore, in the beginning, a cue weak in evoking anxiety is paired with a cue strong in evoking a positive response, and the stronger anxiety-evoking cues are approached gradually.

Further Comments. It is suggested that the view presented here is parsimonious in relating the method of treatment to the theory explaining the development of psychopathology. In contrast, other viewpoints do not seem as consistent. Psychoanalytic theory(2),(7),(11) for example, postulates that the phobia stems from the repressed anxiety arising out of the child's fear of separation from the mother. Treatment, therefore, is necessarily of long duration, because it consists of bringing into consciousness the repressed fears centering about the mother-child relationship. Yet, many psychoanalytically inclined authors advocate quick return of the child to school as a first step in treatment. If therapy consists of uncovering a neurosis, however, is it logically possible to expect the child to be able to return to school (thus eliminating his symptoms) before the neurosis which caused the symptoms is removed?

A ten-year follow-up study of school phobic children(1) treated by traditional psychotherapeutic methods indicates that the majority of such children, although they have returned to school, seem arrested in emotional development. Out of 47 children, 13 were considered to have no limitations, 20 were considered to have moderate limitations and 14 were considered to have severe limitations in their emotional life. These results cast some doubt concerning the success of traditional psychotherapy in most cases beyond that of removing the phobic symptom.

Is it not more economical, then, to employ methods aimed at treating symptoms, if this is all that can be reasonably accomplished, than to engage in psychotherapy over long periods of time and at great expense? The authors know of another case which was treated at their recommendation by desensitization methods, by having a public health nurse accompany the child part-way to school each morning. Although this child had been out of school at irregular intervals during a three-year period, he was able to return to school within two weeks after this procedure was initiated.

The authors suggest that cases of school phobia can be treated relatively quickly and economically by methods based on learning theory principles. When using desensitization procedures, one creates a situation in which a different set of responses may be learned in the presence of the anxiety-evoking cues. It is first necessary to identify what stimuli evoke fear in the patient (these will vary in each case; for example, Jimmy was able to go within a half block of the school by himself, whereas the child in the second case was able to go only one or two blocks from his house by himself). With this information a program of gradual approach to the classroom may be initiated, with care taken never to push the child along too rapidly and by rewarding him at each step along the way. While the child should be accompanied by an adult with whom he feels comforable, apparently, the adult need not be someone the child has known for a long time nor a therapist, as illustrated by the use of the public health nurse in the second case. (Of course, the program should be under the direction of a qualified therapist familiar with learning theory principles.)

Attempting to eliminate only the symptoms may seem superficial to many, but Eisenberg(3) has emphasized the importance and value of this achievement:

It is essential that the paralyzing force of the school phobia on the child's whole life be recognized. The symptom itself serves to isolate him from normal experience and makes further psychological growth almost impossible. If we do no more than check this central symptom, we have none the less done a great deal.

Finally, Grossberg,(5) having reviewed the literature in the area of behavior therapy, concludes that:

. . . the overwhelming evidence . . . is that therapy directed at elimination of maladapted behavior ("symptoms") is successful and long lasting.

REFERENCES

1. Coolidge, J. C., R. D. Brodie and B. Feeney. 1964. A ten-year follow-up study of sixty-six school phobic children. Amer. J. Orthopsychiat. 34(4):675-84.
2. Coolidge, J. C., P. B. Hahn and A. L. Peck. 1957. School phobia: Neurotic crisis or way of life. Amer. 27(2):296-306.
3. Eisenberg, L. 1958. School phobia: a study in the communication of anxiety. Amer. J. Psychiat. 114(8):712-18.
4. Eysenck, H. J., ed. 1960. Behavior Therapy and the Neuroses. Pergamon Press, New York.
5. Grossberg, J. M. 1964. Behavior Therapy: a review. Psychological Bull. 62:73-88.
6. Jones, M. C. 1924. The elimination of children's fears. J. Experiment. Psychol. 7:383-90.
7. Klein, E. 1945. The reluctance to go to school. In Psychoanalytic Study of the Child. Volk International Universities Press, New York. Pp. 263-79.
8. Patterson, G. 1964. A learning theory approach to the treatment of the school phobic child. Mimeographed paper.
9. Shoben, E. J., Jr. 1949. Psychotherapy as a problem in learning theory. Psychologic. Bull. 46:366-92.
10. Solomon, R. L., and L. C. Wynne. 1954. Traumatic avoidance of learning: the principle of anxiety conservation and partial irreversibility. Psychologic. Rev. 61:353-85.
11. Sperling, M. 1961. Analytic first aid in school phobias. The Psychoanal. Quart. 30: 504-18.
12. Wolpe, J. 1958. Psychotherapy by Reciprocal Inhibition. Stanford University Press, Stanford, California.

15. TRANSACTIONAL ANALYSIS FOR NON-TA COUNSELORS

John Mellecker

Peter Schwarzburg

Is Transactional Analysis (TA) for You?

If you are the kind of counselor who wants to help people straighten out their manner of thinking and living, who isn't content to just help people know more about themselves, then TA counseling may be for you.

If, on the other hand, you wish to stay with another counseling modality but are willing to consider using TA as a conceptual system, you will probably find ways to use TA to substantially enhance your comprehension of the complex of factors that cause your counselees to think and function as they do. TA can give you rewarding techniques for graphing characterizations of your counselees which can serve as baselines or charting progress as it occurs. As counselees' life histories unfold, you will be able to determine methodically which early developmental factors contribute most heavily to presently observed distress and behaviors.

TA as a Conceptual System

As a conceptual system, TA is a comprehensive logic of human functioning set on a firm psychoanalytic base by its originator, Eric Berne (1964, 1971). As such, TA not only characterizes thinking and behavior in terms of social appropriateness, but also in terms of developmental antecedents.

The TA conceptual system permits classification of the functioning of the ego through structural analysis; of the historical development of attitudes, thought processes, and behavioral decisions through life script analysis; and of destructive behaviors and social transaction deficiencies through transactional analysis. Each subsystem of analysis is performed discretely but simultaneously with the others. Graphic representations permit establishment of baselines against which progress can be charted.

The TA conceptual system can be utilized while the counselor functions in client-centered, Adlerian, reality, or many other counseling modalities.

TA as a Directive Counseling Modality

As a counseling modality, TA seeks to retrain counselees into heightened awareness of how they function and behave, and why. The goal is appropriateness of social participation guided by a reality-testing intrapsychic process freed from archaic and foreign elements.

What Types of Counselees May Be Expected to Seek and Respond Well to TA Counseling?

Obviously, people who didn't get "straight" messages as children may be expected to ultimately appreciate working with a counselor and fellow counselees (in a TA group) who show high respect for frankness. Then, too, many people appear to be drawn to TA to learn more about themselves, and in some instances to try to learn self-control so as to attempt change.

What Types of Counselors May Prefer to Work in the TA Modality?

Counselors who wish to be involved in the way counselees actually live their lives, who are willing to take responsibility for aiding counselees in evolving a sense of what is real while discarding foreign elements as interferents, and who are capable of such dramatic qualities as may aid counselees in recreating old scenes from the past. The TA counselor is said to need to be *potent* in refusing to accede to seduction and game playing, and in standing up to the retained images of powerful but archaic figures of the developmental past; *permissive* in telling counselees to go ahead and think and do the thoughts and things they have known all along they should be thinking and doing to live appropriately; and *protective* when counselees feel the terror and confusion often associated with any substantial change.

Will This Chapter Describe TA in Detail?

No. The purpose of this chapter is to familiarize readers with what TA can do for counselors and their counselees. To understand the full meaning of TA, one should read certain of the literature as indicated at the end of this chapter, as a start.

Is TA Similar in Any Ways to the Freudian Modalities?

TA is consistent in many ways with its Freudian derivation, particularly in relating all present-day difficulties back to the developmental past. But TA does not become preoccupied with transferences and countertransferences, with oral and oedipal stages of regression.

How Are Some of the Ways TA Diverges from the Freudian Modalities?

For one thing, TA parallels and in its present stage of development encompasses some of Frederick S. Perls' Gestalt Therapy theory, with specific reference to behavior being based on consciously arrived-at decisions. Furthermore, that thought processes are behaviors, and are therefore alterable when original (archaic) decisions are remade.

Another difference lies in the TA policy that each counseling step must be preceded by the making of a "contract" between counselor and counselee, which on one level is a subtle way of training people to themselves make the important decisions about their lives. On another level, placing the matter of

whether to go ahead squarely up to the counselee is a way the counselor protects himself or herself from implications that the counseling is being forced on the counselee. Often, the counselor attaches the condition to his participation in the contract, that the counselee define in advance what advantage might ensue from the joint "work"—the implication being, why do it unless it will be of value to the counselee. Because TA counseling sessions are tape recorded in entirety, contracts as well as all other aspects are readily recallable.

How Does TA Deal with Resistance?

In the TA setting, resistance often is expressed in the negotiations over "contracts," and in the transactions and gamey behaviors observed in TA groups. The TA counselor respects the counselee's right to wait until the time is right before engaging in "work." On the other hand if resistance manifests itself in such acting-out behaviors as disturbing or destructive games or even the possibility of such, the TA counselor firmly stipulates that such behaviors are not permitted and emphasizes this through the potency of his leadership of the TA group.

Counselees assigned to the counselor through some organization such as a school or the police may find the TA approach acceptable in that the counselor is free to begin where the counselor is: with a transactional problem. (Mary Abu-Saba, 1975).

Does TA Assume There Is an "Unconscious?"

Of course. Except that the unconscious is regarded as being available to conscious processes at the beckoning of the so-called "child" ego state; anything that the child decides it can safely produce (for a reason, of course) will be made conscious. Some of the experimental work lending validity to the hypothesis of recall was reported by the neurosurgeon Penfield (1952) who electrostimulated the temporal cortex of subjects awake and able to discuss their recall imagery which was complete with original feelings and colors to one year or so of age!

Why Does TA Place So Much Emphasis on the Ego?

TA is solidly based on the structure and functioning of the ego (as is Gestalt therapy). Through the combined TA/Gestalt focus of the TA counselor, the functioning of the ego may be improved so as to provide a base for the focus made also on social transactions.

How Does TA Define the Structure of the Ego?

This is of crucial importance to anyone attempting to gain understanding of TA, or in making use of it in counseling or as a counselee. Berne (1961), impressed by the postulations of Federn (1952) as to the archeopsyche, neopsyche, and exteropsyche; and the work of Penfield (1952) previously mentioned, made observations that concluded in the presence of *three ego states* which he named: *parent* (value system/anurturing function), *adult* (computer function/reality), and *child* (real self/creative self/relic of past/center for angry, crazy, acting out behavior/center for scared feelings/center for intuition). Berne's ego states are now accepted as existing one at a time, even for a fraction of a second. People, even children, can become accurate ego state identifiers.

The first step of any prospective counseling relationship is for the counselor to observe and begin the classification of ego states, one reason being that a counseling contract—even in a crisis situation—can be made only with the adult ego state. The first step in establishing a TA group is the teaching of the recognition of ego states.

What One Looks for in Ego States

Distinctiveness (particularly in the adult), and *appropriateness*. In health, ego states are clearly discernible and one knows when the healthy person is in the adult, parent, or child. Usually, however, the TA counselor observes *contamination*, or the intermingling of the parent or child with the adult, producing functioning confused by archaic material or prejudiced by foreign material. Here and now reality testing shows some of this; interpersonal transactions shows more. Serious contamination may require referral of a counselee to a TA counselor with training and available time required for decontamination. Decontamination is undertaken

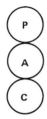

Figure 1. Basic structural diagram of ego states.

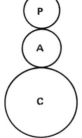

Figure 2. One way of depicting person in child ego state most of time.

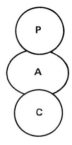

Figure 3. Double contamination of adult by parent and child.

by review of parental injunctions and attributions and the making of redecisions, as will be discussed later.

Structural Diagrams Are the Basic Communications Medium of TA Counseling

They show not only the functioning of the ego, but its stages of development, and the kinds of interpersonal transactions. Dusay (1972) created the useful "Egogram."

What Is the Ultimate Goal of Structural Analysis?

To train and give permission to the counselee to function most of the time under the control of his or her adult, even when having fun and relaxing. Because most of us were never encouraged during childhood to let our own mental capabilities take *full* adult responsibility for our thinking and behavior, starting to do so in TA counseling represents a major opportunity for change, and is an essential step towards achieving change.

Is Structural Analysis Ever the Sole Counseling Intervention Required by a Counselee?

Not likely, because inappropriateness or indistinctiveness of ego states produce so many abberations or strains in one's functioning and behavior. For instance, a bias-contaminated person treats others and becomes "typed" so that mere relief of the bias will not necessarily get the person functioning and accepted. A person with a confused adult not only presents communications problems, but requires potency and persistence from the TA counselor to remain goal oriented in counseling. A person whose internally-conflicted child inhibits natural social functioning may require social transactions retraining.

What Is Meant by "Life Script?"

Life Script Analysis, the second of the three TA submodalities, is based on the observations by Eric Berne (1972) that each person has an existential destiny, in reinforcement of which one repeatedly structures the outcome of situations. Berne stated that a newborn baby is a "prince" who is turned into a "frog" by the family's *injunctions* e.g., don't (do anything that will worry us or that we won't understand") and *attributions*, e.g., "no matter how hard you try, you'll always be a failure" together with the *decisions* the young child makes at critical moments of despair when feeling defeated by the family and realizing that to survive he or she will have to forego what would be normal, healthy aspirations.

So the counselee that appears before you

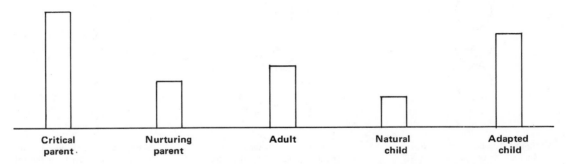

Figure 4. Egogram of a hypothetical counselee before TA counseling (after Dusay, 1972).

may be a "winner," but is more likely a "loser" or "if it weren't for . . ." And as you investigate how the person functions in thought processes and in social transactions, it becomes increasingly evident that the loser manages to keep from winning, and the if it weren't for always places the responsibility for his or her fate on the "appropriate" victim.

Berne also enunciated the four basic existential positions: I'm ok/you're ok ($+/+$); I'm ok/you're not ok ($+/-$); I'm not ok/you're ok ($-/+$); and the worst of all situations to be in, I'm not ok/you're not ok ($-/-$). These are direct products of the injunctions and attributions with the decisions continuing to be remade through adolescence; the injunctions and attributions having produced the basic script by about the age of six.

Thus we can envision the young child who has not yet entered even the outside world of school, being programmed as to what to expect of the world and what his or her place will be in it. That such programming is archaic by the time such a child grows to the age of twenty or thirty, particularly in Western society with its rapid changes, is obvious. What has not been so obvious is the unconscious intent of the programming by the parents, particularly the dominant parent which is usually the mother. Berne's observations, now implemented by other workers, show that the mother is prone to pass along to the offspring qualities which she is afraid to admit in herself, what Fanita English (1969) termed the "Hot Potato" episcript. A crazy mother is prone to attribute craziness to her little prince or princess! Is it any wonder that the TA counselor has to be potent/permissive/ protective if he or she, like in the fairy tales that so intrigued Berne (and still intrigues the modern TA counselor) is to manage to lift

the curse from the poor frog in the counselor's office? TA counseling can be heady stuff!

How Does the TA Counselor Find Out the Life Script?

By being systematic, by knowing what to look for, and by asking the right questions while at the same time not hesitating to guide the development of productive fantasies, the TA counselor readily formulates a tentative script model. But here a word of caution need be emphasized; early indications may be misleading as to script, and particularly to script priorities. So, before the strategy is formulated for reeducation of the value system based on redecisions about injunctions and attributions, the TA counselor should have engaged in all necessary validations to make certain that the most critical factors for change are indeed the most critical.

There are several ways to facilitate investigation of script. Printed aids prepared for use with TA groups have questionnaires which guide group members as to what kind of information is wanted, what kind of early memories should be searched out. Some of these aids provide the counselor with checklists to save time and avoid overlooking important areas. (Jongeward and James, 1973; McCormick, 1971).

The TA counselor continues his script investigation by discussions with a counselee that are initiated by some cue observed or reported in interpersonal transactions (as will be discussed below under "miniscripts.") Whenever appropriate, the TA counselor begins to "work" with the counselee, guiding him or her into recalling where a historic event took place, what was said, how one felt about it, and what decision was made about it.

Another important investigation made

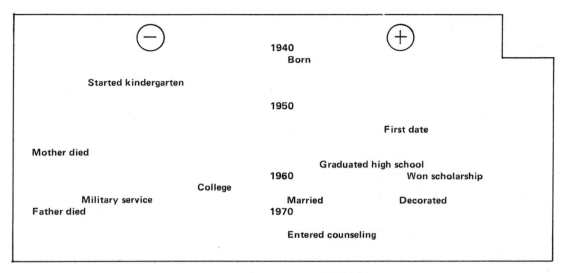

Figure 5. A significant life events chart aiding development of life script.

repeatedly by the TA counselor has to do with the expressed attitudes of others that the counselee remembers, which indoctrinated the developing child or youngster as to what he or she should expect about the world.

Using the Miniscript for Clues as to Not-OK Script Drivers

The miniscript (Kahler and Capers, 1974) is a detention tool that the TA group can use in diagnosing the motives behind negative stroke (attention) generating transactions. Miniscripts are brief transactional sequences, occurring in minutes or even seconds, which reinforce life script patterns. Not-OK miniscripts reinforce not-OK life scripts, and OK miniscripts reinforce OK life scripts. Every second of a day a person is said to be either in his or her OK or not-OK miniscript.

A person with a not-OK life script may engage in a not-OK miniscript that could run something like this: Feeling inadequate, he

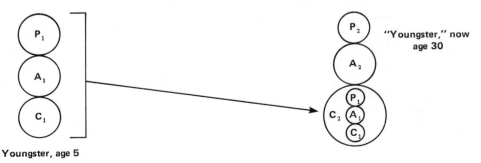

Figure 6. Showing retention of ego state pattern at age 5 in child of grown person.

or she may seize the lead in a conversation and pretend superiority of some function, such as perfection, time-consciousness, devotion to a noble cause, etc. But the pretense doesn't come off; others in the group indicate they don't accept as genuine the pretended quality and this brings the perpetrator to a momentary halt. Then the perpetrator may counter aggressively, and when more negative "strokes" (responses) are had from the group, he or she changes to a sulk.

The initiating feeling of inadequacy is termed the "injunction"; the driver (pretension) is the "counter-injunction" (a "do" performance) which parents demand of their growing children so the parents can be proud of them, such as "work hard." An added benefit to parents is that the counter-injunction absolves them, on a parent level, of the debilitating "injunction" they also laid on the offspring, which might be "no matter how hard you try, you'll never succeed."

So in the not-OK miniscript the dominating injunction triggers the counter-injunction to secure relief. The not-OK counselee then seizes the social opportunity to lord it over others, is put down, reacts aggressively, then gives up in a sulk. The counseling focus is, quite obviously, applied to the injunction, and then to better control of impulsive behavior.

How Are Harmful or Degrading Script Injunctions Neutralized?

As the injunctions, attributions, and related decisions are identified they are classified as to peripheral, central, and core. There is a rule that one doesn't ordinarily attempt to neutralize an outer factor without first getting to the core and putting that in order. The actual neutralization is aided by the "empty chairs" technique (Frederick S. Perls, 1969). The TA counselor trains his

counselee(s) to imagine that anybody or anything concerning him or her can be placed on an empty chair facing the counselee, whereupon the counselee talks to that "object," then takes the empty chair and becomes that object talking back to himself or herself now imagined to be in the formerly occupied chair. Real and formerly living people, dream elements go onto the empty chair for settling what Perls called "unfinished business."

The purpose of talking to an "empty" chair, then having the counselee sit in the empty chair to become the person or object previously imagined as in the chair only to now speak back to himself or herself as imaginarily left behind in the newly vacated chair, is to reexperience in the here-and-now old scenes (anything that has "happened," according to Gestalt therapy theory, is "old") complete with dialog and the feelings that went with the words and presence. The counselee is asked to, first, relive the scene exactly as it took place, then to go over it again from the vantage point of how it all seems at the present instant. Another way of expressing this is, the counselee first reviews what happened and what he or she interpreted at that time as to it significance; then the counselee is in effect asked, "does that interpretation seem appropriate at this moment?" Eventually, as major life events are investigated over and over again by this process, new interpretations come out of it, freeing the counselee from burdens no longer part of his makeup.

Reference has been made to "redecisions." In the case of major events in one's life having resulted in "decisions" that seriously limit one's view of his role in the world, the goal of "chairs" is to evolve new decisions based on a more comprehensive awareness of the world, and one's own qualities for coping with it.

Also, reference is made above to placing

"objects" such as headaches, dream scenery, etc., in the chair. This is done to elucidate what these objects really mean to the counselee, i.e., "what is the headache trying to tell you?" or, "now lets hear the escalator in the dream tell what it symbolizes!" The point to this is, the TA counselor is supposed to objectively *avoid assuming anything* about what is going on within the intrapsychic processes of the counselee. The TA counselor is supposed to ask. Again and again, as necessary.

Will All Counselees Perform Well with Chairs?

No. This is a way counselees can manifest their resistance, by refusing to play chairs, or to go through the motions but doing so without really getting into feelings.

The TA counselor cannot induce anyone to do well with chairs. But like a dramatic coach or director, the TA counselor can train and encourage a willing counselee to emote with greater realism of feelings, with one caution, however; this has to do with aggression. Aggression must be kept under tight rein at all times by enforcement of the working contract which precludes all but small releases under the permission of the TA counselor. The purpose of a "chairs" Gestalt is not to reexperience fury, but to permit the counselee in his experienced maturity of the present moment reevaluate the impact of the original event at that time, thus permitting consideration of redecision to put matters in the perspective of today's realism, under the control of the adult.

One last comment about the counselee who will not role-play with empty chairs, but who appears otherwise cooperative and desirous of self-improvement. Limited Gestalt with persons and objects may be accomplished if the TA counselor simply asks the counselee to practice talking as if oneself at an earlier time, or as if another person or

an object, without making any reference to chair transpositions and the like. Then at some later date, it may be possible to call the counselee's attention to the Gestalt work that has been done, and inquire the real meaning behind the "holdout" from the TA counselor. Not only may it be possible to secure the counselee's full cooperation about Gestalt work; the disclosure of the resistance may open important new channels to the suppressed past.

Is More Than One Chair Ever Used in a Gestalt?

Yes, multiple chairs can represent, for example, a family group—an imaginary psychodrama. Another variant has chairs representing the counselee's ego states.

Are Dramatic, Single-Session Redecisions Ever Possible?

Yes, but not probable except in the case of the counselee who has prepared himself or herself and who knows that once the major roadblock is resolved, functioning will be better. The ultimate criterion, according to Berne, is how the counselee's adult and parent view things.

Is Script Analysis Ever the Sole Solution Required for a Counselee?

Yes. Some people with excellent functioning ego states manage passable interpersonal relationships despite suffering due to injunctions and attributions plus the decisions they had to make as a result. It may be that by resolving these script issues the individual may feel relieved and able to function with far less drain. Which is a way of stating that the TA counselor is trained to keep asking the counselee, repeatedly, what it is that he or she thinks will help make life more livable and rewarding.

Does TA Imply That Actual Mothers and Fathers Are the Sources of the Programming?

No. Berne in his early writings made clear that what is being considered are the parenting forces, whoever has the responsibility and is looked to by the developing child for information and cues. Even "street people" who as children had absentee mothers and maybe never knew who their biological fathers were, do recall individuals who cared for them and taught them what to fear. Cultures do scripting, too. (White and White, 1975; Denton Roberts, 1975.)

The point is, a person remembers only what came from people who were regarded as significant by the developing young child.

What Is Covered in Transactional Analysis (or the Analysis of Transactions)?

In general, how the counselee gets whatever it is he wants in attention from others (such attention is called "strokes"), and how skilled the person is in social transactions to seek goals without being misunderstood.

Stroke hunger is viewed by Steiner (1971) as a basic, essential drive affecting all of us. Stroking is first experienced by the young infant by being held, changed, bathed, fed, and so on. Thirty years later the infant, as a grown person, still needs interaction with other persons to live and be reasonably happy. And as the infant learned to get its strokes, so the grown person will get his or her strokes. If the infant found it got the attention of its mother only by crying, or breaking things, or making messes, when it grows up it is likely to get attention of others by being provoking, antisocial, or at least employing transactional techniques to disturb and perhaps upset others.

So one of the conceptual measures the TA counselor uses, is the Stroke diagram (McKenna, 1974) which depicts the degree to which a counselee seeks and receives positive and negative strokes.

In the TA group, the TA counselor (and other counselees) observe whether or not a counselee generally converses in "parallel" transactions, which are satisfying to others (from one ego state to the other person's

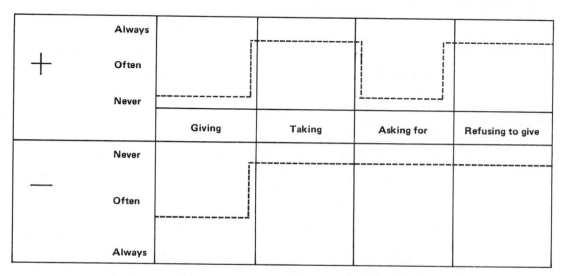

Figure 7. Stroking profile of a hypothetical person before TA counseling.
Copyright © Jim McKenna, 522 N Ballas Road, St. Louis, MO 63141.

identical ego state, back and-forth) or whether the counselee shows a pattern of shifting to another ego state, thus disturbing the other person (such as initiating a conversation from the adult, then later shifting to parent and addressing the child of the other person, as if to say, "why do you say a thing like that?")

If the transactions are observed to sometimes include an ulterior element, the TA counselor (and other group members) know that the counselee is up to some "game."

A "game," according to Eric Berne, and later redefined by Steiner (1974), involves an orderly series of transactions with a beginning and an end, contains an ulterior motive, and results in a payoff for both parties in terms of strong feelings. People play games for many reasons, some being to hurt themselves, to hurt others, to prove once again that people are "just like momma said." People set themselves up to have games perpetrated on them because its exciting, better than being uninvolved, to get hurt, etc.

When Eric Berne's book "Games People Play" (1964) was published, it became an instant success probably because people were able to gain some understanding as to how others engage in gamey behavior. TA became synonymous with Game Analysis (Steiner, 1971.)

Today, games are viewed by TA counselors as extremely important as long as the counselee continues to play them, particularly the "harder," more lethal varieties or any "conning" to make a fool of the TA counselor.

Extinguishing or Attenuating Game Behavior

There are several kinds of situations in which the TA counselor must insist that game playing for all practical purposes cease. One is when it becomes apparent the game playing may disrupt or even destroy the TA group. Another is when games openly involve the TA counselor as would-be victim. And then there are the games which are the reasons why some counselees are referred for counseling by school authorities, police, etc., in which case the immediate, sometimes crisis, goal of counseling is extinguishing games.

TA Counseling for Marital Couples and Families

Game analysis together with game attenuation or extinguishing, and coupled with

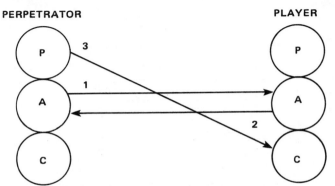

Figure 8. A transactional diagram showing shift from "parallel" (A ⇌ A) to "crossed" (P → C) communication—a putdown for player!

analysis of transactions and stroke economy patterns, are the primary means by which combatant relationships can be stabilized to a degree permitting individual assessment and counseling involving structural and script analysis with redecisioning.

Why Gamey Behavior Is Given Up Reluctantly

Berne (1964) has taught us that people play games to generate "racket" feelings further elucidated by Fanita English (1971, 1972) as replacements for genuine but forbidden, and thus suppressed, feelings. Racket feelings support script injunctions, like "all men are dirty beasts." As the "racketeer" completes a game she (or he) can say, in an internal conversation between child and parent, "they sure are, mom!" whereupon the racketeer pastes another "trading stamp" in her or his collection book. When the book is filled by completion of a series of games the racketeer is entitled to a free blowup, or acting out frenzy by the child with approval of the parent so avidly supported. The blowup may be an orgy, a night in jail, a trip to the emergency ward.

The investigation of gamey behavior focuses on the investigation of racket feelings, a selection of priorities, and Gestalt "work" on the injunctions and attributions which lie behind the games. Little games are important defenses, however, which may remain.

Group or Individual TA Counseling?

Many advantages have been cited of the TA counselor working with a well-trained, disciplined group. That is not to say, however, that individual TA counseling is infeasible; many circumstances may require seeing a TA counselee on only a one-to-one basis. In this case the TA counselor must rely on reports of *outside* transactions, and must struggle in objectifying the feelings the counselee induces in him in attempting to read all signals correctly. It is a difficult, but not altogether insurmountable task.

On the other hand, group counseling of individuals who are in career-competition as employees of an organization may not be feasible or practical. An example would be staff members of an institution where one's revealing in front of a group of such people even quite banal facts about one's functioning and life script might be competitively disadvantageous. A group of teachers from one school might, however, be handled so that activity is focused on learning about TA, with the TA counselor skillfully handling sensitive private matters in one-to-one sessions with individual members.

If, on the other hand, a group of children with the same behavioral problems can be assembled, there can be quite obvious advantages to the sharing not only of knowledge about TA, but also in helping each other resolve the problems. (Jennie Ernst, 1971; Thomas Frazier, 1971)

TA groups in which full-range individual counseling is done in the presence of the group assumes that group members will have no contact outside the group sessions.

TA Can Be Fun

Eric Berne's original concept of the TA group was that it could be a lot of fun. He structured the "language" to be light and humorous, a quality that has carried over into much of the instructional material that has been written since Berne's death. Some TA counselors are skilled at, and carefully conduct their group sessions with a light-heartedness that can be reassuring and supportive, particularly to individuals who tend to view things gloomily.

The "fun" aspect of TA groups can provide a justification for some people to feel socially comfortable to be involved, people who would perhaps be concerned about what their families or friends might think if they were known to be in "therapy."

Another factor about "fun" is that some people seem to progress better in substituting positive thoughts for negative, and in changing their behaviors, if they and their group members can take rather lightly the ways their former selves thought and behaved.

TA Is a Complex System

In the brief, cursory review of highlights of TA covered in this chapter, it has been impossible to convey the serious complexity of this conceptual, directive counseling system. There are many more elements one must use in practice than have been alluded to here. The theory behind the use of the elements, the very diagrammatic representations used have grown far afield from the original texts and early papers. But this is as it must be, for any conceptual system to cover as much breadth of human functioning and behavior as the contemporary TA counselors are doing.

The reason for citing the complexities ahead for the counselor seriously interested in TA is not to discourage one, but instead to offer assurance that TA has come into its own as a serious science. No longer is TA just the "Games that People Play!"

Is TA More Successful Than Other Modalities of Counseling?

Undoubtedly there are TA counselors and counselees who have worked with TA who believe that they could not have achieved what they did with anything less than this broadly conceptual, highly directive system. But the same faith is of course found among practitioners and beneficiaries of all other counseling modalities.

To date, there is little in the literature that supports with hard scientific facts the beliefs and claims of the supporters of the various modalities. That is not to say that good results are not being had; its just that counseling work is not amenable to laboratory types of control and observation.

The few comparative studies that have appeared seem to indicate that competent, skilled counselors working with selected counselees get good results. Perhaps its a bit like Eric Berne hypothesized, that whatever is done, as long as the counselee's adult and parent approve after thinking matters over, then the counseling is "successful." But, added Berne, for a counselor to have the adult and parent so prepared as to be able to think about things like this so positively, takes a good deal of counselor skill!

SELECTIONS FROM THE TA LITERATURE

A recommended reading list implementing the terminology, descriptions, and discussions in this chapter. Most books and the TA periodicals are available from Transactional Pubs, 1722 Vallejo Street, San Francisco CA 94123.

REFERENCES

Abu Abu-Saba, Mary. The female juvenile delinquent. *Transactional Analysis Journal* 5 (1975):62-65.

Berne, Eric. *Games people play* New York: Grove Press, 1964.

———. *Transactional analysis in psychotherapy* New York: Grove Press, 1971.

———. *What do you say after you say hello?* New York: Grove Press, 1972.

Dusay, John M. Egograms and the "constancy hypothesis." *Transactional Analysis Journal* 2 (1972):37-41.

English, Fanita. Episcript and the "hot potato" game. *Transactional Analysis Bulletin* 8 (1969):77-82.

———. Rackets and real feelings, Part l. *Transactional Analysis Journal* 1 (1971):27-32.

—+—. Rackets and real feelings, Part ll *Transactional Analysis Journal* 2 (1972):23-25.

Ernst, Jennie. Using transactional analysis in a high school learning disability grouping. *Transactional Analysis Journal* 1 (1971):11-15.

Federn, P. *Ego psychology and the psychoses* New York: Basic Books, 1952.

Frazier, Thomas. Application of transactional analysis principles in classroom of a correctional school. *Transactional Analysis Journal* 1 (1971):16-20.

Jongeward, Dorothy, and James, Muriel. *Winning with people—group exercises in transactional analysis* Reading, MA: Addison-Wesley, 1973.

Kahler, Taibi, and Capers, Hedges. The miniscript. *Transactional Analysis Journal* 4 (1974):26-42.

McCormick, Paul. *Guide for use of life-script questionnaire in transactional analysis* San Francisco: Transactional Pubs, 1971.

McKenna, Jim. The stroking profile. Application to script analysis. *Transactional Analysis Journal* 4 (1974):20-24.

Penfield, W. Memory mechanisms. *Archives of Neurology and Psychiatry* 67 (1952):178-98.

Perls, Frederick S. *Gestalt therapy verbatim* New York: Bantam Books, 1969.

Roberts, Denton. Treatment of cultural scripts. *Transactional Analysis Journal* 5 (1975):29-35.

Steiner, Claude. The stroke economy. *Transactional Analysis Journal* 1 (1971):9-15.

———. *Games alcoholics play* New York: Grove Press, 1971.

———. *Scripts people live* New York: Grove Press, 1974.

White, Jerome D., and White, Terri. Cultural scripting. *Transactional Analysis Journal* 5 (1975):12-23.

16. THE DEVELOPMENT OF SYSTEMATIC HUMAN RESOURCE DEVELOPMENT MODELS

Robert R. Carkhuff

Peter Schwarzburg

The essential beginning point in the development of systematic human resource development (HRD) programs was with the challenges to the helping profession issued by Eysenck (1965), Levitt (1963) and Lewis (1965). These challenges were to the effect that, for both adults and children, professional psychological treatment did not make a difference. In other words, persons who were in untreated control groups fared as well *on the average* as people assigned professional counselors and therapists. There were several different important answers to these challenges, the first coming from some of the early research studies of counseling and psychotherapy.

Research Studies

Based upon the early naturalistic studies of counseling and psychotherapy, a number of predictive studies were conducted and generalizations were made to other areas of helping. In addition, studies extending and refining the relevant dimensions were conducted. These research studies laid the base for a number of applications in training which, in turn, helped to generate systematic models for HRD programs.

Naturalistic Studies

With some of the original formulation of Rogers (1957) and others (e.g., Shaffer and

Shoben 1956) as the point of origin, a number of studies of counseling and psychotherapy were conducted to identify the effective ingredients of these helping relationships. Two significant findings relevant to the development of HRD models emerged from these efforts.

Helping Effects

The first was the finding that professional counseling and psychotherapy may be "for better or for worse" (Rogers, et al., 1967; Truax and Carkhuff, 1967). That is, when professional counselors and therapists were introduced they tended to have a greater range of effects in the indices of client or patient change or gain. Thus, while there were no differences *on the average* between treated and untreated groups, there was significantly greater variability in the change indices of the treated groups when compared to the untreated groups. With the advent of audio and audio-visual recording devices, it became possible to observe outcome and trace back over process to determine the effective ingredients of helping.

Helper Dimensions

The second significant finding was the finding that we could account in part for the "for better or worse" effects by examining the counselor or therapist's level of functioning on emotional and interpersonal dimensions such as empathic understanding (Rogers, et al., 1967; Truax and Carkhuff, 1967). That is, counselees whose counselors functioned at relatively high levels of certain interpersonal dimensions demonstrated constructive change or gain while counselees of counselors functioning at relatively low levels of these dimensions demonstrated either no change or deteriorative change. At this point of development, the scales employed to measure the interpersonal

dimensions were gross measures of functioning. The dimensions that were assessed included empathy, unconditional regard and congruence as postulated by Rogers (Rogers, et al., 1967) and accurate empathy, nonpossessive warmth and genuineness as modified by Truax (Truax and Carkhuff, 1967). In addition, client involvement in the therapeutic process was also measured by indices of experiencing developed by Gendlin (Rogers, et al., 1967) and exploration developed by Truax and Carkhuff (1967).

In summary, the findings of the early naturalistic studies indicated that HRD may be "for better or for worse" and that these effects can be accounted for in part by the level of the helper's functioning on certain interpersonal dimensions. The implications for counseling were both consoling and distressing. In answer to the challenges to the helping professions, these findings suggest one very consoling implication: these effects may be constructive or destructive. The results of these naturalistic studies led directly to a number of predictive studies.

Predictive Studies

The next logical extension of these efforts was to conduct predictive studies which assessed the helper's level of functioning and predicted their effects upon helpee process and outcome. The first set of these studies focused upon the effects of helper dimensions upon helpee process movement.

Helpee Process

The early predictive studies of helpee process movement involved the experimental manipulation of counselor conditions and the study of their effect upon client self-exploration. A series of studies yielded results that may be divided according to both counselor and client level of functioning. In general, clients of high-level functioning counselors moved toward higher levels of process involvement while clients of low-functioning counselors moved toward lower levels of process involvement (Carkhuff, 1969; Truax and Carkhuff, 1967). There were several important qualifications on this work. When high-functioning counselors experimentally lowered the level of their responses, low-functioning counselees continued to explore themselves. When moderate-functioning counselors experimentally lowered their conditions, both low and high-functioning counselees moved to lower levels of exploration (Carkhuff, 1969). The implications for client outcome over time and with crises were important. If helpees tend to explore themselves differentially according to the level of functioning of their helpers, then over time they should tend to move in the direction of their helper's level of functioning. These hypotheses were investigated in a series of outcome studies.

Helpee Outcome

A number of outcome studies were conducted to assess the differential effects of high- and low-functioning counselors upon indices of counselee outcome. In one series of studies (Carkhuff, 1969; Pagell, Carkhuff and Berenson, 1967), the effects of the level of emotional and interpersonal functioning of counselors and therapists upon the level of emotional and interpersonal functioning of their clients and patients were studied. With both outpatient neuropsychiatric patients and college student counselees similar results were obtained. In general, the helpees moved in the direction of the level of functioning of their helpers. The clients and patients of high-level functioning counselors and therapists demonstrated positive change in the level of their emotional and interpersonal skills as measured by a variety of in-

dices. The clients and patients of low-level functioning counselors and therapists demonstrated no change or negative change in the level of their emotional and interpersonal skills. Indeed, the counselee of the counselor functioning at the highest level was functioning after treatment at levels higher than all other counselors and therapists in the project.

In summary, these studies suggested that the heart of HRD involved the emotional and interpersonal changes in the helpee that were brought about differentially by the level of the helper's emotional and interpersonal skills. These predictive studies suggested a number of studies generalizing the effects to other areas of helpee functioning.

Generalization Studies

The next step in the sequence was to attempt to generalize the effects of helper functioning from the emotional and interpersonal areas to the other areas of HRD, the intellectual and physical areas of helpee functioning. In addition, an attempt was made to assess the effects of the helper's level of functioning in the implementation of a number of systematic programs.

Helpee Functioning

The earliest of these generalization studies was done by Aspy (1969) in the educational realm. Aspy selected teachers functioning at high and low levels of emotional and interpersonal skills and assessed their effect on the educational achievement of grammar and secondary school students. What he found was consistent with the previous work. In general, the students of high-functioning teachers achieved at significantly higher levels than the students of low-functioning teachers. In addition, a variety of other indices of student functioning were related to teacher functioning on emotional and interpersonal dimensions. At the extremes, the students of the highest level functioning teachers gained an average of two and-one— half years of achievement while the students of the lowest level functioning teachers gained an average of six months of achievement. Student tardiness, absenteeism and truancy were also related to teacher functioning. In an attempted extension of this work Kratochvil, Carkhuff and Berenson (1969) studied the cumulative effects of parent and teacher levels of emotional-interpersonal functioning upon the physical and intellectual as well as the emotional and interpersonal functioning of fifth grade students. While they did not find enough variability in the level of functioning of the teachers to elicit differential effects, they did find a significant relationship between the physical, emotional and intellectual functioning of the students. In addition, they found that the effects of the one high-level functioning teacher in the study (two years reading growth in second grade) were washed out by the time the students were in fifth grade. It was this kind of finding that led to the conclusion that it takes only one retarding teacher to neutralize the effects of one facilitative teacher and two facilitative teachers to wash out the effects of one retarding teacher. And the supply of facilitative teachers is extremely limited! Pierce and his associates (1967, 1970, 1971) made a number of generalization studies of the effects of trainer and supervisor level of functioning upon trainee development of skills in helping. His findings were consistent with the earlier evidence: trainees move in the direction of their trainer's level of functioning. While we studied the effects of the teachers' emotional and interpersonal skills, we did not study their teaching methodology or classroom management skills. It now became appropriate to study the differential effects of helper functioning and systematic programs.

Systematic Programs

In path-finding research on the differential effects of people and programs, Vitalo (1970) found that both the helper's level of functioning on the interpersonal dimensions and the systematic program were significant sources of effect in verbal conditioning of personal pronoun emissions by the subject. Examination of the interaction effects revealed that the presence of conditioning was dependent upon the level of the experimenter's functioning. Only the high functioning experimenters elicited learning rates from the experimental group that were different from those produced by a control group. In an extension of this work, Mickelson and Stevic (1971) investigated the effects of verbal reinforcement counseling as a preferred method for increasing high school students' acquisition of information relevant to their educational and/or vocational goals and found that high-level functioning helpers produced a significantly greater amount of helpee information-seeking behavior than functioning helpers. For our purposes, perhaps the most significant result was the finding that while the verbal reinforcement program was effective at the beginning of the session for the helpees of the low-functioning helpers, as the session went on these nonfacilitative helpers had "turned off" their helpee's information-seeking behavior.

In summary, a helper's effectiveness is a function of both his emotional—interpersonal skills and his skills in his specialty program areas. Moreover, his effectiveness generalizes to the intellectual and physical as well as emotional and interpersonal functioning of the helpee.

Extension Studies

The extension studies include the extension of dimensions within the helping relationship as well as the extension to programs which complement the helper's efforts in HRD. Within the helping relationship these extensions include both helper and helpee dimensions.

Helping Dimensions

Perhaps the most important extension within helping has been to expand the helper dimensions from responsive to initiative dimensions. Thus, the original formulations emphasizing helper empathy, unconditional regard and congruence were complemented by the more action-oriented dimensions of helper concreteness (Truax and Carkhuff, 1967) confrontation and interpretations of immediacy (Carkhuff, 1969). We summarize these dimensions as helper responsive (responding to the helpee's experience) dimensions (Carkhuff, 1969). In addition, the original formulations were refined. Empathy was operationalized in five-point scales that were reliable and valid: level 3 empathy was defined in terms of helper responses that were interchangeable with helpee responses in terms of the feeling and meaning expressed by the helpee (this meant that the responses could be laid side-by-side and a determination made if indeed each could have said what the other said); above and below level 3 the determination of the additive or subtractive nature of the responses was made by whether the helpee went on to explore and understand himself at deeper levels or not. In the process, it was found that empathy accounted for the effects of unconditional regard and the dimension of respect was developed to include unconditionality, positive regard and differential regard (conditional and positive as each is

appropriate). Also, genuineness was modified to emphasize that facilitative aspect of this dimension with the thought in mind that helping was for the helpee and not for the helper. In other words, the dimensions were operationalized in an attempt to judge them primarily in terms of their effects (Carkhuff, 1969). The introduction of initiative dimensions led readily to a consideration of program dimensions.

Program Dimensions

Flowing from the initiative interpersonal dimensions, then, were a number of programs calculated to complement the helper's effort. In this regard, as many counselors and therapists have found, the helping relationship is not enough. Other kinds of activities must be developed if the helping relationship is to result in tangible and observable behavioral change (Carkhuff, 1969). These activities include problem-solving activities which emphasize problem and goal definition and the systematic consideration of alternate courses of action in terms of the helpee's hierarchy of values. In addition, these activities include the program development skills necessary to implement a preferred course of action: operationalizing goals; aligning behaviors in terms of degree of difficulty; repetition; review; movement to new behaviors contingent upon the successful completion of all previous behaviors. A number of other necessary programs include program implementation and the use of differential reinforcement; the utilization of teaching methodologies and learning management procedures (Carkhuff, 1972a).

In summary, the extension studies have led to the development of a technology of HRD operationalizing both the people and program variables necessary to effect the constructive change or gain desired. The development of a technology, in turn, led quite readily to a consideration of applications in training.

Application Studies

A number of studies were conducted in which experimental training was introduced and its effects studied in the resultant helping efforts. These studies moved naturally from studies of professions, including those indigenous to the community being serviced, to training entire communities seeking help in the implementation of the concept of "training as a preferred mode of treatment."

Credentialed Professionals

A series of studies of the training of credentialed professionals and the assessment of their effects served to introduce applications in this area. In general the results were to suggest that credentialed professionals could be trained systematically within time limited periods to demonstrate effective HRD efforts.

Counseling Personnel

The first of the series of training applications with professional counselors and therapists (Carkhuff, 1969) demonstrated that they could be trained to function at levels commensurate with outstanding practitioners (Truax and Carkhuff, 1967) or above (Carkhuff, 1969). In the later series, it was established that credentialed professionals could in the brief time of 100 hours or less learn to function above minimally effective and self-sustaining levels of interpersonal skills, criteria that the outstanding practitioners do not measure up to (Carkhuff, 1969). Perhaps most important, they were able to involve their counselees in the helping process at levels of self-exploration and self-understanding leading to constructive change or gain. In one demonstration study in guidance, against a very low base rate of success, the counselors were able to demonstrate success rates of between 74 percent and 91 percent with the introduction of systematic training in interpersonal skills, problem-solving skills and other specialty area skills (Carkhuff, 1972b).

Teaching Personnel

A series of training applications in teaching followed (Carkhuff, 1971). In one of these, Hefele (1971) found student achievement to be a function of systematic training of teachers in interpersonal skills. In addition, he found that the trained group not only succeeded in communicating at higher levels with their students than did the control group, but that it was possible to select those teacher supervisors who could best teach others the specific methodologies involved. The finding that teachers and trainees subsequently exerted a reciprocal impact upon one another in providing a basis for the relationship between subsequent student academic achievement and the interpersonal skills of the teacher was of equal interest. In a more extensive design, Berenson (1971) found that experimentally trained teachers were rated significantly higher in interpersonal skills and competency in the classroom, and that they scored significantly higher on a situation reaction test and utilized significantly more positive reinforcing behaviors in their teaching than a variety of control conditions including a training control group, a Hawthorne Effect control group and a control group proper. The implications for teacher training are obvious.

The implications for the selection and training of credentialed professionals in the helping profession are profound. HRD efforts may be improved enormously by the introduction of systematic interpersonal and specialty area program skills. The success in training credentialed professionals led directly to attempts at training lay personnel.

Functional Professionals

It is clear that dimensions such as interpersonal skills are not the exclusive province of credentialed professionals. In this context, a number of studies utilizing lay personnel were conducted. These included both staff personnel and indigenous personnel. In general, the results suggest that trained lay personnel may serve as functional professionals in effecting significant HRD.

Staff Personnel

In a series of studies, lay staff personnel such as nurses, hospital attendants, prison guards, dormitory counselors and community volunteers were trained and their effects in treatment studied (Carkhuff, 1971). The success of the programs was dramatic in terms of the gains in interpersonal skills of the trainees. In terms of outcome, the trainees were able to elicit significant changes in work behavior, getting and staying out of the hospital and changes in a variety of areas including self-reports, significant other reports and expert reports. Against a backdrop of the crisis in corrections, the results of the implementation of the training model in Atlanta Federal Penitentiary (McGathlin and Porter, 1969) might serve as a timely illustration. In this project, prison guards were systematically trained in interpersonal skills and 12 of them were appointed as correctional officers to counsel and develop courses of action for the inmates. Whereas the prison had been reported to have been in a state of anarchy and at the mercy of the inmates before the model was implemented, reports by Hall (1970) indicated a success rate of between 80 percent and 90 percent depending upon what questions were asked of the inmates. In addition, work attendance and productivity went up and sick leave and work transfers went down significantly. As a consequence two national correctional counseling institutes have been conducted and have served to demonstrate further that much can be done with systematic selection and training of staff in interpersonal skills even against a backdrop of violence. Quite a contrast with Attica! Whereas the utilization of lay personnel initially involved staff members and volunteers, there were implications for direct utilization of members of the community being served.

Indigenous Personnel

The difference between functional professional staff and functional professional indigenous personnel is the difference between the attendant and the patient, the guard and the inmate, the teacher and the student, the policeman and the community member. That is, the use of indigenous personnel involves persons who are part of the community being serviced. It is a natural extension of the earlier work to train indigenous personnel as well as staff personnel in the kinds of skills involved. Here, the emphasis upon selection and training appear particularly critical, although certainly no more critical than for credentialed and functional professionals. However, not just anybody, particularly from the ranks of the physically, emotionally and intellectually immobilized, can serve as helpers. Nevertheless, with selection and training, studies of the use of indigenous functional professionals indicated that they could work effectively with the populations from which they were drawn. A few of the many programs conducted in this area might be mentioned here. In one program human relations specialists were selected systematically from the black community on the basis of their functionality for service in a crisis-ridden school system. They were trained to function in treatment, training and teaching (Black History) capacities, and demonstrated significantly positive results in assessments of their work (Carkhuff, 1971). In another program, new careers teachers were systematically selected from the black community and trained and supervised in the kinds of skills which they needed to teach and guide the development of hard core unemployed from their community. In two programs, six teachers were able to help over 100 people previously considered hard core unemployed hold human service work positions in the community (Carkhuff, 1971).

In summary, lay personnel, whether staff or indigenous, may be selected and trained as functional professional helpers. In these roles, they can effect any HRD that professionals can—and more! There were direct implications of the success of this work for training entire helpee populations.

Helpee Populations

The final logical extension of the HRD model was to cut out the middle man and train the helpee populations directly with the kinds of skills which they need to function effectively in their worlds. Whether for individuals (HRD) or entire communities in general, we have found that training is "the preferred mode of treatment."

Individuals

A number of studies have been conducted with a training theme of servicing individuals. In one series, parents of emotionally disturbed children were systematically trained in the kinds of skills which they needed to function effectively with themselves and with their children. In one

such program (Carkhuff, 1971), it was found that this approach was significantly more effective than all other forms of traditional parental counseling groups. In another series, hospitalized neuropsychiatric patients were trained in the kinds of skills which they needed to function effectively initially on their wards and ultimately in the communities to which they return. In several of these programs (Pierce and Drasgow, 1969) it was found that the systematic training was significantly more effective than all other forms of treatment, individual psychotherapy, group psychotherapy, drug treatment and "total push" treatment involving a combination of all other forms of treatment. Thus, in general, helpees may be trained directly in the kinds of skills which they need to service themselves. The concept of "training as a preferred mode of treatment" led directly to the development of programs to train entire communities.

Communities

The notion of training entire communities stems from the need for training those persons in a helpee's environment who are necessary to sustain his functioning. It culminates in the training of entire institutions from top to bottom. For example, an extension of the aforementioned correctional work and an outgrowth of the national correctional counseling institutes culminated in one program at the Federal Adult Correctional Center in Lompoc, California where staff and inmates at all levels were trained in the kinds of skills necessary to work effectively with each other (Carkhuff, 1972b). All kinds of evidence supports the success of this program but perhaps the most significant are the instances in which it was brought to bear to prevent the occurrence of riots such as that at Attica. In another project, Rhode Island Training Schools were systematically transformed from custodial to treatment orientations (Carkhuff, 1972b). Staff at all levels, beginning with the superintendant, were trained in interpersonal, problem-solving, program development and specialty program skills. In the instance of program development alone, the staff developed over 80 programs ranging from cottage maintenance through field trips to individual and group counseling programs. In addition, students and parents were trained in interpersonal skills and specialty skills such as study methods. The results indicate that runaways and recidivists are down significantly and percent levels for physical, emotional-interpersonal and intellectual functioning are up significantly.

In summary, training is the preferred mode for HRD. When we train people in the kinds of skills which they need to function effectively in their worlds we increase the probability that they will, in fact, function effectively.

Summary and Overview

Research studies of helping relationships developed and validated the helping model; in general, helpees move toward their helpers' level of functioning. The results led readily to large scale applications in HRD with both credentialed and functional professionals.

In general, effectiveness in HRD is a function primarily of two factors: the skills with which the helpers relate to other people (interpersonal skills), and the skills which they have in their specialty areas (program skills). The implications for professional HRD efforts are important. With systematic selection and systematic training, helping personnel may be developed to effect significant and constructive change in individuals or communities of people.

The implication for personal HRD efforts are even more important. In order to accomplish these HRD tasks we must insure our own effective development and translate our own offerings most systematically into effective programs. The most effective modality for developing our own effectiveness as well as that of our helpees is training.

REFERENCES

Aspy, D. The effect of teacher-offered conditions of empathy, positive regard and congruence upon student achievement. *Florida Journal of Educational Research* 11 (1969):39-48.

Berenson, D. H. The effects of systematic human relations training upon the classroom performance of elementary school teachers. *Journal of Research and Development in Education* 4 (1971):70-85.

Carkhuff, R. R. *Helping and human relations.* Vols. I and II. New York: Holt, Rinehart and Winston, 1969.

———. *The development of human resources.* New York: Holt, Rinehart and Winston, 1971.

———. *The art of helping.* Amherst, Mass.: Human Resource Development Press, 1972(a).

———. *People, programs and organizations— The effective ingredients of human and community resource development.* Amherst, Mass.: Human Resource Development Press, 1972(b).

Eysenck, H. J. The effects of psychotherapy. *International Journal of Psychiatry,* 1 (1965):99-178.

Hall, R. *Atlanta correctional and industrial counseling: First annual report.* Washington, D.C.: Federal Bureau of Prisons, 1970.

Hefele, T. J. The effects of systematic human relations training upon student achievement. *Journal of Research and Development in Education* 4 (1971):52-69.

Kratochvil, D.; Carkhuff, R. R.; and Berenson, B. G. The cumulative effects of parent and teacher-offered levels of facilitative conditions upon indexes of student physical, emotional and intellectual functioning. *Journal of Educational Research* 63 (1969):161-64.

Levitt, E. E. Psychotherapy with children: A further evaluation. *Behavior Research and Therapy*, 1 (1963):45-51.

Lewis, W. W. Continuity and intervention in emotional disturbance: A review. *Exceptional Children* 31 (1965):465-75.

McGathlin, W. and Porter, T. *The effects of facilitation training provided correctional officers stationed at the Atlanta Federal Penitentiary.* Washington, D.C.: U.S. Justice Dept., 1969.

Mickelson, D. J. and Stevic, R. R. Differential effects of facilitative and nonfacilitative behavioral counselors. *Journal of Counseling Psychology* 18 (1971):314-19.

Pagell, W.; Carkhuff, R. R.; and Berenson, B. G. The predicted differential effects of the level of counselor functioning upon the level of functioning of outpatients. *Journal of Clinical Psychology*, 23 (1967):510-12.

Pierce, R. M.; Carkhuff, R. R.; and Berenson, B. G. The differential effects of high- and low-functioning counselors upon counselors-in-training. *Journal of Clinical Psychology* 23 (1967):212-15.

Pierce, R. M. and Drasgow, J. Teaching facilitative interpersonal functioning to psychiatric inpatients. *Journal of Counseling Psychology*, 16 (1969):295-98.

Pierce, R. M. and Schauble, P. Graduate training of facilitative counselors: The effects of individual supervision. *Journal of Counseling Psychology* 17 (1970):210-15.

———. Study on the effects of individual supervision in graduate school training. *Journal of Counseling Psychology*, 18 (1971):186-87.

Rogers, C. R. The necessary and sufficient conditions of therapeutic personality change. *Journal of Consulting Psychology* 22 (1957): 95-103.

Rogers, C. R.; Gendlin, E. T.; Kiesler; D. and Truax, C. B. *The therapeutic relationship and its impact.* Madison, Wisconsin: University of Wisconsin Press, 1967.

Schaffer, L. F. and Shoben, E. J. Common aspects of psychotherapy. From Psychotherapy: Learning new adjustments, chapter in *The psychology of adjustment.* Boston: Houghton Mifflin Co., 1956.

Truax, C. G. and Carkhuff, R. R. *Toward effective counseling and psychotherapy.* Chicago: Aldine, 1967.

Vitalo, R. The effects of facilitative interpersonal functioning in a conditioning paradigm. *Journal of Counseling Psychology*, 17 (1970): 141-44.

PART THREE

COUNTERPOINT

A UNIQUE APPROACH

Dear Editor:

"I especially enjoyed Dr. Kirman's article on modern psychoanalytic counseling. I get the idea that this approach really differs quite a bit from the traditional Freudian idea, and that maybe it will offer a revival to efforts at treating the unconscious in the school counseling setting . . . What strikes me as most important is that its methods do not dichotomize between the 'normal' and 'disturbed' client; but rather, it offers ways of dealing with people's needs regardless of their diagnostic category. For this reason, I think it answers forcefully Aubrey's and Tyler's rejection of intensive psychotherapy approaches in the school. . . ."

A.A.H.

•   •   •

Dear Editor:

"Even though the approach is called 'modern psychoanalytic counseling,' it is so much of a humanistic approach, in that it recognizes the uniqueness and special needs of each person, that it seems to me it could be used by counselors of all theoretical persuasions. The concept of trying to understand the *real* meaning of a client's difficulty, in terms of the client's entire psychological orientation (whether it is expressed in terms of 'maturational needs' or 'resistances') and trying to help the client through the dynamic personal relationship (which may be called 'transference') are characteristics of all counseling approaches that work!"

E. A.

LOOKING FOR A SYNTHESIS

Dear Editor:

"In some ways it seems that the Carkhuff paper, strategically placed at the end of this section, is an effort to resolve the many fragmentations that divide counseling theory. Do you think that someday soon we won't have all the so-called 'schools' of counseling, but rather a universal model that can be equally accepted by Freudians, neo-Freudians, existentialists, behaviorists, transactional analysts, etc.?"

B. T. G.

•   •   •

Dear Editor:

". . . As a person who is studying to be a counselor, I would like to know how to use an *eclectic* approach. Do most counselors use different techniques that are taken from different models of helping? Or do they stick mostly to one model, and use that for all of their clients? I would like to see a case that demonstrates the use of different techniques from different approaches, to see how they can be combined effectively. . . ."

N. Y.

•   •   •

Dear Editor:

"A few of the articles in this section gave the impression that a counselor could accept premises or methods from one model while relying primarily on another model. . . . Can a counselor be an existential-psychoanalytic counselor, or a client-centered-Adlerian-behavioral counselor? I thought Mellecker's paper on TA was very strong in this respect, in that it allowed diversity and differences in the application of what he calls a 'counseling modality.' "

R. R., Jr.

Note. These three reactions raise some very worthwhile points. Each writer is looking for a way to synthesize the major emphases of the different positions. A number of exciting papers and books in recent years have attempted to come to grips with these questions; sources which outline positions that make possible a true synthesis of insights that appear in diverse, and often fragmented, orientational disputes. Carkhuff's books (listed in the references), the recent writings of George Gazda, Frederick C. Thorne's work on eclectic psychotherapy (see Thorne's, "Eclectic psychotherapy" in R. Corsini (ed.), *Current psychotherapies* (Itasca, Ill.: F. E. Peacock, 1973, pp. 445-86) or any of Thorne's major works listed at the end of that article) come to mind as immediate examples. An impressive article by Carl Thoresen, "The counselor as an applied behavioral scientist" (*Personnel and Guidance Journal* 47 (1969):841-48) helps to bridge the gap between behaviorism and humanism, in a very practical way. There are also a number of case studies that reveal how counseling *in practice* does combine insights and procedures from different schools of thought. Bennee and Sherman's, "Julien," on pages 000-000, is a fine example of practical eclecticism. The case of "Dee" in Meyer and Meyer's *Counseling psychology; theories and case studies* (Boston: Allyn and Bacon, 1975, pp. 117-35) shows how behavioral counseling and client-centered counseling can be effectively combined in practice. And, finally, "Yes," there probably will be a time, in the not-so-distant future when there will be more agreement, although not *total* agreement, among counselors than there is today.

LOOKING FOR CONTINUITY

Dear Editor:

". . . I was trying in my own mind to relate the articles in the first two parts of the book to the articles in this part. How do counselor qualities (including the counselor's feelings, perceptions, behaviors, and self-actualizing tendencies) relate to any or all of these models? . . . Perry's article also comes to mind: are these models of helping what he would call therapy models, counseling models, or somewhere in the middle? Maybe you are circumventing the question by using the term 'helping,' but I'm not sure. Wouldn't Perry agree that both counseling models and therapy models are models of helping? . . ."

D. S.

BEHAVIORAL COUNSELING APPLAUDED

Dear Editor:

"The section on behavioral counseling offered some very valid insights that can easily be applied in practical situations. What I most admire about the behavioral approach, even if I disagree with some of its assumptions, is that it is concrete; that is, it shows how to go about doing whatever the counselor is supposed to be doing while it explains the reasons for it. The article on extinction and time-out, for instance, really set down some good guidelines that I could use in my own classroom. I think the desensitization approach would be difficult to use in a lot of cases, but some aspects of it might be used in the classroom. The flowcharts in Benoit and Mayer's article make the techniques quite accessible. . . ."

T. B.

THE EFFECTIVENESS OF HELPING MODELS

Dear Editor:

"I wonder if there is any evidence as to which of these models is most effective, or, if the question is broken down, which model is effective for which type of problem. I am sure that there are studies that compare one model with another in terms of which works best. My instructor mentioned, in class discussion, that the decision to use a certain model depends to a large part on the personality of the counselor and her training. But I'm not sure exactly what this means . . . In other words, what I'm trying to find out is which model will be best for me?"

E. Q.

Note. There are hundreds, probably thousands, of studies on the efficacy of different therapeutic approaches, but no clear conclusions can be drawn from the bulk of the literature. Bergin and Garfield's *Handbook of psychotherapy and behavior change* (New York: John Wiley, 1971) is rich in source materials and empirical analyses of the data. Bergin and Strupp's *Changing frontiers in the science of psychotherapy* (Chicago: Aldine, 1972) is a highly readable and very comprehensive discussion of the many problems involved in investigating psychotherapy scientifically.

But what you really want to know is which model is right for you, and this question cannot be answered by reading books. What you might do is explore, under the supervision of your counseling teacher, different approaches through role-playing, videotaping, and so on. In this way, you will learn the right approach by *feeling* it, rather than reading about it.

PART FOUR

CHILD COUNSELING

The models of helping discussed in the preceding section require, at time, special modification when the client is a child. While conceptions of children, and of *childhood* in general, have changed over the years, it has been recognized that the experiential world of the child, as well as the child's ability to deal with the world, are fundamentally different than that of the adult. In just what ways it is different, and what the specific limitations of the child are varies from epoch to epoch, although the spate of research on child development during our century is helping to clarify the issues, if not resolve them. Toby Talbot's comment about childhood pretty well sums up the general conception that prevails at this time:

Childhood, with its lightning changes of mood, its gratifications and deprivations, its fantasies and yearnings, its helplessness and power, is a purgatory to be traversed and a paradise lost, as well as a key to the adult's psychic life. Childhood is a unique stage of man's growth, not merely an anteroom to maturity. (*The world of the child*, ed. T. Talbot. Garder City, N.Y.: Doubleday Anchor, 1968, p. xi)

In this part of the book, we will examine some specific approaches to child counseling. Except for the first article, Freud's classic paper, "The sexual theories of children," which is theoretical in content, each of the other articles will discuss some practical aspects of treating children in the counseling and psychotherapy settings. The Freud paper is included because it is of interest to partisans of the nonpsychoanalytic as well as psychoanalytic approaches. It explicates, in specific terms, the myriad conflicts, rooted in sexual drives and wishes, that precipitate a host of fantasy-reality dilemmas in the child's psychological world.

Janet Finell's "Play therapy approaches to child counseling" combines the basic rationale for play therapy with rich case material. The specific treatment procedures used in the cases of a six-year-old boy and ten-year-old girl illustrate how play therapy is used in the clinical and the school setting. Newman and Stern's "The age game" also uses case material to illustrate the principles of child counseling; only in this case instead of play therapy, "a new therapeutic approach to children's conflicts," unlike any other that appears in the literature, is presented. This original approach is illustrative of the modern psychoanalytic counseling position, derived from the work of Dr. Hyman Spotnitz, and explained in Dr. Kirman's paper, "Modern psychoanalytic counseling," in part 3.

Finally, we come to "Julien," a unique approach to dealing with case study material. The chapter is the result of a cooperative effort between Dr. Fraser Bennee and Dr. Robert Sherman, who are presently developing a casebook using this approach. Dr. Bennee writes the case material, which is presented as a story (but a true story!), with all the drama and realism of the experience itself. Because she recognizes that the counseling process, and more importantly, that the processes of growth, cannot be limited to a single setting, she includes situations which allow us to view the client in a variety of perspectives. In Dr. Sherman's critique, which follows the case, the range of perspectives is used to interpret the underlying dynamics behind the case, and to point out to the reader some general principles which might be helpful in his or her own counseling practice. One of the important contributions of their approach is that it reveals how crucial the counselor's own feelings and perceptions are in the counseling

process, since the counselor, like the client, is also treated dramatically, and presented in vivid reality.

In the following pages, you will come into contact with a wide range of children in conflict. You will feel, along with them, the pains of conflict and frustration, their inability to react to stress in a healthy and appropriate way, the twin terrors of loneliness and emptiness that plague so many of the young people today. And, you will also see in the following pages the seeds of a brighter life germinating in a very special relationship between these children in conflict and other people—counselors, therapists, students—who have come to help them. Through these cases will emerge a picture of that very important, very difficult, very sensitive specialization, that we call child counseling.

SUGGESTED ADDITIONAL READINGS

Axline, V. M. *Dibs in search of self.* New York: Ballantine, 1967.

———. *Play therapy.* New York: Ballantine, 1969.

Dimick, K. M. & Huff, V. E. *Child counseling.* Dubuque: Wm. C. Brown Company Publishers, 1970.

Dreikurs, R. *Children: The challenge.* New York: Meredith, 1964.

Freud, A. *Psychoanalysis for teachers and parents.* New York: Emerson Books, 1947.

Josselyn, I. M. *Psychosocial development of children.* New York: Family Service Association, 1969.

Klein, M. *The psychoanalysis of children.* London: Hogarth Press, 1932.

Murphy, L. B. *et al. Colin: a normal child.* New York: Basic Books, 1956.

Talbot, T. ed. *The world of the child.* Garden City: Doubleday-Anchor, 1968.

17. THE SEXUAL THEORIES OF CHILDREN

Sigmund Freud

Peter Schwarzburg

The material on which the following synthesis is built up is derived from many sources. First, from the direct observation of what children say and do; secondly, from what adult neurotics consciously remember of their childhood and retail during psychoanalytic treatment; and thirdly, from the conclusions, reconstructions and unconscious memories translated into consciousness which result from the psychoanalysis of neurotics.

That the first of these three sources has not alone supplied all that is worth knowing on the subject is due to the attitude of adults towards childish sexual life. Children are not credited with any sexual activities, therefore no pains are taken to observe anything of the kind, while on the other hand any expressions of such a thing which would be worthy of attention are suppressed. Consequently the opportunity of gaining information from this most genuine and fertile source is greatly restricted. Whatever we derive from the uninfluenced communications of adults concerning their conscious childhood is at best subject to the objection that it is perhaps falsified in looking back and, further, has to be estimated in the light of the fact that the persons in question have later become neurotic. The material from the third source is subject to all the attacks that are in general directed against the trustworthiness of psychoanalysis and the reliability of the conclusions drawn from it, so that no justification of it can be attempted here; I will only assert that those who know and make use of the psychoanalytic technique acquire extensive confidence in its results.

I cannot guarantee the completeness of my collection, but I can answer for the care taken in gathering the material.

There remains a difficult question to decide. How far ought one to take for granted what is here reported about children in general as being true of all children, *i.e.*, of every individual child? Pressure of education and the varying intensity of the sexual instinct certainly render possible great individual variations in the sexual behaviour of children, and, above all, these things influence the date at which the childish interest in sexuality appears. Therefore I have not arranged my material according to the successive epochs of childhood, but have included in one recital what applies to various children, in one early, and in another late. It is my conviction that no child—none, at least, who is mentally sound, still less one who is mentally gifted—can avoid being occupied with sexual problems in the years *before* puberty.

I do not think much of the objection that neurotics are a special class of people marked by a degenerative disposition, whose child-life must not be regarded as evidence of the childhood of others. Neurotics are human beings like everyone else, and cannot be sharply differentiated from normal people; in their childhood they are not easily distinguishable from those who later remain healthy. It is one of the most valuable results of our psychoanalytic investigations to have found that their neuroses have no special mental content peculiar to them, but that, as C. G. Jung has expressed it, they fall ill of the same complexes with which we who are healthy also have to contend. The difference is only that the healthy know how to overcome these complexes without great and practically demonstrable harm; while the suppression of these complexes in nervous people only succeeds at the price of costly substitute-formations, thus in practice proving unsuccessful. In childhood nervous and normal people naturally approximate much more closely than in later life, so that I cannot recognize it as an error in method to make use of the communications of neurotics concerning their childhood as analogies for normal child-life. Since those who later become neurotics very frequently include in their constitution an especially strong sexual instinct and a disposition to precocity and to premature expression of this impulse, they enable us in this way to recognize much of the infantile sexual activities more plainly and more correctly than, with our blunted talent for observation of ordinary children, would otherwise be possible. The true value of these communications by adult neurotics can only be estimated, to be sure, when a collection of the childhood-memories of adult healthy people, made after the manner of Havelock Ellis, has also been taken into account.

In consequence of both external and internal unfavourable circumstances, the following remarks apply chiefly to the sexual development of one sex only, namely, the male. The value of a compilation such as I attempt here, however, need not be merely descriptive. The knowledge of the infantile sexual theories in the form in which they appear in childish thoughts can be of interest in various directions—for instance, surprisingly so for an understanding of myths and fairy-tales. They are indispensable for the understanding of the neuroses, where these childish theories are still in operation and have acquired a determining influence upon the form taken by the symptoms.

If, forgetting our mortality and imagining ourselves to be merely thinking beings, gazing, for instance, from another planet, we could apprehend the things of this earth afresh, perhaps nothing would arrest our attention more forcibly than the existence of two sexes among human beings, who otherwise resemble each other so closely and yet emphasize their difference even in the most superficial indications. Now it does not seem

that children also choose this fundamental fact as the starting-point of their investigations concerning sexual problems. Since they have known a father and a mother as far back as they can remember in life, they accept their existence as a reality which needs no further inquiry, and in just the same way does a boy behave towards a little sister from whom he is only separated by a slight difference of age, by one or two years. The child's desire for knowledge does not awaken spontaneously on this point at all, as it would if prompted perhaps by an inborn need to seek for causes, but arises under the goad of a self-seeking impulse which dominates him when he confronted by the arrival of a new child—perchance at the end of the second year. Those children whose own nursery at home does not become divided up in this way are nevertheless able as a result of their own observations to put themselves in the place of others who are in this situation in other homes. The loss of the parents' care and concern, which they actually experience or with justice fear, the presentiment that they must from now and forever share all possessions with the newcomer, have the effect of awakening the emotions of the child and sharpening its thinking capacities. The elder child expresses unconcealed hostility against the newcomer, which finds vent in unfriendly criticisms of it, in wishes that "the stork should take it back again," and occasionally even in attempts at little outrages upon the helpless creature lying in the cradle. A greater difference of age as a rule modifies the expression of this primary hostility; just as in somewhat later years, if brothers and sisters fail to appear, the wish for a playmate like those observed elsewhere obtains the upper hand.

Under the stimulus of these feelings and anxieties the child thus comes to consider the first of the great problems of life, and asks itself the question where children come from, which at first runs, "Where did this particular tiresome child come from?" The after-echo of this first riddle seems to be observable in the innumerable riddles of myths and sagas. The question itself, like all inquiry, is a product of dire necessity, as if to thought were entrusted the task of preventing the repetition of an event so greatly feared. At the same time, we may assume, the child's thinking becomes independent of the stimulus, and continues its activity as a separate impuls towards investigation. Where a child is not already too much intimidated, it takes sooner or later the shortest way by demanding answers from its parents of attendants, who signify for it the source of all knowledge. This way, however, fails. The child receives either evasive answers or a rebuke for its curiosity, or is dismissed with that mythologically significant information which in German runs: "The stork brings the children; it fetches them out of the water." I have grounds for supposing that far more children than parents suspect are dissatisfied with this solution, and respond to it with pronounced doubt, which, however, is not always outspoken. I know of a three-year-old boy who, to the terror of his nurse, was missed after receiving this enlightenment, and found at the edge of the big lake of the castle, where he had run, in order to see the children in the water! I know of another who could allow his disbelief only hesitating expression by saying he knew better, it was not storks who bring the children, but herons. It appears to me from much of the evidence conclusive that children refuse to believe the stork theory, and that from the time of this first deception and rebuff they nourish a mistrust against adults, have the presentiment of something forbidden which is being withheld from them by the "grownups," and consequently conceal their further investigations

by secrecy. With this, however, it comes about that they experience the first occasion of a "physical conflict," in that ideas for which they "by instinct" feel a preference, but which adults consider "naughty," come into opposition with others which are maintained by the authority of the adults without being acceptable to them themselves. Out of these mental conflicts there may soon arise a "mental dissociation"; the one idea which is bound up with "being good," but also with a cessation of thinking, becomes the prevailing conscious one; the other, for which meanwhile the inquiries prosecuted have brought new evidence, which is not supposed to count, becomes suppressed and unconscious. The nuclear complex of neurosis is formed in this way.

Lately, by the analysis of a five-year-old boy[1] which his father undertook and permitted me to publish, I have received an irrefutable proof of a piece of knowledge towards which the psychoanalysis of adults had for long led me. I now know that the changes in the mother during pregnancy do not escape the sharp eyes of a child, and that the latter is very well able subsequently to establish the correct connection between the increase in size of the mother's body and the appearance of a baby. In the case mentioned, the boy was three and a half when his sister was born, and four and three quarters when he showed his better knowledge by the most unmistakable allusions. This precocious knowledge is, however, always kept secret, and later, in connection with the future fate of childish sexual inquiry, is repressed and forgotten.

The stork fable, therefore, is not one of the infantile sexual theories; indeed, the observation of animals, who hide so little of their sexual life and to whom children feel so closely related, strengthens their disbelief. With the knowledge independently obtained that babies grow in the mother's body, a child would be on the right path to solve the problem on which it first tries its thinking powers. Its further progress is stopped, however, by a piece of ignorance which cannot be made good, and by false theories which the condition of its own sexuality imposes on it.

These false sexual theories, which I will now describe, all have one very curious characteristic. Although they go astray in a grotesque way, yet they all, each one of them, contain a bit of the real truth, so that they are analogous to those adult attempts at solution, which we call flashes of genius, of the problems of the universe that are too difficult for human comprehension. What is correct and hits the mark in these theories is to be explained by their origin in those components of the sexual instinct which are already active in the childish organism: for it is not due to an arbitrary mental act or to chance impressions that these notions arise, but to the necessities of the psychosexual constitution, and this is why we are able to speak of typical sexual theories in children, this is why we find the same false ideas in all children whose sexual life is accessible to us.

The first of these theories begins with a neglect of sex-differentiation, the neglect to which we called special attention at the commencement as being characteristic of children. It consists in attributing to everybody, including women, a penis just like the one the boy knows of from his own body. It is precisely in that sexual constitution which we must recognize as a normal one that the penis is already in childhood the governing erotogenic zone, the most important auto-erotic sexual object, and the estimate of its value is logically reflected in the impossibility of imagining a person similar to the self without this essential part. If a little boy obtains a sight of the genitals of a little sister, what he says will show that his prejudice is already strong enough to influence the per-

ception; he does not remark on the lack of the penis but *invariably* says, as if consoling and reconciling: that her "widdler" is still small, but when she is bigger it will soon grow. The idea of a woman with a penis returns still later in the dreams of adults; in a state of nocturnal sexual excitation he throws down a woman, exposes her and prepares for coitus; then on beholding the well-formed penis at the site of the female genitals, the dream and excitation break off. The numerous hermaphrodites of classic antiquity faithfully reproduce this once general infantile idea; one may observe that to most normal people they cause no offense, while actual hermaphroditic formations of the genitals in nature nearly always excite the greatest abhorrence.

If this idea of woman with a penis becomes, "fixated" in a child, it resists all the influences of later life and makes the man incapable of dispensing with a penis in his sexual object, so that such a person, if otherwise he has a normal sexual life, must become homosexual, seeking his sexual object in men who through other physical and mental qualities remind him of women. Real women, as they become known to him later, are excluded from being sexual objects to him because they lack the essential sexual attraction; indeed, in connection with another impression of childhood-life they may become abhorrent to him. A child who is chiefly dominated by penis-excitation usually produces pleasure by stimulation of it with his hand, is detected doing this by his parents or by the persons in charge of him, and is terrorized by the threat that his penis will be cut off. The effect of this "castration threat" is in direct proportion to the value set upon this part of the body, *i.e.*, quite extraordinarily deep-rooted and persistent. Sagas and myths testify to the revolt in the childish feelings, to the horror which is then linked to the castration complex, and this later is remembered with corresponding reluctance by consciousness. The woman's genitalia, seen subsequently and regarded as mutilated, recall this threat, and thus awaken in the homosexual horror instead of pleasure. This reaction is not altered by his learning through science that the childish assumption is not so far wrong after all, namely, that a woman also possesses a penis. Anatomy has recognized the clitoris within the female pudenda as an organ homologous to the penis, and the physiology of sexual processes has been able to add that this little penis which no longer grows behaves in the childhood of the woman like a genuine and real penis, that it is the site of excitations which leads to its being touched, that its excitability gives the sexual activity of little girls a male character, and that it needs an effort of repression in the years of puberty to make the woman develop through discarding this male sexuality. The fact that the sexual function of many women is crippled by their obstinately clinging to this clitoris excitability—so that they remain anaesthetic in coitus, or that repression succeeds so excessively that its action is partly nullified by hysterical compensatory formations—all this shows that the infantile sexual theory that a woman possesses a penis like a man has some truth in it.

One can easily observe that little girls are quite in agreement with their brothers' estimate. They develop a great interest in this part of a boy's body, but this interest is at once dominated by jealousy. They feel themselves injured; they make attempts to urinate in the position that is possible to the boy by his possession of the big penis, and when they express the wish, "I should love to be a boy," we know what lack the wish is to remedy.

If children could follow the hint given them by the excitation in the penis, they would get a little nearer to the solution of their problems. That the baby grows in the mother's body is obviously not a sufficient explanation. How does it get there? What starts it developing there? That the father has something to do with it is probable; indeed, he declares that the baby is also *his* child.[2] The penis, too, certainly also has its share in these mysterious happenings; it testifies to this by the accompanying excitation in it during all this thought-work. Along with this excitation obscure impulses are roused, which the child does not know how to account for—to do something violent, to press in, to knock to pieces, to burst open a hole somewhere. But when the child seems thus in a fair way to arrive at the existence of the vagina, and to attribute to the father's penis an act of incursion into the mother which should create the baby in the body of the mother, the inquiry breaks off helplessly; for at this point there stands in the way the theory that the mother possesses a penis like a man, and the existence of the cavity which receives the penis remains undiscovered to the child. One can readily surmise that the lack of success of this effort of thought facilitates a rejection and forgetting of it. These speculations and doubts, however, become the prototype of all later thought-work on problems, and the first failure has a crippling effect forever after.

Their ignorance of the vagina again makes it possible for children to have a conviction which constitutes the second of their sexual theories. If the baby grows in the body of the mother and is then detached from it, this can only happen by the sole possible way of the anal aperture. The child must be expelled like excrement, like a movement. If in later childhood the same question is the subject of solitary reflection or of a discussion between two children, then the explanations probably are that the baby comes out of the navel, which opens, or that the belly is slit and the child taken out, as happens to the wolf in the tale of Little Red Riding-Hood. These theories are expressed aloud and later consciously remembered; they no longer contain anything shocking. These same children have then completely forgotten that in earlier years they believed another sexual theory, which since then has undergone the subsequent repression of the anal sexual components. At that time an evacuation was something which could be spoken about in the nursery without shame; the child was still not so far distant from his constitutional coprophilic inclinations; it was no degradation then to come into the world like a mass of faeces, which had not yet been attainted by disgust. The *cloaca* theory, which is valid for so many animals, was the most natural and the only one which could force itself upon the child as probable.

Then, however, it was only logical that the child should refuse to grant women the painful monopoly of giving birth to children. If babies are born through the anus then a man can give birth just as well as a woman. A boy can therefore fancy that he too has children of his own without our needing to accuse him of feminine inclinations. It is only his still active anal erotism at work.

If the cloaca theory of birth is preserved in consciousness in later years of childhood, which occasionally happens, it is then accompanied by another solution of the question concerning the origin of children, one which, it is true, is no longer the original one. It is like that in fairy-tales. One eats some particular thing and from this one gets a child. The insane re-animate this infantile birth theory. A maniac, for instance, will lead the visiting physician to a heap of faeces which she has deposited in a corner of her cell, and say to him, laughing, "That is the child I bore today."

The third of the typical sexual theories appears in children when through some unforeseen domestic occurrence they witness parental sexual intercourse, concerning which they are then able to obtain only a very incomplete idea. Whatever detail it may be that comes under their observation, whether it is the position of the two people, or the sounds, or certain accessory circumstances, in all cases they arrive at the same conclusion, that is, at what we may call the *sadistic conception of coitus,* seeing in it something that the stronger person inflicts on the weaker by force, and comparing it, especially the boy, to a fight as they know it from their childish play, in which, by the way, an admixture of sexual excitation is also not wanting. I have not been able to establish whether children recognize this procedure which they observe between the parents as the necessary missing link in the problem of the birth of children; more often it appears that this connection is overlooked by children for the very reason that they had interpreted the love-act as an act of violence. But this sadistic conception itself gives the impression of a reappearance of that obscure impulse towards cruel activity which was linked up with penis-excitation when the child first reflected upon the puzzle of where children come from. The possibility cannot be excluded that that precocious sadistic impulse, which might have led to discovery of the mystery of coitus, itself appeared first under the influence of very dim memories of parental intercourse for which the child had obtained material, without at the time making use of it, when it shared the bedroom of its parents in the first years of its life.[3]

The sadistic theory of coitus, which by itself becomes a false guide where it might have led to enlightenment, is again the expression of one of the inborn components of the sexual instinct, any one of which may be more or less strongly marked in any particular child, and thus the sadistic conception is to a certain extent true; in part it divines the essence of the sexual act and the "antagonism of the sexes" which precedes it. Often, too, the child is in a position to support this conception by accidental observations which it understands in part correctly, in part falsely. In many marriages the wife, in fact, regularly opposes the matrimonial embrace, which to her brings no pleasure and the risk of a fresh pregnancy, and thus to the child who is supposed to be asleep (or pretending to be asleep) the mother might give an impression that could only be explained as meaning warding off an act of violence. At other times the whole marriage presents to the observant child the spectacle of an unceasing quarrel, expressed by loud words and unfriendly gestures, so that the child need not wonder that this quarrel goes on in the night, too, and is finally decided by the very same means which the child himself is accustomed to make use of in its intercourse with its brothers, sisters and companions, that is, by a fight.

The child also regards it as a confirmation of his idea if he discovers spots of blood in the bed or on his mother's linen. These are to him a proof that in the night an attack of this kind by the father on the mother has again taken place, while we should rather take the fresh spots of blood to mean that sexual intercourse for the time being had ceased. Much of the inexplicable "horror of blood" in the nervous finds its explanation in this connection. The child's mistake again covers a small part of the truth, for in certain well-known circumstances a trace of blood is indeed regarded as a sign of initiated sexual intercourse.

In less direct connection with the insoluble problem of where children come from, the child occupies itself with the question of what the nature and the content is of the state called "being married"; and it answers the question differently according to its accidental observations of its parents combined with its own impulses which are still invested with pleasurable feeling. All that these answers appear to have in common is that marriage promises pleasurable gratification, and presupposes a disregard for modesty. The idea I have most frequently met with is that "one urinates before the other"; a variation of this which sounds as if it signified better knowledge symbolically is that "the man urinates into the woman's chamber." On other occasions the meaning of marriage is supposed to be that the two persons show their buttocks to each other (without shame). In one case in which training had succeeded in postponing sexual knowledge especially late, a fourteen-year-old girl who had already begun to menstruate arrived at the idea from reading that being married signified "mixing blood," and since her own sister had not yet had a period the lustful girl attempted to outrage a visitor who confessed that she was just menstruating, so as to compel her to take part in this "mixing blood."

The infantile ideas about the nature of marriage, which are not seldom retained by the conscious memory, have great significance for the symptoms of later neurotic illness. They come into evidence first of all in childish games, in which one does with the other whatever it is that constitutes being married, and then later on the wish to be married can choose the infantile form of expression when it appears in a phobia or some similar symptom which at first sight seemed incomprehensible.[4]

These are the most important of the typical sexual theories that children produce spontaneously in early childhood-years under the influence of the components of the sexual instinct. I know that the material is far from complete and that I have not established a full connection between it and the rest of child-life. I can here add a few supplementary remarks which otherwise every experienced person would have missed in my account. Thus, for instance, the significant theory that one gets a child by a kiss, which obviously betrays a pre-eminence of the erotogenic mouth zone. In my experience this theory is exclusively feminine and is sometimes met with as pathogenic in girls whose sexual curiosity has undergone very strong inhibition in childhood. One of my female patients through an accidental observation happened upon the theory of the "couvade," which is well known among many races as a general practice, and probably has the purpose of contradicting that doubt about paternity that is never quite to be overcome. After the birth of his child, a rather strange uncle of hers remained for days at home and received visitors in his night-shirt, so she concluded that both parents had a share in the birth and must go to bed.

About the tenth or eleventh year information about sexual matters comes to children. A child who has grown up unchecked in its social relations, or who in some other way has found a good opportunity for observation, communicates to other children what he knows, because by doing so he can feel himself to be grown-up and superior. What children learn in this way is mostly correct, that is, the existence of the vagina and its use is revealed to them, but otherwise the enlightenment which they get from one another is frequently mixed with false ideas, and burdened with the remains of older infantile sexual theories. It is scarcely ever complete and sufficient to solve the original problems. Just as formerly with the ignorance of the vagina, so now ignorance of the semen prevents understanding of the whole process. The child cannot guess that out of the male sexual organ another substance can be expelled besides urine, and occasionally an "innocent" girl on her wedding night is still indignant because the man has "urinated into her." This information acquired before puberty links up with a fresh impetus in childish inquiries; the theories which the child now produces, however, have no longer the typical and original stamp, which was characteristic of the early primary ones as long as the infantile sexual components were uninhibited and untransformed and could come to expression in these theories. The later intellectual efforts to solve the sexual puzzle seemed to me not worth the trouble of collecting, nor have they much claim to a pathogenic significance. Their multiplicity is naturally mainly dependent upon the nature of the first information received, their significance consists rather in that they re-awaken the unconscious vestiges of that first period of sexual interest, so that not seldom masturbatory sexual activities and a part of the detachment of feeling from the parents is linked up with them. Hence the condemning judgment of teachers that such information at this age "corrupts" children.

A few examples may show what elements often enter into these later speculations by children about sexual life. A girl had heard from her school companions that the man gives the woman an egg, which she hatches in her body. A boy who had also heard of the egg, identified it with the testicle, which is vulgarly called by the same name, and thereupon puzzled his head how the content of the scrotum could always become renewed. The information given seldom reaches as far as to prevent important doubts on the matter of sexual processes. Thus girls may come to expect that coitus happens only on one single occasion but lasts very long, for twenty-four hours, and that from this one occasion come all the successive children. One would suppose that this child had knowledge of the process of propagation in certain insects: however, this conjecture was not confirmed and the theory appeared to be an independent creation. Other girls ignore the time of gestation, the life in the womb, and suppose that the child appears immediately after the night of the first connection. Marcel Prevost has turned this mistake of young girls into an amusing story in one of his *Lettres de femmes*. Hardly to be exhausted and perhaps in general not uninteresting is this theme of the later sexual inquiries of children, or of adolescents who have been delayed at a childish stage; but it lies further from my purpose, and I must only call special attention to the fact that many errors are invented by children in order to contradict older, better but now unconscious and repressed knowledge.

The way in which the child behaves when he receives information also has its significance. In many children sexual repression has gone so far that they will not hear anything, and these may also succeed in remaining ignorant until even later (apparently, at least) till the knowledge dating from early childhood comes to light in the psychoanalysis of neurotics. I know also of two boys between ten and thirteen years old, who certainly listened to sexual information but gave their informant the averting answer: "It is possible that your father and other people do such things, but I know for certain that my father would never do it." However this later attitude in children towards satisfying their sexual curiosity may vary, we can postulate a thoroughly uniform behaviour in them in early years and believe that at that period they were all eager to find out what it is the parents do with each other to make the babies.

NOTES

1. *Infra*, Freud, "Analysis of a Phobia in a Five-year-old Boy."
2. Freud, *op. cit.*
3. In his autobiographical book entitled *Monsieur Nicolas*, published in 1794, this sadistic misconception of coitus is confirmed by Restif de la Bretonne, who there relates an experience from his fourth year.
4. The games that are significant in later neuroses are the "doctor" game and the game of "father and mother."

18. PLAY THERAPY APPROACHES TO CHILD COUNSELING

Janet Finell

Peter Schwarzburg

Play is to the young child what words are to the adult. Play provides a means through which thoughts and feelings can be communicated, and distressing conflicts resolved. Through play, the child's attention can be captured and maintained as he enacts his inner fears and wishes in the safety and acceptance of the therapeutic relationship.

The use of play in child psychotherapy is a general technique that can be adapted according to the theoretical orientation of the practitioner. Two approaches to play therapy will be discussed in this paper: the psychoanalytic and the client centered approach. Two cases will then be presented: the first conducted in a clinic setting and the second in a school setting.

Child Psychoanalysis

Child psychoanalysts have shown that it is possible to adapt the basic psychoanalytic techniques to the treatment of children. The use of free association, analysis of the transference, resistance and the unconscious are the basic ingredients of psychoanalytic technique (Freud, 1938). The major adaptations of this technique to the treatment of children involve the use of play as an additional means of communication for the child whose verbal and conceptual sophistication make impossible the sole reliance on words that is generally found in the treatment of adults.

Anna Freud (1964) and Melanie Klein (1963) are considered to be founders of child analysis. Klein believed that the child's actions in the analytic setting, including the transference, are expressions of conscious and unconscious wishes. She treated play as the symbolic equivalent of free association, and analyzed it in accordance with psychoanalytic principles.

Unlike Klein, Anna Freud believed that much of the child's play in the analytic set-ting is merely random activity, unrelated to his problems. Although her therapeutic techniques include the use of play, the analysis of dreams and drawings, as well as verbal discussion, are also considered to be of great importance in work with children.

Anna Freud stressed the differences that exist in the treatment of children compared to adults. Children do not come to treatment voluntarily. They may be unaware that they have a problem. Their real need for and dependency on their parents minimizes the possibility of their developing a "transference neurosis," i.e., the re-experiencing of conflicts originally experienced with parents in the relationship with the analyst. Finally, the control that the parents continue to exercise over the child's life can threaten the gains achieved through the treatment. Therefore, in order for analytic work with children to be successful, the analyst must work to capture the child's interest, and to motivate him for the work ahead. Moreover, without parental cooperation, success is highly unlikely.

Case descriptions by child analysts (Baruch, 1952, Bergen, 1958, Gauthier, 1965) show how important the human relationship between child and analyst is in the treatment. However, unlike client-centered therapists' case descriptions, insight and the restructuring of the personality usually receive greater attention than the therapist-patient relationship.

Client-Centered Child Therapy

In contrast to psychoanalytic approaches, client-centered child therapists (Axline, 1967, 1969, Moustakas, 1974) focus on the phenomenological relationship between client and therapist. According to this school of thought, the therapist, above all, should provide a permissive environment in which the child is free to dramatize his conflicts and difficulties. The child is never told that he is in treatment for a particular problem, and no attempt is made to direct, control or structure his play activities. The child is in total command of the situation, and is responsible for his own behavior. Unless his behavior becomes destructive, no limitations are placed upon him. It is believed that an inner drive towards health and maturity provides the motivating force that makes the therapeutic play encounter meaningful.

The nondirective play therapist expresses neither approval nor disapproval of the child's behavior, in order to avoid influencing him in a particular direction. Empathy, acceptance and respect on the part of the therapist are believed to provide the support the child needs in order to gain self-respect, and a sense of his own dignity and worth. Minimal use is made of interpretation, although insight is believed to be necessary in order for the child to behave in a more mature manner. In contrast to Anna Freud's (1964) approach, parental involvement is not believed to be necessary for the maintenance of the therapeutic gains. However, if the parents show that they wish to cooperate with the therapist, their interest is encouraged.

Client-centered child therapists believe that play is the child's most natural means of self-expression. Therefore, play activities in the therapeutic office are the means through which he communicates to the therapist. His freedom to play in any way that he wishes, in an atmosphere of respect and understanding, are believed to foster his self-esteem. In *Dibs in Search of Self*, Axline (1967) provides a detailed description of the manner in which a disturbed youngster's play opened up a world that had formerly been closed by controlling parents.

Case Material

The two cases presented here provide examples of play therapy in the clinical and in

the school setting. The provision of simple toys such as dolls, trucks, cars, as well as paints, drawing materials and clay are sufficient tools for the young child to enact the vivid and anxiety-invoking events of his inner life. The privacy of the therapeutic office, the therapist's interest in the child and his problems, and the promise of confidentiality all contribute to a sense of trust and security in the child.

In the first case, a combination of psychoanalytically oriented play and verbal techniques were utilized in a brief fifteen-session treatment in the clinical setting. In the second case, the approach was basically an eclectic one which encompassed a three-year period, in the school setting.

John. John, aged six was brought to the clinic by his mother because of extreme fears of violence, nightmares and excessively timid behavior. John could not bear to hear the news on radio or television because the frequent broadcasts of stories of war and violence sent him into a panic. In addition, he allowed himself to be intimidated by his peers and made no attempts to defend himself even against children who were smaller than himself.

Although John was prepared for his visit to the therapist by his mother, he was visibly frightened and uncomfortable in the strange situation, and wanted to leave at once. After a few short visits in which no attempt was made to discuss his problems, he relaxed to the point that he began to look forward to the visits. Since his confidence was gained, the time seemed ripe to begin the discussion of his problems. The reason for his being in therapy was discussed, and his cooperation was sought. Being an intelligent and serious youngster, John had no difficulty in grasping the counselor's communication. In fact, he expressed pleasure at the chance he was given to obtain help in overcoming his fears.

During the introductory sessions John had

played with many of the toys. However, no particular pattern was observed in his play. Once the "therapeutic pact" was established, a change occurred in his play. He began to create scenes with a doll family that turned out to be quite repetitious. In practically each scene, the smallest boy doll was repeatedly injured: he fell from his father's shoulders, was hit by a car, etc. At other times, when the family was on an outing, the boy doll was accidentally left behind. The therapist suggested to John that the boy doll was really John, and that for some reason, as yet unknown to both of them, he saw himself as being hurt or left behind. Perhaps John felt he should be punished for something.

John showed that he understood these communications by responding in subsequent sessions with a change in the script. Now it was the father rather than the boy doll who was run over, fell out of the car, etc. This play continued repetitively, and provided some understanding into the meaning of John's fears.

It was now possible to understand John's fear of physical harm as a wish for punishment. He apparently harbored resentful and hostile feelings towards his father, and hoped that his father would be hurt. However, since father was so much stronger than John, retaliation—abandonment and destruction—was feared as the consequence for his wishes. For the child whose sense of reality testing is only partially developed, hostile feelings often seem like real acts. In the immature mind, thoughts are magically powerful, and are indistinguishable from deeds. They are, therefore, subject to punishment.

Play provided the means through which these interpretations were made to John. Just as John had used dolls to communicate his feelings and fears, the therapist now used the dolls to illustrate her interpretations. However, although progress was made in terms of the understanding of John's doll play; the reason for John's intense hostility toward his father was not yet known.

Fortunately, John's mother, Mrs. D, was extremely cooperative, and readily accepted an appointment to see the therapist. The basic groundrule for the therapeutic encounter was discussed—confidentiality. In spite of this, Mrs. D was somewhat reluctant to offer any information concerning intimate family matters. It was not until the third interview that she offered some insight into a home situation that was volatile, and was undoubtedly intensifying feelings in John that, according to Freudian theory, (1905), are universally present in children of his age.

Mother and father were engaged in bitter fights that had become so intense, that on occasion, the father would storm out of the house, threatening never to return. On the evenings of his absences, Mrs. D reported that John would stay up late with her, watching TV. It would seem then, as a result of John's experiences in the home, his Oedipal feelings were intensified and left him with an acute sense of guilt. John's guilt over his rivalrous feelings towards his father, as well as his fear of punishment by him, left him in a state of panic and confusion. The broadcast of violent news reawakened his inner terror. John anticipated attacks from others, and presented a picture of a child whose inner life was one of turmoil and disaster.

Once again, the therapist interpreted the reconstruction of John's psychic life in simple language, illustrating all interpretations with the dolls. Along with this interpretative work, John was assured that his wishes could in no way actually hurt his father, and that it was not his fault that his parents were fighting. Even if they separated, John was not to blame in any way.

The proof that John understood these interpretations was evident when, three weeks later in a telephone interview, Mrs. D reported that John's general panic had begun to subside. John no longer insisted that news broadcasts be shut off. Even more impressive was her observation that, for the first time as far as she could remember, John had pushed another boy in self-defense.

Therapy was discontinued after the fifteenth session, and a follow-up conversation with the mother one year later revealed that John had sustained the gains he had made through the therapy despite the fact that his father had permanently left the home. Mrs. D informed the therapist that after the separation she had decided to seek therapy for herself. She now felt more secure of her role as an independent woman than she had ever felt previously, and believed that she communicated a greater sense of stability to her son, as a result. The fact that she was now building a new life for herself and had become involved in activities outside of the home, made her less dependent on John as a husband substitute. Thus, it would seem that the psychic separation between parent and child so necessary for emotional maturity to be achieved, was now available to John.

Discussion

Without the use of play materials, it would not have been possible for John to communicate his inner fears and wishes to the therapist. For this six-year-old child, the doll family were the toys he chose to dramatize his inner conflicts and fears. Interpretation of his unconscious wishes would not have been possible without the use of the play materials to illustrate them.

Debbie. Debbie, aged ten, was referred for counseling by her teacher because of violent behavior that was characterized by attacks against her peers. Although she was undersized for her age, she often tyranized her classmates by hitting them, stealing their possessions, and hurling insults at them. Academically, although she was in fourth grade and had already been left back one year, Debbie could not read a first-grade reader, and had not mastered any of the basic academic skills. She was extremely hyperactive, and could rarely concentrate on anything for longer than a few minutes. She made inordinate demands on the teacher for attention, and flew into a rage when she couldn't get her way.

The counselor referred Debbie to the school psychologist for testing, and after obtaining permission from her guardian, an aunt, a battery of intelligence and personality tests were performed. The results showed that Debbie was of low normal intelligence, and suffered from intense feelings of anger and rejection.

In consultation with Debbie's aunt, Mrs. S, it was learned that when Debbie was seven years of age, her mother had died as a result of an overdose of drugs. Debbie and her two older siblings had discovered her dead body one morning. They thought their mother was sleeping and shook her to try to awaken her. When she didn't move, they became terrified and rushed to their aunt's and uncle's home, where they were taken in and cared for. Shortly after their mother's death, their father died also.

Mrs. S was quite communicative about the children's past, and offered a considerable amount of information to the counselor. She was quite concerned about the three children, whom she now considered as her own. She knew about Debbie's disruptive behavior and academic failure, but in spite of her pleas and interest in the child, which she considered to be greater than the interest provided by Debbie's natural mother, the child's behavior and work were unchanged.

Debbie was delighted at the prospect of coming to counseling, and responded to the counselor in a very positive manner. She expressed the desire to come for sessions as frequently as possible. Therefore, sessions were scheduled on a twice-a-week basis, and an appointed time was arranged. In the counseling office, Debbie took the lead without prompting, explored the materials, and appeared comfortable with the counselor. Despite her "dull normal" tested IQ, she was quite articulate, and could communicate her needs very clearly.

Debbie made active use of the play materials. She would often play "house," and tended to act as a stern and punitive mother to the dolls and stuffed animals. After she had been coming to counseling for a few months, she began to insist that the toys be left exactly where she had placed them. Although she was told by the counselor that she was free to do anything she wanted to with the toys during her time, no promise could be made that they would be exactly where she had placed them when she returned. Debbie's reasonable ego accepted these limitations, and although she was annoyed when, in subsequent sessions, the toys were not where she had left them, she gradually accepted the fact that the counselor saw other children too.

Debbie was not so reasonable, however, when her sessions came to an end, and it was time to return to her classroom. Her difficulty in accepting limits, and her inordinate need for the counselor's attention reached its height, when after four months of counseling she flew into rages at these times. She kicked the counselor and screamed, "I hate you. I'm not coming here anymore." She would run away, hide, hang onto stairway railings, and had to be carried bodily back to her classroom. Her behavior disturbed nearby classes, and the situation became critical when the principal warned that if the counselor could not control Debbie, her sessions would have to be ended.

The play materials proved to be the means through which Debbie was able to communicate to the counselor what she was feeling at these times. The counselor made the following request of Debbie: "Show me what you are feeling when it's time for you to leave." Debbie responded by wrapping a doll in newspaper, and placed it deep within the counselor's closet. She demanded that no other child be allowed to touch the doll. The counselor understood that Debbie wished to be with her constantly. Separation was painful for this child who had experienced the loss of her parents when she was quite young. If Debbie felt certain that a doll was hidden away in the counselor's closet, she would feel that she herself was symbolically with the counselor even when she had to leave her. Moreover, the demand that no other child be allowed to touch the doll indicated that Debbie regarded the counselor's other clients as rivals for her love.

Debbie's request was granted—the doll would remain in the closet, but Debbie would have to leave at the scheduled time without a tantrum. The counselor reflected Debbie's anguish at separating:

"You get very angry at me when it's time for you to leave. Perhaps you feel that I don't care about you, or that I won't be here for your next visit. But you know that when it's your turn to be here, I always see you. I have never disappointed you."

Thus, the counselor assured Debbie that the relationship was a warm and stable one. Unlike Debbie's mother, the counselor would not suddenly disappear. Debbie could count on her to be there.

In these months of counseling, Debbie had

shown that she could be not only charming and winning, but manipulative and excessively demanding as well. Therefore, the setting of limits was an important part of Debbie's treatment.

In her second year of counseling, Debbie played with the toys in a manner that was quite similar to her earlier game of "house." She frequently set up a mock classroom in which the dolls and stuffed animals were made to represent children. They were given writing materials, and were tested on their knowledge of reading, math and spelling. The dolls and animals generally made mistakes, failed exams, and were threatened by Debbie with being left back. She screamed at them, told them they were bad and stupid, and sometimes hurled objects at them. The counselor was a silent observer of this play. However, before long Debbie insisted that the counselor too must play act that she was one of the children in the "class." Like the others, she had to make mistakes and was insulted and ridiculed for her stupidity. As the "teacher," Debbie was in her glory. She was experiencing the opportunity to master in an active manner what she had experienced passively almost continuously throughout her schooling: failure and humiliation.

This play continued repetitively for a number of months. During this time, the counselor learned that Debbie was now beginning to participate in classroom activities. Her previous stubborn refusal to attempt to read or write had now yielded to persistent attempts on her part to catch up to her classmates. The remedial reading teacher reported that, for the first time, Debbie consented to read aloud in front of other children. She was beginning to overcome her shame at being such a poor reader, and to behave in a manner that opened the way to academic improvement. Thus, through her play, Debbie had managed to overcome, to a considerable extent, the shame and anger that she had experienced in the classroom situation. It is quite possible too, that the mean and punitive teacher symbolized the mother who through her death had abandoned Debbie. Debbie's teacher game may have given her the opportunity to work out some of these feelings as well.

Unfortunately, Debbie's progress was interrupted when, quite suddenly, her uncle died of a heart attack. As surrogate father, Debbie's uncle had been very loving and involved with the children. He and the aunt together provided a sense of security that Debbie had apparently not experienced in her early years. His sudden death left Debbie with feelings that she could not handle. She retreated from all academic efforts, and spent her days in her classroom with her head resting on her desk. In counseling, she was lethargic. She complained of fatigue. It was difficult for her to climb steps, and she had an intense desire to sleep. It appeared that Debbie was depressed, and was retreating into a world where nothing could hurt her anymore. In doing so, however, she was cutting herself off from involvement with her love objects. Such a retreat from the real world can be cataclysmic at any age. For this psychologically delicate and vulnerable child, her retreat from reality was frightening to observe.

During this time, the counselor sat quietly with Debbie, and accepted her retreat. She was not forced to come out of her shell. The hours were quiet ones in which little activity occurred. Debbie knew, however, that the counselor understood how bad, and how frightened she felt. The counselor's facial expression, her acceptance of Debbie's withdrawal, and her sympathetic presence were available throughout this difficult period.

After a few months, Debbie' depression appeared to ease. She began to draw pictures. About a house she had drawn, she said:

"This is a lonely house. I'm going to put a man and woman there to make it a happy house."

Debbie then ripped up the picture into tiny bits. She was apparently trying to deny how lonely and empty she felt inside.

Debbie drew faces, with empty staring eyes, and expressionless mouths. They all looked very much alike. Her comments about some of her pictures were as follows:

Face of a woman: "There ain't a lot of woman, just one. This woman is a nice woman."

Face of a man: The man. This man is a lonely man so you know what I'm gonna do? I'm going to put the man and the woman together so she can be happy."

Her comments about a picture of herself were: "She's sad, skinny. No one likes to play with her. She doesn't have a family."

Thus, the theme of loneliness and sadness pervaded Debbie's pictures, and her comments about them. As she drew these pictures, Debbie expressed certain infantile longings as well as fears of the future. She wished she could be a baby again; everything was nice when she was a baby. She wished she had a mother and father. She remembered her mother's death. It frightened her. She was afraid her aunt would die too. She didn't know how her aunt would have enough money to support them.

The recollection of her past suffering, and her expressions of anxiety about the future apparently unburdened Debbie from some of the anguish that she had been suffering from inwardly. She regained some of her high energy level, and seemed to come out of the depression. An extremely difficult crisis in her life had been mastered.

The final problem in Debbie's long-term counseling revolved around termination. The approach of her graduation to junior high school meant that Debbie and the counselor would be separated. How would this child whose relationship with the counselor had been so intense, and so gratifying, deal with the separation? Would she experience it as another abandonment, and become depressed?

In order to avoid termination being experienced as a sudden shock, the implications of Debbie's graduation were taken up by the counselor many months before it was due to occur. Debbie was frightened at the prospect of her sessions coming to an end. At the same time, she was excited about the thought of going to a new school, and being more "grown-up."

By June, it was obvious that the months of discussion regarding termination had prepared Debbie for the separation. Her behavior had become more mature. Although she was still behind in her school work, she had improved considerably. Her social adjustment was good: she rarely fought and had had no temper tantrums for over a year. A follow-up revealed that Debbie's adjustment to junior high school had gone smoothly; she appeared to be holding her own. Occasional visits to the counselor were joyful occasions for both Debbie and the counselor; Debbie seemed self-confident and happy.

Discussion

The case of Debbie demonstrates the importance of a warm, stable and supportive relationship in the life of a child who had experienced a number of traumatic losses. Play and drawings were combined with verbal discussion in the counseling approach described above. Minimal use was made of interpretation, and the child took the lead in most of the therapeutic encounters. Mature behavior came to replace immature behavior, and Debbie was eventually able to function without the counselor's support.

REFERENCES

Axline, Virginia M. *Dibs in search of self.* New York: Ballantine Books, 1967.

———. *Play therapy.* New York: Ballantine Books, 1969.

Baruch, Dorothy W. *One little boy.* New York: Dell Publishing Company, Inc., 1952.

Bergen, Mary E. The effect of severe trauma on a four-year-old child, *The psychoanalytic study of the child,* V. 13, (1958):407-29.

Freud, Anna. *The psychoanalytical treatment of children.* New York: Schocken Books, 1964.

Freud, Sigmund. *Three essays on the theory of sexuality* (1905). V. 7, *Standard edition.* London: The Hogarth Press, 1964.

———. *An outline of psychoanalysis* (1938). V. 23, *Standard edition.* London: The Hogarth Press, 1964.

Gauthier, Yvon. The mourning reaction of a ten-and-a-half-year-old boy, *The psychoanalytic study of the child,* V. 20, (1965):481-94.

Klein, Melanie, *The psychoanalysis of children.* London: The Hogarth Press, 1963.

Moustakas, Clark E. *Children in play therapy.* New York: Ballantine Books, 1974.

19. THE AGE GAME

Mildred R. Newman and E. Mark Stern

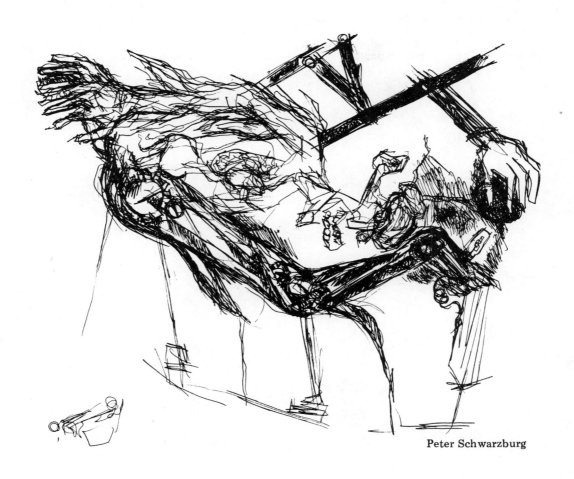

Peter Schwarzburg

This article considers a new therapeutic approach to children's conflicts. It is based on the concept that regression is helpful in the treatment of the emotionally disturbed child. The technique itself, which is called "The Age Game," was conceived spontaneously by one of the authors in response to her own children's complaints about being ages four and five, respectively. She was fascinated by their verbalized wish to be babies.

"Okay," she said, "let's play a game. You can be any age that pleases you, but you must be that age and if you want to be a baby, you must play like you are a baby. If you do anything which is not what a baby does, you are out."

The older child said that she would very much indeed like to be an infant.

"Okay," said mother, "come cuddle in my arms and we'll make believe that you are an infant."

The child sat down on her mother's lap, cuddled up and said, "I am a baby only two weeks old."

"Oh, what a darling baby! You are just lovely. How are you, baby?"

"Fine," replied the five-year-old child, at which point, of course, it was explained that two-week-old babies cannot talk. They probably could coo and they might smile, but they just couldn't talk.

The game was used for a number of years as a diversion when moods seemed to need a little cheering. After a time the children realized how good it was to be their own true age.

This suggested a therapy of reenactment of early wishes in children, where there is a need to get at an "itchy" area of trouble so that there may be growth instead of stagnation. It also seemed possible that it might be of some use in selective moments in the psychoanalysis of adults.

The significance of regression in child therapy has been widely recognized. Melanie Klein(6) reasons that normal and pathological regression causes "the reemergence of early infantile sexuality." She attributes Oedipal fantasies to the very earliest stages of life, and uses these regressive traces in her treatment of children, directly interpreting the Oedipal situation in them. Paula Heimann,(5) in espousing the work done by Kleinian child analysts, makes the following observation:" . . . the analysis of children and adults (has) shown us that the most crucial contents of the Oedipus complex, and the most severe conflicts and anxieties, relate to the primitive impulses and phantasies which form the early states of the Oedipus complex."

Anna Freud(4) infers that the "child's neurotic reactions (remain) grouped around the parents who are the original objects of the pathogenic past." However, Sara Kut(7) describes the phenomenon of "regressed conflicts" which she feels are "repeated in the analysis with the therapist as the actual object, and only resolved and finally given up when these (are) interpreted."

It is our feeling that regression centers not so much about primary outside objects, but is basically an expression of the child's desire for mastery and a conflict-free existence. It is doubtful, in our minds, that children are as concerned with early fears as they are with ideal moments of peace experienced earlier. Even looking back at a difficult infancy, a child might recognize it as an age lived through. The most anxious part of being one's own age is the unpredictability of the future. To look back at a closed book is to know that it began and ended, which makes for the attractiveness of regressive fantasies. Allowing for the fact that the earlier years may be filled with pain, they still, nevertheless, have been dealt with and are past.

Regression to earlier ages is both a fact and a useful tool in psychotherapy. The analytic situation itself creates a climate for behavior characteristic of the most dependent stages in a person's life. The transference experience opens up vistas for the acting-out of early infantile experiences. The couch is not unlike the crib, where the baby is unable to see his mother on demand. It is often reported by patients that the very helplessness and dependency make for a total change in their view of their age positions. In fact, total reliance of the patient on the analyst is the core of the transference neurosis, recommended by Freud as a step toward rehabilitation. To recoup one's self from the transference neurosis is to regain one's age.

Considerable work employing regression has been done by workers in the field of psychotherapy with adult schizophrenics. Sechahaye(12) states that a thorough exploration "into the regressed effective stage is extremely important in the application of symbolic realization, for only in proceeding from the actual level of regression can real contact with the patient be established." Searles(10) emphasizes that:

to join the (schizophrenic) patient more and more often in mutually enjoyable plays on words, contributions of chaotically nonsensical verbalization and uninhibited flights of fancy (has helped restore) what was best and healthiest in the patient's very early relationship with the mother, and it is upon this kind of playful and unfettered interaction, historically traceable to the beginnings of verbal relatedness in the young child's life that the patient's gradual development of firm ego boundaries, and use of more logically organized, adult forms of thought and communication, can be founded. The therapist learns, to his surprise, that there is a kind of chaos and confusion which is not anxiety provoking and destructive, but thoroughly pleasurable—the playful chaos which a mother and a little child can share, or which two little children can share, where mutual trust prevails to such a degree that there is no need for self-defensive organization. (p. 43)

Hypnosis also involves chronological retrogression. The subject becomes fixated to a helpless circumstance in which only the hypnotist has any real authority. His sense of adulthood becomes diminished in the hypnotic condition. Age regression techniques are used in order to arrive at information about early functioning which may be diagnostically or therapeutically helpful. However, in hypnotherapy, as in other techniques, regression is used as an aid to growth. To make the patient potent is to make the present possible.

Regression in psychotherapy, like the transference and the resistance, seeks to acquaint both analyst and patient with areas of expression not always accessible in other relationships. Jules Masserman(5) discusses channels of communication as a road to the understanding of various developmental clusters. For example, in the very young, the most prominent needs are for security and care. Most motives at these early ages are built upon such needs. After adolescence, however, there are fairly strong aggressive drives. Prestige and sexual gratification take on greater importance.

Masserman considers the different age levels as pathways to articulation. He alludes to the various forms of communication which may call up various age levels. The appeal to the "inspirational" and "patriotic" tends to waken a schoolage child. However, the fact that all ages respond to early childhood sentiments shows that no part of our developmental life ever gets completely lost.

Any therapy technique rests on making an individual aware of the rewards of being his own age. Regression, therefore, must always surface those drives within the individual which push forward. To be a child for some patients is inviting, because only during childhood was there any reward, no matter how meager. A brief case in point will help clarify the meaning of this concept:

Jane, now a mother of two young children, was invited to spend the weekend with her parents. Living at her parents' home are two brothers, both of whom are severely disturbed, and suffer from severe helplessness. Jane came back to the city after this weekend enormously despondent. She felt quite unable to cope with her own children and the demands for being a responsible mother. It became clear during the interview that Jane was acting out her own infantile aspirations. Her mother said, during the weekend, that she was too strong, and this created a barrier between them. Jane realized that there was no way of getting close to her mother except by being helpless and emotionally ill. Jane displayed characteristics befitting a youngster who had at least a possibility of deriving some affection from her mother.

Both of Jane's parents were apparently very indulgent to the weak members of the family. Only by weakness could they see themselves as strong. Jane's strength made it impossible for any chance of closeness. Therefore, Jane acted as if she were once again a little child. However, this didn't work out very well for her and she had to sullenly face the prospect of being an adult. The only help the therapist could provide, in addition to pointing up to her the acting out and what it meant, was to reassure Jane about the bittersweet components of being part of one's age group. It might actually mean that she would not have all of the affection she desired from her mother. However, it would insure that she would be a more capable mother and mate. It would mean that she would have to face the pains and pangs of responsibility, but it would insure her a sense of dignity and freedom.

This case illustrates the theme attempted in the age game. The yearning to return to the years of helplessness is probably indicative of the desire for some gratification which was then possible. Now it seems that there is a sense of aloneness and pain in facing one's existential plight. Being alone is the unfortunate consequence of being older. One becomes more aware of aloneness as the years go by and the necessity of separation from the all-caring mother is recognized. Troubling as this may seem it is, by necessity, a step in self-realization and fulfillment. Ideally, to recognize one's aloneness involves new possibilities and choices. The older child is no longer protected by mother, is in fact no longer one with the breast. If he is to have chums, he must do this by choice and effort. How comforting it would be to go back, but one soon learns that there is a price involved. The price is the sacrifice of one's intrinsic desire for freedom and autonomy. No regression can ever be so comforting as to be a final goal. Sternback(14) hinted at some factors which contribute to the therapy of arrested ego development in children. The need for the therapist to wean and guide, a task which he states is essentially "one of upbringing, of training, of encouragement, education and socialization," is obviously based on the assumption that much of the disturbed child's inner core has never been given a chance to develop.

Remembering that the age game was an outgrowth of an informal play technique used by one of the authors with her children, we can now introduce it into the therapeutic arena. Two cases will be presented, treated separately by each of the authors. The illustrations are not so much to focus attention on a specific therapeutic tool as to suggest variations based on the same principles that may be useful to the child analyst.

Case One

Doris, a ten-year-old girl, suffered from a severe school phobia brought on after a weekend trip with her father. The terrors surrounding school attendance were based on a strong suspicion on Doris' part that if she attended school through the day, she would return to find her mother dead. Diagnostically, it was understood through traditional play techniques that Doris' fear was based on an unconscious hostility to her mother. Her anxiety reached a climax when she was alone with her father on a weekend vacation. If her "good" wishes to be with her father could come true her "bad" wishes to kill her mother could also come true.

Most of the "bad" feelings were on an unconscious level. The child was certainly not aware of her fears as such. Her relationship to her father was an extremely close one, in part because of his seductive mode of relating to his daughter. This created guilts in Doris which she was unable to allow herself to deal with. Not only her being a child, but her being frightened of her own sexual attractiveness to her father, destroyed any real impetus for growing. Growing, in a sense, would involve more danger.

No amount of cajoling or bribery could get Doris to return to class. It seemed out of the question to Doris to leave her mother. The therapist was concerned with the possibility that a breakdown might result if any pressures were brought to bear on the child to return to school. One day the therapist mentioned the age game, described it and invited Doris to join her in playing. Doris had a brother who was four years old, and the analyst was aware of Doris' wish to be as young as Tony. This, the therapist felt, would mean both that Doris could be more like her father, and also lose her terror-ridden feelings for her parents.

Doris initially seemed disinterested, but then asked if she might play the game after all, and expressed the feeling that it would be nice to be her four-year-old brother. The therapist discussed the rules with her. She told Doris that she could choose any age she liked, but that if she acted a different age, she would have to be excluded. The challenge to remain in the game became a motivating factor, making it possible for the child to put a great deal of feeling into her newly adopted role.

Doris decided that her first undertaking would be age four. She could now act like Tony. She wanted to play a card game and told the therapist that she was going to cheat, because it was perfectly permissible to cheat at age four. She drew pictures in a haphazard fashion typical of a child four years of age. She was obviously being gratified at this age level. Firstly, she could feel identified with her father, and secondly, she felt freed from her conflict. She was excused from attending school as long as she decided to be age four, giving her a sense of rightness about her behavior.

After some sessions, she decided to be age six. It was apparent that she was learning to trust the analyst, whom she regarded as most helpful in providing the scenery and advantages of a four-year-old and six-year-old, respectively. She was also impressed by the fact that the analyst was consistent in the enforcement of the rules. Doris could, at both ages four and six, learn to face her fears about leaving her parents for any length of time. Six years old created slightly more anxiety than four, but still it was not ten, which was the most troublesome age of all. The six-year-old level seemed best suited to her future plans.

At the next session, she made no mention of the game. Instead she drew a picture of being on a desert island with her father. She was able, at this time, to talk more freely about her desire to be with her father. Both therapist and child were in a better position to discuss the realities of her nonattendance at school and other related problems. Soon school created no problems. She was able to leave her mother for long periods of time during the day. The direction of therapy became more verbal. The girl is now sixteen years-old and has returned to the analyst on rare occasions to report.

Case Two

A seven-year-old boy was seen in therapy because of general behavior problems in school, which threatened to drop him from the rolls. At home he was rebellious, refused to go to bed at night, and when he finally did, invariably wet the sheets. Psychological evaluation pointed to retardation. This evaluation caused the school to discharge him on the basis of inability to learn.

Timmy approached therapy with an avid interest in the toys around the room. He was fascinated by a water fountain and loved to spend hours mixing paints and diluting them as he went along with more and more water. Interpretive material was introduced in relation to water and paint, and his joy in elimination. His mother was so heartbroken about Timmy's asocial behavior that she tended to discourage all play activity at home for fear that it was inappropriate to this age. The therapist made it quite clear that he could play with "messy" paint and water if he chose and that, in fact, he might like to pretend he was a little boy, a very little boy, who had the opportunity to wet his bed without being censured. The therapist enlisted the mother's cooperation. She was asked to extend the rules of the game to the home. This meant that if Timmy chose to be a certain age, she would be informed of this and Timmy would be expected to carry through at this age at home, with all the advantages and disadvantages his choice involved.

Timmy chose to be a little baby, who was permitted to speak only to tell the therapist his wishes. The therapist and Timmy spent some time going over the rules and deciding what a little baby could and could not do. For example, a little baby could go to the park, but he could not walk in the park—he would have to be carried. This brought many smiles to Timmy's face who looked forward to the prospect of being carried across the room to an area the therapist had designated as the park. Once he arrived at the park, he was not permitted to romp around and play, because he could not yet have learned how to walk. To this he agreed, not thinking at the time of the limitations but about the advantages of being carried as a baby is carried.

As was expected, Timmy was titillated with being pampered. He was even informed that if he wanted to urinate and defecate, he would do so in his trousers, since a change of trousers and underwear was available at the clinic. Timmy never took advantage of this permission, but insisted on being carried to the "park" and the "playground." However, he balked at the idea that he could not play when he arrived in the symbolic playground, but had to remain in one place. The therapist explained to him that he could not talk to him very much while at the playground, since the therapist could not expect a little baby to understand more than baby talk. After three sessions of playing at being a baby, and being denied related privileges at home Timmy decided that he would begin to break some of the rules. He was then informed that he could no longer be a baby but would have to choose another age.

He next decided to become an adult, like the therapist. At the same time he chose to be his mother's husband. His mother was separated from Timmy's father and Timmy was enthusiastic about filling his father's place. He began to try to talk like an adult. When riding the subway with his mother, after leaving the clinic, he would take her arm, look for a seat which she could occupy and be, all in all, very attentive. He was, of course, not permitted to play as a baby. If he did, the advantages of adulthood could be taken away, such as a bed hour as late as he chose, and as many portions of food as he wanted. He could no longer drink from a bottle, or be permitted to urinate in his pants. The therapist also told him that he would have to control wetting his bed, as this was typical for a younger child and not for an adult.

Timmy stopped wetting his bed at this point, a pattern which did not return as long as he was in treatment. His behavior at school began to improve. No appreciable change could be seen in his general intellectual development, and it remained doubtful whether he could actually succeed in a regular school. His mother was more inclined to value psychotherapy and more available for cooperative efforts. The therapist had to leave the country at this time and was forced to drop the case. There was no systematic follow-up, since the clinic felt Timmy was doing sufficiently well and he was not, therefore, assigned to another therapist. The therapist heard from Timmy's mother a few years later about resuming treatment, and a suitable referral was made.

Discussion

The age game is primarily acceptable to children precisely because it is both playful and serious. Participation in games is an underlying motivating factor in attracting the youngster to serious business about himself. Involvement in play makes it possible to reach back to feelings and actions of an earlier age. Verbalization itself frequently falls short of presenting a true picture of a child's desire because of the lack of safety words connote during childhood and early adolescence.

Both authors have employed the age game in some form with selected adult patients. Here it takes on the nature of role playing. The patient is encouraged to feel and act as he might have at an earlier stage of his life. He is encouraged to deal with the feelings and thoughts he had then. For example, a therapist might suggest that the patient spend a session or two talking and thinking as he might have on the day he first entered school. Sometimes the patient is asked to act out a condensed twenty-four hour period typical of the time he was a small child. Individuals are encouraged to keep with the age as best they can.

Other workers have used related techniques with adults. Ferenczi(3) expresses his gratitude to workers in child analysis for having inspired a "game" in his analysis of adults. He states:

When you consider that, according to our experience hitherto, and to the premises with which we start, most pathogenic shocks take place in childhood you will not be surprised that the patient, in the attempt to uncover the origin of his illness, suddenly lapses into a childish or childlike attitude. [Ferenczi then asks:] Is there any advantage in letting the patient sink into the primitive state of the child? (p. 137) [He answers somewhat later in his paper:] The analyst's behavior is . . . like that of an affectionate mother, who will not go to bed at night until she has talked over with the child all his current troubles; large and small, fears, bad intentions, scruples of conscience, and has set them at rest. (p. 137)

Coleman and Nelson(2) in their "paradigmatic psychotherapy" in which of "demonstration" rather than interpretation "ten proved valuable in the conduct of the therapy of borderlines" state: "The patient is placed in the position of a growing child who is subject to the impact of many personalities with their disparate temperaments and viewpoints." In acting out many contrasting roles for the patient, the therapist becomes a "paradigm of the world in which the patient must learn to move."

Sechahaye(12) and Searles, (10) mentioned above, are involved in prolonged games with their patients. Sechahaye in one case felt that she became "mama-therapist" to a "schizophrenic child" The careful interpretation of symbolic foods for mother's breasts became a restorative tool in the famous case of Rene.

Moreno(9) in the psychodrama of the patient's conflict helps recreate old situations with new methods of resolution. A return to the past or past event is lived through again, but as in a sometimes optimistic dream, with more power and a more comfortable ending. In still another form Moreno had attempted to eliminate the "interpersonal resistance" in a case of a child who expressed nothing but extreme hostility and disdain for his mother. He had actresses play through experiences in his life, but the significant woman, rather than being a mother was a princess, than a queen—on to a college professor, a mayor's wife, a nurse and finally his own mother. The mother herself did not appear, however, until the therapy helped to "interpolate resistances." The actress who played the queen was asked by the therapist to become more aggressive or more like the child's mother.

In another context one of the authors(13) helped a patient reveal the lost child in herself and thus assisted in the recovery of a classical case of disassociation or "split personality."

In this context we have attempted to point

up the value of a patient acting contrary to his age within the therapeutic experience. One is reminded of Whiting's(15) statement that "If a child were permitted by the rules of his culture to perform the roles of any status he wished (i.e., any envied status), the process of socialization might be quite different from what it is." (p. 121) Why the older child is denied the right to be what he wants, or the right to act like a baby when it would be most helpful to him goes beyond the scope of this paper. We have found that the age game helps restore some of these privileges.

The concept of game makes it clear that much of what is denied in ordinary social process is permitted in the game. Children denied the use of large quantities of money are allowed to speculate on huge real estate ventures in the game, "Monopoly." Adults who dress according to the custom of the community may enter a masquerade contest. But always rules govern these games. Bateson(1) comments that in play and fantasy the player must agree upon rules. Thus for a schizophrenic to talk in a "word salad" within the psychological frame of therapy, is, in a sense, not pathological. After they have ceased to play they are free to discuss the rules and modify them. Thus it is in the age game. The child (or adult) plays his adopted role as does the therapist. If the rules are broken, then they are discussed, and either agreed on for the next role or modified to a point where they become another form of therapy as in the case of Doris where talking and drawing a picture become the new game.

The age game becomes of value as the participants, i.e., patient and therapist, learn the many faceted value of emotional growth from it. Stern(13) found in his work with an older adolescent that growth did not mean extinguishing the child part of a borderline schizophrenic adolescent girl. Instead, he found that helping the personality appreciate the introjected child and using it when needed, will allow for more effective growth than the rigid controls we are too well aware of in our culture. Bateson states that the patient "must learn that fantasy contains truth." (p. 50) Those who help their patients play the age game will learn that the baby in their individual psychodynamic structures has something important to say to the more grown-up portion of the personality.[1] If it is not permitted to have its say then a rage may flare within. The age game is no more than a recognition of the importance of areas of personal expression ordinarily discouraged by social norms. Or to use Whiting's(15) words, ". . . the adult role is to some degree a carry-over of part of the child's role." (p. 124) Whether used in child analysis or adult therapy, the age game can be an aid to the growth and development of an enriched personality.

REFERENCES

1. Bateson, G. A theory of play and fantasy. *Psychiatric Research Reports* vol. 2, 1955, pp. 39-51.
2. Coleman, M. L. and B. Nelson. Paradigmatic Psychotherapy in Borderline Treatment, *Psychoanalysis,* vol. 10, 1957, pp. 28-41.
3. Ferenczi, S. Child Analysis in the Analysis of Adults. M. Balint, ed. *Final contributions and methods of psychoanalysis.* New York: Basic Books, 1955, pp. 126-42.
4. Freud, A. Indications for Child Analysis. *The Psychoanalytic Study of the Child,* vol. 1, 1945, pp. 127-49.
5. Heimann, P. A Contribution to the Re-evaluation of the Oedipus Complex—The Early Stages. M. Klein, P. Heimann and R. Money-Kyrle, eds. *New directions in psychoanalysis.* London: Tavistock Publications, 1955, pp. 23-38.
6. Klein, M. *The Psychoanalysis of Children.* London: Hogarth Press. 1950.

7. Kut, S. The Changing Pattern of Transference in the Analysis of an Eleven-Year-Old Girl. *The Psychoanalytic Study of the Child,* vol. 8, 1953. pp.8 355-78.

8. Masserman, J.*Principles of dynamic psychiatry.* Philadelphia: W. B. Saunders Co., 1946.

9. Moreno, J. L. *Psychodrama* (2nd revised ed.). New York: Beacon House, 1946.

10. Searles, H. F. Schizophrenic Communication. *Psychoanalysis and the Psychoanalytic Review,* vol. 48, 1961. pp. 3-50.

11. ———. Phases of Patient-Therapist Interaction. *British Journal of Medical Psychology,* vol. 34, 1961. pp. 169-93.

12. Sechehaye, M. A. *A new psychotherapy of schizophrenia.* Translated by G. Rubin-Robson. New York: Grune and Stratton, 1956.

13. Stern, E. M. Mirror-Dialogue Approach to the Treatment of a Borderline Psychosis. *Journal of Existential Psychiatry,* vol. 4, 1964.

14. Sternbach, O. Arrested Ego Development and Its Treatment in Conduct Disorders and Neurosis of Childhood. *The Nervous Child,* vol. 6, 1947. pp. 306-17.

15. Whiting, J. W. M. Resource Mediation and Learning by Identification. I. Iscoe and H. W. Stevens, eds. *Personality development in children.* Austin: University of Texas Press, 1960. pp. 112-26.

NOTES

1. Searles(11) highlights this point: "As the patient makes emotional contact with the various previously repressed areas of his past experience, bit by bit, he eventually reaches the realization that, despite all the years of illness, as one patient expressed it with great relief, 'I'm still myself.' " (p. 188).

20. JULIEN: A CASE STUDY

M. Fraser Bennee and Robert Sherman

Peter Schwarzburg

Haitian Family Mores Challenged: Jean-Marie Decides What Man Lives By

Jean-Marie, Julien's mother, wakened at five minutes to six, just before the alarm shrilled. She was a disciplined woman. And proud of being Haitian. Already two years in New York, she still heard the murmuring dawns of Croix des Bouquets, the village where her father was law and she his beloved child. The murderous heat of July lay wet on her gold skin, but as always, early morning brought her childhood back.

"Jean-Marie, get Julien up." Jose, Julien's father, was already on his way to work.

Jose knew men with much book-learning driving hacks in New York. However, to moonlight, from savage necessity, beneath your status, is of no matter. Jose regarded such people with admiration. Also he felt admiration for himself. A Puerto Rican, with four steady jobs, and a high school equivalency diploma, legitimate and fresh, on his bedroom wall—he was content.

Jean-Marie entered the cubicle, off the miniscule kitchenette, where Julien still slept, snoring happily.

His skin was cocoa dark like his father's, and his hair, silky soft and lightly curling, like his mother's.

My treasure, Jean-Marie thinks, my four-year-old son.

Every Haitian believes, she can hear her father saying, that his son is a great possession. That is why we, on this very small, but not unimportant island, are a fine people.

Jean-Marie, looking at Julien, full of tenderness, knows that it is so.

Unfamiliar apprehension touched her. Why? What she had to do this morning was a little thing. Trifling. Hardly to be noticed in Julien's carefully planned day.

Because, of course, she must work. It was demanded to survive in this new land.

She swung Julien high above her head, in a swift, rough movement. He came instantly awake, gurgling deeply. He struggled in her hard delicious grasp. His nose burrowed in her damp neck.

She let him go. And he ran to his table chair. It had his name, Julien, painted across the back. His steaming mug of chocolat-au-lait was not on the table, nor his pain beurre. His mother's plate was empty.

He stared, unbelieving.

"Mommy?"

He was very puzzled.

His hand clutched her skirt, and couldn't let go, so she was unable to get his new jacket on. No matter.

"You will have breakfast with the other children in the nursery today. Not alone with Mommy anymore. Take your fire engine, Julie, with the whistle that blows."

She put it into his hand. He did not feel it, and it dropped to the floor. Jerkily, she shoved it under her arm.

"Oh, Julie, you're not going to be a naughty boy, are you? A big boy now, you are. My son, Julien."

Of course, he is only four. But so quick. So clever. Much more like the six-year-olds, she proudly tells herself. Why can't he understand it is impossible, just impossible, the extra breakfast hour, alone, together?

Impossible, that is, if she was to hold her job. Many others, with more high school than she, wanted it. The foreman had made it quite clear to Jean-Marie.

Julie begins to think of the mornings when Mommy carried him down the steep stairs. And he, yelling and screaming, pretending being mad. The little kids would come out, and stare over the railings. He remembers how Mommy had liked it. But now the game must stop.

Jean-Marie took his hand, and fitted her

pace to his. Today, he walked his own steps down the stairs.

He knew where they were going. The nursery clinic school. The children. And Pierre, the bad one. He had liked Pierre. But that had all been when Mommy and he had breakfast together, first.

The panic was beginning in him as they walked.

"Tiger" and His "Cub":
A Contract Is Sealed in Blood

Tiger Schultz was a physical education major. He had the superlative body of an American trained athlete. He was also the possessor, newly acquired, of a sophomore C+ standing. This was the achievement of a thoroughly mediocre mind, unfalteringly committed to slugging effort.

Tiger was never a wheeler dealer in college baseball. "You deliver the season's ten home runs, hmmm? and the advanced biology, and earth science situation will be taken care of."

No, it was never like that with Schultz. Yet this was 1974, when the sacrosanct New York State Standardized Regent's Exams were selling on street corners and in subways to the highest bidders.

It is important that the moral presence of character which Tiger Schultz possessed, equally, with his superb body and his mediocre mind, be straightaway established, and constantly remembered, as you watch him work magic with Julien.

He appeared in my office promptly on schedule. "My program adviser says to spend two semesters with kids, working with kids."

"Yes?"

"Well, I like kids, I sure do. But they scare me."

"Scare you." I shouldn't have laughed. But he was so huge, and he looked like a thug.

"Dr. Lang!" His voice belonged to the rest of him. So much of it. "Being big, the physical thing of being big, doesn't scare nobody."

True. I think of three large men, the clinic consultants. Each one is a gentle person. My respect for Schultz begins in that moment.

Earnestly, "I've two nephews who are babies. Squawking but not talking yet. You know. I fool around with them a lot. They aren't scared of me. Honest."

He is anxious. Excitement, or is it expectation, in him? Perhaps he is sufficiently intimate with himself, at times, to sense his impact upon another. So few of us are.

"Since you like them young, Tiger, try our nursery school division, for the afternoon. Very young, they are there. And all without their mothers. You may run into Julien. Let me know if he needs someone, like you, nonscary."

I recalled as he left, that several professors felt warmly toward him despite his dismal grades.

Tiger heard the children minutes before he saw them. "Teacher, watch me!"

"Teacher, wait for me, wait now!"

"Teacher, listen, are you listening?"

"You'll come tomorrow, promise, teacher, promise!"

They scrambled about their counselors, strident, demanding. Tiger felt fright in the room. As if each were saying "good-bye" forever.

Must get hold of myself, he thinks, bullshit, what's there to be frightened of here? Kids in a clinic nursery school. Counselors, guys like me, around. And Montessori learning games, and educational toys, and all such crap.

A tall counselor, standing apart, made no

move to leave. Smashed Punch and Judy dolls lay on the floor. A child was pressing, in desperation, against her.

Disgustedly, "—here I go again." In desperation—why in desperation? "Cut it out," Tiger tells himself.

And then, in the emptying room, he saw the child. He was crunched somehow in a wood chair, as if it were rocking him. He was smiling with himself. Tiger knew, at once, it was Julien. Swiftly, he went to him.

"Julien, Julien, they said you'd be here."

Tiger stood above him, bending slightly, very close. He did not touch him. Children are like cats, he knows. You let them take the initiative. He waits, growing eager.

This mysterious child!

Still smiling, Julien twisted forward sharply and caught Tiger's hand tight against his mouth. Tiger felt sudden, wrenching pain. Dazedly, he saw blood, trickling through his fingers.

Julien was still smiling.

"Many doctors agree," I said, watching Tiger's bewildered face as our second conference began, "that love is essential to being alive, When you are not quite four. Julien has love taken away from him, day after day, in the early mornings, before he comes here. It began three months ago."

"I don't know what you are saying." Tiger's voice was loud in anger. He was seeing Julien scrunched on the wood chair.

"Tiger, Julien has a mother, beautiful, loving."

"Bitch." He is outraged.

"Perhaps, you will talk with her, someday?"

"No, Mam! I'd strangle her."

"The time may come, it may come because of Julien, when you will find it necessary to need her, Tiger."

"Julien and she used to begin every day with breakfast together. What a gay one he was then! But they had to stop because of Jean-Marie's work.

And Julien, almost at once, began to go away from us. The psychiatrist tells me he is a very sick little boy. Did you notice he never eats at the table?"

"Is he starving, then?"

"No. After lunch, he rummages in the plastic garbage bags. We make sure he gets lunch. The children pretend not to notice. But I am afraid—soon—"

"He'll stop rummaging?"

I smiled.

"I must warn you, Tiger. He can be suddenly full of screaming hate. Destructive. Vicious. I think it is when love, however briefly, somehow, from somewhere gets through to him." Tiger looked at his bandaged hand. "Yeah. Don't I for sure know!"

Supported Loneliness: Tiger Learns a "Follow the Leader Game"

Julien came home to his childhood slowly, and a second winter was almost past before the journey with Tiger ended.

Doggedly, Tiger reported those early weeks, when Julien was so tortured by his badness that he must hide his eating. Mommy wouldn't eat with him. If anyone else did, she might have to go away, and he'd never see her no more.

At their first nursery breakfast, Tiger told me, Julien sat patiently through the whole meal, his food untouched.

"Man oh man, was he tough!" Tiger looked beaten as he talked, but his voice was loudly admiring. "Never no glance at me. But he darn well knew I was there!"

"He did? How can you be so sure?"

"Because he put a piece of chicken wing on the paper napkin in my lap!"

"Whatever did you do?" My question was sincere. I did not have the answer.

"I threw it on the floor. And he saw that too. Without looking, naturally. And I said, good and loud, 'Bust me, I'm starving! But I can't eat if Julien can't eat.' "

"You really think he heard you?"

"He heard me. He slid off his chair, into his sly trek to the garbage bags in the service hall. I jogged right along, and I stared right at him, while he munched chicken wings, and legs and blueberry cup pie, full of juice."

I must remain constantly objective. To be intrigued confuses judgment. Tiger knows no formal psychology. His transcript, this moment, lies in my desk, unhallowed by a single introductory course in child development.

I had to caution, "Julien is often very far away at mealtimes. The psychiatrist repeatedly emphasizes this to us all. Perhaps he didn't hear you? Never dismiss that perhaps, Tiger. There may be periods still, when he is unaware, as you speak to him or even if you touch him."

Cheerfully, "Could be! But when we got to the second plastic bag, he for sure pushed me—I mean bunted me, head on, in the back. Almost went into the garbage."

"You eat!" he shouted. "And that shout was darn well spoke to me, Dr. Lang!" Tiger waited, meekly subduing his enjoyment.

"And?"

"Well, by gum, I ate."

I was rebuked. I am, I notice, unduly sensitive when wrong. But no chagrin against Tiger Schultz.

Then the gray days came. Brokenly, Tiger confided that he now no more existed for Julien than the children playing about. With them all day long, Julien had forgotten them.

"He scrunches on that wood chair, with his head curled into his stomach. The fetal position, ain't it? Back to the womb. Only safe place, right?"

If Tiger was boning through old physiology notes, he must indeed be desperate. It was a bad time. But the psychiatrist did not suggest Tiger's removal as a counselor. "Let him stay. My feeling is, he may be Julien's last chance."

The inexorable days continued. And Tiger had only their empty passing to report. Julien sat, endlessly, hardly stirring, close to Tiger, touching his hand. But when he spoke, it was always, "Mommy, mommy."

Tiger felt the pain of helplessness. "He doesn't know the difference between a man and a woman, anymore. How horrible it is to watch a child's mind dying. And how wrong." But when he spoke his voice was warm and strong. "Julien, I am Tiger, not Mommy. I am Tiger, your friend. I am here with you. Not Mommy."

"Carry me?"

"No Julien. We carry babies. Never boys, like us, like Julien and Tiger. I will take your hand, and we will walk, close together."

One afternoon, a week later, Tiger suddenly stopped and stooped and threw a red ball at the screen. It bounced back. He threw it harder. Julien's attention seemed to focus. The third time, it hit him in the belly button, and he clutched himself, making a squeak. Or was it a giggle? Tiger, alert, wondered with quick hope. A giggle? It could be. Julien was smiling. But he was always smiling.

Ten sessions more, and a good thing happened. It did not last long, but it happened. Julien climbed the monkey bars, over the slippery iron frame, for the first time, to the highest rung.

Turning, his eyes found Tiger, and in a mobilized flash, he fell. Tiger caught him, gripped him, flung him roughly higher still, and held him firm, once more.

Julien suddenly feels his mother, caught up in shouting laughter, straining him to her, on the steps of their tenement. But it is Tiger who is here, not mommy. Tiger is holding him, not mommy. Julien struggles with the confusion. In these startling moments, for the first time, he is safe. After the empty days, he is not alone.

There was the sound of shrill laughing, off key, and ending in a choke. But it was laughter. Julien's laughter.

Rigid with tension, Tiger appeared for our usual conference. I asked no questions, waiting for his open ease with me to help him. How much he had brought to this day!

"Dr. Lang, I—I've no report—I'm flubbed—not sure what's really happening." He swallowed painfully. "Julien—that kid stoned me—with one word, right at the end of a super hour. He smashed all I had been thinking about him!"

"Yes?"

"It was after five. We had to go. You know how sticky we are about overtime with the kids."

"A generally wise rule, wouldn't you say?"

A silence. I, as yet, had no clue, no signal. Which, of course, Tiger knew.

"Perhaps—I guess—I was wanting to comfort myself, as well as Julien, before we left each other, because I promised. "In the morning, Julie, we'll be together, again, in the morning."

"What a beautifully right thing to say!"

Tiger looked at me, bleakly. "But, Dr. Lang, Julie said, he just said to me like always, like when we first began, 'Mommy!' 'Mommy' had never descended to sympathy with Tiger, nor granted him the false security of directives. But I was human. And on this day, I took the last word."

"So long I have been watching with you, Tiger. And watching Julien use your faith to grow with. Stay a semester longer? And I shall not fear for him."

Tiger looked at me. It was then I learned how much one silent look could say.

He would not leave. Whatever problems the next semester brought, he would not leave.

Imitating Tiger: Julien Accepts a New Role

Again, September. New York's apple-green air spilled an enchanting haze over the complex of univeristy stone and glass.

The last day of the semester. And the last day with Julien. Tiger stood hesitant, in the nursery school doorway, lost in the past two years.

Moving half blindly, he stumbled over a wood chair, splotched with red paint, filthy with sneaker grime and minus one leg. The years vanished as he stared at the chair. For Tiger, it was rocking a mute, shrunken child once again.

An imperious voice banged Tiger into the present.

"You're late," Julien said flatly. "I'm just a kid, so I can't be late. It's the grown-ups are bums. Grown-up bastards as promise things, and don't remember. You, too!" Julien's eyes flashed spite.

Articulate as hell, now days, Tiger notes excitedly, spits out words that slap you silly when he's mad.

"Was thinking of you, Julie," Tiger's steady eyes held him. Steady eyes, that spoke truth. "Had to talk with my friend. He was in trouble."

Julien's pride tingled. Tiger was giving him a confidence. Of course, Tiger trusted him like anything! Julien felt sudden pity for the kids who did't have Tiger. A pity that touched him with healing security. The suspicions that made him want to hurt Tiger, sometimes, even now, died away. He dissolved into forgiveness, that left him a little uncertain, but with his fists unclenched.

Tiger looked at Julien with the love he had never spoken. "Our last day, man, what's it to be?"

Now six years old, and reading exuberantly on a grade four level, Julien had long been prepared for this encounter.

Swiftly, "D'you know about phonics, Tiger?"

"Foniks?" Tiger wondered confusedly if the schools were hipped, in passing, on some exotic sub-dialect.

"You don't know? And you're in college?" Probing sharply, "Tiger, you can read, can't you?" The possibility that he couldn't read was awful. Only dumb pussies don't read. Everybody knows this.

Tiger concluded he had muffed it again. He said, lamely, "Uh, phonics?—a way to learn words by yourself, ain't it?"

"Uh-huh." Still anxious, Julien had to be sure Tiger knew the best gimmicks. "You memorize what a letter says, it's sound that is, and sound it, and put it in a bunch with other sounds, and then you *listen* to the sounds you are sounding—that's just absolutely important—the listening to yourself—and there's the word you didn't know!"

Tiger, in a fog, longs for a reading specialist.

Julien, delightedly teaching him, never noticed his discomfort. "They call it independent reading. It means you don't ask the teacher no more." Curiously, "D'you read this way, Tiger?"

Tiger replied, "Well," cautiously, "not all the time. Tiresome, to go at it that way all the time!"

Julien exuded approval. "I knew you didn't." Impulsively. "I told Miss Ascot yesterday when she was saying island wrong. It should be 'iss-land.'"

"Was Miss Ascot appreciative?"

Jolted, Julien admitted, "not ezzactly, I'm doing phonics drill all next week, 'specially extra, and it ain't me as needs it."

Tiger grinned. "It won't destroy you, Julien," he said comfortably. And Julien's answering grin agreed. Silent, but confused, Julien searched Tiger's face. How had Miss Ascot got mentioned? He never, consciously, misled Tiger. Never. It was just that, sometimes, like now, he found himself saying what he hadn't actually decided, beforehand, to say. He wondered if Tiger had managed it that way.

Julien sighed deeply, but not at all unhappily. He 'preciated Tiger. And understood him more and more. Like learning about yourself, sort of.

After lunch, Tiger walked slowly to the junior activity room. He turned in the direction of caterwauling noises. Julien would probably be there. Somewhere. The new Julien. A you-follow-me game had just stopped, violently.

Kennedy, fat, not quite four, but securely belligerent, was balking. And dictating the entire bedlam, "Me no go! Me no go!" he bellowed. The children bunched tightly, in chaos. "Get up! Get up!" they screeched.

But nobody touched him. Alone he was, safe in defiance. A true Kennedy, already, perhaps?

Tiger's eyes found Julien. But Julien did not see him. Startled, Tiger realized that this was the first time, in their months together, that Julien had not been waiting, tensely expectant, for him. He recognized the moment as an essential development in any child's behavior. And felt morose, almost depressed. Where was the pleasure he should be feeling?

Kennedy sat, unshifting, anchored to the floor, and Julien moved imperceptibly, but shortening the space between them. His eyes, enormous with effort, swept the counselors closing in. He stood between them and the obdurate Kennedy, his hand now firmly on the child's shoulder.

On the group's edge, Tiger stopped, transfixed.

Holding his position, Julien spoke. "I—I fink"—he gulped, mortified. And then, quietly, "I think Kennedy's feeling anti-social." A pause. "It's much more hours than his rest-time," he explained reasonably. Didn't they understand?

Julien gathered them all into his confidence. "Everybody gets irrigated if they're tired."

An hysterical titter pierced the room. His hand still on Kennedy's shoulder, Julien turned to the sound. Today, at the age of six, he was, intellectually, in challenge with a girl of twenty-two.

"Irrigated—I guess, not right." Then, with logical precision, "but I know what it means. It means the way that Kennedy is feeling—why he's squashed like that on the floor. So I used it."

A whisper came from somewhere. "Irritated-irritated."

Julien caught it loudly, "irritated!" and flashed a smile, warm with gratitude.

"Now, we'll go have a pizza. Kennedy won't feel beat, if he gives in for a pizza. He's only tough, if he gets pushed—jist like me," Julian finished, talking to Kennedy.

Kennedy's baby dimples appeared, suddenly, all three of them, in his fat cheeks. He got himself up, off the floor, put his hand in Julien's and walked, proudly, with him, out of the room.

The Lonely World of Second Fiddle: Julien Sees Kenny as an Usurper

Sauntering aimlessly behind the children's swings in the battered playground, Tiger knew he should be at the track tryout. The clinic's first summer session had officially closed. But he was watching the strange woman at the swings, pushing Kennedy. Another aide?

"No stop. You do more."

She pushed again, and the swing swept upwards. Kennedy screeched, "More high. More high."

"That's high enough." Again, she pushed, less vigorously, laughing but firm.

Kenny was mutinous. He jiggled crossly on the wide plank seat, yanking the ropes, and she caught him on the back loop just as his hands let go. He slid to the sand, scowling. "Why you stop?"

"It's lunch time, Kenny."

"No lunch. Me swing." He stamped his foot. They measured each other. Wise in the ways of adult obstruction, Kenny decided not to stamp again. She pro'bly was one of them I-means-it people.

"I'm so hungry." Regretfully, she looked at him. "Good-bye, Kenny." She turned away, walking slowly past the sand piles towards the outdoor cafeteria.

Tiger saw Kenny squirming by the swings. His round face was beet red with indecision.

"Hi, Kenny, want help?" a boy called, halfway across a jungle maze.

Kenny ignored him. "Lady! Lady!" His fat legs took off in a spray of sand, and Tiger caught her smile quite clearly, as she paused, and turned, and took Kenny's hand. He followed them. Lucky for the clinic if she is summer staff, he decided. Engrossed, Tiger quickened his stride, cautiously moving closer.

"How nice of you to come with me, when you aren't hungry." Her voice carried easily, with the slight precision a second language often grants.

"I be hungry most all the times," Kenny conceded, dropping his baby talk coverage for the exciting role her attention invited. "I swings a lot, too," he added hopefully, "as when somebody cooperates." He exuded extra charm, "Like you."

Tiger slid into a folding chair at an empty corner, where he could hear them talking above the table's chatter.

"You're a good swinger." She agreed, "very brave. We'll swing again, soon."

Kenny spooned his soup, noisily, but deftly. "I are brave? How brave?" He was ready to believe, but he had to know why. He had to tell Julien, his first, most own friend.

"Well, let's see."

Kenny put his spoon down to listen better. His china blue eyes gleamed. She counted on her fingers, "One, on the swing, you sit straight and solid. Two, your hands hold strong on the ropes, this way." She closed her fingers around his wrist, and held hard. Kenny chuckled, agreeing. "Three, you lean forward at the top minute, and make the pushes stronger!"

Captivated, Kenny sat, unnaturally quiet, glowing at her.

"Come now, let's finish the soup."

Tiger jumped, and turned to his own bowl, half full and stone cold. Brother, did she have technique!

"Do you like games?"

Last week's play period crackled into Kenny's memory. He could hear them kids yelling and shoving. And him, squatted on the floor, making a scare with his awful mad. "Me no go! Me no go!" He chuckled. His three dimples deepened. "You want we play now?" He looked at her forgivingly. "Let's ride the hobbyhorses. I'm the most young one as does."

She could see them prancing by the sand piles, their long tails and shining manes of real hair lifting in the gusty wind. "I suppose, sometimes, they gallop very fast?"

With an ecstatic whoop, he jumped to the ground, grabbing her hand, "More fast than them swings." Did she really understand? He said slyly, "Fur some kids, they ain't never moved. Some kids ackshully don't know they is alive horses." He waited, scuffing the grass, still holding her hand. If she laughed, like them others, he'd kick her. Yes he would.

She felt Kenny's hand, small and sticky, begin to tremble. "Do you suppose horses, and maybe cats and dogs, know when we are brave?"

She wasn't laughing! Kenny dropped her hand, and stood on his head. He toppled to his knees, snorting, and galloped dizzily, around and around her. Then, hot and happy, he flopped on the grass.

She sat down beside him. The hobbyhorses were forgotten. They looked at each other, both knowing anything could happen.

"It's pretty essasperating, but," Kenny leaned close to her, "My mamma keeps on calling me 'her baby,' and I'm right now in kindergarten! But I onnerstand. I am her most littlest one." The lady had tears in her eyes. Kenny was not disturbed. Mama's were often that way.

He scrambled up. "Wanta see me do a really somersault?" He strutted before her, making a wobbly leap upwards.

Spinning from the sand pit, a pebble grazed his forehead, and he hit the ground in a tangled heap. Children shouted, running confusedly, bunching together. The clinic nurse and two aides pushed through, and carried Kenny off to the emergency room, unhurt, but whimpering with fright.

Julien dropped his sand pebbles. Blind with tears and fury, he stumbled towards his mother, and fell headlong over a hobbyhorse as Tiger raced up. With a half tackle, he scooped Julien under his left arm, looking at Jean-Marie through her son's screaming with mingled wonderment and shame. If only he had talked with her! Talked? What could she have said he would have heard? This negligent woman who had no time for one small boy? He blurted, "You really didn't want to leave him?" Kenny's imagination soaring high in peals of talk, answered his question. He was appalled at himself.

"I was not wise enough. I am learning." Jean-Marie watched Julien, so quiet in Tiger's arms. Julien had burrowed his face out of sight, in Tiger's comforting sweater. She said, "I will go now and take Kenny to his sister."

"But you'll wait? You'll wait for us?"

She felt content and secure. Was that how Julien felt with Tiger? "Oh, yes, I'll wait." Was Julien listening? She looked at the small figure with the hidden face. "Julien?" She moved closer. "Julien?" Tiger stood motionless, holding him, longing, but not daring to help. She touched a thin leg, limp and scratched with sand.

"Go away, you bad woman," Julien said, "You are Kenny's mother now. Go away."

Jean-Marie dropped her hand, and walked quickly across the playground, through the narrow familiar hall where she had so often stood, and into the reception center.

An Adjusted World: Jean-Marie Comes into Focus

"Julien, we are going to talk. Will you walk beside me, if I put you down? Or must I carry you?"

Julien turned, and slid to the ground. "You are mad at me. For what are you mad at?" What had he done? Except slam Kennedy, the sneaky, two bit skunk. His mother and Kenny, talking and playing without him! Julien looked down, concocting vengeance. I'll bloody his nose next time, he thought, soon as I get the chance.

"I'm angry with myself Julien. But you? Why are you angry?"

Julien whirled in front of him, blocking their walk, acting out the defiance of his new self. "My mother stole our private games for Kenny. She never even asted me, which I wouldn't have let her if she had."

"They were having a wonderful time Julien. Your mother and Kenny."

Julien stood, alone and bereft, his world collapsed. Forsaken by his mother. Rejected by Tiger.

Tiger drew him, limp and mute, into the deeper shade, and they sat down, cross legged, facing each other.

"My mother was having a gooder—," he choked. It didn't help any to be a baby again. "She was having a better time with Kenny than with me. Saying more things. Laughing louder."

A flash of pain, and Julien vanished in Tiger's past. He hadn't seen his mother in fourteen years, nor read her fourteen Christmas letters, locked, unopened, in his desk. He said harshly, "Don't behave to your mother as I have to mine, Julien."

Julien's eyes grew enormous with fascination. Instinctively, he knew Tiger had spoken to an equal, as if they were friends. "Your mother isn't dead?"

"Why no. She lives quite near New York." What did he say that for? It wasn't relevant.

Tiger's mother alive, and close, and wouldn't see him? What awful things had he done? Horrified protest flung Julien against his idol, arms in a strangle hold. "You haven't done bad things! You haven't done anything wrong!"

Tiger hugged him hard, then sat back, with the dusty grass between them. Idols powerfully enrich a child's identity when he is learning to love. But they have to be discarded early, Tiger thought. Sometimes they must be smashed.

"Listen carefully, Julien. I need you to listen."

Julien nodded, his heart jumping with fright, and curiousity.

"When my mother left home, I refused to see her anymore!" The conversation made Tiger feel sick. He was not sure he could finish today. "Julien, you won't do this to your mother, will you? Julien?"

"I'm listening, Tiger, like you want."

"Remember what you said before your mother left us today?"

"Yes."

"You do? Then say it Julien. Say it again, to me."

"Your're Kenny's mother now. Go away." Sullenly, "I'm not going to talk to her at all, for the longest time." Julien's face was pinched with furious determination.

"And then?" Tiger wanted nothing left unspoken.

"I'm going to make her decide."

"You are? Decide what?"

"Decide between me and Kenny. She can't have me, till she gets rid of Kenny." He looked scared to death. "Kenny doesn't belong to us. He's not in our family."

"Kenny's such a little fellow. He isn't four yet, is he?"

"He was four five weeks ago," Julien muttered.

"Is that right?" Well, I suppose he must learn to depend on himself. How much he admires you!" Julien gulped. Of course that was true.

"I guess I shouldn't punish my mother," Julien said, after a long minute, with gigantic relief.

"For helping you to look after Kenny?"

Again, Julien accepted the remarkable fact. He had been looking after Kenny.

"Perhaps he needs you a little longer?"

Julien suddenly saw the necessary, important conversations he and his mother would be having because of Kenny. The world was in focus again.

Shadows were filling in across the deserted playground. Coolness, and the mellow carillon from a nearby spire said the day was ending. Tiger walked with Julien through the courtyard to the clinic reception center where Jean-Marie and Kenny were waiting for him.

Julien: Six Months After Counseling

Julien is almost seven now, skittishly awkward, and massively curious. He is a Hawk Scout, a group roller skater, a junior bingo whiz, a scuba diver in a YMCA pool, and he visits three Sunday schools with friends of various faiths.

School is his world. And there he has prophetic moments. There was the afternoon he settled the mauling argument about stone and metal. "They're not the same," he pronounced, "metal's malleable and ductile, and stone ain't."

There are still regressions of omnipotence though. But brief, and tinged with self-amusement. Like a recent comment to his mother, "You tell Pug he's got to play with me when I want him." But Jean-Marie resisted. "You won't let Pug ride your scooter. You tell him." And with the essential adjustments, Julien did. Perhaps the most significant hour in his week is the taxi ride with his father. Sometimes when anxious riders ask confused questions, his father turns to him for information. It is always a proud moment for both of them.

Julien belongs and is using his considerable talents.

Critique: Julien

Julien is utterly panic stricken at being separated from his mother. He feels wiped out as a person and is terrified to do anything. He longs for the safety of oneness with his mother and sits rigidly curled up in his chair in something resembling a fetal position.

Early childhood and child care workers are familiar with children who cling to their mothers and refuse to leave them. They have developed many strategies for attracting the children into stimulating activities so they are too busy to miss mother. But a few children become more sullen or more withdrawn as time goes on and pose a perplexing problem in their acute distress. Julien is such a child. Bright and totally withdrawn he frustrates all efforts of those who would help him.

Meeting the Withdrawn Child

It is difficult to establish a relationship with a boy like Julien because typically he does not overtly respond. This leaves the counselor feeling frustrated, helpless, and rejected. He can see no results of his labor. However, Julien did repsond in the first meeting with Tiger. He bit him and sent Tiger howling in retreat. Fortunately, Tiger has a supervisor to whom he can go for solace and reinforcement.

Tiger realized that Julien valued his privacy and should be approached gingerly. Getting too close too fast or attempting to force Julien tends to raise the child's defenses. Julien's aggression showed that he was aware of the world outside of himself and of Tiger's presence. It is therefore possible for the counselor to communicate to him and perhaps even with him.

Julien expects to be hurt in any relationship with others and so he seeks to avoid it. Any sign of tenderness arouses his anger and feelings of abandonment. He particularly associates tenderness with getting hurt as his mother hurt him. So his interest is to keep the counselor out of his life to maintain some minimal level of safety. If the counselor behaves in any way to make contact he is automatically seen by Julien as an enemy. If the counselor leaves the boy alone, then there is nothing he can do directly to help him. This would seem to be a double bind.

What Tiger does in the early part of their relationship is to accept Julien's behavior and to identify himself with Julien. Julien has a place of his own, the chair he curls up in. Having a territory is part of existing. At home, too, Julien has his special chair marked with his own name on it. Recognizing and accepting his territory is an important step by Tiger in affirming Julien's existence and in making a relationship. Later, at the mealtime Tiger proclaims loudly that he is starved but cannot eat until the hungry Julien eats too. Julien eats from the garbage. Tiger eats with him. Tiger is there mirroring and paralleling Julien. He is there exclusively with Julien. The counselor persists in this parallel existence in spite of frustration and infrequent response. As counseling proceeds he engages Julien in much physical activity plan. He gets to know what Julien is thinking and feeling and is able to interpret it out loud or act to meet the boy's needs. Gradually Julien accepts his presence and begins to trust the person who is so often there and who seems to know him so well. He begins to try to figure Tiger out and predict Tiger's behavior. At this point they are in relationship. Tiger is real. Tiger expresses his feelings and allies them with Julien's feelings.

Tiger is alert to Julien's behavior and whenever Julien does anything, the counselor joins in and capitalizes on it. When Julien deliberately falls off the monkey bars, Tiger catches him and throws him back into the air and makes a game of it. But it is a game of trust because Tiger is always there to catch him securely. When Tiger's ball hits Julien in the stomach and Julien laughs partially, Tiger picks up the cue. Thus is the relationship gradually built until Julien allows himself to speak and then to use his bountiful intelligence to learn to read and write.

The Need to Withdraw

Julien lavishes in the warmth and closeness of his mother's attention. He is happy and contented with her. Apparently he has had little experience being away from her and exploring the world on his own. He is adored and valued. Mother knows just what he likes and what he feels. Julien seldom has to ask for anything. This is evidence of unrecognized parental neglect.

A child like Julien, who is perhaps loved too much, has a difficult time in separating from his mother to enter the wider world. He delights in how well mother tunes in to his needs, feelings and games. He enjoys being so special that she is devoted to him almost exclusively. Her fierce pride in him makes him feel very wanted. This attention is rarely diluted by any third party such as an adoring father who is too busy with four jobs and night school to be present. This wasn't always so. Two years earlier he was plucked from the midst of a large extended family and taken to a strange place where he had only his mother to care for him intensely.

Then suddenly mother leaves him after breakfast and goes to work. And then, even without breakfast, he must be without his mother for very long days in a world of strangers. Mother is not in his safe home waiting for him. She goes away too. He cannot go home if he feels he needs her. Julien feels angry, frightened, not wanted. He feels rejected and betrayed. He doesn't know what to do. How could this happen? It must

be because in some very deep and unfathamable way he is very bad. This false assumption at an early age becomes a major motivating force for Julien's behavior.

Julien hides to avoid the treachery of closeness, for those who are close to him abandon him. Anyone who seeks to approach him is defeated by the fortress he builds to equally protect himself from others and protect others from him. He believes that cutoff from his mother he will wither and die because without her he is nothing. At the same time, characteristic of the "omnipotent" thinking of the young child, he also believes that he is all powerful and very bad. He is so bad that he drove his mother and other relatives away and he can destroy anyone who comes close to him. Certainly he can't eat. "Mommy wouldn't eat with him. If anyone else did, she might have to go away, and he'd never see her no more."

Julien is very angry with his mother. If he acts upon the anger, in his omnipotence he thinks he will kill her. But since he has not yet properly separated his own being from hers he would in effect also be killing himself. Besides, he needs her so very much. His feelings are therefore very dangerous. He must keep them carefully in check at any cost using all the energy at his command. Another false belief that becomes a major motive for Julien. This one renders him helpless.

Julien longs for an earlier time in his life when he and his mother were one and inseparable. He regresses back to the autistic stage which is characteristic of the first three months of life. But his mother continues to send him away and he becomes increasingly angry, upset, and sad. Julien sits in his chair in his corner wearing his thin smile and is lost to the world.

Blanck and Blanck (2) Bettleheim (3) Bowlby (4) Hartmann (6) Mahler (7) and

Spitz (10) have studied the early relationships between mother and child and the developmental processes through which a child develops the ability to leave his parents and define his own identity. Mahler describes the autistic, symbiotic, and separation-individuation phases of early childhood which normally at about age three result in "psychological birth"—the definition of a subjective identity separate from any other person or thing.

Julien's psychological birth is aborted. He is still tied symbiotically to his mother and any major separation finds him with inadequate ego development to differentiate his self and being different from hers.

Mother is so attuned to the pride of her life that Julien's needs and feelings are known to her before he asks. She loves to play with him, hold him close, caress him, feed him, dress him, and carry him down the stairs, even still at the age of four. In her deep love she keeps her son in a dependent state in spite of his quickness and cleverness.

Father is bright and very busy trying to succeed economically. He leaves the house before Julien is fully awake and probably returns long after he is asleep. It's very hard for Julien to really identify with his father and to internalize the many things his father could teach him.

Julien is an only child. He enjoys his mother's exclusive attention and has grown to expect it. He is lost without her. Julien did not have adequate opportunity to wander away from her and try himself out in mastering his world. He did not have a chance to properly rebel and resist his parents' authority and to assert his own individuality because his needs were immediately catered to. Most importantly, he did not learn to internalize a symbolic representation of his mother which he could carry with him and make a part of himself even when she is not physically with him. Nor does he have a

clear internal symbolic representation of himself as a person. In a sense, when mother is not physically there, neither of them exists in Julien's mind. Developmentally he is much like a young child who when he wishes to hide, closes his eyes and firmly believes that no one else can see him.

Julien's early development is incomplete and he does not have the ego resources to be without his mother. Hence his panic when she leaves him.

Julien's response is to withdraw into a tight protective shell where no one can destroy the fragment of identity that he possesses. Any move on his part may upset the precarious existence he is able to maintain.

Withdrawal serves a number of important needs for Julien. (1) It helps him to maintain a semblance of identity; (2) It protects him from further hurt and abandonment; (3) It provides a womblike safe haven; (4) It enables him to keep his own dangerous, destructive feelings in check; (5) It is a safe way to express his anger and aggression since it upsets and frustrates those who let him down; yet he is doing nothing; (6) It is a means of punishing himself for being so bad; (7) It forces others to take care of Julien and preserve his existence, just as a mother cares for an infant.

Julien does not on his own initiative do anything. The autistic relationship of mother and infant is thus recreated.

Withdrawal in no way makes Julien happy. It stunts his growth and leaves him helpless and frightened. But it meets so many of his childish needs that it is a remarkably effective defense against facing what he cannot face.

Getting to Know Julien

At the beginning of their relationship, it is clear to Tiger that Julien isn't going to tell him anything in an interview, reveal himself through play activities or participate voluntarily in any kind of testing. He observes Julien carefully to note even small variations in behavior. Julien bites; he eats; he laughs; he shoves a piece of chicken at Tiger; he climbs; he deliberately falls. All are signs that Julien can be aware of the world around him and even interact with it when he chooses. These examples of intentionality lead to the conclusion that Julien's withdrawal is also to some degree intentional—a defensive posture assumed to meet his needs.

Julien's goal is to protect himself from anger and abandonment. He believes that in some magical way his badness is the cause of his abandonment. As he feels safer with Tiger, gets used to him, and begins to trust him, Julien gradually lets down his protective shield and engages in more and more communication and activity. A major goal of counseling is to enable Julien to feel safe and to show him that he does not have the awesome power that he attributes to himself. He can discover that other people are not demolished when Julien expresses anger, hurt, or demands of any kind.

At the age of four when Julien appears for treatment, we would developmentally expect him to be in the phallic stage, according to Freud (5). This is a time when Julien's sexual drives are surging and his interest in his mother as a sexual object are intense. It is a time when he wants a great deal of narcissistic attention. Julien's demands upon his mother are rejected as she sends him away to nursery school and is separated from him for long periods of time. But he cannot switch his attentions to his father and the male sex role identification because his father is not physically available. The energy that Julien could be devoting toward further development of his own identity is subverted and devoted instead to defending himself through the defense mechanisms of denial

and withdrawal. Under these circumstances, the opportunity for Julien to work with a male counselor can be an advantage, though not a necessity.

Intellectually, Julien is functioning at the preoperational stage in Piaget's schema (8). He is egocentric in his thinking and cannot take the viewpoint of his parents who feel it is a necessity for them to be away from Julien and work hard in order to earn a decent living. He continues to classify objects by single salient features. "Mother is the loving one. If she doesn't love me no one can love me and I am unlovable." And classifying them in the same category he rejects all potential caring others. Though he has learned to use language to represent objects and ideas, he regresses into silence.

Socially, Julien only plays with other children in the presence of his mother. Until she left him in the nursery school, he was never without her. He is apparently quick and able and imaginative in his play but only in the safety of the shadow of his mother. Based on mother's description, he is quick, more like a six-year-old. He is in apparent good health and of normal size and weight for his age.

Julien is a member of an affectionate, highly motivated, hardworking family. If anything, he is pampered and overindulged by his proud mother. Jean-Marie is separated from the fond extended maternal family, who remain in Haiti. She seems to be isolated in New York and until she takes a job, Julien is her principal companion. Her relationship to Julien is exceptionally close. Father Jose also seems to have little contact with his extended family. His goal is to reach an economic and educational level which will satisfy his pride and properly maintain his family. He had little time for the son he loves so well. He probably also has little time for Jean-Marie.

Jean-Marie's close relationship to Julien is

possibly based upon her own need for closeness and she encourages Julien's need to be with her.

The family is new to the country and to the neighborhood and new to the culture. They have much to learn and to adjust to. They are not familiar either with the local customs or available resources. Mother stays at home and it is possible that feeling like a stranger, she may have impressed upon Julien a certain sense of "strangeness" and "not belongingness" outside the immediate home.

Julien has the good fortune of loving parents, sound health, a quick mind, a desire for closeness with others and the experience of being cared for. He wants to control his terrible feelings of anger and hurt and somehow keep a lid on himself. He is young and impressionable. Even though Julien has withdrawn, he is not unaware.

Julien has always gotten what he wanted without effort on his part. Jean-Marie treated his assertiveness and anger as a game and turned it into a game. For example, when he tried to assert himself about walking down the stairs, Jean-Marie picked him up and jokingly carried him down like a baby. Julien's attempts to assert himself and rebel were never treated seriously. Julien never learned anything he could do to accomplish any goals he might have. When his mother left him at the nursery school he did not know how to object and try to influence her to stay with him or take him with her. Julien's passive-aggressive attempt to show her his feelings by dropping his fire engine when they were leaving for school the first day brings the retort that "you are not going to be a naughty boy, are you?" thus shaming his minor attempt at expression. In the end, Julien did the only thing he knew how to do. Nothing. He withdrew and did nothing.

The major problem then is the inability of Julien to separate from his mother and the inadequate development of his own individuality. Withdrawal is Julien's way of facing this problem. The counselor will help Julien to see the uniqueness and durability of each person and the uniqueness of his own being and to value his mother as a separate person.

Working with the Withdrawn Child

A. Enticing Julien into the World as a Separate Person

The process of getting through to Julien and making a relationship with him is slow and painful. The psychiatrist sees Julien as a sick boy facing the dangers of a disabling psychosis. It takes a team effort on the part of the consulting psychiatrist, Dr. Lang, the nurses, school staff, parent volunteers, Jean-Marie and Tiger, two years to get past his defenses and release his great potential. Coming for counseling at the age of four, it takes another one-third of Julien's lifetime to correct the deficiencies of the first few years of life. It appears that the earlier the deficit occurs in a person's life, the greater the damage.

Sequentially, Julien learned to recognize Tiger, to talk with him, to play with other children, to read and write, to play, to become progressively more independent, and finally to recognize his own family and relate to his mother.

1. *Methods.* The major tools used by the staff were expressed faith in Julien, respect for him as a person, deep caringness for him, and consistent positive attention. Tiger came to represent safety and caringness. His ability to accurately empathize with Julien was a major asset in helping Julien become a person in his own right. Like a good parent, and unlike Jean-Marie, Tiger also made increas-

ing demands on Julien to behave in progressively more grown-up ways. "We carry babies. Never boys like us, like Julien and Tiger. I will take your hand and we will walk close together." Tiger became an identification model whom Julien could imitate and learn from.

2. *Becoming a Separate Person.* Julien does not share his fantasies while curled in his chair and Tiger cannot enter that world. Rather, Tiger impacts on the current reality situation waiting for Julien to accept and feel his presence, and ultimately respond to it. Julien, even in his withdrawal, is looking for his own mother. He does not realize that he has rejected her. As Tiger persistently mirrors Julien's acts and joins in them, occasionally Julien recognizes Tiger's existence, at first aggressively. He bites Tiger, he butts him into the garbage, he thrusts a chicken wing in his lap. Later Julien gives vent to his need for a tenderness from his mother. In the depths of his withdrawal he confuses Tiger with mother. He touches Tiger's hand and mutters "Mommy, Mommy." We can only wonder what Julien was thinking. Tiger tries to help Julien recognize reality and says, "I am here with you, not Mommy."

Tiger regularly plays physically with Julien or nearby. Many times there is no reaction. But as the play continues, some sparks are ignited in Julien. For example, when Tiger is throwing a red ball against the screen making a loud noise, Julien fixes his attention on the ball. When the ball bounces back and hits Julien in the stomach he gurgles, enjoying the impact. In a later session, seeking to repeat old joys with his mother, Julien asks to be carried. Tiger says no and takes his hand instead. Another time when Julien is climbing on the monkey bars, he deliberately falls off seeing Tiger close by. Tiger catches him and flings him back into the air. In Julien's confusion it is his mother who is playing with him and hurling him through the air and catching him securely like she used to do. But something new happens. He feels himself and he feels Tiger hurling and holding him. Suddenly, he is not alone and abandoned. Each experience is more active than the one before and in each Tiger tells Julien they are together and Tiger is not mother.

Throughout, Tiger is there talking with Julien, playing nearby, eating with him, sometimes describing and interpreting Julien's behavior and feelings, always making a connection between himself and Julien. Julien grows accustomed to Tiger's presence, attention, active sharing, and eventually playing and talking together.

The counselor's efforts are bent toward enticing Julien into the world around him rather than trying to enter Julien's world. But Julien can't distinguish himself from mother. As Tiger keeps telling Julien that Julien is here and Tiger is here, Julien begins to feel first the connection with Tiger and then his separate existence as a person. Developmentally, one must be part of something before he can become independent and he must be independent before he can transcend separateness to join with another in a mutual cooperative relationship.

3. *Refueling Encourages Greater Independence.* To enter the world and leave his chair and corner, Julien needs to feel that he can return at any time for safety and sustenance. Gradually, he transfers the source to Tiger. As counseling continues, Julien expresses the need for a great deal of attention from Tiger and mother and often seeks comfort in physical closeness to Tiger when he is distressed. Tiger holds him or allows Julien to bury himself in Tiger's body. Knowing that Tiger will be there and he can receive comfort and attention when he needs it, allows Julien increasingly to venture forth

and physically separate himself from Tiger and play by himself or with other children.

4. *Anger and Autonomy.* Part of entering the world for Julien is to become aware of his own feelings of anger. Julien is very angry with his mother and the world and doesn't trust that his needs can be met. As he feels more secure, he is able to give vent to his anger. He attacks Tiger verbally and curses him for being late. Tiger does not retaliate and allows Julien to express his anger. Tiger explains, "Was thinking of you, Julie. Had to talk with my friend. He was in trouble." This increases Julien's feeling of security and reinforces his identity. By being allowed to rebel and be hostile his separateness as a person is confirmed. Tiger appreciates that Julien's anger is a major step forward from his withdrawn state and necessary before he can enter into cooperative relationships involving both giving and taking.

Even Julien recognizes the double edge of aggression. He sees Kenny feeling pushed around by other people, sitting defiantly on the floor refusing to move and asserting his independence rather than submit to the demands of others who do not recognize his needs. He helps Kenny find a satisfying way of getting up and moving on that does not crush his spirit—an important lesson for parents, and others.

Actually, Julien is imitating Tiger. It is clear that he now has a positive identification with Tiger and handles Kenny in the same way as Tiger relates to Julien. He describes Kenny's feelings to Kenny.

As Julien is able to express his anger toward others he eventually finds it possible to know how angry he is with his mother.

On the last day of counseling Julien is very jealous and angry about his mother's attention to Kenny. Julien uses his old defense of withdrawing to punish his mother. He won't speak to her. He certainly knows how well that works. His ability to express this anger,

however, enables Tiger to point out that his mother was carrying out a task of helping Kenny, which Julien also felt was important. He shows Julien how both he and his mother can cooperate to help the younger child. Now feeling included instead of abandoned, Julien looks forward with pleasure to joining with his mother instead of withdrawing from her. This resolution would have been impossible if Julien were unable to express anger initially.

Julien does not have enough faith that his needs will ultimately be met. He can't wait and his frustration tolerance is low. As his needs are consistently met and his own ability to give unto others is reinforced, his ability to wait for gratification and tolerate frustration increases.

B. Learning Self Through Tuning into Another

A major task in counseling is to help Julien become aware of the existence of others, their needs and their value as persons apart from their ability to gratify Julien. Tiger consistently stressed that he is Tiger. Tiger likes to play. Tiger gets hungry. And ultimately Tiger confides he has a mother who he doesn't see and misses.

Julien first grows accustomed to Tiger's presence. Then he feels Tiger's concern for him. Gradually he begins to like Tiger. He looks forward to being with Tiger. Tiger becomes a constant object in Julien's world and Julien realizes Tiger will be there again next time. As this occurs, Julien discovers he is also a constant object, a person of value.

Interacting with Tiger lets Julien know how Julien is behaving and coming across to others. He sees that his behavior has certain effects. He discovers that Tiger has feelings and even problems and it's okay that Julien feels too and has problems too. Other people are like Julien, and Julien is like other people—he is not alone.

C. Separation from the Counselor and Termination

Julien becomes increasingly aware that Tiger trusts and respects him. Tiger leaves the initiative in their relationship to Julien as Julien becomes increasingly active. Tiger confides in him that his friend is in trouble, and that he has rejected his own mother just like Julien did.

Tiger always speaks the truth.

Tiger allows Julien to teach him a little bit of phonics.

When Julien criticizes the teacher on her pronunciation of "island," Tiger doesn't put him down and destroy the confidence that Julien feels in his growing achievement and interaction with others. Tiger accepts Julien's confidences and holds them.

Julien begins to feel increasingly competent, independent, and trustworthy as a person. He knows that Tiger is dependable and therefore, Julien can leave Tiger for longer and longer periods to play with other children, study his reading and vocabulary, and take Kenny as a friend in need.

Another step in preparing Julien for separation is based on the recreation of the family. This occurs when Tiger shows Julien that his mother cares for him and is not abandoning him. Julien rediscovers his mother. He grasps the idea that he has a family. Julien is an important cooperating member of that family. Just as he and Tiger work, play, and talk together and enjoy each other, Julien and his mother can do the same.

Termination is in part appropriate because Julien is now six years old and reading at fourth-grade level. He is ready to perform successfully in school and able to leave his mother to attend school. Tiger has done a long volunteer stint at the clinic and it is time for him to move on to other experiences. Julien is ready to relate to Jean-Marie and get from her the sustenance that Tiger was pro-

viding. Jean-Marie had learned better how to relate to children and awaits Julien's initiative as a separate person, her son.

Finally, Tiger shows Julien he is a real person who can also make terrible mistakes like rejecting his mother. Tiger is not a god. He thereby frees Julien of the fantasy of having a false idol whom he could never successfully emulate.

D. Other Things That Could Be Done

Perhaps progress with Julien could have been improved by counseling with Jean-Marie and Jose. Jean-Marie could be encouraged to get up earlier and the whole family have breakfast together. Jose would have a chance to talk with his son. Jose could be encouraged to do some things with Julien and develop a special time and interests together.

Jean-Marie could learn to give Julien more initiative and stop babying him by dressing and carrying him down the stairs. She could let him play with other children in the house or immediate neighborhood under another parents' supervision when Jean-Marie is at home, such as during weekends.

Both parents could perhaps reassess what their financial needs really are and if so many hours of work are necessary in the immediate future. Perhaps some of their financial goals could be postponed a year or two until Julien matures a little more.

Perhaps Tiger and Jean-Marie could have met early in the counseling relationship to know each other and reinforce each other, especially during the "grey days" of Julien's severe withdrawal.

If Tiger had used a behavior modification model, he would have set up a clearly defined behavior reinforcement schedule and given Julien a reinforcer for each act in a positive direction thereby encouraging and shaping responses toward specified behavioral goals such as eating. For information on how to develop such a program see any good book on behavior modification (11, 12).

Needs of the Counselor

Tiger is a tender, giving man with deep compassion. He has the capacity and patience to make a long-term commitment to Julien. Tiger also has a need to achieve and get some feedback. Julien's progress and regressions fill him with joy and disappointment. For many long months Julien is stingy with feedback. Tiger's supervisor is there to listen and accept his feelings and react to what is happening to him and to Julien. She shares Tiger's excitement and pain and supports him in the often frustrating relationship with Julien.

Tiger identifies with Julien. He too felt abandond by his mother at a young age and is wracked by the anger he feels toward her and the loneliness without her. Tiger, like Julien, must wonder if he were such a bad person that his mother would leave him. Again like Julien, Tiger's response was to cut himself off from his mother and try to deny his feelings. Even being big and strong doesn't protect him from possible hurt from other people. They aren't afraid of him just because he's big.

Tiger instantly projects his unexpressed feelings of anger toward his own mother onto Jean-Marie. To him, Jean-Marie must be a "bitch." But, as he cannot confront his own mother, he is unwilling to see Julien's mother and work with her for Julien's benefit.

Tiger is an untrained college student working in a clinic with trained professionals. As a student his main purpose is to learn something about relating to children and successfully meeting his course requirements. But he is so involved with Julien that he accepts repeated invitations to re- main at the clinic and help Julien far beyond his original assignment. The bond between Tiger and Julien is somewhat similar to the bond that Julien ultimately develops with Kenny. The altruistic relationship and caring for another person helps both to grow and more clearly define their own worth and personhood.

Outcomes

After two years of clinic treatment and relationship with Tiger, Julien is able to make important progress. He has at least one younger friend of his own whom he cares about and cares for—Kenny. He feels respected and able to express his feelings of both anger and affection toward Tiger and Kenny. He realized how much he wants his mother and how he has shut himself off from her. He is able to be away from her all day and to begin to talk with her again.

Julien is eating, reading at an advanced level, showing some leadership skills as he takes over with Kenny, and playing children's games without direct adult and parent involvement. He is a far more independent person.

Julien still has great outbursts of anger and difficulty in controlling his now released feelings. He remains jealous of his mother's attention and bitterly resents Jean-Marie when she is attentive to Kenny. There is still no mention of a satisfying relationship with his father or a complete recognition that Tiger is a man, not a mother. He is not yet really sure that he is a good and worthy person in his own right or that his mother truly loves him when she is not expressively showing it.

Julien is a member of the society of children, achieving academically, and ready for an active role in the family. He no longer requires exclusive attention.

Much of Julien's progress is due to the intuitive and sensitive attention of a non-professional college student under the careful supervision of skilled professionals. For a professional to devote the amount of time to Julien that Tiger was able to give, would put a great strain on the available resources of any clinic. The use of volunteers and para-professionals was certainly rewarding in helping Julien. The power of that relationship seems to have played a major role in Julien's growth and increasing effectiveness as a person.

Tiger and Julien respect, like, and trust each other. Julien copies these characteristics in his friendship with Kenny and imitates what Tiger did with him.

What a marvelous spread of effect!

PART FOUR

COUNTERPOINT

CONSIDERING AGE LEVELS

Dear Editor:

"You mention at the beginning of this section that counseling models require special adaptation when the client is a child. Is it true to assume then that different kinds of adaptations might be necessary depending upon the age of the child. A nine-year-old child may require a different kind of approach than a five-year-old. How specific can we be in designating a certain counseling approach for a certain age level? Also, at which age level would play therapy be invalid as a counseling approach?"

J.J.

Note. A good point is raised in this reaction paper. Because the maturation of the child is so rapid a process, special modifications are required according to age levels. No one has yet answered the questions involved, but there is a wealth of literature on child therapy and child counseling which explains how to deal with children according to their *maturational* levels, rather than chronological ages. Often, the child counselor will rely heavily on his or her experiences with children to determine what types of approaches to use with a specific child.

JULIEN

Dear Editor:

"The case of 'Julien' pointed out two things to me. First, that the counselor's compassion is more important in the long run than any techniques he uses. Tiger really felt for Julien, and that's why he was able to help him. Second, that counseling is not always a smooth process, but one filled with ups and downs. The counselor has to learn to live with that reality, and not become too discouraged when things don't seem to be going well. This is especially true when we work with children, who are always being influenced by their home environments, over which we have little or no control. . ."

A. C.

PUZZLES

Dear Editor:

" . . . . I saw many parallels in the cases in this section. Children are puzzling creatures to adults, but if we try to get into their world and to experience life from the child's perspective things begin to make more sense. In a way, the child is like a slave, in bondage to the stupidity, cruelty, and insensitivity of the parents and other adults around him . . . . What the counselor or teacher seems to do is help the child express his feelings of bondage and overcome the pains that stifle his growth. I think this requires not only a highly sensitive counselor, but one who can look back honestly on his or her own childhood. Once the counselor is able to do that, it doesn't really matter if the counselor probes the child's unconscious, as a Freudian would do, plays games with the child, as the play therapist does, runs a group, or uses educational methods . . . ."

E. W. W.

PART FIVE

COUNSELING SPECIAL GROUPS

We recognize that different clients have different needs, and that counseling approaches which are suitable for Client A may be unsuitable for Client B. In recent years, this appreciation of difference has extended to groups as well as individuals. A rising social consciousness during the 1960s and 1970s has precipitated an increasing interest in counseling applications particular to special groups. Most attention has been paid to the needs of blacks, Hispanic-Americans, Orientals, the lower socioeconomic group, and women. While these recent developments are commendable, we must keep in mind that the client is an individual above all else, and that although group considerations may be important, sensitivity to the needs, interests, abilities, and perceptions of the client-as-individual is still paramount.

In this part of the book, we will look at some recent papers on the special needs of special groups. Robert L. Bell Jr.'s "The culturally deprived psychologist," and Clemmont E. Vontress's "Counseling the racial and ethnic minorities," present the most inclusive coverage of the topic in the literature. Bell's argument, that "the counseling psychologist, be he black, white or otherwise, is likely to function as a culturally deprived person in the black community of his training has taken place in the traditional counselor training program," is more than an admonition: it is a statement of the problem that becomes the central subject-matter of this part of the book. Bell makes some general suggestions how to deal with this problem, but when we turn to Vontress's paper we find very detailed guidelines to help us in our practice with minority group clients. Vontress, who has written extensively on this subject, sums up and sythesizes his positions in this paper, which because of its specificity and perceptiveness deserves special attention.

Each of the following papers deals with a specific "special" group: Blatt's "Counseling the Puerto Rican Client" points out some of the cultural barriers a counselor might encounter working with the Puerto Rican, and suggests some ways of dealing with these problems.Skydell's "Counseling Women in the 1970s" draws from the wealth of literature on this subject some valuable, practical conclusions, which will benefit all counselors, both male and female. One special group that has not been dealt with as fully in the literature as it could be is the single-parent family. The two papers which make up chapter 27, Deanna and Stanley Nass's "Counseling the fatherless child," and Eleanor H. Ruma's "Counseling the Single Parent" pay attention to this special group.

SUGGESTED ADDITIONAL READINGS

Banks, J. A. and Grambs, J. D., eds. *Black self-concept.* New York: McGraw-Hill, 1974.

Brown, D. and Srebalus, D. J. *Contemporary guidance concepts and practices* (section IV), Dubuque, Iowa: Wm. C. Brown Co. Publisher, 1972.

Grier, W. H. and Cobbs, P. M. *Black rage.* New York: Basic Books, 1968.

Nass, S. and Nass, D. R. "Counseling with clients of lower socioeconomic background." In *Foundations of counseling.* edited by G. S. Belkin. Dubuque, Iowa: Kendall/Hunt, 1974.

Riessman, F.; Cohen, J.; and Pearl, A., eds. *Mental Health of the poor.* New York: Free Press, 1964.

Vontress, C. E. "Cultural barriers in the counseling relationship." In *Foundations of counseling,* edited by G. S. Belkin. Dubuque, Iowa: Kendall/Hunt, 1974.

21. COUNSELING THE RACIAL AND ETHNIC MINORITIES

Clemmont E. Vontress

Peter Schwarzburg

Counseling: Racial and Ethnic Factors

The racial and ethnic diversity of people in the United States has never been denied. Early observers characterized the country as a "melting pot," a folksy concept which suggests that culturally different citizens eventually lose the distinct identities separating them. The concept aptly described many assimilated-oriented immigrants who were so committed to becoming "real Americans" that their social and cultural interests, identities and allegiances lay predominantly in the host society rather than in the ethnic community or in the old country. The least assimilated-oriented immigrants confined themselves to their ethnic enclaves, spoke their languages proudly, worshipped in their own ways and, in general, kept alive ethnic subcultures.

As racial and ethnic enclaves grew and became more obvious and often annoying to the dominant cultural group, the concept "cultural pluralism" developed a special appeal for Americans verbally committed to the ideals of democracy and tolerance. It implied cooperation between majority and minority; it suggested mutual respect, appreciation and acceptance of cultural differences; and it inferred that minorities would not have to fear repression or obliteration of their heritages. Cultural pluralism was put to a severe test during the great push for civil rights in the fifties and sixties when the largest and most severely excluded minority in the United States, Americans of African descent, pronounced as never before great pride in their racial and ethnic heritage in the course of demanding equal rights. Concurrently and subsequently, other racial and ethnic groups—American Indians, people of Spanish heritage, Jewish Americans, and others—declared aloud their identities, while decrying simultaneously the inequalities inflicted upon them by dominant group Americans. Their voices and the cries of "Black Power!" announced to all the world that the United States is a country of many subcultures from which constituent minorities acquire language patterns, customs, values, and world views which are often foreign to members of the dominant cultural group. The protests for equal rights caused a variety of reactions from mainstream Americans. These ranged from great humanitarian concern to overt anger and hostility toward the minorities for upsetting the social status quo.

The social phenomenon just described reflects the fact that when human groups exist separately for whatever reasons, voluntarily or forced, in time they develop different language habits and nuances, personalities, perceptions of themselves and others, and values and norms which guide their behavior. They become culturally different. The differences, in turn, become reasons for exclusion by those in power. In the United States, racial and ethnic minorities are excluded from equal opportunity to the degree that they are different from the dominant group. In the case of racial minorities, primary exclusion variables are color of skin, curl of hair, and slave heritage. These are genetically transmitted; that is, if one or both parents have the characteristics, the offspring will have them also—at least to some extent. Although slave heritage is not a biological trait, the fact that one's forebears were slaves is historically indelible. Because of the dominant group's intense reactions to visible and imagined differences, primary variables—singly or interactively—eventuate into numerous potent secondary exclusionary forces, such as differences in language, values, education, income, housing, and general cultural lifestyle. The secondary exclusionary forces are the usual excuses dominant group Americans often give for excluding minorities. One is less apt to be condemned as a bigot when excluding persons for these reasons than when excluding human beings because of color, hair texture, or previous servitude—factors over which the excluded have no control.

Indeed, citizens in the American society are separate and unequal; and this fact is evident throughout the social order. Whenever and wherever majority group members meet and greet members of the minority groups, the likelihood of misunderstanding and ill will is great. Counseling, the largest helping profession in this country, has not gone untouched by the lack of understanding and good will between the majority and minorities. As a process, counseling is a purposeful psychological interaction involving two or more individuals. One or more of the interactants is considered able to help the other person or persons to live and function more effectively at the time of the involvement or at some future time. Specifically, the goal of counseling is to assist the recipient or recipients in adjusting to the various environments which influence his psychological well-being. In order to accomplish this objective, the counselor must be able to relate therapeutically with his client; he must be able to determine the client's state of adjustment; and he must know what ought to be done to help the client maintain or improve his current level of adjustment.

The purpose of this article is to indicate the effects of racial and ethnic factors on the counseling process—that is, to point out how cultural differences affect the ability of the counselor to relate to his client therapeutically, to discuss problems the counselor may encounter in making a diagnosis of the minority group client, and to suggest some difficulties inherent in making recommendations to assist minority group clients.

The Relationship

Counseling is a dynamic process. Elements shift and gain or lose momentum as the interactants are replaced or increased and as problems become more or less demanding of their attention and concern. Even so, an attempt is made here to examine various aspects of the relationship as they relate to assisting minority group clients.

Rapport

As a relationship between two or more individuals, counseling suggests, ipso facto, the establishment of a mutual bond between the interactants. The emotional bridge between the counselor and the counselee is referred to as rapport, a concept which pervades therapeutic literature. Simply defined, rapport connotes comfortable and unconstrained mutual trust and confidence between two or more persons. In a counseling dyad, it implies positive feelings combined with a spirit of cooperativeness. In therapeutic groups, rapport is the existence of a mutual responsiveness which encourages each member to react immediately, spontaneously, and sympathetically to the sentiments and attitudes of every other member.

Rapport should not be misconstrued as just initial "small talk" designed to put the counselee at ease. It is a dynamic, emotional bridge which must be maintained throughout the interview. During the relationship, the participants continuously take stock of each other. They notice how each individual presents himself, what is said, and how it is said. The nature of the communication, spoken and unspoken, can cause the counselee to alternate from trust to tacit reserve or even overt hostility. Exploring content that is threatening to the ego generally requires a more positive relationship bridge than is otherwise needed.

It is a matter of common experience that individuals find it more difficult to establish empathy with those unlike themselves. Differences in racial and ethnic background, in socioeconomic class, and in language patterns—these and other factors, singly or interactively, create rapport problems in the counseling relationship. Often the differences or similarities are so imperceptible that the counselee cannot verbalize them. He can only feel them. For example, he expresses his good feelings toward the counselor by the statement "He talks like us," which is equivalent to saying "He is one of us."

Although minorities differ in a variety of ways throughout the country, it seems possible to offer some general advice in establishing rapport with them—especially with those who have not had a continuing relationship with members of the dominant cultural group. First, the counselor should try to avoid extremes in his behavior. For example, he should refrain from overdressing or underdressing—i.e., he should dress so as not to call undue attention to himself. American reservation Indians appear to be extremely suspicious of too much talking, too many questions, and too much "putting on the dog." Similar attitudes are pervasive among Appalachian whites, who historically have been suspicious of the city slicker with his city clothes and city ways.

In general, the counselor should curtail his small talk at the beginning of the interview, especially if he does not know what small talk is appropriate. Small talk may be perceived as an attempt by the counselor to delay the unpleasant. Thus, it can be anxiety-producing. The counselor should start the interview with a direct but courteous "How can I help you?" This opening allows the *client* the opportunity to chit-chat if he is uncomfortable going immediately into his reason for coming to the counselor. Some Spanish heritage clients may annoy the Anglo counselor with the penchant to pry into his personal life. In such case, the counselor should not be alarmed, but reply to such a question as "Are you married?" He should then get on with the interview.

Structuring

On the whole, minority group members have had limited experiences with counselors and related therapeutic professionals. Their contacts have been mainly with people who tell them what they must or should do in order to receive wages, to get well or to stay out of trouble. Relationships with professionals who place major responsibility upon the individual for solving his own problems

are few. Therefore, the counselor working within such a context should structure or define his role to clients—that is, he should indicate what, how, and why he intends to do what he will do. It is also important to communicate to the client and sometimes to his loved ones what is expected of him or them in the relationship. Failure to structure early and adequately in counseling can result in unfortunate and unnecessary misunderstanding, simply because the counselor's interest and concern are unclear to the client, his parents or significant others.

The counselor of deprived minorities needs to realize that he is working with people who, because of their cultural or experiential backgrounds, are unable or unwilling to participate in introspective explorations. Therefore, techniques such as prolonged silences should be avoided at least until positive rapport has been established, for their use tends to become awkward and to increase the distance between the counselor and his client.

The counselor may find it particularly difficult conducting an interview in which personal issues must be explored. Appalachian whites, for example, find very offensive personal queries which the counselor may perceive to be innocuous. Often parents of counselees are the first to let him know this, especially if he happens not to be "from 'around here."

In general, more than usual attention should be paid to structuring when the subcultural group is typically suspicious of outsiders for whatever reason and when the socialization patterns in the group encourage a structured, well-ordered approach to life. For example, the well-defined roles and expectations for members of the orderly Chinese-American family probably explains why high school and college students from such families prefer concrete and well-structured situations in and out of the classroom. The ambiguity typically inherent in the counseling process is terribly disconcerting to them, to say the least.

Resistance

The counselee's opposition to the goals of counseling is usually referred to as resistance. It may manifest itself in a variety of ways, such as self-devaluation, intellectualization, and overt hostility. Although the counselor may recognize the various manifestations when he counsels a middle-class white counselee, he often fails to recognize the phenomenon in the minority group client probably because he is so overwhelmed by the visible or perceived differences of his client that he fails to follow his usual counseling procedures.

Although many Spanish heritage clients are unable to converse fluently in English, others may reveal to the counselor's subsequent surprise that they are quite adequate in that language. The client's alleged inability to speak English must be viewed, therefore, as resistance—either to the counselor himself, to the Anglo establishment or to both.

It has been observed also that many young blacks, urban or rural, appear to be shy and withdrawn in the counseling dyad or group. The counselor unfamiliar with the nuances of black culture may be quick to assess the behavior as just another unfortunate effect of social and economic deprivation. However, the client's perception of his own behavior may be very different; he's just "cooling it." He knows how to rap beautifully about whatever, but is unwilling to do so until he is convinced that his audience is a person of good will. On the other hand, such clients may be so talkative that they refuse to let the counselor get a word in edgewise. Although such behavior may be perceived as an indication of positive rapport and desire for help, it can also mean that the client is

"playing along" the counselor. It is somewhat similar to a sandlot basketball game in which the ball is being passed to all players but one, the isolate. In this case, the counselor is the outsider.

Other examples of resistance among minorities in the counseling relationship can be cited. A very obvious one is failure to show up for an appointment. American Indians, for example, are very reluctant to disagree or be uncooperative, especially with someone of higher status. Such reluctance may be observed also among many low status Southern blacks, vis-a-vis whites, although perhaps for different reasons. Indians and blacks of all ages may agree to come in for an interview or conference when, in fact, they have no intentions of following through. They promise to do so out of courtesy, respect, or fear.

Transference

Transference refers to an individual's reacting to a person in the present in a manner similar to the way he has reacted to another person in past experience. In other words, transference is a repetition or new edition of an old relationship. It may be conscious or unconscious, positive or negative, and is considered a form of resistance to the goals of counseling. Common in most therapeutic involvements, transference is especially knotty in the majority-minority counseling dyad or group, because minority group members bring to the relationship intense emotions derived from experiences with and feelings toward the majority group.

In counseling, the client either expects the counselor to be succorable and supporting or punishing and controlling. Minority group counselees usually expect the majority group counselor to exhibit the latter attitude, either because of direct experiences with people who remind them of the counselor or because of socialization which teaches them to react to members of the majority group or those who identify with that group with suspicion. For example, preschool Pueblo Indian children know better than to tell the "white man" about anything that is happening in the village. Fear and hostility of Anglos by Mexican-Americans in the barrios of the Southwest are evidenced by four- and five-year-old children who run ahead of any official-looking car entering their neighborhood screaming "La migra, la migra" (the migration officials). Such behavior implies that these children learn before they enter school that Anglos are not to be trusted. It is easy to understand why many of them associate a counselor in a private office with the "policia" or some other official who does not have their best interest at heart.

Black children also learn at an early age, very often at the feet of their parents, that white people are not to be trusted. As they mature in decaying ghettos of great cities, they have other experiences which lead them to approach whites with resentful anxiety, distrust, hostility and ambivalence. In a similar way, many Appalachian children learn that outsiders, whatever color they happen to be, are people who "mean you no good." Thus, their school counselors, especially those perceived as outsiders, find that mountain children appear to be fearful, shy, and reluctant to talk.

Countertransference

Countertransference is the transference of the counselor to the counselee. The counterpart of transference, it leads to persistent inappropriate behavior toward the counselee and results in untold strains in the counseling relationship. Although counselors are quick to recognize transference as a reality, they find it difficult to consider the possibility that they may not accept, respect or like many of their counselees. Their professional training has tended to inculcate in them the idea that they should be imbued with Rogerian ingredients of empathy, positive regard, unconditionality of positive regard, and congruence. They, therefore, fail to admit that they are also parents, voters, property owners, taxpayers, Northerners or Southerners, Republicans or Democrats— in a word, that they are human beings with a variety of beliefs, values, and attitudes (conscious and unconscious) which invariably affect the counseling relationships which they establish with minority group people.

As products of a society which has been characterized as racist, counselors bring to the therapeutic relationship preconceived attitudes and ideas about racial and ethnic minorities. The preconceptions manifest themselves in numerous ways. Because majority group members occupy the most powerful and prestigious positions in society, they are often perceived rightly or wrongly by minority group people as "Ugly Americans," as authoritarian and condescending. In counseling, this phenomenon may be described as the "great white father" syndrome. The counselor communicates to minority group clients not only that he is omnipotent (probably because he is a member of the majority group) but also that he means them nothing but good as well. He literally guarantees them that he will "deliver" if only they will put themselves in his hands. Simultaneously he communicates, albeit unconsciously, the implication that if they do not depend on him they will be doomed to catastrophe. The great white father syndrome may be interpreted as countertransference, because it suggests that the counselor is anxious not only to demonstrate his power and authority but also to prove that he is not like all the other majority group people the minority group clients may have known.

Another general manifestation of countertransference is the counselor's tendency to be excessively sympathetic and indulgent with minority clients. For example, his definition of achievement for them may be in wide variance with his achievement yardstick for members of the majority group. Does he view achievement for minorities as that level of attainment—educational, social, occupational, and economic—considered meritorious, laudable, acceptable or desirable as measured by criteria, explicit or implicit, which are established or espoused by the dominant cultural group? Or does he consider it appropriate to use a different set of achievement criteria for minorities, simply because they are minorities? If the latter is the case, he is guilty of saying, thinking or implying that his minority group client is pretty good for a black, a Mexican-American, or an Indian.

Language

Language is a part of an individual's culture or subculture. Failure to understand his culture is failure to comprehend much that he communicates in his language. In order to communicate effectively with minority group clients, the counselor must be able to understand the verbal and nonverbal language of his counselees, for each aspect is dependent on the other. If a counselor listens only to the speaker's words, the counselor may get as much distortion as if he "listened" only to body language. To understand the meaning of gestures, postures and inflections, it is important to know a people, their institutions, values and lifestyle.

The counselor encounters varying degrees of difficulty communicating with racial and ethnic minorities. For example, on Indian reservations variations in facility to use English can be illustrated on the one hand by some of the Pueblos of New Mexico where no English is spoken in everyday life, and on the other by the Fort Berthold Reservation Indians of North Dakota where almost everybody speaks English. On the Choctaw Reservation in Mississippi, about four percent of the families use excellent English; fifty-seven percent, good English; and thirty-nine percent, poor English. Although this description is fairly typical of English facility among reservation Indians in general, young Indians having gone to school in English use that language with greater facility than do their elders. Even so, Indians of whatever age communicate with great economy of language; and they are given to the use of concrete as opposed to abstract words. Therefore, counselors find that Indian clients are limited in the ability to express personal feelings, which is considered necessary by most counselors.

In the Southwest, Spanish heritage people customarily live in enclaves isolated from the English-speaking community. In many counties in Texas and New Mexico, the children enter the English-speaking world for the first time when they enroll in public schools. In classrooms children unable to speak English are often threatened with punishment if they speak in their native language. Badly needed to assist these children and their parents are bilingual counselors who speak Spanish natively, because many Anglo counselors who have studied Spanish in school find that they are still unable to communicate with alingual or biculturally illiterate children who speak neither English nor Spanish that is standard.

The counselor is less handicapped in communicating with Appalachian whites than he is with American Indians and Spanish heritage clients. Even so, he usually finds therapeutic communication difficult, because mountain people tend to use simple Anglo-Saxon words as opposed to long Latinate words. Their speech is characterized by a reduction in qualifiers, adjectives, and adverbs, especially those which qualify feelings. Therefore, the counselor expecting his Appalachian clients to talk a great deal about how they feel is apt to be disappointed. Unique idioms and pronunciations also may constitute communication barriers, at least until the counselor's ears become attuned to the language patterns.

Among lower-class blacks, the counselor (black or white) often experiences difficulties in understanding not only slurred pronunciations, but also idioms and slang endemic to the community. Some counselors, not wanting to indicate that they cannot or do not understand the counselee's argot, continue the dialogue hoping to catch up later. Unfortunately, they often discover that the more they allow the client to talk without clarification, the more confused they become as to what he is saying. If the counselor fails to understand the client for whatever reason, the most honest thing to do is to ask him for an explanation or repetition of his statement.

The counselor probably experiences more difficulty understanding nonverbal language in the lower-class black community than he does comprehending the verbal. Individuals speak not just with their voices alone; they use their entire bodies either to make a complete statement or to punctuate one. For example, the "hip" shuffle of the young black male, his slouched sitting position with chin in hand, his erect stance with genitals cupped, the apparently unconscious wipe at the chin or mouth with his hand when there is nothing visible to wipe away—all of these nonverbal expressions are filled with significant meaning if the counselor can interpret them. To arrive at the correct interpretation, the counselor must understand both their general and contextual meanings. He needs to recognize that the more emotionally charged the verbal language, the less definite its meaning and the more important the accompanying nonverbal expressions.

Occasionally, the counselor may need to use an interpreter with Indian and Spanish heritage clients. If an interpreter is needed when counseling or communicating with Hispanic people, it is important to use someone whom the individual can respect. For example, the Anglo counselor would be advised not to ask a third or fourth grade Spanish-speaking student to interpret for him when he consults with a Spanish-speaking parent. Because of the demand for respect so characteristic among the Spanish speaking, the counselor should obtain someone whom the parent can respect as he respects him, the counselor.

Knowledge of the client's language and its nuances are important in counseling because so many customary counseling techniques demand fluency in this area. Paraphrasing, reflection, and interpretation presuppose understanding the client's language. In order to reflect accurately what the client is experiencing and feeling, the counselor should be able to interpret nonverbal language. He must not allow skin color or accent to blind him to cues which would be otherwise obvious if he were counseling a majority group client.

Psychosocial Barriers

Several psychosocial characteristics of racial and ethnic minorities constitute, singly or interactively, barriers to the achievement of therapeutic goals in the counseling relationship. These barriers are usually unconscious aspects of the personality and are derived primarily from the American culture which both socializes and oppresses its minorities simultaneously. Occasionally, current behavior patterns can be traced back to the old country. Some of the barriers are discussed below.

1. *Self-disclosure.* Self-disclosure, or the willingness to let another person know what you think, feel or want, is basic to the

counseling process. It is particularly crucial in the rapport-establishment phase of the relationship because it is the most direct means by which an individual can make himself known to another person and is, therefore, prerequisite to achieving the goals of counseling. People of African descent are especially reluctant to disclose themselves to others, probably because of the hardships which they and their forebears have experienced in the United States. Many of them, especially the males, are devoid of confidence in human relations.

Reluctance to disclose is a problem in the white-black dyad, because few blacks initially perceive whites as individuals of good will. The client discloses himself when he feels that he can trust the target person, not necessarily when he feels that he is being understood. In fact, the black client fears being understood, for understanding carries with it the idea of engulfment, of loss of autonomy, of being destroyed in a society which he perceives as racist. Obviously, the fear of being understood has grave implications for individuals and group counseling. It is conceivable that, in the case of the black client, the counselor who understands too much is to be feared and even hated.

2. *Self-hatred.* When one is a member of an ostracized, excluded or oppressed group, he tends not only to despise his group, but also to hate himself for being a member of the group. In the United States, blacks more than any other minority have unconsciously identified with the majority group (their perceived oppressors) and, consequently, have developed contempt for and hatred of themselves. In view of the generally acknowledged positive correlation between self-rejection and the rejection of others, the counselor may expect repulsion, passive or overt, from the black client for this reason alone. The counselor's helping the black counselee to accept himself more positively

should result in the client's progressive acceptance of the counselor.

3. *Machismo.* When counseling the Hispanic male, it is important to understand the meaning of machismo which refers to one's manhood, to the manly traits of honor and dignity, to the courage to fight, to keeping one's word and to protecting one's name. It also refers to a man's running his home, to "controlling" his women and to directing his children. Therefore, machismo which provides respect from a male's peers is not to be taken for granted. It also suggests rather clear-cut separation of the sexes. The male, ipso facto, enjoys rights and privileges denied women, who are generally reluctant to demand equality. It is probably because of machismo that Spanish heritage boys and girls are often more uncomfortable and uncommunicative in coed group counseling than are members of groups who are entirely Anglo. Another implication of machismo is that Anglo female counselors should not be too aggressive or forward in the counseling interview with Hispanic males, not even with preadolescents. The right amount of deference must be shown at all times.

4. *Personalism.* Personalism is a rather stubborn counseling barrier among Appalachian whites, Spanish heritage people and blacks. Although a precise definition is difficult, personalism suggests that individuals are more interested in and motivated by considerations for people than they are by bureaucratic protocol. The mountaineer derives self-identification mainly from his relationships with others. Therefore, he puts a lot of stock in being neighborly. For him, it is more important to pass the time of day with a friend encountered en route to an appointment than it is to arrive at the destination punctually.

Refusing to be enslaved by clocks, mountain people transact their business by feelings—not protocol. People adherent to appointments, promptness, planning and protocol are suspect. In counseling, personalism encumbers the counselor in getting his clients to make and keep appointments. They continue to just drop by to "pass a spell" and "visit" and *may* get around to discussing something that has been "on my mind."

As suggested earlier, asking a counselor personal questions may be the Hispanic person's way of getting close to an individual who might otherwise remain impersonal. Although the lower-class black is reluctant to ask a counselor direct questions, he is generally more comfortable relating to him after he has obtained at least a modicum of information about the counselor as a human being—i.e., he is apt to "check out" the counselor before "spilling my guts" to him.

5. *Listening.* Among other things, counseling requires listening, an area in which many lower-class blacks and Appalachian whites have little experience, probably because of their early socialization in large families. Often their homes are filled with din and confusion, with everybody talking simultaneously. In such an environment, young people soon learn not to listen to what words mean, but to emotions speakers convey. This is why the observant counselor may discern a blank stare on the face of his client, even when he perceives himself to be providing the youngster with much needed insight. The empty facial expression indicates that the client has tuned out the counselor until he stops talking. The inability of black and mountain people to attend to a speaker may help to explain why their conversation seems to have little continuity of ideas. Inability to listen hampers more directly group counseling than it does dyadic relationships.

6. *Modesty.* Modesty in the presence of superiors is a relationship barrier in counseling Japanese-Americans. The phenomenon may be attributed to the total respect customarily paid the father, whose authority in the family is beyond question and toward whom one is forbidden to express overt negative feelings. Many young Japanese-Americans are so imbued with awe of authority that they hesitate to express their feelings on any subject when they are in the presence of higher status individuals or when they are expected to articulate their views in groups. It is easy to understand how their hesitancy intrudes in the counseling relationship, dyadic or group.

Characteristic reserve in the Japanese-American personality makes it difficult to determine where cultural patterns end and psychologically debilitating symptomatology begins. The counselor must have two perceptual yardsticks for measuring normal behavior—he must be able to determine what is deviant behavior in the Japanese-American subculture as well as what is aberrant in the culture at large.

Reserve among many Puerto Rican females and rural lower-class blacks in general corresponds closely to that of Japanese-Americans. The well-bred Puerto Rican girl often avoids eye-to-eye contact, especially with men, a fact which may cause the Anglo counselor to draw false conclusions about her character and personality. Her hesitancy to voluntarily interact in group counseling may be attributed to socialization in the Puerto Rican culture in which boys are expected to assert their manhood, while girls remain retiring. Traditionally, Southern blacks were expected by Southern whites to be nonassertive and passive. The residue of such expectations remains today, especially among lower-class blacks in the South and probably helps to explain why black youngsters are often hesitant to interact in interracial counseling groups.

These, then, are but a few psychosocial

barriers the counselor may experience in therapeutic relationships with racial and ethnic minorities. Others could be cited to illustrate the importance of the counselor's being cognizant of subcultural factors when relating to culturally different clients.

Diagnosing

In order to accomplish the goals of counseling, the counselor must be able to relate to, and communicate with, his client; he must be able to determine the client's state of adjustment; and he should know what needs to be done to help the client maintain or improve his level of adjustment. Although relating to minority group people is problematic, making an accurate diagnosis of culturally different counselees is probably fraught with more difficulties. Albeit his clients are racially and ethnically different, the counselor perforce relies on the same assessment tools and procedures used in counseling majority group clients.

Diagnostic Techniques

Commonly used diagnostic techniques, whether standardized or unstandardized, are generally questionable for assessing minority group clients. The ones most used today are standardized and objective—their procedure, apparatus, and scoring have been regularized to allow replicated administration; and every observer of performance arrives at the same report. Included in this category is a variety of commercially available instruments labeled proficiency, achievement, developmental, intelligence and personality tests, and a limited number designated interest inventories.

There are several problems inherent in using these instruments with minorities. The first can be described as situational. For disadvantaged minority group individuals, extended structured situations demanding assiduity are physically and psychologically annoying. Unusual surroundings, formal procedures, and unfamiliar people so characteristic of large group testing environments (individually or combined) aggravate their annoyance and often account for anxiety sufficient to depress scores of the reluctant examinees. In the case of blacks, examiners with regional accents which put them on guard can influence performance. In general, white people with Southern accents are associated with prejudice and discrimination; therefore, as test administrators they are apt to produce in blacks anxiety which may affect test performance.

Steps can be taken to assure an environment most conducive to optimum performance of minority group individuals on standardized tests. First, test administrators should prepare the examinees in advance for the test. Individual and group counseling is one vehicle which can be used not only to allay apprehension about test taking, but to motivate toward optimum performance as well. Secondly, in order to insure the most favorable testing conditions, the size of the testing group should be kept small, ten or twenty examinees to a room. Herding groups of fifty, a hundred, or two hundred students into a large testing arena is most undesirable. Thirdly, test batteries requiring from six to eight hours to administer should be given in segments extending over several days. Finally, examiners and proctors of the same racial and ethnic background as the examinees should be used whenever possible.

In general, language constitutes a handicap for minorities taking standardized tests, not necessarily because it serves as a people's vehicle for communication, but because of its role in the transmission of culture from one generation to another. As a major aspect of culture, it is also a barometer which reflects changes in cultural demands and expectations, however subtle. Those who observe that minorities are verbally destitute and somehow connect the destitution with depressed scores on standardized tests overly simplify a complex problem. Language differences are simply indicative of more global and significant differences, the cultural.

The more assimilated a minority group, the fewer problems its members are apt to experience in taking standardized tests. Groups may lose their total cultural identity as many ethnics have done; they may do as Jewish and Japanese-Americans have done, accept selectively achievement related aspects of the host culture while simultaneously retaining many components of the old; they may become equicultural, moving comfortably back and forth across the line separating the old culture from the new; or they may remain essentially cultural isolates. The majority of American Indians, Americans of African descent, and Mexican-Americans can be classified as cultural isolates, because they are excluded physically and psychologically from the cultural mainstream of the American society. The language difficulty which they experience in taking standardized tests is but one of the manifestations of their exclusionary status.

In view of this problem, counselors should determine informally the degree to which the individual is assimilated in the American culture before administering him a standardized test. If he is a cultural isolate, insisting that he take a standardized test in the idiom of the host culture is questionable. The examiner also should determine the reading level of the examinee before subjecting him to a test which demands reading facility. If the readability level of a test is beyond the individual's reading ability, there is little to be gained by using the test.

Because of the cultural barriers encountered in using standardized tests with racial and ethnic minorities, it is often felt that substitute procedures should be em-

ployed. The obvious alternative is the impressionistic approach—the counselor looks for significant cues by any means available and integrates them into a total impression of the individual's ability, personality, aptitude, or other traits. The unstandardized procedures include observations, anecdotal records, and interviews—analytic techniques well known to counselors. Unfortunately, for minorities, these assessment approaches are probably more unreliable than the objective, standardized techniques because of cultural stereotypes which impair the counselor's ability to diagnose individuals from subcultural groups of which he is not a member. For example, white counselors generally find it difficult to determine through an impressionistic interview where the usual Japanese-American modesty and reserve end and psychological malady begins. Majority group counselors also generally are inept in assessing psychological problems in blacks, mainly because for so long whites have accepted, expected or demanded bizarre behavior of Negroes.

Recurring Problems

Although each minority group counselee should be perceived and counselled as an individual, several common problems plague identifiable minorities in the United States. The severity of each problem depends on, among other things, geographic location and level of assimilation and deprivation. Three recurring problems are economic deprivation, educational deficiencies, and negative self-concept.

In general, the unemployment rates of minorities far exceed that of the majority group. On countless reservations and in many ghettos and barrios, more able-bodied people are unemployed than are employed. Economic deprivation resulting from unemployment and low-paying jobs in turn leads to a complex of psychosocial problems. For example, inadequate and high-density housing fast give rise not only to family dissension but to increased morbidity as well. Life becomes so difficult that short-run hedonism necessarily becomes one's goal.

Intertwined with economic disability are educational deficiencies so much in evidence in black, Mexican-American, and Indian communities. Although there is no concensus on the causation of educational bankruptcy among minorities, it seems clear that a complex of factors such as poor nutrition, inadequate housing, insufficient or improper familial stimuli and role models, poor teachers, and limited school resources interact to constitute a formidable barrier to equal education.

Members of subcultural groups enduring victim status in a country over an extended period of history soon come to view themselves negatively. Illustrative are blacks who were abducted to this country, stripped of their language, heritage and religion, and assigned an inferior status from which few have been able to escape. Their lack of identity and consequential self-contempt help to explain their lack of academic achievement, interpersonal conflicts, intragroup hostility, and drug abuse—especially among young black males.

Among American Indians, confusion over cultural identity also leads to interpersonal problems that are expressed in terms of jealousy and suspiciousness of others. Envy and distrust of one's peers are reflected in the school performance of many Indians who are reluctant to surpass the achievements of their classmates; in their hesitancy to assume leadership roles which might lead to insidious comparisons; and in hostility and conflict between adolescents and their elders. Widespread alcoholism among Indians, even teenagers, may also be attributed to loss of cultural identity and the accompanying institutional and ritualistic restraints which provided significant meaning and direction in life.

Intervention

Deciding what preventive or corrective action should be taken and by whom and for what reason is more difficult for the counselor of minority group members than being able to relate to them or to diagnose their problems. Unlike majority group clients, the problems which minorities encounter in almost every area of life are somehow related, directly or indirectly, to the subordinate status to which they are assigned in the American society. Viewing their problems so globally is overwhelming and frustrating to counselors, some of whom are provoked to "fight the system." However, probably the majority of them will work as best they can to help the client "make it" in spite of his minority group status.

In order to accomplish this goal, the counselor will find that for the most part he must use the same counseling theories, tools, and procedures available for use in counseling members of the majority group. To use them is to experience a great deal of frustration, because they, as presently constructed and used, are not very effective with culturally different clients. Therefore, it is understandable if the counselor abandons what he has learned in graduate school and does "what comes naturally." Unfortunately, such desperate behavior can lead only to further desperation.

Importantly, the counselor should view his clients as human beings. Then he ought to consider that the theories he learned and which now presumably give him direction in counseling are theories of human behavior. The tools and techniques which he learned are also designed to be used to help human beings. Therefore, if he concedes that blacks, Chicanos, Indians, and other minorities are human beings firstly and members of subcultural groups secondly, he should conclude that whatever problems he encounters in his work are not due to what he has learned already. They are probably due to what he has yet to learn—more about himself and more about the minority group client, and more about the psychosocial forces which shape both their lives, forces which cause them to perceive and understand each other with distortion.

Conclusions

Numerous problems exist in counseling minority group counselees. They derive primarily from cross cultural barriers which cause communication static and distortion in interactions involving individuals from culturally different backgrounds. The fact that the client comes from a distinct subculture impairs the counselor's ability to determine not only what difficulties he may be experiencing but also leaves him at loss as to what to do to prevent or alleviate them.

Now that the impediments have been described, what should be done? Concerned counselors ask for special techniques to use with minorities. Others want to know whether it is better for minorities to be counselors to other minorities, since racial and ethnic barriers are so threatening and difficult to penetrate. Few counselors ever ask what they can do to change themselves; few want to know how they can become better human beings in order to relate more effectively to other human beings who, through the accident of birth, are racially and ethnically different. The failure of counselors to ask these questions indicates essentially why counseling minorities continues to be a problem in this country. Counselors are products of a culture which has been characterized as racist. They, in spite of a few graduate courses in guidance and counseling, are shaped by that culture.

Counselors in service and in training need to be exposed to new experiences if they are to become effective counseling minorities. Although a course in counseling racial and ethnic minorities may be another exciting and rewarding cognitive exposure, needed most are affective experiences designed to humanize counselors. Therapeutic group activities extending over long periods, practicums and internships in minority group communities, living in subcultural environments, and individual therapy—these are just a few suggestions for helping counselors grow as human beings. However, these experiences presuppose that counselor educators and supervisors have achieved enough personal insight and knowledge of minorities to help others develop in the manner suggested.

22. COUNSELING THE PUERTO RICAN CLIENT: SPECIAL CONSIDERATIONS

Irwin Blatt

Peter Schwarzburg

The United States is a nation that has been continually expanded through waves of immigration. The most recent large group of people to arrive have come from the island of Puerto Rico. The Puerto Ricans, as all previous groups have encountered various social and economic problems of adjustment, but, in addition, the Puerto Rican faces some unique problems. Politically, the native Puerto Rican is an American, but culturally, he is a Latin American. His native ties are often reinforced by his ability to return frequently to Puerto Rico. This ambiguity often causes a serious identification crises which he must face. This article deals with these culture conflicts and some possible counseling approaches.

The Puerto Rican's Culture Conflict

Among the Puerto Rican's problems, poverty ranks high. The Board of Education's study of Puerto Ricans in New York, *Puerto Rican Profiles*, (Board of Education, 1969) indicates that the number of Puerto Ricans on welfare increased from 28.5 percent in 1957 to 31.5 percent in 1964. In a project supported by the U. S. Public Health Service and published by the Research Foundation of the City University of New York in 1969, it was found that the percentage of Puerto Ricans on welfare increased again to 40 percent and from the surveys taken, the trend is still upward (Podell, 1969). The Puerto Rican comes seeking better economic opportunity and finds that he is an agrarian worker in a technical economy. His language barrier also contributes to his socioeconomic difficulties.

Puerto Ricans are insecure about their social identity in relations with North Americans. Because the Puerto Rican's mixed ancestry is translated into the American "code book" as being an inferior race, comparable to the black social identity, the Puerto Rican feels insecure and immobilized. He feels he cannot be accepted into "White" America. Even in Puerto Rico the people often can feel out of place in a group with a white majority (Seda-Bonilla, 1961).

The family is considered to be the single most important element in Puerto Rican culture. Yet, along with its many strengths, there exist many weaknesses. According to Elena Padilla, "Young or old, the individual is oriented toward placing his family's interests before his own and toward subordinating his own individual needs to the demands of family life." (Stycos, 1955). The male is believed to be superior to the female in both strength and intellect. This belief in the male's superiority is shared by the female. The extent to which a man is considered masculine is measured by the number of children he has fathered and the masculine mannerisms he demonstrates (Stycos, 1955).

Elena Padilla defines the "good husband" as one who, "Provides for his family's needs and exercises his authority to maintain order and good behavior in children" (Mussen and Beytagh, 1969). The inability of the father, on the mainland, to find work, puts him and his family in often painful psychological conflict. When the effects of his unemployment are combined with the fact that the women in the family find work more easily than do the men, the impact is still more devastating.

Another conflict that the Puerto Rican must deal with is his rural-urban dilemma. The Puerto Rican migrant, for the most part, is a semiskilled farm laborer who comes with rural skills as well as social values. The child in rural Puerto Rico is subjected to a restrictive set of responsibilities that can often interfere with his personal freedom, as well as his education. David Landy, Professor of psychiatry at Harvard Medical School, in his study of child rearing practices in a small Puerto Rican village, notes that the free play for rural children is generally very short (Landy, 1959). Children are introduced into the working force at a very early age. Often between the ages of four and seven, the child's responsibilities for the maintenance of the family are increased sharply. On the mainland the children will often see school as deterring their adulthood and will attend poorly with the determination to leave or dropout as rapidly as possible. Girls in the Puerto Rican family from the age of two or three are taught their roles. They are encouraged to imitate their mothers doing household chores and receive affection in recognition of their progress (Lewis, 1968).

The psychological character of the Puerto Rican has historically been a passive one. The island has been dominated by foreign powers since the coming of Columbus. The people have a propensity to obey, to follow others, and to refrain from aggressiveness. They do not tend to be competitive. This apparent lack of drive is often interpreted as laziness on the part of the Puerto Rican by the mainlander, but it is certainly not. The value persists that a Puerto Rican's financial income must not interfere with sociability, hospitality, or recreational activities. It is not important for the Puerto Rican male to be the "entrepeneur" and sacrifice his cultural mores. In fact, the "doing" orientation of Americans often leads to a comparison and competition with others which is intense and extreme. This competitiveness can become a source of compulsion that is neurotic in itself.

It is difficult for one to evaluate the Puerto Rican by his outward appearance. Puerto Ricans are typically defensive. They tend to be on guard against any person that they might be suspicious of strangers and over-sensitive to criticism. These reactions are often interpreted by strangers to the culture as characterizing aloofness and evasiveness, when they actually initiate from insecurity and shyness (Brameld, 1959).

A counterpart of this defensiveness is aggressiveness both to others and to the self. The lack of rebelliousness in Puerto Rican history can be explained by the masochistic tendency to channel this aggression inward. This phenomena can explain the high rate of suicides among Puerto Ricans. Explosive anger and flightiness are similarly further expressions of aggression (Brameld, 1959).

All interpersonal treatment in Puerto Rico is guided by respecto (Cordasco and Bucchioni, 1968). Respecto is a quality which is ascribed to properties. It demands proper attention to the ceremonial order of behavior. The other person's respecto must also be considered at all times so that in social relationships, dignidad (dignity) must not be offended (Cordasco and Bucchioni, 1968). Even when a superior enjoys the prestige of giving orders, he is obligated to express his deference to the subordinate's ego through the proper symbolic acts. It is most insulting when this does not occur. It is for this reason that the peasant in Puerto Rico tends to avoid the use of state sevices since the clerks do not express the proper respecto (Cordasco and Bucchioni, 1968).

An extensive repertoire of vocabulary, speech and gesture are used to define a situation. Tones and laughter are used to convey the impression that a particular statement is not meant as an affront. These subtle facets of interpersonal relations are often implicit and therefore missed by foreigners and mainlanders. Subtle jokes called relajos are often exchanged among friends. This is usually a sign of friendship and of trust. It is an important part of expression of familiarity between islanders (Cordasco and Bucchioni, 1968). But, the literal words could be an extreme insult if not related properly.

Socializing among the young people of rural towns is also quite formal. The "paseo" is still practiced. On weekends, and on holidays, the young people of the towns congregate in the town plaza, while young men sit on the stone benches and observe them. Some men also walk around and chat with the girls. The paseo is the accepted practice for sweethearts to meet and exchange words before marriage (Steward, 1956). Social events are not school sponsored or held in school facilities as they often are on the mainland (Brameld, 1959). In contrast, the comparatively looser mores of the mainland often tend to bring the Puerto Rican parent into conflict over the apparent erosion of their children's morals, especially where the young daughters are concerned. The Puerto Rican male, on the other hand, is expected to be sexually aggressive. Even after marriage, it is acceptable for a man to see other women. Rich men often keep mistresses. This dual standard is not easily accepted on the mainland. The Puerto Rican woman becomes aware of her husband's infidelity and responds to it negatively. This can often cause the family to disintergrate. On the island, the practice is accepted and the family preserved.

Gambling is often considered to be a major problem within the Puerto Rican community by mainland authorities. On the island, dice, cards and dominos are played all around, on roadsides, in cafes, in houses and in front of stores. Formal gambling in the casinos is done only once per week (Steward, 1956).

The church is a major source of psychological security on the island. The Puerto Rican on the mainland faces religious anomie. He can find little salvation because sitting in the pews, is a white Catholic audience and addressing them from the pulpit, is a white English speaking priest. The Puerto Rican is almost forced to form his own religious sects and open storefront churches. These little congregations with their painted windows are often frowned upon by the surrounding communities. They are, in fact, as equally unsatisfying to their occupants who are accustomed to the beautiful Spanish churches of Puerto Rico.

The Puerto Rican is also placed into discomfort by his tradition of congregating in the warm streets of his home village. Men would sit for hours at cafes and sip coffee while chatting about politics and social issues. In New York, Puerto Rican men can no longer easily congregate in large groups (on the steps of houses) and chat leisurely, as they had done in Puerto Rico. Even when the weather permits it, their neighbors often react to these large gatherings of people speaking Spanish with irrational fear that the group might be plotting some antisocial behavior. The unreceptive attitude on the part of the community, often contributes to the migrant's forming "Barrios" within various sections of the cities. It is only within these "Barrios" that their social lives can in any way resemble the way it was in Puerto Rico (Suttles, 1968).

The schools, however, never do become a total part of the "Barrio." They remain a source of difficulty for the children of the Puerto Rican communities who are caught between two cultures. Eugene Bucchioni (1960) feels that for the most part, Puerto Rican children behave well in school. They show respect for their teachers and do what they are asked to in most situations. They attempt to be "good" in the general use of that word by teachers. They seldom show extreme disorderly behavior or go out of control. There are few fights and fewer attacks on teachers. Children tend to obey the school's rules and do not deviate far from them. They fear the possibility of punishment by their teachers and their parents if they do not follow the set behavior guidelines of the classroom. Concerning the rare instances when Puerto Rican children do act out, Eugene Bucchioni states: "Teachers do encounter some difficulties, however, and Puerto Rican children are frequently reprimanded. There are for example, occasions of minor disorder, usually consisting of talking and noise resulting from movement in and about the classroom; sometimes obscenities in Spanish are heard."

To a great extent, these difficulties encountered by the teacher derive from the conflict arising from differences in the values of middle-class teacher and those of her slum dwelling pupils. The elementary school teacher teaches lower-class pupils, as Miss Dwight does, value conflicts are likely to occur. The educational process then reflects the conflict in values both within the school and the social and cultural milieu of the surrounding community. (Cordasco and Bucchioni, 1968).

The school guidance counselors encounter a similar problem to the one faced by the classroom teacher, namely value conflict arising out of culturally unfamiliarity. The counselors, therefore, have equal difficulty in meeting the needs of the "ego alienated" child. Their compassionate and understanding attempts to help the child to "come around" to the way of thinking of the school authorities, further frustrates the situation.

Puerto Ricans and the Mental Health Professions

Often Puerto Rican families seek help with their problems of staying together, or controlling a child they fear is becoming delinquent, but there has been a lack of adequate family service agencies. Agustin Gonzalez of the Puerto Rican family institute states, "The frustration that these agencies experienced in not being able to understand the cultural patterns of the Puerto Ricans, communicated itself to the migrant. This situation added to his burden, and made him feel even more rejected. . . ." (New York City Puerto Rican Com. Conf., 1967). All of these social workers had dealt with greatly deteriorated families, who previous to their arrival in New York City had possessed an "innate" desire for home and for family life. Unfortunately, these strengths became distorted in the process of shifting from their culture to another.

Psychotherapists and counselors tend to represent the dominant values of their own culture. They often overlook the importance of the belief systems of their clients and try to influence people to adjust to society-at-large, rather than their own subculture. Therapists are hard put to disguise their culturally biased communications to the client. Wilfred Quaytman states, "We all know that patients soon come to know what kind of person the therapist is, what he or she believes in, what kinds of people the therapist respects and admires. This can and does have an enormous influence over the patient" (Quaytman, 1964). Surely to be totally effective, the therapist must also deal with the moral and the existential conflicts faced by the patient.

The problem of racial identification in therapy is not as significant among the Puerto Ricans as it might be among other minorities since the Puerto Rican is accustomed to dealing with all racial types. As long as there is no language problem, so that affective as well as effective communication can take place, the counselee should be able to develop a positive identification with a white counselor.

All people are, to a very great extent, the products of their culture. It would be most difficult for a therapist or counselor to effect significant cultural change or value orientations upon his client over the short period of several one hour interviews. It is also not for the counselor to decide that the mores of his client are inappropriate. Attempts at restructuring of a client's value system usually result in the client feeling greater conflict, and less relief. A good counseling approach would be to reconcile the conflicts created by the meeting of the two cultures by helping the client adapt to his new environment. This will not involve the total abandonment of all of his previous values. Every culture has some valuable and "worthwhile" values that can be easily modified so that acculturation to the new society can take place with a minimum of trauma.

A counselor who imposes his value system, either consciously or unconsciously is apt to increase the conflict faced by his client rather than eliminating it or even relieving it. The counselor must practice culture related counseling by which he understands his client in relation to the clients culture. The feelings, attitudes, and emotional expressions will be based upon the client's culture, just as much as the client's beliefs are. It is only within the context of the cultural perspective that effective counseling can take place. One cannot speak of such counseling cliches as ego ideal, self-concept, or self-actualization until the counselor himself is cognizant of his client's value system. Again, attempts to "correct" their client's conflicts by counselors who are culturally biased, can often result in increased feelings of alienation on the part of their clients.

Cultural Training for Professionals

It is quite understandable that some counselors feel that the most significant discipline for the training of counselors is cultural anthropology. This study can lead to the identification of the characteristics of social behavior within a society and the negative as well as the positive affects they have upon the individual (Gibson, 1973).

In order to deal more effectively with Puerto Rican families on the mainland, it would be very advisable for counselors to obtain specific cultural training regarding their clients. Among the many possible suggestions has been a required course for counselors dealing with Puerto Rican clients, taught as part of their guidance curricula or an in-service course for counselors already in practice. Such a course would not only reduce the possibility of cultural prejudice, but it would also increase the empathy of the counselor for his client's dilemma. Another effect of such a course would be to define for the professional just what is neurotic behavior on the part of his client and what is perfectly within the clients cultural norms. It must be realized that attempts as being "liberal" by untrained or unacquainted counselors (often trying to compensate for their own real prejudices) can lead to the acceptance or condonment of behavior that should be exposed as irrational in any culture.

Internships are another possibility. Any counselor who will deal in a Spanish-bilingual setting should be exposed to such experience as part of his supervised training. Experience has proven itself to be a valuable teacher if the learner is guided along simultaneously so that the negative aspects of the interpersonal conflict and failures that occur will not be internalized in the form of a permanent prejudice. Internships also acquaint individuals who will eventually wish to remain there as professional staff at the completion of their training. They also serve to help individuals decide if they have made the correct choice in the type of population they wish to work with.

Encounters are still another type of training that can be provided, both on-the-job or as part of the academic curricula. Middle-class, urban counselors will often need more than intellectual educational experiences to resolve their long held personal negative feelings. Encounter workshops have proven to be very valuable avenue for ventilating feelings, which if left untouched, prevent affective therapeutic communications. They will again serve to inform those counselors that should not be dealing in a minority centered milieu of their own "professional" barriers to servicing the needs of their clients.

There are certain fundamental and universal human problems that all cultures face. There is also a great variability within a range of possible solutions to them. Counseling can only be effective when the counselor and client share mutual respect for each other. A counselor's sincerity and commitment to his client's successful resolution of his conflicts is still a most important variable in the process of directed emotional growth, called counseling.

Suggestions for Counseling Puerto Ricans

When dealing with Puerto Rican clients, it is important for counselors to recognize their own attitudes toward poor, rural, racially mixed and culturally alien clients (Christensen, 1975). Counselors who have been practicing for many years with urban middle-class populations might find difficulty in the abandonment of some well entrenched modes of functioning, but it will be advantageous, at times, for them to reach out to their clients in a less traditional way. The best methods are, no doubt, those that work, and the good counselor's loyalties are to his client, rather than his own theoretical framework. Below are outlined some specific suggestions that might be employed by counselors working primarily or partially with Puerto Ricans.

It must be remembered that Puerto Ricans are often ill at ease or at least intimidated by bureaucratic and institutional settings. It would be helpful for the counselor to present as human and as "unofficial" a side to the client as is possible. The normal professionalism that would help to establish the working relationship with a middle-class urban client would often tend to alienate the rural Puerto Rican further. The cool and objective nonjudgmental approach might also be seen as a lack of concern.

Sitting behind a desk in a padded chair while the client sits in a lesser chair similarly communicates a distant and somewhat humiliating role to the client. The counselor can then encounter a resistance based upon the client exerting his need to reinforce his own dignity (dignidad) and self-respect respecto). Talking down to the client in an attempt to reassure him further complicates the problem.

The counselor should establish himself as a warm and concerned human being with a sincere interest in being of assistance. He should be demonstrative and work on an affective level (affecto). When the client enters the office, the counselor should come out from behind his desk and greet him. If possible he should use two equal size chairs and a cocktail table or no table at all, rather than the desk as a barrier. Serving coffee, or offering candy would be extremely well taken. This is a common practice in Puerto Rico and a sign of trust and friendship. Do not be totally the receptive listener. Show interest and enthusiasm. Offer feedback and a reaction to what is being discussed.

Recognize the value of the family in counseling and to the Puerto Rican culture on the whole. Individuals will often place their families interests before their own. A bright student will at times even leave school to help earn money at home. The counselor cannot logically convince him to stay by indicating where his best interests lie. Often the client hesitates to express his actual reason for dropping out since he feels it will be misunderstood. The counselor here faces a family problem and working with the family is the best approach.

The counselor must also consider the Puerto Rican client's masculine-feminine conflict. Puerto Rican males often feel that their role is to be superior to the female economically and physically. "Women's rights" are not only ignored by most husbands, but are seen as a threat to their masculinity (machismo). Acceptance of new values and roles come slowly to any people with an established culture. The counselor must show patience and understanding of these conflicts that emerge in the family when women gain social and economic independence.

Puerto Ricans also tend to be fatalistic (fatalismo). They accept their positions in life and the daily problems that they face. What might be seen as a lack of desire for change or lack of ambition can really be seen in terms of a cultural perspective that is different from the one the counselor is used to working with. The client and counselor need mutual trust and belief in each others commitments. Puerto Ricans will not value increased income over increased pleasure. This must be accepted by the counselor. The competitiveness of the counselor's culture must not be projected as an achievement need of the client. It is as necessary for the counselor to make a conscious effort to learn from his client and to be open to change as it is for the client to be receptive to the efforts of the counselor.

REFERENCES

Board of Education City of New York. *Puerto Rican Profiles.* Curriculum Bulletin no. 5. New York: The Board, 1964.

Brameld, T. *Remaking of a culture.* New York: Harper and Brothers, 1959.

Christensen, E. W., "Counseling Puerto Ricans: Some Cultural Considerations," *The Personnel and Guidance Journal,* vol. 53, no. 5, January, 1975. pp. 349-56.

Cordasco, Francesco and Bucchioni, eds. *Puerto Rican children in mainland schools.* New Jersey: The Scarecrow Press, Inc., 1968.

Gibson, Robert L., Marianne Mitchell, Robert Higgins, eds. *The development and management of school guidance programs.* Dubuque, Iowa: Wm. C. Brown Company Publishers, 1973.

Landy, David. *Tropical childhood.* North Carolina: North Carolina University Press, 1959.

Lewis, Oscar. *La Vida: A Puerto Rican family in the culture of poverty: San Juan and New York.* New York: Random House, 1966.

Mussen, Paul and Luz Beytagh. "Industrialization, Child Rearing Practices and Children's Personality," *The Journal of Genetic Psychology,* vol. 115, part II, December, 1969.

New York City Puerto Rican Community Conference *Puerto Ricans Confront Problems of the Complex Urban Society: A Design for Change.* New York: 1967.

Podell, Lawrence. *Families on Welfare in New York City.* New York: City University of New York, 1969.

Quaytman, Wilfred. "What Makes a Creative Psychotherapist, "*Journal of Contemporary Psychotherapy.* vol. 6, no. 2, Summer, 1974. pp. 168-72.

Seda-Bonill, Edward. "Social Structure and Race Relations," *Social Forces,* vol. 40, December, 1961, pp. 141-48.

Steward, Julian, Robert A. Manners, Eric R. Wolf; Elena Padilla; Elena Mintz; Sidney W. and Raymond L. Scheele. *The people of Puerto Rico: A study in social anthropology.* Urbana: University of Illinois Press, 1956.

Stycos, J. M. *Family and fertility in Puerto Rico.* New York: Columbia University, 1955.

Suttles, Gerald D. *The social order of the slum.* Chicago: University of Chicago Press, London W.C. 1, 1968.

23. COUNSELING WOMEN IN THE 1970s

Ruth H. Skydell

Peter Schwarzburg

Out of the turbulence and turmoil of the sixties, there emerged one movement that is having a profound impact on our traditional ways of thinking. As a result of the powerful and effective drive for women's liberation, the beliefs about women once shared by most members of our society are no longer accepted as universal truths, and our world will never be the same again.

In the wake of this disintegration of old values has come a new freedom for women—a freedom of choice. No longer is marriage the *only* option for every woman; no longer does a woman have to have children to consider herself "fulfilled"; no longer does she have to take "feminine" courses in school and be content with low level jobs. It's a brand new, brave new world!

But while some women have already taken advantage of their new options— remaining unmarried, having fewer children and returning to school in middle age— many of them are frightened at the prospect of making choices. For, where there are so many options, life can be intimidating.

Today's woman is living with one foot in the past, the other in the future. It is a time of transition, a time of learning who she is. It is difficult because marriages aren't going to be the same and social relationships aren't going to be the same—the old, familiar patterns are changing rapidly. Many women are feeling a little lost in this strange, uncharted territory, with no historical referents to guide them. In trying to find their way, they are seeking help, looking to the counseling profession for guidance.

Like most of us, however, counselors are products of a culture which has always assigned women specific roles that are now in the process of being changed. Can counselors be of help if they, too, are finding many of their long-held beliefs shaken? Can they meet the challenge of the 1970's—the decade of transition?

Before we attempt to answer this question, let us first look at some of these beliefs and values which have been sanctified throughout the ages and are now being reevaluated.

The first of these is the belief that since men and women have different physical characteristics, they differ in many other important respects as well. Among these are status, role, temperament and abilities. Because of their greater physical strength, men were believed to be superior; therefore they were given a higher status in society, while women were relegated to inferior positions.

The female role was limited to domestic service and care for her husband and children; males were given all other interests and were expected to be achievers. The family, with the male regarded as its head and the female in a subservient role, was accepted as the basic unit in society.

In temperament, men were said to be aggressive, forceful, and efficient, while women were believed to be passive, docile, sensitive, emotional and impulsive. Studies have shown that such stereotyping is learned early by both sexes, increases with age, and holds true for all socioeconomic levels (Smith, 1939; Tuddenham, 1952; Broverman et al., 1972; Schlossberg and Goodman, 1972).

These sexist stereotypes are learned from parents and reinforced by the educational system. A recent content analysis of the most widely used textbooks in the United States (Weitzman and Rizzo, 1974) led to the conclusion that children are being warped by the latent messages in these books. For example, the researchers found that females (who represent 51% of the population) comprise a mere third of the illustrations in second grade books and that this number drops to a fifth of the total number of illustrations on the sixth grade level. In other words, as textbooks increase in sophistication, women become less numerous and, by implication, less significant as role models. Covertly, then, a young girl is told that she, a female, is less important, as the textbook world shifts to the world of adults. Furthermore, the study revealed, boys are shown as active, skilled and adventuresome; girls as passive, watching, and waiting for the boys. Adult men are shown in over 150 occupational roles, while almost all adult women are shown as housewives. In science books, boys are shown looking through microscopes and pouring chemicals, while girls stand and watch them, and in arithmetic books, men are shown earning money, while women are pictured slicing pies.

Literature is replete with examples which help to perpetuate the stereotypes. Kate Millett (1969) criticizes D. H. Lawrence, Henry Miller and Norman Mailer for poor treatment of women in literature, while Betty Friedan (1963) notes that women's magazines assume that women are "brainless fluffy kittens" (p. 58).

One area in which women have experienced blatant discrimination over the years, is the world of work. This discrimination is reflected in the amount of pay they receive, as well as in the limited job opportunities for women. Although their situation today has improved in some respects, women still earn considerably less than men in all occupations. As recently as 1972, according to United States Department of Labor Statistics, the average annual salary for men was $10,538, while the average for women was $6,053. In other words, for every dollar a male worker earned, a working woman earned only 57 cents in 1972, *down* from 60 cents in 1969.

Women are heavily clustered in low-paid, low-skill jobs. Opportunities for advancement are denied them. Many unions exclude them from apprentice programs and large industrial concerns often will not enroll them in their executive training programs. Women occupy relatively few high prestige positions in government, business, or in the key professions.

A number of rationalizations have been put forth for denying women the opportunity to work in so-called "male" jobs. Discriminatory hiring practices are attributed to the belief that some jobs are "men's work," such as those requiring the lifting of heavy objects; or that it is a "masculine" field, such as engineering (although in the USSR, every third engineer is female). Family responsibilities, the fear of high rates of absenteeism of married women, or the belief that they will leave the job if their husbands relocate, are often cited by employers as deterents to occupational advancement of women.

Why do women tolerate this situation? Why have they for so long accepted the notion that the world is divided into two parts—men's work and women's work?

One answer may be found in the statement by Weisstein that "what a person does or who he believes himself to be will in general be a function of what people around him expect him to be and what the overall situation in which he is acting implies that he is." (1971, p. 70).

Is it at all surprising then, since the male stereotype is regarded more positively, that studies have shown women to have more negative self-concepts than men (Broverman et al., 1972)? Or that college women, when asked to evaluate a professional article, valued the identical material more highly when they thought it was produced by a man than when they believed it was written by a woman. (Goldberg, 1971).

This acceptance of their inferior status in the work world also stems from the widely held notion that for women, intellectual achievement is equated with loss of femininity and popularity. Wolfe (1969) observed that sex role identity is established at the same time that careers are chosen. Young women, therefore, may be reluctant to choose careers that detract from their femininity. Because high levels of achievement are not considered appropriate for females, the price of career success might be social failure. Bright women often find themselves in a double bind. They must achieve in order to live up to their own standards, but must avoid success in order to retain their femininity.

On the basis of her doctoral research, Horner (1970) states "When the fear of success interferes with the desire to be successful, the result is an inhibition of achievement motivation." This "motive to avoid success" may be operating within some women, interfering with their intellectual and professional accomplishments. She concluded that many young women faced with a conflict between their need for achievement and their female image will conform to the sex role stereotype, with possible negative emotional consequences for the individual (1972).

Thus, although women today have many options available to them, many of them are in conflict. Times of change are very stressful and many difficult challenges to the counseling profession have emerged. In particular need of creative counseling are women who find themselves in the following situations: (1) the woman presently in her thirties, forties or fifties, who was brought up with the old sexual stereotypes and is now having real difficulty trying to resolve the conflict between newly awakened strivings and early social learning, (2) the woman who has reached the stage (usually between the ages of 35 and 40) when her husband and children are busy and she finds herself less needed or useful. She faces what Brandenburg (1974) calls "a renewed identity crisis"; (3) the woman who knows what she wants to do with her life—who wishes to continue her education or reenter the work world—but does not known how to go about it; (4) the woman who faces a conflict between career and marriage; (5) the woman who has a poor self-image, and (6) the young woman in high school who must make educational and vocational decisions that will affect her entire life.

As we noted at the outset, counselors, no matter how dedicated they may be to the goal of helping their clients become self-actualizing human beings, are themselves products of society's value system. As a consequence, both male and female counselors hold biases about women (Thomas and Stewart, 1971, Pietrofesa and Schlossberg, 1970.) In what has become a classic study of clinician's attitudes, Broverman et al. (1970) have established that "a double standard of health" exists. This stems from the clinicians' acceptance of an "adjustment" notion of health. They equate masculine rather than feminine behavior with what they consider to be normal and adult. They generally agree that the healthy woman is more submissive, less independent, less adventuresome, more excitable in minor crises, more emotional, and less objective than man. They state: "For a woman to be judged healthy, from an adjustment viewpoint, she must adjust to and accept the behavioral norms for her sex, even though these are generally less healthy for the mature adult." (p. 6).

Extensive research on the phenomenon of experimenter bias, which demonstrated that a person's expectations about another person's behavior come to act as a self-fulfilling prophecy (Rosenthal, 1963), leads us to an inevitable conclusion: if a counselor enters the counseling relationship with a built-in bias, of which he may not even be aware, it cannot help but affect his counseling stance. For example, if counselors believe that certain behaviors are appropriate for men and others for women, this may influence their advice to a particular client to choose a career which in her case might not be the one for which she is best suited. There are many stories of discouragement of girls for professional careers by guidance counselors unaware of their own biases.

Other ways in which counselors may show their bias in the counseling relationship include depreciating the importance of a woman's career, using a client's attitude toward child-bearing as an index of emotional maturity, and making her feel she must adjust better to her role as a wife and mother, instead of encouraging her to become an independent person. A scene in a 1974 television special, "Growing up Female," shown on the Public Broadcasting System, graphically illustrates this last point. A high school guidance counselor, talking to a young girl who is pregnant and about to marry the father of her child, says: "A girl should be neat, clean, attractive, kind, courteous and have a good attitude toward life. The husband should make the major decisions and the wife should understand and go along with his decision. . . . Don't expect him to do housework. Give him time to do his studies—he must compete and he must strive to be successful and you want him to be a success, so you must do the laundry and the housework. . . . The wife has an obligation to take care of his meals and help him to be a healthy, happy and successful man."

Sex role stereotypes are also reflected in some of the materials used by counselors in the counseling interview. Interest inventories, college catalogues and career brochures often contain biased statements which would influence a client in one direction rather than another (Cole, 1973; Schlossberg and Goodman, 1972; Tittle, 1974). To encourage qualified women to consider nontraditional careers, the Career Education Program at the National Institute of Education (NIE) has released a set of "Guidelines for Assessing Sex Bias and Sex Fairness in Career Interest Inventories." These new guidelines are a valuable tool for test developers and users of career interest inventories who wish to overcome the problem of sex bias. Specific suggestions on detecting and minimizing sex bias are given.

It is generally agreed (Schlossberg and Pietrofesa, 1973; Rice and Rice, 1973; Gardner, 1971) that counselors must accept counseling bias as a fact and try to bring their biased feelings into the open so that they are better able to deal with them and remove them from the counseling encounter. Counselors must critically examine their own sex-role stereotypes and ask themselves if their counseling and/or the materials they use tend to perpetuate sexism. One method of discovering one's personal sex role bias is through sensitivity training.

In a course conducted by the writer, a number of techniques were used to help counselors-in-training become aware of their unconscious biases and of the feelings of women today. Among these were a consciousness-raising session, role playing, lectures, and an up-to-date bibliography of reading materials, dealing with the history of the women's liberation movement, discrimination, and other problems encountered by women. By far the most successful device was the "rap session" or consciousness-raising period, in which six women students sat in a circle in front of the class and talked freely about their experiences in school and in the world of work. Most of the men in the class were shocked to hear, at firsthand, accounts of blatant discrimination against these obviously highly-qualified individuals. When one woman, a high school teacher who had received her B.A. degree with honors in mathematics, expressed her resolve to do battle in the forthcoming year for the right to teach an advanced math course, rather than the home economics course she had been assigned for years, the entire class burst into spontaneous applause.

Role playing of various situations, in which women with different problems come for counseling, was also very successful in sensitizing the would-be counselors to the unconscious bias that exists in most people and to the needs and problems of women. A questionnaire dealing with attitudes toward significant women's issues, given to the trainees at the outset of the semester and again at its conclusion, revealed a significant change in participants' expressed opinions, as compared with those of a control group of counselor-trainees who did not take this course. Those who completed the course showed a heightened awareness of the needs and problems of women and greater sensitivity to their struggle for equality.

But, as Oliver (1975) points out, becoming aware of one's bias is not enough. This awareness must be accompanied by constant monitoring and corrective action on the part of counselors. For example, they must be careful not to discourage a client, even subtly, who expresses a nontraditional career choice, and to suggest a wider range of career options for the client who does not express a nontraditional choice, but who is obviously suited for such a career.

After becoming conscious of one's biases and learning to deal with them, what can counselors do to help women who come to them with one or more of the problems mentioned earlier in this paper?

Case 1

The woman who is in conflict over the variety of choices open to her in the 1970s because she has been brought up with the old cultural stereotypes. Although she knows intellectually that the world is a different place today, she is torn emotionally between her old stereotyped beliefs and the new values. Perhaps the most helpful thing the counselor can do is to arrange for her to participate in group discussions with other women who are in the same situation, at which they can air their fears and doubts. Bringing in women who have successfully resolved this type of problem can be very effective. The counselor should also suggest that she read some of the literature put out by the National Organization for Women and help her, through the use of nonsex-biased instruments, to find out what her vocational interests and abilities are. On the basis of these, the counselor may recommend a positive plan of action for her to pursue, while continuing to participate in the group sessions until she has achieved a resolution of her conflicts.

Case 2

The woman, between the ages of 35 and 40, who is facing her second "identity crisis." Brandenburg (1974) notes that this period is getting increasing attention as a critical period for women. It is often a second important time for career exploration. Because her children are in school and her husband is preoccupied with his career, she feels less useful and may even become depressed as a result. The counselor should attempt to deal with the woman's feelings of dependency, and must be prepared to give her immediate academic and vocational counseling. Counselors should keep a file of material dealing with careers and a list of part-time employment agencies and placement services just for women. They must be able to assist women in coping with possible resistance from their family and friends to their going back to work or school.

Case 3

The woman who wishes to go back to school or reenter the world of work, but who doesn't know how to go about it. Since she may need to brush up on rusty study habits or work skills, the counselor may have to direct her to places where such retraining is available. He or she may suggest that she contact the local college, where she can be put in touch with other mature students who have returned to school and are willing to share the benefits of their experience with her.

It is important that the counselor inform the client of the realities of the job market with respect to her age. Awareness of the existing conditions should not limit her choices, as Brandenburg (1974) points out, but rather it should encourage her to make realistic decisions and suggest strategies for gaining employment in areas where difficulties exist. The counselor should acquaint her with a list of employment agencies specializing in positions that meet the special needs of women.

Case 4

The woman in conflict over her dual role as wife and career woman. There are no easy solutions to this problem, but the counselor should be able to convince her that marriage, child raising and a career can be combined successfully. She can be shown that, with the availability of excellent day care facilities which provide an enriched environment for the child, motherhood no longer precludes pursuit of a career. Incidentally, the counselor should work with local agen-cies to provide top flight child care centers in the community. It is important, however, to advise the young woman who is contemplating combining marriage and a career that there are many problems involved in filling this dual role so that she can be prepared to cope with them as they arise.

Case 5

The woman who has a poor self-image. The counselor must help her redefine herself in the face of role stereotypes and help her improve her concept of herself as a woman. He or she can give her reading material on the contributions of women in history, literature, the arts and sciences. To help her modify her attitude toward herself, the counselor may also employ assertiveness training, urge her to take female studies courses and help her, through various instruments designed to reveal her skills and aptitudes, to become aware of her potentialities and start to fulfill them. Use of Rogerian techniques is also recommended as an aid in enhancing her self-image.

Case 6

The young girl in need of career guidance. Because women are remaining unmarried longer, having fewer children and returning to work when their family responsibilities have lessened, early career guidance is assuming crucial importance, and the counselor must really be an expert on changing developments in the occupational world.

Since women, as a rule, follow much more complex career and life patterns than men, who follow a relatively simple and straightforward pattern (Ginzberg et al., 1966), counseling women has a somewhat different aspect from counseling men. Oliver (1975) suggests that the counselor emphasize career counseling for women "within a life-planning context, taking into consideration the developmental stages involved" (p. 435). It is important to reach a girl at an early stage, going back as far as the junior high or even the elementary school level, if she is to be encouraged to consider nontraditional careers. Early expert counseling can also help to forestall later problems which may arise when a woman reaches the age at which her family responsibilities decrease, or when she is left alone, through divorce or the death of her spouse. In order to be effective, the counselor must take the initiative—he or she must reach out to the girl and not wait for her to ask for help. She might not be aware that she needs it.

The counselor must keep an up-to-date file on occupations that are available to women—which are changing from week to week—and make sure that the counselees are aware of changing qualifications within a field. When planning a program for a high school girl, counselors must plan with an eye to the future. They should try to get girls to aim high. They should advise high school girls to seek the maximum education to enable them to qualify for high level jobs, if they have the ability. Inviting a successful career woman—a doctor, for example—to speak to the high school students, to provide a career model for them, is an excellent device for raising their aspirations.

The counselor should work with the curriculum committee to see that changes are made so that boys and girls may enroll in any course available at the school, in accordance with the rules recently issued by the Department of Health, Education and Welfare, for enforcing the ban on sex discrimination in public schools and colleges. The counselor should also see to it that the school library purchases books about the women's liberation movement and equality for women. Information concerning the National Organization for Women and the special issues of popular magazines dealing with college and careers should be made available in the library as well.

Finally, the counselor should encourage high school girls to form discussion and consciousness-raising groups to air their mutual problems. The mothers of the girls should also be encouraged to form such groups so that they will be receptive to the new ideas being discussed by their daughters.

These suggestions for today's counselors who must face the many challenges of a society in transition are by no means all-inclusive. In addition to adopting some or all of them, truly creative counselors will bring their own ingenuity to bear, improvising, experimenting with many approaches, always keeping in mind the goal of helping each woman to follow the course most appropriate for her so that she may function to the best of her ability in a mature and healthy society.

REFERENCES

Brandenburg, J. B. The needs of women returning to school. *Personnel and Guidance Journal,* 53 (1974):11-18.

Broverman, I. K.; Broverman, D. M.; Clarkson, F. E.; Rosenkrantz, P. S.; and Vogel, S. R. Sex role stereotypes and clinical judgments of mental health. *Journal of Consulting and Clinical Psychology,* 34 (1970):1-7.

Broverman, I. K.; Vogel, S. R.; Broverman, D. M.; Clarkson, F. E.; and Rosenkrantz, P. S. Sex-role stereotypes: A current appraisal. *Journal of Social Issues,* 28 (1972):59-78.

Cole, N. S. On measuring the vocational interests of women. *Journal of Counseling Psychology.,* 20 (1973):105-12.

Friedan, B. *The feminine mystique.* New York: Norton, 1963.

Gardner, J. Sexist counseling must stop. *Personnel and Guidance Journal,* 49 (1971):705-13.

Ginzberg, E. et al. *Life-styles of educated women.* New York: Columbia University, 1966.

Goldberg, P. Are women prejudiced against women? In *Sex differences in personality: Readings,* D. K. Schaeffer, ed., Belmont, Calif: Brooks/Cole, 1971, 62-66.

Horner, M. S. Femininity and successful achievement: A basic inconsistency. In *Feminine personality and conflict,* J. Bardwick, ed., Brooks/Cole, Belmont, Calif., 1970.

Horner, M. S. Toward an understanding of achievement-related conflicts in women. *Journal of Social Issues,* 28 (1972):157-75.

Millett, K. *Sexual politics.* New York: Doubleday, 1969.

Oliver, L. W. Counseling implications of recent research on women. *Personnel and Guidance Journal,* 53 (1975):430-37.

Pietrofesa, J. J. and Schlossberg, N. K. Counselor bias and the female occupational role. Detroit: Wayne State University, 1970. ERIC document CG006 056. (Cited in N. K. Schlossberg and J. J. Pietrofesa, Perspectives on counseling bias: Implications for counselor education. *Counseling Psychologist,* 4 (1973):44-54.

Rice, J. K. and Rice, D. G. Implications of the women's liberation movement for psychotherapy. *American Journal of Psychiatry,* 130 (1973):191-96.

Rosenthal, R. On the social psychology of the psychological experiment: The experimenter's hypothesis as an unintended determinant of experimental results. *American Scientist,* 51 (1963):268-83.

Schlossberg, N. K. and Goodman, J. Imperative for change: Counselor use of the Strong Vocational Interest Blanks. *Impact,* 2 (1972):26-29.

Schlossberg, N. K. and Pietrofesa, J. J. Perspectives on counseling bias: Implications for counselor education. *Counseling Psychologist,* 4 (1973):44-54.

Smith, S. Age and sex differences in children's opinions concerning sex differences. *Journal of Genetic Psychology,* 54 (1939):17-25.

Thomas, H. and Stewart, N. R. Counselor response to female clients with deviate and conforming career goals. *Journal of Counseling Psychology,* 18 (1971):352-57.

Tittle, C. K. Sex bias in educational measurement: Fact or fiction? *Measurement and Evaluation in Guidance,* 6 (1974):219-26.

Tuddenham, R. D. Studies in reputation: I, Sex and grade differences in school children's evaluation of their peers. *Psychological Monographs,* 66 (1952):1.

U.S. Department of Labor. Bureau of Labor Statistics. Washington, D.C. U.S. Government Printing Office, 1973.

Weisstein, N. Psychology constructs the female, or the fantasy life of the male psychologist. In *Roles Women Play: Readings Toward Women's Liberation,* M. H. Garskof, ed., Belmont, Calif., Brooks/Cole, 1971, 68-83.

Weitzman, L. J. and Rizzo, D. *Images of males and females in elementary school textbooks.* National Education Assn. and Resource Center on Sex roles in Education. Washington, D.C. 1974.

Wolfe, H. *Women in the world of work.* Unpublished doctoral dissertation, University of the State of New York, 1969.

24. COUNSELING THE SINGLE PARENT

Eleanor H. Ruma

Peter Schwarzburg

There are over 3.5 million families headed by a single parent in the United States today and over 85 percent of these parents are women (1, p. 498). The largest portion of these women are single parents through separation or divorce. This article will discuss single parenthood from the perspective of women although many of the issues will also be relevant to men.

Women traditionally have defined themselves primarily through their relationships with their husbands and children. The experience of separation and divorce creates important changes in these relationships, changes which invariably affect the ways she sees herself. She is faced with the fact that her life has not followed the expected pattern of personal fulfillment through marriage. Frequently, sources of satisfaction in being a parent become more complicated. The crisis of separation and divorce presents women with issues which they may not have encountered if they had remained married. The manner in which the woman copes with these issues determines whether the crisis has a progressive or regressive effect on her life.

The issue of work and its meaning and place in a woman's life assumes a different kind of importance after separation or divorce. Seventy percent of such women work, as compared with 41 percent married women (1, p. 501). A sizeable percentage of fathers fail to continue in child support after the first year of divorce (1, p. 501). Typically both the husband and the wife have a lower standard of living after divorce. The hard reality of economic necessity requires women to take work outside the home more seriously than while they were married. The woman, then, often must consider issues which previously were the concerns of men, such as the family's economic stability, and the future potential and meaningfulness of employment. Previously the woman re-

garded her work as a supplementary source of income or at least pooled it with her husband's income. After divorce this attitude is apt to be challenged. Financial problems are extensive for the majority of single parent women. She has to deal with the impact of economic changes on not only her own life but also on the lives of her children. The woman must face the issue of whether her standard of living is going to depend on the actions of someone else or if she is going to assume greater responsibility in this regard. To consider herself responsible for the economic well-being of herself and her children requires a fundamental revision of self-definition for most women. Viewing one's work more seriously also provides the context for evaluating its meaningfulness more carefully. A woman who is facing working for the rest of her life may begin to consider that what she is doing is satisfying in a way which is not possible when there are other options.

Divorce also raises issues regarding the experience of parenthood. Certainly the experience becomes more demanding in some ways. Most often the woman has increased responsibilities, frequently without supplementary sources of help. Our social structure is based on the two-parent family and has yet to deal adequately with the reality of extensive divorce and of the breakdown of the extended family. Day care services are available to only a small percentage of women. While homemaker services are provided for single fathers the same type of help is not available to employed mothers.

The single mother has to deal with her own feelings of loss as well as these feelings in her children. Frequently children increase demands and expression of aggression toward the person with whom they have most frequent contact, which usually is the mother. Available evidence suggests that father absence is associated with greater dependence on the mother, behavior and conduct disturbances and academic difficulties (2). While the studies on which these findings are based did not consider characteristics of the mother and the mother-child relationship, and are thus limited, nonetheless it seems likely that some disruption in the child's functioning will occur—temporarily if not permanently. Thus at a time when the woman's sense of self in relation to a man has been disturbed there is also the likelihood that her sense of self as a parent will also be disturbed. However, if she can meet and cope effectively with the problems that emerge in her children she has the opportunity for eventually establishing a greater sense of competence in her parent self-definition. Particularly in instances where she has previously relied on the man to make important decisions and has been forced to take on some of these responsibilities, she has the context for developing resources which otherwise may not have become manifest.

Counseling Implications

As in all counseling situations, a careful evaluation of the client's resources and limitations is important in order to establish a treatment plan. Areas both of general concern and of specific concern to the single-parent woman need to be explored. The questions asked point to what the counselor considers important and thus ultimately to the counselor's values concerning what is seen as sources of meaning in a woman's life. Listed and discussed below are areas that need to be explored.

1. *Reason for Seeking Counseling at This Time.* What prompted the client to seek help? What were the circumstances in her life leading to this decision? It is necessary to explore the areas of her life—work, relationships with adults, relationships with her children—to determine the context in which the presenting problem occurred. The most commonly encountered presenting problems are the emergence of symptoms in the child and personal feelings of unhappiness, depression, and worry about being able to cope alone. It is very important to keep in mind the concerns of the client. Her conerns may not be the only concerns but certainly they must be given careful consideration. One way in which this consideration is shown is in the questions asked, that is, in the emotional understanding and psychological knowledge they reflect. It is important that the counselor have some kind of previous experience on an emotional level with persons with children who have gone through divorce or separation. Also, the counselor needs to know about the mourning process and clinical manifestations of depression. The psychoanalytic perspective, as represented by Fenichel (3) for example, is especially enlightening in the areas of depression and mourning.

2. *Sources of Stress and Support in the Client's Life.* In order to work optimally on psychological issues with a client the client needs to have a stabilized life. To the degree that her life is not stabilized the counselor will have to help her to achieve such stabilization. Therefore, it is important to know from the beginning in what specific areas the client needs help and what resources are available. There is no point in planning to work on the client's feelings about her sexuality, no matter how concerned she is about it, if she must deal with such reality issues as, for example, not knowing if she will receive this month's child support payments, a dying mother, or loss of a babysitter. The counselor will need to explore her economic situation, including

major expenses, sources of income, and additional means of financial help. Are there any urgent problems, such as unexpected expenses or indecisions regarding priorities of payments (debts, medical needs, recreation, moving)? The counselor also needs to know about her relationship with her husband: what is the extent of contact and its nature; what is the degree of support as compared with stress the relationship provides? Additionally, it is necessary to explore the quality of her relationships with friends and relatives. Studies show that single parents who receive financial help from relatives, have sources of emotional support through relatives and friends make more successful adjustments than when these resources are not present (1, p. 502). Thus it is important to communicate interest in these areas of the client's life. If stability in these areas is not present you must expect to spend time exploring resolution of problems through personal and community resources.

3. *Past History.* What are some memories the client has of life in her family, at the preschool, elementary, junior high and highschool time periods in her life? The presence of clear positively toned memories suggests the capacity for positive interactions in the present. Research shows that one good predictor of parenting ability is the quality of relationship the parent had with her own parents (4). Loss of one or both parents (physically or psychologically) early in life is associated with disruptions in parenting skills. If such loss or limitation is part of the history of the client, she will need special support. The counselor will at times need to serve as a parent substitute in those areas in which the client has received inadequate parenting. Relationships with siblings can sometimes compensate for qualities lacking in the relationship with parents. Similarly, relationships with peers provide such an opportunity as well as for learning the give and take of more equal relationships. Investigation of the client's functioning in school provides insight regarding how she relates to authority and handles responsibility and frustration, and areas of interest which may offer actual or potential avenues of expression in her present work. Frequently parents' attitudes about school are reflected in the child's attitude. Thus, this area is particularly important to explore if the client's child is manifesting difficulties in school.

4. *Work Experience.* What are the client's attitudes about her work? What does she consider to be her important achievements and accomplishments? The woman who does not see her primary accomplishments in the homemaker role will find the transition to working outside the home easier than the woman who considers her natural role to be at home caring for her children. It is important to inquire in detail to discover some thread of meaning in working outside the home that will assist in making plans in this area. Such inquiry communicates the expectation that the counselor sees the area of work as a potential contributor to your client's sense of self. This is important, although in somewhat different ways, whether the counselor is a man or a woman. If a man, his attitude may offer an important contrast to other men in the client's life who have regarded a wife's (or a mother's) work as a peripheral interest. If the counselor is a female, the fact that she works and is asking the client about her work puts the counselor in an important position as a role model.

5. *Evaluation of the Child's Functioning.* Inquiry into the child's functioning indicates that the counselor is aware that the client is a parent and consequently needs to be concerned with her child as well as with herself. In some instances, persons going through separation and divorce have so many press-

ing issues regarding themselves to deal with that they do not discuss their children in counseling sessions. At other times there is so much anxiety concerning the children's reactions that a parent avoids approaching the subject in fear that she will feel overwhelmed. If the client does not spontaneously mention her child, then the counselor needs to initiate exploration in this area.

There are a number of behaviors which occur in children that suggest disturbance to a degree that if the behavior persists, the child's development may be hampered. In order to adequately understand the client's description of her child's functioning you need a background in child development and child psychopathology and certainly should at least be well acquainted with introductory texts on those topics before working with any adult with children. Behaviors associated with various stages of development can be intensified by separation and divorce and a single-parent family situation and their presence or absence in a child should be noted. Areas of the child's behavior which need to be explored include:

a. Disruption in relationship. How did the child respond to the parents' separation and to the father's absence? If there is a strong attachment between father and child a normal reaction to the disruption is some direct or indirect expression of loss. If the child shows no reaction, it suggests denial is operating, no doubt in response to a communication from the mother. The way the child handles the loss will give the counselor an idea of the way in which strong emotions are handled in the family, particularly by the mother. If the child becomes more active, showing behavior which is disruptive to a degree uncharacteristic of his age, it may be that the mother also uses activity to avoid dealing with feelings. If the child openly ex-

presses sadness and distress, it suggests that the mother also allows herself to do this.

b. Separation from the mother; increased demands on the mother. One of the problems associated with loss of one parent is fear of loss of the other parent. If a child shows no reaction to separation from the mother or an intensely negative reaction, the presence of such a fear is suggested. Single-parent situations typically lead to a stronger bond between mother and child than exists in a two-parent situation. Evaluation of the quality of this bond is important. The mother may look to the child to compensate for the loss of the spouse and teach the child to be a substituting mate. The child certainly will go through a period of time of increased demands on the remaining parent. Evaluation of how the mother handles such demands will give valuable information relevant not only to the mother's functioning as a parent but also to how she handles extensive demands from other people in her life.

c. Over and underexpression of aggression. One of the ways of dealing with loss is to become angry either at the parent who has left or at the parent who remains, thinking she caused the father to leave. Some conduct problems in children represent masked depression. The other disturbance in aggressive feelings is in inhibition of such feelings for fear of abandonment by the parent. This, too, is more likely to occur in a single-parent family situation, particularly if the mother also has difficulty in recognizing and expressing aggressive feelings. Overexpression of aggression is more common among male children and underexpression of aggressive feelings is more common in female children.

d. Inhibition in the area of achievement. Another modality for expressing feelings associated with loss is in the area of achievement. If the child has not settled the developmental issues of the preschool period he will not have the necessary energy available for adequate functioning in school. Anxiety about relationships within the family can diminish the child's ability to invest in activities in school, sports, hobbies, peer relationships, etc. Failure to invest in such areas keeps the child tied to the mother in developmentally inhibiting ways. Parents' attitudes towards their own work is influential in forming the child's attitude toward his work. Fathers and working mothers play a very important role in the formation of this attitude. Thus in a single-parent family situation a working mother provides an important model for both male and female children in the area of work.

After evaluation in the above areas of functioning, a treatment plan can be devised based on the concerns of the client as well as those considered central by the counselor. Including the child in the treatment plan has preventative implications, for in working with the parent, the counselor is indirectly influencing the child. In addition to general counseling goals, here are some specific to the situation of the single parent:

1. *Assisting in the Mourning Process.* If the loss due to separation has been denied (as indicated by complete lack of anger or by anger so intense as to disrupt her life), the parent must be helped to experience the loss and to work through the feelings associated with it so that she can go on to build a new life. Until this occurs the client will in some respects be tied to the past. The same is true of the person who persists in the mourning process by holding on to her feelings of loss and sorrow (often expressed as the helplessness and low self-esteem seen in depressed states) beyond a resonably expected period of time: she, too, is tied to her past and must be helped to let go in order to find new sources of satisfaction. Mourning usually

takes a considerable length of time and cannot be accomplished in short-term counseling unless the mourning is already partially completed or the client has already given up defenses against the loss. The parent must be helped to deal with the child's sense of loss and to differentiate her feelings from her child's.

2. *Meeting Some of the Needs Once Met by the Husband/Father.* One of the most important functions of the counselor is to provide the client a context for discussing everyday issues, including those involving her children. Frequently the single parent does not have anyone in her life with whom she can discuss child-rearing issues, financial concerns, and the joys and frustrations of her life. Although counseling goals should include establishment of such relationships outside the counseling relationship, until this occurs it should be considered a valuable aspect of the treatment. The counselor's responses to the client need to include a sensitivity to her being a woman and commenting on areas of competence and attractiveness much as a good mate would. Although one would hope for the client to become increasingly less dependent on the counselor for such support over time, certainly in the beginning and middle stages of the process such interventions serve an important function. In the case of a male counselor, it might be particularly important for him to have some form of continuing relationship with the client's children in order to provide ongoing, concerned contact with an adult male.

3. *Pointing Out Realities of the Single-Parent Situation.* Too often standards based on two-parent situations are applied to the lives of individuals who do not fit that mold. It is important to provide a context where the client can recognize that some of the issues with which the struggles are common

to persons in her life situation. Financial problems, problems in allocation of time, and problematic interactions with children are more common among single-parent family situations. It is important for the counselor to be familiar with the lives of single parents in order to prevent communicating inappropriate expectations based on either single, nonparent situations or two-parent married situations. Again the counselor serves as an important model in this regard, teaching the client realistic self-expectations.

4. *Participating in Arrangements to Provide Substitute Male-Adult Relationships for the Client's Children.* Research on father-absent male and female children suggests that growing up without a close relationship with a father has a notable negative effect on the child's functioning. In males the primary effect seems to be in the areas of achievement and sex-role identification. In females the effect seems to be in difficulty in establishing satisfactory relationships with males. Work with the single parent should include planning for relationships with adult males for her children—either with male relatives, babysitters, teachers, tutors, camp counselors, or other concerned men.

5. *Presenting Singlehood as a Viable Life Style.* The value of being married as a goal to be sought runs deep in our culture, particularly in women and even more so for those with children. Yet as a group, single women report higher degrees of life satisfaction than married women. Until we have information suggesting otherwise, it seems important to communicate to the single-parent client that she has options regarding remarriage and can consider remaining single with the expectation of a satisfying life. Frequently women prematurely get involved in new love relationships as much because they expect it and so do others as out of more personal considerations. To have someone in

their lives who presents singlehood as a life option to consider provides an important perspective which most likely otherwise would be lacking. The degree to which the counselor is aware on a personal level of the possibility of a rich and meaningful life without the presence of a primary love relationship and/or marriage will determine how successfully this option is communicated to the client.

As has been continually emphasized in this article, the ability that you, the counselor, have to understand and help your client will depend as much on your appreciation of her life's issues and communication of options open to her as on formal knowledge and techniques. Such appreciation ultimately comes from awareness of those parts of yourself that paralled her own life. To the degree that you can be aware of your own conflicts in love relationships, achievement, and caring for and appropriately guiding someone who is dependent on you, you will bring to the counseling situation a useful perspective in working with the single parent. If you have no personal experience with these issues perhaps at this time it would be more rewarding to choose to work with some other client population. A compensating resource may be your relative inexperience and young adult status, which is likely to make you more open to life's options and more aware of feelings of self-doubt and conflict—useful feelings in working with the single-parent client.

Case Illustration

Ms. W., age 27, mother of two children, a boy eight and a girl six, sought counseling a few months after separating from her husband. She expressed feelings of concern that she might "go off the deep end." These feelings seemed to relate to a sense that she might not be able to manage working and caring for her children adequately and would lose control of her life. She was greatly afraid of going back with her husband, who she said beat her in fits of rage and in general behaved in a restrictive, infantile manner. At the same time, she depended upon him for economic support and babysitting with the children. She was having trouble sleeping, was tempted to drink during times of being without male companionship on weekends, and generally felt without energy and on the verge of tears.

Inquiry into Ms. W.'s relationship with her husband revealed that she felt that she had stopped loving him several years ago but had been afraid to leave him. It was not until she had begun to work, initially so they could buy a home, that she started to consider the possibility of separation. She had become somewhat more assertive against his aggressive outbursts but still felt unable to prevent him from hitting her unless she was willing to sever all contact with him. Her son has begun to show aggressive outbursts in school and she had been contacted in this regard. Neither child had said much about their father's no longer living in the home. Ms. W. reported difficulty in openly verbalizing feelings of sadness and anger about the relationship in the presence of the children. Despite her moderate depression, she was able to work most of the time. On occasion she would call in sick when she was feeling that she could not handle things.

Ms. W. was the eldest of four, the three younger children were all males. Her father was an alcoholic and her mother worked and did the major portion of raising the children. Ms. W. assumed a maternal role in interaction with her younger brothers. She did not like school and as an adolescent had been truant a great deal. She married after getting pregnant before graduating from high school. She and her husband were drug addicts during the early years of their marriage. She managed to take adequate care of her children despite her addiction. Her mothering skills were one of her most important areas of strength.

She had more difficulties in the areas of work and relationships with adults. Her characteristic work pattern was to have periods of effective functioning and then periods of nonfunctioning due to feeling resentful over excessive demands. Her pattern in relationships with both men and women was to form alliances where she played the nurturant role. She picked persons who were more confused and needy than she and then felt resentful when they did not reciprocate her concern for their needs. She had been having an affair with a man who also was unhappily married. Despite her awareness that there was no long-term possibility in the relationship she continued to see him because she could not deal with her sexual and emotional needs in other ways. She had a degree of support from her relationship with her mother, who appeared to be a strong although harsh figure, and her mother was available for some financial as well as emotional assistance.

It is obvious from the material presented that Ms. W. had a number of serious limitations in her present situation and past history which would lead to a treatment plan of limited goals over a long-term counseling process. In view of her pattern in relationships where she played the maternal role but underneath had considerable unmet needs from childhood, it would be difficult for her to deal with a relationship where she was being given to and no longer had to be the strong one. Since her characteristic ways of dealing with stress was through withdrawal, one would expect that as the relationship began to become more meaningful to her and she was about to make some significant changes, she might respond to these stresses through withdrawing from the relationship.

Her work pattern of alternating periods of adequate and inadequate functioning plus the reality factors of lack of a high school degree, limited skills and a tight job market made the possibility of preparing herself for more meaningful and enjoyable work a difficult task. She had extensive financial, time allocation, and babysitting problems which would require a good deal of attention in the therapy sessions, and would limit the energy and flexibility for arriving at a more satisfying life situation. She had strong needs for a relationship with a man but not any long-term satisfying experiences. Her major strengths were in being able to care adequately for persons less mature than herself, the desire to make a better life for herself and some manifestations of being able to start doing this, and a degree of psychological awareness, as reflected in her concern about the self-destructive aspects of her behavior.

Therapy goals were to (1) work on the mourning process, enabling her and her children to become more aware and more expressive of their loss; (2) develop more awareness of and appropriate outlets for aggressive feelings so that she did not so readily get into burdensome situations and so that her daughter could learn that females can express aggression. Work in the areas of loss and anger would alleviate Ms. W.'s depression, and help her deal even more effectively with her children in expressing emotion and setting limits; (3) establish better balance in areas of her life by helping her to establish the ability to avoid overextending herself in work situations and to be concerned with her own needs as well as those of others, by helping her to find alternative ways to meet sexual and emotional needs so that she has more choice about the relationships she enters, and by helping her to find some time to do things she personally enjoys in the context of a very busy, demanding life.

Work with Ms. W. has been intermittent over the last year, due to disruptions because of reality factors (sick children, death of relatives, work schedules, etc.) as well as Ms. W.'s fear of a close, satisfying relationship. She still has some manifestations of depression but less so since she has become more aware of her feelings of loss and better able to express anger. She has achieved somewhat greater regularity on her job and has begun going to night school. She handles her son with greater firmness and has arranged for him to have regular meetings with a male assistant teacher. She has been able to be assertive so that her husband no longer beats her and comes to the home infrequently but at agreed upon times. Her daughter is now less passive and more able to express feelings openly. Both her son and daughter are doing well in school although her son still infrequently has aggressive outbursts. She still has not formed any satisfying relationships with women and men. She has, however, established a better relationship with her mother and is more able to deal with the mother's limits and accept her help. She is somewhat more open to seeing a life as single as having some value, at least for a period of time, although she continues to have difficulty staying out of transitory, unsatisfying relationships. She has not found the time for activities of personal enjoyment, like the dance class she would like to take, but perhaps will soon. She is considering moving closer to work in order to spend less time commuting and to have more time with her children and for herself. She arranged for the children to go to a summer camp program staffed by male counselors. Despite the limitations, she has made progress and will probably continue to do so in the future.

REFERENCES

1. Brandwein, Ruth A.; Brown, Carol A.; and Fox Elizabeth. Mothers and their families.

Journal of Marriage and the Family 36, no. 3, (1974):498-515.

2. Ruma, Eleanor H. The dynamics of the single parent child: a review of empirical research and clinical literature. Unpublished paper, 1975.

3. Fenichel, Otto. *The psychoanalytic theory of neurosis* New York: W. W. Norton & Company, (1945):387-414.

4. Frommer, Eva A., and O'Shea, Gillian. The importance of childhood experience in relation to problems of marriage and family building. *British Journal of Psychiatry* (1973):23, 157-60.

COUNSELING THE FATHERLESS CHILD

Deanna R. Nass
Stanley Nass

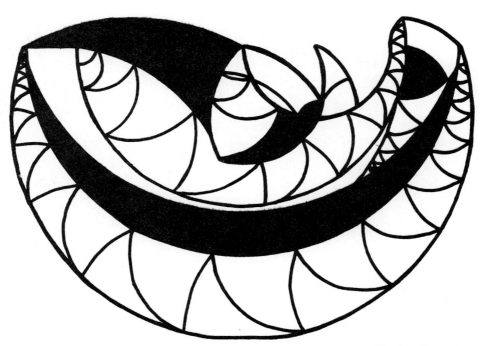

Vasilije Knezevic

According to recent statistics on one parent families, this social phenomenon is on the rise in the United States. For those individuals who hope to do family counseling, the youngster of a parent without a partner shall become the increasing focus of concern for many such professionals. In order to assist these children, the counselor must familiarize himself with the services that are presently offered to these families.

Counseling services to one parent families have often attempted to fill social, educational, and economic gaps resulting from the absence of a mate. The first pioneer movement to help the single parent and his family was made by Parents Without Partners, Inc., an organization with an educational focus. Programs of lectures, debates, forums, and recreational activities are offered to parents and their children. While the principal concern of such programs is to address the distinctive problems of incomplete households, the incidental effect of drawing people together in a common cause is to furnish them with social opportunities.

Day care centers for the children of working mothers provide one parent families with economic, as well as educational advantages. While children are coached in whatever preschool skills a lay staff can offer, mothers are relieved of child rearing responsibilities long enough to earn a living. Although full-time employment necessitates daily separation between a mother and her child, the negative effect of these separations on a youngster can be overcome by satisfying, albeit limited, maternal contact.

The aim of several community programs is to reinforce sex role identification in half orphaned children by providing them with surrogates of the missing parent. While teachers, T.V. and movie heroes, even military superiors, may supply children of one parent families with a much needed substitute, the contact with such grownups is usually not sustained or direct enough to fill the gaps in the youngster's experience. One program that does attempt to place fatherless boys in an enduring, on-going relationship with an adult male is the Big Brother Plan. Under this program, young boys are accompanied by men on weekend camping trips. Gradually, over the course of several such trips, the boy typically develops an emotional bond with a favorite scout master.

Unless a greater number and variety of community projects are designed for the one parent household, family life for the people of this background will eventually break down. In a prosperous country such as ours, there is no excuse for ignoring the problems and special needs of this growing segment of our population. Since we are a nation undergoing change in its cultural norms, the one parent family may soon gain acceptance as it gains prominence on the American scene. Certainly the counselor hoping to work effectively with this unit must develop a more sensitive appreciation of this phenomenon than that demonstrated by him in the past.

To offer assistance and understand the unique circumstances surrounding the child of the widowed, divorced, or separated parent, the counselor must review the extensive literature devoted to this area of human relationships.

Generally speaking, one finds that the bulk of material gathered on this subject is concentrated on fatherless, rather than on motherless, homes. For this reason, it is important to understand the unique role played by the father in the family structure and the period in the life of the offspring when the paternal influence is most needed. In addition to focusing on the matriarchal quality of most one parent families, the literature also stresses the behavioral differences manifested by children of one and two parent households. The traits most often discussed in the literature are as follows:

1. masculine-feminine identification;
2. dependency of the young child on adults and/or peers;
3. aggressiveness (including deliquent behavior) versus passivity;
4. tendency of the young child to select immediate or delayed gratification;
5. educational aspirations.

The variables which contribute to the differences in the children of split and intact families are the following:

1. the age at which a child is deprived of a parent;
2. the sex of the single parent who rears him;
3. the family attitudes and social values of the parent in charge of the household;
4. the economic consequences of the split household;
5. the circumstances which deprive a child of either parent (i.e., death,

divorce,   separation,   illegitimacy, military leave, etc.);

6. the race and cultural norms of any particular one parent household;

7. the sibling composition of a one parent family.

Prior to engaging in an analysis of a one parent household, the researcher should know the extent of the phenomenon as indicated by current statistical evidence.

Statistics

Over six million American children under the age of eighteen live in one parent homes,[1] many of them the victims of divorce. Nine times out of ten the mother has custody of the children when the courts intervene.[2] Of all the divorce rates in the world, the American rate ranks among the highest.[3] While divorced women outnumber men by about two to one, the statistical differences between the two sexes are largely attributable to higher death and remarriage rates among male partners of unsuccessful marriages.[4] Half the divorced persons are between their midthirties and their midforties, many of them the partners of unsuccessful marriages dating from the teenage years.[5]

While the one parent household is largely the result of divorce, many such family compositions derive from the untimely death of one partner, usually the husband. Although the majority of widows are past the age of seventy-five and no longer need care for dependent children, a goodly number are below the age of forty-five with the responsibility of providing for a young offspring.[6] Of this population of families headed by women, forty percent are classified as belonging to the poverty bracket.[7] When death or abandonment separates the male from his family, the mother, often too unskilled to become the breadwinner, is forced to rely on welfare funds for the support of her household. The highest rate of mother dominated families reliant on welfare is among the black population.

What the Findings of Various Studies Suggest

Having examined the statistical data which quantifies the problem of one parent families, a researcher is drawn to the theories of cause and effect posited by numerous studies on the subject. Certainly many studies are chiefly preoccupied with the sexual identification and development of offspring from fatherless homes.

Sexual Development

Sex typed behaviors, as defined in the literature, are actions linked to male-female self-image, dependency, and aggressiveness. The development in the young child of various sex-related behavior is largely attributable to the father's role in the family structure.

According to Anna Freud, the infant's emotional relationship to his father begins later in life than that to his mother. His emotional need for a father begins from about the second year onward, his feelings for this parent being bound up with admiration for the father's superior strength and power. Although the young child has a more immediate relationship with his mother than with his father, he recognizes that the man in authority provides the material advantages upon which the entire family relies. It is the "bigness" and forcefulness of the father that inspire the fantasies of power and the imitative behavior of the young child.[8]

Studies assessing differences in the sex-related behavior of offspring from fatherless and two parent homes are generally inconclusive or contradictory. While some researchers discover great contrasts in behavior between the two groups of children, others find no differences solely related to the variable of father absence. It seems that masculine identification in young boys operates in situations with complex and numerous inconstants.

Certainly the age of a young boy at the time of father loss is an important factor in the development of his sexual identity.[9] Although exaggerated manifestations of masculine traits (a phenomenon known as overcompensation) may occur in boys who lose a father after age five, this situation is less serious than the confused sexual identity that frequently prevails in boys deprived of paternal contact before age five.[10] However, even for the boy deprived of paternal influence from infancy onward, a masculine indentity may develop in him by means of peer influence and surrogate father figures.

A second chief factor in the development of sexual identification is the attitudes manifested by the remaining parent, usually the mother. While maternal attitudes play an important role in every child's life, even for children in two parent households, they are doubly influential in the life of a child lacking a father. The image of the lost father that is presented by the mother can greatly affect the young boy's strivings for manhood. If the image of the lost father is a negative one, the son may favor a feminine identity over a masculine one in order to win his mother's approval.

In addition to the attitudes projected about her lost mate, the mother also reacts to the results of his absence. The mother without a husband usually finds herself in poor economic circumstances, living in a depressed neighborhood, and lacking social, emotional, and physical assistance in child rearing. How husbandless mothers accommodate themselves to these circumstances can have important consequences for their children.

"A consequence of particular social concern is the educational handicap which children from fatherless families seem to suffer. There is evidence that such children have lower IQs, are retarded in school, and complete fewer years of study than do children of complete families."[11] In view of numerous findings to the contrary, however, there is certainly no clear cut indication that father absence, of itself, necessitates poor academic achievement. What does seem to contribute to school performance in young people are maternal attitudes about education. While husbandless mothers appear quite concerned about the marks of their school age youngsters, often exerting pressure in situations that do not demand it, they seem somewhat less interested in study beyond high school than about grades.[12] The level of educational aspiration seems especially modest in families characterized by meagre economic circumstances.

In short, while husbandless mothers are often concerned about the well-being of their children, the harshness of their circumstances often prevents them from acting in the youngster's best interest. Rather than providing the kind of emotional support and encouragement condusive to high educational achievement in their children, these mothers frequently manifest an anxiety that discourages academic success.

Sibling Composition and Father Absence

A question raised by many researchers is whether father absence is equally deleterious for children from different sibling statuses and family sizes. In a study of this theme,[13] four variations were explored:

1. the psychological traits of a girl living with two parents and a younger brother;
2. the psychological traits of a girl living with a husbandless mother and a younger brother;
3. the psychological traits of an only female child living with a husbandless mother;
4. the psychological traits of an only male child living with a husbandless mother.

Oddly enough, experimental findings indicate that the girl living with a younger brother engages in a healthy rivalry when the father is present in the home, but that she is negatively affected by the younger brother when the father is absent. Of an even more surprising nature are the findings concerning only children. Several studies of only children in fatherless homes indicate that the male without siblings suffers fewer adverse effects from father absence than does the fatherless female without siblings. For both, however, there is a tendency of only children in fatherless homes to be feminine in their sex role orientation, while the converse is true for only female children deprived of paternal contact. Speaking generally then about family size and membership, the negative effect of father absence may be modified by sibling composition.

Racial and Cultural Norms

The one parent household of many black Americans is a topic of great concern to laymen and professionals alike. Although the problems of such a family have much in common with its white counterpart, it is unique in its relationship with black cultural norms. To sense the distinctive quality of the black household, one must carefully examine the various elements of this institution.

Kardiner's studies of lower class black homes reveal that father absence in families with preschool children is a common social pattern.[14] The matriachal structure of the typical black family, regardless of whether the father is absent or is only minimally present, inhibits the development of a strong masculine identity in the son.[15] Despite the fact that black boys deprived of their fathers during the preschool years frequently act masculine in their overt behavior, especially as manifested by their involvement with aggressive, competitive sports, their underlying sex role orientation often seems somewhat confused or decidedly feminine.[16]

In cases of extreme overcompensation by male youths anxious to prove their masculinity, delinquent acts may promote an image of toughness while concealing traits of effeminacy.[17] In studies of black gang members from lower class, fatherless homes, results indicate that many such boys obtain high scores on indirect measures of feminity, feel victimized and unable to control their environment, choose small immediate gains over large, but delayed, gratifications, and perpetuate in their adult lives patterns of divorce and abandonment experienced by them in early childhood.[18]

Conclusion

Despite the extensive research in one parent families, particularly fatherless homes, findings are generally fragmentary and inconclusive. There is not even general agreement among the studies that father absence, in itself, creates adverse consequences for the child of such environments. Many of the negative behavioral traits found in children of one parent homes are often due to the tensions indirectly resulting from an individual's absence, rather than being the direct outcome of the absence itself.[19]

For example, juvenile delinquency is more often the result of family bickering that precedes divorce than of the loss of a parent which follows a breakup. In fact, statistics on rates of juvenile delinquency in one and two parent homes seem sbout equal.

The false assumptions of good and bad attributed to two and one parent homes respectively may be disproven by comparison studies of conflict-ridden, two parent households and harmonious, one parent families. This area of research has not yet been thoroughly investigated. Even fewer studies inquire about how the image of an absent father is presented to his children; almost no studies relate father absence to availability of other relatives or to the economic consequences of his absence.

Another area of weakness in the current research on fatherless homes concerns conclusions drawn from male-female ratings. When a boy scores low on these sexual identity tests he is considered feminine; when he scores high, he is regarded as overcompensating. Perhaps the items on these tests and interpretations drawn from them are not entirely valid. Given the ambiguity of male-female test items and the sexual revolution presently occurring in America wherein traditional sexual roles are being rapidly abandoned, children should not be restricted in their actions to stereotypes associated with the two sexes. A more important consideration than male-female roles may be the child's conception of what it means to be a human being and what to expect from and offer other human beings.

Because the findings on fatherless homes are so often conflicting and inconsistent, especially where sex related behavior is the focus of study, programs based on such evidence are often meaningless. Too often the fatherless home is regarded by counselors as a mutilated form of normal family life rather than as a separate structure with its own set of strengths and weakness. Until refined analysis is made of the various versions of this institution, appropriate community supports to it will not be forthcoming.

NOTES

1. Herzog, E.; and Sudia, C. E. Fatherless homes. *Children*, XV, 5, (September-October 1968):177.
2. Gould, E. P. Special report: The single parent family benefits in Parents Without Partners, Inc. *Journal of Marriage and the Family*, XXX, 4, (November 1968):669.
3. *Ibid.*
4. *Ibid.*
5. *Ibid.*
6. *Ibid.*
7. *Ibid.*
8. Freud, Anna; and Burlingham, Dorothy. *Infants without families.* New York, N.Y.: International University Press, 1944, 101-06.
9. Brofenbrenner, U. The psychological costs of quality and equality in education. *Child Development*, XXXVIII, (December 1967):915.
10. Hetherington, E. M. Effects of paternal absence on sex-typed behaviors in Negro and white preadolescent males. *Journal of Personality and Social Psychology*, IV, 1, 87.
11. Kreisberg, Louis. Rearing children for educational achievement in fatherless families. *Journal of Marriage and the Family*, XXIX, 2, (May 1967):288.
12. *Ibid.*, 291, 300.
13. Sutton-Smith, B.; Rosenberg, B. G.; and Landy, F. Father absence effects in families of different sibling composition. *Child Development*, vol. 39, (1968):1217-21.
14. Kardiner, A.; and Ovessey, L. *The mark of oppression.* Cleveland, Ohio: The World Publishing Company, August 1962.
15. Biller, H. B. A note on father absence and masculine development in lower-class Negro and white boys. *Child Development*, XXXIX, 3, 1003.
16. Hetherington, E. Effects of paternal absence on sex-typed behaviors in Negro and white preadolscent males. *Journal of Personality and Social Psychology*, IV, 1, 88.
17. Bronfenbrenner, U. The psychological costs of quality and equality in education. *Child Development*, XXXVIII, (December 1967):915.
18. *Ibid.*
19. Herzog, E.; and Sudia, C. E. Fatherless homes. *Children*, XV, 5, (September 1968):179.

PART FIVE

COUNTERPOINT

WHO ARE THE MINORITIES?

Dear Editor:

". . .In addition to the 'minorities' cited in this section, I am sure that there are virtually hundreds of other groups that consider themselves minorities, but are not treated that way in the literature. What does a group have to do to become a special minority, and deserve special attention including generous federal funds and lots of academic research? They have to speak out, to riot, to complain and ballyhoo—that's what! I think it's grossly unfair to the vast majority of people in our country, that these special minorities get all the attention they do, and I would like to see an article on counseling the member of the *majority* group. I'm proud to be a member of that group, but I'm always neglected in books like yours."

R.S.

Note. You might glance at parts one, two, three, four, and six of this book if you feel neglected as a "majority-group" member. Also, since you are studying counseling, you might want to work out in therapy some of these feelings.

UNDERSTANDING THE CLIENT

Dear Editor:

"It seems to me, from what I've read and observed, that the crux of all counseling is understanding the client. If the client is a member of one of these special groups mentioned, and if the counselor is not a member, then there certainly does exist a barrier between them. But fortunately, it is not an immovable barrier; but one that can be chipped away, bias by bias, if the counselor is open to learning about the client's world. I, personally, found these articles extremely helpful in my efforts to gain insight about those people around me, and with whom I work, who are a little different than myself, or whose backgrounds differ from mine."

W. E., III

• • •

Dear Editor:

"I think that perceiving a client as part of a special group, in the long run, is an injustice to the client and an ineffective way to approach the counseling task. Let's face it, people are fundamentally different: each person is a unique creature who, although he shares many common characteristics with his fellow man, is strikingly singular. If Jose Rodriquez or Mary Smith, or Bob Thompson come to me for counseling, I don't want to think of them as Puerto Rican, female, and black—but rather as three individual people that have to be understood for what they are. True, the counselor has to be sensitive to special group differences, but must at all costs avoid the temptation to categorize which, no matter how noble the intentions, is the foundation of stereotyping."

C. P.

A SPECIAL CASE

Dear Editor:

"I was recently working with a client who was a black, hispanic, culturally different woman who came from a fatherless home and now was a single parent with two children. I found these articles very helpful in understanding some of the problems she faces, and in better appreciating some of the things she's been telling me. But I think that knowing her as a person is more important than the social factors discussed in the articles."

J. M.

Note. A number of these reactions make the point, which I fully agree with, that the individuality of the client has precedence of the nonvoluntary affiliation of the client with a "special" group. However, just as a basic understanding of personality development, psychodynamics, and social psychology can help the counselor better organize and articulate his or her perceptions of the client—*without diluting the personal dimension of the relationship*—understandings about the specialized problems and specialized needs of these groups should not be used in lieu of personal involvement with the client.

APPLYING A MODEL OF HELPING

Dear Editor:

"I am thinking back to the articles on models of helping which were in part three. I wonder if there are any specific models which can be more helpful to these minorities or special groups. My impression is that the Adlerian model, which emphasizes the social dimension of the client, can be used very effectively with minorities and "special" groups. Also, in the TA model, the client's feelings about his minority group status may be analyzed in terms of transactional analysis—especially between a minority group person and a nonminority group person."

A. Z.

• • •

Dear Editor:

"In the school where I teach, over half the children are black and from families where no father is present at home. Since I work both with the children and with their mothers, I am involved with the fatherless child and the single parent. Looking at all these articles together, I see so many things that are true in my school. I think it is important for teachers, as well as counselors, to be sensitive to the problems that arise from such social situations. I would like to point out three things I've found to be true, which may be helpful to others:

1. Children who come from homes where there is no father, if encouraged to speak about their feelings, usually relate some very strong feelings about not having a man in the house. While these feelings are different from child to child, I've always found that it helps the child to be able to express the feelings openly in an empathic, uninhibited environment.

2. The mothers of my children often attribute their child's school problems to the father-absence. I've found that while there may be a grain of truth to this, it is often an excuse for the problem rather than a cause. I try to help the mothers understand what they can do to enrich their child's education, rather than relying on an excuse.

3. I found the points made in Dr. Vontress's article extremely helpful and very valid for me, even though I myself am black. I think that often black counselors, more than white ones, forget the difficulties that their black clients may be experiencing because of their race, and feel that "If I made it as a black, then there's no reason why these kids can't."

G. J.

PART SIX

COUNSELING SERVICES

This concluding part of the book will be used to briefly look at some of the specific services counselors perform. Each of these services usually demands more intense study, and the reading list at the end of this introduction will help the counselor pursue any topics he or she wishes to explore in more depth.

Carkhuff, Alexik, and Anderson's "Do we have a theory of vocational choice?" elucidates some of the major theories of career choices, and then challenges these theories with some penetrating insights. A more specific problem, of using appraisal tools in vocational counseling is dealt with in Norman Fredman's "The use of inventories in vocational counseling." These two papers serve as a brief, but stimulating, introduction to the always evolving field of career counseling.

Drug counseling and group counseling with disruptive adolescents are treated in the next two papers, by Donald J. Wolk and Lester J. Schwartz, respectively. These two topics, of special interest to the secondary school teacher, also have application on the elementary school level, with certain modifications.

Gerald H. Zuk's "Family therapy," deals comprehensively with one of the fastest growing areas of counseling. Zuk's treatment, while primarily practical, also offers a strong theoretical base. Finally William J. Kirman's "Counseling in the classroom," translates the principles of modern psychoanalytic counseling (see chapter 10) to the classroom setting.

SUGGESTED ADDITIONAL READINGS
Belkin, G. S. ed. *Foundations of counseling* (chapters 6, 7, 8). Dubuque, Iowa: Kendall/Hunt, 1974.

———. *Practical counseling in the schools* (chapters 17-22). Dubuque, Iowa: Wm C. Brown Company Publishers, 1975.

Erickson, G. D. and Hogan, T. P. *Family therapy: an introduction to theory and technique.* Monterey, Ca.: Brooks/Cole, 1972.

Gazda, G. M. *Group counseling: a developmental approach.* Boston: Allyn and Bacon, 1972.

Perrone, P. A., Ryan, T. A. and Zeran, F. R. *Guidance and the emerging adolescent.* Scranton, Pa.: International Textbook, 1970.

Tolbert, E. L. *Counseling for career development.* Boston: Houghton Mifflin, 1974.

25. DO WE HAVE A THEORY OF VOCATIONAL CHOICE?

Robert R. Carkhuff
Mae Alexik
Susan Anderson

Peter Schwarzburg

The curious blend of approaches attempting to elaborate and elevate the vocational choice processes above an "accident theory" of occupational choice and development reflect in large part the different beginning points and levels at which the aspiring theorists operate. The very real question confronting the counseling and guidance professions today is: Do we have a "theory" of vocational choice? This paper might best be viewed as a tentative formulation of a possible way of viewing and organizing contemporary vocational "theories" in light of this question.

A Schema of Theory

The many views of what is involved in theorizing (Bergman, 1953; Boring, 1953; Feigl, 1945; Harré, 1960; Koch, 1951; Spence, 1944) converge upon a fundamental purpose of science: explanation. An understanding of the phenomena that the science seeks to describe is accomplished by bringing under the fewest possible assumptions, concepts, and principles the greatest number of facts and observations. It has been suggested (Hemple / Oppenheim, 1953) that there exists a continuum that incorporates, at its one end, the level of description that involves fairly simple accounts of immediately observable facts and moves through empirical laws to first-order theories and finally to higher order constructs of even greater generality.

Much controversy has surrounded the issues involving the inductive and deductive functions of theory (Hull, 1943; Skinner, 1950), and some of the logical problems involved in equating the two processes (Harre, 1960) have been established. However, at the risk of appearing naive to the sophisticated and perhaps sophisticated to the naive, we will assume the view of theory

serving both an inductive and deductive function (Underwood, 1957) and present a simplified schema to this effect. To better understand this view of theory, we might begin inductively at the point of the raw data. (See figure 1.)

The stability and reliability of the phenomena and the relationships which obtain between and among independent variables and these phenomena would appear to be logical determinants of theoretical readiness (Level A). Of course, cross-validation of results and all that this implies is an important consideration at this empirical level. From these raw data, certain propositions of a singular nature (facts) or general nature (laws) may be established (Level B). In turn, these functional relationships between observed events interact with each other, resulting in first-order theories which relate and "interpret" the relationships (Level C). First-order theories may also interact in the production of higher-order generalizations. Viewed from another stance, these theories and higher-order constructs may also serve to produce certain expectations about as yet unobserved data, i.e., serving the deductive function of theory.

The interrelationship of laws and facts accomplished in theory permits the deduction of theorems or abstract generalizations from which hypotheses or inferential statements of a tentative nature may be derived and empirically tested (Level D). That statement of relationships in the "if. . . then" form are confirmed, or not, by the significance of the raw data (Level E). The results (again cross-validation is important), in turn, serve neither to prove nor disprove theory but rather either to support it or not.

An investigation may, then, begin at several points, but in all probability it will begin with either, the stable body of empirical data (point A), from which it may

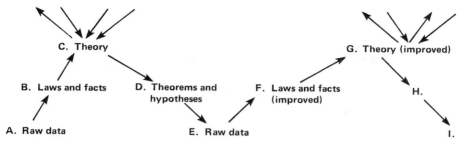

Figure 1. A schematic representation of the inductive and deductive functions of theory.

operate inductivity, or with an already existing theory (point *C*), from which systematic deductions might be made. The usual flow would be inductively from *A* to *C* or from *C* to *E*. Having arrived at the predetermined objectives, one might find the theory inadequate to the task of explaining some of that data. An obligation to reflect back and qualify, re-organize, or dismiss the theory (the movement from *E* to *G* in an attempt to improve the system) now becomes apparent. The interactional process of theory-building continues in perpetuity (*H, I, J, K, L,* etc.). In this regard, Hebb (1959) has stated succinctly the mandate incumbent upon the investigator:

theory is not an affirmation but a method of analysis and can't produce any belief. Knowledge progresses by stages, so the theory one holds today must be provisional, as much a formulation of one's ignorance as anything else, to be used as long as it is useful and then discarded. Its function is to organize for better evidence. It is really only a working assumption which the user may actively disbelieve.

This schema of theory will be employed and elaborated upon in the works of Roe, the Michigan Group, Tiedeman and O'Hara, Super, and Holland in an attempt to obtain some perspective on these theories, especially in terms of how these various vocational choice approaches relate to the inductive-deductive process of theory-building.

Roe

Anne Roe and her associates (1956, 1964, 1966) begin by viewing occupational choices as a process of "self-categorization." Roe looks upon the individual, as does Maslow, as an "integrated, organized whole," whose classification should be based upon his goals or needs, whether conscious or unconscious. Thus, Roe sees an occupation as a primary source of need satisfaction. In an apparent attempt to come to some immediate closure, she seeks to arrange these goals or needs in a hierarchy of protency and makes what appears to be a somewhat arbitrary choice of Maslow's somewhat arbitrary hierarchical system. Roe, then, relates her "empirical approach" wherein she proceeds to select representatives from various vocational fields and to differentiate their personality characteristics and needs. In this regard, her choice of perhaps the least empirical of measuring instruments, the Rorschach Ink Blot Test, is an interesting one, again revealing Roe's analytic bias.

Roe's most meaningful contribution remains her very useful level-and-group classification of occupations. Her later attempts to relate vocational choice to family background (home atmosphere and parental attitudes) have, sadly, met with little empirical support. Thus, in her schema, she finds that those arriving at Level One in her classification schema are strongly driven, absorbed in their work, superior in intelligence, and from favorable social climates. She suggests that those freed for creative work through lower-need gratification can produce more effectively and with infinitely greater end-satisfaction than those whose creativity is in spite of, or perhaps partly marshalled by, a hunt for substitute gratifications. Roe's group findings include descriptions of the physical scientist as withdrawn, compulsive, rigid and anxious; biologists, as restricted and nonsocial; psychologists, as disinterested in intellectual controls and interested in people; and artists as tending to think abstractly. Further, Roe's studies of the differences between "experimentalists" and "theorists" demonstrate that theorists come from more professional backgrounds, liked school, and developed more adequate social contacts than the experimentalists.

Unfortunately, instead of attempting to generalize her findings into a unique and comprehensive system, Roe apparently seeks to "rationalize" her results by drawing from analytic theory and Maslow's postulates to support her findings. She has neither systematically deduced her hypotheses from these systems nor does she work inductively to these systems. While Roe feints in the direc-

tion of higher-order inductive generalizations (E to F, figure 2), she falls back upon analytic theory and the need hierarchy (F to C) which she apparently had in mind all the while and from which, to be consistent, she should have operated deductively in the first place. It appears entirely possible that she would have made the connections with these systems no matter what her empirical findings were. Roe neither makes systematic derivations from the theories that she proposes nor is the theory with which she deals a generalization of her findings, serving to organize the available evidence and guide the search for better evidence. Rather, she appears to seek entrance to already existing systems. She does not make sufficient attempt to qualify the existing theories in terms of her findings and, thus, provides no unique theory of her own to encompass her results. In summary, then, according to the schema, Roe makes no justifiable generalizations from her data above the level of what has been defined as laws.

The Michigan Group

The Michigan Group (Nachmann, 1960; Segal, 1961; Galinsky, 1962; Bordin, Nachmann, / Segal, 1963; Beall / Bordin, 1964;

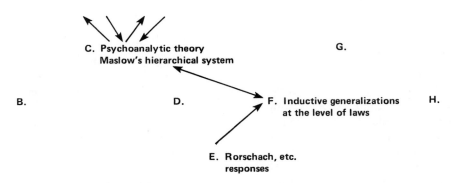

Figure 2. A suggested schematic representation of Roe's approach.

Segal / Szabo, 1964; Galinsky / Fast, 1966; Beall, 1967) has proposed a series of dimensions traceable to infantile physiological functions, which will account for all of the gratifications that work can offer. Any occupation can be described in terms of the relative strengths of these component dimensions and their relation to a series of modifying characteristics. The theoretical formulations had their original stimuli in studies applying psychoanalytic assumptions regarding personality development to the explanation of occupational activity patterns of accountants and creative writers; lawyers, dentists, and social workers; clinical psychologists and physicists; and engineers. In all of these studies occupational analyses were made to identify what needs might be gratified, through what modes of expression. While they make passing mention to the effect that this expression occurs within the framework of the environmental pressures and opportunities with which the individual is confronted, Roe (1963), herself, is critical of the inability of the Michigan school to incorporate "persons . . . whose occupational motivation is constrained mainly by external forces—economic, cultural, geographical, and other— and persons who have little capacity to get gratification from their work." Because of time and space limitations, we might attend primarily to the first of the studies (Segal, 1961), which initiated a program of research and theory under Bordin's direction.

Segal suggests that analytic concepts such as identification, the development of defense mechanisms, and sublimation in conjunction with the process of role implementation can be used to understand the personality characteristics of individuals who make a specific vocational choice. First, he ascertains the behavioral demands made of practitioners in various fields by an evaluation of occupational information sources. He then selects the vocational fields of creative writing and accounting because they represent widely divergent occupational activities and social stereotypes. He proceeds to determine analytically the personality characteristics expected and employs primarily the Rorschach in testing his hypotheses.

While Segal presents himself as having proceeded directly from theory, systematically deducing his hypotheses, there are many questions as to whether this is a test of psychoanalytic theory as it has been related by Segal to the vocational process. Segal seems to have engaged in a two-step process here: (1) moving from the occupational stereotypes to psychoanalytic theory in an *ad hoc* fashion in order to "explain" how the stereotypes may have come about and to determine analytically the implications of the stereotype (D to C, figure 3); (2) predicting Rorschach and other responses from the occupational stereotypes (D to E). In general, the main effect of the two steps is to preclude any possibility of testing the theory as related by Segal. The predictions seem to be made according to the stereotypes, not according to the theory, and while an *ad hoc* attempt is made to relate psychoanalytic theory with the stereotypes, there is no direct line deduction. Thus, it appears that Segal is testing essentially one of two things: (1) how accurate the stereotyped descriptions and their implications are, or (2) how sensitive to these characteristics his instrument is.

In addition, on some of the Rorschach indices that would be critical to his study Segal does not get expected differences. If, as is claimed by Segal, the hypotheses were directly derived from theory, then, unless he is severely critical of the sensitivity of the instrument employed, Segal is obliged to reflect back upon the original theory as he in-

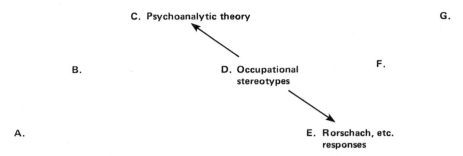

Figure 3. A suggested schematic representation of Segal's approach.

terprets it to qualify or reorganize it, since in some way it has been deficient. (Thus, he should have moved from *E* to *G* in the schematic representation.) The question must be raised as to whether or not Segal is taking for granted the essential truth of his theory in not looking at the implications of all of his findings.

While Segal's work suggests the possibility that aspects of analytic theory might someday be deductively related to the vocational process, it appears that he has completed only the first step in the process of finding the best system to organize the available evidence and guide the quest for better evidence. His efforts seem quasi-empirical. He appears only to have supported Roe's essential finding that on some of the Rorschach indices that instrument supports the concept of occupational stereotypes.

Tiedeman and O'Hara

Tiedeman and O'Hara (1961, 1962, 1963) view career development as part of a continuing process of differentiating ego-identity: just how a person's identity evolves is dependent upon his early childhood experiences with the family unit, the psychosocial crises encountered at various developmental stages, the congruence between society's meaning system and the individual's meaning system (including his needs, aptitudes, and interests), and the emotional concomitants of each of these factors. They have borrowed heavily from the thinking of Freud, Erikson, from Super, Ginzberg, and Roe, and from the social psychologists in developing highly complex, mathematical, and sometimes esoteric formulations of career development: ". . . a concatenation of concepts that seem to be needed as primitive terms in a science of career development relating personality and career through the mechanisms of differentiation and integration as a chooser chooses and experiences the evolution of his life problem."

Their all-inclusive attempt, then, views career development as a sequence of developmental life stages or events. Related to the *aspect* of *anticipation* or *preoccupation* (of career goals) are the *sub-aspects* (or steps) of *exploration, crystallization, choice,* and *clarification.* During the *aspect* of implementation or *adjustment,* the steps of *social induction, reformation,* and *integration* occur. Accompanying each of these developmental stages are certain personality or psychosocial crises, such as the "autonomy versus shame" crisis characteristic of the "anal" period, or the "identity versus role diffusion" crises of early adolescence. In addition, Tiedeman and O'Hara have concentrated on the developmental crises of later life occurring in school and the world of work, since they feel there is less of a biological and more of an "integrated, or in-balanced, conjunction of the emotional and the rational elements of the personality." Much of their research has characteristically centered on the vocational decision-making processes of children, adolescents, and young adults in school counseling situations, making extensive use of tape-recorded transcripts of counseling or standardized interview sessions, which they analyze and describe in terms of their preconceived paradigm of career development. Each case is presented in terms of the differentiation and integration model, with reference to both career choice and personality development. The vocational choice processes of each are described, with particular emphasis upon the psychosocial crises relevant to the situation. As an example, in citing the case of Bob, a bright third-grader who identifies with his uncle rather than his father in his present vocational choice, Tiedeman and O'Hara state that this "transference to another adult in the environment with the same role" may lead to an easy resolution of a potential oedipal crisis. It is apparent that Tiedeman and O'Hara, while contributing

little of their own, have attempted an integration of a number of theories and approaches into a coherent and comprehensive theory of career development.

What Tiedeman and O'Hara *do* have, then, is a massive collection of laws, facts, and theorems, some of which have been derived from systematic research into the career development process and others that have been borrowed from existing theories. They begin with the theoretical systems of the psychoanalytic and the trait-and-factor analysts. From here they proceed deductively toward the establishment of a developmental paradigm at the level of theorem (C to D, figure 4). They have collected a great deal of research evidence, which has also led them to postulate similar developmental paradigms (E to F), that they relate to the deduced theorems (F to D and D to F). However, both their own research and their assumptions based upon other theories have led them to develop similar, theorems, apparently independently of each other, the only logical linkage being that they continuously relate their findings back to the preconceived theories with which they began

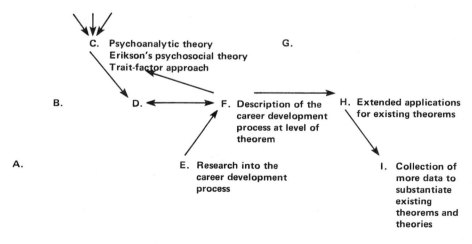

Figure 4. A suggested schematic representation of the approach of Tiedeman and O'Hara.

(*F* to *C*, figure 4). Their theoretical modifications consist only of extending the specific instances to which their theorems apply (*F* to *H*) and never of any real changes in their previous formulations (*E* to *F* to *G*). As a result, their theory cannot emerge beyond the status of a collection of lower-level generalizations. Instead of streamlining and simplifying their theorems, they seem to be moving in the opposite direction—toward encompassing as diverse data as possible, hoping that in the future, out of the midst of chaos, order will emerge.

Super

Super and his associates (Super, 1957, 1963; Super / Bachrach, 1957; Super et al., 1957; Super, Overstreet, et al., 1960; Super et al., 1963) are perhaps most candid in accepting as valid the criticism that much of the work in the occupational area lacks an adequate theoretical framework. In particular, Super derides the trait-and-factor people who, with their isolated and fragmentary research, forego the rewards of a systematic, developmental approach that offers the potential for a well-organized theory. Super views each of the major orientations, the trait-and-factor approach, the social-systems view, and the personality approach, as partial analytic systems incomplete in and of themselves. His proposal, then, is an integrative one, stressing the interactive nature of the process of vocational development, i.e., the interaction of personal and environmental variables. His own unique contribution involves an attempt to synthesize the different orientations with vocational, sociological, industrial, and psychometric learnings. In order to establish the lawful determinism of career patterns, Super borrows heavily from the developmental principles of Ginzberg et al. (1951) and others in order to view vocational development as an ongoing, continuous, and generally irreversible process. While such formulations have been criticized as resting upon a catalogue of stages of development for all personalities (Kitson, 1951; O'Hara / Tiedeman, 1959), Super puts them to good use in characterizing the career process as a process of compromise within which his key construct, the development and implementation of the self-concept, operates. The individual chooses occupations whose characteristics will allow him to function in a role that is consistent with his concept of himself, which, in turn, is a function of his own developmental history.

Unfortunately, Super's formulation of the *formation, translation,* and ultimate *implementation* of the self-concept in education and work suffer from his attempt to integrate all possible theoretical and research considerations into one system. While this is laudable in the sense that there are many obvious factors that others have neglected, the product is a too loosely, too general, too inclusive set of propositions, all of which seem to be fighting for equal weight and none of which allow for any systematic and meaningful theoretical derivations. The reader is overwhelmed by the proliferation of considerations and the difficulties involved in operationalizing many of these considerations.

Perhaps more interesting than his formulations per se is the lack of relationship between the longitudinal and very valuable, though sometimes fragmentary, studies of career patterns and those formulations. While he claims to employ a developmental framework, Super gets involved in very low-level, empirical kinds of expectations that bear little relationship to his "theoretical" formulations. It must be said that Super has not explicitly stated that his intention is to relate his theory with his investigation. However, he *does* operate at two different levels and these *are not* related. On the one hand, he has taken it upon himself to attempt to integrate all available knowledge or lack of knowledge into one general and loosely connected system where the weights of the various factors are indiscernible, and on the other hand he is operating at a strictly empirical level with no logically deduced hypotheses but, rather, having many low-level and probationary expectations limited by the realities of the studies in terms of design, methodology and instruments, etc. He operates inductively up to the level of laws (*A* to *B*, figure 5) but does not establish the connection between his two processes, although he may yet relate *B* to some future *C*.

It would seem, then, since very little connection has as yet been established between the two phenomena, that the longitudinal work offers the most immediate potential since great difficulty is encountered in implementing his all-inclusive theoretical formulations. Super's most worthwhile contributions are included in his longitudinal work in collecting his data and establishing the presence of stable phenomena.

Holland

Holland and his associates (1959, 1962, 1964., 1966a, 1966b; Stockin, 1964; Osipow et al., 1966) attempt to delineate a theory of vocational choice "comprehensive enough to integrate existing knowledge and at the same time sufficiently close to observables to stimulate further research." Evident in Holland's formulations are the general influences of need theory, role theory, self theory, social learning theory, psychoanalytic theory, and sociology.

The theory assumes, in accordance with general psychological theory, that at the time a person chooses his vocation he is a product of his heredity and environment. Out of his experiences he develops a hierarchy of habitual or preferred methods for dealing with necessary social and environmental tasks, i.e., his life-style. This hierarchy or pattern of personal orientations directs the individual toward an occupational environment that will satisfy his particular hierarchy. That is, various classes or occupational groups furnish different kinds of gratifications or satisfactions and require different abilities, identifications, values, and attitudes, and a person's choice of an oc-

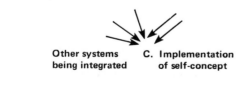

Other systems   C. Implementation
being integrated   of self-concept   G.

B.   D.   F.

A. Longitudinal study   E.

Figure 5. A suggested schematic representation of Super's approach.

cupation is an expressive act reflecting his motivations, his knowledge of the occupation in question, his insight and understanding of himself, his personality, and abilities. In viewing one's occupation as a "way of life, an environment rather then a set of isolated work functions or skills," Holland describes both the working environment and the person in the same terms; out of his own experience he arrived at six major classes of occupational environments and six corresponding personal orientations: the realistic, the intellectual, the social, the conventional, the enterprising, and the artistic. His categorizations bear a heavy trait-factor quality, but his inclination to offer a clinically flavored analysis carries him beyond that approach. One other aspect of Holland's work deserves mention—his attention to extra-individual factors, whose influence is usually recognized, though side-stepped, by most theorists. Thus, he has found that "persons with particular personality patterns achieve in some environments but not in others." Yet, despite his attention to such factors, Holland has, in the past, confined his research in large part to persons functioning at higher levels, populations whose members not only aspire to vocations that require professional training but also have maximal freedom in their vocational choice.

Thus, we find Holland at Level B, implicitly influenced by his own experience, integrating empirical data from previous research and operating with a general "set" indicative of contact with a number of different theories. He has generalized from accumulated raw data and simple facts to the level of laws, which, while they serve to integrate a good deal of existing research and suggest testable hypotheses, do not provide explanations for specified consequences of the interaction of data and laws (B to D, figure 6). For example, Holland hypothesizes that the level within an occupational area that an individual chooses is a function of that individual's self-evaluation and intelligence. Whereas theory would offer some explanatory principle from which this formula might have been derived, Holland merely presents the formula, which, because it is testable, may be verified or modified, but which has yet to be placed within the logical context of theory. Thus, Holland's research efforts do not flow deductively from theory but rather consist of a series of cross-sectional analyses and longitudinal studies that are attempts to relate subjects'

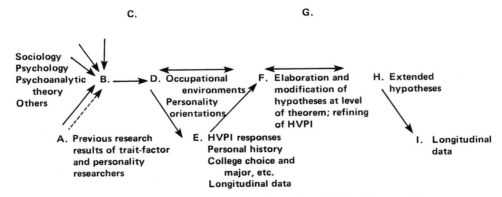

Figure 6. A suggested schematic representation of Holland's approach.

high-point codes on his preference inventory to a number of other variables: SAT scores, the famous people they would like to emulate, self-ratings, teacher ratings, nonacademic activities, choice of college major, background. In addition, Holland has added a great deal of interesting and valuable information to the area of vocational choice and has been open to reformulations of original hypotheses (*E* to *F*, figure 6). However, his predictions are made from descriptive stereotypes, not theory, and, his results support, add to, or modify his descriptive categories, not theory. Holland neither logically deduces his hypotheses, nor does he make generalizations from his data above the level of laws.

Summary

There does not appear to be any theory of vocational choice that meets the inductive-deductive model of theory-building. The general situation may be represented as one in which we have two sets of constructs: (1) low-level generalizations which offer the potential of being interrelated with one another, and each with rules of correspondence connecting it to observables; (2) those constructs, also offering the possibility of interrelationship with one another, but of logical or pseudological definition. Notably lacking, but indispensable to adequate theory-building, are the appropriate inductive-deductive connections between these two sets of constructs.

For the most part, preconceived theoretical structures, in that they are not modified by empirical results, promote circularity of formulation and inhibit our efforts at theoretical breakthrough. Illustrative here are many of the efforts to transpose psychodynamic theory from the realm of personality to that of vocational choice. Rather than

(1) developing lower level generalizations from the data in the ultimate hope of interrelating these generalizations, or (2) employing the data to modify or qualify the higher order constructs from which they were derived, these "theorists" all too often restrict their use of new data to that supporting the original theoretical framework. However, while their efforts, and thus their results, are wanting in independent, internally consistent direction, unencumbered and systematic attempts, such as those of the Michigan school, to discern the potentially unique contributions of the ego-analytic position to vocational development must be applauded.

At the other extreme are efforts, such as those of Super, that appear to make no attempt to bridge the gap between laws and theory. His theoretical formulations are often difficult, although by no means impossible, to operationalize. While beginning with theoretical formulations based upon self-heory, he has become primarily involved in empirical research which, because it often bears little or no direct relationship to his elaborated formulations, avoids entanglement in a closed theoretical network. However, while his system has not emerged beyond the level of low-level generalizations, his efforts to accumulate longitudinal data contribute to the establishment of a basis for theoretical readiness.

Similarly, Holland's large-scale empirical efforts are in large part free from delimiting theoretical bias; the tightly knit quality of his prolific research is supplemented by a continuous process of reformulation and speculation at the level of laws. Because his concepts and measurements are often almost one and the same, he manages to assure the relevance of his research to that supposedly being researched; however, the parsimony of his methodology, while it avoids duplication, must not become a handicap to theoretical aspirations.

A comprehensive attempt, drawing both inductively from new bodies of stable data and deductively from already existing formulations, is necessary: the dimensions held in common by the various orientations and the potentially unique contributions of each orientation must be discerned and systematically investigated. In this manner, we can work toward assigning differential weights to the potentially huge number of forces influencing vocational choice and development (Stefflre, 1966). It is hoped that the model presented in this paper will lead to a more complete understanding of the theory-building process and facilitate the integration of an otherwise bewildering mass of vocational constructs and data.

REFERENCES

Beall, L. Vocational choice: the impossible fantasy and the improbable choice. *Journal of Counseling Psychology*, 14, (1967):86-92.

Beall, L., and Bordin, E. S. The development and personality of engineers. *Personnel and Guidance Journal*, 43, (1964):23-32.

Bergman, G. Theoretical psychology. In *Annual Review of Psychology*, 4, (1953):435-58.

Bordin, E. S., Nachmann, B., and Segal, S. J. An articulated framework for vocational development. *Journal of Counseling Psychology*, 10, (1963):107-16.

Boring, E. G. The role of theory in experimental psychology. *American Journal of Psychology*, 66, (1953):169-84.

Erikson, E. Identity and the life cycle. *Psychological Issues*, 1959, 1-171.

Feigl, H. Operationism and scientific method. *Psychological Review*, 52, (1945):250-59.

Galinsky, M. D. Personality development and vocational choice of clinical psychologists and physicists. *Journal of Counseling Psychology*, 9, (1962):299-305.

Galinsky, M. D., and Fast, I. Vocational choice as a focus of the identity search. *Journal of Counseling Psychology*, 13, (1966):89-92.

Ginzburg, E., Axelrod, and Herma. *Occupational choice*. New York: Columbia University Press, 1951.

Harre, R. *The logic of the sciences*. London: Macmillan, 1960.

Hebb, D. O. Intelligence, brain function and the theory of the mind. *Brain*, 182, (1959):260-75.

Hemple, C. G., and Oppenheim, P. The logic of explanation. In H. Feigl and M. Brodbeck eds. *Readings in the philosophy of science*. New York: Appleton-Century-Crofts, 1953.

Holland, J. L. A theory of vocational choice. *Journal of Counseling Psychology*, 6, (1959):35-44.

———. Some explorations of theory of vocational choice: I. One- and two-year longitudinal studies. *Psychological Monographs*, 76, (1962):No. 26 (Whole No. 545).

———. *The psychology of vocational choice: a theory of personality types and environmental models*. New York: Ginn, 1966. (a)

———. A psychological classification scheme for vocations and major fields. *Journal of Counseling Psychology*, 13, (1966):278-88. (b)

Holland, J. L., and Nichols, R. C. Explorations of a theory of vocational choice: III. A longitudinal study of change in major field of study. *Personnel and Guidance Journal*, 43, (1964):235-42.

Hull, C. L. *Principles of behavior*. New York: Appleton-Century-Crofts, 1943.

Koch, S. Theoretical psychology, 1950: an overview. *Psychological Review*, 58, (1951): 295-301.

Kitson, H. D. Review of Ginzberg's *Occupational choice*. *Occupations*, 29, (1951):611-13.

Nachmann, B. Childhood experience and vocational choice in law, dentistry, and social work. *Journal of Counseling Psychology*, 7, (1960):243-50.

O'Hara, R. P., and Tiedeman, D. V. Vocational self concept in adolescence. *Journal of Counseling Psychology*, 6, (1959):292-301.

Osipow, S. H.; Ashby, J. D.; and Wall, H. W. Personality types and vocational choice: a test of Holland's theory. *Personnel and Guidance Journal*, 45, (1966):37-42.

Roe, A. *The psychology of occupations*. New York: Wiley, 1956.

———. Comment. *Journal of Counseling Psychology*, 10, (1963):117.

Roe, A., Hubbard, W. D., Hutchinson, T. and Bateman, Studies of occupational history. Part

I: Job changes and the classification of occupations. *Journal of Counseling Psychology*, 13, (1966):387-93.

Roe, A., and Siegelman, M. *The origin of interests*. Washington, D.C.: American Personnel and Guidance Association, 1964.

Segal, S. J. A psychoanalytic analysis of personality factors in vocational choice. *Journal of Counseling Psychology*, 8, (1961):202-10.

Segal, S. J., and Szabo. R. Identification in two vocations: accountants and creative writers. *Personnel and Guidance Journal*, 43, (1964): 252-55.

Skinner, B. F. Are theories of learning necessary? *Psychological Review*, 57, (1950):193-216.

Spence, K. W. The nature of theory construction in contemporary psychology. *Psychological Review*, 51, (1944):47-68.

Stefflre, B. Vocational development: ten propositions in search of a theory. *Personnel and Guidance Journal*, 44, (1966):611-16.

Stockin, B. C. A test of Holland's occupational level formulation. *Personnel and Guidance Journal*, 42, (1964):599-602.

Super, D. E. *The psychology of careers*. New York: Harper, 1957.

———. The definition and measurement of early career behavior: a first formulation. *Personnel and Guidance Journal*, 41, (1963):775-80.

Super, D. E., and Bachrach, P. B. *Scientific careers and vocational development theory.*

New York: Bureau of Publications, Teachers College, Columbia University, 1957.

Super, D. E.; Crites, J. O.; Hummel, R. C.; Moser, H. P.; Overstreet, P. L.; and Warnath, C. F. *Vocational development: a framework for research*. New York: Bureau of Publications, Teachers College, Columbia University, 1957.

Super, D. E.; Overstreet, P. L.; et al. *The vocational maturity of ninth-grade boys*. New York: Bureau of Publications, Teachers College, Columbia University, 1960.

Super, D. E., Starishevsky R.; Matlin, N.; and Jordaan, J. P. *Career development: self-concept theory*. Princeton, N.J.: College Entrance Examination Board, 1963.

Tiedeman, D. V. Decision and vocational development: a paradigm and its implications. *Personnel and Guidance Journal*, 40, (1961):15-21.

Tiedeman, D. V., and O'Hara, R. P. *Differentiation and integration in career development*. Cambridge, Mass.: Harvard Graduate School of Education, 1962.

———. *Career development: choice and adjustment*. New York: College Entrance Examination Board, 1963.

Underwood, B. J. *Psychological research*. New York: Appleton-Century-Crofts, 1957.

THE USE OF INVENTORIES IN VOCATIONAL COUNSELING
Norman Fredman

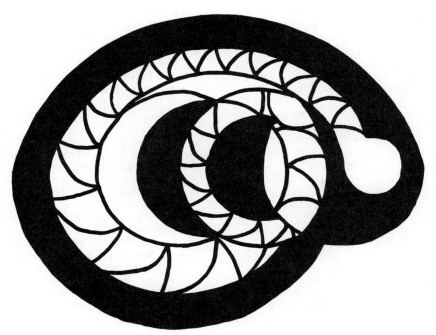

Vasilije Knezevic

The marriage between tests and counseling has been a stormy one for many reasons. Everyone is afraid of tests: "the biggest fool can ask questions the wisest man cannot answer." Testing has been a technique often beyond the abilities and interests of counselors. Counselors see themselves as humanists only too glad to acknowledge a weakness with numbers. Testing is inconsistent with that school of counseling that stresses the need for a nonjudgmental, nonthreatening atmosphere of acceptance. The objectivity tests provide is usually redundant, often irrelevant. True, Rogers and Rogerians use tests in research, but research is rarely the job of the practitioner, regardless of the usefulness of its results. Tests are seen as an invasion of privacy and justification of the status quo. Test results promote an elitism that occasionally contains a whiff of racism and seems to militate against the "counselor as change-agent." Despite criticisms of Rosenthal and Jacobson's research, most counselors remain fairly convinced that teachers, principals, and counselors other than themselves are easily biased by tests into labeling students in such a way that a subtle atmosphere is created so that the tests, even if originally invalid, become "self-fulfilling prophecies." Tests very often do not add to what is already known about the student. They are merely used to make decisions that would otherwise be too painful, decisions about grading, tracking, and selection—activities that counselors generally oppose.

But vocational inventories do have certain charms that make them appealing to counselors. Their questions can be answered. Usually a sixth or seventh grade reading level suffices to answer all questions though occasional words or activities may draw a blank. In a real sense, they are not tests, what Cronbach calls measures of best performance, but inventories or measures of typical performance. The subject matter, though reported in numbers, intrigues the counselor. Interests are something we all can have and interest inventories deal with those nonpathological aspects of personality that counselors feel comfortable with. True, interest inventories can be faked. But, so what? They are counseling tools, not selection weapons. Minorities have interest patterns as fascinating and as interpretable as anyone else, though, as we shall note, the majority—women—can be discriminated against.

Possibly the major criticism against interest inventories is that they may not tell us any more than we might otherwise learn by simpler and less costly methods. The single best vocational interest question is simply to ask the client: "If you could become anything, what would you like to become?" The second best question is, "If you can't be that, what would be your next choice?" The third best question is, "And if you can't be that, what would be your next choice?" It is necessary, by the way, to separate the three choices, and not ask, "What three things would you like to become?" By the third question you might have to smile pleasantly, which is one minor advantage inventories have; they can ask as many as 399 questions without smiling and still usually retain cooperation. But these three questions are so powerful that if their result contradicts the printout of the standardized inventory you dare not dismiss them. Moreover expressed interests will predict future vocations as well as inventoried interests.

If so, who needs interest inventories? Edward Strong tells of counseling a client who wanted to become a doctor, whose father and grandfather were doctors, but whose inventoried interests showed a dissimilarity of interests with those engaged in medical and biological sciences and a similarity of interests to those engaged in business. Knowing that the medical profession did not consist simply of healing, Strong did not lead the client into an exploration of his feelings about the contradiction between his expressed (and his parents) interests and his inventoried interests. The client could see a synthesis and indeed a decade or so later became a successful hospital administrator. The inventories may be used to explore possibilities the client had not thought of before because of a limited exposure to occupations.

The truth is that three only slightly related measurements are necessary for a proper vocational self-understanding. Ability is probably the single best predictor of vocational success. Expressed interests are definitely not the same as ability; but they do tell us what the client consciously wants to be. Inventoried interests are measures of the degree to which the client's interests are similar to those presently engaged in certain vocations. They correlate significantly with how long a person remains with a job. As the many interviews of Terkel's *Working* made clear, having a job is not the same as being happy with a job.

One theorist has suggested that group

membership is something like a card game in which each player is entitled to just so many idiosyncratic chips. You don't have to be exactly like everybody else. Indeed you should be different. But there are just so many chips you are allowed to spend on your differences. At a certain point you're out of the game. This is probably a key reason why counselors find interest inventories useful. That, and the relationship between interests and personality—and, of course, the possibility of thinking about activities and one's self in ways one had never thought of before.

There is a phrase each counselor should add to his vocabulary: "You scored like." This is especially true of interest inventories. It is false to say, "You are not interested in medicine," or "You are interested in business." It is honest to say, "Your interests are not the same as several hundred doctors this inventory polled," or, "Your interests are like those of several hundred businessmen this inventory surveyed." This is the underlying logic of inventoried interests: if your interests are like those of people already in the field you will have something more in common with your colleagues and will probably be more satisfied with that line of work. Moreover, there are probably some personality variables that correlate a person's many interests with the type of job he'd be happiest with.

Where do you begin? First of all, take the inventories yourself. As a rule of thumb, that makes as good sense practically as it does ethically, never administer a test or an inventory until you take it first. This will give you some knowledge about its practicality, how long it really takes, its offensiveness, and the sheer boredom of answering the questions. The *Edwards Personal Preference Schedule* is fun to score and interpret but many find it tedious to take. If you score high on the homosexual scale of the *MMPI* you will be less likely to point an accusing or limp finger at some client who scores similarly.

If you are less than twenty-five and you take the *Strong Vocational Interest Battery (SVIB)* you will probably have interests like a musician performer. Repeat those last six words. This does not mean that you can play or sing a note. These are inventories of interest, not tests of ability. It is quite possible, and for the young quite likely, to have interests like musician performers regardless of musical talent.

It is necessary to have your inventory evaluated or at least watch someone else experienced in inventory interpretation. Although they are a bit expensive, and eventually unnecessary computer readouts of the *Strong-Campbell Interest Inventory (SCII)* do give an intelligent evaluation. You will see, among other things that inventory results do not become a grocery list of occupations where the client comes out saying, "The dumb test says I should become a physical therapist."

Probably till twenty-five, people are still exploring possible professions. By then heavy commitments of money, time and effort have made it difficult to change vocational plans. So we want inventories that can be of use considerably before twenty-five. Fortunately or unfortunately, the question, "What are you going to be when you grow up?" when addressed to children will bring answers usually limited to fantasy. High school measures of interest are probably best if they concentrate on basic interest patterns. A *Kuder Occupational Interest Survey (OIS)* was administered to forty-four ninth graders, half in an intellectually gifted class, half in a slow class. About 75 percent of the "gifted" children produced results that were interpretable. Despite having the instrument read to them only 25 percent of the "slow" children produced interpretable results. The best age for taking the inventories (old enough to be interpretable, young enough to be usable) is high school senior through college.

Certain patterns of response will produce related vocational choices that need to be viewed with caution. In our society, clients who dislike everything score like people who work with ideas: scientists, lawyers, journalists. Clients who like everything score like people who work with people: social workers, teachers, salesmen. Clients who are indifferent to everything score like people who work with things: hard hats and skilled laborers. This might explain why news media are filled with bad news or why intellectuals seem to agree with Chicken-Little: the sky *is* falling. It might also explain the immense gap between the academic psychologist who is trained to be critical and the practicing counselor who can find nothing wrong, except perhaps with the system. The interpreter of such instruments as the *SVIB* is warned however not to confuse grumpiness with criticism, acquiescence with enthusiasm, or apathy with independence. A high percentage of responses in one direction (say, like) regardless of the question asked (this is called "response set") may mean that you need to give another type of test.

The Kuder *OIS* is a forced-choice inventory and has the advantage of eliminating response set. The client must choose which of three activities he likes best and which he likes least. In effect he ranks three activities. It is inevitable that some choices will be difficult. Which do you like best: delivering mail, collecting garbage, or sorting mail? For some this is a choice between losing one's feet, one's dignity, or one's mind—not a choice between outdoor and clerical activities. Nor does the inventory amply distinguish between the overenthused client

who can't make up his mind because he likes everything and the underenthused client who can't make up his mind because he likes (and dislikes) nothing. These two different approaches—forced choice and free response—may be one of the reasons the results on the *OIS* and *SVIB* do not correlate with each other higher. For many clients it may be necessary to give both instruments.

Women have been discriminated against vocationally since the dawn of history. Their essential employment as mothers generally meant that they would not seek any other full-time careers. But the realities of zero population growth, increased day care opportunities, women's liberation, and government affirmative action programs have meant that women increasingly regard careers other than housewife as part of their life-style. As late as the 1960s a profession could be defined accurately, if cynically, as a line of work employing few women or minorities. No more!

The *OIS* was the first to toe the line. Women were compared with male as well as other female employees and professionals. Eventually men were compared with females as well as males. Not that men were being terribly discriminated against, but the need to break down sexist vocational stereotypes was felt. How to take instruments that describe the world as it is and replace them with something that describes what should be is basically an insoluble problem. Only compromises could be offered, compromises and astute counseling.

The *SVIB* was slower in adjusting to the women's movement demands. At first the Male *SVIB* was printed in blue and the Female *SVIB* was printed in pink for easy identification. But that was too much. So the Female *SVIB* was printed in green. In 1974 a combined male-female *SCII* was published. The old *SVIB*'s had areas that lended themselves to better counseling. Rather than simply look at one job—surgeon or counselor, for instance—the counselor would encourage the client to look at areas—biological sciences and socially oriented activities. But this technique had to go. Skilled labor and nursing areas were sexist enough but that last area on the female *SVIB* that grouped together such occupations as executive housekeeper, beautician, telephone operator, elementary school teacher and stewardess could only be called "unliberated women." In the place of areas went Holland's theory that organized all activities into six scales. It is a pity that John Holland had to use good English words in his own way. A whole generation of counselors will be brainwashed into calling scientists, "Intellectual", white collar workers, "conventional" and skilled labor, "realistic."

There are, of course, other vocational inventories besides the various Strongs and Kuders. The emergence of computer scoring has produced sophisticated statistical results that go far beyond counting up the raw score and looking up the percentile. Fortunately these tests do not require as much statistical background as good sense in their interpretation, although jagged profile lines and numbers with decimals will create an initial shock. Some inventories include measures of the clients value system: his need for prestige, economic return, or intellectual stimulation. Our theories of intelligence have grown beyond the belief in a global general intelligence. It therefore became necessary to give an aptitude battery rather than one test. Our theories of vocational guidance might similarly grow beyond the single dimension of interest or need or economic opportunity to include the many dimensions of vocational behavior. It may therefore become necessary to give a vocational battery rather than just one interest inventory.

It is usually agreed that IQ and achievement tests are more reliable and valid than electrocardiograms and electroencephalograms. But rarely is a good word spoken about the former tests or a bad word about the latter. Why? Because of test interpretation. Clients sense the IQs and achievement tests are being used against them; the medical tests, for them. One group of tests is being used to select and condemn, too often without using other information available. The other group is used to understand and heal and is combined with every other bit of knowledge available.

The vocational inventories are less reliable and valid than IQ and achievement tests though they are unquestionably the best personality inventories available. True, they too can be misused by squelching the client or numbing him with numbers, by sexism or justification of the status quo, and by trying to create self-fulfilling prophecies. Yet, if used to help the client in his struggle for self-understanding, to supplement his expressed interests, and to stimulate thought and new horizons they might well bring the client to that vocation.

> where love and need are one,
> and the work is play for moral stakes.

26. YOUTH AND DRUGS: GUIDELINES FOR TEACHERS

Donald J. Wolk

Peter Schwarzburg

An atmosphere of acceptance for the use of drugs has developed. Increasingly more drugs are prescribed by overworked physicians; mass media advertise the virtues of popping a pill and patients often demand tangible treatment for real or imagined illness. "This nation has become so medicine-oriented that patients demand antibiotics of physicians for the treatment of virus infections even though such infections are unaffected by antibiotics."[1]

And we wonder why the younger generation has turned to drugs.

Instant relief and instant gratification have become desirable goals for many people. The effort to hastily satisfy needs and to relieve tension and anxiety may result in moving us away from introspection and self-discipline. It becomes easier to ingest a change agent—a chemical remedy—than to expend the effort to understand the difficulties

Is this the world of the future—a brave new world in which we are feeding an increasing inability to tolerate smaller and smaller amounts of physical and emotional discomfort? Might future drugs throw entire societies into "a sort of painless concentration camp of the mind in which people will have lost their liberties in the enjoyment of a dictatorship without tears"?[2]

Inasmuch as drugs are influencing the structure of society, the topic is of special significance for the social studies class. The emphasis must be on individual attitudes, societal values, changing styles of life and implications for the future. "The task is . . . to educate, not about the evils of heroin, LSD, and the dangers of specific stimulants and depressants, but about people, about chemicals and how they interact with people, about social control, about the positive and negative consequences of drug use for the individual and for society, to the extent that we know rather than imagine them. We must help young people make informed decisions on the basis of broad general principles."[3]

The youth of today are not the only ones caught in an age of accelerated scientific advancement, social upheaval and family and religious turmoil. Adults are constantly confronted with contradictory information and theory concerning child rearing—a *predicament* that has led to feelings of uncertainty, helplessness and inadequacy. They are torn between setting limits and establishing guidelines for their children (or students) or allowing them the freedom to discover the world around and within themselves. One pattern is often experienced as too restricting and inhibiting, while the other is felt to be overly-permissive. All too often the resolve is to avoid establishing and enforcing rules and discipline. "Resignation? Perhaps; but we must keep in mind that these adults are also responding to their own needs and motivations. Not the least of these may be a conscious or unconscious desire for more freedom for themselves. This type of need may result in vicariously living through their children (or students), unconsciously encouraging deviant, exciting, freedom-seeking behaviour."[4]

Moreover, organized religion has lost ground to humanism, reality, science and technology. Though still cherished as a precious heirloom, religion has failed to keep pace with today's needs with today's attitudes and values, and with today's beliefs. People tend to turn inward and outward, but not upward.

The loss of symbols, authority, and established guidelines has abandoned youth to the steel tempered world of reality—a cold world of logic and hypocrisy. In the remaining void, personal involvement and group belongingness become essential. For some, drugs become the means to this end. "The less strongly a person is already committed to a set of beliefs, values, and goals, the more likely he is to accept as valid those he finds via the drug experience."[5]

The Drugs of Concern

"Ups" (amphetamines, including Methedrine or "speed"), "Downs" (barbiturates), marijuana, and LSD are the major drugs used and abused by students. Heroin and glue-sniffing are special drugs used by selective groups within the drug world. Glue is primarily confined to high school grades and below; heroin is usually restricted to ghetto areas, rarely being seen on the college campus and occasionally in middle-middle and higher socioeconomic noncollege groups (both white and black).

Marijuana ("Pot," "tea," "mary jane," etc.)

Special emphasis will be devoted to marijuana, since this drug appears to be the most widely used by youngsters, and the most controversial.

Although marijuana has been used for nearly 5,000 years, much needs to be learned about its chemical composition and its long-term physical and mental effects. Within the last several years the chemical component believed to be the potent element of the plant, cannabis sativa (marijuana), has been synthesized; this active ingredient is known as tetrahydrocannabinol (THC). Research is being conducted through the auspices of the National Institute of Mental Health, the primary legal dispenser of the drug. Thus far, the results remain unclear and tentative. High dosages of THC have been found to produce severe emotional reactions in every person tested, and psychotic reactions have been observed in some individuals.[6] However, THC is known to be many times more potent than the marijuana usually smoked outside the laboratory setting. Therefore, the generalization that "marijuana" is dangerous because it produced psychotic reactions in the laboratory is totally unjustified.

One must be careful in reading and teaching the "facts" regarding drugs. Zinberg and Weil reported an experiment they had conducted in the spring of 1968 in which the subjects were given marijuana cigarettes ("joints") to smoke—replicating as much as possible the "real world" in which the drug is used. Their conclusions are enlightening although, for some, frightening. Concerning physical effects:

> Marijuana caused a moderate increase in heart rate, but not enough to make subjects conscious of a rapid pulse, and it reddened whites of eyes. It had no effect on pupil size, blood sugar, or respiratory rate. Possibly the drug has a few other effects on the body. . ., but it is unlikely that other major effects will be found. [It is] unlikely that marijuana has any seriously detrimental physical effects in either short-term or long-term usage.

> All in all, we think it is fair to say in terms of medical dangers only, marijuana is a relatively harmless intoxicant.[7]

Moreover, the two researchers concluded that "marijuana seems to affect little in the brain besides the highest centers of thought, memory and perception. It has no general stimulating or depressive action on the nervous system—no influence in our lower centers like those controlling the mechanical aspects of speech and coordination. As a result it seems possible to ignore the effects of marijuana on consciousness, to adapt to them, and to control them to a significant degree."[8]

Psychologically, Zinberg and Weil state ". . . in short-term usage only. . .usual doses of marijuana do not impair a user's ability to carry out successfully a wide range of tasks of ordinary complexity. But higher than usual doses, especially in novice smokers, might be expected to cause performance decrements."[9]

Based on my own studies and clinical experience (on the college level), I can readily support the "psychological effects" cited by Zinberg and Weil. However, we must also consider that the effect of the drug is dependent on several circumstances:

1. the mood of the individual (joyous, depressed, angry, etc.),
2. motivation of the smoker (to tranquilize, to become happier, to become more outgoing, to have sexual relationships, etc.),
3. the environment (setting) in which the individual finds or places himself.

These factors are crucial in evaluating and understanding the effects of drugs on the individual.

Many youngsters experiment, that is, take marijuana once, twice, or even several times, in order to satisfy their curiosity, and then discontinue use. Some take "pot" on occasion, from one to two times per month, to several times per year. Still another group smokes the drug on a regular weekly basis. Why do students, especially those in the last two groups, use marijuana?

Students' reasons for smoking marijuana were cited in a previously published paper by this author. Moreover, through clinical counseling and teaching contact with students, I have learned that there are usually "other" underlying reasons for the drug-taking, reasons that are not readily apparent to the smoker.

The reason most students cite is for a feeling of "relaxation" or tranquility. In this sense, marijuana serves as a relief from tensions and anxieties stemming from various academic, social and personal pressures. For some, the drug becomes a necessary tranquilizer, relieving discomfort. For many other students, marijuana is a temporary "escape" from reality, and students readily admit this. What then occurs is not an increased tolerance for the drug, but an increased intolerance for anxiety and frustration . . . two ingredients in our lives which, within limits, serve a useful purpose in motivating us toward constructive goals and accomplishments.

The second most cited reason is a combination of increased sensitivity and awareness of others and the environment and increased insight into oneself. Students who are practiced in taking marijuana find that they are better able to appreciate art, music, nature and a myriad number of mundane, often overlooked objects (such as tables, chairs, ashtrays, pencils, water, bubbles, etc.). Their senses, most usually sight, sound and touch, become more acute, and meaning is found in what was previously taken for granted. Sensitivity to other people is heightened. Students report that they become more understanding and perceptive of the other person's communications (both overt and covert), and they may fully relate their feelings and interpretations to another person. These "therapy sessions" could be beneficial; but, more often than not, I suspect they are either innocuous or harmful. In some instances the "insightful" smoker projects (attributes) to others feelings and attitudes which lie within himself but of which he is not aware. Or, he picks up bits of information from talking with another person, formulates hypotheses, and believes that because he is high on marijuana his insights must be true. It is important to recognize that, as a result of his relaxed, euphoric state, the individual who uses marijuana is more suggestible; he is, therefore, more easily influenced to believe something which may be clear distortion. This is where the danger is: he will either convince himself or be convinced by others that the ideas and so-called insights he attained while using "pot" are valid. He may then proceed to react to and act on them; if these are false conclusions he will eventually increase his discomfort and move further from the truth, rather than closer. Moreover, the personal insight he gains is very often superficial and difficult to maintain once the drug effect wears off.

Other reasons mentioned by users of the drug include loss of inhibitions, a feeling of inner freedom to express himself in a relatively unrestrained manner, and the desire and ability to work in a more effective manner (not cited very often). In regard to freedom of expression, the individual must consider the possiblity that he may simply be rationalizing liberal behavior while under the influence of a drug. He will thus blame the drug for his behavior, removing the responsibility from himself. In terms of becoming more effective in work or study, most regular users state that it neither increases their creativity nor their productivity.

Other reasons have been expressed, some of which include a challenge to authority, a desire to be caught and stopped (an unconscious wish for external care and control), and several others which are highly idiosyncratic.[10]

Finally, the need and pressure to belong to and identify with a "hip" group, or with a group that offers the freedom to "be oneself," is tantalizing. This same sense of belongingness and of identification is a significant factor causing the regular user to feel bound to the drug-oriented group.

Once attachments are formed, especially those in which there is a strong common bond (such as drugs), separation from the group becomes extremely difficult. . .even if desirable. For example, if the student decides that marijuana is detrimental for him, he must ultimately choose between remaining or leaving the drug-oriented group. If he remains, he will eventually resume using drugs to some degree. If he truly decides to discontinue with this pattern of life, he will undergo much inner conflict, experiencing feelings of guilt, detachment and loneliness. He will probably, for a time, lose his sense of belongingness to any group . . . and especially to the one with which he so strongly identified. It is not easy or pleasant to relinquish established bonds, even if the original, overt objective (in this example, drugs) is no longer desired.[11]

Since the psychological and sociological implications far outweigh the physical effects of marijuana, this should be the main area of discussion.

LSD (D-Lysergic Acid Diethylomide)

LSD is a special drug. Under its influence a person may rise to the heights of ecstasy, gaining sensitivity and insight, or he may fall to the depths of despair, feeling extreme loneliness and dread. For some, the experience may be beneficial; for others, the LSD trip may lead to further problems.

LSD use has sharply decreased. Widespread publicity about the severe psychotic reactions resulting from it and the possibility of chromosome damage generated sufficient anxiety to turn younsters off and away from the drug. "Acid" has become too hot to handle, although its complete demise may not be seen for quite some time.

What is LSD? A synthesized drug of almost unbelievable potency, the "normal" LSD dosage (100-250 micrograms) can produce an 8-12 hour trip. This tremendous potency is dramatized by realizing "that an amount of LSD equivalent to two aspirin tablets would provide 6,500 100 microgram doses."[12]

The questionable value of these "trips," or "psychedelic journeys," provides material for discussion. Simmons and Winogard, in their interesting and provocative book, *It's Happening*, expand on Dr. Timothy Leary's five major dilemmas arising from psychedelic journeys.[13] The series of fears are "balanced against the series of yearnings." My own "balanced" commentary follows the listed dilemmas.

1. *"The terror of loss of rational control is balanced by the hope of transcending one's hidebound ways of thought and freeing oneself from programmed ruts."*

We are fully aware that the "terror" is an occasional happening, even to those who have used the drug many times. Brief (acute) psychotic episodes and anxiety reactions resulting in a "loss of rational control" while under the direct influence of LSD have been reported numerous times. Moreover, the phenomena known as "flashbacks" have been related more often as the years go by. A flashback is a spontaneous recurrence of sensations from an LSD trip experienced weeks or even months before. Suddenly, the individual, who had his last trip three or four months ago, becomes unexplainedly anxious or depressed while reexperiencing some of the terror of that trip. This occasionally results in prolonged, severe anxiety or depressive symptoms, loss of emotional control, a fear of going crazy and/or panic (an overwhelming experience of dread). The most frightening feeling as related to me by several students to whom this had occurred was that of losing control of one's emotions and thinking, and, therefore, of one's mind.

2. *"Fear of acting shamefully is balanced by the hope of casting off one's social fetters and behaving as one truly wants to."*

For many, the task of casting off an undesirable and uncomfortable social mask is extremely difficult. However, becoming more of one's self can also be accomplished by self-examination and requested feedback from others. In my opinion, deep and trusted interpersonal relationships become more meaningful, freeing, and satisfying than those emerging from a drug experience. However, the necessity of a chemical catalyst is a thought to ponder and discuss—if a "safe" drug is eventually marketed.

3. *"The terror of perhaps really seeing yourself is balanced by the hope of really finding yourself."*

4. *"The fear of disenchantment with one's society and one's position within it is balanced by the hope of insight into the inner workings of one's social environment and of seeing more creative alternatives."*

The "hope" within each dilemma is one that, I am sure, most of us desire. The question is whether to risk the danger of the drug and the experience or seek other means to achieve the same goals. "Haste makes waste." "A stitch in time saves nine." Which shall it be? What are the alternatives for seeking self and of better understanding one's environment? These are the questions that need discussion.

5. *"And, the fear of discovering a 'supernormal' realm so pleasant that one will never return is balanced by the hope that one can reach a level of awareness which will transform everything into splendor."*

Who will deny the secret desire for a utopia of one's own making? How long does "splendor" last? It will remain as long as one continues to strive for openness, honesty and spontaneity or as long as one is sufficiently tranquilized so as to block all unpleasant realities. Alas, all too often, students I have seen have had to continue on either LSD or other drugs to relive the splendor of the moment. It is too easy to become dependent on a chemical that promises the secret of contentment. Is this type of existence delusional or real? Who is to decide? The individual or the society?

These five dilemmas and the commentary following them are grist for the social education mill. To discuss the effects and uses of LSD, such as in psychotherapy or in treating alcoholics, for terminal disease cases, and for autistic children, would not be within the realm of this paper. Of importance here is having students think through the personal and societal meaning of drug use.

Amphetamines

Amphetamines (stimulants, otherwise known as "ups" or pep pills) are a pick-me-up. They offer relief from depression and fatigue, a feeling of alertness and wakefulness, and an increased ability to concentrate, think and speak more effectively. Sleep is not necessary so long as the individual continues taking his "bennies" or "dexies." Of course, the user of pep pills cannot continue this behavior indefinitely; his body, if not his mind, requires rest.

The set or motives of the individual determines, to a large extent, the nature of his later feelings and his behavior. However, the person using the drug is not always cognizant of his underlying motives nor does he or she always want to be aware of his or her desires. Behavior which would ordinarily not be acted out can always be excused (rationalized) as having occurred because of the drug. You cannot be responsible for the actions of a pill!

The drug of prime concern in the amphetamine category is "speed" (methamphetamine or Methedrine). This drug is usually taken intravenously for a quick, potent boost. The individual experiences a feeling of mental and physical alertness and power, a wild, joyous attitude, and the capability of talking and working till all hours of the morning and night. It is a high feeling, very often an avoidance of or escape from unpleasant sensations of inadequacy, depression, loneliness and alienation. The world is too cold, gray and demanding; it is more pleasant to float on the billowy clouds of "speed." But, the fall (coming down) is painful; depression and fatigue quickly set in, and it becomes increasingly more difficult to remain on the ground, that is, without outside support, understanding and guidance. Although amphetamines do not produce physical dependence, a tolerance to these drugs does develop so that larger and larger doses are required to feel the effects.

Barbiturates

Barbiturates (sedatives, otherwise known as "downs," "goofballs," and by many other names) are the quieting-down drugs. They are taken by youngsters to alleviate the tension and anxiety, to induce sleep, and to experience a fast, pleasant "drunk." In higher dosages the effects and the experience are usually those of confusion, slurred speech, uncoordinated walking, and an inability to think and work effectively. Heavy users may eventually show signs of instability, anger and combativeness.

Barbiturates are addictive, that is, the body develops a need for higher and higher doses of the drug which, when discontinued, may result in withdrawal pains. This "abstinence syndrome" is primarily experienced as cramps, nausea, and delirium. Convulsions and death may occur in some cases.[14] Moreover, "users may react to the drug more strongly at one time than at another. They may become confused about how many pills they have and die of an accidental overdose. Barbiturates are a leading cause of accidental poison deaths in the United States."[15]

The free use of barbiturates and amphetamines once again points out the desire and urge to resolve all problems through a pill or an injection. This is a social phenomenon and problem which is not easily accepted or resolved.

Glue—or Solvent—Sniffing

Many of the reasons youngsters sniff glue and inhale other solvents (such as gasoline, lighter and cleaner fuids, lacquer thinners, etc.) are similar to some already cited for marijuana use, namely: curiosity, to experience a fast "high," to have pleasant sensations, rebellion and/or escape from an unpleasant reality. Glue and other solvents are used by younger teenagers because they are inexpensive and readily available.[16]

Inhalation of glue may produce feelings of exhilaration, drunkenness, omnipotence, and general euphoria. Some individuals experience pleasant emotions and have peaceful thoughts and imagery; others undergo unpleasant, anxiety-laden experiences in which terrifying thoughts and hallucinatory material emerges.

. . . for most individuals, solvent-sniffing is indulged in transiently and, except for occasional instances of injury, suffocation or violence, no permanent scar is left. A small number of individuals will become severely habituated, and for them glue- or gasoline-sniffing is a very serious problem which often results in aggression, violence or delinquent behavior, increases psychological isolation, accentuates personality defects, and may result in permanent brain dysfunction.[17]

Heroin

Heroin (an opiate commonly referred to as "H," "smack," "horse," etc.) is a total escape drug. The relief and joy experienced reinforces its repeated use. The desire and necessity of involving oneself with the mundane affairs of the "straight" world gradually decrease; the user becomes primarily interested in and concerned with himself and his drug—his major goal and challenge is in acquiring the drug and turning himself off.

For those persons who develop a psychological dependence on heroin, it also becomes addicting. This results in physical withdrawal symptoms (the "abstinence syndrome") when the drug is discontinued. However, these symptoms are not as debilitating as they were thought to be. Expectations to undergo great physical pain when withdrawing from heroin create an anxious, tense attitude. Expectancy then leads to the actual experience of unbearable pains. Apparently this is more psychologically and socially induced than physically necessary. In describing an average withdrawal scene at one of the more successful treatment centers, Daytop Village, Alexander Bossin writes:

He [the addict] goes through withdrawal on a couch in the living room with residents all about him, laughing, playing cards, listening to music, dancing. He is too ashamed to put on the expected exhibition of wall climbing and swinging from chandeliers. He knows that these people will not be impressed by his performance. He knows there will be no payoff for his histrionics from these wise, hardnosed critics. And somewhat to his own surprise, he kicks the remnants of his [physical] habit in record time with no more discomfort than the average guy with a mild case of flu.[18]

The major problem concerning heroin addiction is the individual, his needs, goals and outlets. Undoubtedly, heroin is an insidious, self-destructive drug, and it needs a human hand to inject it. Most of those who become addicted have psychological problems, but this is not to say that addiction can be viewed only from the point of view of the individual and his family background. The problem is a sociological one as well.

"At present only 30 percent of all addicts in the United States are Caucasian. Heroin abuse is primarily a disease of repressed minorities; 50.4 percent of the users are Negro, 13.6 percent Peurto Rican and 5.4 percent Mexican."[19]

Heroin is a ghetto drug. It is readily available and all too easily accepted as one means of escaping from an impoverished, depressing environment. For the affluent, drugs serve as a means to immediate pleasure, relief and gratification. For the people in the ghetto, the need is to escape from a "blighted reality." In one population we find a lack of discipline and an overly-permissive attitude; in the other we see deplorable social conditions which produce blind alleys and endless frustrations.

It is well to consider that the major influence on an individual's use of drugs is the peer group. The prestige of key figures and the power of group approval, identification, and belongingness are tremendous motivating factors. So great are these needs that the adolescent "is willing to sacrifice his individual preferences and convictions for group acceptance."[20]

Conclusions

The topic of drug usage often causes teachers (and parents) to feel uncomfortable and defensive. Contradictory theories, inconclusive research findings and uncertain "facts" are plentiful. Moreover, the teacher is weighted down with the task of telling students to stay away from drugs—not to educate them about the effects of drugs (good and bad) on individual and society. He is placed in a straightjacket of administrative and parental pressures, a difficult position if one is to educate in an unbiased manner. All too often, one-sided scare tactics are ineffective, especially for those youngsters who have already used drugs, and for those who are still walking the fence.

The teacher cannot afford to become a preacher—not in this day and age. Today, information about drugs, politics, sex, social class, racial inequities and international affairs, is disseminated by a variety of media—only *one* of these being the classroom teacher. The teacher is no longer the indisputable authority. To delude himself with the belief that his word will be heeded or to indulge in self-pity and frustration if his teachings are ignored can be fatal to communication. He "must be prepared to take a flexible approach, maintaining, at the very least, an open mind to the range of student feelings and attitudes. If HE accepts or condemns too quickly, without knowledge or feeling, HE only perpetuates the anxiety, the resentment and the defensiveness of the younger generation."[21] When discussing the topic of drugs the teacher must be a student in his own class; he must become a participant-observer, a guide or a facilitator—but not *The Teacher!*

Following are four basic rules that can serve as a guide to thinking through the problem of teaching about drug use:

1. *Although the topic is drug use, drugs, per se, are not always of prime concern.* Major areas for discussion are: (a) The personal meaning in taking drugs, (b) implications for one's lifestyle (c) one's interpersonal relationships, and (d) future goals.
2. *Know the facts, fantasies and uncertainties about drugs and drug use.* A thorough knowledge of chemical and physical effects is not as necessary as a concerned awareness of the psychological and sociological effects and reasons for use.
3. *Present an objective view of drug use and abuse.* Do not limit discussion to the dangers or negative side and avoid anything remotely positive; present as fair a picture as possible. Avoid moralizing and making quick judgments (positive or negative).

However, do not inhibit the expression of your own opinions and values. Carefully think through and then express and discuss the rationale for your way of thinking; offer this as simply another point of view.

Allow discussion from all sides, requesting questions and comments, both written and oral. If an attempt is made to "brainwash," you will lose those students you most want to reach, and who probably want to be reached.[22]

4. *Finally, learn from your students.* Do not regard yourself as the authority or as the only teacher in the room. In an atmosphere of openness and inquiry, you are apt to learn more about drug use and student feelings and attitudes than you may believe possible.

NOTES

1. D. B. Louria, *The Drug Scene.* New York: McGraw-Hill Book Company, 1968, p. 16.
2. J. B. and C. R. Saunders, quoted in B. Barker, *Drugs and Society.* New York: Russell Sage Foundation, 1967, p. 160.
3. H. H. Nowlis, *Drugs on the College Campus.* A publication of the Drug Education Project of The National Association of Student Personnel Administrators, December 1967, p. 18.
4. D. J. Wolk, "Why Marihuana?" *University of Bridgeport Quarterly,* Spring, 1968, pp. 8-11.
5. W. P. McGlothlin, "Toward a Rational View of Hallucinogenic Drugs." Paper distributed at National Association of Student Personnel Administrators Drug Education Conference, Washington, D.C., November 7-8, 1966.
6. "Students and Drug Abuse." *Today's Education,* March, 1969.
7. N. E. Zinberg and A. T. Weil, "The Effects of Marijuana On Human Beings." *The New York Times Magazine,* May 11, 1969, p. 89.
8. *Ibid.,* p. 92.
9. *Ibid.,* p. 94.
10. D. J. Wolk, *op. cit.,* pp. 9-10.
11. *Ibid.* p. 11.
12. H. H. Nowlis, *op. cit.,* p. 9.
13. J. L. Simmons and B. Winogard. *It's Happening.* Santa Barbara, California: March-Laird Publications, 1966, pp. 50-51.
14. For a detailed description of the physical and mental effects of these drugs, refer to N. B. Eddy, *et al.,* "Drug Dependence: Its Significance and Characteristics." *Bulletin of the World Health Organization,* 1965, 32, pp. 721-33.
15. "Students and Drug Abuse," *op. cit.,* p. 44.
16. E. Press and A. K. Done, "Solvent Sniffing." *Pediatrics,* vol. 39, no. 3-4, March and April, 1967.
17. D. B. Louria, *op. cit.,* p. 52.
18. A. Bossin, "Daytop Village." *Psychology Today,* December, 1968, p. 51.
19. D. B. Louria, *op. cit.,* p. 4.
20. D. P. Ausubel, *Drug Addiction: Physiological, Psychological and Sociological Aspects,* New York: Random House, 1958, pp. 51-52.
21. D. J. Wolk, *op. cit.,* p. 11.
22. For a worthwhile, refreshing view of the "case" for inquiry teaching, read O. A. Hagen and S. T. Stansberry, "Why Inquiry?" *Social Education,* vol. 33, no. 5, May, 1969, pp. 534-37.

27. GROUP COUNSELING WITH DISRUPTIVE ADOLESCENTS

Lester J. Schwartz

Peter Schwarzburg

Group counseling with adolescents has been modeled on the group techniques used with adults. With some modification, these techniques have been successful with many adolescents. There are, however, adolescents who have not responded well to these traditional modes of group counseling. Among such are adolescents who are generally described as "disruptive."

In school, disruptive adolescents are unable to comply with the minimal rules. The term antiachiever aptly describes their school behavior. They are often truant, unprepared in their work and, consequently, poor students. They seriously interfere with the education of all; their own no less than others.

Outside of school, disruptive adolescents may be at the fringes of trouble with the law, if not already involved in delinquent acts. They commonly engage in such antisocial acts as vandalism, petty thievery and disturbing the peace of the community. Often, the only difference between disruptive and delinquent adolescents is that the latter have been caught or the former have received more protection from their families and communities.

Because the basic problem of disruptive youngsters is their inability to function constructively in social settings, group counseling is a logical therapeutic approach. Group counseling is particularly appropriate for modifying the behavior of disruptive adolescents because it provides a miniature but highly compacted social setting. A group creates the climate in which social behavior can be examined and understood and it affords an opportunity to practice change.

The dilemma for the group counselor, however, is that the very behavior that disruptive adolescents need to change can destroy the group in its early stages, or worse yet, cause the group members to act destructively towards each other. There is nothing more harmful to a group than all its members acting out their antisocial feelings promiscuously and without restraint. Such groups are doomed to failure.

Generally, it is wise for a group to be well balanced without one personality type dominating. Ideal conditions, however, seldom exist and counselors must often work with people who have very similar personality dynamics. Beyond the problem of homogeneity of group composition, other writers (Redl and Wineman, 1951) have pointed out the need for using different approaches with children who act out. Indeed, disruptive adolescents cannot be expected to respond positively to traditional group counseling because such counseling is based on assumptions which apply to youngsters who have a reasonable degree of internalized social controls. To account for the differences between the disruptive and the more socialized adolescents, the group counseling process must be modified in relation to these assumptions.

The Basic Assumption of Group Counseling

The first such assumption is that individuals possess enough latent capacity to trust and to be concerned about other group members, to permit group cohesion. This cohesion cannot be achieved without mutual concern on the part of group members and is essential to successful group process. It provides the atmosphere of support and security in which problems can be aired, shared, and worked through. In disruptive adolescents, however, the capacity for trust and appropriate social guilt has been severely damaged, (Persons, 1970). Whatever the etiology—prolonged experience with harsh authority, an absence of any real affectional relationships, or impossible conditional standards for acceptance—the disruptive adolescents often feel that they can't trust others. Nor do disruptive adolescents feel that it pays to be concerned about others, because they are sure they will be disappointed or betrayed.

A second assumption made about group participants is that each individual has the potential to take responsibility for self-change. Although he may come to the group with strong defenses it is expected that eventually he can understand that he can modify events and experiences in his life if he takes responsibility for his behavior. Kahn (1971) pointed out that acting out adolescents can not conceputualize this kind of responsibility. Disruptive adolescents perceive their life-style as fixed and necessary; they feel powerless to deal with the social environment. They feel that restraints, selfishness, and the control exerted by others leave them with no alternative but to deal with people by fighting, stealing, and deception. They do not say, "something is wrong or missing inside of me and I must try to do something about it"; rather they say, "the rotten world forces me into the situation I'm in and I'm going to beat them at the game." The only kind of responsibility disruptive adolescents may take for themselves is to try to be disruptive in the cleverest or in the most overpowering way.

The third assumption is that group members can learn and understand the objectives and methodology of group process in rather short order. This means that the group members can soon come to appreciate that the group process can be helpful, that personal goals can be set, that other group members have similar feelings and problems, and that affective interaction within the group is conducive to growth. These aspects of the group process, however, are beyond the ken of most acting out youngsters

(Truax, Wargo, and Volksdorf, 1970). Instead of being goal oriented, they are impulsive. Instead of being interdependent, they act only in immediate self-interest. Instead of being empathetic, they feel insulated. Instead of being in touch with their feelings, they avoid and deny.

In summary, the difficulties that disruptive youth have in being successful group participants are:

1. They have great difficulty in trusting and feeling concern for others.
2. They are unwilling to take responsibility for their own behavior and its modification.
3. They are unfamiliar with the skills and process of interpersonal and intrapersonal problem solving.

A group leader anticipates these problems in any group and he deals with them continuously, along with all the other problems that the group generates. The normal group process accommodates the problems and they are worked through in due course. The same can happen in a group of disruptive adolescents led by a skilled leader; but in this kind of group, the degree of distrust, irresponsibility, and past defective social learning is so great that progress proceeds at a snail's pace, if at all.

A Didactic-Affective Approach

An effective means for dealing with these problems is through a combined didactic-affective approach during the initial phase of a group's life. The problems, in fact, become the content of the initial phase. The following five points constitute the basic concepts employed by a group leader in using this approach during the initial phase of group counseling with disruptive youth.

1. *Expectations Must Be Dealt With.*

Disruptive youth approach the group with distortions, confusion, or ignorance about the group process. Many of them feel that the leader's objective is to reform them or to try to make them conform. The participants' expectations must not be unrealistic. To correct the misperceptions, the group leader teaches the group that each member must decide for himself what he wants to get out of the group and that each member has absolute control over the kind and degree of his own participation. The possible kinds of individual goals and participations are explained and discussed. The leader, also at this time, imposes a limitation on the behavior of every member. The group is told that no one may behave in any way that may seriously injure the group or any member of the group. This announced limitation helps the members feel less vulnerable to attack. It also helps contain dangerous acting out behavior. A discussion may then follow of goals and behaviors that are consistent with group enhancement and those that are group destructive.

2. *Didactic Instruction Facilitates Affective Learning.* Although interpersonal psychology is the major determinant of social behavior, cognitive and verbal learning play an important role. In counseling, insights are usually intellectually understood before they are integrated affectively. Similarly, didactic instruction does not in itself change behavior, but in group counseling with disruptive youth, it makes the process and goals of therapy explicit and provides the referents which mark the course to be taken by the group.

3. *Dealing with Mistrust Takes Precedence.* Mistrust is an inhibiting force to group cohesiveness and whenever it emerges, it takes precedence. In the preparatory phase distrust is spelled out as a basic problem both in its etiology and how it influences behavior. The leader should impress the group with the importance and meaning of distrust in the group members' lives. This does not mean that the distrust can be dispelled or worked through at this point. In fact, in the preparatory phase, little would be gained by attempting to establish trust artificially. It is proper, however, for the leader to point out the elements of distrust that he observes within the group. He should also point out, without attempting to convince or assure, that he, as well as the group members, will have to earn each others' trust.

The issue for concern for others is the other side of trust. The leader helps the group to examine how trust and concern are related and how the presence of one leads to and then relies on the presence of the other. Again, the group members should not be urged to feel concern for others but they should begin to see why it is important and how it can develop.

4. *Self-Responsibility Is a Primary Goal.* The most difficult aspect of group work with disruptive youth is the learning of self-responsibility. The use of the existential concepts of choice, guilt, and anxiety is a helpful approach in this respect (de Beauvoir, 1946). The group members can be taught that guilt and anxiety are a normal and, in fact, necessary condition in interpersonal situations where choices must be made. This concept can be conveyed to the group through illustration. For example: suppose one had to choose between visiting a sick friend in the hospital or keeping a date to go to a movie with a girlfriend. Whatever decision is made, and no matter how understanding the girlfriend and the sick friend are, one of them would have to be disappointed. The appreciation of this disappointment is guilt; but this kind of guilt is not pathological and it is something one must learn to accept. In the

example cited the guilt is quite mild and not troublesome but when the choices are more difficult, the guilt becomes more intense. Without the guilt we are sociopaths, an incipient problem of disruptive adolescents. Consequently, a group leader attempts to help the group members not to be afraid of the guilt and anxiety that accompany human decisions. This is accomplished during the initial phase of the group's life by using choice points as they come up: When should the sessions be scheduled? What should the ground rules be? Where should people sit? etc. The objective is for the members to learn that there is always a choice to be made, that the choice involves others, and most importantly, that an individual can control the choice he makes. Like the other points that are made during the preparatory phase, the process of what is happening is made explicit didactically.

5. *Problem Solving Skills Are Learned.* Disruptive adolescents' problem solving skills, generally, are inappropriate and self-defeating. To make good choices in conflict situations, they must relearn the method of problem solving. A number of techniques can be used towards this end. Two such techniques are problem joining and stop action. Problem joining is demonstrating that a group member can assist other members with problems because he has or had problems with similar elements. As individuals talk, the leader delineates, compares, distinguishes, and summarizes with an emphasis on the similarities among the group members' experiences. Stop action is role playing a problem to the point of critical action. The group then discusses possible solutions and the rationales for each proposed

alternative. The proposed solutions are then role played with an ensuing discussion of how each solution felt. Whatever techniques are used, the important point is to help the members understand the skills and their use.

It is a mistake to assume that disruptive youth have the necessary social attitudes and skills to function effectively but can't or won't use them merely for psychological reasons. These skills and attitudes must be learned. The use of the process described above, during the early stages of group counseling, can shortcut the otherwise long, arduous, and often frustrating task of social relearning that disruptive youth must go through if they are to change. These social handicaps must be recognized and the gaps filled if the group and its members are to grow. Such a preparatory phase—which focuses on handicaps and which employs a combined didactic and process approach—can be an effective way of shortening the relearning process.

REFERENCES

de Beauvoir, S., Le Sang des autres. New York, N.Y.: French and European Publications, 1946.

Kahn, R., The delinquent's ability to use information to modify his goals, British Journal of Criminology, 2 (1) (1971):63-72

Persons, R. W., The Mosher Guilt Scale: Theoretical formulation, research, review and normative data, Journal of projective techniques and personality assessment, 34(4) (1970) 266-70.

Redl, F. R. and Wineman, D. Children Who Hate. Glenco, Ill.: The Free Press (1951).

Truax, C. B.; Wargo, D. G.; Volksdorf, N. R., Antecedents to outcome in group counseling with institutionalized juvenile delinquents, Journal of Abnormal Psychology. 76 (1970):2 35-42.

28. FAMILY THERAPY
Gerald H. Zuk

Peter Schwarzburg

Family therapy studies of the past dozen years, as a recent review establishes,[1] have predominantly reflected the psychoanalytic viewpoint, even though striking departures from psychoanalytic theory and technique have been made by family therapists. For the most part, writers on technique[2,7] have essentially adhered to the view that to promote beneficial change in patients the therapist must formulate and communicate insights and work through unconscious resistances. Even such departures from psychoanalytic technique as those described by Satir[8] and Minuchin[9] recently seem to this writer fundamentally insight-centered.

Among major contributors to family therapy theory and practice today, only Haley[10] has offered a clear alternative to the "insight-centered model," although he is joined to an extent by Jackson[11] and Brodey,[12] using somewhat different approaches. Haley maintains that the therapist secures beneficial change when he enforces a dominant *position* vis-a-vis patient; that is, to the extent he controls the relationship, decides what its goals shall be, and parries the patient's attempts to undermine his control. The therapist is skillful at setting up paradoxical situations in which the patient thinks he can "win" against the therapist, but loses. In the losing, the patient comes to accept the therapist's control and direction and changes accordingly.

As a result of experience in family therapy over the past five years, I am convinced that beneficial change, as Haley suggests, is a creative outcome of a struggle for control between the therapist and family members, but I believe that the skillful setting-up of paradoxical situations is not sufficient as an explanation of change in family therapy, although it does provide a useful basis to consider what does bring about change. This paper will describe a technique which uses

sources of therapeutic leverage believed unique to family therapy, although applications are possible in marital and, to a lesser extent, in group therapy. The technique arises specifically from the fact that family therapy is the transaction of a therapist with at least two or more persons who have had an extensive history of relating to one another.

Preliminary descriptions of technique and theoretical framework have been given elsewhere.[13,14] A cornerstone of the technique is a definition of family therapy as follows: *it is the technique that explores and attempts to shift the balance of pathogenic relating among family members so that new forms of relating become possible.* This definition presumes Jackson's notion[15] that the family is a homeostatic system in which change in one part is likely to effect changes in other parts.

Another cornerstone of the technique that will be described in this paper is the fact that the expression of conflict in family therapy is like that in no other form of therapy, and that conflict generates the energy required to shift fixed patterns of relating among family members. The therapist must be an expert in searching out the main issues in the family, in keeping these issues in focus, and in exploring the sources and intensity of disagreement. Only in family therapy do patients come with an established history of conflict and with well-developed means for expressing or disguising it.

In the more comprehensive of the preliminary papers,[14] I described go-between process in family therapy in four variations rather commonly encountered. In two of the variations the initiative in conducting go-between process rests with the therapist. In the other two variations the initiative resides with the family members; that is, they conducted go-between process "against" the therapist as a means to forestall his attempts to control and direct the treatment. In this paper I hope to take up in much greater detail the steps in the go-between process and describe the theoretical structure in which the process is grounded.

Go-Between Process: Its Terms and Some Dimensions

In the sections to follow, terms and some dimensions of go-between process will be elaborated: (1) from the point of view of the therapist vis-a-vis family; (2) in the context of the family's defensive tactics; and (3) in the context of "phases" of treatment, specifically onset and termination.

From the Viewpoint of Therapist vis-a-vis Family

The therapist conducts go-between process when: *Term 1*—(*a*) He probes issues in the family, establishes the existence of conflict by eliciting expressions of disagreement, and encourages the open expression of disagreement. (*b*) He exposes and otherwise resists the family's efforts to deny or disguise disagreement. (*c*) He encourages the expression of recent or current disagreement rather than rehashes of old. (*d*) He encourages expression of conflict between members who are *present* rather than absent from the treatment session.

Term 1 sets conditions for the therapist's encouragement of expression of conflict. Families differ greatly in the extent to which they will express it: some appear only too eager to do so; others are most reluctant. The therapist must be as wary of the first type of these families as the second, for the first type often generates a lot of superficial "noisy" disagreement, and frequently deeper sources are disguised. In these families, members will engage in a great deal of

mutual recrimination—bitterness, anger, and hostility are openly expressed. But the process might be labeled a "pseudohostility." "Wynne[16] has used this term and means by it a shared defense against recognizing feelings of tenderness, affection, or sexual attraction, but I use it here to mean the expression of hostility as a mask for a more pervasive, deeper-lying hostility. A "pseudohostility" may be directed by one family member against another toward whom the first does not really feel the greatest animosity, but who is a convenient scapegoat.

A second, contrasting group of families will deny disagreements and even develop elaborate means for disguising them. Some of these families will appear genuinely puzzled when the therapist calls attention to sources of conflict. Family members appear confused, pained, even deeply hurt if the therapist persists in pointing out conflict. The members pride themselves on their rational approach to the solution of family problems, on their ability to find answers acceptable to all. Even from themselves they skillfully hide the fact that they simply have failed to deal with major problem areas—have swept them under the rug, as it were.

Because memory for detail is likely to be still fresh and emotions running high, the therapist conducting go-between process encourages families to talk about recent conflict as opposed to old. Sometimes therapists will encounter families whose members prefer to talk about their past problems, but this may be a skillful gambit to introduce doubt and uncertainty into the treatment situaon—i.e., members have difficulty recalling precisely what was said, who was present, and so on. The therapist will have to judge how much of this "recollection" to allow, and in general will tend to discourage its expression.

Therapists will also encounter family

members who prefer to talk about their conflict with a family member, relative, or friend who is not present in the treatment session. Since this process also tends to introduce doubt and uncertainty, the therapist conducting go-between process will in general tend to discourage its expression. Too much control is left in the hands of the member who presents his side of the disagreement. There will be times, to be sure, when the therapist will allow this expression, but only if he thinks it will "open up" sources of conflict between family members who are present.

The therapist conducts go-between process when: *Term 2(a)*— He selects specific disagreements as especially worthy of discussion, rejects others as unworthy, and resists the family's expected efforts to establish its own rules of priority. (*b*) This selection is part of his move into the role of the go-between. He then seeks to establish his authority in the role and resists the family's expected efforts to displace him.

In a previous paper[14] on the topic it was stated that

In family therapy the go-between may be very active, intrusive and comfronting or inactive and passive. He may move into the role of go-between by the device of attacking two parties he hopes to make into principals; or he may move into the role by calmly pointing out a difference between two parties. On the other hand, he may become a go-between by refusing to take sides in a disputed; that has erupte or he may become one by presenting a new point of view in a dispute (p. 165).

The point here is that in the role of go-between the therapist is constantly structuring, and directing, the treatment situation.

A case will be presented to illustrate the terms of go-between process, but Term 2 in particular. A family was referred for therapy on the basis that a young daughter's poor school performance seemed to have origins in disturbed family living. The family was composed of the daughter, 9 years old, her brother, 13 years old, her 40-year-old mother, and 56-year-old father. The family was of Catholic, Irish-German, and upper-lower religious, ethnic, and social status origins. The mother had completed high school, but the father only the fourth grade, and the difference in educational level was a serious source of conflict between them. The father was a steady job holder who was married previously and had been involved in sexual misconduct with other women in his marriages. He considered his main problem to be his explosive temper and the fact that he could not get his children to be respectful to him. The mother began drinking heavily in her late teens, and referred to herself as an alcoholic up until five years ago, when she gave up drinking and joined Alcoholics Anonymous. There was also evidence of some sexual promiscuity on her part before her marriage to her husband 14 years ago, but none since.

The mother reported that at times she believed she was losing her mind. She expressed bitterness toward her husband, who she said deserted her for another woman about the time she was pregnant with her now 13-year-old son. She believed the marriage started to deteriorate since that time. She expressed fear of her husband's quick temper, as did the children. Her son openly expressed bitter resentment of his father and hoped that his mother would separate.

A special source of resentment of the father was that his wife had taken their son into their bedroom, avowedly to attend to him more effectively during an illness, and had not moved him out in several months. She asked her husband to sleep in another room and he complied. Another source of the father's resentment was the chaotic condition of the home, although as it turned out he contributed to the chaos by bringing and storing in the house all sorts of odd, useless objects.

The therapist had little difficulty getting family members to verbalize conflict. (This was one of the "noisy" type families referred to earlier which seem only too eager to express their feelings.) But the conflict did not seem to go anywhere for the first few sessions: each member expressed opposition to another in such a way as to put the other in a bad light, and each seemed to know the means to put the other on the defensive. However, in the fourth session there was a "break" which the therapist was quick to take advantage of, and which will illustrate how the therapist conducting go-between process selects certain types of disagreements as especially worthy of discussion and rejects other types.

A week or so prior to the fourth session the father brought home a bicycle that was given to him by a friend. He told his daughter the bike was hers, that he had bought it from his friend for $10 and that he had had it repaired at an additional cost. His daughter accepted the bike and rode it, but it soon broke down. She took the bike for repair but it broke down again, and again she returned the bike for repair, threatening the repairman that if he did not fix it properly this time or if he refused to fix it he would start screaming at the top of her voice right there in his shop. The man fixed the bike. But later it broke down again and the girl decided to give it to her brother. Her brother repaired the bike and rode it for awhile before it again broke down and was put away in storage. In the meantime, the daughter got her mother to promise to buy her a new bike as a Christmas present.

As this incident was related mainly by the daughter to the therapist, it was apparent that it met the criteria of Term 1 of go-between process in that disagreement was expressed about how the bike was purchased and who was to use it, all members involved were present and capable of telling their versions, and the incident had occurred recently and was still fresh in the memory. Because these criteria were met and because the incident seemed to epitomize so well the way conflict was handled (or rather mishandled) in the family, the therapist selected it for special attention. (A not insignificant factor influencing his decision was that the incident was one about which the father could talk with some show of control, that is, without such excitement or emotion that he would frighten other family members into quiet submission.)

The therapist specifically moved into the role of go-between by stating that he was puzzled by what actually happened in the bike incident and that in order to clear up the confusion he would ask each member to tell his version of the story. The therapist then acted to establish his *authority* as the go-between by indicating that he would not allow interference in the telling of stories. He was thus introducing an unusual structure for the family: they were not used to letting each talk without frequent interruption, for one thing, and without efforts at intimidation, for another.

First, the fuller details of the daughter's story were elicited. When she came to the point at which she threatened the bike repairman with screaming if he did not agree to fix the bike again, the therapist said he thought she was using one of her father's favorite tactics of intimidation. Then the son was directed to relate his story. (He counter-suggested that his father should speak next, but this was disallowed since it was believed by the therapist that it would have helped to subtly undermine the type of procedure he had established.) The son voiced his resentment that the bike was not given to him originally. He said he knew he would get it eventually because it was bound to break down, his sister would come to him to fix it, and then he would be able to claim at least part ownership. He complained that his father never gave him anything—giving the bike to his sister was just another example of the father's stinginess toward him.

In telling his story, the father stressed his good intentions and expressed resentment that they were doubted. He told how he had bargained skillfully with the original owner of the bike to get it for the lowest price, and, if possible, for nothing. He told how he had taken the bike for renovation to a place he knew would do it for little money. He said he fully supported his daughter when she insisted the bike should be repaired properly by the repairman.

When it came the mother's turn to tell her story, she ruefully stated it was incidents such as this one that sometimes made her doubt her sanity. She said she actually felt relieved and reassured that the therapist had also expressed doubt and uncertainty about what really happened. In the following excerpt from the fourth session, the mother relates how her husband and children frequently befuddle her.

Therapist: You've said that two or three times—that you were losing your sanity. What do you mean by that?

Mother: I told you when I first came here I had questions about my own sanity. When you live under these conditions and you hear it morning, noon and night, after a while you do question your own sanity. Am I hearing this, or am I imagining it?

Therapist: What's the worst part of the whole thing? A lot is going on. A lot of it looks to be kind of harmless.

Daughter: (referring to her brother) He teases me—with the cat.

Therapist: Teasing is teasing. I'm asking your mother.

Mother: You mean of this bickering back and forth?

Therapist: Whatever it is that drives you crazy.

Mother: Well, they'll tell me one thing and then there's a twist to the story. You saw it yourself. Each one told a slightly different version. After a while you just can't follow it. All these thoughts get in my head and I think, Oh my God, am I imagining this or is this so? I find that the three of them—my husband the children—are very much alike in this bit. Like even the interruption! I don't think you could say I interrupted here today, but they do and it's constant. Nobody shows each other courtesy enough to hear each other out. . . . They all have to get heard and they all consider their own feelings more important than anybody else's.

This excerpt and the description of the bike incident should show that the therapist as go-between provides the family with a new context in which to express and examine their conflicts. As go-between he acts as the "broker" in the context—for example, he insures that all parties understand his rules for examining the conflict, and he insures that all parties are fairly dealt with. He aims to fashion a context that is different from the established pathogenic patterns of relating among family members. Temporarily freed by the therapist's action from a vicious repetitive pattern, the family may experience the good feeling of more positive and productive relating and explore the possibility of new means to relate in the future.

In his excellent paper on marriage therapy, Haley[17] notes that the therapist is unavoidably a go-between or "broker." He states that the mere presence of the therapist as a third party requires that the spouses deal differently with each other than they have in the past—particularly because the therapist is a third party who is a presumed expert in unraveling the meaning of human interaction. He points out that the marriage therapist may relabel or redefine the activities of the spouses with each other, and he may label the treatment situation as unique in other respects—e.g., as having rules which would not hold in ordinary situations.

The therapist conducts go-between process when: *Term 3*—(*a*) He sides, either by implications or intentionally, with one family member against another in a particular disagreement. (*Siding is unavoidable,* for even if the therapist thinks he is maintaining a strictly neutral or objective position, the family still judges him to be partial. The problem of the therapist is to decide when and with whom to side *intentionally*—i. e., as a therapeutic tactic—and to decide with whom the family *believes* him to be siding.) (*b*) He may side with or against the entire family unit in a disagreement, as well as with or against single family members.

Haley, in his paper on marriage therapy, notes that a therapist cannot make a neutral statement:

. . . his voice, his expression, the context, or the mere act of choosing a particular statement to inquire about introduces a directiveness into the situation (p. 225). (Haley continues) When the therapist is being directive, coalition patterns are being defined and redefined, and a crucial aspect of this type of therapy is continually changing coalition patterns between therapist and each spouse.

This statement is equally true of family therapy: the therapist's most innocuous-sounding comment will be judged by family members as clear evidence that he favors the "position" of one member agains another. Family members will *act* toward the therapist as if he were siding, and even *interpret* him as siding, however he may choose to deny that such was his intention. (It is also true, to be sure, that therapists are rarely fully aware of all the ways in which they *actually may be siding* with one member against another, and may become defensive when this is *fairly* brought to their attention.)

In my opinion, not only is siding

unavoidable in family therapy, it is a legitimate tactic of therapeutic value in shifting the balance of pathogenic relating among family members. *By judicious siding, the therapist can tip the balance in favor of more productive relating, or at least disrupt a chronic pattern of pathogenic relating.* By siding with one family member in a disagreement with another, the therapist throws weight to the position of the former. The effect of the therapist siding *against* all members often is for the members to minimize the extent of the disagreement, but it also moves them to examine more carefully the bases of the disagreement. The effect of the therapist siding *with* all members is often subtly disorganizing, for then they will become confused as to what their own position should be vis-a-vis the therapist—in other words, it tends to undermine any stubborn shared family resistance to the therapist's interventions.

It is probably unwise for the therapist to give the message that he consistently sides with one member against others. It is advantageous for him to keep the family guessing as to *whether* he will engage in siding and *what* the tactics of his siding will be. The therapist must retain flexibility in the face of strenuous efforts by the family to get him to side predictably with one member or another with the result that he becomes, in my opinion, a less effective therapeutic agent.

In the fourth treatment session with the family that has been described here, there were several instances of intentional siding by the therapist. For instance, he engaged in siding when enforcing his rule that family members could not interrupt each other in telling the story of the bike incident, for he did not enforce the rule *with equal vigor* for all members. For example, the therapist tended to halt the attempted interruptions of the father with considerably more vigor than such attempts of other family members, particularly when his attempts were directed against his son. In this the therapist showed an inclination to side against the father. One reason for this type of siding was that it seemed necessary to the therapist to guard against the danger that the father would undermine the therapist's rules of procedure by means of an outburst of temper. A correlated reason was to encourage other family members to speak their feelings more freely, especially the son, who was furious at his father for being continually browbeaten by him. In brief, the therapist was intentionally siding *against* the father and *with* other family members in enforcing his rules of procedure for the exposition of the bike incident.

In the fifth treatment session with the family there was a good example of the therapist siding first with one member and then another in a disagreement as a therapeutic tactic to tip the balance of pathogenic relating. The father had accused his wife, in a typically inferential manner, of sexual misconduct with other men in the course of her work in Alcoholics Anonymous. The therapist encouraged the father to talk about his feelings of anger and jealousy which he, again characteristically, strenuously denied having. Turning then to the wife, the therapist asked her to respond to her husband's feelings of anger and jealousy based on suspicion. In confirming the husband's *feelings*, despite his lack of confirmation of actual promiscuity by the wife, the therapist was implicitly siding with the husband against his wife. He was suggesting, in effect, that the husband's feelings were genuine and valid, and that the wife was bound to consider and respond to them. The following excerpt from the fifth session is relevant.

Therapist: The question is—your husband is showing jealousy.

Mother: Right. I've said this from the beginning.

Therapist: And you are responding in a funny kind of way. I don't know whether you're encouraging it or discouraging it.

Mother: You would have to understand AA. I don't know if you do, but each and every one of us help each other out in maintaining sobriety.

Father: But a man don't help no woman, and the woman don't help no man! A man helps a man and a woman helps a woman!

Therapist: Yes! Your husband is raising the question of men in particular: jealousy of the men. And you are not responding to that. You're putting it in terms of humanity. . . .

Mother: I've given in to every whim about jealousy. I've stopped kissing my kids and stopped hugging them.

Therapist: But you're still sleeping with your son.

Mother: He's in my bedroom, yes. . . .

Therapist: Maybe you've stopped kissing him, but you haven't stopped sleeping with him.

Father: Her son is not sleeping with her; he's sleeping in a twin bed.

Therapist: Are you defending her too now? (Laughs) Whose side are you on? I'm not implying anything. . . . This has been something that you brought up here today.

Father: That's right.

Therapist: You're angry about it.

Father: I'm not angry about it.

Therapist: You say you're not and I say you are.

Shortly after this exchange in which, by encouraging the husband to express his jealousy and by confronting the wife with her evasiveness, the therapist appears to side with the husband, the therapist then turns the tables: he now confronts the husband in such a way as to appear to side with the wife.

Therapist: . . . Is that what you're saying to him: "I need companionship. I need somebody"?

Mother: I certainly do need somebody . . .

Therapist: "I need my son close to me because I get something from him that I don't get from somebody else." This I think is what your wife seems to me to say. She says, "I need something too. And whether you're jealous about it— well, that's just too bad. I need those things." That's what she's saying. . . .

Father: Well, I understand that and I want to try my best to give her what she wants!

By siding alternatively with father and then mother, the therapist believed he "shook up" their relationship and facilitated open expression of a bitter conflict between them that had been raging for some time, but in a rather devious form. In the case of the father, the therapist insisted that he acknowledge his anger and jealousy in the presence of his family. In the case of the mother, the therapist insisted she express her yearning for warmth and emotional closeness. The therapist made it difficult for the parents to employ their usual techniques to avoid confronting each other with their actual feelings and attitudes. He promoted a more direct confrontation than was typical for them in their relationship, i.e., forced them to put aside the usual means both had developed to keep each other at a distance, and opened up the possibility of relating in a new way.

This discussion of siding and the illustrations given should make it quite evident how complex an issue it is in family therapy. Certainly related to it, for example, are the issues of transference and countertransference, although siding is not simply to be explained by either or both of these concepts because as conceived here, it means an *intentional* alignment of the therapist with the position of one family member against another for the purpose of tipping the balance of the relationship between them.

The Family's Defensive Tactics vis-à-vis Therapist

Families exhibit a marvelous array of tactics which serve to forestall the therapist in his conduct of go-between process. The therapist must be alert to these tactics and act to circumvent them. Three major defensive tactics may be listed. In the first, family members seek to lead the therapist astray by subtle denials or evasions of his allegations of conflict. For example, the therapist may call attention to an issue between two members on which there seems latent conflict. The members deny the allegation; they say they have never disagreed on the issue. (Technically, they may be telling the truth in the sense that they may never have actually *openly* disagreed on the issue.) The therapist is called on to either hit on some device to "split the team'" or give up the issue he introduced—an often not insignificant loss of face. As a face-saving device, I sometimes return to the issue introduced when it seems less anxiety-provoking. This is a kind of therapeutic oneupmanship in that it defines the fact that the members have formed a coalition against the therapist, informs them of his awareness of the fact, and implies a sympathetic understanding of the needs that caused them to join forces against him.

A second defensive tactic of the family vis-a-vis therapist is encountered when a member assumes the role of spokesman and consistently comments on or explains the meaning of the family to the therapist. This role seems most often assumed in families by the mother, but sometimes it is assumed by the father, and infrequently by one of the children. In effect, the family spokesman is in the role of a go-between as long as he occupies a go-between role, the therapist's capacity to assume it is impaired. Sometimes the therapist will decide early in treatment to prohibit a member from taking the role of family spokesman; sometimes, however, he will temporize and permit the member to be the spokesman in the hope of learning more about the key dynamics of the family. In either case, it is necessary for the therapist to identify the family spokesman early and restrain or check him at some time in the course of treatment.

A third defensive tactic is encountered when family members act toward the therapist as if he was a particular type of go-between, or when they act toward him as if he were consistently siding with a particular member against others. As an example of this type of tactic, the father in the family whose case has been presented would accuse his wife of some misconduct, then turn to the therapist and ask, "Am I right or am I wrong?" He addressed the therapist as he might a judge who would decide a case, somewhat rigging his question to get the answer he wanted, which was to be in effect. "Yes, Mr. ———, you are perfectly right."

My practice, as therapist, was to respond to the father in one of three ways: (1) state that I was not a judge and that the purpose of family therapy was not to decide who in the family was right and who was wrong; (2) ignore the father's question and change the subject: or (3) not answer the question directly, but turn to the wife and ask her to comment on the husband's accusation. By means of these responses the therapist takes steps to turn aside the father's attempt to cast the therapist in the role of the family judge, a particularly inflexible type of go-between in family therapy. In the third response, in which the therapist asked the wife to comment on her husband's accusation, there was an implicit message given, to the effect: "There may be something to your husband's accusation and I would like you to defend yourself." The message could be interpreted as evidence that the therapist was mildly siding with the husband against the wife, but evidence not nearly so strong as that initially desired by the husband in his aim to cast the therapist as the family judge.

Change at Onset and Termination of Family Therapy

Go-between process constitutes, in the writer's opinion, an alternative to the psychoanalytical insight-centered model to explain the beneficial changes that may occur in family therapy. Onset and termination are key phases in relation to the issue of change. At onset two points at issue between the family and therapist are the questions "Is there something wrong with us?" and "If there is something wrong, how will you treat us as a family?" The family and therapist may be viewed as opponents on these questions. The therapist begins to conduct go-between process when he explores them with the family for areas of expected disagreement.

Some families, in their eagerness to convince the therapist at the onset that there is nothing wrong with them as units, will actually bring about some improvement. The change need not be perceived as the result of insight, but as a function of the "bargaining" transaction between family and therapist on the question, "Is there something wrong with us?" The family changes *in order to achieve a change* in the therapist's expected position. The change is calculated to be the least necessary to secure a change in the expected position of the therapist. By means of judicious siding, by taking the role of go-between, or by shifting between these two positions, the therapist hopes to control the "bargaining" transaction in accordance with his therapeutic goals.

By the tenth therapy session in the case of the family described in this paper, beneficial symptomatic changes had already begun to occur. In the tenth session the mother reported she had begun to clean up the mess in her house and had requested the cooperation of her husband and children in doing so. The mother also reported that she had moved her son back into his own bedroom and that her husband was once again occupying the bed that adjoined hers. It also became evident that her husband had been less verbally abusive to her and her children during the preceding couple of weeks.

I suggest that these beneficial changes in

the onset phase constituted moves to try to move the therapist from a position the family members believed he was occupying, and that the mother considered the therapy a means to punish her husband for his past misdeeds, and a means to persuade the therapist of the righteousness of her "cause" vis-à-vis her husband. When in the early sessions it became apparent that the therapist was not easily being sold on her viewpoint, she was compelled to introduce a more subtle means of persuasion. She would show the therapist that *she* could change but her husband could not, and thus the lack of a true foundation for the marriage would become even more apparent. It did not quite enter into her calculations that her husband *would* change in relation to (or as a result of) her own change, and that this change would also be of a positive nature.

It has been my experience that sometimes dramatic improvement may follow upon *the therapist's notice of intention to terminate treatment because there has been no significant progress.* When the therapist puts the family on such notice, he is using go-between process in the sense that he is siding against the family as a whole. He employs this powerful confrontation because he is convinced that only by means of it can he undercut a powerful family resistance to change.

I have had the privilege of seeing, both in cases of my own and of colleagues, dramatic improvement—even including the clearing-up of bizarre symptoms in schizophrenics—following the therapist's notice of intention to terminate. It may be speculated here also that *what has produced the change is actually the family's strenuous effort to prevent change;* that is, a strenuous effort by the family to frustrate the therapist's avowed intention to withdraw from treatment. In confronting the family with his intention to terminate, the therapist conducts go-between process in accordance with Term 3 stated in this paper: i.e., siding against the whole family as a means to shake up the system.

Summary

Family therapy is defined in this paper as the treatment that examines and attempts to shift the balance of pathogenic relating among family members so that new forms of relating become possible. Go-between process is described as a technique that may be employed in family therapy to promote the shift of pathogenic relating. This process is grounded in the fact that the unique aspect of family therapy is that the so-called patients have had an extensive history of relating to one another.

The three terms of go-between process as conducted by the therapist are: (1) his definition of issues on which the family is in serious conflict and the expression of that conflict; (2) his taking the role of go-between or "broker" in conflicts; (3) his siding with or against the family members in conflicts. As the therapist moves from one step to the next and back again, he exerts a critical leverage on the fixed patterns of relating among family members.

Families display a number of tactics which seem aimed at forestalling the therapist in his conduct of go-between process—in effect, they are a kind of counter go-between process conducted by the family. Three such tactics are: (1) the family denies or is evasive about the therapist's allegations of conflicts;(2) with the complicity of other family members, one becomes the family spokesman and thus a kind of go-between who blocks the therapist's access to his critical role; and (3) the family attempts to trap the therapist into becoming an over-rigid type of go-between, such as the family judge, or accuses him of siding unfairly with one family member against others.

It is a main hypothesis of this paper that families change in order to forestall the therapist's expected demands for much greater change, or in order to foil his other attempts to control the relationship. Illustrations of such change are given in which the *phase* of treatment seemed also a critical factor; that is, whether treatment was at the onset phase or termination. The notion of change entertained here is believed consonant with Haley's,[10],[17] which was designed to contrast with the insight-centered psychoanalytic model.

REFERENCES

1. Zuk, G. H., and Rubinstein, D.: "A Review of Concepts in the Study of Treatment of Families of Schizophrenics," in Boszormenyi-Nagy, I., and Framo, J. L. eds.: *Intensive Family Therapy.* New York: Paul B. Hoeber Inc., Medical Division of Harper & Row 1965, pp. 1-31.

2. Ackerman. J. W.: "Family-Focused Therapy of Schizophrenia," in Scher, S. C., and Davis, H. R. eds.: *Out- Patient Treatment of Schizophrenia.* New York: Grune & Stratton Inc., 1960, pp. 156-73.

3. Bell, J. E.: *Family Group Therapy.* Washington, D.C.: Public Health Monograph No. 64, Department of Health, Education, and Welfare, 1961.

4. Bowen, M.: Family Psychotherapy. *Amer. J. Orthopsychiat* 31 (161):42-60.

5. Jackson, D. D., and Weakland, J. H.: Conjoint Family Therapy: Some Considerations on Theory, Technique and Results. *Psychiatry* 24 (1961):30-45.

6. Whitaker, C. A.; Felder, R. E.; and Warkentin, J.: and "Countertransference in the Family Treatment of Schizophrenia," in Boszormenyi-Nagy, I., and Framo, J. L. eds.: *Intensive Family Therapy.* New York: Paul B. Hoeber Inc., Medical Division of Harper & Row, 1965, pp. 323-41.

7. Wynne, L. C.: "Some Indications and Contraindications for Exploratory Family Therapy," in Boszormenyi- Nagy, I., and Framo, J. L. eds.: *Intensive Family Therapy,* New York: Paul B. Hoeber Inc., Medical Division of Harper & Row, 1965, pp. 289-322.

8. Satir, V.: *Conjoint family therapy.* Palo Alto, Calif.: Science and Behavior Books, Inc., 1964.

9. Minuchin, S.: Conflict-Resolution Family Therapy, *Psychiatry* 28 (1965):278-86.

10. Haley, J., *Strategies of psychotherapy,* New York: Grune & Stratton Inc., 1963.

11. Jackson, D. D.: "Aspects of Conjoint Family Therapy." in Zuk, G. H., and Boszormenyi-Nagy, I. eds.: *Family Therapy and Disturbed Families* Palo Alto, Calif: Science and Behavior Books, Inc., to be published.

12. Brodey, W. M.: "A Cybernetic Approach to Family Therapy," in Zuk, G. H., and Boszormenyi-Nagy, I. eds.: *Family Therapy and Disturbed Families,* Palo Alto, Calif: Science and Behavior Books, Inc., to be published.

13. Zuk, G. H.: "Preliminary Study of the Go-Between Process in Family Therapy," in *Proceedings of the 73rd Annual Convention of the American Psychological Association,* Washington, D.C.: American Psychological Association, 1965, pp. 291-92.

14. Zuk, G. H.: The Go-Between Process in Family Therapy, *Family Process* 5 (1966):162-78.

15. Jackson, D. D.: The Question of Family Homeostasis, *Psychiat. Quart.* 31 suppl. (1957) :79-90.

16. Wynne, L. C.: The Study of Intrafamilial Alignments and Splits in Exploratory Family Therapy, in Ackerman, N. W.: Beatman, F.; and Sherman, S. N. eds.: *Exploring the Base for Family Therapy.* New York: Family Service Association of America, 1961, pp. 95-115.

17. Haley, J.: Marriage Therapy, *Arch. Gen. Psychiat.* 8 (1963):213-34.

29. EMOTIONAL EDUCATION IN THE CLASSROOM
A Modern Psychoanalytic Model

William J. Kirman

Vasilije Knezevic

It is becoming increasingly clear that pro-phylactic as well as remedial emotional education for the vast majority of students in our schools will not take place in a practitioner's office—indeed not even in the Guidance office. The number of students is too great and the number of available professional clock hours too small to permit popular experience of a one-to-one counseling relationship.

There is, however, one professional person who comes in contact with virtually every child in our communities—namely the school teacher. The teacher is ideally suited by virtue of his relationship with both students and parents to help promote emotional growth and maturity.

Accordingly, a theory of emotional education is here presented along with specific techniques for its implementation that will be of interest to the classroom teacher.

Emotional Education in the Ongoing Classroom

Modern psychoanalysis, with a greater flexibility than classical analysis and a more sophisticated structure than other psychotherapies is ideally suited for application to the classroom. With certain modifications in the analytic model and some elaboration in technique, modern psychoanalysis is extremely useful in helping students on the road to emotional maturity. Abandonment of the curriculum is not advocated since it is not our goal to encourage emotionally healthy but intellectually deficient students. The application here envisioned calls upon the teacher to sustain a sensible role in the cognitive development of the student while at the same time promoting emotional growth in the classroom

When modern psychoanalysis is correctly applied to the ongoing classroom situation both students and teachers should accelerate their intellectual and emotional growth. While classes in emotional education are valuable and should be included in the curriculum as separate courses, our aim is more broadly defined. We are not advocating a simple application of group therapy nor a special class in emotional education for students in a school or college setting. In the best sense of the word we are dealing with the "whole" student—intellectually, physically, socially, morally. He is encouraged to develop and maximize his potential in these areas while in the classroom. We are proposing to accomplish what educators have been advocating for many years. And we propose to accomplish this within the framework of a tested and comprehensive system—modern psychoanalysis.

Transference

The existence of transference in the student-teacher relationship has been insufficiently appreciated in theorizing about how and why people learn. Just as Freud saw transference as the wind which drives the therapeutic mill, so the motivation to stay in school or drop out, to score high grades or low, to learn out of love or fear, is often determined by the emotional significance the teacher has for the student. The question we need to ask ourselves as teachers is not whether we wish our students to develop a transference, but rather how we can deal with it effectively once it develops, since it occurs automatically to a greater or lesser degree in most students.

To many teachers transference might seem to interfere with teaching. Freud, himself, originally thought that transference in the analytic setting was a hindrance—that it distracted patients from the job at hand of recalling memories. Yet, over the years analysts have increasingly come to recognize that transference manifestations are important forms of communication that should be utilized to expedite the therapeutic process. The same is true of transference manifestations in the classroom. They are the sine qua non for the teacher if he is to gain a significant role in influencing the student's thinking and feeling. If there is little transference then little will be meaningful in the classroom and little can generalize to the outside. It is important to recognize that once the transference is established the teacher has the most powerful tool ever discovered to influence the lives of students.

This influence can be brought to bear upon students in a variety of positive and negative ways. It is a two-edged tool that can be used to corrupt and hurt as well as to help and build. While under the influence of a positive transference students may flood the teacher with warmth and admiration, offer to perform any number of personal services and at times appear a willing partner to a master-slave relationship.

It is equally important that the teacher like the analyst employ the transference to achieve a constructive, long-range goal for the student and not yield to the wish for personal exploitation. It is the teacher's responsibility to help the students to utilize their positive feelings for him, in a way that enables them to maximize their affective and cognitive functioning.

Transference feelings toward the teacher are similar if less intense than in the analytic situation. Due to the teacher's actual role in evaluation and the fact that his actions outside the classroom proper (grading, passing, failing) do affect the student's life, the teacher is more likely, at first, to represent the more powerful of the two parents. This, of course, may vary with the actual personality of a teacher. Accordingly, the challenge to his authority may come early in

the relationship, often thinly disguised as a wish to learn. This challenge must be met head on and the teacher's authority clearly established. Otherwise students will rightly feel that their hostile impulses will damage the teacher and fellow students. If the teacher can meet this challenge effectively and at the same time set an example of controlled behavior himself an atmosphere is established where it is safe to deal with angry feelings.

A. *Types of Transference*

The patterns of transference follow the level of ego development of the individual members of the class. Some students whose lives have been emotionally more fortuitous demonstrate *object transference* from the start and perceive the teacher as mother, father, or an other significant adult from childhood. This capacity for predominantly object transference is restricted to the more emotionally mature members of the class. The majority of students, however, like the majority of patients in our experience, demonstrate the kind of transference that modern psychoanalysis has stressed in its research investigations namely, *narcissistic transference*. These students, due to their emotional inability to clearly differentiate ego and object field, attribute their own feelings about themselves to the teacher and their classmates. (See Spotnitz reference.) Since the origin of these resistances is during the first two years of life (the *pre-Oedipal stage*) the techniques of modern analysis are particularly well suited to deal with them effectively. Very frequently the teacher (who must reveal himself much more than the analyst) comes to represent an aspect of the despised and idealized self for the student and is detested and worshipped accordingly. This *negative narcissistic transference* is handled as in modern analysis; namely, helping the student to accept his despised self in the teacher which in turn leads to self-acceptance. The *idealizing narcissistic transference,* however, is not analyzed; instead the student is helped to become the kind of person he admires in the teacher and the *cathexis* is encouraged to generalize from the teacher to the subject matter of the course as well. This idealizing narcissistic transference if properly utilized by the teacher can effect great influence on the students' life. It entails the most basic type of learning—learning by identification—a situation where the teacher's character, values, goals, and knowledge exert a significant influence on the student. Contrary to the suggested dictum the student emulates the teacher on the basis of "do as I do—not as I say." Students identify with what they experience—not with what they are told.

B. Facilitating the Transference Relationship

There are certain attitudes and behavior on the part of the teacher that can facilitate the development of transference. Since it is generally recommended that a positive transference be encouraged early in the term, the teacher, like the analyst, should reveal little information about himself. He should set an emotional climate of acceptance and understanding, while remaining clearly in control of the class. When a teacher loses control of a class it is very difficult to establish a meaningful transference relationship.

Most importantly, the teacher must indicate, by his manner and words, that in this class the student's life and feelings are important and that the subject matter to be covered is significant but SECONDARY. This can be done by having the students tell about themselves at the outset and by asking nonprobing neutral questions to elicit details about their daily routines and hobbies. Students will generally react with surprise and

pleasure when a teacher asks questions about how they spend their leisure time, what they eat, what movies they see, who their friends are, and why they like them. With an athletic boy the teacher may ask, not only what sports he prefers but additionally where he plays them and who are the other members of the team. After all, a good parent is interested in all details of a child's life.

A music student can be asked if he heard a particular record or stereo broadcast. A student interested in Westerns can be asked if he would like to tell about the latest episode of "Gunsmoke." It is important that these questions be asked out of genuine interest and not be insincere if a meaningful transference is to develop. The genuineness of the teacher's emotional communications are as crucial as the analyst's with his patients. The teacher should communicate that he cares, as a good parent does, about the total life of the student—his physical and emotional functioning as well as his cognitive.

In order to encourage the transference, the teacher, like the analyst, must exaggerate his own importance to the class and its importance to him and to each other. This focuses attention on the here-and-now and relegates outside events to second place. Lecturing or advising the student on how to make friends, improve relations with his father or how to be more assertive with the biology teacher all have limited value. The classroom, like the group in group therapy, must be the major laboratory experience. Fred's rule of dealing with transference before content is relevant here. The teacher must concentrate on investigating why the student cannot interact differently with his current teacher and fellow classmates and be helped to develop the necessary skills. The world outside the classroom must be seen as secondary in importance. *If the teacher wishes to help a student he must help him to change with the teacher in this particular class and at this particular time.* The interpersonal knowledge thus gained in the context of a strong transference is long remembered and generalized to the outside world as is the knowledge which occurs in analysis. If the teacher is to effect real change in his students he must renounce preaching and persuasion and concentrate on working with the transference. There should be a free climate of emotional interchange between students and teacher. All feelings are legitimate emotional interchanges within the limitations here suggested, spanning the range from hostility to love.

Initially it is important for the teacher to defer serious consideration of subject matter for a while. This does not mean the subject matter cannot be presented from the outset, but simply that emotional responses must receive their greatest priority early in the term. Premature emphasis on intellectual material discourages the development of a strong transference. Still, serious lecture material can be presented almost immediately, providing the teacher takes the emotional temperature of the class immediately following the presentation.

In the discussion that follows, however, all student communications must be responded to in terms of their affective message rather than their cognitive ones. This clearly establishes the priority in this classroom. The student correctly receives the message that while intellectual learning is proper and important, in this particular class the students' feelings are given preference. A demonstration of this kind is more convincing than explanations and reassurances about the teacher's philosophy of education.

The old argument that the home is a more powerful influence than the school and can cancel out its effectiveness is invalid. So,

too, is the argument about the limited amount of time spent in school. Since many patients have been shown to make significant progress in a one and one-half hour weekly group therapy session, the student can surely improve his functioning in a greater period of time with a teacher trained in modern analysis. It is the nature of the emotional interchange that occurs and the skill of the teacher that determines the impact of the class on a student's life—not the duration of time. A short period of time spent in a relationship that is emotionally charged and that conveys a feeling of psychological understanding has a greater impact on one's life than a longer time period lacking in these essentials.

Students should be allowed to communicate with the teacher at any time during the week, on weekends, or during vacations by letter. This freedom to communicate with the teacher during nonscheduled, nonpaid time seems to have a maturational effect and students become convinced that the teacher really cares. It also allows quiet students who do not choose to speak in class a comfortable opportunity to communicate. A useful adjunct to the classroom interacton is to encourage students to keep a daily log or reaction sheet. It is important that this activity be voluntary if it is to be therapeutic. Keeping the daily log and writing reactions to each class session serves as a kind of psychological diary which students can turn in to the teacher and receive comments back. With some students who avail themselves of this opportunity the letters may be viewed as comparable to communications in individual therapy which are complimented by the group therapy aspect of the classroom. The time the teacher devotes to this can be very rewarding in terms of student growth both emotionally and intellectually. This is a particularly effective technique for upper grade and college level students and permits the student to communicate all those important personal feelings which limited classroom time doesn't allow. In fact, some students choose letters as the major avenue of emotional communication with the teacher and are primarily interested in intellectual discussions in class. These written communications allow the student with a strong transference to "be with" the teacher even when the teacher is not physically present. In college classes this kind of detailed self-examination is sometimes a prelude to psychotherapy. The teacher's caring helps develop "basic trust" in emotionally deprived students and they often generalize it to the outside world. If one person is viewed as caring, the student may take a chance with others as well.

No student should be coerced into having an emotional experience in the classroom or into revealing anything about himself he doesn't wish to. Indeed, a small number of students are not able to tolerate the emotionally charged atmosphere that permeates the classroom here described. These students should be excused from class and encouraged to transfer into more traditionally oriented experiences since their continued presence may be nonproductive for themselves and the group. This kind of classroom experience is not good for everybody. But it seems to be good for the vast majority of people.

Resistances and Interventions

As in analysis, the student's customary defenses are brought into the classroom and, being charged with transference, become resistances, the only difference being the nature of the resistances. In psychoanalysis what is resisted is talking freely about one's life story while in the classroom the resistance serves a different function. Whereas the "cured" patient can say everything that occurs to him easily and with appropriate affect and can function the way he chooses, reality permitting, the hypothetically "ideal" student has a separate set of goals. He can come to class regularly, feel comfortable in asking and answering questions of fact, feeling, and opinion, accept mistakes in himself, his peers and his teacher and cooperate with his peers and teacher in making the class a more meaningful and enjoyable experience for all. In addition he is able to master the cognitive material of the course, earn a good grade, and move on comfortably to the next course. Though such an ideal student is undoubtedly as rare as the truly "cured" patient, it is nevertheless the goal we are striving for.

Admirable as these classroom goals may be, they are generally opposed with a good deal of energy by most students. Although there is a challenge in learning new material, and curiosity and interest are present, opposing feelings are also awakened in the classroom and these opposing forces have to be dealt with effectively.

The resistances that emerge in a class taught from the modern psychoanalytic viewpoint can be described as resistances to cognitive learning, emotional learning, forming a cooperative relationship with teacher and classmates, earning a good grade, and class termination.

A student's questions indicate his method of making contact with the teacher just as the analytic patient demonstrates his contact functioning by his questions. It would seem that only a small proportion of questions students ask indicate a genuine desire for knowledge or information. The great majority of questions are asked largely in the service of resistance. And just as in modern psychoanalysis, resistance patterns are met initially by joining and psychological reflection; so should the resistance to cognitive learning be similarly dealt with in the classroom.

The teacher must carefully distinguish between the *content* of a question and the *intent* of the questioner. Very frequently the *intent* and *content* of a student communication are at variance and thus pose a problem for the analytically trained educator. To ignore the intent of the question is to ignore the resistance and diminish the transference. *Only when the intent of the student question is to gain knowledge and information which the class is eager to hear should the teacher respond to the content.* At other times the teacher should treat the student communication in terms of the underlying resistance. He must understand why this student is asking this particular question in this particular way at this particular time. What is he trying to accomplish beyond his ostensible quest for knowledge? Does he wish to demonstrate his superiority to other students? To the teacher? Is he trying to annoy or frustrate the teacher? Is he asking to be reassured? Appreciated? Hated? Does his question have the effect of disrupting the class or of helping the class work together? Is he expressing negativism or cooperation? Is he asking the question at a time the teacher wishes to give information or is he provoking an already frustrated teacher? Is he demonstrating pitiable ignorance or does he want some personal opinion confirmed to bolster his self-confidence? Or does he genuinely wish to know the answer to his question so that he can learn?

Since much of life is routine the student must be equipped to function properly even when he is not intensely motivated. Just as a loving child eats his spinach to please his mother because he knows that she cares for him, so a student in a state of positive transference should be encouraged to learn necessary cognitive material even if it is

somewhat boring, to please the teacher. If the material is important for the student's immediate or long-range goals the protest that it is boring is to be viewed as a resistance. The teacher should dispense with lectures about its importance and value and simply say "learn it for me and just believe that I won't mislead you." The teacher should not overlook the student's transference as a primary motivation since it often supersedes intrinsic subject matter interest.

Another resistance to cognitive learning employed by classes is to create an atmosphere where it is impossible to teach. The substitute teacher is frequently faced with this situation. The following classroom illustration of psychological reflection (mirroring the resistance) is an effective modern analytic approach to resolving this resistance.

The substitute teacher walked into an unruly, chaotic class that was determined to resist any efforts on the part of the teacher to teach them a thing. After ten minutes of frustration and no results, he intervenes in the following way: he tells the children that he wishes their teacher wasn't absent today. The principal woke him up with his phone call early in the morning. He says that he was planning to sleep late and then to take advantage of the unusually nice weather, going to the park. He really didn't feel like teaching at all and since he is only a substitute teacher, they certainly should not have to cooperate. In fact, if they don't behave he can sit at his desk all day and study for a very hard course that he is taking at graduate school. If they do behave, it would spoil his day and make him work hard to teach them. One child who was forward and aggressive demanded that the teacher give the class work to do or he would go to the principal and have the teacher fired. Since the student insisted and the class agrees, he gave the class an assignment but only if they promised not to annoy him while he sits at his desk and studies. After the students had eagerly finished the assignment (this took about three-fourths of an hour), they wanted him to mark it for them. They seemed intent on making him work. One student then complained that the work was too easy for the class. He then purposely gave them a very difficult assignment too advanced for their level which they had difficulty completing. They asked him to teach it to them since it sounded so interesting. He agreed to teach it to them though reluctantly and they settled down for a lesson—all ears. In mirroring this pre-Oedipal group resistance, the teacher is appealing to the negative suggestibility of the class and getting them to do what Kesten refers to as "learning for spite." (reference)

In the following situation the teacher attempts to resolve the resistance to forming a cooperative peer relationship by mirroring the student's unconscious and thereby promoting a narcissistic transference: John, a seventh-grade student, is like a shark; he pounces on other students in the class when he senses they are weak. He has a leer on his face like a hyena moving in for the kill. When a student gives an incorrect answer, John calls him a "retard"; if someone trips and falls, John laughs in glee; if a member of the class has a cold and sneezes, John gloats that he is very healthy. He also goads the teacher to laugh with him—to have contempt for these inferior creatures, too. The teacher intervenes to interrupt John's destructive interpersonal patterns:

Teacher: "You're very lucky to be so healthy—I am often sick and feel terribly weak—sometimes I think I shouldn't even come to school.

John: "Why shouldn't you come to school, teach"?

Teacher: Because they'll all laugh at me when they see how weak I am—and besides when I feel sick I also feel stupid—they might find out how stupid and weak I am and fire me.

John: (laughing wildly) Teacher is a retard! Teacher is a retard! But why tell all the kids if you're so stupid, teach? Once they find out—boy, are you gonna get it!

Teacher: Well, I thought you should know about it—perhaps you can help me. What do you suggest I do?

The teacher here, by mirroring John's repressed feelings, enables the student to deal with his own dreaded feelings in terms of the teacher's ego. At the same time the hostility is deflected from the more vulnerable students to the teacher. And if the "important" teacher himself is weak, then weakness cannot be quite so despicable. Of course many such interventions are necessary over a long period of time before this student can gain the ego strength to face his own feelings of weakness and inadequacy.

The following illustration indicates a special situation where the resistance to emotional learning is resolved by the techniques of mirroring the unconscious and devaluing the object. It must be kept in mind that the relationship between intellectual and emotional learning is complimentary and when emotions are liberated and under control, intellectual performance often improves. Therefore, resolving a resistance to emotional learning often implicitly resolves the resistance to cognitive learning as well.

A very slow CRMD class in a typical lethargy, bored, disinterested and restless, finds it difficult to learn anything. These students have been in slow classes all their lives. When the teacher asks how they feel about coming to the "slow class" year after year carrying different books, not being able to read well and being laughed at, the students begin to express their frustrations and feelings of humiliation. They blame themselves instead of the school. The teacher then states that it must be his fault too. After all they gave him the slow class to teach and he must be a slow teacher. Other teachers have college bound classes and special projects. But not he. They all laugh at him when he passes in the hall. They say there goes Mr. Jones, the slow class teacher. He guesses the slow class and he really belong together. A slow class, and a slow teacher. A student asks "Do you mind being with a slow class?" and he responds, "Do you mind being with a slow teacher?" The teacher continues if the class is responsive. "I don't blame you for feeling all this. School has been a terrible experience for you. You're getting nothing out of school, all these years and you can't even read. Other students are ahead of you. Even in my class. I have taught you very little." After several class experiences with this approach the students begin to unburden themselves of their anger and fury. They deflect the bottled up feelings from ego to object and if they can be taught to behave properly while expressing these negative feelings, they can often go on to a higher level of cognitive learning.

If the explanations and assignments are appropriate and the student's ability is adequate then he is expected to earn a good grade. Not to do so indicates resistance and should be dealt with accordingly. Failing a final exam or not handing in required work may be an attempt to force the teacher to be punitive in the evaluation. This self-destructive behavior is often repetitive and if the teacher responds by giving a poor or failing grade the student's paranoia may be reinforced and he may feel justified in hating authority. The teacher can many times deal with this situation by withholding the grade (or in college giving an "incomplete"), while at the same time interpreting to the student his self-destructiveness and the teacher's wish for him to succeed. In the college set-

ting, at least, the "incomplete" grade can be more unsettling than a low grade. But it often mobilizes the student to produce for the moment and deprives him of secondary gain of provoking failure or near failure.

It is important that the teacher help free the student from compulsive, stereotyped ways of behaving and responding in the classroom situation. Alternative modes of behavior are explained and illustrated and the student's resistances to these are studied. It is precisely in the routine classroom interaction (attendance, seating, asking and answering questions, responding to other students, homework) that resistances manifest themselves and can be resolved.

Since the classroom experience, unlike the analytic one, does not intend to frustrate students into remembering the past and putting it into words, the teacher's interventions may differ from the analyst's. The teacher's primary aim is to improve the student's current functioning in the classroom. To this end the teacher may intervene appropriately other than through resistance analysis. It is proper for the teacher to meet maturational needs even though this intervention, at times, may not be intended to resolve a resistance. The teacher must project an image of a gratifying, helpful, real person as well as a willing transference object. This means that trips, surprises, and parties are quite appropriate. It is the teacher's ability to move easily between these differing roles as he does between emotional and cognitive teaching that determines his overall effectiveness. The classroom is an important part of a person's ongoing life experience as well as a place to correct faulty interpersonal patterns from the past.

Countertransference and Counterresistance

The teacher in response to student transferences and resistances, like the analyst, develops countertransference and counter-resistances.

This countertransference can be understood in terms Spotnitz (reference) has outlined as subjective or objective— subjective when the teacher's feelings are a function of his own idiosyncratic past life experiences, and objective when the feelings are induced by the reality of the current experience. An objective countertransference can be confirmed if any teacher, given this situation, would feel very much the same way.

Countertransference feelings may be directed at individuals or at the class as a whole. The entire range of countertransference feelings present in the analytic office are potentially present for the teacher in the classroom. The provocative student induces the wish to punish; the helpless student the wish to protect; the achieving student the wish to praise, etc. As does the modern analyst, the teacher must come to regard countertransference as an important form of communication. The teacher must learn to recognize objective countertransference feelings and view them as originating in the student's ego rather than his own. They are a clue to the student's past and often represent unconscious feelings the student has developed toward himself or that a significant adult felt toward him. These countertransference feelings of the teacher must be studied and an appropriate maturational communication made on the basis of understanding rather than current feeling.

The group resistance of the class often mobilizes powerful counterresistance on the part of the teacher. In the course of a semester a teacher may variously feel exhilarated, tired, stimulated, bored, angry, hopeless, ill, sexually stimulated, competitive, sadistic, masochistic, etc. For example, when a class has a powerful resistance to learning, a teacher may experience a wish to go home, to go to sleep or eat. Or he may wish to respond negatively and force the students to learn against their will (a reenactment of the anal power struggle). All of these feelings are acceptable but the actions they suggest should be controlled. Instead the teacher can recognize the nature of the group resistance and work toward resolving it with modern analytic techniques. Teachers need to be trained to understand the feelings students induce in them and to inhibit action on their part unless the action will clearly produce constructive results. *So often in the classroom a teacher's responses are a function of countertransferences acted out without awareness.*

Teachers may sometimes resist dealing with students' feelings by claiming the class time is inadequate to cover all the cognitive material. The principal, supervisor, or Regent's exam is used as the rationalization for maintaining this resistance. The teacher resists knowing that he has the responsibility for deciding when the material is "covered."

The teacher can variously hand out mimeographed material, put the work on the board, have a student put it on the board, assign reading, or reading lists, drill the same thing 150 times, give a brief verbal summary, have the students discuss the material in small groups, etc., as a part of covering a lesson. It is much easier to feel helpless in the hands of an authority who has outlined a master plan which interferes with a proper integration of intellectual and emotional education. In effect, when resistances to learning are resolved academic work can be covered in much less time and remembered longer.

Group Resistance

Group resistance is a crucial concept for the teacher to understand if he is to apply modern psychoanalytic findings to the classroom situation. It refers to the total impact of the class upon the teacher in making known its will to resist being a mature class. This is indeed a powerful resistance and must be dealt with on a priority basis. Even important individual resistances must be relegated to second place. This means, for example, that in a potentially out of control class the needs of the shy, quiet student cannot be met; instead the teacher must concentrate on the potentially destructive group resistance and insist on strict self-control.

Individual members of the class are responded to when their comments are seen to embody the group resistance. In ostensibly responding to an individual student the teacher can effectively communicate to the class as a whole without explicitly doing so. *In effect the group resistance should at all times be uppermost in the teacher's mind and he should try consistently to respond first to those students who at a given moment represent the current group resistance.* When the group resistance is resolved or weakened the teacher may then turn his attention to individual maturational needs.

It is by no means the number of students in a class that determine the nature of the group resistance. A class of six may mobilize much greater group resistance at a given point than a class of sixty. It is primarily the group resistance that determines what a teacher can and cannot accomplish with a class—not the number of students in it. It would be more productive to learn how to group students optimally than to concentrate exclusively on reducing class size.

It is often true that the more a teacher structures a class at the outset the greater will be the group resistance. Therefore, since a moderately structured class generally produces moderate resistance this is often a good way to start. A temporary set of moderate rules can be proposed to the class as the need arises and these can later be modified depending upon group needs.

It is important that the entire class share in the responsibility for individual student behavior. When only a few students belligerently attack the teacher the rest of the class is also held responsible for sitting back silently and enjoying the teacher's discomfort. The repressed id impulse is interpreted in an accepting way while the students failure to come to the teacher's aid is investigated. Such arguments as, "Oh, I thought you could handle it alone" or "I was sorry for you but was afraid to speak," are consistently rejected.

If the resistance persists the teacher may offer that he is human too, that sometimes he likes to see students get picked on. Yet when the students gang up on one class member he generally helps even though he may like to watch the destructiveness. How come he feels one way and acts another? The teacher here can make the vital distinction between feeling and doing while at the same time moving the students from narcissism to object orientation. It frequently comes as a distinct "surprise" to the students that they should be responsible for the teacher's welfare. When a class proceeds to annoy a teacher in the myriad ways that students' ingenuity can dream up, with incessant and picayune questioning about homework assignments, tests, and grading, confusion, continuous and persistent disagreement or talking with each other, the teacher may feel as if he is being backed up against the wall and an invading army is about to march. If at this point the teacher tries to intervene by explaining to the class what they are doing, his interpretations will usually be met with massive denial and an intensification of the teacher torment. An effective technique to resolve this "pre-oedipal" group resistance is to mirror it definitively. The teacher must proceed to "annoy" the class in a very similar way and continue with a similar denial when the class accuses the teacher of tormenting them. The teacher may casually interrupt the lesson to say in a very calm, misleading voice, by the way, he feels in all fairness that he should tell the class about the test he promised them next week. It really will be very difficult and he supposes many of them may not pass. But if they wish, additional books are available they can look at, although he understands the library does not have them in this week.

Evaluation

The concept of evaluation is a complex one in terms of its philosophy, implementation and impact both on teacher and student. Regardless of the teacher's point of view, evaluation must be viewed as an integral part of the course and not a necessary but unimportant addendum. Even if the teacher views it as insignificant, its emotional meaning for the student is sometimes greater than that of the course itself.

From the modern psychoanalytic point of view, evaluation of a student's performance, progress, and potential must be viewed not only in terms of the "objective facts" but in terms of transference, countertransference and repetition compulsion. Many modern educators, as evidenced by the increased use of the "P" in colleges and universities, wish to avoid making evaluations. They feel that evaluation is, at best, a necessary evil that interferes with the basic purpose of the course and is a detriment to a constructive student-teacher relationship. This is no solution to the problem. On the contrary, evaluation can play a constructive role in promoting emotional and intellectual growth. Unconsciously, students wish to be evaluated and wish the evaluation to be of help to them in their efforts to grow and develop.

Frequently evaluation is experienced by the student as reinforcing existing attitudes. The student's "value" as seen in the teacher's

low grade may be taken as confirmation of an already established negative self-concept. This negative evaluation can then become a self-fulfilling prophecy. Because of his need to repeat typical family patterns in class and often to replay his relationship with his parents with the teacher, a student may behave and perform in such a way as to induce negative feelings in the teacher. These feelings are often a repetition of the very feelings the student's parents felt towards him. If the teacher acts on these induced feelings via a negative evaluation, the student's self-concept of "bad" is more firmly established.

Evaluation, on the other hand, may act as a reinforcement of an existing overly positive attitude for the bright and lazy student. Objectively good performance based on innate ability and minimal effort is frequently praised and held up for emulation to other students. The positive evaluation such a student receives acts as a reinforcement of emotional fixation and encourages the student to continue functioning according to the pleasure principle, i.e., why bother frustrating oneself and working harder when one is rewarded for minimal effort? Accordingly, this evaluation fails to move the student toward more mature functioning in line with the reality principle.

From the evaluative point of view, there is in most courses a large gray area where the perception of objective truth fades into countertransference. It is insufficiently acknowledged that the evaluative role has been, over the years, a "legitimate" way for the teacher to act out his transference and countertransference feelings toward the student. So firmly established is the respectability of this concept—that the teacher has a right to judge (almost a "droit du seigneur")—that even practicing psychoanalysts who would, of course, deal with resistances therapeutically in a patient, feel perfectly free to punish and devaluate students who manifest the identical resistances in the classroom. It is very difficult for the teacher to forget the way his teachers handled his resistances as a student and not relate to his students in a like manner. The mechanism described by Anna Freud as "identification with the aggressor" seems to sum up the behavior of many teachers.

Let us illustrate the above by examining the performance of a given student in a graduate psychology class. The registrar stated the class was closed; Miss X approached the instructor and pleaded to be admitted in spite of the overenrollment. The instructor asked Miss X why he should allow her in the class since it would mean additional work for him. Miss X convincingly stated that the instructor would not regret admitting her—as she would be an asset to the course (a discussion course on unconscious communication in psychotherapy), that she would support the instructor if verbally attacked by other students, and would generally contribute to a friendly and constructive classroom atmosphere. This student then proceeded to attend the class sessions and remained silent and uninvolved. When the instructor was embroiled in controversy and verbally attacked, the student would quietly smile and say nothing. When called upon to help out and reminded of her promise, she implied that she never promised any such thing. The written work handed in at the end of the term was to form only a small part of the course evaluation, the major part being class participation.

Miss X's behavior produced in this particular instructor a number of countertransference reactions. On a subjective countertransference level the student evoked a feeling of vindictiveness. The teacher had experienced this feeling in the past for people whom he had helped and who had not appreciated his efforts. He felt used and manipulated and had a strong wish to retaliate. On an objective countertransference level, the student's behavior made the teacher feel that the student was untrustworthy, that she did not deliver on a promise, and was not a desirable, productive member of the group. The written report handed in at the end of the term was viewed by outside observers as satisfactory and indicated adequate intellectual understanding of the course material. How should the teacher evaluate this student?

Should he say that Miss X has not made a real intellectual contribution to the class (which is true enough since she was silent) even though her written work appears adequate? Should he allow himself to dwell on the errors in her written work, its perception being colored by negative feelings? Should he recognize that it is impossible for someone to make an intellectual contribution when she is caught up in the wish to betray and the fear of imminent punishment for it? Should the teacher also recognize that her fear of punishment is the obverse of the wish? Should he say to himself that this is a student and not a patient or client and that she must pay the consequences for her performance regardless of motivation? What really was her performance? That she was immobilized by a major resistance and unable to resolve it? That her transference to this particular instructor was a function of his personality as well as of hers? How would she have performed if the instructor had responded differently? Suppose he had required nothing of her and smiled and communicated that one more person would be no burden? Or suppose he said that the class was absolutely closed and refused to admit her and then she persuaded the Dean to grant her admittance after all? Wouldn't the student's transference and the instructor's countertransference be very different under these conditions? What if the student had verbally regretted her promise and indicated she was not really able to carry it out? How would that have affected the countertransference? In each of the above options the final evaluation of the student is contingent upon a series of countertransference feelings that blend into whatever objective measures of performance are available.

The major difference between a clinical diagnosis and an educational evaluation is the greater opportunity for the teacher to include judgmental statements. It is difficult to make an educational evaluation without implicitly conveying some judgment about the student's desirability or undesirability. That most subjective area of student evaluation described as "character," or "moral attitude" is particularly fertile ground for the teacher to act out his transference and countertransference feelings with impunity.

It is interesting as well to examine the student's reaction to the evaluation he receives This reaction is largely a function of the student's emotional makeup which in turn determines the nature of his transference reactions toward the teacher. A high school teacher trained in modern analytic procedure gave his English class a multiple choice test covering only major concepts of the course in which the correct answer was clearly apparent—in other words, a very easy test. When the test was scored and graded on a percentage basis, most of the class had received eighty-five or better with half of the class scoring over ninety. The test was discussed in class and student reaction elicited. The mood of the class was euphoric, manic with a good deal of laughter and talking out. The students would eagerly argue with the teacher and demand that another answer be viewed as correct. They complained that the test was too ambiguous, that the grades should have been higher since the students were of excellent caliber.

The same teacher gave the same class a second test consisting of the same number of questions. This time only ambiguous multiple choice items were included which dealt only with very minor points of the course material—in other words, a very difficult test. When the test was scored and graded on a percentage basis, most of the class had received seventy-five or lower with half of the class scoring below seventy. The test was again discussed in class and student reaction was again elicited. The mood of the class was subdued and depressed. The students were noncommunicative, passive and glum. None of the test items were questioned and students made self-depreciatory remarks indicating the feeling that they were not sufficiently prepared for the test and had only themselves to blame. They felt the grades were fair and pleaded for another test where they could do better.

These two examples of students' attitudes toward evaluation clearly demonstrate the subjective nature of their response. When the teacher is in effect generous and giving, he is attacked and criticized; when he is punitive and frustrating, the students attack and criticize themselves. This is, of course, the way small children would react to corresponding parental attitudes and behavior. In other words, the students' transference reactions to the teacher who provided these two different evaluative experiences are a function not of the reality but of the degree to which depression or mania had been induced by the teacher's behavior. While there was some small variation in the student reaction, the above pattern was clearly the general trend.

When the nature of the above evaluation experiments was explained to the class, anxiety and confusion resulted. The students evidenced resistance to seeing the subjective nature of evaluation and of their reactions. The teacher's explanation presented a world too chaotic for the students' egos to master. After the second test, they were reluctant to blame the teacher even after realizing how unfair the test was. They preferred to blame themselves rather than view the teacher as a "malevolent giant" (Bergler) just as the neurotic child prefers to blame himself rather than see the all-powerful parent as bad. The test is seen as something special—not as a subjective creation of the teacher but as a pronouncement "ex cathedra" of the student's worth. The teacher is viewed as right and his judgment as just. Thus "judge" and "justice" achieve a magical merger in the student's transference reaction toward the teacher, thereby allowing the teacher wide latitude to act and react, to project and deny, to help or destroy as he sees fit.

The Need for Insulation in the Classroom

It is of the utmost importance that the teacher feel comfortable with the class and that he talk and behave in such a way as to put himself at ease and to make the experience enjoyable and interesting. The teacher should develop the attitude of remaining somewhat apart from the emotional interchanges that may occur. Harry Stack Sullivan's concept of the "participant-observer" has validity for the classroom (reference). If emotional education is to proceed smoothly, the teacher must develop a degree of insulation from the bombardment of intense feelings which the students will generate, be it anger, jealousy, sexual stimulation, or love, the teacher needs to maintain a corner of his personality as the objective observer. He can participate in the interchanges and still remain clearly in control of the degree and nature of emotional stimulation.

The students likewise need to maintain or develop the necessary amount of emotional insulation from the feelings of the teacher and their fellow students. They too must be helped to develop an observing part of their personality that is not continually caught up in the flow and exchange of feelings. The teacher should learn to control the intensity of emotional exchanges so that the students are not overstimulated. An effective way to dampen a heated emotional interchange is to ask an object-oriented question—that is a question that deals with the academic material or the realities of the world. This will often have the effect of bringing the student abruptly back to reality and providing breathing space for him to master too intense feelings. Likewise, students should be discouraged from revealing too much about themselves. The need to pour out personal information in a tactless inappropriate manner is an indication of a personality lacking insulation. It is a disservice to the student to encourage or allow him to talk so freely under the guise of cartharsis; rather he must be helped to suppress these feelings and learn appropriate social functioning in a classroom setting. Very frequently this type of student will protest any efforts to help him establish controls, since his emotional outbursts tend to be gratifying. The teacher must, however, engage in object-oriented communication and help the student to frustrate himself into appropriateness.

Mutual Resistance

Finally there is an insidious resistance that both teachers and students share. This makes it all the more destructive and difficult to resolve. Namely, the situation arises when the teacher needs to feel he has covered his material and taught the students well and the students need to feel they have done their work and learned something worthwhile. The reality may be in barren contrast; nothing really may have been communicated by the teacher and nothing valid may have been learned by the students. This apparent "Folie a deux" where each side plays out its assigned role of denial to assuage the superego prevents relevant, permanent and useful learning. The student here may also be fearful to know the reality since this knowledge may stimulate anger which he may be impotent to discharge in his role as a student. His denial is comparable to that of the child who will not see his parent as inadequate but is quick to see inadequacy in himself. The teacher, on the other hand, needs to maintain his professional self-esteem. The knowledge that he may be an ungiving, uncaring authority could produce anxiety and self-hate; he is on safer ground indeed to *feel* he has taught well and to see any inadequacy as originating in the students.

This educational paradigm of the Emperor's clothes can only be dispelled when both students and teacher develop sufficient ego strength to tolerate unpleasant aspects of reality.

PART SIX
COUNTERPOINT

ALIENATION AND THE JOB MARKET

Dear Editor:

"It seems to me that, in part at least, the rising rate of drug and alcohol addiction among young people today is linked to their lack of sound career counseling. What does an adolescent today have to look forward to: a depressed economy, a scarcity of jobs, or four years of college and then the unemployment line? Perhaps if the schools, beginning with the elementary schools which have been most deficient in this, were to give children more of a sense of purpose in the world, as well as a sense of their own worth, we wouldn't need the remedial career counseling as we do now. . . . I hope someday we reassess our priorities and place the education of our children at the top of the list."

P. W.

THE PERSON IN THE FAMILY

Dear Editor:

"Dr. Zuk's article on family counseling brought together a lot of the points mentioned in Dr. Ruma's article on the single parent and Nass's paper on the fatherless child. I think that while we are only beginning to understand the complexity of family dynamics, Zuk's point about the importance of the 'struggle for control between the therapist and family members,' shows in many ways what the family unit is all about. . . . The family is a miniature social unit, but a very special type of social unit. In other social units, such as the nation, the organization, or even the committee, reason and logic play a more important part in the formation of rules and the treatment of each of the constituents. In the family, on the other hand, where the sometimes devastating proximity and intimacy of daily contact brings out the worst in each family member, feelings and conflicts are likely to reign over reason and logic. Looking at these three articles together, we can see how social insights and dynamic psychology can be applied to help the *person*, who happens to be, as all of us are, a member of a family, which he neither chose in the first place nor can disaffiliate himself from, even if he thinks he wants to."

C. U.

NEW HORIZONS FOR TEACHERS

". . . I think that the Kirman article, 'Emotional education in the classroom' opens up new horizons for teachers, who often feel confined by the burdens of subject-matter, and stifled by the need to teach people who are not emotionally ready to be taught. Educational psychologists and school administrators often forget that the education of emotions is as important—if not *more* important—than the inculcation of subject-matter, and what Kirman makes clear in his paper is that the two goals invariably go hand-in-hand."

S. W.

Note. As we begin to recognize our increasing failures in our efforts to educate the students in our charge, we will be compelled to acknowledge more and more the type of insights Dr. Kirman provides in his paper. Dr. Kirman is currently at work on a book elaborating the position presented in this paper.

WHAT IS VOCATIONAL COUNSELING ALL ABOUT?

"As a person who has never sought the assistance of a vocational counselor, nor felt the need to, I've never been too sure what vocational counseling is all about, and how it relates to psychological counseling, which is my primary interest at this point in life. The two articles on the subject have clarified for me what I'm beginning to recognize is an important part of counseling. Taken together, the two papers amply show the limitations and strengths of the vocational counseling position. "Do we have a theory of vocational choice?" shows that while we do not really understand at this point in time how people make career decisions there is hope that such a view will be achieved in the near future. Dr. Fredman's article gives a well-balanced view of vocational inventories—tests I've never really considered too important, but which I can now see in proper perspective. I'm still not certain what vocational counseling is all about, but these two papers did raise some interesting questions and stimulate my thinking so that perhaps I will find some relevant and valid answers."

Y. A.

• • •

Dear Editor:

I think the Carkhuff, Alexik and Anderson article puts all these vocational theories in their place, but does it too gently for my taste. When I took my first course in vocational counseling and had to learn all these theories, I thought there was something wrong with me—they made so little sense to me. The more I studied them and the more I considered the evidence, the less valid they seemed. Now I'm beginning to see that I'm not the only one who rejects these theories as valid explanations of why people make the career choices they do."

G. E. E.

With Thanks

The preparation of book such as this involves the cooperation of many individuals. My editor inspired this project and guided it through its various stages of preparation. He suggested "field testing" the material on students and reviewers, and from this experiment emerged the *Counterpoint* sections at the end of each part of the book. The authors who were kind enough to contribute original material, or to permit reprinting of other material, made the skeleton outline of a book into a reality. My father, as usual, contributed generously of his time and talent, helping me with the bits and pieces every editor dreads doing alone. After dozens of trips to the post office, countless days of numbering pages and checking and rechecking details, he suggested that I should have listened to him years ago and become a poet!

Melanie, my wife assisted in the preparation of indexes, reviewed all the material, and made the many important suggestions that were central in the evolution of this book.

Name Index

Subject Index